The Fielding Bible

Volume IV

Praise for previous editions of
The Fielding Bible from readers:

"The biggest leap forward in defensive metrics ever."

"Information you need to fully understand the game of baseball."

"A must for the thinking baseball fan and an essential for any credible baseball library."

"Another validation that statisticians looking objectively at data can reach conclusions that 'experts' never could."

"Doing to baseball what W. Edwards Deming did to business analysis: get rid of 'opinion' and replace it with 'facts.'"

"Will teach you about the part of baseball that is underappreciated: defense."

"These guys really go the last mile to make sure everything is explained appropriately."

"A very valuable analysis of Major League Baseball players' fielding abilities."

"The individual write-ups for each player create a nice overview of their strengths and weaknesses."

The Fielding Bible

Volume IV

John Dewan & Ben Jedlovec

with Joe Rosales & Scott Spratt

Baseball Info Solutions

www.baseballinfosolutions.com

Published by ACTA Sports

A Division of ACTA Publications

www.actasports.com

Cover by Tom A. Wright

Cover Photo by Daniel Shirey, USA TODAY Sports

First Edition: March 2015

Published by:
ACTA Sports, a division of ACTA Publications
4848 North Clark Street
Chicago, IL 60640
(800) 397-2282
www.actasports.com www.actapublications.com

ISBN: 978-0-87946-541-4
ISSN: 1946-7524

Printed in the United States of America

Table of Contents

Dedication

To Juliet Jedlovec, the youngest stat-checker in the history of *The Fielding Bible*. You and Amy are my greatest passions in life. I hope that you are lucky enough to find the people and activities that fulfill your life the way that you, Amy, and baseball have impacted mine.

Ben Jedlovec

Introduction

Welcome back to *The Fielding Bible*. Has it been three years already? We hope you've been well. Boy, that Andrelton Simmons fellow is really something, isn't he?!? And how about those shifts!!!

If you're anything like us, you probably agree that there is never a shortage of questions to be answered when it comes to baseball. Every time we dig into a new study we find ourselves asking more questions than we've answered.

At Baseball Info Solutions, we are fortunate in many ways. First of all, our company's mission is to collect and provide the most accurate, in-depth, and timely professional baseball data, including cutting-edge research and analysis, striving to educate major league teams and the public about baseball analytics. What does that mean? Well, we get to collect information about baseball that no one else has, and then we get to analyze it. We expand our data collection efforts every year, and of course, major league teams are kind enough to play 162 games over the course of six months every season. Even if we thought we'd ever get bored analyzing the information already at our disposal, the fire hose of new data is running faster than we can lap it up.

On top of the fact that we like to continuously improve our understanding of the game of baseball, we like to tell people about everything we've learned. Thus, we'll keep coming to you with our latest research.

That's exactly what you'll find in this book. We prepare monthly research updates, called our "Team Newsletters", that we send out to major league teams. These Newsletters include updates to previous research, analysis of new BIS data, and even analytically driven reactions to various trends around baseball (such as The Shift!). We've updated each of these Newsletters and published them here in book form for your perusal. You'll find chapters on Strike Zone Plus/Minus (our catcher framing analysis), Defensive Projections, and a new stolen base algorithm.

Of course, a *Fielding Bible* book wouldn't be complete without a couple of articles about The Shift! Shift usage has increased over 500 percent since we suggested more shifting in *Volume II* and then even more strongly advocated for its increased usage in *Volume III*. No, that's not a typo. Five hundred percent. We like to think that we had a small role in that, but we have no doubt that the primary reason for the explosion is the success of a handful of progressive coaches, players, and organizations who saw the shift as a way to get an extra edge over the competition. There's no way we could have expected the shift to become the biggest strategic change in baseball since the creation of the closer's role; but it's certainly exciting!

We've cut back on some of the data sections this time because we wanted to showcase the abundance of research. In addition to the remaining data sections in this book, you can find the data with daily updates published in a number of places, including Bill James Online, Baseball-Reference, and FanGraphs.

Thanks again for joining us. We hope you enjoy the book, and we hope to hear from you soon!

John Dewan and Ben Jedlovec
February 2015

Defensive Runs Saved

In The *Fielding Bible—Volume III* we introduced some significant enhancements to Defensive Runs Saved. In 2009, we began timing every ball in play, which allowed us to more accurately group balls in play for the purposes of calculating the likelihood of successfully making a play. This hit timer data also allowed us to improve our evaluations of outfielders' throwing arms. We introduced an entirely new component of Runs Saved based on a system for classifying Good Fielding Plays (GFP) and Defensive Misplays (DM) and Errors (E) devised by Bill James, Good Play/Misplay Runs Saved. And we presented significant upgrades to our GDP Runs Saved and Bunt Runs Saved methodologies. All told, there were eight components of Defensive Runs Saved.

For *Volume IV*, we continue to move forward. We now have nine components of Defensive Runs Saved. The newest is Strike Zone Runs Saved, our method for quantifying pitch framing skills. We are also constantly re-evaluating the existing techniques that we use to quantify defensive performance. As a result, we have made accounting changes to several metrics that have improved their accuracy.

Before we get into all the new stuff, we need to address a point of confusion that has come to our attention in recent years.

Same Stat, New Name

The foundation for Defensive Runs Saved has always been the Plus/Minus System. The Plus/Minus System was developed as a way to measure how many outs a player made relative to the average player at his position. It serves as a way to evaluate how a player combines his range with his positioning to turn batted balls into outs, and can be expressed in units of Plays Saved. Then, in order to determine the value of those Plays Saved to a team, we converted them into runs to get Defensive Runs Saved. However, over the years, Baseball Info Solutions has developed ways of measuring many more aspects of defense, including outfielders' throwing arms, infielders' skill at turning double plays, catchers' ability to control the running game, among others. There are now nine different components of Defensive Runs Saved, one of which, until now, was called Plus/Minus Runs Saved.

However, because the concept of measuring defensive prowess by giving positive and negative credit to a player based on his success or failure on many different types of game events (not just balls in play) had become so closely associated with Defensive Runs Saved, a lot of people have come to consider the Plus/Minus System to be synonymous with the Defensive Runs Saved System. Therefore, in order to try to clarify the fact that Plus/Minus Runs Saved and the measurement of a player's range and positioning is just one of nine components of Defensive Runs Saved, we have decided to rename that component.

From now on, the Plus/Minus System will now be called the *Range and Positioning System*. Accordingly, Plus/Minus Runs Saved will be called *Range and Positioning Runs Saved*, Basic Plus/Minus will be called *Plays Saved*, and Enhanced Plus/Minus will be called *Bases Saved*. It will feel a little strange at first to not use such an established term as Plus/Minus, but once we all get used to the new names, we feel that it will be more straight forward and understandable for everyone.

Also New in Volume IV

There are five major upgrades to Defensive Runs Saved that BIS has made in the past three years.

1) Strike Zone Runs Saved—This is a brand new methodology. We developed a system that divides the credit for a pitch being called a ball or a strike among the pitcher, catcher, batter, and umpire. The system measures each party's ability to get extra strikes or extra balls and converts that into Runs Saved. The system is unique from other publicly available "catcher framing" metrics because it treats each party as an active participant on the outcome of the pitch—e.g., catchers with their receiving skills, pitchers with their ability to locate the pitch, batters with their body language or other mannerisms, and umpires with their personal standards—and because it utilizes BIS Command Charting data (the distance between where the catcher sets his initial target and where the pitch ends up). Strike Zone Runs Saved is only included as a component of Defensive Runs Saved for catchers, but it still serves as a tool for evaluation for all the other parties. To read more about how the system works, see the Methodology section on page 344.

2) Range and Positioning Runs Saved—We made an accounting change to how the system handles shallow, medium, and deep balls in calculating an outfielder's Runs Saved. In *The Fielding Bible—Volume II*, we introduced a system that converted Plays Saved into Bases Saved, then Bases Saved into Runs Saved. However, the conversion of bases to runs relied on a slightly oversimplified assumption. Therefore, we decided to cut out the middle man and go straight from plays to runs for outfielders. For more information on what this accounting change entails, see page 324.

3) Shift Runs Saved—This is an extension of Range and Positioning Runs Saved applied at the team level. In 2012, we discovered that the way the Range and Positioning System handled balls in play, third basemen positioned in short right field as part of a shift were getting an inordinate amount of positive credit for making a play because of how far outside of their normal jurisdiction they were when making that play. Therefore, we removed shift plays from the calculation of an individual player's Range and Positioning Runs Saved and created Shift Runs Saved to measure how successful a team has been in employing its shifts. The calculation is the same as for Range and Positioning Runs Saved, but

instead of looking at an individual player at a specific position, it treats the whole infield as a unit. For more details on the methodology behind Shift Runs Saved, see page 350.

4) Catcher Blocks of Home Plate—This is one of the categories of Good Fielding Plays. In calculating Good Play/Misplay Runs Saved, as with many other categories of Good Fielding Plays (GFP) and Defensive Misplays (DM), we compare the number of times a catcher successfully blocks the plate to the number of opportunities that he had to do so. We used to define those opportunities as the number of "touches" that a catcher had in a season, but we found that it was much more accurate to define opportunities to block the plate as the number of runs that cross the plate with a given catcher on the field (excluding home runs).

5) Catcher Blocks Runs Saved—This refers to catcher blocks of pitches in the dirt, and is a component of Good Play/Misplay Runs Saved. In the past we handled catcher blocks (a type of GFP) separately from potential wild pitch catches (another type of GFP) and wild pitch misplays (a type of DM). However, we realized that the two GFPs are natural opposites to the one DM, and passed balls are also a related piece. By accounting for them all as part of the same calculation, we do a better job of accurately representing a catcher's skill behind the plate. For more details on the revised system, see page 93.

Nine Components of Defensive Runs Saved

1) Range and Positioning System – measures range and positioning

2) OF Arm Runs Saved – measures outfielder arms

3) GDP Runs Saved – measures double play ability

4) Bunt Runs Saved – measures ability to field bunts

5) Good Play/Misplay Runs Saved – measures the run impact of good plays and misplays that are not accounted for in other components of Runs Saved

6) Catcher Stolen Base Runs Saved – measures the catcher's ability to control the running game

7) Pitcher Stolen Base Runs Saved – measures the pitcher's ability to control the running game

8) Adjusted Earned Runs Saved – measures the catcher's handling of pitchers

9) Strike Zone Runs Saved – measures the number of extra strikes drawn by a catcher because of his framing ability.

Here's a grid by position showing which methodologies are used for which positions:

Component	Position								
	P	C	1B	2B	3B	SS	LF	CF	RF
Range & Pos	x		x	x	x	x	x	x	x
OF Arms							x	x	x
GDP			x	x	x	x			
Bunts	x	x	x		x				
GFP/DME	x	x	x	x	x	x	x	x	x
Catcher SB		x							
Pitcher SB	x								
Adj. ER		x							
Strike Zone		x							

Year-by-Year Summary of Enhancements

Here is a year-by-year summary of enhancements we've made over the years. Sometimes it's all new methodologies and sometimes it's a tweak to improve an existing one. During upcoming seasons, you'll find all the updated numbers on BillJamesOnline.com, BISData.com, FanGraphs.com, and Baseball-Reference.com.

2004

- Baseball Info Solutions (BIS) team clients get the first "Specialized Fielding Report" based on the in-depth coding of batted ball locations by BIS
- The Plus/Minus System debuts in this report

2005

- Distinction made between liners and flyballs in the Plus/Minus System, instead of just a velocity coding of soft, medium and hard. Data changed back to 2003
- Team clients get the second "Specialized Fielding Report" through the 2004 season. It is renamed to the *Team Fielding Bible*, exclusive to BIS customers

2006

- New defensive analysis goes public with the publication of the first volume, *The Fielding Bible*
- Plus/Minus System introduced to the public
- Outfielder Arm, GDPs and Bunts – methodologies for each introduced
- Revised Zone Rating – an upgrade to the old Zone Rating system
- After the release of the book, "fliners" added as new category to outfield plus/minus
- After the book, vector system changed to polar coordinates allowing for use of the standard 360 circle for measurement
- After the book, we modified the Plus/Minus System to consider all outfielder balls in the air that are caught or land within five feet to be the same, and all infield balls in the air within three feet to be the same
- BIS team clients receive updated information based on new techniques added after the book

2007

- Manny Adjustment added – removing balls hit high off the wall from consideration as a fieldable ball in the Plus/Minus System
- BIS team clients get the Manny Adjustment included with their new information

2008

- Catcher Adjusted Earned Runs Saved introduced
- Catcher SB Runs Saved, Pitcher SB Runs Saved introduced
- All methodologies converted to Runs Saved
- BIS team clients continue to receive updated information and techniques

2009

- *The Fielding Bible—Volume II* comes out providing updates to the public
- Defensive Runs Saved introduced to public
- Home Run Saving Catches become the first Good Play or Misplay to be converted to Runs Saved
- Batted Ball Timer started by BIS
- After the book, outfield Plus/Minus revised to include batted ball timer
- After the book, GDP Runs Saved revised to include timer and hit location
- BIS team clients receive all adjustments

2010

- Infield Plus/Minus revised to include batted ball timer
- Outfield Arm Runs Saved revised to include timer and hit location
- Outfield Plus/Minus modified to consider all outfielder balls in the air that are caught or land within about ten feet to be the same, and all infield flyballs and line drives within about eight feet to be the same.
- BIS team clients now receive all updated techniques and adjustments as part of the new system for them to access information on a daily basis

2011

- Good Plays/Misplays Runs Saved developed and added back to 2004
- BIS team clients receive this new technique as well

2012

- Centering of all runs saved methodologies takes place
- Bunts Runs Saved recalculated for all players back to 2003
- Pitcher SB Runs Saved recalculated and centered for all players back to 2003
- *The Fielding Bible—Volume III* is published
- Improved the handling of wall balls in Good Fielding Plays
- Changed the accounting for shifts to the team level

2013

- Revised the way opportunities for catchers to block the plate are estimated in calculating Good Plays/Misplays Runs Saved
- BIS team clients receive this new adjustment

2014

- Strike Zone Plus/Minus Runs Saved developed and added back to 2010
- Improved Plus/Minus Runs Saved with an accounting change on shallow and deep balls that more accurately measures outfielders who consistently make either shallow or deep plays
- Catcher Block Runs Saved (a part of Good Play/Misplay Runs Saved) is streamlined with a plus/minus methodology that includes catcher blocks of pitches in the dirt, catches of potential wild pitches, passed balls on non-knuckleballs, and wild pitch misplays
- BIS team clients receive these new adjustments

2015

- Changed the name of the Plus/Minus System to the Range and Positioning System
- *The Fielding Bible—Volume IV* is published

Infield Runs Saved Leaders

First Basemen 3-Year Leaders		Second Basemen 3-Year Leaders		Third Basemen 3-Year Leaders		Shortstops 3-Year Leaders	
Gonzalez,Adrian	38	Barney,Darwin	49	Machado,Manny	48	Simmons,Andrelton	88
Rizzo,Anthony	26	Pedroia,Dustin	43	Arenado,Nolan	46	Hardy,J.J.	36
Votto,Joey	20	LeMahieu,DJ	34	Donaldson,Josh	36	Cozart,Zack	35
Teixeira,Mark	19	Kinsler,Ian	32	Uribe,Juan	36	Ryan,Brendan	31
Alonso,Yonder	18	Ellis,Mark	29	Wright,David	34	Barmes,Clint	28
Napoli,Mike	17	Cano,Robinson	21	Lawrie,Brett	24	Crawford,Brandon	22
Goldschmidt,Paul	15	Casilla,Alexi	19	Beltre,Adrian	17	Florimon,Pedro	22
Pujols,Albert	15	Phillips,Brandon	18	Headley,Chase	15	Peralta,Jhonny	16
Morneau,Justin	13	Goins,Ryan	15	Frazier,Todd	15	Pennington,Cliff	14
Belt,Brandon	12	Pennington,Cliff	13	Prado,Martin	10	Aviles,Mike	13

First Basemen 3-Year Trailers		Second Basemen 3-Year Trailers		Third Basemen 3-Year Trailers		Shortstops 3-Year Trailers	
Moss,Brandon	-20	Weeks,Rickie	-62	Johnson,Chris	-31	Reyes,Jose	-36
Fielder,Prince	-19	Murphy,Daniel	-34	Castellanos,Nick	-30	Jeter,Derek	-35
Dunn,Adam	-18	Altuve,Jose	-28	Cabrera,Miguel	-23	Lowrie,Jed	-31
Howard,Ryan	-17	Hill,Aaron	-18	Freese,David	-21	Nunez,Eduardo	-28
Konerko,Paul	-14	Schumaker,Skip	-17	Nelson,Chris	-19	Cabrera,Asdrubal	-28
Encarnacion,Edwin	-14	Uggla,Dan	-17	Gillaspie,Conor	-19	Rutledge,Josh	-20

First Basemen 2014 Leaders		Second Basemen 2014 Leaders		Third Basemen 2014 Leaders		Shortstops 2014 Leaders	
Gonzalez,Adrian	11	Kinsler,Ian	20	Donaldson,Josh	20	Simmons,Andrelton	28
Alonso,Yonder	9	Pedroia,Dustin	17	Uribe,Juan	17	Cozart,Zack	19
Pearce,Steve	9	LeMahieu,DJ	16	Arenado,Nolan	16	Peralta,Jhonny	17
Morneau,Justin	8	Schoop,Jonathan	10	Wright,David	13	Hardy,J.J.	10
Adams,Matt	8	Barney,Darwin	10	Headley,Chase	13	Mercer,Jordy	9
Davis,Chris	8	Wong,Kolten	9	Rendon,Anthony	12	Crawford,Brandon	8
Napoli,Mike	7	Kendrick,Howie	7	Seager,Kyle	10	Tulowitzki,Troy	7
Rizzo,Anthony	6	Phillips,Brandon	6	Beltre,Adrian	9	Amarista,Alexi	7
Pujols,Albert	6	Sogard,Eric	5	Prado,Martin	8	Owings,Chris	5
Duda,Lucas	5	Hicks,Brandon	5	Harrison,Josh	8	Rollins,Jimmy	4

First Basemen 2014 Trailers		Second Basemen 2014 Trailers		Third Basemen 2014 Trailers		Shortstops 2014 Trailers	
Abreu,Jose	-10	Weeks,Rickie	-17	Castellanos,Nick	-30	Escobar,Yunel	-24
Howard,Ryan	-10	Odor,Rougned	-11	Chisenhall,Lonnie	-14	Reyes,Jose	-16
Freeman,Freddie	-7	Kipnis,Jason	-11	Johnson,Chris	-13	Andrus,Elvis	-13
Encarnacion,Edwin	-5	Cabrera,Asdrubal	-10	Gillaspie,Conor	-12	Jeter,Derek	-12
Singleton,Jon	-5	Murphy,Daniel	-10	Valbuena,Luis	-10	Lowrie,Jed	-10
Jones,Garrett	-5	Gyorko,Jedd	-9	Freese,David	-9	Rutledge,Josh	-9

Outfield Runs Saved Leaders

Left Fielders 3-Year Leaders		Center Fielders 3-Year Leaders		Right Fielders 3-Year Leaders	
Gordon,Alex	67	Lagares,Juan	52	Heyward,Jason	56
Marte,Starling	30	Gomez,Carlos	35	Reddick,Josh	41
Cespedes,Yoenis	15	Cain,Lorenzo	35	Parra,Gerardo	39
Yelich,Christian	13	Martin,Leonys	29	Victorino,Shane	24
Blanco,Gregor	13	Gentry,Craig	26	Suzuki,Ichiro	19
Lough,David	13	Dyson,Jarrod	23	Byrd,Marlon	17
Murphy,David	11	Bourn,Michael	21	Cain,Lorenzo	15
Pearce,Steve	11	Span,Denard	20	Cowgill,Collin	14
Joyce,Matt	9	Pollock,A.J.	19	Bautista,Jose	13
Heisey,Chris	9	Marisnick,Jake	17	Schierholtz,Nate	13

Left Fielders 3-Year Trailers		Center Fielders 3-Year Trailers		Right Fielders 3-Year Trailers	
Ibanez,Raul	-20	Fowler,Dexter	-35	Cuddyer,Michael	-24
Willingham,Josh	-20	Saunders,Michael	-27	Arcia,Oswaldo	-15
Holliday,Matt	-20	Kemp,Matt	-26	Hunter,Torii	-15
Quentin,Carlos	-18	De Aza,Alejandro	-21	Pence,Hunter	-15
Morse,Michael	-16	Revere,Ben	-21	Murphy,David	-14
Coghlan,Chris	-14	Pagan,Angel	-19	Choo,Shin-Soo	-13

Left Fielders 2014 Leaders		Center Fielders 2014 Leaders		Right Fielders 2014 Leaders	
Gordon,Alex	26	Lagares,Juan	26	Heyward,Jason	26
Yelich,Christian	13	Martin,Leonys	16	Kiermaier,Kevin	13
Cespedes,Yoenis	11	Bradley Jr.,Jackie	15	Nava,Daniel	13
Ackley,Dustin	8	Hamilton,Billy	14	Reddick,Josh	10
Marte,Starling	7	Cain,Lorenzo	14	Schierholtz,Nate	10
Lough,David	7	Dyson,Jarrod	13	Byrd,Marlon	9
Young,Chris	6	Inciarte,Ender	13	Saunders,Michael	7
Young,Eric	5	Eaton,Adam	11	Venable,Will	7
Guyer,Brandon	5	Ozuna,Marcell	8	Stanton,Giancarlo	6
Davis,Khris	4	Pollock,A.J.	8	Craig,Allen	3

Left Fielders 2014 Trailers		Center Fielders 2014 Trailers		Right Fielders 2014 Trailers	
Coghlan,Chris	-11	Fowler,Dexter	-19	Hunter,Torii	-17
Morse,Michael	-10	Crisp,Coco	-18	Murphy,David	-12
Choo,Shin-Soo	-9	Revere,Ben	-17	Arcia,Oswaldo	-9
Gomes,Jonny	-8	McCutchen,Andrew	-13	Garcia,Avisail	-8
Viciedo,Dayan	-7	Trout,Mike	-12	Viciedo,Dayan	-8
Davis,Rajai	-7	Jones,James	-9	Myers,Wil	-8

Pitcher/Catcher Runs Saved Leaders

Pitchers 3-Year Leaders		Catchers 3-Year Leaders	
Dickey,R.A.	18	Molina,Yadier	66
Greinke,Zack	18	Lucroy,Jonathan	51
Buehrle,Mark	18	Martin,Russell	44
Kershaw,Clayton	17	Posey,Buster	40
Cueto,Johnny	16	Gomes,Yan	29
Leake,Mike	15	Hanigan,Ryan	29
Keuchel,Dallas	13	McCann,Brian	27
Alvarez,Henderson	11	Maldonado,Martin	27
Kendrick,Kyle	11	3 tied with	25
Teheran,Julio	11		

Pitchers 3-Year Trailers		Catchers 3-Year Trailers	
McAllister,Zach	-13	Rosario,Wilin	-45
Hughes,Phil	-12	Iannetta,Chris	-42
Lincecum,Tim	-12	Suzuki,Kurt	-36
Feldman,Scott	-12	Santana,Carlos	-35
Burnett,A.J.	-12	Doumit,Ryan	-34
Volquez,Edinson	-11	Pierzynski,A.J.	-28

Pitchers 2014 Leaders		Catchers 2014 Leaders	
Keuchel,Dallas	10	Lucroy,Jonathan	25
Kershaw,Clayton	7	Martin,Russell	19
Alvarez,Henderson	6	Conger,Hank	17
Cueto,Johnny	6	Rivera,Rene	15
Greinke,Zack	5	Joseph,Caleb	14
Wainwright,Adam	5	Flowers,Tyler	11
Kendrick,Kyle	5	Montero,Miguel	10
Maness,Seth	5	4 tied with	8
Teheran,Julio	5		
Dickey,R.A.	5		

Pitchers 2014 Trailers		Catchers 2014 Trailers	
Hughes,Phil	-8	Saltalamacchia,J	-22
Feldman,Scott	-7	Suzuki,Kurt	-17
Petit,Yusmeiro	-5	Pierzynski,A.J.	-14
Lackey,John	-5	Rosario,Wilin	-14
Burnett,A.J.	-5	Iannetta,Chris	-14
McAllister,Zach	-4	Navarro,Dioner	-14

Catchers - 3-Year Runs Saved

Player	Adj ER	Stolen Bases	Bunts and GFP/DME	Strike Zone	Total
Yadier Molina	13	15	19	19	66
Jonathan Lucroy	-6	-5	19	43	51
Russell Martin	3	15	2	24	44
Buster Posey	3	-1	4	34	40
Ryan Hanigan	4	7	4	14	29
Yan Gomes	-1	9	5	16	29
Brian McCann	5	0	0	22	27
Salvador Perez	10	15	8	-8	25
Jeff Mathis	4	6	4	11	25
Jose Molina	-2	6	-9	29	24
Chris Stewart	-4	3	2	23	24
Tyler Flowers	8	5	-4	13	22
Miguel Montero	-5	-1	-3	26	17
Wilson Ramos	1	5	1	3	10
Mike Zunino	-3	-2	-8	21	8
Alex Avila	5	-3	2	1	5
Carlos Ruiz	0	1	11	-7	5
Josh Thole	3	-4	-5	10	4
Jose Lobaton	-1	-3	3	4	3
Derek Norris	2	-5	-1	6	2
J.P. Arencibia	7	-8	-1	2	0
Matt Wieters	-9	7	4	-3	-1
Welington Castillo	-2	10	8	-25	-9
Jason Castro	0	-3	-1	-7	-11
Devin Mesoraco	-2	-8	7	-9	-12
Dioner Navarro	1	0	2	-15	-12
A.J. Ellis	3	4	-3	-20	-16
John Buck	-3	-2	1	-13	-17
Nick Hundley	-8	1	4	-16	-19
Jarrod Saltalamacchia	-3	-10	-4	-5	-22
A.J. Pierzynski	-4	-3	-6	-15	-28
Carlos Santana	-3	2	-10	-24	-35
Kurt Suzuki	-7	-7	12	-34	-36
Chris Iannetta	-9	-5	-2	-26	-42
Wilin Rosario	1	1	-21	-26	-45

Catchers - 2013 Runs Saved

Player	Team	Adj ER	Stolen Bases	Bunts and GFP/DME	Strike Zone	Total
Yadier Molina	StL	6	2	8	14	30
Russell Martin	Pit	5	9	0	7	21
Yan Gomes	Cle	4	7	0	10	21
Buster Posey	SF	5	-1	3	9	16
Salvador Perez	KC	4	4	4	-1	11
Jonathan Lucroy	Mil	-5	-2	3	14	10
Chris Stewart	NYY	-5	2	2	11	10
Wilson Ramos	Was	3	2	1	4	10
Jeff Mathis	Mia	3	2	1	4	10
Jose Molina	TB	1	2	-4	10	9
J.P. Arencibia	Tor	6	-4	-1	7	8
Hank Conger	LAA	2	-1	-2	9	8
Joe Mauer	Min	5	3	0	-1	7
Brian McCann	Atl	2	-1	0	5	6
Welington Castillo	ChC	4	4	6	-11	3
Ryan Hanigan	Cin	1	2	-2	1	2
Tyler Flowers	CWS	3	0	-2	0	1
Carlos Ruiz	Phi	0	-2	4	-2	0
Derek Norris	Oak	-1	-1	-1	2	-1
Miguel Montero	Ari	-4	1	-3	4	-2
Alex Avila	Det	3	-7	-1	3	-2
Jose Lobaton	TB	-1	-3	1	1	-2
A.J. Pierzynski	Tex	-2	0	1	-3	-4
A.J. Ellis	LAD	1	4	-4	-5	-4
Jarrod Saltalamacchia	Bos	-2	-4	-1	2	-5
Jason Castro	Hou	0	0	-1	-4	-5
Devin Mesoraco	Cin	-1	-2	2	-4	-5
Kurt Suzuki	2 tms	-3	-6	6	-5	-8
Matt Wieters	Bal	-12	2	2	-2	-10
Nick Hundley	SD	-6	1	0	-7	-12
Wilin Rosario	Col	2	-2	-4	-9	-13
Rob Brantly	Mia	-3	0	-2	-8	-13
John Buck	2 tms	-7	-1	1	-9	-16
Carlos Santana	Cle	-3	-2	-6	-8	-19
Chris Iannetta	LAA	-4	-4	0	-14	-22

Catchers - 2014 Runs Saved

Player	Team	Adj ER	Stolen Bases	Bunts and GFP/DME	Strike Zone	Total
Jonathan Lucroy	Mil	1	-1	11	14	25
Russell Martin	Pit	3	6	2	8	19
Hank Conger	LAA	3	-2	0	16	17
Rene Rivera	SD	0	6	0	9	15
Caleb Joseph	Bal	4	5	0	5	14
Tyler Flowers	CWS	5	1	-3	8	11
Miguel Montero	Ari	-1	-4	0	15	10
Mike Zunino	Sea	-4	1	-5	16	8
Yan Gomes	Cle	-5	2	5	6	8
Buster Posey	SF	0	-2	-1	11	8
Brian McCann	NYY	0	2	0	6	8
Salvador Perez	KC	5	4	2	-4	7
Yadier Molina	StL	4	5	4	-6	7
Jose Lobaton	Was	1	1	3	1	6
Ryan Hanigan	TB	2	-1	3	0	4
Alex Avila	Det	-1	2	4	-3	2
Jason Castro	Hou	-3	-2	3	4	2
Wilson Ramos	Was	-2	4	1	-1	2
Carlos Ruiz	Phi	4	2	1	-6	1
Robinson Chirinos	Tex	-1	5	1	-4	1
Jose Molina	TB	-2	0	-3	6	1
Evan Gattis	Atl	2	-2	-3	2	-1
Yasmani Grandal	SD	0	-4	-2	5	-1
Derek Norris	Oak	1	-4	0	0	-3
Nick Hundley	2 tms	-1	-3	1	0	-3
Devin Mesoraco	Cin	1	-3	4	-7	-5
A.J. Ellis	LAD	0	-2	3	-7	-6
Welington Castillo	ChC	-6	6	1	-9	-8
Travis d'Arnaud	NYM	-5	-4	-6	7	-8
Dioner Navarro	Tor	0	-1	4	-17	-14
Chris Iannetta	LAA	-4	0	-4	-6	-14
Wilin Rosario	Col	-5	0	-4	-5	-14
A.J. Pierzynski	2 tms	-4	-5	0	-5	-14
Kurt Suzuki	Min	0	-5	3	-15	-17
Jarrod Saltalamacchia	Mia	3	-3	-6	-16	-22

Catchers - 2012 Runs Saved

Player	Team	Adj ER	Stolen Bases	Bunts and GFP/DME	Strike Zone	Total
Yadier Molina	StL	3	8	7	11	29
Ryan Hanigan	Cin	1	6	3	13	23
Buster Posey	SF	-2	2	2	14	16
Jonathan Lucroy	Mil	-2	-2	5	15	16
Jose Molina	TB	-1	4	-2	13	14
Matt Wieters	Bal	3	6	1	3	13
Brian McCann	Atl	3	-1	0	11	13
Martin Maldonado	Mil	1	1	2	7	11
Josh Thole	NYM	4	-1	-1	8	10
Miguel Montero	Ari	0	2	0	7	9
Salvador Perez	KC	1	7	2	-3	7
Jeff Mathis	Tor	0	3	1	3	7
Alex Avila	Det	3	2	-1	1	5
Jarrod Saltalamacchia	Bos	-4	-3	3	9	5
Jesus Flores	Was	1	-1	1	4	5
Russell Martin	NYY	-5	0	0	9	4
Carlos Ruiz	Phi	-4	1	6	1	4
Kelly Shoppach	2 tms	5	2	-3	-1	3
John Buck	Mia	4	-1	1	-3	1
Geovany Soto	2 tms	0	-2	-4	6	0
Chris Snyder	Hou	-3	0	0	2	-1
J.P. Arencibia	Tor	1	-3	3	-5	-4
Joe Mauer	Min	-2	-3	0	0	-5
Michael McKenry	Pit	-1	-2	2	-4	-5
A.J. Ellis	LAD	2	2	-2	-8	-6
Miguel Olivo	Sea	-4	4	-1	-5	-6
Chris Iannetta	LAA	-1	-1	2	-6	-6
Jason Castro	Hou	3	-1	-3	-7	-8
A.J. Pierzynski	CWS	2	2	-7	-7	-10
Kurt Suzuki	2 tms	-4	4	3	-14	-11
Mike Napoli	Tex	-3	-2	1	-8	-12
Lou Marson	Cle	0	-4	-3	-5	-12
Carlos Santana	Cle	0	3	-4	-14	-15
Wilin Rosario	Col	4	3	-13	-12	-18
Rod Barajas	Pit	1	-10	-4	-8	-21

First Basemen - 3-Year Runs Saved

Player	Range & Pos	Bunts	GDP	GFP/DME	Total
Adrian Gonzalez	28	3	1	6	38
Anthony Rizzo	25	-4	1	4	26
Joey Votto	17	-3	-1	7	20
Mark Teixeira	13	1	1	4	19
Yonder Alonso	10	4	0	4	18
Mike Napoli	16	1	0	0	17
Paul Goldschmidt	15	-3	0	3	15
Albert Pujols	11	1	0	3	15
Justin Morneau	7	0	1	5	13
Brandon Belt	12	4	1	-5	12
Adam LaRoche	-1	3	2	5	9
James Loney	0	1	2	6	9
Matt Adams	8	1	0	-2	7
Nick Swisher	4	-1	1	3	7
Lucas Duda	2	0	0	4	6
Lyle Overbay	2	0	0	3	5
Freddie Freeman	-2	-4	1	8	3
Eric Hosmer	-5	1	1	4	1
Mitch Moreland	1	0	0	0	1
Mark Trumbo	2	1	0	-2	1
Gaby Sanchez	5	-2	0	-3	0
Logan Morrison	3	0	0	-3	0
Chris Davis	0	-1	0	-2	-3
Allen Craig	-6	1	0	1	-4
Mark Reynolds	-7	0	0	2	-5
Carlos Pena	-2	-2	0	-1	-5
Ike Davis	-4	0	0	-2	-6
Adam Lind	-11	1	-1	2	-9
Garrett Jones	-8	1	0	-4	-11
Justin Smoak	-10	-1	-2	1	-12
Edwin Encarnacion	-12	-1	-1	0	-14
Paul Konerko	-13	0	-1	0	-14
Ryan Howard	-7	0	-1	-9	-17
Prince Fielder	-14	-3	1	-3	-19
Brandon Moss	-20	1	-1	0	-20

First Basemen - 2013 Runs Saved

Player	Team	Range & Pos	Bunts	GDP	GFP/DME	Total
Anthony Rizzo	ChC	16	-3	0	3	16
Paul Goldschmidt	Ari	11	0	0	2	13
Adrian Gonzalez	LAD	11	-1	0	1	11
Mike Napoli	Bos	9	1	0	0	10
Freddie Freeman	Atl	6	-1	0	2	7
Yonder Alonso	SD	8	0	0	-1	7
Joey Votto	Cin	7	-1	-1	1	6
Nick Swisher	Cle	5	-1	1	1	6
Justin Morneau	2 tms	2	1	0	2	5
Lyle Overbay	NYY	3	0	0	2	5
James Loney	TB	-1	1	1	3	4
Brandon Belt	SF	7	1	0	-4	4
Eric Hosmer	KC	3	0	1	-1	3
Mark Trumbo	LAA	3	1	0	-2	2
Adam LaRoche	Was	-2	1	0	2	1
Mitch Moreland	Tex	1	1	0	-1	1
Ike Davis	NYM	1	1	0	-1	1
Todd Helton	Col	-5	1	0	4	0
Allen Craig	StL	-2	1	0	0	-1
Ryan Howard	Phi	0	0	0	-1	-1
Garrett Jones	Pit	-3	1	0	1	-1
Matt Adams	StL	-1	1	0	-2	-2
Paul Konerko	CWS	-3	0	0	0	-3
Gaby Sanchez	Pit	-1	-2	0	0	-3
Juan Francisco	Mil	-1	0	0	-2	-3
Logan Morrison	Mia	-2	0	1	-3	-4
Mark Reynolds	2 tms	-4	0	0	-1	-5
Chris Carter	Hou	-5	1	0	-1	-5
Chris Davis	Bal	-6	-1	0	0	-7
Adam Lind	Tor	-8	0	0	1	-7
Justin Smoak	Sea	-6	0	-1	-1	-8
Edwin Encarnacion	Tor	-6	1	-1	-2	-8
Brandon Moss	Oak	-12	1	-1	0	-12
Adam Dunn	CWS	-9	0	0	-3	-12
Prince Fielder	Det	-13	-1	0	1	-13

First Basemen - 2014 Runs Saved

Player	Team	Range & Pos	Bunts	GDP	GFP/DME	Total
Adrian Gonzalez	LAD	6	2	1	2	11
Yonder Alonso	SD	4	2	0	3	9
Steve Pearce	Bal	6	0	0	3	9
Matt Adams	StL	7	1	0	0	8
Justin Morneau	Col	4	0	1	3	8
Chris Davis	Bal	6	0	0	2	8
Mike Napoli	Bos	7	0	0	0	7
Anthony Rizzo	ChC	6	-1	0	1	6
Albert Pujols	LAA	5	0	0	1	6
Lucas Duda	NYM	3	0	0	2	5
Joey Votto	Cin	4	0	0	1	5
Joe Mauer	Min	4	0	-1	1	4
Eric Hosmer	KC	-1	0	0	4	3
Brandon Belt	SF	2	1	0	0	3
Mark Teixeira	NYY	1	0	0	1	2
Mark Reynolds	Mil	3	0	0	-1	2
Paul Goldschmidt	Ari	3	-1	0	-1	1
Adam LaRoche	Was	-2	0	1	1	0
Logan Morrison	Sea	1	0	-1	0	0
Brayan Pena	Cin	1	0	0	-1	0
James Loney	TB	-5	1	0	3	-1
Miguel Cabrera	Det	-2	0	1	0	-1
Lyle Overbay	Mil	-2	0	0	1	-1
Gaby Sanchez	Pit	-2	0	0	-1	-3
Ike Davis	2 tms	-2	0	0	-2	-4
Carlos Santana	Cle	-5	1	0	0	-4
Justin Smoak	Sea	-3	0	-1	0	-4
Brandon Moss	Oak	-5	0	0	1	-4
Nick Swisher	Cle	-4	0	0	0	-4
Garrett Jones	Mia	-2	0	0	-3	-5
Jon Singleton	Hou	-5	1	0	-1	-5
Edwin Encarnacion	Tor	-4	0	0	-1	-5
Freddie Freeman	Atl	-9	-2	1	3	-7
Ryan Howard	Phi	-5	0	0	-5	-10
Jose Abreu	CWS	-6	0	0	-4	-10

First Basemen - 2012 Runs Saved

Player	Team	Range & Pos	Bunts	GDP	GFP/DME	Total
Mark Teixeira	NYY	12	1	1	3	17
Adrian Gonzalez	2 tms	11	2	0	3	16
Joey Votto	Cin	6	-2	0	5	9
Adam LaRoche	Was	3	2	1	2	8
Albert Pujols	LAA	6	0	0	2	8
James Loney	2 tms	6	-1	1	0	6
Gaby Sanchez	2 tms	8	0	0	-2	6
Brandon Belt	SF	3	2	1	-1	5
Anthony Rizzo	ChC	3	0	1	0	4
Freddie Freeman	Atl	1	-1	0	3	3
Yonder Alonso	SD	-2	2	0	2	2
Casey McGehee	2 tms	0	1	0	1	2
Paul Goldschmidt	Ari	1	-2	0	2	1
Todd Helton	Col	0	1	0	0	1
Adam Lind	Tor	2		-1	0	1
Carlos Pena	TB	3	-1	0	-2	0
Justin Smoak	Sea	-1	-1	0	2	0
Justin Morneau	Min	1	-1	0	0	0
Mitch Moreland	Tex	-1	0	0	1	0
Casey Kotchman	Cle	0	0	-1	0	-1
Edwin Encarnacion	Tor	-2	-2	0	3	-1
Mark Reynolds	Bal	-6	0	0	4	-2
Ike Davis	NYM	-3	-1	0	1	-3
Allen Craig	StL	-5	1	0	1	-3
Ty Wigginton	Phi	-2	0	0	-1	-3
Prince Fielder	Det	-2	-1	1	-2	-4
Bryan LaHair	ChC	-4	1	0	-1	-4
Eric Hosmer	KC	-7	1	0	1	-5
Carlos Lee	2 tms	-4	0	0	-1	-5
Corey Hart	Mil	-5	0	0	0	-5
Garrett Jones	Pit	-3	0	0	-2	-5
Chris Carter	Oak	-3	1	0	-3	-5
Brett Wallace	Hou	0	-2	0	-3	-5
Ryan Howard	Phi	-2	0	-1	-3	-6
Paul Konerko	CWS	-10	0	-1	0	-11

Second Basemen - 3-Year Runs Saved

Player	Range & Pos	GDP	GFP/DME	Total
Darwin Barney	42	2	5	49
Dustin Pedroia	37	1	5	43
DJ LeMahieu	30	1	3	34
Ian Kinsler	31	2	-1	32
Mark Ellis	23	0	6	29
Robinson Cano	20	0	1	21
Brandon Phillips	20	-4	2	18
Dustin Ackley	12	3	-1	14
Eric Sogard	11	-4	5	12
Brian Dozier	7	-2	4	9
Chase Utley	13	-4	-1	8
Kelly Johnson	11	-1	-3	7
Emilio Bonifacio	7	0	-1	6
Howie Kendrick	2	0	3	5
Danny Espinosa	2	3	0	5
Donovan Solano	7	0	-3	4
Chris Getz	0	2	2	4
Neil Walker	0	0	3	3
Ben Zobrist	8	-2	-3	3
Omar Infante	6	2	-6	2
Matt Carpenter	-1	2	-2	-1
Brian Roberts	0	-1	-2	-3
Scooter Gennett	-1	-2	0	-3
Dee Gordon	-2	0	-2	-4
Gordon Beckham	-13	5	2	-6
Logan Forsythe	-4	-2	-1	-7
Jason Kipnis	-1	-2	-6	-9
Jedd Gyorko	-5	-5	0	-10
Marco Scutaro	-8	-4	-2	-14
Jemile Weeks	-14	-1	-1	-16
Dan Uggla	-13	2	-6	-17
Aaron Hill	-19	-4	5	-18
Jose Altuve	-31	3	0	-28
Daniel Murphy	-24	-4	-6	-34
Rickie Weeks	-55	-3	-4	-62

Second Basemen - 2013 Runs Saved

Player	Team	Range & Pos	GDP	GFP/DME	Total
Dustin Pedroia	Bos	13	0	2	15
Mark Ellis	LAD	10	0	2	12
Darwin Barney	ChC	11	0	0	11
Ian Kinsler	Tex	8	2	1	11
DJ LeMahieu	Col	7	1	2	10
Emilio Bonifacio	2 tms	9	0	1	10
Elliot Johnson	2 tms	8	1	1	10
Brian Dozier	Min	11	-2	0	9
Neil Walker	Pit	8	-2	3	9
Ben Zobrist	TB	6	-1	2	7
Robinson Cano	NYY	6	-2	2	6
Eric Sogard	Oak	3	-1	3	5
Chris Getz	KC	3	1	1	5
Donovan Solano	Mia	3	0	1	4
Ryan Flaherty	Bal	0	2	1	3
Scooter Gennett	Mil	2	0	0	2
Brandon Phillips	Cin	5	-3	-1	1
Matt Carpenter	StL	0	2	-2	0
Nick Franklin	Sea	1	-2	1	0
Brian Roberts	Bal	-1	1	0	0
Jason Kipnis	Cle	1	-1	-1	-1
Jedd Gyorko	SD	1	-2	0	-1
Jose Altuve	Hou	-7	3	1	-3
Howie Kendrick	LAA	0	-1	-2	-3
Gordon Beckham	CWS	-2	1	-2	-3
Chase Utley	Phi	-3	-1	0	-4
Omar Infante	Det	-3	1	-3	-5
Anthony Rendon	Was	-5	1	-1	-5
Derek Dietrich	Mia	-7	0	1	-6
Marco Scutaro	SF	-7	-1	1	-7
Aaron Hill	Ari	-8	-2	1	-9
Josh Rutledge	Col	-9	0	0	-9
Daniel Murphy	NYM	-10	0	-3	-13
Rickie Weeks	Mil	-14	-1	0	-15
Dan Uggla	Atl	-15	2	-6	-19

Second Basemen - 2014 Runs Saved

Player	Team	Range & Pos	GDP	GFP/DME	Total
Ian Kinsler	Det	23	-1	-2	20
Dustin Pedroia	Bos	19	-2	0	17
DJ LeMahieu	Col	15	1	0	16
Jonathan Schoop	Bal	5	5	0	10
Darwin Barney	2 tms	9	0	1	10
Kolten Wong	StL	7	2	0	9
Howie Kendrick	LAA	4	2	1	7
Brandon Phillips	Cin	5	0	1	6
Eric Sogard	Oak	7	-3	1	5
Brandon Hicks	SF	1	2	2	5
Chase Utley	Phi	6	-2	-1	3
Gordon Beckham	2 tms	-2	2	3	3
Brian Roberts	NYY	7	-2	-2	3
Ryan Goins	Tor	1	1	1	3
Logan Forsythe	TB	1	0	1	2
Omar Infante	KC	3	-1	-1	1
Ben Zobrist	TB	5	-1	-3	1
Brian Dozier	Min	-4	0	4	0
Robinson Cano	Sea	-3	2	1	0
Danny Espinosa	Was	-3	2	0	-1
Joe Panik	SF	-3	2	0	-1
Donovan Solano	Mia	1	0	-2	-1
Neil Walker	Pit	-5	2	1	-2
Munenori Kawasaki	Tor	-3	0	0	-3
Tommy La Stella	Atl	-7	1	2	-4
Dee Gordon	LAD	-3	0	-2	-5
Scooter Gennett	Mil	-3	-2	0	-5
Jose Altuve	Hou	-10	2	1	-7
Aaron Hill	Ari	-9	0	2	-7
Jedd Gyorko	SD	-6	-3	0	-9
Daniel Murphy	NYM	-6	-3	-1	-10
Asdrubal Cabrera	Was	-11	1	0	-10
Jason Kipnis	Cle	-6	-2	-3	-11
Rougned Odor	Tex	-12	1	0	-11
Rickie Weeks	Mil	-15	-1	-1	-17

Second Basemen - 2012 Runs Saved

Player	Team	Range & Pos	GDP	GFP/DME	Total
Darwin Barney	ChC	22	2	4	28
Robinson Cano	NYY	17	0	-2	15
Alexi Casilla	Min	10	2	3	15
Dustin Ackley	Sea	9	2	0	11
Brandon Phillips	Cin	10	-1	2	11
Dustin Pedroia	Bos	5	3	3	11
Mark Ellis	LAD	8	0	2	10
Chase Utley	Phi	10	-1	0	9
Jamey Carroll	Min	5	2	1	8
DJ LeMahieu	Col	8	-1	1	8
Freddy Galvis	Phi	3	2	2	7
Omar Infante	2 tms	6	2	-2	6
Kelly Johnson	Tor	9	-1	-3	5
Robert Andino	Bal	4	2	-1	5
Dan Uggla	Atl	3	0	1	4
Jason Kipnis	Cle	4	1	-2	3
Danny Espinosa	Was	3	0	0	3
Ryan Roberts	2 tms	0	1	2	3
Ian Kinsler	Tex	0	1	0	1
Howie Kendrick	LAA	-2	-1	4	1
Donovan Solano	Mia	3	0	-2	1
Daniel Descalso	StL	0	0	0	0
Ramon Santiago	Det	-1	0	0	-1
Skip Schumaker	StL	0	0	-1	-1
Aaron Hill	Ari	-2	-2	2	-2
Chris Getz	KC	-4	1	1	-2
Neil Walker	Pit	-3	0	-1	-4
Ben Zobrist	TB	-3	0	-2	-5
Gordon Beckham	CWS	-9	2	1	-6
Marco Scutaro	2 tms	0	-3	-3	-6
Daniel Murphy	NYM	-8	-1	-2	-11
Logan Forsythe	SD	-8	-2	-1	-11
Ryan Theriot	SF	-11	0	-1	-12
Jemile Weeks	Oak	-12	-1	-1	-14
Jose Altuve	Hou	-14	-2	-2	-18
Rickie Weeks	Mil	-26	-1	-3	-30

20

Third Basemen - 3-Year Runs Saved

Player	Range & Pos	Bunts	GDP	GFP/DME	Total
Manny Machado	46	3	1	-2	48
Nolan Arenado	40	2	1	3	46
Josh Donaldson	29	0	1	6	36
Juan Uribe	40	1	-1	-4	36
David Wright	34	2	-1	-1	34
Brett Lawrie	25	-1	0	0	24
Adrian Beltre	8	5	2	2	17
Chase Headley	21	-2	-2	-2	15
Todd Frazier	17	-1	-1	0	15
Martin Prado	13	-4	2	-1	10
Mike Moustakas	15	-7	2	-1	9
Evan Longoria	6	1	0	1	8
Anthony Rendon	-2	7	2	0	7
Matt Dominguez	-1	1	-1	5	4
Luis Valbuena	0	2	0	-1	1
Alberto Callaspo	1	0	0	0	1
Matt Carpenter	-1	2	1	-1	1
Trevor Plouffe	-3	-1	2	0	-2
Ryan Zimmerman	-15	5	2	5	-3
Kyle Seager	-4	-1	2	-2	-5
Casey McGehee	-4	-3	1	1	-5
Pablo Sandoval	5	-6	-1	-4	-6
Pedro Alvarez	6	-7	-2	-4	-7
Cody Asche	-10	0	0	0	-10
Juan Francisco	-8	-2	0	0	-10
Eric Chavez	-9	-1	-2	0	-12
Aramis Ramirez	-7	0	-3	-3	-13
Will Middlebrooks	-11	0	-1	-4	-16
Lonnie Chisenhall	-20	-1	0	4	-17
Conor Gillaspie	-25	-1	0	7	-19
Chris Nelson	-18	-1	0	0	-19
David Freese	-25	0	1	3	-21
Miguel Cabrera	-28	1	3	1	-23
Nick Castellanos	-29	0	-2	1	-30
Chris Johnson	-26	1	-3	-3	-31

Third Basemen - 2013 Runs Saved

Player	Team	Range & Pos	Bunts	GDP	GFP/DME	Total
Manny Machado	Bal	36	0	1	-2	35
Nolan Arenado	Col	27	2	0	1	30
Juan Uribe	LAD	18	0	-1	-2	15
Josh Donaldson	Oak	10	1	0	1	12
Evan Longoria	TB	10	1	0	1	12
Matt Dominguez	Hou	6	1	-1	2	8
Luis Valbuena	ChC	4	2	0	0	6
Todd Frazier	Cin	5	-1	0	1	5
Chase Headley	SD	6	-2	0	1	5
David Wright	NYM	7	1	0	-3	5
Brett Lawrie	Tor	3	-1	0	2	4
Ed Lucas	Mia	3	0	0	1	4
Pedro Alvarez	Pit	6	-1	-1	-1	3
Placido Polanco	Mia	3	0	0	0	3
Lonnie Chisenhall	Cle	-3	1	1	2	1
Trevor Plouffe	Min	1	0	1	-2	0
Martin Prado	Ari	1	-2	0	1	0
Ryan Zimmerman	Was	-8	2	1	4	-1
Yuniesky Betancourt	Mil	1	-1	-1	0	-1
Mike Moustakas	KC	-3	0	1	-1	-3
Chris Nelson	3 tms	-3	0	0	0	-3
Conor Gillaspie	CWS	-7	0	0	3	-4
Adrian Beltre	Tex	-7	1	0	1	-5
Pablo Sandoval	SF	-3	-2	0	0	-5
Alberto Callaspo	2 tms	-5	-1	0	0	-6
Mark Reynolds	2 tms	-4	-2	0	0	-6
Chris Johnson	Atl	-6	0	-1	0	-7
Cody Asche	Phi	-8	0	0	1	-7
Kyle Seager	Sea	-10	1	1	0	-8
Will Middlebrooks	Bos	-5	0	-1	-2	-8
Eric Chavez	Ari	-7	-1	-1	-1	-10
Aramis Ramirez	Mil	-9	-1	-1	-1	-12
David Freese	StL	-17	1	1	1	-14
Miguel Cabrera	Det	-19	1	1	-1	-18
Michael Young	2 tms	-17	0	-1	-2	-20

Third Basemen - 2014 Runs Saved

Player	Team	Range & Pos	Bunts	GDP	GFP/DME	Total
Josh Donaldson	Oak	15	-1	1	5	20
Juan Uribe	LAD	17	1	1	-2	17
Nolan Arenado	Col	13	0	1	2	16
David Wright	NYM	13	1	-1	0	13
Chase Headley	2 tms	14	0	0	-1	13
Anthony Rendon	Was	3	6	2	1	12
Kyle Seager	Sea	10	0	1	-1	10
Adrian Beltre	Tex	6	1	1	1	9
Martin Prado	2 tms	11	-2	1	-2	8
Josh Harrison	Pit	6	1	0	1	8
Todd Frazier	Cin	6	1	0	0	7
Trevor Plouffe	Min	5	-1	1	1	6
Manny Machado	Bal	4	2	0	0	6
Justin Turner	LAD	5	0	0	1	6
Pablo Sandoval	SF	5	-1	0	0	4
Brett Lawrie	Tor	1	0	0	-1	0
Mike Olt	ChC	-1	0	0	0	-1
Casey McGehee	Mia	-4	-1	1	2	-2
Matt Carpenter	StL	-2	1	1	-2	-2
Mike Moustakas	KC	3	-2	0	-3	-2
Yangervis Solarte	2 tms	0	-1	0	-1	-2
Danny Valencia	2 tms	-1	-1	0	0	-2
Cody Asche	Phi	-2	0	0	-1	-3
Matt Dominguez	Hou	-6	0	0	2	-4
Evan Longoria	TB	-5	0	0	0	-5
Aramis Ramirez	Mil	-2	-1	-1	-1	-5
Pedro Alvarez	Pit	2	-4	-1	-2	-5
Will Middlebrooks	Bos	-6	1	0	0	-5
Juan Francisco	Tor	-7	-1	0	1	-7
David Freese	LAA	-9	-2	0	2	-9
Luis Valbuena	ChC	-8	-1	-1	0	-10
Conor Gillaspie	CWS	-16	1	0	3	-12
Chris Johnson	Atl	-10	1	-1	-3	-13
Lonnie Chisenhall	Cle	-12	-2	-1	1	-14
Nick Castellanos	Det	-29	0	-2	1	-30

Third Basemen - 2012 Runs Saved

Player	Team	Range & Pos	Bunts	GDP	GFP/DME	Total
Brett Lawrie	Tor	21	0	0	-1	20
David Wright	NYM	14	0	0	2	16
Mike Moustakas	KC	15	-5	1	3	14
Adrian Beltre	Tex	9	3	1	0	13
Alberto Callaspo	LAA	6	1	0	0	7
Manny Machado	Bal	6	1	0	0	7
Brandon Inge	2 tms	4	3	0	-1	6
Ryan Roberts	2 tms	4	0	0	2	6
Luis Valbuena	ChC	4	1	1	-1	5
Aramis Ramirez	Mil	4	2	-1	-1	4
Josh Donaldson	Oak	4	0	0	0	4
Todd Frazier	Cin	6	-1	-1	-1	3
Ian Stewart	ChC	1	1	0	1	3
David Freese	StL	1	1	0	0	2
Jack Hannahan	Cle	4	0	0	-2	2
Placido Polanco	Phi	-1	2	0	1	2
Kevin Frandsen	Phi	0	1	-1	2	2
Chipper Jones	Atl	-4	1	0	3	0
Scott Rolen	Cin	1	0	-1	0	0
Ryan Zimmerman	Was	-7	3	1	2	-1
Kevin Youkilis	2 tms	-3	0	1	1	-1
Alex Rodriguez	NYY	0	-2	1	-1	-2
Eric Chavez	NYY	-1	0	-1	0	-2
Chase Headley	SD	1	0	-2	-2	-3
Will Middlebrooks	Bos	0	-1	0	-2	-3
Miguel Cabrera	Det	-8	0	2	2	-4
Pedro Alvarez	Pit	-2	-2	0	-1	-5
Pablo Sandoval	SF	3	-3	-1	-4	-5
Wilson Betemit	Bal	-6	1	0	-1	-6
Kyle Seager	Sea	-4	-2	0	-1	-7
Trevor Plouffe	Min	-9	0	0	1	-8
Chris Johnson	2 tms	-10	0	-1	0	-11
Hanley Ramirez	2 tms	-13	0	1	1	-11
Jordan Pacheco	Col	-14	1	0	0	-13
Chris Nelson	Col	-17	-1	0	0	-18

Shortstops - 3-Year Runs Saved

Player	Range & Pos	GDP	GFP/DME	Total
Andrelton Simmons	74	6	8	88
J.J. Hardy	20	7	9	36
Zack Cozart	37	-3	1	35
Brendan Ryan	22	4	5	31
Clint Barmes	27	1	0	28
Brandon Crawford	19	3	0	22
Pedro Florimon	23	0	-1	22
Jhonny Peralta	13	2	1	16
Cliff Pennington	12	2	0	14
Mike Aviles	13	1	-1	13
Alexei Ramirez	2	7	2	11
Pete Kozma	10	3	-2	11
Jordy Mercer	10	0	-2	8
Troy Tulowitzki	6	1	0	7
Elvis Andrus	5	4	-3	6
Marwin Gonzalez	1	2	3	6
Jean Segura	9	-2	-2	5
Didi Gregorius	4	-2	-2	0
Alcides Escobar	-3	0	1	-2
Ruben Tejada	-4	-1	2	-3
Adeiny Hechavarria	-4	-2	2	-4
Everth Cabrera	3	-7	0	-4
Stephen Drew	-4	-2	1	-5
Brad Miller	1	-4	-2	-5
Yunel Escobar	5	-4	-7	-6
Erick Aybar	-12	0	5	-7
Jonathan Villar	-2	-1	-4	-7
Ian Desmond	-7	3	-4	-8
Starlin Castro	-2	0	-10	-12
Hanley Ramirez	-9	0	-4	-13
Jimmy Rollins	-24	-2	7	-19
Asdrubal Cabrera	-27	1	-2	-28
Jed Lowrie	-24	-5	-2	-31
Derek Jeter	-34	-3	2	-35
Jose Reyes	-37	3	-2	-36

Shortstops - 2013 Runs Saved

Player	Team	Range & Pos	GDP	GFP/DME	Total
Andrelton Simmons	Atl	37	2	2	41
Pedro Florimon	Min	12	0	0	12
Clint Barmes	Pit	13	0	-1	12
Elvis Andrus	Tex	8	2	1	11
J.J. Hardy	Bal	3	3	2	8
Pete Kozma	StL	8	2	-2	8
Troy Tulowitzki	Col	7	0	-1	6
Brendan Ryan	2 tms	5	-1	2	6
Alcides Escobar	KC	4	1	-1	4
Yunel Escobar	TB	5	0	-1	4
Zack Cozart	Cin	5	-2	1	4
Jean Segura	Mil	3	1	-1	3
Hanley Ramirez	LAD	6	-1	-2	3
Brandon Crawford	SF	4	-1	-1	2
Alexei Ramirez	CWS	0	2	-1	1
Jhonny Peralta	Det	0	0	0	0
Jose Iglesias	2 tms	-4	1	3	0
Didi Gregorius	Ari	2	-1	-2	-1
Stephen Drew	Bos	-2	-1	1	-2
Jordy Mercer	Pit	0	-1	-1	-2
Brad Miller	Sea	3	-2	-3	-2
Ian Desmond	Was	-2	1	-2	-3
Adeiny Hechavarria	Mia	-2	0	-1	-3
Everth Cabrera	SD	-4	0	1	-3
Jose Reyes	Tor	-7	2	1	-4
Ronny Cedeno	2 tms	-5	0	0	-5
Jonathan Villar	Hou	-2	0	-3	-5
Ruben Tejada	NYM	-7	1	0	-6
Erick Aybar	LAA	-5	-2	0	-7
Starlin Castro	ChC	-5	0	-3	-8
Omar Quintanilla	NYM	-6	-2	0	-8
Jimmy Rollins	Phi	-18	1	2	-15
Asdrubal Cabrera	Cle	-16	0	0	-16
Jed Lowrie	Oak	-17	-3	2	-18
Eduardo Nunez	NYY	-25	-1	-2	-28

Shortstops - 2014 Runs Saved

Player	Team	Range & Pos	GDP	GFP/DME	Total
Andrelton Simmons	Atl	21	3	4	28
Zack Cozart	Cin	20	-1	0	19
Jhonny Peralta	StL	13	2	2	17
J.J. Hardy	Bal	3	4	3	10
Jordy Mercer	Pit	9	1	-1	9
Brandon Crawford	SF	5	3	0	8
Troy Tulowitzki	Col	5	1	1	7
Alexi Amarista	SD	7	-2	2	7
Chris Owings	Ari	6	0	-1	5
Jimmy Rollins	Phi	4	-2	2	4
Marwin Gonzalez	Hou	1	0	3	4
Ruben Tejada	NYM	6	-2	-1	3
Everth Cabrera	SD	7	-4	0	3
Jean Segura	Mil	7	-3	-2	2
Ian Desmond	Was	2	1	-2	1
Didi Gregorius	Ari	1	-1	0	0
Jonathan Villar	Hou	0	-1	-1	-2
Erick Aybar	LAA	-6	1	2	-3
Adeiny Hechavarria	Mia	-4	-2	3	-3
Brad Miller	Sea	-2	-2	1	-3
Andrew Romine	Det	-4	0	1	-3
Alcides Escobar	KC	-4	-1	1	-4
Alexei Ramirez	CWS	-10	3	3	-4
Eugenio Suarez	Det	-6	2	-1	-5
Eduardo Escobar	Min	-3	-2	-1	-6
Starlin Castro	ChC	-6	2	-3	-7
Asdrubal Cabrera	2 tms	-5	-1	-1	-7
Hanley Ramirez	LAD	-10	1	0	-9
Xander Bogaerts	Bos	-6	-3	0	-9
Josh Rutledge	Col	-7	-2	0	-9
Jed Lowrie	Oak	-6	-2	-2	-10
Derek Jeter	NYY	-9	-2	-1	-12
Elvis Andrus	Tex	-12	1	-2	-13
Jose Reyes	Tor	-16	1	-1	-16
Yunel Escobar	TB	-17	-3	-4	-24

Shortstops - 2012 Runs Saved

Player	Team	Range & Pos	GDP	GFP/DME	Total
Brendan Ryan	Sea	21	4	2	27
Andrelton Simmons	Atl	16	1	2	19
J.J. Hardy	Bal	14	0	4	18
Alexei Ramirez	CWS	12	2	0	14
Yunel Escobar	Tor	17	-1	-2	14
Mike Aviles	Bos	14	2	-2	14
Clint Barmes	Pit	11	1	1	13
Zack Cozart	Cin	12	0	0	12
Brandon Crawford	SF	10	1	1	12
Elvis Andrus	Tex	9	1	-2	8
John McDonald	Ari	4	0	3	7
Cliff Pennington	Oak	4	1	0	5
Paul Janish	Atl	3	-1	2	4
Starlin Castro	ChC	9	-2	-4	3
Erick Aybar	LAA	-1	1	3	3
Brian Dozier	Min	-2	2	1	1
Ruben Tejada	NYM	-3	0	3	0
Ben Zobrist	TB	-3	1	2	0
Jhonny Peralta	Det	0	0	-1	-1
Alcides Escobar	KC	-3	0	1	-2
Jed Lowrie	Hou	-1	0	-2	-3
Rafael Furcal	StL	-4	0	0	-4
Everth Cabrera	SD	0	-3	-1	-4
Asdrubal Cabrera	Cle	-6	2	-1	-5
Ian Desmond	Was	-7	1	0	-6
Elliot Johnson	TB	-3	0	-3	-6
Troy Tulowitzki	Col	-6	0	0	-6
Stephen Drew	2 tms	-5	-1	-1	-7
Hanley Ramirez	LAD	-5	0	-2	-7
Jimmy Rollins	Phi	-10	-1	3	-8
Willie Bloomquist	Ari	-9	-2	0	-11
Josh Rutledge	Col	-8	-1	-2	-11
Dee Gordon	LAD	-11	-3	0	-14
Jose Reyes	Mia	-14	0	-2	-16
Derek Jeter	NYY	-20	-1	3	-18

Left Fielders - 3-Year Runs Saved

Player	Range & Pos	OF Arm	GFP/DME	Total
Alex Gordon	27	24	16	67
Starling Marte	25	0	5	30
Yoenis Cespedes	-7	20	2	15
Christian Yelich	23	-8	-2	13
David Murphy	9	1	1	11
Ryan Braun	8	1	0	9
Martin Prado	3	4	2	9
Matt Joyce	6	1	2	9
Eric Young	9	-1	0	8
Daniel Nava	-3	6	5	8
Dustin Ackley	5	2	1	8
Bryce Harper	-1	5	2	6
Michael Brantley	-8	7	6	5
Seth Smith	5	-2	1	4
Carl Crawford	9	-5	-2	2
Khris Davis	8	-4	-2	2
Josh Hamilton	1	1	-2	0
Alejandro De Aza	5	-2	-5	-2
Nate McLouth	3	-3	-3	-3
Alfonso Soriano	-2	-2	0	-4
Rajai Davis	-7	3	0	-4
J.D. Martinez	-10	1	3	-6
Melky Cabrera	-20	8	5	-7
Carlos Gonzalez	-6	-2	0	-8
Dayan Viciedo	-16	5	2	-9
Jonny Gomes	-13	0	3	-10
Ryan Ludwick	-10	-2	1	-11
Domonic Brown	-21	8	1	-12
Justin Upton	1	-6	-7	-12
Jason Kubel	-21	2	6	-13
Michael Morse	-13	-2	-1	-16
Carlos Quentin	-6	-9	-3	-18
Matt Holliday	-6	-12	-2	-20
Josh Willingham	-16	-6	2	-20
Raul Ibanez	-8	-9	-3	-20

Left Fielders - 2013 Runs Saved

Player	Team	Range & Pos	OF Arm	GFP/DME	Total
Starling Marte	Pit	17	-1	2	18
Alex Gordon	KC	5	6	6	17
Carlos Gonzalez	Col	3	4	4	11
David Murphy	Tex	3	2	1	6
Andy Dirks	Det	5	1	0	6
Gregor Blanco	SF	5	1	0	6
Chris Heisey	Cin	6	0	-1	5
Michael Brantley	Cle	-4	4	4	4
Bryce Harper	Was	-1	4	1	4
Vernon Wells	NYY	0	4	0	4
Alfonso Soriano	2 tms	1	0	2	3
Yoenis Cespedes	Oak	3	3	-3	3
Juan Pierre	Mia	9	-5	-1	3
Ryan Braun	Mil	0	2	1	3
Eric Young	2 tms	4	-1	-1	2
Nate McLouth	Bal	3	-1	-1	1
Jason Kubel	2 tms	-3	2	2	1
Carl Crawford	LAD	5	-3	-2	0
Jonny Gomes	Bos	-6	4	2	0
Christian Yelich	Mia	4	-3	-1	0
Daniel Nava	Bos	-1	-1	2	0
Kelly Johnson	TB	-3	3	0	0
J.B. Shuck	LAA	-4	1	2	-1
Andres Torres	SF	4	-1	-4	-1
Alejandro De Aza	CWS	2	-1	-3	-2
Dayan Viciedo	CWS	-11	4	3	-4
Melky Cabrera	Tor	-6	0	2	-4
Domonic Brown	Phi	-11	4	2	-5
Carlos Quentin	SD	2	-5	-2	-5
Josh Willingham	Min	-7	-1	2	-6
Justin Upton	Atl	-3	-3	-3	-9
Oswaldo Arcia	Min	-10	1	-1	-10
Lucas Duda	NYM	-8	-1	-2	-11
Matt Holliday	StL	-4	-7	-2	-13
Raul Ibanez	Sea	-11	-5	-2	-18

Left Fielders - 2014 Runs Saved

Player	Team	Range & Pos	OF Arm	GFP/DME	Total
Alex Gordon	KC	15	9	2	26
Christian Yelich	Mia	19	-5	-1	13
Yoenis Cespedes	2 tms	-7	14	4	11
Dustin Ackley	Sea	5	2	1	8
Starling Marte	Pit	4	1	2	7
David Lough	Bal	7	-1	1	7
Chris Young	2 tms	5	2	-1	6
Eric Young	NYM	4	0	1	5
Brandon Guyer	TB	3	1	1	5
Khris Davis	Mil	8	-3	-1	4
Brett Gardner	NYY	3	-1	1	3
Robbie Grossman	Hou	3	1	-1	3
Matt Joyce	TB	1	1	0	2
Nelson Cruz	Bal	2	0	0	2
Michael Brantley	Cle	-4	3	2	1
Seth Smith	SD	4	-2	-1	1
Carl Crawford	LAD	3	-1	-1	1
Alejandro De Aza	2 tms	3	-1	-2	0
Bryce Harper	Was	-2	1	1	0
J.D. Martinez	Det	-2	0	2	0
Matt Holliday	StL	4	-4	-1	-1
Corey Dickerson	Col	2	-3	-1	-2
Josh Hamilton	LAA	-2	0	0	-2
Josh Willingham	Min	-5	0	3	-2
Justin Upton	Atl	4	-3	-4	-3
Melky Cabrera	Tor	-11	6	2	-3
Ryan Ludwick	Cin	-6	-1	2	-5
Carlos Gonzalez	Col	-2	-4	0	-6
Domonic Brown	Phi	-8	3	-2	-7
Rajai Davis	Det	-4	-2	-1	-7
Dayan Viciedo	CWS	-5	-1	-1	-7
Jonny Gomes	2 tms	-6	-3	1	-8
Shin-Soo Choo	Tex	-6	-2	-1	-9
Michael Morse	SF	-9	-1	0	-10
Chris Coghlan	ChC	-10	-2	1	-11

Left Fielders - 2012 Runs Saved

Player	Team	Range & Pos	OF Arm	GFP/DME	Total
Alex Gordon	KC	7	9	8	24
Martin Prado	Atl	3	5	3	11
Desmond Jennings	TB	9	1	-1	9
Shane Victorino	LAD	7	0	0	7
Ryan Braun	Mil	8	-1	-1	6
David Murphy	Tex	7	-1	0	6
Mark Trumbo	LAA	2	1	2	5
Daniel Nava	Bos	-2	5	1	4
Juan Pierre	Phi	2	0	1	3
Dayan Viciedo	CWS	0	2	0	2
Andy Dirks	Det	5	-3	0	2
Seth Smith	Oak	0	1	1	2
Johnny Damon	Cle	1	0	1	2
Rajai Davis	Tor	-6	5	2	1
Vernon Wells	LAA	4	-5	2	1
Josh Hamilton	Tex	1	1	-1	1
Yoenis Cespedes	Oak	-3	3	1	1
Melky Cabrera	SF	-3	2	1	0
Casper Wells	Sea	-1	2	-1	0
Raul Ibanez	NYY	3	-3	-1	-1
Quintin Berry	Det	0	-1	0	-1
J.D. Martinez	Hou	-4	1	1	-2
Alex Presley	Pit	6	-6	-2	-2
Jason Bay	NYM	-4	0	2	-2
Shelley Duncan	Cle	-3	0	1	-2
Ryan Ludwick	Cin	-3	1	-1	-3
Nate McLouth	2 tms	0	-2	-1	-3
Alfonso Soriano	ChC	-2	-1	-2	-5
Jason Kubel	Ari	-11	2	4	-5
Michael Morse	Was	-3	-1	-1	-5
Matt Holliday	StL	-6	-1	1	-6
Logan Morrison	Mia	-4	-1	-1	-6
Carlos Quentin	SD	-6	-3	-1	-10
Josh Willingham	Min	-4	-5	-3	-12
Carlos Gonzalez	Col	-7	-2	-4	-13

23

Center Fielders - 3-Year Runs Saved

Player	Range & Pos	OF Arm	GFP/DME	Total
Juan Lagares	31	17	4	52
Carlos Gomez	20	8	7	35
Lorenzo Cain	32	0	3	35
Leonys Martin	9	18	2	29
Craig Gentry	17	3	6	26
Jarrod Dyson	23	2	-2	23
Michael Bourn	16	3	2	21
Denard Span	20	-4	4	20
A.J. Pollock	14	1	4	19
Peter Bourjos	16	0	-1	15
Colby Rasmus	6	6	1	13
Jacoby Ellsbury	15	-4	1	12
Austin Jackson	11	-3	1	9
Marcell Ozuna	5	3	0	8
Adam Eaton	9	-2	1	8
Brett Gardner	6	-1	3	8
Cameron Maybin	9	-7	2	4
Desmond Jennings	3	-4	0	-1
Mike Trout	4	-11	5	-2
Drew Stubbs	-1	2	-3	-2
Michael Brantley	-5	-2	5	-2
Chris Young	3	-4	-1	-2
Jon Jay	2	-5	-1	-4
Curtis Granderson	-4	-3	1	-6
Adam Jones	-20	10	-1	-11
B.J. Upton	-11	1	-3	-13
Andrew McCutchen	0	-7	-7	-14
Coco Crisp	-8	-10	2	-16
Shin-Soo Choo	-16	1	-3	-18
Angel Pagan	-12	-3	-4	-19
Ben Revere	-12	-6	-3	-21
Alejandro De Aza	-10	-4	-7	-21
Matt Kemp	-33	7	0	-26
Michael Saunders	-26	-1	0	-27
Dexter Fowler	-21	-12	-2	-35

Center Fielders - 2013 Runs Saved

Player	Team	Range & Pos	OF Arm	GFP/DME	Total
Carlos Gomez	Mil	19	6	7	32
Juan Lagares	NYM	11	11	4	26
Lorenzo Cain	KC	10	4	3	17
Leonys Martin	Tex	9	6	-1	14
Jacoby Ellsbury	Bos	12	0	1	13
Colby Rasmus	Tor	8	2	2	12
A.J. Pollock	Ari	11	1	0	12
Gregor Blanco	SF	8	0	-1	7
Craig Gentry	Tex	7	0	0	7
Jarrod Dyson	KC	7	0	-1	6
Andrew McCutchen	Pit	3	3	-1	5
Brett Gardner	NYY	3	-1	3	5
Brandon Barnes	Hou	1	4	0	5
Austin Jackson	Det	3	2	-1	4
Will Venable	SD	6	-1	-1	4
Denard Span	Was	5	-4	2	3
Coco Crisp	Oak	7	-4	0	3
Michael Bourn	Cle	2	0	0	2
Aaron Hicks	Min	-5	2	5	2
B.J. Upton	Atl	1	0	-1	0
Adam Jones	Bal	-8	7	0	-1
Ben Revere	Phi	-3	0	0	-3
Andre Ethier	LAD	-4	1	0	-3
Dexter Fowler	Col	0	-4	0	-4
Justin Ruggiano	Mia	-2	0	-2	-4
David DeJesus	3 tms	-2	-3	0	-5
Matt Kemp	LAD	-8	2	1	-5
Alexi Amarista	SD	-5	-1	1	-5
Desmond Jennings	TB	-2	-2	-2	-6
Angel Pagan	SF	-7	-1	-1	-9
Jon Jay	StL	-3	-5	-2	-10
Mike Trout	LAA	-5	-3	-3	-11
Michael Saunders	Sea	-13	-1	0	-14
Alejandro De Aza	CWS	-6	-4	-5	-15
Shin-Soo Choo	Cin	-16	1	-3	-18

Center Fielders - 2014 Runs Saved

Player	Team	Range & Pos	OF Arm	GFP/DME	Total
Juan Lagares	NYM	20	6	0	26
Leonys Martin	Tex	1	12	3	16
Jackie Bradley Jr.	Bos	11	4	0	15
Billy Hamilton	Cin	8	4	2	14
Lorenzo Cain	KC	15	-3	2	14
Jarrod Dyson	KC	12	1	0	13
Ender Inciarte	Ari	11	1	1	13
Adam Eaton	CWS	11	-2	2	11
Marcell Ozuna	Mia	6	2	0	8
A.J. Pollock	Ari	4	0	4	8
Peter Bourjos	StL	9	0	-2	7
Jon Jay	StL	2	2	1	5
Sam Fuld	2 tms	3	1	1	5
Desmond Jennings	TB	4	-2	2	4
Adam Jones	Bal	-2	4	1	3
Cameron Maybin	SD	6	-3	-1	2
Carlos Gomez	Mil	2	-1	0	1
Charlie Blackmon	Col	2	-1	0	1
Drew Stubbs	Col	2	1	-3	0
Danny Santana	Min	-2	2	0	0
Austin Jackson	2 tms	3	-4	0	-1
Denard Span	Was	-1	-1	0	-2
Jacoby Ellsbury	NYY	-2	-1	0	-3
Michael Bourn	Cle	-6	1	1	-4
Gregor Blanco	SF	-7	1	2	-4
Angel Pagan	SF	-5	0	0	-5
Andre Ethier	LAD	-4	-1	0	-5
Colby Rasmus	Tor	-5	0	-1	-6
B.J. Upton	Atl	-9	3	-2	-8
James Jones	Sea	-6	-2	-1	-9
Mike Trout	LAA	-8	-6	2	-12
Andrew McCutchen	Pit	-2	-7	-4	-13
Ben Revere	Phi	-9	-6	-2	-17
Coco Crisp	Oak	-12	-5	-1	-18
Dexter Fowler	Hou	-15	-4	0	-19

Center Fielders - 2012 Runs Saved

Player	Team	Range & Pos	OF Arm	GFP/DME	Total
Michael Bourn	Atl	20	2	1	23
Mike Trout	LAA	17	-2	6	21
Denard Span	Min	16	1	2	19
Craig Gentry	Tex	7	3	5	15
Bryce Harper	Was	10	3	0	13
Justin Maxwell	Hou	10	-1	1	10
Peter Bourjos	LAA	7	2	0	9
Colby Rasmus	Tor	3	4	0	7
Cameron Maybin	SD	6	-3	4	7
Austin Jackson	Det	5	-1	2	6
Chris Young	Ari	6	0	0	6
Justin Ruggiano	Mia	6	0	-1	5
Andres Torres	NYM	4	1	-1	4
Jarrod Dyson	KC	4	1	-1	4
Carlos Gomez	Mil	-1	3	0	2
Jacoby Ellsbury	Bos	5	-3	0	2
Drew Stubbs	Cin	-1	2	0	1
Jon Jay	StL	3	-2	0	1
Michael Brantley	Cle	-4	0	4	0
Shane Victorino	2 tms	-4	3	1	0
Coco Crisp	Oak	-3	-1	3	-1
John Mayberry	Phi	0	0	-1	-1
Emilio Bonifacio	Mia	0	-2	-1	-3
Angel Pagan	SF	0	-2	-3	-5
B.J. Upton	TB	-3	-2	0	-5
Jordan Schafer	Hou	-3	0	-2	-5
Andrew McCutchen	Pit	-1	-3	-2	-6
Alejandro De Aza	CWS	-3	-1	-2	-6
Curtis Granderson	NYY	-7	-1	1	-7
Yoenis Cespedes	Oak	-8	2	-1	-7
Josh Hamilton	Tex	-5	-3	-1	-9
Matt Kemp	LAD	-15	4	1	-10
Michael Saunders	Sea	-11	0	0	-11
Dexter Fowler	Col	-6	-4	-2	-12
Adam Jones	Bal	-10	-1	-2	-13

Right Fielders - 3-Year Runs Saved

Player	Range & Pos	OF Arm	GFP/DME	Total
Jason Heyward	61	-5	0	56
Josh Reddick	25	11	5	41
Gerardo Parra	25	13	1	39
Shane Victorino	19	3	2	24
Ichiro Suzuki	16	-1	4	19
Marlon Byrd	10	7	0	17
Jose Bautista	-11	20	4	13
Nate Schierholtz	15	-3	1	13
Chris Denorfia	5	6	2	13
Cody Ross	13	0	0	13
Jay Bruce	-1	4	6	9
Giancarlo Stanton	18	0	-9	9
Nori Aoki	6	5	-2	9
Yasiel Puig	5	5	-1	9
Will Venable	15	-10	-2	3
Nick Swisher	2	-1	2	3
Justin Upton	8	-4	-2	2
Alex Rios	-1	-3	3	-1
Andre Ethier	3	-3	-1	-1
Curtis Granderson	8	-9	0	-1
Travis Snider	-3	1	1	-1
Kole Calhoun	-5	0	1	-4
Carlos Beltran	-3	-1	-1	-5
Matt Joyce	-2	-4	-1	-7
Ryan Braun	-5	-2	-1	-8
Jeff Francoeur	-21	11	1	-9
Jayson Werth	-9	-2	1	-10
Wil Myers	-6	-4	-1	-11
Nelson Cruz	-10	0	-2	-12
Nick Markakis	-25	3	9	-13
Shin-Soo Choo	-12	-1	0	-13
David Murphy	-8	-4	-2	-14
Hunter Pence	-8	-3	-4	-15
Torii Hunter	-23	7	1	-15
Michael Cuddyer	-23	1	-2	-24

Right Fielders - 2013 Runs Saved

Player	Team	Range & Pos	OF Arm	GFP/DME	Total
Gerardo Parra	Ari	20	10	2	32
Shane Victorino	Bos	18	4	1	23
Jay Bruce	Cin	9	4	3	16
Josh Reddick	Oak	7	3	3	13
Jason Heyward	Atl	17	-3	-1	13
Nori Aoki	Mil	7	5	-2	10
David Lough	KC	6	2	2	10
Yasiel Puig	LAD	7	1	1	9
Chris Denorfia	SD	6	3	0	9
Marlon Byrd	2 tms	4	3	1	8
Ichiro Suzuki	NYY	4	1	3	8
Jose Bautista	Tor	-2	9	-1	6
Chris Parmelee	Min	-2	4	2	4
Andre Ethier	LAD	2	1	0	3
Nate Schierholtz	ChC	3	-3	1	1
Travis Snider	Pit	0	1	0	1
Jayson Werth	Was	1	-2	1	0
Jeff Francoeur	2 tms	-4	3	1	0
Daniel Nava	Bos	-3	0	1	-2
Nelson Cruz	Tex	-1	-2	0	-3
Wil Myers	TB	-1	-2	0	-3
Will Venable	SD	-1	-3	1	-3
Alex Rios	2 tms	-8	2	2	-4
Drew Stubbs	Cle	-3	0	-1	-4
John Mayberry	Phi	-2	0	-2	-4
Giancarlo Stanton	Mia	1	-2	-5	-6
Matt Joyce	TB	-4	-1	-1	-6
Nick Markakis	Bal	-12	0	5	-7
Carlos Beltran	StL	-3	-3	-1	-7
Hunter Pence	SF	1	-6	-3	-8
Josh Hamilton	LAA	-6	-1	-1	-8
Delmon Young	2 tms	-10	0	1	-9
Torii Hunter	Det	-9	0	-1	-10
Michael Morse	2 tms	-9	-2	-2	-13
Michael Cuddyer	Col	-11	-3	-1	-15

Right Fielders - 2014 Runs Saved

Player	Team	Range & Pos	OF Arm	GFP/DME	Total
Jason Heyward	Atl	23	1	2	26
Kevin Kiermaier	TB	15	-1	-1	13
Daniel Nava	Bos	9	3	1	13
Josh Reddick	Oak	8	2	0	10
Nate Schierholtz	2 tms	8	1	1	10
Marlon Byrd	Phi	6	4	-1	9
Michael Saunders	Sea	5	0	2	7
Will Venable	SD	9	-3	1	7
Giancarlo Stanton	Mia	7	0	-1	6
Allen Craig	2 tms	3	1	-1	3
Gerardo Parra	2 tms	1	2	-1	2
Chris Denorfia	2 tms	0	2	0	2
Nick Markakis	Bal	-6	3	4	1
Jose Bautista	Tor	-6	5	2	1
Kole Calhoun	LAA	-4	1	4	1
Ichiro Suzuki	NYY	4	-2	-1	1
Yasiel Puig	LAD	-2	4	-2	0
George Springer	Hou	2	-1	-1	0
Charlie Blackmon	Col	1	-1	0	0
Hunter Pence	SF	-2	0	1	-1
Curtis Granderson	NYM	6	-8	0	-2
Gregory Polanco	Pit	-6	2	2	-2
Matt Kemp	LAD	-2	0	-1	-3
Jayson Werth	Was	-5	1	0	-4
Alex Rios	Tex	2	-4	-2	-4
Oscar Taveras	StL	-4	0	0	-4
Jay Bruce	Cin	-8	-1	3	-6
Nori Aoki	KC	-6	0	-1	-7
Ryan Braun	Mil	-5	-2	-1	-8
Wil Myers	TB	-5	-2	-1	-8
Dayan Viciedo	CWS	-6	-1	-1	-8
Avisail Garcia	CWS	-7	-1	0	-8
Oswaldo Arcia	Min	-12	2	1	-9
David Murphy	Cle	-7	-3	-2	-12
Torii Hunter	Det	-14	-2	-1	-17

Right Fielders - 2012 Runs Saved

Player	Team	Range & Pos	OF Arm	GFP/DME	Total
Josh Reddick	Oak	10	6	2	18
Jason Heyward	Atl	21	-3	-1	17
Torii Hunter	LAA	0	9	3	12
Ben Revere	Min	11	-1	1	11
Ichiro Suzuki	2 tms	8	0	2	10
Ben Zobrist	TB	6	2	2	10
Giancarlo Stanton	Mia	10	2	-3	9
Alex Rios	CWS	5	-1	3	7
Carlos Beltran	StL	2	3	2	7
Nori Aoki	Mil	5	0	1	6
Jose Bautista	Tor	-3	6	3	6
Gregor Blanco	SF	6	-1	-1	4
Brian Bogusevic	Hou	-1	4	0	3
Nick Swisher	NYY	3	-2	1	2
Chris Denorfia	SD	-1	1	2	2
Jose Tabata	Pit	2	0	0	2
Nate Schierholtz	2 tms	4	-1	-1	2
Justin Upton	Ari	6	-3	-2	1
Cody Ross	Bos	1	0	0	1
Matt Joyce	TB	2	-2	0	0
Jay Bruce	Cin	-2	1	0	-1
Andre Ethier	LAD	4	-4	-1	-1
Will Venable	SD	7	-4	-4	-1
Bryce Harper	Was	-3	2	0	-1
David DeJesus	ChC	3	-4	-2	-3
Garrett Jones	Pit	1	-2	-3	-4
Hunter Pence	2 tms	-7	3	-2	-6
Brennan Boesch	Det	-7	-1	2	-6
Jayson Werth	Was	-5	-1	0	-6
Nick Markakis	Bal	-7	0	0	-7
Michael Cuddyer	Col	-10	3	-1	-8
Jeff Francoeur	KC	-17	8	0	-9
Shin-Soo Choo	Cle	-9	-1	0	-10
Nelson Cruz	Tex	-11	2	-2	-11
Lucas Duda	NYM	-11	-4	0	-15

Pitchers - 3-Year Runs Saved

Player	Range & Pos	SB	Bunts	GFP/DME	Total
R.A. Dickey	12	5	1	0	18
Mark Buehrle	6	7	3	2	18
Zack Greinke	10	5	2	1	18
Clayton Kershaw	7	10	0	0	17
Johnny Cueto	6	8	1	1	16
Mike Leake	11	2	1	1	15
Dallas Keuchel	12	0	-1	2	13
Kyle Kendrick	8	1	1	1	11
Henderson Alvarez	10	1	0	0	11
Julio Teheran	3	5	2	1	11
Wei-Yin Chen	8	1	1	-1	9
Hector Santiago	7	2	-1	1	9
Brad Ziegler	8	0	1	0	9
Adam Wainwright	4	2	1	1	8
David Price	3	5	0	0	8
Jordan Zimmermann	4	1	2	1	8
Madison Bumgarner	5	5	-5	2	7
Hiroki Kuroda	3	3	0	1	7
Homer Bailey	5	0	1	1	7
Jose Quintana	3	4	0	0	7
Travis Wood	4	1	2	0	7
Hisashi Iwakuma	5	2	0	0	7
Eric Stults	8	-1	-1	1	7
Alex Cobb	9	-2	0	0	7
Wade Miley	-2	8	0	0	6
Bronson Arroyo	3	2	1	0	6
Francisco Liriano	9	-1	0	-2	6
Dillon Gee	4	1	1	0	6
Nathan Eovaldi	-1	4	1	2	6
Alfredo Simon	4	1	1	0	6
Andrew Cashner	7	-3	1	1	6
Jake Peavy	4	3	0	-2	5
Doug Fister	4	4	-3	0	5
Jon Niese	2	3	1	-1	5
Chris Capuano	3	3	-1	0	5
Joe Saunders	6	2	-2	-1	5
John Danks	3	1	1	0	5
Bruce Chen	2	2	1	0	5
Hyun-Jin Ryu	4	1	0	0	5
Jhoulys Chacin	2	2	2	-1	5
David Phelps	-1	5	1	0	5
Sonny Gray	1	2	1	1	5
Jose Fernandez	3	1	-1	2	5
Mike Fiers	4	0	0	1	5
Justin Verlander	3	-1	1	1	4
Kyle Lohse	2	1	2	-1	4
C.J. Wilson	6	0	-1	-1	4
Jason Vargas	4	1	-1	0	4
Justin Masterson	7	-2	-2	1	4
Jorge de la Rosa	4	1	0	-1	4
Tommy Hunter	2	2	0	0	4
Bud Norris	2	1	2	-2	3
Chris Tillman	-3	5	0	1	3
Ryan Vogelsong	3	1	0	-1	3
Tommy Milone	3	3	-3	0	3
Josh Collmenter	0	1	2	0	3
Tanner Roark	0	1	2	0	3
Alex Wood	-1	4	0	0	3
Gavin Floyd	2	1	0	0	3
Matt Cain	2	-3	1	2	2
Jeremy Hellickson	-1	2	0	1	2
Paul Maholm	2	2	-1	-1	2
Jordan Lyles	2	-1	1	0	2
Hector Noesi	1	1	0	0	2
Anthony Swarzak	-1	2	0	1	2
Jarred Cosart	1	1	0	0	2
Jeanmar Gomez	3	-1	0	0	2
Kyle Gibson	0	1	0	1	2
Jaime Garcia	2	1	-1	0	2
Josh Tomlin	-1	2	1	0	2
Lance Lynn	-2	5	1	-3	1
Yovani Gallardo	-3	1	2	1	1
Edwin Jackson	2	1	-2	0	1
Jerome Williams	1	1	-1	0	1
J.A. Happ	2	-1	0	0	1
Jeff Locke	-2	4	-1	0	1
Drew Smyly	2	1	-2	0	1
Charlie Morton	0	1	0	0	1
Matt Harrison	-3	2	1	1	1
Tyler Clippard	2	-1	0	0	1
Martin Perez	0	3	-1	-1	1
Erasmo Ramirez	0	0	0	1	1
Ian Kennedy	-4	3	2	-1	0
Ervin Santana	2	0	-1	-1	0
Yu Darvish	3	-4	0	1	0
Bartolo Colon	1	3	-3	-1	0
Cliff Lee	-2	2	1	-1	0
Trevor Cahill	4	-3	-1	0	0
CC Sabathia	0	1	1	-2	0
Jason Hammel	0	1	-1	0	0
Derek Holland	-1	3	0	-2	0
Lucas Harrell	-1	-2	1	2	0
Scott Kazmir	1	-2	0	1	0
Matt Moore	2	-2	1	-1	0
Randall Delgado	-2	0	2	0	0
Gerrit Cole	2	-2	0	0	0
Matt Belisle	0	0	0	0	0
Brett Oberholtzer	0	1	-1	0	0
Luke Gregerson	4	-4	0	0	0
Jeremy Guthrie	-2	2	-1	0	-1
Jered Weaver	0	-1	0	0	-1
Dan Haren	2	-2	-1	0	-1
Mike Minor	-1	2	-1	-1	-1
Clay Buchholz	-2	2	0	-1	-1
Corey Kluber	-2	0	1	0	-1
Marco Estrada	0	-2	0	1	-1
Wily Peralta	-5	1	2	1	-1
Tyson Ross	2	-3	1	-1	-1
Roberto Hernandez	2	-3	0	0	-1
Joe Kelly	-1	1	-1	0	-1
Juan Nicasio	-2	2	-1	0	-1
Vance Worley	-4	3	0	0	-1
Wade Davis	-1	1	0	-1	-1
Franklin Morales	-1	1	0	-1	-1
Brian Duensing	-3	2	0	0	-1
James Shields	-6	5	1	-2	-2
Cole Hamels	0	0	-1	-1	-2
Stephen Strasburg	-1	-2	1	0	-2
Aaron Harang	-1	-1	0	0	-2
Mat Latos	1	-2	0	-1	-2
Miguel Gonzalez	-3	1	0	0	-2
Tom Koehler	-2	2	-1	-1	-2
Jake Arrieta	2	-4	0	0	-2
Ivan Nova	-3	1	0	0	-2
Dan Straily	-2	0	0	0	-2
Carlos Torres	-5	0	2	1	-2
Nick Tepesch	-4	2	0	0	-2
Kelvin Herrera	-1	-2	1	0	-2
Bryan Shaw	-1	0	-1	0	-2
Fernando Rodney	-2	-1	1	0	-2
Chris Sale	-3	1	0	-1	-3
Shelby Miller	-3	0	-1	1	-3
Erik Bedard	0	0	-3	0	-3
Carlos Villanueva	0	-1	-1	-1	-3
Ross Detwiler	-4	1	0	0	-3
Esmil Rogers	-3	0	0	0	-3
Drew Hutchison	-2	-3	2	0	-3
Brandon Morrow	-3	0	0	0	-3
Kenley Jansen	0	-2	-1	0	-3
Rick Porcello	-3	0	0	-1	-4
Gio Gonzalez	-3	1	-1	-1	-4
Brandon McCarthy	-2	-2	0	0	-4
Felix Doubront	-1	-3	0	0	-4
Garrett Richards	-3	-1	0	0	-4
Jesse Chavez	-4	1	-1	0	-4
Brad Peacock	-1	-3	0	0	-4
Felix Hernandez	-2	-3	0	0	-5
Kevin Correia	-5	2	-3	1	-5
Chris Archer	-3	-1	-1	0	-5
Josh Beckett	-1	-3	-1	0	-5
Jacob Turner	-2	-1	-2	0	-5
Zack Wheeler	-5	0	1	-1	-5
Colby Lewis	-2	-1	-2	0	-5
Jon Lester	-2	-1	-1	-2	-6
Max Scherzer	-9	3	-1	1	-6
Jeff Samardzija	-3	-1	-1	-1	-6
Anibal Sanchez	-1	-6	2	-1	-6
Tim Hudson	-6	0	0	0	-6
Wandy Rodriguez	1	-1	-6	0	-6
Craig Stammen	-1	-3	-1	-1	-6
Adam Ottavino	-3	-3	1	-1	-6
Jamey Wright	-3	-2	-2	1	-6
Ricky Nolasco	-4	-1	-1	-1	-7
Ubaldo Jimenez	1	-7	-1	0	-7
Samuel Deduno	-3	-2	-1	-1	-7
Chris Young	-3	-3	-1	0	-7
Tom Wilhelmsen	-3	-5	0	0	-8
Matt Garza	-6	2	-5	-1	-10
John Lackey	-3	-7	0	0	-10
Edinson Volquez	-7	-3	-1	0	-11
A.J. Burnett	-3	-8	-1	0	-12
Phil Hughes	-10	0	0	-2	-12
Tim Lincecum	-3	-8	0	-1	-12
Scott Feldman	0	-11	1	-2	-12
Zach McAllister	-7	-3	-3	0	-13

Pitchers - 2014 Runs Saved

Player	Team	Range & Pos	SB	Bunts	GFP/DME	Total
Dallas Keuchel	Hou	7	1	1	1	10
Clayton Kershaw	LAD	6	2	-1	0	7
Johnny Cueto	Cin	4	2	0	0	6
Henderson Alvarez	Mia	6	0	0	0	6
Adam Wainwright	StL	3	0	1	1	5
Julio Teheran	Atl	1	2	2	0	5
R.A. Dickey	Tor	4	1	0	0	5
Zack Greinke	LAD	4	0	1	0	5
Kyle Kendrick	Phi	3	2	-1	1	5
Seth Maness	StL	4	1	0	0	5
Jose Quintana	CWS	2	1	0	1	4
Nathan Eovaldi	Mia	0	2	1	1	4
Tanner Roark	Was	1	1	2	0	4
Alfredo Simon	Cin	3	0	1	0	4
Kyle Gibson	Min	2	1	0	1	4
Travis Wood	ChC	3	0	1	0	4
J.A. Happ	Tor	4	0	0	0	4
Charlie Morton	Pit	2	1	0	1	4
Edwin Jackson	ChC	3	1	0	0	4
Masahiro Tanaka	NYY	2	0	0	2	4
Andrew Cashner	SD	3	0	1	0	4
Brad Hand	Mia	3	0	1	0	4
Sonny Gray	Oak	0	1	1	1	3
Stephen Strasburg	Was	2	0	1	0	3
Mike Leake	Cin	2	1	0	0	3
Lance Lynn	StL	3	1	0	-1	3
Jon Niese	NYM	2	1	0	0	3
Vidal Nuno	2 tms	2	1	0	0	3
Hyun-Jin Ryu	LAD	3	0	0	0	3
Marco Estrada	Mil	3	-1	0	1	3
Hector Santiago	LAA	1	2	0	0	3
David Phelps	NYY	1	1	1	0	3
Carlos Martinez	StL	2	0	1	0	3
Dan Otero	Oak	2	1	0	0	3
Chris Tillman	Bal	0	2	-1	1	2
Cole Hamels	Phi	0	1	1	0	2
Jake Peavy	2 tms	2	1	0	-1	2
Bartolo Colon	NYM	0	1	1	0	2
Mark Buehrle	Tor	0	2	1	-1	2
Wade Miley	Ari	-1	3	0	0	2
Jordan Zimmermann	Was	1	1	0	0	2
Kyle Lohse	Mil	2	0	1	-1	2
Ervin Santana	Atl	1	1	0	0	2
Jason Vargas	KC	5	-1	-2	0	2
Wei-Yin Chen	Bal	3	0	-1	0	2
Ryan Vogelsong	SF	3	0	-1	0	2
Yordano Ventura	KC	1	1	0	0	2
Hisashi Iwakuma	Sea	0	2	0	0	2
Eric Stults	SD	2	-1	0	1	2
Hector Noesi	3 tms	2	0	0	0	2
Doug Fister	Was	1	1	0	0	2
Roenis Elias	Sea	1	1	0	0	2
Homer Bailey	Cin	1	1	0	0	2
Yu Darvish	Tex	2	-1	0	1	2
Dillon Gee	NYM	2	0	0	0	2
Matt Shoemaker	LAA	1	1	0	0	2
Jeff Locke	Pit	0	2	0	0	2
Justin Masterson	2 tms	2	0	0	0	2
Jordan Lyles	Col	2	-1	1	0	2
Chase Anderson	Ari	1	1	0	0	2
Michael Wacha	StL	-1	1	1	1	2
Chris Capuano	2 tms	1	1	0	0	2
James Shields	KC	-2	3	0	0	1
Madison Bumgarner	SF	-1	4	-2	0	1
John Danks	CWS	1	0	0	0	1
Edinson Volquez	Pit	-1	1	1	0	1
Josh Collmenter	Ari	0	0	1	0	1
C.J. Wilson	LAA	3	0	-1	-1	1
Chris Sale	CWS	0	1	0	0	1
Alex Cobb	TB	1	0	0	0	1
Collin McHugh	Hou	1	1	0	-1	1
Nick Martinez	Tex	-1	1	1	0	1
Carlos Carrasco	Cle	1	0	0	0	1
Marcus Stroman	Tor	1	0	0	0	1
Tommy Milone	2 tms	2	0	-1	0	1
Danny Salazar	Cle	-1	1	1	0	1
Josh Tomlin	Cle	-1	1	1	0	1
Rubby de la Rosa	Bos	0	0	1	0	1
Dustin McGowan	Tor	0	0	1	0	1
Kyle Hendricks	ChC	1	0	0	0	1
Corey Kluber	Cle	-2	2	0	0	0
Jered Weaver	LAA	1	-1	-1	1	0
Justin Verlander	Det	1	0	-1	0	0
Rick Porcello	Det	-1	1	0	0	0
Ian Kennedy	SD	-1	0	1	0	0
Brandon McCarthy	2 tms	1	-1	0	0	0
Dan Haren	LAD	1	-1	0	0	0

Player	Team	Range & Pos	SB	Bunts	GFP/DME	Total
Shelby Miller	StL	-1	0	0	1	0
Jarred Cosart	2 tms	0	1	0	-1	0
Alex Wood	Atl	-2	2	0	0	0
Jake Odorizzi	TB	-2	2	0	0	0
Roberto Hernandez	2 tms	2	-2	0	0	0
Francisco Liriano	Pit	2	-2	1	-1	0
Drew Smyly	2 tms	0	1	-1	0	0
Gerrit Cole	Pit	2	-2	0	0	0
Scott Carroll	CWS	-1	0	0	1	0
Ubaldo Jimenez	Bal	2	-2	-1	1	0
David Buchanan	Phi	-1	0	0	1	0
Kevin Gausman	Bal	-1	1	0	0	0
Mat Latos	Cin	0	0	0	0	0
Odrisamer Despaigne	SD	0	-1	1	0	0
Matt Cain	SF	0	0	0	0	0
Bronson Arroyo	Ari	0	0	0	0	0
Anthony Swarzak	Min	0	0	0	0	0
Daisuke Matsuzaka	NYM	1	-1	0	0	0
Cliff Lee	Phi	0	0	0	0	0
Scott Baker	Tex	0	0		0	0
Adam Warren	NYY	0	1	-1	0	0
David Price	2 tms	-1	1	-1	0	-1
Jeff Samardzija	2 tms	-1	0	0	0	-1
Aaron Harang	Atl	-1	0	0	0	-1
Jeremy Guthrie	KC	-1	1	-1	0	-1
Hiroki Kuroda	NYY	-2	1	0	0	-1
Wily Peralta	Mil	-1	-1	1	0	-1
Yovani Gallardo	Mil	-3	1	0	1	-1
Tom Koehler	Mia	-1	0	0	0	-1
Scott Kazmir	Oak	1	-2	0	0	-1
Zack Wheeler	NYM	-3	1	1	0	-1
Jorge de la Rosa	Col	0	-1	0	0	-1
Jason Hammel	2 tms	0	0	-1	0	-1
Clay Buchholz	Bos	-2	1		0	-1
Garrett Richards	LAA	-1	0		0	-1
Bud Norris	Bal	0	0		-1	-1
Matt Garza	Mil	0	1	-1	-1	-1
Gio Gonzalez	Was	-1	1	0	-1	-1
Kevin Correia	2 tms	-1	0	-1	1	-1
Trevor Bauer	Cle	0	-1	0	0	-1
Danny Duffy	KC	-1	3	-3	0	-1
Franklin Morales	Col	0	-1	0	0	-1
Jacob deGrom	NYM	-1	0	1	-1	-1
Nick Tepesch	Tex	-3	2	0	0	-1
Anibal Sanchez	Det	1	-1	0	-1	-1
Josh Beckett	LAD	0	-1		0	-1
Jerome Williams	3 tms	-1	0	0	0	-1
Vance Worley	Pit	-2	1	0	0	-1
Juan Nicasio	Col	0	0	-1	0	-1
David Hale	Atl	-1	-1	1	0	-1
Cesar Ramos	TB	-1	0	0	0	-1
Felix Doubront	2 tms	0	-1	0	0	-1
Felix Hernandez	Sea	0	-2	0	0	-2
Tyson Ross	SD	2	-2	-1	-1	-2
Tim Hudson	SF	-1	-1	0	0	-2
Chris Young	Sea	0	-1	-1	0	-2
Ricky Nolasco	Min	-1	-1	1	-1	-2
Tim Lincecum	SF	0	-2	0	0	-2
Jesse Chavez	Oak	-3	1	0	0	-2
Brett Oberholtzer	Hou	-1	0	-1	0	-2
Brad Peacock	Hou	-1	-1	0	0	-2
Tyler Matzek	Col	-1	0	-1	0	-2
T.J. House	Cle	-2	0	0	0	-2
Carlos Torres	NYM	-4	0	1	1	-2
Joe Kelly	2 tms	-2	0		0	-2
Dellin Betances	NYY	-1	-1		0	-2
Brandon Workman	Bos	0	-1	-1	0	-2
Tom Wilhelmsen	Sea	0	-2	0	0	-2
Jon Lester	2 tms	-1	-1	0	-1	-3
Miguel Gonzalez	Bal	-2	-1	0	0	-3
Jake Arrieta	ChC	0	-3	0	0	-3
Tyler Skaggs	LAA	-1	1	-2	-1	-3
Trevor Cahill	Ari	0	-2	-1	0	-3
Shane Greene	NYY	-3	0		0	-3
Max Scherzer	Det	-4	1	-1	0	-4
Chris Archer	TB	-4	0	0	0	-4
Drew Hutchison	Tor	-2	-3	1	0	-4
Colby Lewis	Tex	-1	-1	-2	0	-4
Mike Minor	Atl	-2	0	-1	-1	-4
Jacob Turner	2 tms	-3	-1	0	0	-4
Samuel Deduno	2 tms	-2	-2	0	0	-4
Jenrry Mejia	NYM	-3	-1	0	0	-4
Zach McAllister	Cle	-2	-1	-1	0	-4
A.J. Burnett	Phi	-3	-2	0	0	-5
John Lackey	2 tms	-2	-2	-1	0	-5
Yusmeiro Petit	SF	-3	-2	0	0	-5
Scott Feldman	Hou	-1	-5	0	-1	-7
Phil Hughes	Min	-6	-1	0	-1	-8

Pitchers - 2013 Runs Saved

Player	Team	Range & Pos	SB	Bunts	GFP/DME	Total
Patrick Corbin	Ari	4	3	1	0	8
R.A. Dickey	Tor	5	1	1	0	7
Zack Greinke	LAD	3	2	1	1	7
Hiroki Kuroda	NYY	4	2	0	0	6
Mike Leake	Cin	6	0	0	0	6
Julio Teheran	Atl	2	3	0	1	6
Hector Santiago	CWS	5	1	-1	1	6
Hisashi Iwakuma	Sea	5	0	0	0	5
Madison Bumgarner	SF	4	2	-2	1	5
Andrew Cashner	SD	5	-1	0	1	5
Jorge de la Rosa	Col	4	2	0	-1	5
Bruce Chen	KC	2	2	1	0	5
Adam Wainwright	StL	2	1	1	0	4
Clayton Kershaw	LAD	0	3	1	0	4
Mark Buehrle	Tor	0	3	0	1	4
David Price	TB	1	2	0	1	4
Kyle Kendrick	Phi	3	-1	2	0	4
Francisco Liriano	Pit	5	1	-1	-1	4
Wei-Yin Chen	Bal	3	1	0	0	4
Jake Westbrook	StL	3	1	0	0	4
Jordan Zimmermann	Was	1	0	1	1	3
Mike Minor	Atl	1	2		0	3
Eric Stults	SD	4	0	-1	0	3
Jose Quintana	CWS	1	2	0	0	3
Dillon Gee	NYM	1	1	1	0	3
Andy Pettitte	NYY	3	0	0	0	3
Jose Fernandez	Mia	2	1	-1	1	3
Dallas Keuchel	Hou	2	0	0	1	3
Trevor Cahill	Ari	3	-1	1	0	3
Jeremy Hefner	NYM	3	0	0	0	3
Tony Cingrani	Cin	1	2	0	0	3
Alex Wood	Atl	1	2	0	0	3
Cliff Lee	Phi	1	1	0	0	2
Chris Tillman	Bal	-2	3	1	0	2
Bronson Arroyo	Cin	0	1	1	0	2
Jhoulys Chacin	Col	0	1	1	0	2
Hyun-Jin Ryu	LAD	1	1	0	0	2
Bud Norris	2 tms	1	0	2	-1	2
Miguel Gonzalez	Bal	0	1	1	0	2
Jeff Locke	Pit	0	2	0	0	2
Matt Moore	TB	2	-1	1	0	2
Jordan Lyles	Hou	2	0	0	0	2
Ivan Nova	NYY	1	1	0	0	2
Martin Perez	Tex	2	1	0	-1	2
Jason Marquis	SD	2	0	0	0	2
Alexi Ogando	Tex	1	1	0	0	2
Henderson Alvarez	Mia	1	0	1	0	2
Alfredo Simon	Cin	1	1	0	0	2
David Phelps	NYY	0	2	0	0	2
Tom Gorzelanny	Mil	3	0	0	-1	2
Shaun Marcum	NYM	0	1	1	0	2
Brandon Kintzler	Mil	2	0		0	2
Max Scherzer	Det	0	1	-1	1	1
CC Sabathia	NYY	1	1	1	-2	1
Homer Bailey	Cin	0	-1	1	1	1
Doug Fister	Det	0	1	0	0	1
Travis Wood	ChC	0	1	0	0	1
Kyle Lohse	Mil	0	0	1	0	1
Kris Medlen	Atl	-1	2	0	0	1
Justin Masterson	Cle	1	0	0	0	1
Matt Cain	SF	1	-2	1	1	1
Joe Saunders	Sea	3	0	-2	0	1
Jeremy Hellickson	TB	-1	1	0	1	1
Jerome Williams	LAA	1	1	-1	0	1
Scott Kazmir	Cle	0	0	0	1	1
Corey Kluber	Cle	0	0	1	0	1
Alex Cobb	TB	1	0	0	0	1
John Danks	CWS	0	1	0	0	1
Esmil Rogers	Tor	1	0	0	0	1
Barry Zito	SF	0	1	0	0	1
Tyson Ross	SD	0	0	1	0	1
Randall Delgado	Ari	0	0	1	0	1
Nathan Eovaldi	Mia	-1	1	0	1	1
Anthony Swarzak	Min	0	1	0	0	1
Kevin Slowey	Mia	0	1	0	0	1
Brandon Maurer	Sea	1	0		0	1
Carlos Torres	NYM	0	0	1	0	1
Jeanmar Gomez	Pit	1	-1	1	0	1
Adam Warren	NYY	1	0	0	0	1
Tanner Scheppers	Tex	1	1	0	-1	1
Ryan Pressly	Min	1	0	0	0	1
James Shields	KC	-2	2	1	-1	0
Derek Holland	Tex	-1	1	0	0	0
C.J. Wilson	LAA	1	-1	0	0	0
Ervin Santana	KC	1	0	-1	0	0
Yu Darvish	Tex	0	-1	1	0	0

Player	Team	Range & Pos	SB	Bunts	GFP/DME	Total
A.J. Griffin	Oak	0	0	0	0	0
Ricky Nolasco	2 tms	0	1	-1	0	0
Jarrod Parker	Oak	-1	1	-1	1	0
Ian Kennedy	2 tms	-2	2	1	-1	0
Matt Harvey	NYM	-2	1	0	1	0
Felix Doubront	Bos	0	0	0	0	0
Paul Maholm	Atl	0	0	0	0	0
Mike Pelfrey	Min	-2	0	1	1	0
Scott Diamond	Min	2	1	-2	-1	0
Carlos Villanueva	ChC	1	0	-1	0	0
Gerrit Cole	Pit	0	0	0	0	0
Clay Buchholz	Bos	-1	1	0	0	0
Justin Grimm	2 tms	0	1	-1	0	0
Luis Mendoza	KC	0	0	0	0	0
Josh Collmenter	Ari	0	0	0	0	0
Tommy Hunter	Bal	-1	1	0	0	0
Justin Verlander	Det	0	-1	0	0	-1
Jeremy Guthrie	KC	-2	0	1	0	-1
Wade Miley	Ari	-3	2	0	0	-1
Wily Peralta	Mil	-4	1	1	1	-1
Scott Feldman	2 tms	3	-4	1	-1	-1
Yovani Gallardo	Mil	0	-1	0	0	-1
Juan Nicasio	Col	-1	0	0	0	-1
Tommy Milone	Oak	0	0	-1	0	-1
Dan Straily	Oak	-1	0	0	0	-1
Roberto Hernandez	TB	0	-1	0	0	-1
Garrett Richards	LAA	-1	0	0	0	-1
Jake Peavy	2 tms	0	0	0	-1	-1
Aaron Harang	2 tms	0	-1	0	0	-1
Jon Niese	NYM	-2	1	1	-1	-1
Tom Koehler	Mia	-1	2	-1	-1	-1
Wade Davis	KC	-1	1	0	-1	-1
Chris Archer	TB	1	-2	0	0	-1
Joe Kelly	StL	0	0	-1	0	-1
Charlie Morton	Pit	-1	0	0	0	-1
Chris Capuano	LAD	-1	0	0	0	-1
Ryan Vogelsong	SF	-1	0	0	0	-1
Jonathan Pettibone	Phi	0	-1	0	0	-1
Nick Tepesch	Tex	-1	0	0	0	-1
J.A. Happ	Tor	0	-1	0	0	-1
Freddy Garcia	2 tms	-1	-1	0	1	-1
Nate Jones	CWS	-1	0		0	-1
Todd Redmond	Tor	0	-1		0	-1
Cole Hamels	Phi	0	-1	0	-1	-2
Mat Latos	Cin	1	-1	-1	-1	-2
Gio Gonzalez	Was	-3	1	0	0	-2
Bartolo Colon	Oak	-1	1	-1	-1	-2
Dan Haren	Was	-1	-1	0	0	-2
Lucas Harrell	Hou	-2	-1	0	1	-2
Erik Bedard	Hou	0	0	-2	0	-2
Jason Vargas	LAA	-4	1	0	1	-2
Phil Hughes	NYY	-1	0		-1	-2
Brandon McCarthy	Ari	-2	0	0	0	-2
Tyler Chatwood	Col	0	-1	0	-1	-2
Samuel Deduno	Min	-1	0	0	-1	-2
Chad Gaudin	SF	-2	1	-1	0	-2
Brad Peacock	Hou	0	-2	0	0	-2

28

Player	Team	Range & Pos	SB	Bunts	GFP/DME	Total
Ryan Webb	Mia	0	-2	0	0	-2
A.J. Ramos	Mia	-1	0	0	-1	-2
Kenley Jansen	LAD	-1	-1		0	-2
Chris Sale	CWS	-1	-2	0	0	-3
Jon Lester	Bos	-2	0	0	-1	-3
Felix Hernandez	Sea	-2	-1	0	0	-3
Lance Lynn	StL	-5	2	1	-1	-3
Stephen Strasburg	Was	-2	-1	0	0	-3
Edwin Jackson	ChC	0	-1	-2	0	-3
Shelby Miller	StL	-2	0	-1	0	-3
Ryan Dempster	Bos	0	-2	-1	0	-3
Jered Weaver	LAA	-1	-2	0	0	-3
Jason Hammel	Bal	-3	0	0	0	-3
Zach McAllister	Cle	-2	0	-1	0	-3
Joe Blanton	LAA	-1	-2	0	0	-3
Tim Hudson	Atl	-2	-1	0	0	-3
Dylan Axelrod	CWS	-2	-1	0	0	-3
Marco Estrada	Mil	-2	-1		0	-3
Jacob Turner	Mia	-1	0	-2	0	-3
Adam Ottavino	Col	-3	-1	1	0	-3
A.J. Burnett	Pit	-1	-2	-1	0	-4
Kevin Correia	Min	-4	1	-1	0	-4
Ubaldo Jimenez	Cle	-1	-1	-1	-1	-4
Rick Porcello	Det	-3	0	0	-1	-4
Matt Garza	2 tms	-4	0	0	0	-4
Zack Wheeler	NYM	-2	-1	0	-1	-4
Craig Stammen	Was	-2	-1	0	-1	-4
John Lackey	Bos	-1	-5	1	0	-5
Josh Johnson	Tor	-4	-1	0	0	-5
Jeff Samardzija	ChC	-5	0	-1	0	-6
Anibal Sanchez	Det	-3	-3	0	0	-6
Edinson Volquez	2 tms	-2	-3	-2	0	-7
Tim Lincecum	SF	-3	-3	-1	-1	-8

Pitchers - 2012 Runs Saved

Player	Team	Range & Pos	SB	Bunts	GFP/DME	Total
Mark Buehrle	Mia	6	2	2	2	12
Jake Westbrook	StL	7	3	0	1	11
Johnny Cueto	Cin	0	6	1	1	8
Randy Wolf	2 tms	4	1	1	1	7
R.A. Dickey	NYM	3	3	0	0	6
Clayton Kershaw	LAD	1	5	0	0	6
Zack Greinke	2 tms	3	3	0	0	6
Ricky Romero	Tor	2	3	1	0	6
Mike Leake	Cin	3	1	1	1	6
Justin Verlander	Det	2	0	2	1	5
David Price	TB	3	2	1	-1	5
Wade Miley	Ari	2	3	0	0	5
Alex Cobb	TB	7	-2	0	0	5
Jake Peavy	CWS	2	2	0	0	4
Jason Vargas	Sea	3	1	1	-1	4
Homer Bailey	Cin	4	0	0	0	4
Bronson Arroyo	Cin	3	1	0	0	4
Chris Capuano	LAD	3	2	-1	0	4
Joe Saunders	2 tms	2	2	0	0	4
Luis Mendoza	KC	2	2	0	0	4
Chad Billingsley	LAD	4	0	0	0	4
Tommy Hunter	Bal	2	1	1	0	4
Jason Hammel	Bal	3	1	0	0	4
Jeff Francis	Col	2	0	1	1	4
Patrick Corbin	Ari	3	1	0	0	4
Aaron Laffey	Tor	3	0	1	0	4
Clayton Richard	SD	1	2	0	0	3
Matt Harrison	Tex	-1	2	1	1	3
Yovani Gallardo	Mil	0	1	2	0	3
C.J. Wilson	LAA	2	1	0	0	3
Jordan Zimmermann	Was	2	0	1	0	3
Wei-Yin Chen	Bal	2	0	2	-1	3
Jon Niese	NYM	2	1	0	0	3
Tommy Milone	Oak	1	3	-1	0	3
Henderson Alvarez	Tor	3	1	-1	0	3
Luke Hochevar	KC	4	0	0	-1	3
Ryan Dempster	2 tms	5	-2	0	0	3
Gavin Floyd	CWS	2	1	0	0	3
Kris Medlen	Atl	0	1	1	1	3
Mike Fiers	Mil	3	0	0	0	3
Hiroki Kuroda	NYY	1	0	0	1	2
CC Sabathia	NYY	0	0	1	1	2
Lucas Harrell	Hou	1	-1	1	1	2
Ryan Vogelsong	SF	1	1	1	-1	2
Jered Weaver	LAA	0	2	1	-1	2
Jeremy Hellickson	TB	0	1	1	0	2
Derek Holland	Tex	2	1	0	-1	2
Bud Norris	Hou	1	1	0	0	2
Doug Fister	Det	3	2	-3	0	2
Kyle Kendrick	Phi	2	0	0	0	2
Francisco Liriano	2 tms	2	0	0	0	2

Player	Team	Range & Pos	SB	Bunts	GFP/DME	Total
Travis Wood	ChC	1	0	1	0	2
Carlos Zambrano	Mia	0	1	0	1	2
Joe Kelly	StL	1	1	0	0	2
Drew Smyly	Det	2	1	-1	0	2
Eric Stults	2 tms	2	0	0	0	2
Josh Collmenter	Ari	0	1	1	0	2
Josh Roenicke	Col	0	1	1	0	2
Matt Cain	SF	1	-1	0	1	1
Kyle Lohse	StL	0	1	0	0	1
Madison Bumgarner	SF	2	-1	-1	1	1
Justin Masterson	Cle	4	-2	-2	1	1
Anibal Sanchez	2 tms	1	-2	2	0	1
Paul Maholm	2 tms	1	2	-1	-1	1
Barry Zito	SF	2	1	-1	-1	1
Jeremy Guthrie	2 tms	1	1	-1	0	1
Dan Haren	LAA	2	0	-1	0	1
Lance Lynn	StL	0	2	0	-1	1
Jeff Samardzija	ChC	3	-1	0	-1	1
Scott Diamond	Min	0	0	1	0	1
James McDonald	Pit	1	-1	1	0	1
Ross Detwiler	Was	0	1	0	0	1
Blake Beavan	Sea	2	-1	0	0	1
Jerome Williams	LAA	1	0	0	0	1
Nathan Eovaldi	2 tms	0	1	0	0	1
Johan Santana	NYM	0	0	1	0	1
Dillon Gee	NYM	1	0	0	0	1
Travis Blackley	2 tms	-2	3	0	0	1
Josh Tomlin	Cle	0	1	0	0	1
Anthony Swarzak	Min	-1	1	0	1	1
Aaron Cook	Bos	-1	1	0	1	1
Randall Delgado	Atl	-1	1	1	0	1
Jeanmar Gomez	Cle	2	0	-1	0	1
Brad Lincoln	2 tms	2	-1	0	0	1
Alfredo Aceves	Bos	2	0	-1	0	1
A.J. Griffin	Oak	0	1		0	1
Felix Hernandez	Sea	0	0	0	0	0
Mat Latos	Cin	0	-1	1	0	0
Ian Kennedy	Ari	-1	1	0	0	0
Jon Lester	Bos	1	0	-1	0	0
Trevor Cahill	Ari	1	0	-1	0	0
Bruce Chen	KC	0	0	0	0	0
Edwin Jackson	Was	-1	1	0	0	0
Clay Buchholz	Bos	1	0	0	-1	0
Aaron Harang	LAD	0	0	0	0	0
Mike Minor	Atl	0	0	0	0	0
Rick Porcello	Det	1	-1	0	0	0
Kevin Correia	Pit	0	1	-1	0	0
Bartolo Colon	Oak	2	1	-3	0	0
Jose Quintana	CWS	0	1	0	-1	0
Hisashi Iwakuma	Sea	0	0	0	0	0
Carlos Villanueva	Tor	-2	1	1	0	0
Jaime Garcia	StL	0	1	-1	0	0
Hector Noesi	Sea	-1	1	0	0	0
David Phelps	NYY	-2	2	0	0	0
Nick Blackburn	Min	0	0		0	0
Cole DeVries	Min	0	0	0	0	0
Dallas Keuchel	Hou	3	-1	-2	0	0
Brandon Beachy	Atl	0	0	0	0	0
Gio Gonzalez	Was	1	-1	-1	0	-1
Adam Wainwright	StL	-1	1	-1	0	-1
Chris Sale	CWS	-2	2	0	-1	-1
Joe Blanton	2 tms	-1	1	0	-1	-1
Tim Hudson	Atl	-3	2	0	0	-1
Roy Halladay	Phi	-1	0	0	0	-1
Marco Estrada	Mil	-1	0	0	0	-1
Vance Worley	Phi	-2	1	0	0	-1
Jason Marquis	2 tms	-2	-1	1	1	-1
Erik Bedard	Pit	0	0	-1	0	-1
Brandon Morrow	Tor	-1	0	0	0	-1
Shaun Marcum	Mil	0	-1	0	0	-1
Chris Volstad	ChC	2	-2	-1	0	-1
Miguel Gonzalez	Bal	-1	1	-1	0	-1
Colby Lewis	Tex	-1	0	0	0	-1
Alex White	Col	2	-1	-2	0	-1
Anthony Bass	SD	0	-1	0	0	-1
Jeremy Hefner	NYM	-1	0	0	0	-1
Craig Stammen	Was	1	-2		0	-1
Chris Tillman	Bal	-1	0	0	0	-1
Kelvin Herrera	KC	-1	-1	1	0	-1
Samuel Deduno	Min	0	0	-1	0	-1
Cole Hamels	Phi	0	0	-2	0	-2
Cliff Lee	Phi	-3	1	1	-1	-2
Yu Darvish	Tex	1	-2	-1	0	-2
Phil Hughes	NYY	-3	1	0	0	-2
Tim Lincecum	SF	0	-3	1	0	-2
Jarrod Parker	Oak	-2	-1	0	1	-2
Ervin Santana	LAA	0	-1	0	-1	-2
Matt Moore	TB	0	-1	0	-1	-2
Stephen Strasburg	Was	-1	-1	0	0	-2

Player	Team	Range & Pos	SB	Bunts	GFP/DME	Total
J.A. Happ	2 tms	-2	0	0	0	-2
Jordan Lyles	Hou	-2	0	0	0	-2
Jake Arrieta	Bal	-1	0	-1	0	-2
Brandon McCarthy	Oak	-1	-1	0	0	-2
Liam Hendriks	Min	-1	0	-1	0	-2
Christian Friedrich	Col	-3	1	0	0	-2
Esmil Rogers	2 tms	-2	0	0	0	-2
James Shields	TB	-2	0	0	-1	-3
A.J. Burnett	Pit	1	-4	0	0	-3
Max Scherzer	Det	-5	1	1	0	-3
Ubaldo Jimenez	Cle	0	-4	1	0	-3
Ivan Nova	NYY	-3	0		0	-3
Felix Doubront	Bos	-1	-2	0	0	-3
Brian Duensing	Min	-3	0	0	0	-3
Brian Matusz	Bal	-4	1	0	0	-3
Drew Pomeranz	Col	-2	-1	0	0	-3
Jeff Karstens	Pit	-2	-1	0	0	-3
Will Smith	KC	-3	0	0	0	-3
Matt Belisle	Col	-2	0	-1	0	-3
Adam Ottavino	Col	0	-2	0	-1	-3
Josh Johnson	Mia	0	-3	-1	0	-4
Josh Beckett	2 tms	-1	-2	-1	0	-4
Kevin Millwood	Sea	-1	-2	-1	0	-4
Scott Feldman	Tex	-2	-2	0	0	-4
Freddy Garcia	NYY	-2	-2	0	0	-4
Tom Wilhelmsen	Sea	-2	-2	0	0	-4
Ricky Nolasco	Mia	-3	-1	-1	0	-5
Edinson Volquez	SD	-4	-1	0	0	-5
Chris Young	NYM	-3	-2	0	0	-5
Matt Garza	ChC	-2	1	-4	0	-5
Philip Humber	CWS	-2	-2	-1	0	-5
Wandy Rodriguez	2 tms	-2	-1	-3	0	-6
Tommy Hanson	Atl	-2	-2	-2	0	-6
Zach McAllister	Cle	-3	-2	-1	0	-6
Derek Lowe	2 tms	-6	0	-1	-1	-8

Catcher Pop Times

Baseball Info Solutions' attempt to measure and account for every aspect of a catcher's attempt to throw out basestealers began in 2011 with the most obvious piece, his throws to second and third base. As is the industry standard for measuring those throws—which are called catcher pop times—we start the clock the instant the pitch hits the catcher's mitt and stop it as the ball hits the infielder's glove at a base. The complicated process of quickly transferring the ball from the mitt to the free hand, standing up, and accurately throwing, is a skill that not all catchers can perform at the same speed. A catcher may have the strongest raw arm in the game, but if he can't quickly and consistently transfer and release, he won't be able to throw out very many baserunners.

There are several factors that contribute to whether a team is able to throw out the runner or not on a stolen base attempt. The benefit of measuring catcher pop times is that we can isolate the catcher's throw from the contributions of the pitcher, the runner, and the receiving infielder.

Pop Times Relative to Catcher Caught Stealing Rates

It stands to reason that the quicker the catcher is able to get the ball to the base that he is throwing to, the more likely he is to throw the runner out. To verify whether this is true, we took a look at attempted steals of second base with a right-handed pitcher on the mound. We grouped our catcher pop times into intervals of 0.10 seconds and looked at the corresponding catcher caught stealing rates. Just as we expected, the quicker the catcher gets the ball down to second base, the more likely he is to throw the runner out.

Catcher Pop Times vs. Caught Stealing Rates

2014, With Right-Handed Pitchers

Pop Time	Catcher Caught Stealing %
1.70-1.79	46%
1.80-1.89	34%
1.90-1.99	32%
2.00-2.09	31%
>2.10	26%

It should be noted that the caught stealing percentages in this table only reflect catcher success on stolen base attempts on which we were able to record a valid pop time. If no throw was made, or if the catcher had to double-clutch, or if the video did not allow us to record an accurate time, those stolen base attempts were not considered.

The Quickest

So when it comes down to it, who is able to deliver the ball to second base the quickest? From 2014 and with a minimum of 25 valid pop times to second base, here are the five quickest catchers in baseball.

Fastest Average Catcher Pop Times to 2B

2014, Minimum 25 Valid Pop Times

Catcher	Avg. Pop Time (sec)	CS% on Timed Throws	Overall CS%	Catcher SB Runs Saved
Yan Gomes	1.84	37%	29%	2
Russell Martin	1.88	44%	32%	6
Rene Rivera	1.88	42%	33%	6
Salvador Perez	1.90	45%	29%	4
Caleb Joseph	1.90	35%	38%	5

Note: Our overall caught stealing rates do not match most other sources because most other sources do not separate catcher caught stealings from pitcher caught stealings. A pitcher caught stealing is any play in which a runner is charged with a caught stealing without a pitch having been thrown to the plate (i.e., the pitcher made the throw to catch the runner stealing).

Having the fastest pop times in baseball, these catchers are accordingly among the most successful in throwing basestealers out, which in turn allows them to save their team runs.

The Slowest

The catchers in the previous table all save runs for their teams by throwing out significantly more basestealers than the average catcher. But what about the catchers on the other end?

Slowest Average Catcher Pop Times to 2B
2014, Minimum 25 Valid Pop Times

Catcher	Avg. Pop Time (sec)	CS% on Timed Throws	Overall CS%	Catcher SB Runs Saved
Kurt Suzuki	2.03	19%	15%	-5
Hank Conger	2.02	29%	20%	-2
John Baker	2.01	16%	12%	-3
Tyler Flowers	2.00	33%	26%	1
Miguel Montero	1.98	31%	24%	-4

Four of these five catchers are below average at throwing out basestealers, if not among the very worst in the league. As a result, they have cost their team runs when it comes to controlling the opposition's running game.

Throwing to Third Base

Understandably, catchers can throw the ball to third base quicker than they can throw to second, due to the shorter throwing distance. But even though the pop times are quicker, the top catchers on the previous list rank highly on this one, indicating that proficiency at throwing to second base plays as well as it does when throwing to third base. Here are the fastest throwers to third base among the catchers who qualified for the second base leaderboards.

Fastest Average Catcher Pop Times to 3B
2014

Catcher	Avg. Pop Time (sec)	Rank on 2B List
Rene Rivera	1.43	3 of 29
Welington Castillo	1.44	8 of 29
Russell Martin	1.46	2 of 29
Mike Zunino	1.48	11 of 29
Buster Posey	1.49	15 of 29

Small Differences Do Matter

Our data shows that in 2014, with a minimum of 25 throws to second base, the quickest arm in baseball from behind the plate belongs to Indians catcher Yan Gomes. His average pop time of 1.84 seconds was 0.10 seconds better than league average last season, and while a difference of a tenth of a second may seem inconsequential and trivially small, consider this: the average basestealer covers the 90 feet from first to second base in 3.53 seconds. At that speed (and holding the pitcher's delivery time constant), the 0.10-second difference between an average catcher's throwing arm and Yan Gomes' throwing arm is the difference between a runner being safe and a runner being out by an entire arm's length.

Catcher Arm Accuracy

When considering how good a catcher's mechanics are in controlling the running game, people tend to think only about his Pop Time—how quickly he gets the ball down to second base on a stolen base attempt. However, the accuracy of his throw can be very meaningful as well. Baseball Info Solutions began collecting Catcher Arm Accuracy data during the 2014 season, making it possible to analyze how catchers combine quickness and arm strength with throwing accuracy to control the running game.

Best and Worst Throwing Catchers, Combining Pop Time and Accuracy

In trying to determine how to accurately analyze Catcher Arm Accuracy data, the question that we asked ourselves was: "What are the processes the defense employs when trying to throw out an opposing baserunner?" In the end, the pitcher is trying to get the ball to home plate as quickly as possible, the catcher is trying to get the ball down to second base as quickly as possible, and the infielder's tag needs to be applied to the runner as quickly as possible (or, more importantly, before he touches the base).

This can be broken into a simple math equation:

(1) [Baserunner Time] is greater/less than [Pitcher Delivery Time + Catcher Pop Time + Tag Time]

The Baserunner Time is straightforward and measurable, as are the Pitcher Delivery Time and the Catcher Pop Time. Baseball Info Solutions tracks all three of these using its frame-by-frame software. The final piece of the equation that is needed is the Tag Time. While Tag Time can differ based on the infielder, our research has shown that the accuracy of the catcher's throw is the most significant factor in determining the time it takes for the infielder to get the tag down. Therefore, we will translate our Catcher Arm Accuracy data into "expected" Tag Times for the purpose of evaluating the accuracy of catchers' throws.

It makes sense when you think about it with specific examples. When a catcher throws a ball high and to the third base side of the second base bag, the second baseman must reach up and across his body to catch the ball and then pull his glove diagonally down to his other side to make the tag. That creates a lengthy Tag Time, and that's what makes the throw inaccurate. In contrast, a throw that hits the fielder's glove just off the ground and on the first base side of the second base bag is already perfectly positioned for the tag, and that's what makes it perfectly accurate.

We looked at the catchers that had the best combined average Pop Time and Tag Time with at least 25 throws in 2014. Fast Pop Times paired with accurate throws result in catchers that are better than average in throwing baserunners out at second base.

Best Throwing Catchers, 2014

Minimum 25 Throws

Catcher	Avg Pop Time	Avg Tag Time	Combined Time	CS%	Throws
Y. Gomes	1.84	0.228	2.07	29%	40
R. Rivera	1.88	0.214	2.09	33%	43
R. Martin	1.88	0.227	2.10	32%	46
B. Holaday	1.91	0.206	2.11	28%	28
A. Avila	1.92	0.214	2.13	27%	42

Rene Rivera, Bryan Holaday, and Alex Avila claimed three of the top five spots for having the best throwing arm (Combined Pop plus Tag Time), partly because they were also the top three most accurate catchers according to their average Tag Time in 2014. In contrast, Yan Gomes and Russell Martin do not rate that well in terms of their accuracy, but they are so quick with their release and throw with such velocity that it's less important where the ball winds up in proximity to the second base bag.

Worst Throwing Catchers, 2014

Minimum 25 Throws

Catcher	Avg Pop Time	Avg Tag Time	Combined Time	CS%	Throws
K. Suzuki	2.03	0.234	2.26	15%	34
H. Conger	2.02	0.237	2.25	20%	41
J. Baker	2.01	0.227	2.24	12%	31
T. Flowers	2.00	0.221	2.22	26%	45
M. Montero	1.98	0.228	2.21	24%	44

Kurt Suzuki leaves a lot to be desired defensively. He shows up here as having the worst Combined Pop plus Tag Time in baseball among catchers that made at least 25 throws down to second base in 2014, and he also shows up as the third-worst pitch framing catcher in 2014 based on our Strike Zone Runs Saved data.

Catcher Arm Accuracy: Methodology

We wanted to take the approach of translating Catcher Arm Accuracy data into Tag Times for the purpose of comparing pop time and accuracy on the same scale. Surveying a sample of plays with throws grouped according to the grid shown below (the bottom row of the grid indicates throws that bounced), and using our frame-by-frame timing software, we found that the average Tag Times in each zone varied from 0.175 to 0.314 seconds.

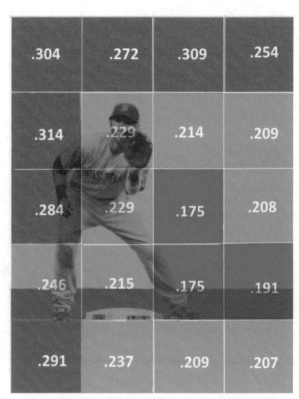

Tag Time Average by Accuracy Sector

As you can see, an accurate throw from the catcher can save the infielder up to 0.139 seconds (the difference between the slowest and fastest sectors) compared to an inaccurate throw, and that differential can determine whether the runner is safe or out on his steal attempt.

Catcher Arm Accuracy: Tag Times

We looked at all major league catchers with a minimum of 25 throws to second base in 2014 and calculated the average expected Tag Time for each catcher. The most and least accurate catchers are listed in the following tables.

Most Accurate Catchers, 2014

Minimum 25 Throws

Catcher	Avg Tag Time	Throws
B. Holaday	0.206	28
A. Avila	0.214	42
R. Rivera	0.214	43
R. Chirinos	0.220	31
T. Flowers	0.221	45

The Detroit Tigers' tandem of Holaday and Avila led the way for catchers having the most accurate arms in 2014.

Least Accurate Catchers, 2014

Minimum 25 Throws

Catcher	Avg Tag Time	Throws
E. Gattis	0.243	39
T. d'Arnaud	0.238	33
H. Conger	0.237	41
Y. Grandal	0.236	30
S. Perez	0.235	40

Evan Gattis, who in 2015 may primarily play in left field for the Houston Astros, had the least accurate arm in 2014. Salvador Perez, known for intimidating runners with his cannon arm behind the dish, sometimes struggles to locate those cannon shots.

Catcher Arm Accuracy: Wild Throws

All of the data discussed above does not account for wild throws, throws that are wide or high of the infielder and sail into the outfield.

Catchers with the Most Wild Throws, 2014

Catcher	Wild Throws
Y. Gomes	9
H. Conger	8
J. Saltalamacchia	7
R. Chirinos	6
E. Gattis	5

As demonstrated in the first table, our data shows that Yan Gomes had the best throwing arm in 2014 based on his Combined Pop plus Tag Times. However, Gomes also led all of baseball with nine throws that completely missed their mark. His Combined Time does not take into account all of the throws that he made in which a pop time could not be recorded because the throw was uncatchable for the infielder. Gomes is a player that takes many risks at trying to throw baserunners out on the basepaths. Even though he may be one of the best in the game by this analysis, he can still make improvements by reigning in his sometimes wild throws.

Conclusion

The approach that we have taken to translate our Catcher Arm Accuracy data into Tag Times allows us to evaluate a catcher's Pop Time and Accuracy simultaneously and on the same scale (and to explore the trade-off between the two). Overall, catchers who are quicker at releasing the ball, may not have the most accurate throws. For these players in particular, the lack of accuracy at times may be insignificant due to how strong the throws are. However, for players that don't have elite Pop Times, the variations in their accuracy can be meaningful. For example, Salvador Perez would jump five spots from ninth to fourth in Combined Pop plus Tag Time if his accuracy was similar to that of Robinson Chirinos.

Moving forward, this approach will also provide us the ability to do a couple of other things. It will allow us to develop all-encompassing catcher stolen base ratings independent of the pitcher, infielder, and baserunner. Further, it will allow us to enhance the algorithm we use as a basis for the prediction of stolen base success as explained in the next section.

Expected Stolen Base Success

As offense has declined in Major League Baseball over the last several years, and power numbers with it, teams do not have the same luxury of simply getting runners on base and waiting for the three-run homer that they once did. As such, the importance of the stolen base has increased as teams have needed to rely more heavily on alternative methods of advancing baserunners.

In 2011, Baseball Info Solutions began collecting Catcher Pop Times. That was followed in 2012 by the addition of Pitcher Delivery Times. Then, in 2013, we started recording baserunner Stolen Base Times. With this data available to us, we have developed a model by which we can predict the expected stolen base success rate of a specific baserunner going up against a given pitcher-catcher battery on stolen base attempts of second base.

Pitcher Delivery Times

There are several tactics that pitchers can use to help control the running game. They can vary their looks over to first base, they can vary the time that they take between coming set and starting their delivery, and they can vary their delivery time to the plate. The first two have more to do with gamesmanship and keeping the runner off balance. The pitcher's delivery time, however, has a more direct correlation to how likely it is that a runner will be able to successfully steal a base. The quicker the pitcher gets the ball to the plate, the less time the runner will have to get to second base safely.

Now, the significance of a pitcher's delivery time in controlling the running game is different for right-handed and left-handed pitchers. A lefty's delivery time is obviously less of a factor because he can still throw over to first base after a leg-lift, which affords him an element of deception that a right-hander doesn't have at his disposal. For this reason, when looking at the relationship between pitcher delivery times and runner caught stealing rates, we began by focusing only on right-handed pitchers. The way that we deal with left-handed pitchers as it applies to our overall algorithm will be discussed later in the article.

Here is how pitcher delivery times affect runner caught stealing rates for right-handed pitchers.

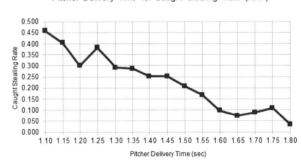

The chart confirms what we expected to see, namely that the quicker the pitcher is to the plate, the more likely the basestealer is to be thrown out. Specifically, this shows that a pitcher who can get the ball to the plate in 1.1 seconds is about 40 percent more likely to see the basestealer thrown out than a pitcher who takes 1.8 seconds.

Catcher Pop Times

As with pitchers and their delivery times, the quicker the catcher is with his pop time, the more successful we would expect him to be in throwing out basestealers. With pop times and their relationship to caught stealing rate, we again looked only at stolen base attempts with right-handed pitchers on the mound. There is a larger variation in the jumps that runners might get off a left-handed pitcher because of their tendency toward slower, more deceptive deliveries, and we wanted to remove as much of the noise this creates from the study as possible. Again, we will discuss how we deal with left-handed pitchers later in the article.

Here is how catcher pop times affect runner caught stealing rates with right-handed pitchers on the mound.

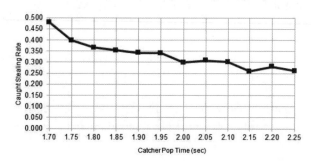

Again, this matches our expectations. The quicker a catcher gets the ball down to second, the more likely he is to throw the runner out. It is interesting to note, however, that the drop off in caught stealing rate from the fastest to the slowest pop times is not as dramatic as it is with pitcher delivery times. While we are not accounting for the accuracy of the catcher's throw with this data, this would suggest—and would support other research that we have done—that the pitcher has more of an impact on controlling the running game than the catcher does.

Stolen Base Times

Stolen base times also conform to expectations. Faster is better, of course. The quicker that a runner gets down to second base, the more likely he is to be safe.

As with the other individual pieces of this study, we have focused on stolen base attempts versus right-handed pitchers only.

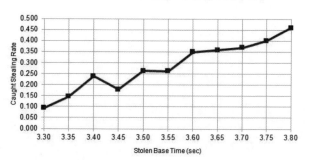

It should be noted that BIS collects its stolen base times by starting the clock on the pitcher's first move and stopping the clock when the runner touches second base. By recording stolen base times this way, a runner's jump is built in to his time. Therefore, our stolen base times capture more than a runner's pure speed. They are a combination of his speed and efficiency getting out of the blocks.

Net Times

Each of the charts above helps to confirm information that we intuitively know. When it comes to the race to second base between the baserunner and the battery (via their combined efforts of throwing the baseball), being faster leads to more success. However, beyond that basic point, those charts may be a bit misleading.

Yordano Ventura offers us a fascinating example. Ventura nearly made it to 200 career innings before anyone even attempted to steal a base against him—he now has two, one who was successful and one who was caught. While the fact that Ventura has one of the fastest average delivery times in baseball (1.21 seconds) obviously serves as something of a deterrent to baserunners, the pitcher delivery times chart above suggests that runners attempting to steal off of Ventura should succeed more than 50 percent of the time. If there really was better than a coin flip's chance of stealing second off of Ventura, then one would think that more adventuresome baserunners would have given it a shot by now. But only the two have. So, Ventura's delivery time can't be the only thing preventing runners from trying to steal off him.

There are two things that the pitcher delivery times chart does not tell us: 1) what kind of pop times were associated with the delivery times, and 2) what kind of stolen base times were associated with the delivery times. Similarly, the catcher pop times chart and the stolen base times chart lack the information on the other two players involved to inform any proper decision-making. In order to get a true sense of how successful a stolen base attempt might be, we need information on all three parties involved.

With that in mind, we took every stolen base attempt for which we have a recorded delivery time, pop time, and stolen base time and looked at the caught stealing rate as a function of the net time between the pitcher/catcher duo and the baserunner. Again, we did this only for instances where there was a right-handed pitcher on the mound. The chart below shows the resulting relationship. The open circles represent the actual results according to our data, while the solid line represents the best-fit line on which we have based our model.

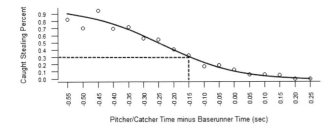

The chart shows that there is a non-linear relationship between Net Time and caught stealing rate. In order to develop an algorithm that would model the non-linearity of these results, we opted to apply a best-fit curve to the data through logistic regression.

The far left of the curve represents the instances where the throw beat the runner by a substantial amount. The data sample is small at the left most extreme, which is why the caught stealing rates there fluctuate the most. In general, the more the throw beats the runner by, the more likely the runner is to be thrown out. However, the caught stealing rate never quite gets to 100 percent because, no matter how well the pitcher and catcher do, the infielder does not always receive the throw cleanly at second base.

Moving to the right, as the margin by which the throw beats the runner diminishes and then transitions over to the runner getting in ahead of the throw, a change

in the Net Time results in larger changes in the caught stealing rate. Then things taper off again at the far right of the curve, eventually reaching the point where runners get in so far ahead of the throw that they are always safe.

A baserunner needs to be successful on approximately 70 percent or more of his stolen base attempts for his efforts to be beneficial to his team. Based on this model, we find that a 70 percent stolen base success rate—which would be a 30 percent caught stealing rate according to the previous chart—corresponds to a net time of -0.15 seconds (shown by the dashed lines in the chart). That means that, even if the baserunner slides in to second 0.15 seconds after the throw arrives, because of the lag between the infielder catching the throw and applying the tag, the baserunner is likely to be safe often enough to justify his having attempted the steal.

The Net Time chart only includes instances when there was a recorded catcher pop time on the play. On about 27 percent of all stolen base attempts of second base, we don't have a recorded pop time either because the catcher did not make a throw or because the catcher's throw was errant. Thus, our model currently assumes an on-target throw when determining the likelihood of success of the stolen base attempt.

Getting back to the example of Yordano Ventura, more often than not he is throwing to Salvador Perez, who has one of the fastest average pop times in the league at 1.90 seconds. Combining Ventura's average delivery time with Perez's average pop time gives us 3.13 seconds. The average stolen base time in BIS's database is 3.53 seconds. That means that the average basestealer only has about a 27 percent chance of successfully stealing against that duo, assuming Perez gets off a catchable throw. Now it makes more sense why runners would opt not to test themselves against Ventura.

Left-Handed Pitchers

Up to this point, we have focused on stolen base attempts that occur with right-handed pitchers on the mound because there is a higher degree of certainty in the meaningfulness of the discrete times. The runner is going to take off for second base as soon as a right-handed pitcher begins his delivery to the plate. We have confidence that both parties are starting the race at the same time, and thus we have confidence in our model.

With a left-handed pitcher on the mound, we cannot model the deception of his pickoff move to first nor a baserunner's decision-making process on when to break for second. Therefore, in order to incorporate lefties into the model, we have made a simplified assumption. If we assume that a runner is going to take off for second on the pitcher's first move, then all aspects of deception and gamesmanship are taken out of the equation, and we can fall back on the same model that we use for right-handed pitchers.

However, there is still one adjustment that we have to make to our model to account for left-handed pitchers. If the runner goes on the lefty's first move, there is always the possibility that the pitcher throws over to first base. Using the play-by-play data that we collect at BIS, we calculated that lefties throw over to first (rather than go home with the pitch) 22 percent of the time that there is a runner on first base with second base open. And of the times that a runner decides to attempt a steal on a pickoff attempt by a lefty, the runner reaches second base safely 22 percent of the time (coincidentally, both numbers are 22 percent). Therefore, the way that our algorithm addresses left-handed pitchers is to apply these percentages as adjustments to the logistic regression model that we came up with for right-handed pitchers.

Let's use a couple of Braves pitchers from 2014 as an example, hypothetically facing the Marlins. Aaron Harang is a right-handed pitcher who had an average delivery time in 2014 of 1.47 seconds. When Harang was paired with Evan Gattis and his 1.93 second average pop time, Adeiny Hechavarria and his 3.56 second average stolen base time had a 69 percent chance of successfully stealing a base off them. If Mike Minor, a left-handed pitcher with an average delivery time of 1.61 seconds, was the pitcher instead of Harang, Hechavarria would have had a 72 percent chance of stealing second safely if he were to take off on Minor's first move. While Minor's delivery time is much slower than Harang's, Hechavarria's expected success rate against the two is almost the same because there is that possibility that Minor might throw over. If a right-handed pitcher had a delivery time as slow as Minor's, we would expect Hechavarria to be safe about 85 percent of the time.

Other Factors for Consideration

There are several other factors that can potentially affect the success of a stolen base attempt that we have not accounted for in our model. We are at various stages of investigating the degree to which each affects the likelihood of a runner being thrown out and whether incorporating each into our model will improve its predictive accuracy.

The first thing that we considered is pitch type. As one might expect, because of the difference in velocity and movement of the various pitch types that make up the arsenals of major league pitchers, some pitches are easier to steal against than others. The table below shows how caught stealing rates vary by pitch type.

Pitch Type	Caught Stealing Rate
Cut Fastball	27%
Fastball	26%
Splitter	22%
Slider	21%
Changeup	21%
Curveball	16%
Knuckleball	33%

Cut fastballs hold a slight edge over normal fastballs probably because most cutters received by catchers are thrown by right-handed pitchers, meaning that the ball is actually moving in a direction that makes the exchange from glove to hand for the catcher the easiest. Otherwise, as velocity decreases and movement increases, it becomes more and more difficult to throw out a basestealer, with caught stealing rates bottoming out with the curveball. While the caught stealing rate on knuckleballs seems to buck this trend, the number of knuckleballs in the sample are actually very small, limited mainly to the offerings of R.A. Dickey. And Dickey actually has one of the fastest average delivery times in the league at 1.24 seconds, plus a harder-than-typical knuckleball, so the results for that pitch type probably aren't that instructive.

Another factor to consider is pitch location. The following diagram shows how caught stealing rates vary based on pitch location (the diagram is shown from the pitcher's perspective).

Caught Stealing Rate by Pitch Location

Caught Stealing Rate by Catcher Throw Sector

As is probably not a surprise to anyone, pitches thrown below the strike zone are the most difficult to throw out a basestealer on, while pitches thrown up in the zone, especially those high and away to right-handed hitters (where a pitchout will most often be thrown to) result in the highest incidence of the runner being gunned down. This probably isn't entirely independent of pitch type, actually. For example, curveballs usually end up low in the strike zone (often in the dirt) while fastballs are more often thrown higher in the strike zone.

Considering how much the location of the pitch affects the likelihood of a runner being caught stealing, it stands to reason that the location of the catcher's throw when it reaches second base will be significant as well. Beginning with the 2014 season, BIS started collecting data on Catcher Arm Accuracy. We plot where the catcher's throw ends up relative to the base and relative to the receiving infielder's body, as well as whether the throw bounced and whether the throw was received in front of the bag, behind the bag, or at the bag. The following diagram shows how caught stealing rates vary based on the catcher's throw location, with the bottom most row representing bounced throws.

There are also considerations to be made for the aggressiveness and/or speed of the baserunner. Through some preliminary studies that we have done, there appears to be a discernible tendency for many pitchers to speed up their delivery time when more aggressive basestealers are on first base. As it stands, our model uses a pitcher's average delivery time (as well as the catcher's average pop time and the runner's average stolen base time) to determine the likelihood of the runner being able to steal second. However, if a pitcher is more likely to speed up his delivery when there is a more aggressive runner on base, then there might be an opportunity for us to improve the accuracy of our model by using a runner-adjusted delivery time for the pitcher.

Similarly, there appear to be some catchers in the league who will speed up their pop times if there is a faster runner on base. Again, this is something worth further investigation to see if our model might be improved by using a runner-adjusted pop time for catchers.

Shift or Get Off the Pot

We have now come full circle.

In 1946, Lou Boudreau intuitively knew that he can increase the likelihood of getting an out by rearranging his defense. In 2015 we now use analytics to demonstrate this.

In 1946, Indians manager Lou Boudreau put on the first Ted Williams Shift, against Ted Williams, on July 14. He not only put three infielders to the right of second base, he put four!

In 2014, Cardinals manager Mike Matheny put on the Ted Williams Shift, against Lucas Duda, on April 24. It was no ordinary Shift. Like the original, Matheny had four players to the right of second base!

Compare the positioning of players between the two pictures. How unique it is to see all four infielders to the right of second. On top of that, their positioning is so similar. Both Boudreau and Matheny put the second baseman in short right field. Plus all the other infielders

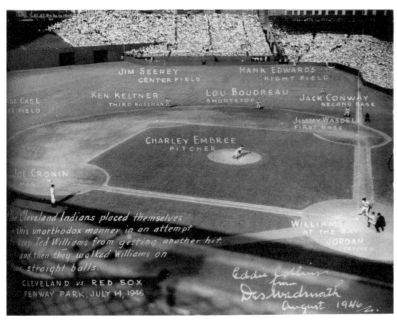

1946

2014

2014

Five-man infield, four-man shift, infield in

are playing very deep in the infield. Looking closer, the dirt part of the infield in 1946 looks smaller. That means the 2014 players are playing deeper than the 1946 players. But still, the 1946 players are playing deeper than they ordinarily would.

Mike Matheny's four-man Ted Williams shift was the only one of its kind in all of 2014. Not one other manager, not even Matheny himself, had the guts to do an extreme shift like this the rest of the year. With one exception.

It's a five-man infield, with a four-man shift, with the infield in. How cool is that? Someone needs to make up a clever name for that! The Seth Smith Super Shift? It's August 29 and Seth Smith is batting for the Padres in the bottom of the 12th of a tie game with the bags loaded and one out. It's the extremest of extreme situations. They have to do anything they can to stop that man at third from scoring. Any medium to deep flyball wins it. Dodger manager Don Mattingly knows Smith is an extreme pull hitter on grounders. So he brings in centerfielder Andre Either to play first base... er, what should we call it, to man the area near first base. Regular first baseman Adrian Gonzalez is to his right. Then it's regular second baseman Dee Gordon to Adrian's right. Then shortstop Miguel Rojas. Regular third baseman Justin Turner is at the normal third base position. So what happens? It works like a charm. A groundball right to Dee Gordon and he nabs the runner at the plate. Mattingly wins the battle... But he loses the war as the next batter singles to end the game.

Will we see this kind of extreme shifting again? Probably, but the point is that there is a revolution in baseball right now to experiment with defense and it's not going to stop. Just like defenses in other sports, most notably football, baseball defenses have begun to take on different shapes. Analytics are helping shape these defenses, and the shapes will continue to change as analytics continue to shed more light on the subject.

Let's walk through the recent history of The Shift.

Recent History of The Shift

Prior to **2006** – We don't have records but most fans will remember that a three-man Ted Williams shift was used for years on lumbering left-handed sluggers like David Ortiz, Jim Thome, Adam Dunn and Ryan Howard. This goes back to the 60's when teams occasionally shifted on similar players like Willie McCovey and Willie Stargell. While it is a strategy that has a long history, it was only sporadically used.

2006 – Just after publication of the first *Fielding Bible*, Baseball Info Solutions develops a software package to analyze defensive positioning called BIS-D. The general purpose is to help teams with defensive positioning by providing separate "smart charts" for infielders and outfielders against each batter they might face. But more specifically, the software identified players for whom a shift should be considered. Instead of the handful of players that were being shifted prior to that point, the software suggests that there are dozens of players that are shift candidates.

Brandon Moss
Bats Left
Last 120 grounders and short liners

Shift candidate! (92% right of 2B)

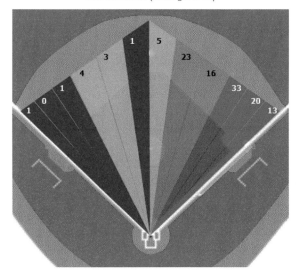

38% of last 250 balls in play were grounders and short liners.
2 bunt attempt(s) in last 300 plate appearances.

2007 and **2008** – Baseball Info Solutions presents BIS-D software to major league teams. While several teams show interest, only one or two teams subscribe to the BIS-D daily update product. It is not an overwhelming success.

2009 – *The Fielding Bible—Volume II* is published. BIS-D is introduced to the public showing examples of shift candidates. Charts for Ortiz, Thome, Howard and Dunn are shown demonstrating how they pull balls on the infield. Dunn is mentioned as only a marginal shift candidate. But other players are mentioned that are never shifted like Chase Utley and Brian McCann. More significantly, the shift is suggested by BIS-D software on several right-handed hitters like Jason Bay, Garret Atkins and Ben Francisco.

2010 – BIS starts counting shifts. Specifically, it's any play where a ball was hit while a shift is on. The Tampa Bay Rays lead MLB with 242 shifts. No other team is close (Mets are second with 169). With a minuscule payroll by comparison, the Rays beat out the Yankees and Red Sox and win the division.

2011 – The Rays do it again. They deploy 240 shifts and make the playoffs again with a limited payroll. The next closest team is Cleveland with 177 shifts.

2012 – This is where the Shift hits the fan and spreads all over baseball.

- *The Fielding Bible—Volume III* is published
- Analytics in the book show that shifting saves about 30 points on batting average (groundballs and short liners)
- Analytics show further that when deploying shifts, the type of pitch (fastball vs. breaking pitch) and the count should be a consideration
- BIS presents these analytics at the SABR Analytics conference in March
- BIS also presents shift analytics privately with many more teams.
- By the end of March, at least 20 teams in baseball have seen the BIS shift analytics showing the success of shifting
- We at BIS like to think the analytics we developed were instrumental in teams shifting more often
- But the most important reason that teams started to shift more often in 2012 was:
- Teams around baseball saw the Rays deployed more shifts than any other team in baseball the last two years and saw their overall success despite their limited payroll. The copycat strategy is a major strategy throughout sports – copying the strategies of the most successful teams. While the copycat strategy is not always successful, it very often has merit. "The shift works for the Rays – it can work for us."
- In the middle of the season BIS revises its Defensive Runs Saved calculations and develops Shift Runs Saved at the team level because shifting is a team strategy, not an individual player strategy. The Rays shifting saved 10 runs in each of 2010 and 2011. No other team was in double digits in either year.
- By the end of the 2012 season the Rays once again lead all of baseball in shifts, but now they've nearly doubled their output to 463 shifts. But now two other teams (Blue Jays and Indians) have over 400 shifts as well and MLB as a whole nearly doubles the number of shifts deployed over the 2011 season.
- The Rays save 10 runs for the third year in a row with their shift defense, but the Blue Jays edge them out for the shifting crown with 12 shift runs saved.

2013 – Now there are eight teams that surpass 400 shifts, with five of them over 500. The Rays have 561, but come in second to the Orioles' 599 shifts. The MLB total nearly doubles again from 2012. The Rays up the ante with 16 Shift Runs Saved. Three other teams have double-digit run-saving totals on the shift: Red Sox (15) runs, Orioles (11) and Reds (11).

2014 – MLB shifting increases again, by 63% over 2013. The Astros explode for 1,341 shifts. 15 teams surpass 400 shifts. In 2010 and 2011, the Rays were the *only* team that shifted more than 200 times. In 2014, every team *except* one (Rockies) shifted more than 200 times. The Astros save a whopping 27 runs utilizing the shift. Here's a chart that shows the number of teams with double-digit shift runs saved by season.

Number of Teams with Double-Digit Runs Saved

Season	Total Teams
2010	1
2011	1
2012	2
2013	4
2014	9

Shift Analytics Today

Now as we write this in January 2015, Lou Boudreau's intuition can be measured and demonstrated. Or, as my fellow actuaries would say, we can now substitute facts for appearances, and demonstrations for impressions. More shifts correlates to fewer hits, and more shifts translates into more runs saved on defense. Here are some of the analytics.

The Shift Lowers Batting Averages

In *The Fielding Bible—Volume III* we looked at the then 10-most-shifted hitters in baseball. They all faced the shift at least 100 times in 2010 and 2011 (or, the better way to say this, they all put a ball in play against the shift at least 100 times). The study showed that the shift lowered batting averages on grounders and short liners for these 10 hitters by 30 points, from .238 to .208.

Collectively, over two years, these 10 hitters faced 2,660 shifts. In 2014, teams deployed 13,296 shifts against all batters. The shift dropped the batting average by 32 points in 2014.

MLB Batting Averages, 2014

Grounders and Short Liners

Number of Shifts	No Shift	Shift	Difference
13,296	.266	.234	32 points

For more on this topic, including a breakdown on right-handed and left-handed hitters, see "The Shift Works" on page 57.

The Shift Saves Runs

In 2012, when shifting was taken to another level, we discovered a flaw in the Defensive Runs Saved (DRS) system. Brett Lawrie, third baseman for the Toronto Blue Jays, was on track for the highest single-season total of defensive runs saved ever recorded. This was happening because he was making quite a few plays that no other third baseman ever made. Namely, in a new shift strategy deployed by the Toronto Blue Jays, Lawrie was playing on the first-base side of second base and getting huge credit for plays he made there. To correct this problem BIS revised the DRS system to fit the new shift climate. Shift Runs Saved was developed.

Since shifting is a team strategy, Shift Runs Saved is solely a team metric. Brett Lawrie no longer gets credit for all the plays he was making. Instead, the team gets credit. But the credit only turns into a positive value of Shift Runs Saved if more outs are saved when the shift is on than when it is not on. Shift Runs Saved looks at all plays in the infield where the shift is deployed. It then compares how often outs are made when the shift is on relative to how often outs are made on all plays overall. Just like the rest of the DRS system for infielders, plays are categorized by how hard the ball was hit and the direction of the batted ball.

Thanks to their new strategy, the Toronto Blue Jays saved the most runs with the shift in 2012:

Most Shift Runs Saved, 2012

Team	Shift Runs Saved
Toronto Blue Jays	12
Tampa Bay Rays	10
Cleveland Indians	8
Baltimore Orioles	8
Boston Red Sox	7

Using the rule of thumb that 10 runs is worth one win, each of these teams improved themselves in the standings by about one game utilizing the shift.

Now look where we are just two years later:

Most Shift Runs Saved, 2014

Team	Shift Runs Saved
Houston Astros	27
Toronto Blue Jays	16
Boston Red Sox	13
Texas Rangers	12
St. Louis Cardinals	12
San Francisco Giants	12

A lot more runs are being saved with the shift. Here are the league-wide Shift Runs Saved totals since 2010:

MLB Shift Runs Saved, 2010-14

Year	Number of Shifts	Shift Runs Saved
2010	2,464	36
2011	2,357	42
2012	4,577	76
2013	8,180	135
2014	13,296	195

The answer is simple: the more you shift, the more you save.

Here is a complete chart of all the teams in 2014.

Shift Runs Saved by Team, 2014

Team	Number of Shifts	Shift Runs Saved
Astros	1,341	27
Blue Jays	686	16
Red Sox	498	13
Rangers	490	12
Cardinals	367	12
Giants	361	12
White Sox	534	11
Athletics	488	10
Phillies	291	10
Mariners	411	9
Tigers	205	8
Orioles	705	7
Indians	516	7
Twins	478	7
Padres	241	6
Pirates	659	5
Mets	221	5
Brewers	576	4
Diamondbacks	252	4
Reds	212	4
Cubs	316	3
Braves	213	3
Rays	824	2
Angels	347	2
Dodgers	208	2
Nationals	201	1
Rockies	114	1
Yankees	780	0
Royals	543	0
Marlins	208	-7
Total	**13,296**	**195**

Every team in baseball is shifting way more often than they did as few as three years ago. And it is paying off. But there are 10 teams (a third of the league) who shifted less than 260 times each for the season. Collectively they saved 27 runs (less than three runs per team). The other two thirds of the teams more than doubled their effectiveness, averaging over eight Shift Runs Saved per team.

Shift Runs Saved, 2014

Grouping	Shifts per Team	Shift Runs Saved per Team
Top 20 Shifting Teams	561	8.4
Bottom 10 Shifting Teams	208	2.7

I would give these 10 teams the same advice we gave in *The Fielding Bible—Volume III* after the 2012 season:

"If I were running a Major League Team, I would employ The Shift far more often…", or as the title of this article says, "Shift or Get Off The Pot."

When BIS developed its BIS-D defensive positioning software in 2006, very little interest was shown by major league teams. Now in 2015, more than half the teams in MLB subscribe to at least one of the many defensive-oriented products provided by Baseball Info Solutions.

One final graphic to enjoy. In 1959 the Fleer Corporation, a gum company who began producing baseball cards in 1923, made a special baseball card that depicted the Ted Williams Shift from 1946:

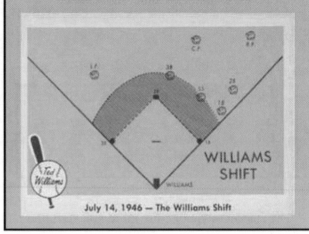

GETTING SHIFTY WITH TED

When Ted Williams came to the plate against Cleveland on July 14, Indian manager Lou Boudreau ordered a radical defensive alignment in which almost everyone on the field played right of second base, as exhibited on this 1959 Fleer baseball card. The alignment would forever be known as "The Williams Shift."

WILLIAMS SHIFT

July 14, 1946 — The Williams Shift

Defensive Alignment

There is now a continually increasing understanding throughout baseball that teams can improve their run prevention by positioning their fielders according to a hitter's ball-in-play tendencies. For some hitters, those trends may simply dictate subtle shading by the infielders relative to where they would normally play. Other hitters' approaches may require a full Ted Williams shift, where three infielders are positioned to one side of second base.

In each of the past three seasons, the total number of defensive shifts employed across the league has nearly doubled over what it had been the year before. And, just as the number of shifts that teams employ has increased, so too has the diversity of those shifts.

Shifts on Balls in Play by Season, 2010-14

Season	2010	2011	2012	2013	2014
Shifts	2,464	2,357	4,577	8,180	13,296

Traditionally, Baseball Info Solutions has relied on descriptive classifications of infield defensive alignment: No Shift, partial Ted Williams Shift, full Ted Williams Shift, and Situational Shift (the Situational Shift is an alignment in which the defense plays in to cut off a run at home, defends for a possible bunt, or brings in an outfielder to function as a fifth infielder). However, the way one team executes a partial or full shift can be very different from the way another team does in terms of where they place their infielders. Similarly, even if a team is not aligned in what we would classify as a shift, there can still be subtle differences between the way two teams approach the same hitter.

Therefore, in order to provide more insight into any given team's approach to defensive alignment, we began plotting the starting position of all visible infielders on all groundballs and short line drives (the ball-in-play types most affected by infield alignment). Now, in addition to the descriptive classifications of defensive alignment, we can also provide a detailed depiction of how a team positions its infielders in specific situations.

The Shift Decision

While many batters throughout the league are considered to be obvious shift candidates, others bring up an interesting philosophical decision for teams about how extreme a batter's tendencies must be in order to implement a shift. That decision is most important when considering a divisional opponent, as the team's defensive alignment can have a huge impact on the success of a pull-heavy hitter who they may face for upwards of 70 plate appearances over the course of a season. Some batters' division rivals disagree as to the optimal way to position their defense.

Take Adrian Gonzalez as an example. Gonzalez is capable of using the entire field, and he falls short of the 80 percent pull threshold on his grounders and short liners BIS frequently uses to identify potential shift candidates. However, Gonzalez has a couple of sections of the infield to which he hits the majority of his balls. One is in the hole between the traditional first and second basemen positions—which a full Ted Williams shift is effective at taking away—and the second is just to the third base side of the second base bag—which a full shift often leaves open.

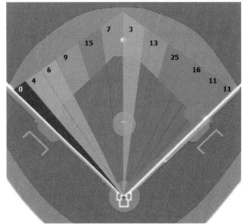

Adrian Gonzalez
Bats Left
Last 120 grounders and short liners

41% of last 250 balls in play were grounders and short liners.
0 bunt attempt(s) in last 300 plate appearances.

The Giants were the NL West team that best addressed Gonzalez's batted ball tendencies in 2014. They deployed 36 partial shifts—which put a defender in both of the sections of the infield that Gonzalez tends to hit the ball—along with 5 full shifts and 12 no shifts (traditionally aligned defenses). Not surprisingly, they also had the most success, limiting Gonzalez to a .097 batting average on grounders and short liners. The Rockies also shifted Gonzalez more often than not, deploying 7 partial shifts and 18 full shifts against 16 no shifts. They also had success, holding Gonzalez to a .192 average on his balls to the infield. Neither the Padres nor the Diamondbacks were as committed to shifting. Collectively, they shifted 23 times against 72 no shifts, and Gonzalez hit .286 on his grounders and short liners against them combined.

The following image displays those teams' defensive alignments against Gonzalez over the course of the season. Each dot represents the starting position of an infielder on a grounder or short line drive. Black X's represent first basemen, green triangles are second basemen, red circles show shortstops, and blue squares are third basemen. You can see the Giants tendency to use partial shifts in the first chart. Their biggest cluster of shortstop dots against Gonzalez are just to the third base side of the second base bag, but they still deploy their second basemen in shallow right field more often than not. In contrast, the Rockies used mostly full shifts when they shifted Gonzalez, so most of the time their shortstops were positioned across second base. Both San Diego and Arizona stuck to a traditional defensive alignment most of the time.

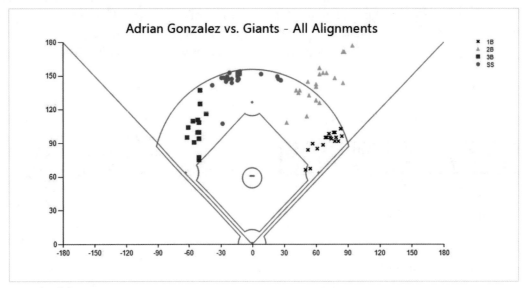

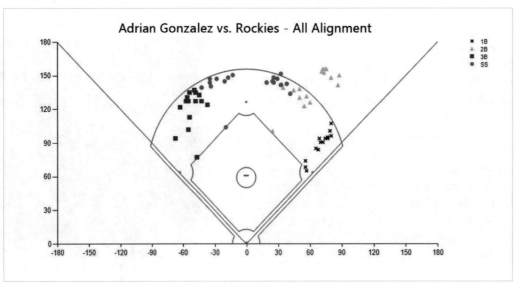

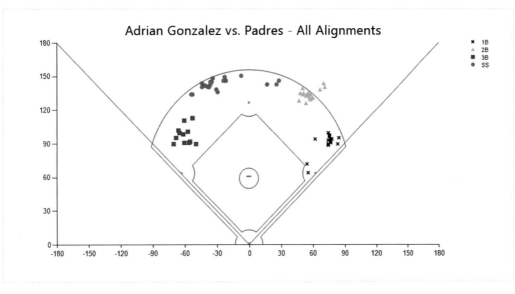

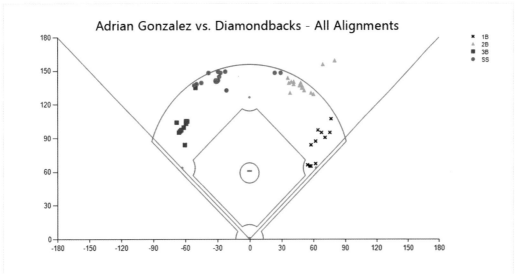

Shift Deployment and Positioning

Even when two division opponents do agree that a player is a prime shift candidate, they still can differ greatly in how they align their defense against him. Adam Dunn, who played the bulk of the last two seasons for the White Sox, is a dead-pull power hitter and a classic shift candidate. Since the start of the 2013 season, teams have shifted Dunn 746 times, third most of any batter in MLB. As you'd expect, his AL Central rivals were some of the more aggressive teams in their defensive alignment against Dunn. Cleveland, traditionally a very shift-heavy club, earned that characterization with their alignment against Dunn, full shifting him in 61 of 64 available plate appearances over the two seasons. Kansas City's defense against Dunn was nearly as extreme, as they deployed a full Ted Williams shift on 48 of the 54 available occasions.

However, comparing those two teams' alignments when they did shift produces some interesting conclusions. Even when both teams used a full shift, there were some differences between their alignments. The most dramatic difference is at third base. On all but one occassion, Indians' third basemen played near the traditional shortstop postition in their full shift against Dunn. In contrast, the Royals' third basemen regularly played near the third base line, opening up a hole between the shortstop position and the second base bag.

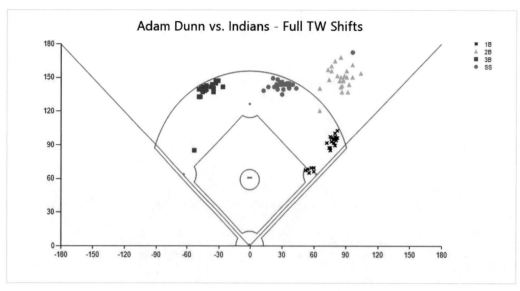

Adam Dunn vs. Indians - Full TW Shifts

Legend: ✕ 1B, ▲ 2B, ■ 3B, ● SS

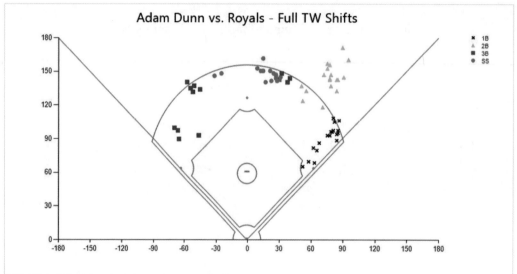

Adam Dunn vs. Royals - Full TW Shifts

Legend: ✕ 1B, ▲ 2B, ■ 3B, ● SS

Dunn was much more successful against Kansas City's version of the shift than he was against the more compact Cleveland alignment. His batting average on grounders and short liners (balls likely to be affected by the infield alignment) into the shift was .370 against the Royals, his second-best mark against any team in the AL. Meanwhile, his batting average on grounders and short liners was .148 against the Indians' shifts, his second-worst performance against any team that shifted him 25 or more times.

Given the small sample, we can't definitively declare the Indians' alignment to be superior, but it makes sense given that Dunn hits few balls near the third baseline.

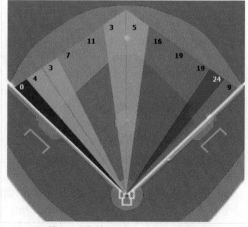

Adam Dunn

Bats Left

Last 120 grounders and short liners

40% of last 250 balls in play were grounders and short liners.
0 bunt attempt(s) in last 300 plate appearances.

The defensive alignment data also allow us to compare how teams deploy shifts in general. While the Ted Williams Shift against left-handed batters is well established, shifting against righties became commonplace for the first time in 2014. The two most prolific shifters against right-handed hitters, Houston and Tampa Bay, have displayed some subtle differences in how they arranged their defenders in those situations.

The following images display the two teams' full shift alignment charts against right-handed batters from 2013-14 with no runners on base.

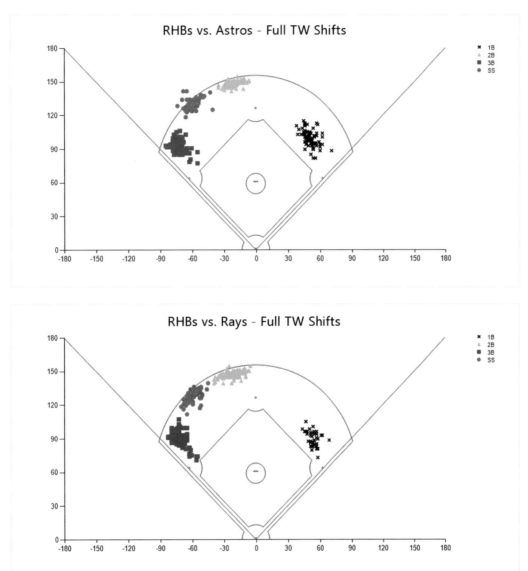

As you can see, there are interesting differences in the deployment of this shift. Notably, Houston first basemen tend to move with the shift, positioning themselves between first and second, while in Tampa's case the first basemen stayed closer to the bag. Additionally, Houston's shortstops lined up in the outfield grass on multiple occassions, which none of Tampa's infielders ever did. Finally, Tampa's third baseman was positioned more shallow on average.

Houston's shift defense against right-handed batters has been more effective, limiting them to a .249 batting average on grounders and short liners compared to .281 for Tampa Bay. This is a small difference but possibly significant.

Shading and Standard Positioning

Even when a team decides to employ a standard defensive alignment against a batter, infielders must make vitally important decisions about their positioning. With each batter, defenders adjust their depth and vary their positioning to compensate for the hitter's handedness and pull tendencies. Using the Defensive Alignment dataset, we are now able to analyze these subtle movements, understanding which fielders make the largest and the smallest batter-to-batter adjustments and how that affects their ability to field the balls a specific batter puts into play.

Two teams that rely on different degrees of defensive shading are the Mets and the Royals. Let's start by looking at how Ruben Tejada and Wilmer Flores of the Mets positioned themselves on non-shifts versus right-handed hitters in 2014.

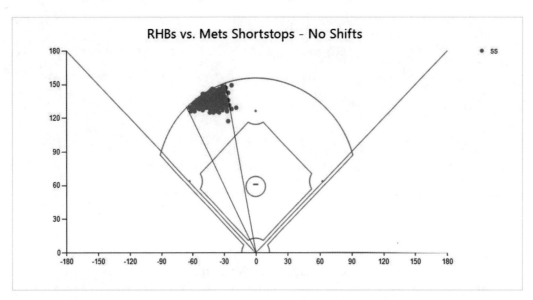

Using those two lines from home plate to the left and right boundaries of their positioning, we can then compare it to how they positioned themselves versus left-handed hitters.

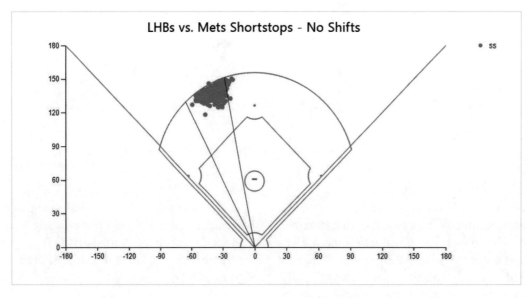

While there is some slight movement toward the second base bag, which is the pull side for left-handed hitters, Tejada and Flores use fairly consistent positioning regardless of the hitter's bat side. Contrast that with Alcides Escobar of the Royals, who makes more significant shading adjustments. First, here is his positioning versus right-handed hitters using the same boundary markers.

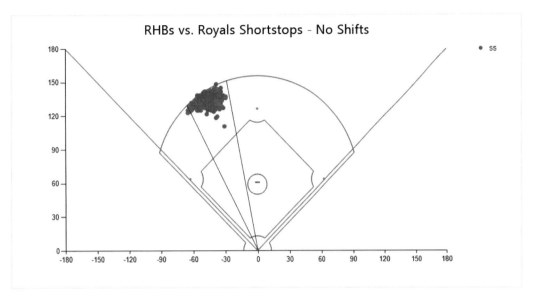

Compared to the Mets, Escobar's distribution of alignments is skewed more toward the third base side, albeit with fairly similar extremes. Against left-handed hitters, the differences are more stark.

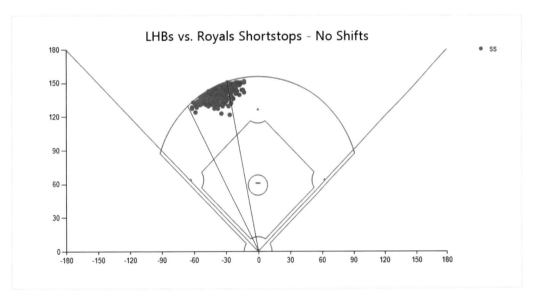

Here, Escobar shows a clear tendency to shade himself toward the second base bag, so much so in fact that he is right on the border of a partial Ted Williams shift in a lot of cases.

The differences between the Mets and Royals with the shading of their shortstops reflect their overall team strategies. In 2014, the Royals shifted on 543 balls in play, more than twice as many as the Mets (221). It stands to reason that their shading tendencies would match those shifting tendencies. Of course, it could also be the case that Escobar is individually motivated to alter his positioning based on the batter and Tejada and Flores are not, perhaps because of differences in their comfort levels with backhanded plays or sight lines.

Conclusion

The explosion in the number of defensive shifts across baseball in recent seasons is clear evidence that a blind commitment to traditional defensive alignments is a thing of the past. Defensive Alignment data allows us to take the modern approach to defense a step further. There is no reason that baseball cannot soon mirror a sport like football, where teams deploy a variety of different defensive alignments based on an offense's tendencies for a specific situation, be that based on a specific hitter, a count, a pitcher's sequence, and more.

No Matter How You Slice It, The Shift Works

Back in 2010, when Baseball Info Solutions began tracking defensive shifts, only a handful of batters received the shift treatment. It was power-hitting left-handers like Adam Dunn, Ryan Howard, and David Ortiz and that's it. Since, as shifting has nearly doubled across baseball every season, teams have started to use the shift against less and less obvious shift candidates. As such, it's fair to wonder whether shifting has continued to be an effective defensive strategy.

To answer that question, we thought we would take a look at various breakdowns of our shift data. We will use splits by batter handedness as well as pitcher handedness and will look at the Batting Average on Grounders and Short Liners (BAGSL) of hitters within each split category in order to determine whether the shift has been effective in preventing hitters from reaching base. We have chosen to look at grounders and short liners because those are the ball-in-play types that are most affected by The Shift. Previous research has demonstrated that defensive shifts do not typically have any bearing on the outcome of flyballs or line drives hit to the outfield.

We will be looking at the data in aggregate from 2010-14, as well as for 2014 only. For the five-year totals, we chose only hitters with 25 or more shifts. For the 2014 season totals, we instead used a 20-shift minimum.

Left-Handed Batters

Let's begin with lefty swingers, since lefties remain the most commonly shifted batters. Starting with how they fared against right-handed pitchers, defenses have held down batting averages by 40 points over the time period ranging from 2010-14.

Batting Average of Shifted LHB against RHP

2010-14

Alignment	Hits	At-Bats	BAGSL
Shifted	1,952	8,968	.218
Not Shifted	7,935	30,762	.258

Likewise, if we look only at what shifted lefties did against right-handed pitchers in 2014, we see similar results. Defenses limited batting averages by 43 points in that situation last year.

Batting Average of Shifted LHB against RHP

2014

Alignment	Hits	At-Bats	BAGSL
Shifted	723	3,297	.219
Not Shifted	867	3,304	.262

The Shift has not been quite as effective when a left-handed pitcher has faced a left-handed hitter from 2010-14. In this instance, defenses have been able to reduce batting averages by 23 points.

Batting Average of Shifted LHB against LHP

2010-14

Alignment	Hits	At-Bats	BAGSL
Shifted	499	2,283	.219
Not Shifted	2,483	10,278	.242

If we look at 2014 on its own, employing The Shift against lefty batters with left-handed pitchers on the mound shows a similar difference of 25 points.

Batting Average of Shifted LHB against LHP

2014

Alignment	Hits	At-Bats	BAGSL
Shifted	155	726	.213
Not Shifted	252	1,057	.238

While this greater level of effectiveness in 2014 comes with the caveat of featuring a smaller sample size of at-bats, the numbers still tell us that teams are more effective in using The Shift than in not using it.

Right-Handed Batters

Part of the reason for the significant increase in defensive shifts in recent seasons is that teams have realized the benefit of shifting more often against certain right-handed hitters. While righties still are not shifted nearly as frequently as lefties, defenses have recognized that The Shift can be utilized just as effectively against them.

Looking at right-handed hitters against right-handed pitchers from 2010-14, defenses have managed to lower batting averages by 30 points.

Batting Average of Shifted RHB against RHP
2010-14

Alignment	Hits	At-Bats	BAGSL
Shifted	311	1,286	.242
Not Shifted	3,886	14,293	.272

Of those 1,286 potentially shift-affected at-bats from 2010-14, more than half came in 2014 alone (677). As would be expected, the reduction in batting averages looking just at this season has been a very similar 39 points to the results that include the last five years combined.

Batting Average of Shifted RHB against RHP
2014

Alignment	Hits	At-Bats	BAGSL
Shifted	163	677	.241
Not Shifted	548	1,956	.280

With right-handed hitters facing left-handed pitchers, the trend holds, but it is lessened. From 2010-14, defenses held righties in this situation to a batting average that is 15 points lower when they use a shift compared to when they do not.

Batting Average of Shifted RHB against LHP
2010-14

Alignment	Hits	At-Bats	BAGSL
Shifted	136	521	.261
Not Shifted	1,409	5,111	.276

And, just as we have seen with the other splits, when we restrict ourselves to righty hitters versus lefty pitchers in 2014 alone, The Shift continues to demonstrate its effectiveness, reducing batting averages by 11 points.

Batting Average of Shifted RHB against LHP
2014

Alignment	Hits	At-Bats	BAGSL
Shifted	77	286	.269
Not Shifted	177	633	.280

Conclusion

By splitting the shift data up into the various combinations of batter and pitcher handedness, it can be seen that no matter how you slice it, the shift works. Whatever arm the pitcher throws with, and whatever side the batter steps in on, the use of defensive shifts has consistently improved the ability of team defenses to prevent certain hitters from reaching base on grounders and short liners.

Possible Drawbacks of Shifting

The last few years have seen a complete transformation in the role of the shift in baseball. Once an oddity employed by just a few of the most statistically-minded clubs, the shift is more prevalent in today's game than ever before and has been accepted as a component of a winning strategy by nearly every decision-maker in baseball. The most shift-heavy team in baseball in 2014, the Astros, more than doubled the 2013 Orioles' record for shifts on balls in play in a season. In addition to Houston, five other teams outpaced Baltimore's short-lived record in 2014. The Rockies shifted less than any team in baseball, but even they reached a total of 114 shifts, which would have ranked sixth in MLB in 2010. Overall, teams are aggressively pushing to discover how valuable the shift can be to their defensive efforts; 28 of the 30 clubs shifted more in 2014 than they did in 2013.

However, the widespread deployment of the shift does not mean that the strategy doesn't have its detractors. Many argue that the value of the shift is diminished by a combination of several factors that together markedly reduce the value of utilizing a non-traditional alignment. We will examine Defensive Misplays/Errors, Double Plays, Foul Flyouts, and Bunts and quantify their impact on the shift to determine how these variables might impact a team's defensive strategy.

Defensive Misplays and Errors

In a shift, fielders are frequently challenged to make different plays than they're accustomed to. For instance, third basemen are used to playing near the third base line, where groundballs and liners have a typical bounce, curvature, and reaction time. However, when a shift is on, the third baseman might be playing near the shortstop's typical position or on the other side of the field entirely. The third baseman (and any other shifted infielder) is tasked with fielding balls in an area of the infield they're not used to and making a throw at an angle and distance that is not a part of their traditional job description. Do fielders make more mistakes when they're taken out of their respective comfort zones by a shift?

That is something we can measure using Defensive Misplays and Errors (DMEs). DMEs are discrete fielding events where a fielder makes a negative play that results in a tangible consequence, such as a base lost or an out lost. They cover a broad spectrum of plays such as failures to hit the cutoff man, bad routes taken to balls in play, and failures to catch in-reach throws. Changes in defensive alignment clearly affect the chances fielders can reach certain balls in play, and any changes in DME frequency would potentially illustrate the effect of the unfamiliar positioning on fielders.

For this study, we calculated a weighted average of the 25 batters who had seen the most shifts from a specific side of the plate since 2010. This allows us to limit confounding factors, including the possibility that the defender's misplays might be impacted by a particularly speedy batter putting pressure on the play. Then, we compared how frequently defenses made misplays and errors both when they shifted those hitters and when they did not as a ratio of how frequently putouts were made on those plays. We further restricted the data to include only groundballs and short line drives, which are the balls in play defensive shifts impact most directly.

Here are the results:

DMEs Per Putout with and without Shifts, 2010-14

Top 25 Shifted Hitters

	No Shift		Shift		
	Plays	Plays/Putout	Plays	Plays/Putout	Diff.
DMs	517	0.077	302	0.058	0.019
Errors	196	0.029	139	0.027	0.002
DMEs	713	0.106	441	0.084	0.022

The error rate of fielders with and without the shift is similar, and in fact fielders make 0.2 percent fewer errors per play when in the shift, which runs counter to the perception that fielders might be worse playing out of their typical positioning. Meanwhile, fielders have made Defensive Misplays much less frequently while in the shift, on just 5.8 percent of plays compared to 7.7 percent with no shift.

This result is the opposite of the perception that fielders should struggle playing out of their normal positioning, but it seems reasonable. The goal of shifting is to put your fielders in the best positions to make plays. That isn't just increasing the likelihood of making a play, but it's also increasing the frequency of routine plays. When a left-handed hitter hits a hard grounder up the middle and a shifted fielder is there waiting for it, he has plenty of margin for error. Even if he bobbles it or pulls the first basemen off the bag, there will be a better chance to recover and still record an out compared to an unshifted second basemen trying to dive and throw to first against his momentum.

The advantage defensive teams are seeing on Defensive Misplays and Errors with the shift are captured by our Shift Runs Saved calculations. Those measurements are more accurate than our commonly cited Batting Average on Grounders and Short Liners (BAGSL) because they include errors as a negative result. According to Shift Runs Saved, defenses have saved 289 runs against these 25 hitters since 2010 because of the shift.

Turning the Double Play

Another potential drawback of the shift is that it could make it more difficult for infielders to successfully turn a double play. The traditional defensive alignment features the shortstop and second baseman positioned on either side of second base, ready to cover the bag should a grounder be hit to their middle infield counterpart or another infield glove. The shift will often result in only one fielder being in the vicinity of second base, or in the third baseman being shifted toward the traditional shortstop area and forced to act as the pivot man. Either situation naturally may lead to concerns over whether the shift reduces the team's ability to effectively turn the double play, costing the defense outs that would be recorded were they playing in a traditional alignment.

These concerns came to fruition for the Mets in their May 15, 2014 game against their crosstown rivals. In the top of the seventh, the Mets deployed a full shift with Brian McCann in the box, a runner on first, and one out in a scoreless ballgame. Jacob deGrom induced a groundball to Daniel Murphy that should have resulted in an inning-ending double play. Murphy threw to second, where David Wright was covering. Wright's footwork lacked the fluidity of a seasoned middle infielder in attempting to complete the pivot, and his throw failed to retire McCann at first base. Two pitches later, deGrom hung a slider to Alfonso Soriano, whose double to left-center scored McCann for what would prove to be the only run of the ballgame. While McCann's grounder may very well have been a single against an unshifted defense, Wright's issues making this pivot anecdotally support the idea that the shift could weaken a defense's double play chances.

To investigate whether those concerns had an impact on the field in a more general sense, we measured how frequently double plays were successfully turned since 2010. We again looked at only the 25 batters who had been shifted the most from a specific bat side in that time frame.

Double Play Completion Rate, 2010-14
Top 25 Shifted Hitters

Alignment	DP Opps	DP Successes	DP Completion Rate
No Shift	1,167	808	69.2%
Shift	454	303	66.7%

When we examine all of the double plays that were started (an out is recorded on a groundball in double play situations, which we define as situations with a runner on first and less than two outs), then the concerns about the shift reducing a defense's ability to turn the double play seem well-founded. A lower percentage of double plays are converted in the shift, with 66.7 percent of potential double plays being successfully completed in the shift compared to 69.2 percent in traditional defensive alignments.

As suspected, third basemen seem to be the primary culprits. Tasked with the responsibilities of the pivot man on double play attempts in a shift, third basemen turn a lower percentage of double plays than their middle infield teammates. This supports the notion that the third baseman might be better off on the right side in a shift, leaving the left side and the double play pivot responsibilities to the shortstop.

Double Play Opportunities in the Shift, 2010-14

Pivot Man	DP Completion Pct
2B	63.2%
3B	62.7%
SS	64.8%

However, it's vital to note that if the shift is doing its job, there will be more double plays started with a shift on than without it. It's possible that even though double plays are turned less successfully there may still be more double plays turned than in a non-shifted alignment. Using a weighted average of the top shift candidates on groundballs in all double play situations:

Groundballs in Double Play Situations, 2010-14

Top 25 Shifted Hitters

Alignment	No Outs	One Out	Two Outs
No Shift	28.5%	35.1%	36.4%
Shift	23.2%	39.9%	36.9%

When we include all grounders in double play situations, we see that shifts increase the number of plays resulting in both one and two outs. While the shift does make it slightly more difficult to turn the double play, it counteracts that effect by providing additional opportunities to turn double plays by increasing the number of fielded grounders. As a result, more double plays, along with fielder's choices and other one-out results, are completed overall.

Our Shift Runs Saved calculation gives the defense credit for getting one out on the play, but it does not credit or penalize the defense for turning/not turning the double play. To appropriately account for the extra benefit of the shift, we need to multiply this small 0.5 percent difference (36.9 – 36.4) by the run value difference (0.57, as calculated in *The Fielding Bible—Volume III*). From this calculation, we estimate that defenses saved two additional runs since 2010 against these 25 batters due to the slightly increased likelihood of turning the double play.

Foul Flyouts

In the fifth inning of the Red Sox game against the Reds on May 6, 2014, David Ortiz hit a ball into foul territory along the third base line at Fenway Park. Third baseman Todd Frazier, ideally the best player to make the catch, was watching the play from his shifted position on the other side of the diamond. Shortstop Zack Cozart chased the foul flyball but came up short as the ball dropped harmlessly to the ground a few feet short of the box seats. On the very next pitch, Ortiz lined a ground-rule double to right field, where he was stranded at the end of the inning.

That fifth inning at-bat suggests that pop fouls to the infield's weak side might be caught less frequently when a shift is employed. However, that is not always the case. Two innings later, Ortiz hit a similar pop foul slightly

closer to the third base line that Cozart had time to get underneath for the catch. In addition, having an extra infielder cheating towards the pull side foul line might boost the chance of catching a foul ball down that line. So what is the net impact?

From 2010 to the present, 78 percent of foul flyouts were hit to the opposite side. As a result, we might expect that the shift costs the defense more foul flyouts than it saves.

To determine if that is the case, we looked at foul flyout rates (per ball in play) with and without the shift for the top 25 shifted hitters since 2010. For the most part, hitters were largely consistent in their foul flyout rates with and without the shift. For example, Jose Bautista fouled out more than any other hitter with the shift (6.1 percent) and the second most without a shift (6.0 percent). On the other end of the spectrum, Ryan Howard flew out in foul territory 0.7 percent of his shifted balls in play and 1.8 percent of his unshifted balls in play, the fewest and second fewest among the top 25 shifted batters, respectively.

We calculated the weighted average of the foul flyout rates with and without the shift for these 25 hitters. Sure enough, there were fewer foul flyouts with the shift on than without it, dropping the foul flyout rate by 1.1 percent from 3.2 percent to 2.1 percent.

Foul Flyouts Per Ball in Play, 2010-14

Top 25 Shifted Hitters

	Foul Flyouts	Shift	No Shift
Foul Flyout Rate	1,047	2.1%	3.2%

Using the run expectancy matrix, a foul flyout is worth about -0.28 runs for the offense, while a foul ball (a strike) is worth about -0.06 runs for the offense. The difference between the two is about 0.22 runs. Multiplying the decrease in foul flyout rate (1.1 percent) by the difference in run values (0.22 runs) yields 0.00242 runs per ball in play, which translates to a difference of about 2.4 runs per 1,000 balls in play. This translates to about 31 runs lost since 2010 due to lost foul flyouts.

Bunts

Perhaps the most obvious potential drawback to using a defensive shift is that it leaves the defensive team vulnerable to the batter bunting for a single. With the defense mostly vacating one side of the infield, particularly the area down the batter's opposite field foul line, it can seem like the batter is basically being invited to take first base.

However, the decision for the batter to bunt against the shift is not quite that straightforward. First, it depends on how skilled the hitter is at getting the bunt down in the first place. Many of the most shifted players are power hitters and have never had to bunt with any regularity in their careers. While there is obviously more margin for error when bunting against a shift, there is still a certain skill required in getting the bunt down with the proper weight and direction to be able to reach first base safely. Second, the batter's decision also depends on how extreme his pull tendency is. He might have a better chance of beating a shift than another hitter by swinging away because he can more easily hit the ball up the middle or to the opposite field.

We looked at the 25 most shifted hitters since the start of 2010, and generally speaking they do not try to bunt against the shift very often. Collectively, they have laid down a bunt on about 6 out of every 1000 balls in play against the shift, and that rate has remained consistent from year to year despite the significant increase in the number of shifts that defenses have deployed. That said, when they do bunt against the shift, they are generally pretty successful, with 67 percent of their non-sacrifice attempts going for hits. For comparison, the league as a whole, when facing a non-shifted defense, has laid down a non-sacrifice bunt on about 13 out of every 1000 balls in play over that same time frame with a 33 percent hit rate.

Despite those 25 hitters not attempting to bunt very often, there is still the question of whether defenses have cost themselves runs by exposing themselves to the shifted bunt single.

The table below shows a breakdown of their non-sacrifice bunt attempts.

Bunt for Hit Attempts, 2010-14

Top 25 Shifted Batters

Alignment	All BIP	Bunt Strikes*	Bunt Outs	Bunt Hits	Bunts Per 1000 BIP
No Shift	22,720	49	19	11	1.3
Shift	15,251	114	31	63	6.2

*Includes missed bunts and foul bunts.

As little as these hitters bunt when they are being shifted against, they almost never bunt when they are not being shifted.

Using the run expectancy matrix, a bunt strike is worth about -0.06 runs to the hitter, a bunt out is worth about -0.28 runs, and a bunt hit is worth about +0.47 runs. Applying those run values to the results these hitters have seen translates to about 0.9 runs per 1000 balls in play when bunting against the shift and -0.1 runs per 1000 balls in play when bunting against a non-shifted defense. That amounts to about 1.0 runs per 1000 balls in play lost by teams through their use of the defensive shifts, or about 16 total runs lost since the start of 2010.

Conclusion

We've quantified several aspects of the shift and need to sum their collective impact against these 25 hitters since 2010:

Shift Runs Saved	+289 runs
Double Plays	+2 runs
Foul Flyouts	-31 runs
Bunts	-16 runs
Total	+244 runs

In total, the shift remains a comfortably positive event for the defense. However, there are a handful of additional variables that one should account for when considering a shift for an opposing hitter.

- Depending on the infielders' skill sets in a double play situation, the shortstop should stay near his normal positioning so he can act as the pivot man rather than the third baseman.
- Depending on the ballpark and the flyball tendencies of a given hitter and pitcher, it might make sense to reduce the shift or at least cheat towards the opposite foul line to cover potential foul flyballs.
- Though few batters have shown both the willingness and ability to lay down a bunt against a shift, it can be an effective strategy at beating the shift. Defenses should check their advanced reports to be aware of a shift candidates' bunt frequency and adjust accordingly.

Shifts Have Limited Effect on Run Scoring

The Shift is a useful defensive strategy in baseball, but not a major factor in league-wide run scoring. The concept of eliminating shifting because it affects run scoring is like a doctor saying to a patient that he is going to treat his broken leg by giving him a Tylenol. But the idea of banning defensive shifts in an effort to inject more offense into the game keeps coming up. Most recently, new MLB Commissioner Rob Manfred suggested that he would be in favor of eliminating shifts in an interview he gave this past January. We at Baseball Info Solutions (BIS), as well as other analysts, have made this point before, but it's worth making again. There is an edge to be gained for teams by employing the shift against certain hitters, but the overall effect on the offensive environment of the game is minimal because the number of batted balls on a shift is still a small percentage of all batted balls put in play.

In 2014, with shifts skyrocketing to new heights across the league, BIS has calculated that the league as a whole saved an estimated 195 runs through the use of defensive shifts. That's 6.5 runs per team for the entire year. For comparison, back in 1969, when the pitcher's mound was lowered to increase offense, run scoring went up by 105 runs per team. Shifts are a drop in the bucket by comparison.

Another way to evaluate this is to look at the league-wide Batting Average on Balls in Play (BABIP). Even as shifting has increased, there hasn't been any visible effect on league-wide BABIP. The table below shows what

league-wide BABIP has been over the last 10 years, as well as the shifts data that we have been collecting at Baseball Info Solutions since 2010.

Season	BABIP	Shifts
2014	.299	13,296
2013	.297	8,134
2012	.296	4,577
2011	.295	2,357
2010	.297	2,464
2009	.299	-
2008	.300	-
2007	.303	-
2006	.301	-
2005	.295	-

Here is what we wrote in John Dewan's Stat of the Week (www.statoftheweek.com) in July 2014:

Based on research that we have done at BIS, we know that the shift lowers the batting average on grounders and short liners (the ball in play types most affected by the shift) by about 30 points. In 2014, the batting average on grounders and short liners on shifted plays was .234, and on non-shifted plays it was .266. That's a significant difference. However, despite the shift being employed far more often in 2014 than any previous season, it was still only used about 10 percent of the time. Therefore, the overall batting average on all grounders and short liners in baseball has been .264, only a 2 point difference from the .266 average on non-shifted plays.

And that's just grounders and short liners. If you factor in ALL balls in play, that 2 points gets diluted even further, because the infield shift has no effect on balls hit to the outfield. The league-wide BABIP in 2014 was .299, but it would have been .300 without the shifting. So, in general the shift is only going to lower the overall BABIP by about 1 or 2 points, and that gets lost in the noise when looking at year-to-year BABIPs.

However, just because it might be difficult to see the impact that shifting has had when looking at year-to-year numbers doesn't mean that shifting hasn't had a meaningful impact. In 2014, teams saved 195 runs throughout baseball by shifting. If we assume all those runs would have been earned, that means the league's overall ERA of 3.74 would actually have been 3.78 if teams weren't shifting. So, the shift does make a difference.

As the data shows, the shift is just a small part of run prevention. Regulating it isn't going to reverse recent run-scoring trends. A difference of 6.5 runs per team and 1 or 2 points of league-wide BABIP would barely make a difference.

Team Defense

The 2014 postseason proved to be an excellent barometer of the importance of defensive play to team success. In the regular season, 17 teams saved at least 10 runs based on the combined defensive efforts of everyone on the team as well as their defensive shifting. Of those 17 teams, 8 were playoff teams, including the St. Louis Cardinals, who led all of baseball with 71 Runs Saved, and the Baltimore Orioles, who led the American League with 64 Runs Saved.

In contrast, the Detroit Tigers were the only playoff team with double-digit negative Runs Saved. Their -62 Runs Saved total was second-worst in all of baseball, ahead of only the Minnesota Twins (-83 Runs Saved). The Tigers made a concerted effort to improve themselves defensively prior to the 2014 season. That included trading for both shortstop Jose Iglesias and second baseman Ian Kinsler and trading away offensive stalwart and defensive liability Prince Fielder, which allowed the team to move Miguel Cabrera back to first base.

Clearly, the plan didn't work since the Tigers were three runs worse in 2014 than they were in 2013. However, some of the original pieces of the plan did work as intended. Specifically, Ian Kinsler saved 20 runs, the most among second basemen, and Miguel Cabrera cost the team just one run at first base after costing them 18 the year before at third base. Unfortunately, Cabrera's replacement, Nick Castellanos, cost the team 30 runs defensively, more than any other player at any position in baseball. In addition, former gloveman Torii Hunter declined further to -17 Runs Saved in right field, and Jose Iglesias missed the entire season with stress fractures in his shins, creating a massive hole on the left side of their infield.

Other teams were more successful in filling their holes. For example, the Cardinals enjoyed a career defensive season from their free agent signing, shortstop Jhonny Peralta. Peralta had been up and down in his career, previously, but his 17 Runs Saved at shortstop in 2014 were 15 more than his previous best season at the position. The Orioles finished atop the AL in Runs Saved despite losing three of the best defensive players—Manny Machado, Matt Wieters, and Chris Davis—in season. Several of their replacement players were able to fill those voids, specifically Steve Pearce, who saved nine runs at first base and nine more in the corner outfield, and rookie catcher Caleb Joseph, who saved 14 runs behind the plate in large part because of his excellent 38 percent caught stealing rate.

And, of course, no discussion of 2014 defense could be complete without mentioning the Royals. Kansas City orchestrated one of the most impressive defensive turnarounds ever in 2013, saving 93 runs defensively, which were 84 more than in 2012. They were able to continue that defensive success this season with 34 Runs Saved, third best in the American League. They were at their best in the outfield, where Alex Gordon, Lorenzo Cain, and Jarrod Dyson combined for 61 Runs Saved.

Description of the Team Defense Charts

Looking at the Team Defense charts has always been a good way to see which teams have collected the best group of defensive talent and where a team's defensive strengths and weaknesses lie. However, with teams increasing their use of hitter tendency data in a deliberate effort to align its fielders on a hitter by hitter basis, team defense is taking on more of a collective significance.

With that in mind, we have created a separate calculation to measure each team's collective performance when using defensive shifts. Treating the entire infield as one unit, we devised a system similar to our Range and Positioning evaluation to estimate how many hits and runs each infield saves as a result of shifts, and we have added the results of this team Shift Runs Saved calculation to the Team Defense charts.

On the following pages, we break down each team's defense by Runs Saved at each position and their collective Shift Runs Saved for each of the last three years.

Team Defensive Runs by Position - 2014

Team	Pitcher	Catcher	First Base	Second Base	Third Base	Shortstop	Left Field	Center Field	Right Field	Shifts	Total
St Louis Cardinals	20	-7	7	16	-4	13	3	14	-3	12	71
Cincinnati Reds	15	0	4	6	9	18	3	14	-6	4	67
Baltimore Orioles	-2	3	15	8	6	5	9	7	6	7	64
San Diego Padres	-2	14	9	-10	11	9	-5	10	10	6	52
Boston Red Sox	-7	0	6	15	-18	-8	2	18	31	13	52
Pittsburgh Pirates	11	20	-8	0	4	12	18	-15	-3	5	44
Arizona Diamondbacks	-2	10	-2	-3	2	6	-6	21	6	4	36
Kansas City Royals	1	2	-1	-2	-6	-4	24	23	-3	0	34
Oakland Athletics	0	-4	1	4	20	-9	9	-11	13	10	33
Los Angeles Dodgers	10	-3	12	-3	29	0	-3	-17	-6	2	21
San Francisco Giants	2	8	6	1	5	6	-6	-12	-1	12	21
New York Mets	-6	-12	7	-11	12	0	7	26	-9	5	19
Houston Astros	-3	4	-3	-8	-8	6	8	-14	9	27	18
Seattle Mariners	-10	9	-6	-2	11	2	5	-6	3	9	15
Milwaukee Brewers	2	31	0	-22	2	1	7	-5	-5	4	15
New York Yankees	1	11	-1	10	9	-12	2	0	-8	0	12
Washington Nationals	4	11	0	-4	10	3	-6	-2	-5	1	12
Atlanta Braves	-2	-13	-7	-12	-12	32	-3	-11	27	3	2
Colorado Rockies	-7	-21	8	10	9	2	-6	1	5	1	2
Los Angeles Angels	3	3	1	8	-21	-4	3	-13	9	2	-9
Tampa Bay Rays	-13	5	0	1	-4	-24	11	0	3	2	-19
Toronto Blue Jays	5	-13	-8	4	-2	-14	-3	-6	-1	16	-22
Miami Marlins	-9	-14	-8	-13	-2	-1	13	10	6	-7	-25
Texas Rangers	-16	-11	-1	-9	10	-11	-8	9	-6	12	-31
Chicago Cubs	7	-14	6	4	-9	-9	-17	-4	0	3	-33
Philadelphia Phillies	-10	3	-10	3	-8	-1	-7	-20	7	10	-33
Chicago White Sox	-3	1	-16	2	-12	-5	-8	9	-17	11	-38
Cleveland Indians	-5	10	-10	-7	-19	-5	-6	-8	-13	7	-56
Detroit Tigers	-7	-7	-6	21	-32	-9	-2	-8	-20	8	-62
Minnesota Twins	-13	-28	2	-3	3	-2	-22	-5	-22	7	-83

Team Defensive Runs by Position - 2013

Team	Pitcher	Catcher	First Base	Second Base	Third Base	Shortstop	Left Field	Center Field	Right Field	Shifts	Total
Kansas City Royals	2	6	2	18	-2	5	22	21	16	-1	89
Arizona Diamondbacks	12	-5	14	4	-10	5	3	11	47	4	85
Pittsburgh Pirates	7	11	-3	13	5	9	22	6	-5	9	74
Milwaukee Brewers	3	20	-4	-12	-5	8	7	33	9	9	68
Texas Rangers	-2	0	1	5	-7	14	11	20	-3	8	47
Atlanta Braves	15	6	8	-20	-4	42	-17	-1	17	0	46
Tampa Bay Rays	3	7	4	8	12	7	6	-7	-11	16	45
Cincinnati Reds	9	-1	7	5	3	8	-4	-16	18	11	40
New York Yankees	13	8	7	6	3	-23	9	9	2	3	37
Los Angeles Dodgers	3	-4	13	-2	21	6	5	-13	6	0	35
Baltimore Orioles	-1	-9	-10	7	35	9	-2	0	-7	11	33
Boston Red Sox	-13	0	6	15	-18	-4	-4	10	21	15	28
Toronto Blue Jays	12	1	-15	10	-1	-4	1	13	4	5	26
San Francisco Giants	1	13	4	-11	3	-2	13	3	-8	2	18
Chicago Cubs	-3	4	16	9	5	-6	-4	-8	-2	-1	10
San Diego Padres	10	3	14	1	0	-13	-9	-2	3	3	10
Miami Marlins	-5	-8	3	0	4	-5	2	2	-2	9	0
New York Mets	0	-14	2	-16	3	-12	-6	19	8	5	-11
Colorado Rockies	-1	-15	-3	3	23	5	5	-13	-21	2	-15
Washington Nationals	-18	5	0	0	-6	-4	-3	3	5	2	-16
Minnesota Twins	-6	-13	8	10	-7	19	-11	-5	-18	1	-22
St Louis Cardinals	-4	26	-5	-3	-10	0	-14	-5	-8	0	-23
Cleveland Indians	-8	1	-1	-1	-12	-16	7	-1	-5	9	-27
Houston Astros	3	2	-14	-4	6	-8	-7	-1	-22	-1	-46
Oakland Athletics	-14	-12	-15	-13	12	-21	2	-5	6	9	-51
Chicago White Sox	-2	2	-16	-12	-6	5	-4	-14	-5	-3	-55
Detroit Tigers	-21	-5	-10	-7	-15	6	1	0	-11	3	-59
Los Angeles Angels	-14	-14	0	-9	-4	-12	-1	-9	-14	6	-71
Philadelphia Phillies	-5	-3	-2	-6	-26	-16	-7	-17	-15	-1	-98
Seattle Mariners	0	-18	-11	0	-8	1	-18	-32	-17	2	-101

Team Defensive Runs by Position - 2012

Team	Pitcher	Catcher	First Base	Second Base	Third Base	Shortstop	Left Field	Center Field	Right Field	Shifts	Total
Atlanta Braves	-5	20	4	5	3	9	12	23	14	0	85
Toronto Blue Jays	10	3	-3	5	21	17	-4	10	1	12	72
Boston Red Sox	-3	5	14	13	-7	25	6	-2	6	7	64
Cincinnati Reds	23	22	1	7	2	9	-4	-1	-2	6	63
Tampa Bay Rays	10	14	-1	-1	9	-4	11	-5	9	10	52
Los Angeles Angels	2	-3	8	3	4	-7	3	28	6	-3	41
Arizona Diamondbacks	16	7	2	-2	2	-8	0	7	7	1	32
St Louis Cardinals	15	28	-4	-9	3	-8	-4	0	4	1	26
Milwaukee Brewers	8	24	1	-28	4	-1	6	5	4	1	24
Minnesota Twins	-6	-24	-4	22	-6	11	-12	18	15	1	15
San Francisco Giants	1	14	7	-18	-9	3	5	-5	11	2	11
Philadelphia Phillies	-7	13	-7	17	1	-5	3	-2	-4	1	10
Chicago White Sox	1	0	-13	1	5	12	5	-8	4	0	7
Oakland Athletics	-5	-5	-8	0	12	-3	2	-14	25	2	6
Baltimore Orioles	7	9	-7	-3	-7	18	-1	-13	-7	8	4
Seattle Mariners	-3	-23	1	13	-4	28	-1	-19	10	1	3
New York Yankees	-14	15	23	16	-6	-21	-3	-9	-3	0	-2
Kansas City Royals	1	2	-8	-15	14	-5	25	-3	-11	-3	-3
Los Angeles Dodgers	10	-9	4	1	12	-21	7	-12	1	1	-6
Chicago Cubs	-9	-7	-6	25	1	4	-4	-10	-7	5	-8
Texas Rangers	-3	-21	-1	-3	9	8	7	5	-13	0	-12
Washington Nationals	-1	-4	8	2	1	-3	-16	5	-7	-1	-16
San Diego Padres	-16	12	3	-17	-3	-5	-8	6	-1	5	-24
Detroit Tigers	0	-6	-5	-8	-3	-3	3	2	-14	5	-29
New York Mets	-2	5	-1	-16	15	-5	-6	-2	-23	2	-33
Pittsburgh Pirates	-17	-26	-1	-2	-3	10	8	-6	-5	0	-42
Cleveland Indians	-13	-27	-4	6	-6	-12	1	2	-13	8	-58
Miami Marlins	5	-9	4	7	-24	-16	-21	-12	6	-2	-62
Houston Astros	-15	-3	-8	-22	-14	-9	-7	8	-2	4	-68
Colorado Rockies	-7	-33	1	1	-32	-24	-8	-1	-13	1	-115

The Predictive Power of Defensive Projections

For 13 years, Baseball Info Solutions has been advancing the state of defensive analytics. Much of the reason for publishing *The Fielding Bible—Volume IV* is to share those advancements with everyone. But it is also important to look backwards. Since defensive metrics are so much a part of our day-to-day work at BIS, we have developed a trust in their accuracy and predictive power that is not always matched by the public perception. One of those perceptions is that a fielder needs three full seasons in the major leagues before his defensive metrics provide a true indication of his defensive abilities. With that in mind, we aim to quantify the consistency and projectability of defensive metrics, and specifically Defensive Runs Saved, to foster greater trust in defensive metrics as a whole.

First, we ran a series of correlation studies to test whether one year or three years of defensive data better predicted the subsequent year's DRS totals. Then, we tested various regression levels to optimize correlation strength. Finally, we compared those correlation values to similar tests of various offensive statistics like batting average, OPS, and home run rate.

Our results suggest not only that defensive metrics are predictive, they are more predictive than we might have guessed. Defensive Runs Saved correlated as well as many of the offensive metrics and stabilized with similar sample sizes. In fact, once a fielder has played at least 350 innings in the field, his DRS total is a better predictor of his future DRS totals than batting average and OPS are predictors of themselves following an equivalent time frame.

Projecting Defensive Runs Saved

Before each season, BIS puts together projected Defensive Runs Saved based on two separate components. First, we project DRS per inning for all players. Then, we project how many innings they will play and apply that rate to produce a projected DRS total.

BIS has compiled its own playing time projections before each season in order to produce the defensive projections. These are estimates of how much time fielders will see at each position, not how well they will perform there. Therefore, this study will focus specifically on the projected quality of play.

Traditionally, the rate portion of our defensive projections has been based on players' DRS totals from the previous three seasons. It has also included a regressor of 667 innings of neutral defense, which was done in an attempt to better forecast players with small samples of innings played. Frequently, fielders with large positive or negative DRS totals in limited innings have reached those outlier totals because of unsustainable play over the small sample, and their ensuing defensive performances have then regressed to less extreme true talent levels. It is the same principle that drives every offensive projection system.

The choices to use three years of recent production instead of one, and to use 667 innings of regression instead of some other number make intuitive sense—typically, statistics become more meaningful over larger samples—but they were still somewhat arbitrary decisions. To truly evaluate how well we can predict future DRS totals, we set up a series of tests using different lengths of historical DRS performance, different innings regressors, and different thresholds of innings for players to qualify for the study. To start, we used only position players because they shared the same potential number of innings played per season. We'll circle back to pitchers later.

Test 1 - 100 Minimum Innings

To systematically examine each of those three parameters, we ran a series of correlation studies. We began by setting a fixed threshold of innings played. We used the same minimum for both the dependent variable—which we tested with both the previous year and the previous three years—and the independent variable, which was the following year. Test 1 uses 100 innings as the minimum threshold for both the sets of data.

For a position player, 100 innings are not very many. A full-time player will surpass 1,400 innings in a healthy season playing every day, so 100 innings represents something close to two weeks of playing time. Because the threshold is so low, we did not expect to see strong correlation coefficients. However, it is still a useful threshold to test because often the most important players to project are those that have not yet had much playing time.

For example, catcher Roberto Perez debuted in 2014 and saved the Indians five runs in just 232.1 innings. Kennys Vargas cost the Twins one run in 107 innings at first base. If one simply prorates their totals over a full 1,400 innings, Perez looks like one of the league leaders and Vargas looks like one of the league trailers. But is that fair to say?

DRS Rate Correlations

Position Players, 2013-14
100 Minimum Innings in Both Samples

Period	Regressor	n	R
Previous Season	None	788	0.33
Previous Season	567 Innings*	788	0.37
Previous Season	700 Innings	788	0.37
Previous Season	1,400 Innings	788	0.36
Last 3 Seasons	None	919	0.34
Last 3 Seasons	558 Innings*	919	0.39
Last 3 Seasons	700 Innings	919	0.39
Last 3 Seasons	1,400 Innings	919	0.38

Maximum R achieved with these inning regressors

Correlation coefficient—represented by **R** in the tables—is on a scale of -1 to 1 such that a 0 indicates no relationship between the two data sets, a 1 indicates a strong positive relationship between the two data sets, and a -1 indicates a strong inverse relationship between the two data sets. In the table, **n** represents the sample size of the study.

Our most basic tests, the one-year and three-year samples with no regressors, still show moderately strong correlations at 0.33 and 0.34. Meanwhile, each three-year sample slightly outperforms its corresponding one-year sample. That supports our traditional decision to rely on three years of DRS totals in our projections as opposed to the most recent season alone.

The tests using no regressor, a regressor of 700 innings of neutral defense, and a regressor of 1,400 innings of neutral defense are arbitrary choices meant simply to decide whether adding regression to the mean is worthwhile. In this case, it is. With the one-year samples, the regressors we tested produced correlations between 0.36 and 0.37, a bit better than the DRS rate with no regressor at 0.33. The same is true with the three-year samples, which ranged between 0.38 and 0.39 with various regressors but was 0.34 with no regressor.

Now that we have established that regression added strength to the correlations, we wanted to figure out which regressors were the best. To do so, we used a tool to test every potential regression value between 0 and 1,667 innings with a goal of maximizing the R values. For Test 1, those optimal regressors were 567 innings for the one-year sample and 558 innings for the three-year sample. The latter produced a 0.39 correlation that was the strongest of Test 1. It was also the closest to the parameters we had been using in our traditional defensive projections. It turns out that three years and 667 regressed innings that were used are not far off from the ideal solution, assuming a 100-inning minimum for the samples.

Test 2 - 350 Minimum Innings

For Test 2, we ran the same series of regression models as in Test 1, but we did so using 350 innings as the minimum threshold for the players to qualify for the sample. Here is how they fared:

DRS Rate Correlations

Position Players, 2013-14
350 Minimum Innings in Both Samples

Period	Regressor	n	R
Previous Season	None	419	0.53
Previous Season	2 Innings*	419	0.53
Previous Season	700 Innings	419	0.52
Previous Season	1,400 Innings	419	0.51
Last 3 Seasons	None	503	0.55
Last 3 Seasons	223 Innings*	503	0.55
Last 3 Seasons	700 Innings	503	0.55
Last 3 Seasons	1,400 Innings	503	0.54

Maximum R achieved with these inning regressors

DRS Rate Correlations

Position Players, 2013-14
700 Minimum Innings in Both Samples

Period	Regressor	n	R
Previous Season	None	244	0.53
Previous Season	0 Innings*	244	0.53
Previous Season	700 Innings	244	0.53
Previous Season	1,400 Innings	244	0.52
Last 3 Seasons	None	300	0.59
Last 3 Seasons	511 Innings*	300	0.60
Last 3 Seasons	700 Innings	300	0.60
Last 3 Seasons	1,400 Innings	300	0.59

Maximum R achieved with these inning regressors

The increase in minimum innings from just 100 to 350 led to a dramatic increase in the strength of the correlation results. In fact, each correlation in Test 2 finished with a coefficient stronger than 0.50, which is often considered a threshold of stabilization. **In other words, you can feel confident in your assessment of a defender's abilities as measured by DRS once he has played something close to 350 innings—about one fourth of a season—whether or not those innings are in the previous season or over the previous three seasons and whether or not you regress his DRS total.**

For the one-year sample, Test 2 produces the strongest correlation with a 2-inning regressor—which essentially means no regressor. Over the three-year sample, it optimizes with a regression of 223 neutral innings. However, the optimal regressor produces the same R value as no regression, which again essentially means no regressor.

Test 3 - 700 Minimum Innings

Our final test used a minimum of 700 innings in both samples, and it produced the best correlation results yet:

Similar to Test 2 with 350 minimum innings, Test 3 with a one-year sample performed best without any regressor at all. With the three-year period, the correlation coefficient was maximized by adding 511 innings of neutral defense. That is again very close to our traditional method of defensive projections.

Comparison to Offensive Statistics

The notion that DRS stabilizes as a predictive measurement somewhere near 350 innings provides some context to the statistic, but the best way to provide context is to compare those study results to the results of similar tests run on some of the offensive statistics that are more familiar to the public and more commonly trusted. The challenge there is that most offensive statistics are calculated as a rate of at-bats rather than innings played, so we would need to find at-bat thresholds analogous to our minimum innings thresholds of 100, 350, and 700 in order to ensure we are comparing apples to apples.

There is no foolproof way to translate innings in the field to at-bats because some fielders play multiple positions and some hitters do not play in the field at all. We approximated a similar threshold by picking out examples of fielders who barely exceeded the 100 innings minimum but did so at a single position as a full-time player. For example, Cameron Maybin played just 120.1 innings, all in center field, in 2013 because of a wrist injury and had 51 at-bats. Kevin Kouzmanoff filled in for Adrian Beltre when he went on the DL in 2014, and Kouzmanoff reached 108 innings, all at third base, and 47 at-bats. We split the difference to estimate that about 50 at-bats are the equivalent of 100 innings in the field, which also means that 175 at-bats corresponds to 350 innings and 350 at-bats corresponds to 700 innings.

From there, we ran similar correlation studies for various offensive statistics to what we did for DRS and regressed DRS. Here is the first set, which compares the DRS and regressed DRS correlation values based on a 100 inning minimum to hitter statistics for position players with a 50 at-bat minimum:

Offensive Statistic Comparisons

Position Players, 2013-14
50 Minimum At-Bats in Both Samples

Statistic	Period	n	R
Line Drive %	Previous Season	806	0.31
DRS	Previous Season	788	0.33
AVG	Previous Season	806	0.36
K/BB	Previous Season	803	0.36
Regressed DRS	Previous Season	788	0.37
OPS	Previous Season	806	0.42
HR/AB	Previous Season	806	0.59
GB/FB	Previous Season	806	0.69
Line Drive %	Last 3 Seasons	850	0.31
DRS	Last 3 Seasons	919	0.34
Regressed DRS	Last 3 Seasons	919	0.39
AVG	Last 3 Seasons	850	0.40
K/BB	Last 3 Seasons	847	0.40
OPS	Last 3 Seasons	850	0.47
HR/AB	Last 3 Seasons	850	0.63
GB/FB	Last 3 Seasons	850	0.73

For the lowest threshold, you can see that DRS performs better when you add a regressor to it. With just the previous year of data, DRS itself has a 0.33 correlation coefficient, which outperforms line drive rate but trails all other offensive statistics we tested. However, with the added regressor, DRS increases to a 0.37 correlation and beats a few offensive measurements that are commonly trusted like batting average and strikeout-per-walk rate.

With three years of data as the independent variable, both the defensive and offensive statistics make some small improvements, as expected. Batting average and strikeout-per-walk rate actually increase a bit more than regressed DRS, which allowed them to edge it in correlation strength 0.40 to 0.39.

Next up, here are the correlations with a 175 at-bat minimum in both samples, analogous to 350 innings for the fielding statistics:

Offensive Statistic Comparisons

Position Players, 2013-14
175 Minimum At-Bats in Both Samples

Statistic	Period	n	R
Line Drive %	Previous Season	546	0.35
AVG	Previous Season	546	0.46
OPS	Previous Season	546	0.50
DRS	Previous Season	419	0.53
Regressed DRS	Previous Season	419	0.53
K/BB	Previous Season	546	0.59
HR/AB	Previous Season	546	0.67
GB/FB	Previous Season	546	0.79
Line Drive %	Last 3 Seasons	605	0.37
AVG	Last 3 Seasons	605	0.46
OPS	Last 3 Seasons	605	0.52
K/BB	Last 3 Seasons	605	0.54
DRS	Last 3 Seasons	503	0.55
Regressed DRS	Last 3 Seasons	503	0.55
HR/AB	Last 3 Seasons	605	0.70
GB/FB	Last 3 Seasons	605	0.80

This is the approximate threshold that both DRS and regressed DRS stabilize, finishing with correlation coefficients above 0.50 with both the one-year and the three-year samples of data. The two measurements with the strongest correlations—home runs per at-bat and groundball-to-flyball rate—each crossed the 0.50 benchmark with just the 50 at-bat minimums. They continue to have the strongest relationship with the 175 at-bat threshold, as well. However, none of the other offensive statistics beats DRS and regressed DRS with this threshold and a three-year sample.

Finally, here are the correlation values with a 350 at-bat minimum (and 700 inning minimum for the fielding statistics):

Offensive Statistic Comparisons

Position Players, 2013-14
350 Minimum At-Bats in Both Samples

Statistic	Period	n	R
Line Drive %	Previous Season	293	0.42
AVG	Previous Season	293	0.47
OPS	Previous Season	293	0.52
DRS	Previous Season	244	0.53
Regressed DRS	Previous Season	244	0.53
K/BB	Previous Season	293	0.66
HR/AB	Previous Season	293	0.71
GB/FB	Previous Season	293	0.82
Line Drive %	Last 3 Seasons	369	0.44
AVG	Last 3 Seasons	369	0.47
OPS	Last 3 Seasons	369	0.51
DRS	Last 3 Seasons	300	0.59
Regressed DRS	Last 3 Seasons	300	0.60
K/BB	Last 3 Seasons	369	0.69
HR/AB	Last 3 Seasons	369	0.73
GB/FB	Last 3 Seasons	369	0.85

With the highest threshold we tested, both DRS and regressed DRS continue to stack up well against the offensive statistics we tested. For both the one-year sample and the three-year sample, it finished behind groundball-per-flyball rate, home runs per at-bat, and strikeout-per-walk rate and ahead of line drive rate, batting average, and OPS.

Pitchers

With our traditional method of defensive projections, we used the same 667 inning regressor for pitchers that we did with hitters. But even though pitchers play far fewer innings in the field than position players do, they tended to be more consistent year to year.

We ran a similar series of correlation tests for pitchers using thresholds of 14 innings, 50 innings, and 100 innings, which are roughly equivalent to one fourteenth, one quarter, and one half of a full season for starting pitchers. Here are those results:

DRS Rate Correlations

Pitchers, 2013-14
Last 3 Seasons

Minimum	Regressor	n	R
14 Innings	364 Innings	836	0.23
50 Innings	214 Innings	537	0.34
100 Innings	71 Innings	237	0.47

Even with a minimum of 14 innings, which is more or less just two starts, pitchers showed some correlation strength. As the innings minimum increased, so too did the correlation values. With a 100 inning minimum, pitchers produced a 0.47 correlation coefficient that was actually much higher than position players with a 100 inning minimum (0.39).

Conclusion

With our battery of tests, we saw strong correlations between seasons of DRS using both three-year and one-year samples of historical data even with small minimum qualifications of innings played. Specifically, our defensive metrics stabilized after about 350 innings of play in a season and beat several offensive metrics—such as line drive rate, batting average, and OPS—in the majority of our tests.

Those results suggest one should have similar confidence in DRS as in most offensive statistics, even with less than a full season of data to work with. However, in our defensive projections going forward, we will continue to rely on three years of sample data, which our tests demonstrated showed stronger correlations than those run with only the previous season.

The final question is just how much we should regress those defensive projections. Previously, we used 667 innings of neutral defense as a regressor. However, the tests we ran using 100, 350, and 700 innings as the qualification thresholds all maximized their correlation strength with fewer innings. With the three-year samples for position players, their optimal levels were 558, 223, and 511 innings, respectively. For pitchers, they were 364, 214, and 71 innings.

It is a testament to the quality of DRS as a statistic that the optimal regression totals were so consistent for the different thresholds. Because of the similarity of the results from both the 100-inning test and the 700-inning test for position players, we decided on a 500-inning regressor for our defensive projections moving forward. The tests showed that threshold was effective in projecting both veteran players who have played every day and new players with few major league innings to their names. The pitcher regressors were less similar, so we opted for a 200-inning regressor. It is close to the midpoint of the three optimal values.

2015 Defensive Projections

The 2014 postseason showed how important defense is to a team's championship aspirations. One of the major storylines during the World Series was how amazing the Kansas City Royals' outfield was, especially in the late innings when Jarrod Dyson would enter the game in center field to join Alex Gordon in left field and push Lorenzo Cain over to right field. Both Gordon and Cain won Fielding Bible Awards in 2014, and Dyson may have been good enough to do so as well if he had played a full season's worth of innings. Cain was named the ALCS MVP, partly because of the great series he had offensively, but also because he made one outstanding play after another in the outfield to keep the Orioles from putting together any rallies. Even Nori Aoki, who had a disappointing season defensively but had been an above average right fielder in seasons past, got into the act when he robbed the Angels of two extra-base hits in Game 1 of the ALDS. Defense may not have won the Royals the World Series, but it helped get them darn close.

But the Royals are not the only example. Their opponents in the World Series, the San Francisco Giants, benefited greatly from their defensive efforts as well. In the 5th inning of Game 7, with the Giants leading 3-2 and Bumgarner having just entered the game, Aoki came to the plate with a runner on second and one out. Aoki hit a line drive that was slicing hard toward the left field line that looked like a sure double off the bat, except that Juan Perez was right there to catch it without much trouble. If that ball had fallen in, it would have changed the entire game and the series. Instead, because of the effort that the Giants made to understand the tendencies of their opposing hitters, they put themselves in a position to win the World Series.

And we could go on. The two teams that the Royals and Giants defeated in the Championship Series to reach the World Series were also two of the best defensive teams in baseball. The Cardinals led the National League in 2014 with 71 Defensive Runs Saved, and the Orioles led the American League with 64 Runs Saved. The point is that the teams that put together the best defenses were well rewarded for their efforts.

So, which teams look like they are the best positioned (no pun intended) defensively to give themselves a chance to reach the World Series in 2015? We have defensive projections for that. In the previous chapter, we discussed our process for putting together our defensive projections, as well as their reliability (see Predictive Power of Defensive Projections on page 69). In the following pages, you will find projections for each team broken down by position, as well as leaderboards and trailerboards of the best and worst projected players at each position for 2015.

Before we get to those, let's look at the top projected infield and outfield units for 2015.

Top Projected Infield in 2015

It may be surprising to think about because of the struggles that this team has been through in the past few years, but the team that is projected to have the best infield defense in 2015 is the Colorado Rockies. What is more surprising is how they get to such a projection. The biggest name in that infield, and understandably so, is Troy Tulowitzki. Tulo has won three Fielding Bible Awards at shortstop and would be a perennial MVP candidate if he didn't get injured so often. However, his defensive projection is not the one pacing the Rockies' infield. In fact, of the four players expected to get the bulk of the playing time at each position, Tulo has the lowest total of Defensive Runs Saved projected.

Colorado Rockies Infield

Pos	Player	2015 Proj DRS	2014 DRS
1B	Justin Morneau	3	8
2B	DJ LeMahieu	13	16
3B	Nolan Arenado	19	16
SS	Troy Tulowitzki	2	7

The two players that are driving the Rockies' projection are Nolan Arenado and DJ LeMahieu. Both are projected to be the best defensive players in baseball at their position in 2015. For Arenado, that is not that surprising. He has ranked second and third in Defensive Runs Saved at third base in 2013 and 2014, respectively, and has won the NL Gold Glove Award both years that he has been in the major leagues. It is not hard to imagine him meeting or exceeding the 19 Runs Saved he is projected for in 2015.

For LeMahieu, while his projected Runs Saved total of 13 makes sense given his level of play since entering the league, it is a bit surprising to see him showing up ahead of defensive stalwarts like Dustin Pedroia (winner of three of the last four Fielding Bible Awards at second base) and Ian Kinsler. However, LeMahieu has always shown great defensive abilities, and now that he has established himself as a full-time player, he has put himself in a position to gain more recognition.

At shortstop and first base, Tulowitzki's and Justin Morneau's projections are not quite as impressive. Those projections are held down somewhat by each player's injury history and by the fact that they each had a lackluster defensive season within the recent past. However, both actually looked very solid last year. If they can both stay healthy and play at the level they did last year, then Rockies opponents will wish they could adjust their swings to get as much lift on the ball as they can, because it is going to be tough to get a groundball through this infield.

Top Projected Outfield in 2015

Much less surprising than the best infield, the team projected to have the best outfield in 2015 is the Kansas City Royals, and it isn't even close. As a unit, the Royals outfield is projected to save 39 runs in 2015. The next highest total is 15 runs for the Oakland A's. The Royals will still be employing the services of Alex Gordon, Lorenzo Cain, and Jarrod Dyson as three of their four main outfielders, but instead of Nori Aoki, who has moved on to the Giants, they will have Alex Rios helping hold things down in right field.

Kansas City Royals Outfield

Pos	Player	2015 Proj DRS	2014 DRS
LF	Alex Gordon	19	26
CF	Jarrod Dyson	5	13
CF	Lorenzo Cain	10	14
RF	Lorenzo Cain	5	8
RF	Alex Rios	0	-4

The Royals have the unique pleasure of employing the best left fielder and two of the best center fielders in game. Alex Gordon has won the last three Fielding Bible Awards in left field, and his 26 Defensive Runs Saved in 2014 is the highest total that we have recorded at the position since we starting keeping track of DRS in 2003. His metrics are strong across the board, from his range to his throwing arm to his ability to make special plays and avoid mistakes. There's just no one better.

In center field, we could potentially be talking about either Lorenzo Cain or Jarrod Dyson in similar terms, except that they split time with each other. Or, more accurately, Cain splits time between center field and right field, as he moves over when Dyson gets the occasional start or comes in late in games. The leading center fielder in 2014 was Juan Lagares with 26 DRS. Together, Cain and Dyson had 27 DRS. They are both outstanding defenders. The one thing tempering their projections for 2015 is that they are still young and building up a track record.

In right field, Alex Rios is projected to be about average. His last couple of seasons have been slightly below average, so he is the one player that might drag this outfield down a bit. However, the Royals did great in 2014 with Aoki having a sub-par season, so they should be able to carry Rios as well. Or if they decide to trust in Dyson's offense a little more, the Royals may even be able to expand the time on the field that their three best outfielders share.

Projected Infield Defensive Runs Saved Leaders

First Basemen Projected 2015 Leaders		Second Basemen Projected 2015 Leaders		Third Basemen Projected 2015 Leaders		Shortstops Projected 2015 Leaders	
Gonzalez,Adrian	11	LeMahieu,DJ	13	Arenado,Nolan	19	Simmons,Andrelton	31
Rizzo,Anthony	7	Pedroia,Dustin	12	Machado,Manny	14	Cozart,Zack	10
Teixeira,Mark	6	Kinsler,Ian	11	Uribe,Juan	12	Hardy,J.J.	9
Votto,Joey	5	Schoop,Jonathan	6	Donaldson,Josh	11	Franklin,Nick	6
Napoli,Mike	5	Wong,Kolten	6	Wright,David	9	Crawford,Brandon	6
Pujols,Albert	4	Cano,Robinson	6	Lawrie,Brett	8	Semien,Marcus	4
Alonso,Yonder	4	Phillips,Brandon	5	Harrison,Josh	7	Peralta,Jhonny	4
4 tied with	3	Goins,Ryan	5	Beltre,Adrian	4	Ramirez,Jose	3
		Dozier,Brian	4	Rendon,Anthony	4	8 tied with	2
		2 tied with	3	3 tied with	3		

First Basemen Projected 2015 Trailers		Second Basemen Projected 2015 Trailers		Third Basemen Projected 2015 Trailers		Shortstops Projected 2015 Trailers	
Abreu,Jose	-7	Murphy,Daniel	-10	Castellanos,Nick	-22	Reyes,Jose	-12
Howard,Ryan	-7	Altuve,Jose	-9	Johnson,Chris	-11	Lowrie,Jed	-11
Fielder,Prince	-6	Weeks,Rickie	-9	Gillaspie,Conor	-9	Rollins,Jimmy	-6
Singleton,Jon	-5	Cabrera,Asdrubal	-8	Chisenhall,Lonnie	-8	Galvis,Freddy	-6
Lind,Adam	-5	Odor,Rougned	-8	Freese,David	-6	Bogaerts,Xander	-5
Encarnacion,Edwin	-4	Callaspo,Alberto	-7	Asche,Cody	-6	Castro,Starlin	-4
3 tied with	-3	Rutledge,Josh	-6	2 tied with	-5	Flores,Wilmer	-4

Projected Outfield Defensive Runs Saved Leaders

Left Fielders Projected 2015 Leaders		Center Fielders Projected 2015 Leaders		Right Fielders Projected 2015 Leaders	
Gordon,Alex	19	Lagares,Juan	24	Heyward,Jason	19
Marte,Starling	9	Cain,Lorenzo	10	Reddick,Josh	12
Yelich,Christian	6	Martin,Leonys	9	Kiermaier,Kevin	11
Cespedes,Yoenis	5	Gomez,Carlos	8	Cain,Lorenzo	5
Blanco,Gregor	4	Hamilton,Billy	7	Cowgill,Collin	5
Fuld,Sam	3	Dyson,Jarrod	5	Bautista,Jose	4
Gentry,Craig	3	Inciarte,Ender	5	Puig,Yasiel	4
Ackley,Dustin	3	Pollock,A.J.	4	Pearce,Steve	3
Lough,David	3	Bourn,Michael	4	Betts,Mookie	3
12 tied with	2	3 tied with	3	Stanton,Giancarlo	3

Left Fielders Projected 2015 Trailers		Center Fielders Projected 2015 Trailers		Right Fielders Projected 2015 Trailers	
Coghlan,Chris	-8	Fowler,Dexter	-12	Cuddyer,Michael	-11
Arcia,Oswaldo	-8	Revere,Ben	-11	Garcia,Avisail	-8
Holliday,Matt	-7	McCutchen,Andrew	-7	Choo,Shin-Soo	-8
Upton,Justin	-7	Pagan,Angel	-7	Trumbo,Mark	-6
Gattis,Evan	-5	Crisp,Coco	-7	Braun,Ryan	-5
Brown,Domonic	-5	Upton,B.J.	-6	6 tied with	-4
Gomes,Jonny	-5	Jones,Adam	-6		

Projected Pitcher/Catcher Runs Saved Leaders

Pitchers Projected 2015 Leaders		Catchers Projected 2015 Leaders	
Buehrle,Mark	5	Molina,Yadier	16
Greinke,Zack	5	Lucroy,Jonathan	13
Dickey,R.A.	4	Gomes,Yan	11
Teheran,Julio	4	Rivera,Rene	10
Leake,Mike	4	Posey,Buster	9
Cueto,Johnny	3	Martin,Russell	9
Alvarez,Henderson	3	Vazquez,Christian	8
Kershaw,Clayton	3	Conger,Hank	8
10 tied with	2	Flowers,Tyler	7
		4 tied with	6

Pitchers Projected 2015 Trailers		Catchers Projected 2015 Trailers	
Feldman,Scott	-3	Iannetta,Chris	-14
Lackey,John	-3	Rosario,Wilin	-13
Lincecum,Tim	-3	Suzuki,Kurt	-13
8 tied with	-2	Jaso,John	-10
		Saltalamacchia,Jarrod	-8
		Laird,Gerald	-7
		3 tied with	-6

Team Defensive Runs by Position - 2015 (Projected)

Team	Pitcher	Catcher	First Base	Second Base	Third Base	Shortstop	Left Field	Center Field	Right Field	Total
Kansas City Royals	0	6	-2	1	2	-2	19	15	5	44
Los Angeles Dodgers	7	2	11	4	14	-6	4	-2	5	39
St. Louis Cardinals	-2	13	2	8	0	4	-7	-1	19	36
Boston Red Sox	3	14	4	12	-4	-7	0	4	8	34
Cincinnati Reds	8	-7	4	3	4	11	2	7	2	34
Baltimore Orioles	1	2	-1	7	15	8	3	-7	4	32
Oakland Athletics	2	0	-5	3	8	3	7	-4	12	26
Pittsburgh Pirates	-1	5	-1	2	7	2	12	-7	-1	18
New York Yankees	1	6	5	1	1	1	3	2	-4	16
Toronto Blue Jays	9	8	-6	3	11	-12	1	-3	5	16
Colorado Rockies	1	-21	3	13	19	1	-3	-6	2	9
Tampa Bay Rays	-1	1	2	-10	2	4	2	-2	11	9
Arizona Diamondbacks	1	-4	3	-2	-1	4	-1	9	-3	6
Miami Marlins	3	-4	-2	-4	3	-2	5	2	4	5
San Francisco Giants	0	8	4	-2	-3	5	3	-7	-4	4
Milwaukee Brewers	-1	17	-4	-12	-5	1	2	8	-3	3
Washington Nationals	-3	3	-3	4	4	-3	1	3	-4	2
Cleveland Indians	-1	11	-4	-2	-10	4	1	4	-2	1
New York Mets	-1	-8	3	-10	9	-4	-3	24	-11	-1
Seattle Mariners	-4	1	-1	6	-3	-2	3	-1	-1	-2
Texas Rangers	-2	1	-6	-7	4	1	-2	8	-8	-11
Atlanta Braves	4	-15	0	-5	-11	31	-6	-6	-5	-13
Detroit Tigers	0	-5	-3	11	-22	1	4	-1	-5	-20
Chicago Cubs	0	2	7	-3	-6	-5	-6	-13	3	-21
Chicago White Sox	1	2	-6	1	-9	2	-4	2	-10	-21
San Diego Padres	1	-2	5	-4	-4	2	-10	-2	-7	-21
Los Angeles Angels	3	-14	2	-8	-6	-5	1	-4	3	-28
Houston Astros	-3	2	-6	-9	-1	-10	-6	0	0	-33
Minnesota Twins	-3	-17	1	4	-2	-7	-8	-3	-6	-41
Philadelphia Phillies	-3	-3	-7	3	-8	-7	-5	-11	-2	-43

Fielding Bible Awards 2014

The final four teams competing to win their respective league championships this year were the St. Louis Cardinals against the San Francisco Giants in the National League and the Kansas City Royals and the Baltimore Orioles in the AL. What is the most common element that sets these teams apart compared to the other 26 teams in baseball? It's defense. The Orioles and Cardinals had the best defense in each of their leagues (based on Defensive Runs Saved). The Royals were third best in the AL while the Giants were above average in the NL. Looking at batting and pitching, only one team ranked as high as third in any category (Baltimore, third in the AL in pitching). Defense matters.

The importance of defense and using analytics to measure it has become part of baseball's culture. Baseball highlights involving defense are a mainstay of baseball recap shows. Using defensive metrics such as Defensive Runs Saved and Ultimate Zone Rating has become well accepted. Even the Gold Glove voting has come around to using analytics as a component for determining the Gold Glove Awards.

In 2014, eight of the ten winners of The Fielding Bible Award were also the MLB leader in Defensive Runs Saved. The other two came in second. It is clear that today's baseball experts trust and rely on the fact that the new defensive metrics can truly measure defense.

We've added a 10th Fielding Bible Awards this year: the Multi-Position award. Defensive excellence at multiple positions and the value of versatility to play multiple positions is now being recognized. The inaugural winner of this award is Kansas City's Lorenzo Cain.

In this, the ninth year of The Fielding Bible Awards, five other players join Cain as first time winners: Adrian

Gonzalez (Dodgers) at first base, Josh Donaldson (A's) at third, Juan Lagares (Mets) in center field, and a pitcher-catcher battery combination of Dallas Keuchel of the Astros and Brewer Jonathan Lucroy. Atlanta teammates Andrelton Simmons (shortstop) and Jason Heyward (right field) win their second awards. Third time winners are Dustin Pedroia at second base and Alex Gordon with his third consecutive award in left field.

Here's a short refresher course on how the awards are determined: We asked our panel of twelve experts to rank 10 players at each position on a scale from one to ten. We then use the same voting technique as the Major League Baseball MVP voting. A first place vote gets 10 points, second place 9 points, third place 8 points, etc. Total up the points for each player and the player with the most points wins the award. A perfect score is 120.

One important distinction that differentiates our award from most other baseball awards, including the Gold Gloves, is that we only have one winner for all of Major League Baseball, instead of separate winners for each league. Our intention is to continue to stand up and say, "This is the best fielder at this position in the major leagues last season."

Here are the Fielding Bible Awards for the 2014 season:

First Base – Adrian Gonzalez, LAD

Adrian Gonzalez has been the best defensive first baseman in baseball over the last six seasons but somehow he has never won a Fielding Bible Award. Until now. Gonzalez wins his first Fielding Bible award, leading all of baseball's first basemen by saving 11 runs defensively for the Dodgers in 2014. That brings his six-year total to 61 runs saved, 13 more than Albert Pujols' second-place total of 48. Every aspect of Gonzalez' defensive game is superb. He fields his position well, does a great job with difficult throws, and handles bunts and double plays with the best of them. But he's not flashy. Just consistently excellent.

Previous Winners:

2013	Paul Goldschmidt	2009	Albert Pujols
2012	Mark Teixeira	2008	Albert Pujols
2011	Albert Pujols	2007	Albert Pujols
2010	Daric Barton	2006	Albert Pujols

Second Base – Dustin Pedroia, Bos

This is classic Dustin Pedroia: in a game early in the season J.J. Hardy hits a ball sharply up the middle that literally goes through the legs of the pitcher. Pedroia ranges a long way from the normal second base position and dives to field the ball as it enters the grass in short center field. He gets up in less than the blink of an eye while his momentum carries him to the shortstop side of second base. He makes an incredibly difficult and accurate off-balance throw from the outfield grass that would be a huge challenge for a strong-armed shortstops, let alone a second baseman. And the throw has enough velocity to nab Hardy at first base by an eyelash. That one play shows so many of Pedroia's skills: excellent speed, great range, willingness to lay out for anything within reach, incredible quickness getting back up to his feet, quick reactions and a strong arm. This is Pedroia's second consecutive Fielding Bible Award and third overall.

Previous Winners:

2013	Dustin Pedroia	2009	Aaron Hill
2012	Darwin Barney	2008	Brandon Phillips
2011	Dustin Pedroia	2007	Aaron Hill
2010	Chase Utley	2006	Orlando Hudson

Third Base – Josh Donaldson, Oak

Josh Donaldson led all MLB third basemen with 20 Defensive Runs Saved. Here's another way to measure Donaldson's excellence. Baseball Info Solution tracks a stat invented by Bill James called Good Fielding Plays (GFP). It's not as easy as it sounds to define a Good Fielding Play - there are 28 different categories of GFPs. Donaldson's total of 77 GFPs is 13 more than the 64 good plays handled by Colorado's Nolan Arenado. Donaldson is especially good making plays to his right where his excellent reaction time and strong arm really stand out. Nolan Arenado was second in the voting: Donaldson 114 points, Arenado 104.

2013	Manny Machado	2009	Ryan Zimmerman
2012	Adrian Beltre	2008	Adrian Beltre
2011	Adrian Beltre	2007	Pedro Feliz
2010	Evan Longoria	2006	Adrian Beltre

Shortstop – Andrelton Simmons, Atl

For the second consecutive year Andrelton Simmons wins the Fielding Bible Award with a unanimous vote, first on all 12 ballots for a perfect score of 120 points each year. That expression of how good Simmons is, as rated by the expert Fielding Bible Award panel, might actually fall short of how good he really is. His range is incredible. His reaction time is incredible. His hands are incredible, on backhand plays and on transfers from his glove hand to his throwing hand. And he has the strongest, most accurate throwing arm in the game. Simmons' three-year total of 88 runs saved are the most in baseball by 21 runs (Alex Gordon has 67), and blows away the second-best shortstop total of 36 runs saved by J.J. Hardy by a huge margin.

Previous Winners:

2013	Andrelton Simmons	2009	Jack Wilson
2012	Brendan Ryan	2008	Jimmy Rollins
2011	Troy Tulowitzki	2007	Troy Tulowitzki
2010	Troy Tulowitzki	2006	Adam Everett

Left Field – Alex Gordon, KC

It's a three-peat for Alex Gordon. Three Fielding Bible Awards in three years. And it was unanimous. Every voter had Alex Gordon ranked first. Gordon saved 26 runs for the Royals on the year. This is the highest total ever recorded for a left fielder since the tracking of Defensive Runs Saved began in 2003. Christian Yelich of Miami was a distant second with 13. Gordon's converted third-baseman arm has always set him apart. It counted toward nine of his runs saved in 2014, but his excellent range also makes a huge difference. His range in left field has been above average every year since he started playing there in 2010, but this year he had his career high with 15 Range and Positioning Runs saved.

Previous Winners:

2013	Alex Gordon	2009	Carl Crawford
2012	Alex Gordon	2008	Carl Crawford
2011	Brett Gardner	2007	Eric Byrnes
2010	Brett Gardner	2006	Carl Crawford

Center Field – Juan Lagares, NYM

In 2013, Juan Lagares started only 88 games in center field, yet he saved 26 runs there defensively for the Mets. He finished second in the 2013 Fielding Bible Award voting. This year he started 105 games, blew away the field with another 26 runs saved, and won his first Fielding Bible Award. His throwing arm in center field is superb and deeply respected by baserunners; he had six Outfield Arm Runs Saved in 2014. But it's his ability to cover ground that sets him above the rest. He made nine more plays on deep balls than an average center fielder (+20 Range and Positioning), the highest total among all center fielders. This is true despite the fact that, generally speaking, he plays on the shallow side. He had a +9 total on shallow balls, tied for second best among center fielders. His +4 on medium hit balls was tied for fifth best. Lagares finished first on every ballot except one.

Previous Winners:

2013	Carlos Gomez	2009	Franklin Gutierrez
2012	Mike Trout	2008	Carlos Beltran
2011	Austin Jackson	2007	Andruw Jones
2010	Michael Bourn	2006	Carlos Beltran

Right Field – Jason Heyward, Atl

The Fielding Bible Award voters were unanimous about Jason Heyward as well. Heyward is the best defensive right fielder in baseball, bar none. He has had double-digit runs saved totals in every season of his five-year career. What makes him so consistently good? He refuses to allow an extra-base hit. Over his career he has been a bit above average on shallow hit balls (+13 in the Range and Positioning System) and on medium hit balls (+15). On deeply hit balls he is phenomenal. +67! That means he has made 67 more plays making catches on deeply hit balls than an average right fielder. He was +19 on deeply hit balls in 2014 alone. Think of it like this: he saved 19 doubles last year! He excels at picking the ball up quickly off the bat and he always takes a good route to the ball. Overall, he had 26 Runs Saved for the Braves defensively in 2014, which tied for the highest total at any position in 2014 and was a career high for Heyward.

Previous Winners:

2013	Gerardo Parra	2009	Ichiro Suzuki
2012	Jason Heyward	2008	Franklin Gutierrez
2011	Justin Upton	2007	Alex Rios
2010	Ichrio Suzuki	2006	Ichiro Suzuki

Catcher – Jonathan Lucroy, Mil

It is high time that catchers become recognized defensively for more than just their throwing arm. Jonathan Lucroy is another first-time winner of a Fielding Bible Award and the first of a new breed. Lucroy has an average throwing arm, but his other skills are so much better than everyone else, the expert panel rated him the best overall defensive catcher in baseball in 2014. One area that he excels is in handling pitches thrown in the dirt and other potential wild pitches. Baseball Info Solutions calculates a stat called Catcher Block Rate. It's based on how often a catcher successfully handles difficult pitches. Lucroy's 96% rate in 2014 was the best in baseball. The panel also received a preview version of the new Strike Zone Plus/Minus system from Baseball Info Solutions, previously available only to major league teams. The system measures the ability of a catcher to frame pitches, to get strike calls on borderline pitches. Since 2010 Lucroy has gotten the most extra strikes called of any catcher in the game: 715 extra strikes, saving an estimated 85 runs. The next best total is a distant second: Miguel Montero with 407 extra strikes and 48 runs saved. The voting for the award was close. Lucroy garnered 105 voting points to 102 for Russell Martin of the Pittsburgh Pirates.

Previous Winners:

2013	Yadier Molina	2009	Yadier Molina
2012	Yadier Molina	2008	Yadier Molina
2011	Matt Wieters	2007	Yadier Molina
2010	Yadier Molina	2006	Ivan Rodriguez

Pitcher – Dallas Keuchel, Hou

Dallas Keuchel out-Buehrle'd Mark Buehrle. He one-upped the World's Best Pitcher, Clayton Kershaw. And he duked it out with last year's Fielding Bible Award winner, R.A. Dickey, and won his first Fielding Bible Award for defensive excellence at the pitcher position. Keuchel led all major league pitchers with ten Defensive Runs Saved, better than the second-best total of seven runs saved by Kershaw. The dynamic defensive duo of R.A. Dickey and Mark Buehrle, who've won the last five Fielding Bible Awards at pitcher, saved five runs and two runs, respectively, for the Toronto Blue Jays. Keuchel is channeling Mark Buehrle as he allowed only one runner to steal a base all season, but his ability to cover his position (seven runs saved based on the Range and Positioning System) is where he excels. Keuchel received 109 voting points. Kershaw was second with 95.

Previous Winners:

2013	R.A. Dickey	2009	Mark Buehrle
2012	Mark Buehrle	2008	Kenny Rodgers
2011	Mark Buehrle	2007	Johan Santana
2010	Mark Buehrle	2006	Greg Maddux

Multi-Position – Lorenzo Cain, KC

This is the first year of the Multi-Position Fielding Bible Award. The goal of this new award is to recognize players who bring versatility to their teams with their ability to play multiple positions, and who play those positions well defensively. Lorenzo Cain was so good in 2014 that if he played full-time in either center field or right field, he might have won the Fielding Bible Award at either position. He saved 14 runs in center field in 93 games he started there for the Royals on the season, and another 8 runs in right despite only 29 games started there. Cain's ability to play right field give the Royals the best outfield defense in baseball by a wide margin with fellow FBA winner Alex Gordon in left field and baseball's fastest player, Jarrod Dyson, in center. In the closest of margins in this year's balloting, Cain edged out Mr. Versatility, Ben Zobrist of the Tampa Bay Rays, by three points, 92 to 89.

Background of the Fielding Bible Awards

While the four volumes of *The Fielding Bible* put a lot of emphasis on the numbers, especially Defensive Runs Saved and the Range and Positioning System, we feel that visual observation and subjective judgment are still very important parts of determining the best defensive players. Also, we believe people have a right to know who is voting and all the players they are voting for. Therefore, in setting up the Fielding Bible Awards, we took the following steps:

1. *We appointed a panel of experts to vote.* We have a panel of twelve experts plus three "tie-breaker" ballots. (See below.)

2. *We rate everybody in one group.* The Gold Glove vote is divided into National League and American League. We make ours different by putting everybody together. Besides, is playing shortstop in the American League one thing and playing shortstop in the National League a different thing, or are they really very much the same thing? A few years back we had a great example of this decision. Without the Fielding Bible Award, Jack Wilson wins *nada*, because he switched leagues in mid-year. According to our panelists (and unlike the Gold Glove voters), Jack was the best fielding shortstop in baseball in 2009. Period. He deserved to be recognized for that.

3. *We use a ten-man ballot and a ten-point scale.* We use a ten-man ballot. We give ten points for first place, nine points for second place, etc, down to one point for tenth place. We feel strongly that a ten-man ballot with weighted positions leads to more accurate outcomes.

4. *We defined the list of candidates.* Only players who actually were regulars at the position are candidates. This eliminates the possibility of a vote going to somebody who wasn't really playing the position.

5. *We are publishing the balloting.* We summarize the voting at each position, clearly identifying whom everybody voted for. Publishing the actual vote totals encourages the voters to take their votes more seriously. Also, we feel the public will have more respect for the voting if they have more insight into the process. You can find the voting totals in the Bill James Handbook or by visiting FieldingBible.com.

A perfect score is 120 points. If all 12 voters place one player first on their ballot, he scores 120. Three players had perfect scores of 120 in 2014: Andrelton Simmons, Alex Gordon, and Jason Heyward.

Here are the tie-breaker rules (which came into play in our very first year, and did so again last year, as well as in 2010). They are applied one at a time until we have a winner:

1. Most first-place votes wins.
2. Count the tie-breaker ballots, highest point tally wins.
3. Award goes to player with the higher Range and Positioning Runs Saved total.

Ballots were due four days after the end of the regular season. Here is this year's panel:

Since you have this book, you probably know **Bill James**, a baseball writer and analyst published for more than thirty years. Bill is the Senior Baseball Operations Advisor for the Boston Red Sox.

The **BIS Video Scouts** at Baseball Info Solutions (BIS) study every game of the season, multiple times, charting a huge list of valuable game details.

As the MLB Network on-air host of *Clubhouse Confidential* and *MLB Now*, **Brian Kenny** brings an analytical perspective on the game of baseball to a national television audience. He also won a 2003 Sports Emmy Award as host of ESPN's *Baseball Tonight*.

Dave Cameron is the Managing Editor of FanGraphs. He resides in Winston-Salem, North Carolina, where the local minor league team once forced him to watch Michael Morse play shortstop for an entire season. He has appreciated defensive value ever since.

Doug Glanville played nine seasons in Major League Baseball and was well known for his excellent outfield defense. Currently, he is a baseball analyst at ESPN on *Baseball Tonight* and ESPN.com, as well as a regular contributor to *The New York Times*.

The man who created Strat-O-Matic Baseball, **Hal Richman**, continues to lead his company's annual in-depth analysis of each player's season. Hal cautions SOM players that his voting on this ballot may or may not reflect the eventual fielding ratings for players in his game. Ballots were due prior to the completion of his annual research effort to evaluate player defense.

Named the best sports columnist in America in 2012 by the National Sportswriters and Sportscasters Hall of Fame, **Joe Posnanski** is the National Columnist at NBC Sports.

For over twenty-five years, BIS owner **John Dewan** has collected, analyzed, and published in-depth baseball statistics and analysis. He has authored or co-authored four volumes of *The Fielding Bible*.

Mark Simon has been a researcher for ESPN Stats & Information since 2002 and currently helps oversee the Stats & Information blog and Twitter (@espnstatsinfo). He is a regular contributor on baseball (often writing on defense) for ESPNNY.com and ESPN.com.

Peter Gammons serves as on-air and online analyst for MLB Network, MLB.com and NESN (New England Sports Network). He is the 56th recipient of the J. G. Taylor Spink Award for outstanding baseball writing given by the BBWAA (Baseball Writers Association of America).

Rob Neyer has been a working writer for 25 years, and currently is best-known as FOXSports.com's Senior Baseball Editor. His seventh book, *Untitled*, will be published after he writes it.

The **Tom Tango Fan Poll** represents the results of a poll taken at the website, Tango on Baseball (www.tangotiger.net). Besides hosting the website, Tom writes research articles devoted to sabermetrics and is the co-author of *The Book: Playing the Percentages in Baseball*.

Our three tie-breakers are **Ben Jedlovec**, president of Baseball Info Solutions and co-author of *The Fielding Bible—Volumes III and IV*, **Dan Casey**, veteran Video Scout and Operations Analyst at BIS, and **Sean Forman**, the founder of Baseball-Reference.com.

Donaldson vs. Seager

The "hot corner" is slowly becoming a position filled by many young and athletic stars. For many years, third base was the bailiwick for veterans such as David Wright, Evan Longoria and Adrian Beltre. However, with the new crop of stars making a major impact with their gloves, a changing of the guard at third base across the Major Leagues is in full effect.

The new, young generation of players includes Nolan Arenado, Manny Machado, Todd Frazier and Anthony Rendon, all of whom made a major impact for their teams over the past few seasons. Two other individuals who were significant in their teams' success (especially in 2014) were Josh Donaldson of the Oakland Athletics (who was traded to the Toronto Blue Jays during the off-season) and Kyle Seager of the Seattle Mariners.

The best defensive third baseman in baseball last year according to The Fielding Bible Award panel was Josh Donaldson. Donaldson saved the Athletics 20 runs with his defense in 2014 and captured his first Fielding Bible Award. The seventh-best third baseman in baseball last year according to Defensive Runs Saved was Kyle Seager, who saved the Mariners 10 runs with his defense in 2014 and finished ninth in the Fielding Bible Award ballot. However, Kyle Seager did win his first American League Gold Glove Award. Both Donaldson and Seager are defensive wizards, but there are differences in how they get the job done. And so the question needs to be asked, how does a player win a Gold Glove at his position but finish ninth on the Fielding Bible Award ballot?

Josh Donaldson vs. Kyle Seager

2014

Statistic	Donaldson	Seager
Games	150	157
Innings	1,320.2	1,402.0
Errors	23	8
Fielding Pct.	.952	.981
GFPs	77	23
DMs	23	28
Plays Saved	16	12
DRS	20	10
DRS Rank	1	7

Let's compare their skills one at a time.

Who Has The Better Arm?

When we dig deeper into the data, there are two glaring differences between these two infielders. The first major difference is the number of errors committed in 2014. Josh Donaldson committed the second-highest number of errors among all third basemen in 2014. In contrast, Kyle Seager was one of baseball's best with only eight errors. Donaldson struggled the most with his arm. Of his 23 errors, 17 of them were because of a bad throw. He has committed the second most throwing errors among all Major League players since 2013, trailing only the notorious Pedro Alvarez, and he is tied with Alvarez for the biggest difference between his throwing misplays and errors (DMEs) and his throwing good plays (GFPs) over the same period.

Net Throwing Related GFP/DME by 3B

2013-14

Player	Net GFP/DME
Josh Donaldson	-24
Pedro Alvarez	-24
Anthony Rendon	-15
Lonnie Chisenhall	-11
Adrian Beltre	-11

On the opposite side of the spectrum is Kyle Seager, who only committed two throwing errors in all of 2014 and only seven in total since 2013. He is known for being one of the most accurate third basemen in the majors. He has ranked second in Infield Good Throw Rate—which accounts for both his throwing misplays and errors as well as instances when the first baseman had to make a good play to catch his errant throw (see page 119)—for each of the past two seasons with a 96.7 percent and 96.6 percent rate, respectively, and has been the most accurate third baseman over the past two seasons combined.

Infield Good Throw Rate

2013-14, Minimum 200 Throws

Player	Good Throw Rate
Kyle Seager	96.6%
Juan Uribe	95.8%
Pablo Sandoval	93.9%
Chris Johnson	93.3%
Todd Frazier	92.9%

Arm: Donaldson   **Seager** ✔

Who Covers More Ground?

The second major difference between these two players is their range. Josh Donaldson is a web-gem machine and covers way more ground than your average third baseman. He saved 16 more plays than the average third baseman in 2014, which ranked second among all third basemen. The number of Good Fielding Plays (GFP) Donaldson accumulated this year was superb. His 77 GFPs in 2014 were the best among all third basemen.

Most GFPs in a Season by a 3B

2011-14

Player	Season	GFPs
Ryan Zimmerman	2012	85
Ryan Zimmerman	2013	78
Josh Donaldson	2014	77
Nolan Arenado	2013	76
Manny Machado	2013	69

Seager improved his range dramatically after an abysmal 2013 campaign. After costing the Mariners 15 runs in 2012-13, he made a major defensive turnaround saving the Mariners 10 runs at the position in 2014. He showed great improvement ranging towards the hole, where he saved seven more plays compared to the average third baseman. One of Seager's weaknesses is handling balls hit straight at him, where he cost his team six plays, whereas Donaldson saved his team five plays.

Most Plays Saved on Groundballs, 3B

2014

Player	To His Right	Straight On	To His Left
Juan Uribe	8	9	2
David Wright	-6	14	12
Chase Headley	11	6	-1
Nolan Arenado	-1	8	6
Kyle Seager	12	-6	7
Josh Donaldson	8	5	0

Range: **Donaldson** Seager

The Scout's Eye

Throughout the season, BIS Video Scouts scrutinize every single ball in play and assign a primary responsibility to one fielder on each ball. Then, they assign a 1-5 rating of the difficulty of each play, from a "1" representing a routine play that every fielder is expected to make, to a "5" representing a play that the fielder had zero chance at making.

There are many young athletic third basemen that caught our scouts' eyes in 2014. Leading the pack in Scout's Defensive Rating—which awards credit or penalty for making plays relative to how frequently players at a position convert plays of similar difficulty—was Nolan Arenado, who has been one of the most impressive defensive third basemen for the past couple of years. Rounding out the top five were Josh Donaldson, Pablo Sandoval, Josh Harrison and Kyle Seager.

3B Scout's Defensive Rating

2014

Player	Scout's Defensive Rating
Nolan Arenado	25.2
Josh Donaldson	17.3
Pablo Sandoval	12.1
Josh Harrison	10.3
Kyle Seager	10.2

None of the players on the list above rated close to Arenado. Donaldson was the closest player because of his ability to make difficult plays. He flourished at flashing the leather at opportune moments within a game. In contrast, Seager is not the flashy player people love to watch on television. He makes all the routine and easy plays that a third baseman is expected to make. However, his relative inability to make the more difficult plays is reflected in his rating.

3B Conversion Rate on "Difficult" Plays

2014

Player	Total Opps	Difficult Opps	Difficult Conversion Rate
Nolan Arenado	389	69	44.9%
Josh Donaldson	506	65	33.8%
Pablo Sandoval	415	62	29.0%
Josh Harrison	189	30	33.3%
Kyle Seager	461	49	16.3%

Scout's Eye: **Donaldson** ✔ Seager

Final Verdict

In the end, we have to side with the Fielding Bible Award voters and give the edge to Josh Donaldson. Seager has displayed above-average range and the ability to avoid fielding or throwing mistakes, but he is not as likely to make the more difficult play. Furthermore, Donaldson outperformed Kyle Seager in Defensive Runs Saved, Good Fielding Plays and Scout's Defensive Rating and that more than compensates for his mistakes. That said, no team will go wrong in having either one of these players guarding the hot corner.

The Art of Pitch Framing
(Or, How Can Lucroy Be Anywhere Near As Good As Yadier?)

Yadier Molina is a great catcher. Running through the analytics that Baseball Info Solutions has been developing since 2002 shows a player that is good at every aspect of what is required of a catcher on the defensive side. Molina has always been a menace to basestealers, recording 3 of the 12 best individual seasons in Stolen Base Runs Saved since 2002. He has two of the six best individual seasons in Good Play/Misplay Runs Saved (which, for catchers, mainly consists of blocking balls in the dirt and preventing wild pitches). He is tied for the best single season of fielding bunts among catchers with the four Bunt Runs Saved he had in 2012. His handling of the pitching staff, as measured by Adjusted Earned Runs Saved, has not been quite as superlative, but he has generally been above average by that measure as well. He is just good at everything.

None of this is news to anybody, though. Everyone is pretty clearly aware of how great Molina is. Of the nine Fielding Bible Awards that have been given out to catchers since 2006, Molina has won six of them. He has also won the last seven National League Gold Gloves. Even his offensive skills have been recognized as part of a complete package, as he has garnered MVP votes in four different seasons, including third and fourth place finishes in 2013 and 2012, respectively. We can all see how great he is and has been for a long time.

However, until recently, something that we didn't have a handle on, and something that we couldn't fully appreciate, was how good catchers are at pitch framing. In order to try to quantify that skill, and improve our insight into catcher defense, BIS developed the Strike Zone Plus/Minus system.

To be clear, Strike Zone Plus/Minus is a system that measures more than just "pitch framing." While a catcher's receiving skills certainly have a lot to do with whether a borderline pitch ends up being called a ball or a strike, our research found that the other parties involved on the pitch—the pitcher, the batter, and the umpire—have a significant impact as well. Therefore, the methodology that we developed divides the credit for getting extra strikes or extra balls between all four. For a detailed explanation of how the system works, see the Methodologies section on page 344.

Besides the fact that Strike Zone Plus/Minus treats all four of the catcher, the pitcher, the batter, and the umpire as active participants on a pitch, the other feature of the system that makes it unique from other methodologies is that it incorporates BIS's Command Charting data as a variable. BIS has been charting pitchers all the way back to its start in 2002, but in 2010 we began charting where the catcher sets up his target before each pitch as well. In our research, we found that the distance between where the catcher sets his target and where the pitch ends up has a significant impact on whether the pitch is called a strike or not. Because this Command Charting data is so integral to the system, Strike Zone Plus/Minus data only goes back to 2010.

When we look at Strike Zone Plus/Minus as it relates to Yadier Molina, guess what? He's good. No surprise there. However, the data does shed some light on the talents of another player that hasn't garnered quite as much attention over his five year career so far: Jonathan Lucroy.

The table below shows Molina's and Lucroy's statistical totals from 2010-14.

Player	Adjusted ER Saved	Stolen Base Runs Saved	Bunt Runs Saved	GFP/DME Runs Saved	Strike Zone Runs Saved	Total Runs Saved
Yadier Molina	13	21	6	24	33	97
Jonathan Lucroy	-7	-7	-1	22	85	92

Lucroy hasn't been entirely overlooked in that time period. In 2014, Lucroy was honored with his first Fielding Bible Award, and he also finished fourth in the National League MVP voting (though, Molina still won the NL Gold Glove). However, Lucroy has added just about as much defensive value to his team as Molina has over the last five years, not just in 2014. Molina and Lucroy are the top two catchers in all of baseball with their 97 and 92 Defensive Runs Saved, respectively, since 2010. The reason that Lucroy hasn't received as much attention in that time is that most of his value is comprised of his pitch framing abilities and less so the defensive skills that catchers have traditionally been celebrated for.

There are two reasons that Lucroy's pitch framing skills are able to make up for his deficiencies in other areas of his game. First, he has been the best catcher in baseball at getting extra strikes called during the five years that he has been in the league. Specifically, his 23 and 19 Strike Zone Runs Saved in 2011 and 2010, respectively, are the two highest single season totals that BIS has recorded. In the last few years his totals have come down, but he still led the league with 15 Strike Zone Runs Saved in 2012, tied for the league lead (with Molina) with 14 Strike Zone Runs Saved in 2013, and finished fourth in the league with 14 Strike Zone Runs Saved in 2014.

The second reason is that pitch framing as a skill offers more of an opportunity to save runs defensively than any other defensive skill associated with catchers. This makes sense if you think about it. By BIS's calculations, converting a pitch from a ball to a strike is worth 0.12 runs on average. Despite that miniscule value, catchers can see upwards of 10,000 called pitches over the course of a season. Compare that to 100 opportunities to throw out a basestealer, 20 opportunities to field a bunt, or even 700 opportunities to block a potential wild pitch in the dirt. Even though each of those types of events has a greater run value associated with it, and is thus more impactful as a singular event within a game, the sheer volume of pitches that a catcher sees over the course of a game trumps them all.

One of the major criticisms of publicly available catcher framing metrics is that they overstate the value of pitch framing as a skill. However, by factoring in the other participants on a pitch, Strike Zone Plus/Minus is much more moderate than other publicly available methodologies in evaluating catchers. For example, in 2011, when we measured Lucroy as having saved 23 runs with his framing, other systems valued him at upwards of 40 runs. Many of the other systems focus on giving the credit for an extra strike being called all to the catcher, then sometimes use the pitcher, the umpire, and the batter as context to be adjusted for. However, by dividing the credit among all four parties, Strike Zone Plus/Minus does a more accurate job of appropriately valuing each. To be sure, valuing a catcher at about four wins the way other systems value Lucroy's 2011 season, just on his pitch framing alone, is difficult to believe. But with Strike Zone Plus/Minus, Lucroy's 23 and 19 Runs Saved from 2011 and 2010, respectively, are the outliers. Every other year, the best catchers in the game have been worth about 15 Strike Zone Runs Saved, and no catcher besides Lucroy has ever surpassed 16 Strike Zone Runs Saved. Given the number of pitches that catchers see over the course of a season, those numbers seem entirely reasonable.

Yadier Molina is a much more well-rounded catcher than Jonathan Lucroy. Molina excels at all facets of the game defensively and is absolutely deserving of all the accolades that have been bestowed upon him. However, Lucroy's abilities as a pitch framer should not go overlooked. He excels at a singular skill, but it is perhaps the most important mechanical skill for a catcher to have. Now that we have a reliable way of quantifying that skill, hopefully more people will take notice of his defensive value as a catcher.

Catcher Blocks of Pitches in the Dirt

Baseball Info Solutions has been accounting for a catcher's ability to prevent wild pitches in the Good Play/ Misplay component of Defensive Runs Saved since 2009, though we've tracked Catcher Blocks and Wild Pitch Misplays back to 2004. However, we have found that we could improve the accuracy of our accounting and include one previously neglected data point: Passed Balls.

BIS Video Scouts record every time a pitch hits the dirt with runners on base. If the catcher gets down and successfully blocks the pitch and prevents baserunner advancement, we record a Catcher Block. If the catcher is not able to block the Wild Pitch well enough to prevent advancement, he receives a Wild Pitch Misplay (Defensive Misplay #53). Similarly, if a pitcher throws a pitch well wide or high of the plate and the catcher is able to catch it, we record a Potential Wild Pitch Catch (Good Fielding Play #27). Finally, if the pitch is so wild that the catcher never had a shot (less than one percent of all Wild Pitches), we record the Wild Pitch but not a Defensive Misplay on the catcher.

In our most recent accounting, we treated Catcher Blocks, Potential Wild Pitch Catches, and Wild Pitch Misplays independently. However, the two Good Fielding Plays and the Defensive Misplay are natural opposites, and treating them as such can improve our calculation. To put it another way, every Wild Pitch Misplay is a failed Catcher Block or Potential Wild Pitch Catch and should receive the counteracting credit. If we do not compare one directly to the other, we risk mis-crediting catchers who face a relatively large or small number of possible wild pitches or pitches in the dirt, as some pitchers and entire pitching staffs tempt hitters to chase more often than others.

We also updated the run values for these plays. We calculated the average run expectancy change for Catcher Blocks and Potential Wild Pitch Catches as well as Wild Pitch Misplays. The two GFPs, which usually result in no change but occasionally result in a pickoff or caught stealing, average -0.040 runs for the offense, while Wild Pitch Misplays average 0.257 for the offense. The difference, 0.297, is the number of runs we attribute to each Catcher Block above average.

Using Alex Avila as an example, he faced a total of 598 potential Wild Pitches or pitches in the dirt (adding Catcher Blocks, Potential Wild Pitch Catches, and Wild Pitch Misplays). Catchers blocked 93.4 percent of such pitches in 2014, so we'd expect Avila to block 559 of them. He actually blocked 576 of them, 17 more than expected. Those 17 extra blocks, multiplied by 0.297 runs apiece, results in about 5.0 runs he's saved with his blocking.

The other related piece is Passed Balls, pitches that should have been caught in the estimation of the official scorer but were not. The problem comes from assuming that all pitches are equally catchable. For instance, Passed Balls are highly correlated with knuckleballs. In previous years, the Passed Ball leader was always whichever poor Red Sox catcher was tasked with catching Tim Wakefield. Obviously, that isn't fair to them, as knuckleballs are substantially more difficult to receive. In order to include Passed Balls in our updated catcher blocks metric, we decided to throw out all knuckleballs in our analysis.

For Passed Balls, we compare a catcher's rate per "received pitch" to the league average. We define a "received pitch" as any pitch with runners on base which is not put in play or fouled off. We performed a similar run expectancy analysis to find the average run value of a Passed Ball, and we multiplied by the number of Passed Balls above or below expected based on the league average rate.

So returning to the Avila example, he had 4,564 "received pitches" in 2014. Based on league-wide rates of Passed Balls, we would expect Avila to have a little less than eight in that number of opportunities. In actuality, he has had just three Passed Balls. Therefore, using a run value of -0.240 for Passed Balls, Avila saved 1.3 runs with his sure-handedness. Putting those numbers together with the 5.0 runs he has saved with his catcher blocks, he has a total of 6.3 Catcher Block Runs Saved.

Now, here are more of the results!

Most Catcher Block Runs Saved, 2014

Catcher	Catcher Block Runs Saved
J. Lucroy	8.6
A. Avila	6.3
Y. Gomes	3.6
Y. Molina	3.2
C. Ruiz	2.7

Least Catcher Block Runs Saved, 2014

Catcher	Catcher Block Runs Saved
T. d'Arnaud	-4.5
W. Rosario	-4.3
E. Gattis	-4.0
M. Zunino	-3.0
J. Saltalamacchia	-2.7

Jonathan Lucroy leads the way and maintains a convincing margin over his peers in 2014, adding to his already strong all-around campaign which earned him a fourth place MVP finish. However, defensive stalwart Yadier Molina has been the most consistently dominant catcher in this regard in recent years, saving an MLB-best 42.0 runs through his exceptional blocking since entering the league in 2004. The bottom of the list may be no surprise either. Wilin Rosario has struggled with both pitches in the dirt and Passed Balls since arriving in the majors.

Runs saved on Catcher Blocks, Potential Wild Pitch Catches, and Passed Balls are all included in the broader Good Play/Misplay Runs Saved category of Defensive Runs Saved. However, we've included just the runs saved on these particular components in the leaderboards above.

Catcher Block Runs Saved is the most accurate way we evaluate a catcher's ability to block potential wild pitches and pitches in the dirt, but if you prefer a simpler format to get the gist of the information, we can also present the information as a "Catcher Block Rate". We simply divide a player's Catcher Blocks and Potential Wild Pitch Catches total by the sum of his Catcher Blocks, Potential Wild Pitch Catches, Passed Balls, and Wild Pitch Misplays. The resulting percentage is essentially the ratio of pitches blocked to those not blocked or caught. The following table shows the leading and trailing catchers in this stat for 2014.

Best Catcher Block Rate, 2014
Minimum 200 Catcher Block Attempts

Catcher	Catcher Blocks	Potential Wild Pitch Catches	Passed Balls	Wild Pitch Misplays	Catcher Block Rate
A. Avila	571	5	3	22	0.958
J. Lucroy	804	1	5	31	0.957
J. Lobaton	292	2	1	14	0.951
Y. Molina	382	0	3	18	0.948
J. Mathis	313	0	3	16	0.943

Worst Catcher Block Rate, 2014
Minimum 200 Catcher Block Attempts

Catcher	Catcher Blocks	Potential Wild Pitch Catches	Passed Balls	Wild Pitch Misplays	Catcher Block Rate
T. d'Arnaud	383	3	12	39	0.883
A. Nieto	189	2	6	19	0.884
Y. Grandal	311	1	12	26	0.891
W. Rosario	473	0	12	44	0.894
C. Vazquez	197	1	8	15	0.896

The lists are very similar to the previous ones, as we'd expect.

The Fielding Jones

By Bill James

Editor's Note: The following are Chapters I to XX of a larger research piece written by Bill James for BillJamesOnline.com. As we go to print, Chapters I to LV have been published online.

I. Catchers Deserving of the Gold Glove, 1900-1919

Year	League	Player	City	Team
1900	National	Chief Zimmer	Pittsburgh	Pirates
1901	American	Billy Sullivan	Chicago	White Sox
1901	National	Malachi Kittridge	Boston	Braves
1902	American	Lou Criger	Boston	Red Sox
1902	National	Johnny Kling	Chicago	Cubs
1903	American	Lou Criger (2)	Boston	Red Sox
1903	National	Johnny Kling (2)	Chicago	Cubs
1904	American	Lou Criger (3)	Boston	Red Sox
1904	National	John Warner	New York	Giants
1905	American	Ossee Schreckengost	Philadelphia	A's
1905	National	Red Dooin	Philadelphia	Phillies
1906	American	Billy Sullivan (2)	Chicago	White Sox
1906	National	Johnny Kling (3)	Chicago	Cubs
1907	American	Ossee Schreckengost (2)	Philadelphia	A's
1907	National	Johnny Kling (4)	Chicago	Cubs
1908	American	Billy Sullivan (3)	Chicago	White Sox
1908	National	George Gibson	Pittsburgh	Pirates
1909	American	Ira Thomas	Philadelphia	A's
1909	National	George Gibson (2)	Pittsburgh	Pirates
1910	American	Fred Payne	Chicago	White Sox
1910	National	George Gibson (3)	Pittsburgh	Pirates

Year	League	Player	City	Team
1911	American	Oscar Stanage	Detroit	Tigers
1911	National	Chief Meyers	New York	Giants
1912	American	Bill Carrigan	Boston	White Sox
1912	National	Chief Meyers (2)	New York	Giants
1913	American	Ray Schalk	Chicago	White Sox
1913	National	Chief Meyers (3)	New York	Giants
1914	American	Ray Schalk (2)	Chicago	White Sox
1914	Federal	Art Wilson	Chicago	Whales
1914	National	Chief Meyers (4)	New York	Giants
1915	American	Ray Schalk (3)	Chicago	White Sox
1915	Federal	Bill Rariden	Newark	Peppers
1915	National	Frank Snyder	St. Louis	Cardinals
1916	American	Ray Schalk (4)	Chicago	White Sox
1916	National	Hank Gowdy	Boston	Braves
1917	American	Ray Schalk (5)	Chicago	White Sox
1917	National	Bill Killefer	Philadelphia	Phillies
1918	American	Steve O'Neill	Cleveland	Indians
1918	National	Walter Schmidt	Pittsburgh	Pirates
1919	American	Ray Schalk (6)	Chicago	White Sox
1919	National	Bill Killefer (2)	Chicago	Cubs

II. General

In certain things I have written about fielding statistics, in the past, I may have been too harsh in judging the work of those who went before me. Traditional fielding statistics have very serious limitations. However, at times in the past, I may have attributed those limitations to failings by the 19th century record keepers who created baseball's statistical universe, in ways that were not accurate or were lacking insight.

About the work of the 19th century stat fathers, there are three things that I think should be kept in mind, which I did not focus on when I was more critical of the outlines of fielding records. Those three things are:

1. Changes in the game which undercut what the original statisticians were trying to do with fielding statistics,

2. The inherent difficulty of record-keeping without computers, and

3. The development of baseball statistics as language.

I'll give each of those its own little essay here.

III. The Changes in the Game

In 1870, when professional baseball began, errors were on the same level of commonality as hits, in the general sense in which Chicago is on the same level of population as New York. In 1876, the first year of the National League, there were 5,338 hits in the league, and 3,124 errors. For every 100 hits, there were 59 errors.

Errors decreased in frequency rapidly after that, but for as much as 50 years, this continued to be true in a general way—that errors were on the same level of commonality as hits, in the same sense that Jacksonville and Los Angeles are both cities. In 1915 Ollie O'Mara made 78 errors as the shortstop for the Brooklyn Dodgers. In 1916 Whitey Witt made 78 errors as the shortstop for the Philadelphia A's.

If you back it up ten years, the numbers are even larger. In 1903 Johnny Gochnauer made 98 errors in 134 games for the Cleveland Indians—and that was after fielding percentages had been improving rapidly for at least 25 years, probably 30 years. In 1901 Bill Keister made 97 errors in 112 games for Baltimore. In 1892 Herman Long made 102 errors for the Boston Braves; in 1893 he made 100 more. In neither season was he the only major league player to make 100 errors.

In the 1880s many players made more than one error per game played. Pop Smith made 89 errors in 83 games in 1880. Bob Ferguson made 88 errors in 87 games in 1883, and was regarded as a legendary defensive standout. In the 1870s the numbers are smaller because teams didn't play 100 games a year, but the numbers per game are even larger.

Errors, and also passed balls. Pop Snyder in 1881 had 44 errors in 62 games—and also 99 Passed Balls. Emil Gross in 1883 had more than one error per game played at catcher, and also more than one Passed Ball.

Several things happened in the early years to make errors less common, of which the largest, of course, was the development of fielding gloves. But my point is that given the game as it was played when the first statistics were being developed, it was not at all unreasonable to evaluate fielders based on their ability to deal with routine plays, to evaluate them by their success in avoiding a bad outcome on "routine" plays—given that they were catching line drives bare-handed, given that the fields on which they played were maintained at a level far below that of a modern T-Ball game, fields on which bad hops were more the norm than the exception and a twisted ankle was a normal outcome of running full speed.

But over time, errors became less common and less common and less common. In 1876 the National League Fielding Percentage was .866; in 1896, it was .938, a disappearance of one-half of the errors. By 1916 the National League Fielding Percentage was up to .963; by 1936, to .969. By 1956 it was up to .977. By 1976 it was still .977, but by 1996 it was up to .979. In 2014 it was .984. This has occurred despite the fact that, as fielding expectations have improved, official scorers have become ever stricter and less tolerant in assigning errors. In 2014, for every 100 base hits there were 7 errors. It's not New York and Chicago anymore; it is more like New York and Des Moines.

Passed Balls have diminished at essentially the same pace. But the disappearance of errors cut the heart out of traditional fielding statistics, and undermined the traditional concept of fielding excellence. As errors disappeared, the measured differences between the best fielders and the worst became smaller and smaller and smaller, until eventually, almost nothing was being measured by fielding percentages.

But the first generation of baseball statisticians, the Henry Chadwick generation, cannot be faulted for this failure, because they had no way of knowing that this evolution would occur. They set up a system to measure something, and then the thing they were measuring went away. Suppose that NBA players stopped missing shots, so that rebounds disappeared. Would we fault the NBA statisticians for failing to anticipate this, thus setting up a system to measure something that no longer happened? Of course we would not.

IV. Catchers Deserving of the Gold Glove, 1920-1939

Year	League	Player	City	Team
1920	American	Ray Schalk (7)	Chicago	White Sox
1920	National	Mickey O'Neil	Boston	Braves
1921	American	Patsy Gharrity	Washington	Senators
1921	National	Walter Schmidt (2)	Pittsburgh	Pirates
1922	American	Ray Schalk (8)	Chicago	White Sox
1922	National	Bob O'Farrell	Chicago	Cubs
1923	American	Johnny Bassler	Detroit	Tigers
1923	National	Frank Snyder (2)	New York	Giants
1924	American	Muddy Ruel	Washington	Senators
1924	National	Zack Taylor	Brooklyn	Dodgers

Year	League	Player	City	Team
1925	American	Ray Schalk (9)	Chicago	White Sox
1925	National	Gabby Hartnett	Chicago	Cubs
1926	American	Luke Sewell	Cleveland	Indians
1926	National	Bob O'Farrell (2)	St. Louis	Cardinals
1927	American	Muddy Ruel (2)	Washington	Senators
1927	National	Gabby Hartnett (2)	Chicago	Cubs
1928	American	Mickey Cochrane	Philadelphia	A's
1928	National	Gabby Hartnett (3)	Chicago	Cubs
1929	American	Bill Dickey	New York	Yankees
1929	National	Jimmie Wilson	St. Louis	Cardinals
1930	American	Rick Ferrell	St. Louis	Browns
1930	National	Gabby Hartnett (4)	Chicago	Cubs
1931	American	Bill Dickey (2)	New York	Yankees
1931	National	Jimmie Wilson (2)	St. Louis	Cardinals
1932	American	Mickey Cochrane (2)	Philadelphia	A's
1932	National	Gabby Hartnett (5)	Chicago	Cubs
1933	American	Luke Sewell (2)	Washington	Senators
1933	National	Gabby Hartnett (6)	Chicago	Cubs
1934	American	Mickey Cochrane (3)	Detroit	Tigers
1934	National	Gabby Hartnett (7)	Chicago	Cubs
1935	American	Rick Ferrell (2)	Boston	Red Sox
1935	National	Gabby Hartnett (8)	Chicago	Cubs
1936	American	Luke Sewell (3)	Chicago	White Sox
1936	National	Gus Mancuso	New York	Giants
1937	American	Bill Dickey (3)	New York	Yankees
1937	National	Al Lopez	Boston	Braves
1938	American	Bill Dickey (4)	New York	Yankees
1938	National	Al Todd	Pittsburgh	Pirates
1939	American	Bill Dickey (5)	New York	Yankees
1939	National	Al Lopez (2)	Boston	Braves

V. They Had No Computers

It is very difficult for a modern person to understand how difficult it was to keep track of a wide variety of statistical categories without computers. These modern statistical categories we have are wonderful—but there is no way that an army of statisticians could have kept track of all of these things without computers—an Army, a Navy, an Air Force and a Marine Corps. And the Coast Guard and the Merchant Marines.

I have some understanding of the problem, because I started the Baseball Abstract, and produced the Baseball Abstract for about five years, before I had a personal computer. My wife would help me; she would sit down and search box scores for notes like "SB—Moreno" and "DP—Cleveland, 1" and make totals of those, so that we would have counts of things like the number of stolen bases allowed by Ted Simmons and the number of Double Plays turned behind Tommy John. It was damned hard work, consumed many, many hours, and we made a lot of mistakes.

You have to understand: for a 19th century statistician to add three categories to the statistical record was a major undertaking, adding many, many hours to his workload—and everything is supposed to balance. A hit for a batter is a hit allowed by a pitcher. Sometimes, in the early records of the game, they *don't* balance, which is wrong, but when you add categories to the statistical record, the number of "contact points" where things are supposed to match increases exponentially. If you double the number of records, you don't double the number of points that are supposed to balance; it is more like an 8-fold increase. And computers haven't made record-keeping 10% easier, or even 99%, but more like 99.999% easier. It's almost impossible for anyone born after 1965 to understand how difficult it would have been to have kept track of more things.

VI. Baseball Statistics As Language

The way in which baseball statistics are generally understood is not as numbers at all, but as a peculiar kind of language. Batting and pitching statistics have a wide array of standards associated with excellence. 20 home runs means "power", 30 home runs means "real power", and 40 home runs means "unusual and unique power, possessed by only a few players at a time." 50 home runs means "historic power" or "steroid user".

There are standards like this all over the map. 20 stolen bases is a mark of some speed; 40 stolen bases, real speed, 60 stolen bases, singular and unique speed, possessed by only a few players at a time; 80 stolen bases, historic speed. A .300 batting average, of course, is a mark of excellence, but in the world of traditional batting statistics the fan's eye was so finely tuned that .290 looked very different from .280, over course of a career, and even .288 was different from .285 in some small but meaningful way.

It doesn't have anything to do with 288 of anything; a .288 batting average has no connection at all to 288 items or .288 items. The math has been buried so far beneath our conscious consumption of the data that for all practical purposes it doesn't exist. What exists is the standard, and the relationship between the standard and the player's number.

Because this is true, it is entirely possible to create fiction out of baseball statistics, in a way that it is impossible to create fiction in numbers in almost any other endeavor. I have done that before, and I will do it

again, but we'll skip it right now. I could show you a player who you would immediately know looks like Darrell Evans or Graig Nettles, and who you would immediately place in a category with Darrell Evans or Graig Nettles, even though he never actually played. My point is that this wealth of standards—magic numbers, if you will—combined with just the slightest bit of extraneous information such as a player's race and height and one or two anecdotes, will create complex and nuanced images of human beings, based essentially on numbers.

In hitting and pitching there are thousands of "magic numbers" or numbers which are standards of excellence—20 wins, 200 strikeouts, a sub-3.00 ERA, 30 Saves, 200 hits, 40 doubles, 100 runs scored, 100 RBI. They exist almost without limit. Because 100 RBI is a standard of excellence, 90 RBI is a meaningful standard of productivity, and 80, and 70, each number indicative of quality at a slightly different level.

In fielding, however, there are no magic numbers—literally none. There is not one fielding statistic of any kind which has resonance in the imagination of the typical baseball fan, none which conveys any image, none which conjures up images of Del Ennis or Darrell Evans or Joe Charboneau or Marty Barrett or any other phantom from the magical cabinet of our youth.

Fielding statistics lack this "numbers as language" facility essentially because the numbers are so different from one position to the next that, to interpret them in the same way we do hitting and pitching stats, we would have to maintain an entirely different set of standards for each position. The normal fielding statistics of a regular third baseman don't look anything like the normal statistics of a shortstop. Each must be interpreted by its own standards. This is more work than the human mind can easily do. To maintain two sets of carefully calibrated standards, one for pitchers and one for hitters, is a manageable task; to erect an additional eight sets of standards is too much—so we don't do it, so we don't have any "magic numbers" for fielders.

The consequence of this is *fielding statistics, to make any sense, must be studied as numbers*, rather than being simply assimilated as language, as are batting and pitching statistics.

In the past, when I was younger and less careful, I may have been critical of early baseball statisticians for failing to give us numbers that just "make sense" in the way that batting and pitching numbers make sense. But when I think about it, I realize how wrong-headed that judgment was. The development of this "numbers as language" facility for hitting and pitching numbers was serendipity. It was just a happy accident. It was not anticipated by the 19th century statisticians, and it could not have been anticipated, since it is unique to baseball (although a few other sports are also starting to gain this function, as are investments.) To suggest that 19th century statisticians should have anticipated this numbers-as-language function and should have created something similar for fielding statistics is just silly—rather like suggesting that Abraham Lincoln should have had the foresight to wear a helmet to Ford's Theater.

VII. Catchers Deserving of the Gold Glove, 1940-1957

Year	League	Player	City	Team
1940	American	Rollie Hemsley	Cleveland	Indians
1940	National	Harry Danning	New York	Giants
1941	American	Bill Dickey (6)	New York	Yankees
1941	National	Mickey Owen	Brooklyn	Dodgers
1942	American	Bill Dickey (7)	New York	Yankees
1942	National	Mickey Owen (2)	Brooklyn	Dodgers
1943	American	Buddy Rosar	Cleveland	Indians
1943	National	Ray Mueller	Cincinnati	Reds
1944	American	Paul Richards	Detroit	Tigers
1944	National	Ray Mueller (2)	Cincinnati	Reds
1945	American	Mike Tresh	Chicago	White Sox
1945	National	Phil Masi	Boston	Braves
1946	American	Buddy Rosar (2)	Philadelphia	A's
1946	National	Ray Mueller (2)	Cincinnati	Reds
1947	American	Jim Hegan	Cleveland	Indians
1947	National	Walker Cooper	New York	Giants
1948	American	Jim Hegan (2)	Cleveland	Indians
1948	National	Del Rice	St. Louis	Cardinals
1949	American	Jim Hegan (3)	Cleveland	Indians
1949	National	Roy Campanella	Brooklyn	Dodgers
1950	American	Jim Hegan (4)	Cleveland	Indians
1950	National	Wes Westrum	New York	Giants
1951	American	Yogi Berra	New York	Yankees
1951	National	Roy Campanella (2)	Brooklyn	Dodgers
1952	American	Yogi Berra (2)	New York	Yankees
1952	National	Del Rice (2)	St. Louis	Cardinals
1953	American	Yogi Berra (3)	New York	Yankees
1953	National	Roy Campanella (3)	Brooklyn	Dodgers
1954	American	Yogi Berra (4)	New York	Yankees

Year	League	Player	City	Team
1954	National	Del Crandall	Milwaukee	Braves
1955	American	Sherm Lollar	Chicago	White Sox
1955	National	Roy Campanella (4)	Brooklyn	Dodgers
1956	American	Sherm Lollar (2)	Chicago	White Sox
1956	National	Del Crandall (2)	Milwaukee	Braves
1957	American	Yogi Berra (5)	New York	Yankees
1957	National	Roy Campanella (5)	Brooklyn	Dodgers

VIII. Traditionalists vs. Analysts

The conflict between traditional baseball fans and sabermetric analysts may also be seen as a conflict between statistics as math, and statistics as language. The traditional fan interprets baseball statistics as a form of language, measuring each player against the standards of excellence. This is not ANY less true now than it was in 1975, and it will not be any less true in 50 years. Many people have no real capacity to deal with numbers as math, and are almost entirely blind to whatever can be learned in that way, except that they may be gracious enough to take our word for it in certain cases.

We, on the other, deal with baseball statistics *as numbers*. We interpret them by mathematical processes; we perform computations with them, we use them to measure things that were previously unmeasured. This is the essential conflict between the two camps—the difference in how we interpret statistics. It isn't one camp using numbers and the other not using numbers; it is, instead, a vast difference in HOW we use the numbers.

To a traditional baseball fan, .300 is .300; it is a standard of excellence, and one definition of a "standard" is that it is a measurement which does not change. A foot is a standard measurement, meaning that it is a measurement that does not change; it may be used as a standard for other measurements. But to us, .300 is +.025 if the league batting average is .275, and +.050 if it is .250.

When we ignore standards, when we diminish things like a Triple Crown, a batting title or 20 wins, we offend those in the other camp, because in doing that we are trying to take their touchstones away from them. This is not necessary or productive. We can argue our points without doing that.

Ignorance—like racism—does not vanish like a fart in the wind; rather, it pours out constantly from the rotting carcasses of old misunderstandings. You can't banish it with a grand gesture; you can only clear it away a little bit at a time.

IX. 100 Double Plays

The closest thing there is to a magic number in fielding statistics is a consecutive-game errorless streak. There is one thing, however, that should be a magic number for fielders: 100 double plays for a middle infielder.

Which is more common: for a hitter to drive in 100 runs, or for a middle infielder to turn 100 double plays?

In the history of baseball there are 1,855 hitters who have driven in 100 runs; not 1,855 different hitters, but you know what I mean. There are a little less than 400 second basemen who have turned 100 double plays (I expected to be able to give you an exact number there, but there is a little glitch in my data.) There are just over 300 shortstops who have participated in 100 double plays. For a middle infielder to participate in 100 double plays is less than one-half as common as for a player to drive in 100 runs.

Of course, there is the problem that playing on a bad team helps a player turn more double plays, since bad teams have more runners on base against them than good teams. The winning percentage of teams who have had a second baseman with 100 double plays is .517; a shortstop, .518. I don't know what it is for 100-RBI men; I'm sure it is higher than that, since playing on a good team helps a hitter pile up RBI.

I'm just saying...did you ever see a press note, "Johnny Fasthands is just six double plays away from turning 100 double plays for the second time in his career." We see those notes every day, late in the season. . .Jack Brewer is just 3 doubles away from hitting 30 doubles for the fifth consecutive year, etc." There are no similar notes about fielding. But there should be this one.

X. Catchers Who Won the Gold Glove and Were Deserving Of It

Beginning in 1957 there are actual Gold Gloves, and thus no need to speculate as to who might have or should have won the Award, had the Award been around.

I have a new Fielding Analysis here, Win Shares and Loss Shares for everybody, which I am explaining a little bit at a time; it may take me a month to get them all explained. Since the Gold Gloves began in 1957 (beginning in both leagues in 1958), there have been 56 catchers who are seen by my new method as the best defensive catchers in the league, and who also won the Gold Glove in that season:

Year	League	Player	City	Team
1958	National	Del Crandall	Milwaukee	Braves
1959	National	Del Crandall	Milwaukee	Braves
1961	National	John Roseboro	Los Angeles	Dodgers
1962	American	Earl Battey	Minnesota	Twins
1962	National	Del Crandall	Milwaukee	Braves
1963	American	Elston Howard	New York	Yankees
1963	National	Johnny Edwards	Cincinnati	Reds
1964	American	Elston Howard	New York	Yankees
1965	American	Bill Freehan	Detroit	Tigers
1966	National	John Roseboro	Los Angeles	Dodgers
1970	National	Johnny Bench	Cincinnati	Reds
1972	National	Johnny Bench	Cincinnati	Reds
1973	American	Thurman Munson	New York	Yankees
1973	National	Johnny Bench	Cincinnati	Reds
1974	American	Thurman Munson	New York	Yankees
1974	National	Johnny Bench	Cincinnati	Reds
1975	American	Thurman Munson	New York	Yankees
1975	National	Johnny Bench	Cincinnati	Reds
1976	American	Jim Sundberg	Texas	Rangers
1976	National	Johnny Bench	Cincinnati	Reds
1977	American	Jim Sundberg	Texas	Rangers
1978	American	Jim Sundberg	Texas	Rangers
1980	National	Gary Carter	Montreal	Expos
1981	American	Jim Sundberg	Texas	Rangers
1981	National	Gary Carter	Montreal	Expos
1982	American	Bob Boone	California	Angels
1982	National	Gary Carter	Montreal	Expos
1984	National	Tony Pena	Pittsburgh	Pirates
1985	National	Tony Pena	Pittsburgh	Pirates
1986	American	Bob Boone	California	Angels
1986	National	Jody Davis	Chicago	Cubs
1988	National	Benito Santiago	San Diego	Padres
1989	American	Bob Boone	Kansas City	Royals
1991	American	Tony Pena	Boston	Red Sox
1995	American	Ivan Rodriguez	Texas	Rangers
1996	American	Ivan Rodriguez	Texas	Rangers
1997	American	Ivan Rodriguez	Texas	Rangers
1997	National	Charles Johnson	Florida	Marlins
1998	American	Ivan Rodriguez	Texas	Rangers
1999	American	Ivan Rodriguez	Texas	Rangers
2000	National	Mike Matheny	St. Louis	Cardinals
2001	National	Brad Ausmus	Houston	Astros

Year	League	Player	City	Team
2002	National	Brad Ausmus	Houston	Astros
2004	National	Mike Matheny	St. Louis	Cardinals
2006	American	Ivan Rodriguez	Detroit	Tigers
2006	National	Brad Ausmus	Houston	Astros
2007	National	Russell Martin	Los Angeles	Dodgers
2008	American	Joe Mauer	Minnesota	Twins
2009	National	Yadier Molina	St. Louis	Cardinals
2010	National	Yadier Molina	St. Louis	Cardinals
2011	National	Yadier Molina	St. Louis	Cardinals
2012	American	Matt Wieters	Baltimore	Orioles
2012	National	Yadier Molina	St. Louis	Cardinals
2013	National	Yadier Molina	St. Louis	Cardinals
2014	American	Salvador Perez	Kansas City	Royal
2014	National	Yadier Molina	St. Louis	Cardinals

The 56 players who have won the Gold Glove at catcher and are also seen by this analysis as the most deserving candidates for that award are just short of one-half of the Award winners.

Before, I was giving you running totals of "Deserved Gold Gloves"; let me finish that. These are the catchers who are shown by this method as the best defensive catchers in their leagues the most times:

Player	Total
Ray Schalk	9
Gabby Hartnett	8
Bob Boone	7
Bill Dickey	7
Brad Ausmus	6
Johnny Bench	6
Yogi Berra	6
Gary Carter	6
Yadier Molina	6
Thurman Munson	6
Ivan Rodriguez	6
Roy Campanella	5
Del Crandall	5
Jim Hegan	4
Johnny Kling	4
Chief Meyers	4
John Roseboro	4
Jim Sundberg	4
Mickey Cochrane	3
Lou Criger	3
George Gibson	3
Elston Howard	3
Sherm Lollar	3
Ray Mueller	3
Tony Pena	3
Mike Scioscia	3
Luke Sewell	3
Billy Sullivan	3
Earl Battey	2
Rick Ferrell	2
Ramon Hernandez	2
Randy Hundley	2
Bill Killefer	2
Al Lopez	2
Javier Lopez	2
Mike Matheny	2
Joe Mauer	2
Bob O'Farrell	2
Mickey Owen	2
Del Rice	2
Buddy Rosar	2
Muddy Ruel	2
Benito Santiago	2
Walter Schmidt	2
Ossee Schreckengost	2
Frank Snyder	2

Player	Total
Matt Wieters	2
Jimmie Wilson	2

I don't believe there are ANY surprises on the list. Ray Schalk is in the Hall of Fame based almost entirely on his defensive reputation, and my previous analysis similar to this have also scored him very well, so his position at the top of the list is not a Schalk. Hartnett, Berra, Bench, Dickey, Carter and Campanella are in the Hall of Fame as well. Boone, Ausmus, Molina, Munson and Ivan Rodriguez are, I think, all universally accepted as outstanding defensive catchers.

XI. Taking another look at Traditional Fielding Statistics

I maintain several very large Excel Files that I use to study different problems. I have a "spreadsheet encyclopedia" for hitting statistics, and I have one for pitching statistics. These are enormously useful to me, and they enable me to answer a good many questions that I would otherwise be entirely unable to answer.

However, I have never had a parallel encyclopedia for Fielding Statistics, until now. Over the past month I have spent most of my time creating a spreadsheet encyclopedia for traditional fielding stats, and I have that mostly in place now.

The Fielding Encyclopedia lacks modern analytic fielding data. But this Fielding Encyclopedia enables us to re-visit questions about fielding as they pertain to the many years of major league baseball which predate modern analysis. I will have many points related to that in this long series of articles that I am beginning here, but the big takeaway is this: that, in the past, I may have underestimated what could be done in evaluating fielders, based just on traditional fielding numbers. I underestimated it because I was trying to interpret fielding statistics in traditional ways. But a great deal can be known, from the fielding statistics, by way of careful, organized analysis.

XII. Season Scores for Fielders

The first thing I did, once I had a Fielding Encyclopedia sort of in place, was to create a system of Season Scores for fielding. I have a system of Season Scores for hitters and one for pitchers, and these are very useful to me although I think I can accurately say that the rest of the analytic community is unanimous in that they Don't See the Point In That. I like them, anyway, and I use them regularly, and so I created a system of Season Scores for Fielders.

That was interesting and useful, but I'm not going to say any more about it right now, because after I did that, I pushed on for two more weeks to create an organized, systematic analysis of fielding statistics by Win Shares and Loss Shares. I think of these two as the naïve analysis—Season Scores—and the sophisticated analysis—Win Shares and Loss Shares. I've got about 10,000 things I want to tell you from doing the Win Shares and Loss Shares, but it would just be confusing to simultaneously introduce ANOTHER new set of Fielding Metrics, particularly since the two would not always agree.

XIII. Trivial Disparities Between the Gold Glove and the Win Shares List (Catcher)

Since the Gold Gloves were introduced there have been 115 Gold Glove catchers—56 of them also seen by the Win Shares System as the best in the league, and 59 not seen. Most of the 59 disparities or disagreements are trivial disagreements...close calls that just didn't happen to go the same way. The first Gold Glove in 1957, for example, went to Sherm Lollar, who is not seen as the most valuable defensive catcher of 1957, but is seen as deserving of the Gold Glove in 1955, 1956 and 1960, and who is near the top of the list in 1957. This continues to happen to the present day. My system agrees with all of the Gold Gloves at catcher from 2012 to the present, except the American League in 2013. The Gold Gloves at catcher the last three years have gone to Wieters, Salvador Perez and Perez again, whereas my system would have chosen Wieters, Wieters, and Perez—a trivial difference, since the two methods agree that Perez and Wieters are the best defensive catchers in the league, but just split on the 2013 award. In 2011 my system would have chosen Alex Avila as the best catcher in the American League, Wieters fifth, Wieters won the Award, so that is a real and substantial disagreement.

In addition to the 56 players who won the Award and also led the league in Win Share Value at catcher, there are 32 others who won the award and were second or third in the league in Win Share value. Many of the others were guys like Bench, Rodriguez and Sundberg, who won the Award in seasons in which they missed some games with injuries, and consequently finished 4th or 5th in Win Share value. I would say that there are nine cases in which there is a substantial disagreement between Win Shares and the Gold Glove voting at catcher. I'll discuss those nine the next time this comes around, which I guess will be point XVI.

XIV. New Fielding Win Shares and Loss Shares

The new system of Fielding Win Shares and Loss Shares is not the same as the Fielding Win Shares and Loss Shares that I have discussed here in the past; it is a new system. It is a new system which is similar to the old one, of course, and which in most cases reaches at least somewhat similar conclusions, but...it is a new and different approach.

One way in which it is different is that I have abandoned the "causal link" between outs made and defensive responsibility. The number of innings that a TEAM must play in the field depends directly on how many outs they make at bat. For every three outs you make at bat or on the bases, you have to play one inning of defense.

For that reason, I had (in the past) a "link" in my defensive analysis which placed additional responsibility on a defensive player if he made more outs at bat. Gary Sheffield, for example, ranked better in my defensive analysis than in anyone else's defensive analysis, because Sheffield, with his very high On Base Percentages, didn't make very many outs, Since he didn't make outs, he was not placing a defensive responsibility on the team. Conversely, Aurelio Rodriguez or Ozzie Guillen or Jerry Adair would look worse in my system than in others, because the number of outs that they made as a hitter creates additional responsibility to play defense.

It is an entirely logical link, and I would defend that link today as I would have two months ago. What is true of the team must be true of the individuals on the team. The failure to represent this in the statistical model is a failure of the statistical model.

Nonetheless, it is almost impossible to explain to a third party why Gary Sheffield should receive a higher *defensive* value than another player based on the fact that he has a good on base percentage as a hitter. That's one serious problem, and another is that this "link"—like all links—makes the analysis more complicated, more time-consuming, more...awkward. When you make a line of analysis more awkward, you limit what you can do with that line of analysis. I decided that, regardless of what I might think, I needed to disconnect that link in order to make the analysis work better.

Related to that issue but in ways that may not be apparent right off the cookie, the old analysis would not and could not deliver a player's defensive won-lost record at any one position. Suppose that a player—let's call him Craig Biggio—plays 428 games in his career at catcher, 1,989 games at second base, 255 games in center field, and 111 games in left and right. It is natural, in that situation, to ask what his defensive won-lost record was as a catcher, as a second baseman, as a center fielder, and as an outfielder.

In my old system I could not answer that question. The old system was set up to assign defensive *responsibility*, on the one hand, and defensive *credit* on the other, by a separate pathway. The two merged at the end of the process, but they did not merge for each position, so there was no way to say what a player's defensive won-lost record was at any one position.

This was occasionally useful—for example, with regard to Vic Power. Vic Power, a great defensive first baseman, would have a better defensive won-lost record than any other player who was essentially a first baseman, because he would play games almost every year at second base and third base, and sometimes he would play games at shortstop and in the outfield. This tended to make his defensive won-lost record better, so that he would come out ahead of the other first basemen.

Entirely logical, in a way; Vic Power WAS a better defensive player than the other first basemen, and he played second base and third base and sometimes shortstop because he was a dramatically better fielder than the other first baseman. The system was not lying.

Still, it was awkward and in a certain sense illogical not to be able to say what his defensive won-lost record was simply as a first baseman, as a second baseman, as a third baseman or as a bench jockey. Certainly it was limiting not to be able to do this. So in my redesign of Defensive Win Shares and Loss Shares, following from the construction of my spreadsheet Fielding Encyclopedia, I set it up so that each player has a Defensive Won-Lost record (each season) at each position.

XV. The Structure of Win Shares and Loss Shares

For each game that a team wins, there are three Win Shares, three shares of that win. For each game they lose, there are three Loss Shares. I will explain in another little article, Point XVII, why 3 to 1 is the best ratio to use.

In original Win Shares, published a little more than ten years ago, the ratio of Team Wins to Win Shares was absolutely three to one in all cases, no matter what; the system was forced through after-the-fact adjustments to ensure that this would be true. In this version of Win Shares and Loss Shares, the intention of the system is that there will be a 3-to-1 ratio of Wins to Win Shares, and the general outcome is that there will be a 3-to-1 ratio, but this is not an absolute, unyielding requirement of the system, there is no end-of-the-process adjustment to ensure that this is true, and there will be some cases where a team might have 90 wins but 264 Win Shares, or something of that nature. I would still guess that the ratio of Wins to Win Shares is "tighter" and more consistent in this system than it is in any parallel system such as WAR or JAWS, although I don't know for certain that it is.

In any case, Win Shares is in essence a process of assigning the Wins and Losses of a team to individual players. We start the Won-Lost record of the team. Let us say that a team had a won-lost record of 100-62. That makes 300 Win Shares, 186 Loss Shares.

First, we assign those from the team to Offense and Defense. The 2005 St. Louis Cardinals went 100-62, so let's use them to illustrate the process. They have 300 Win Shares, 186 Loss Shares.

First, we break that down into "Offensive" Wins and Losses and "Defensive" Wins and Losses, "Defensive" at this stage including pitching. In their case it breaks down as 146-97 on offense, and 154-89 on defense. This split is made based on the team's runs scored and runs allowed, park adjusted, compared to the league averages.

I'm not going to fully explain every formula as we go, because there are hundreds of formulas that interlock and interact to create the end product; the process of explaining every formula would slow us down so much that it would stretch out this series of articles to the length of a book, and also, that stuff is not at all interesting. You'll just have to trust me with some of the details for now; at some point I will need to explain them, but for the moment you're just going to have to trust me, that my formulas do what I tell you I am doing.

So the Cardinals Pitching-and-Defense have a won-lost record of 154-89 in 2005, and their batters have a won-lost record of 146-97. Add that together, it is 300-186, which is 100-62 times three. Focusing on the 154-89 record of the team's fielder's and pitchers, the next task is to divide those between pitchers and fielders.

In Win Shares (and Loss Shares), Wins (and Losses) are assigned from the team to the offense or defense, from the defense to pitching or fielding, from "fielding" to specific defensive positions, and from the defensive position to the individual fielder. All of those transfers are tricky; all of them are, to a certain extent, speculative. I divide them up as seems most reasonable and most consistent with what I know, but the evidence for many of the transfers could not be called logically compelling. The same is true of all parallel systems: there are always arbitrary decisions hidden in there, waiting to be exposed.

Of the 243 Win Shares and Loss Shares which are attributed to pitchers and fielders on a team, 162-game schedule, about 60 to 70 typically are assigned to fielders. The percentage used to be much higher, because fielding used to be more central to the game. The split between pitchers and fielders depends on the team's strikeouts, walks, hit batsmen, home runs, errors and double plays. Strikeouts, walks and home runs make the fielders irrelevant; there is nothing the fielder can do about those things. As those things increase, the "pitcher's percentage" increases. Similarly, errors and double plays are actions essentially of the defense, to an extent outside the control of the pitcher, so as those things increase, the "fielding percentage" increases.

In modern baseball strikeouts are, of course, at a historic high, and errors are (always) at historic lows. Home Runs are not at the level of ten years ago, but they're not at the level of the 1920s, either; in 1925 the average major league team hit 73 home runs, whereas in 2014 the average team hit 139 home runs. The three-cornered battle between hitter, pitcher and fielder is gradually being smushed into a two-man battle between pitcher and hitter, with the fielders increasingly taking on the role of innocent bystanders.

The 2005 St. Louis Cardinals had 69 Win Shares and Loss Shares assigned to fielders, which was the second-highest total of any team in 2005; actually 69.36, but we are wary of the decimal points, although we carry them along. The Cardinals were last in the National League in walks allowed, near the bottom in strikeouts, and below average in home runs allowed. The pitchers kept the ball in play, which allowed the defense room to work.

At this point in writing up this process, I have already discovered three significant mistakes that I made in implementing the new Win Shares and Loss Shares, which will mean that I have to go back and re-do about

10 days work, so you can imagine how chipper I feel about that. It will also mean that there may be some delay in my continuing the publication of this series, and also, it means that a whole bunch of notes that I had about cool things I learned from the data are no longer trustworthy.

XVI. Cases of Substantial Disagreement between Gold Glove Voting at Catcher and the Win Shares System

Joe Torre won the Gold Glove at catcher in the National League in 1965, but is seen by my system as the 12th-best catcher in the league (actually the 12th most valuable catcher.)

Occasionally, historically, the Gold Glove voting system just goes haywire and somebody wins the award who obviously shouldn't. I think that's happened about six times in the history of the award, not counting pitchers, and...this is one of them. Torre was never regarded as an outstanding defensive catcher, and Whitey Herzog said in one of his books that his friend Joe Torre was the worst defensive catcher he ever saw. He was the best *hitting* catcher in the league, and apparently the vote split wildly and allowed the "attention effect" of Torre's bat to pull in enough voters to carry a split vote. As to who should have won the award: John Roseboro in a landslide.

Roseboro won the Award in 1961 and 1966. You may remember that on August 22, 1965, Roseboro was involved in the most memorable incident of the 1965 season, when Juan Marichal cracked him over the head with the bat. That incident may have played into the voting in some way. We're not always right; the Gold Glove voters aren't always wrong because they don't agree with me. But in that case, I think most people would agree that the vote was a clunker.

Ray Fosse won the American League Award in 1970 and 1971. My system mildly disagrees with the 1970 Award—we have Fosse third, behind Thuman Munson and George Mitterwald—but strongly disagrees with the 1971 Award, placing Fosse sixth behind Munson, Ellie Rodriguez, Bill Freehan, George Mitterwald and Elrod Hendricks. The collision with Rose was in 1970.

Mike LaValliere won the National League Award in 1987. You know the expression "Built like a catcher"? LaValliere was built so much like a catcher that it was actually funny; if you met him on the street you would say "That guy is built like a catcher." We have LaValliere with a very high Winning Percentage at catcher in 1987 (.804), as opposed to Torre, 1965, (.554) and Fosse, 1971, (.637), but there are other catchers with more playing time and similar Winning Percentages in 1987: Mike Scioscia (.776), Gary Carter (.704), Bob Brenly (.799), and Bo Diaz (.719), all with more playing time. Maybe it's not a "serious" disagreement, because LaValliere has the highest Defensive Winning Percentage in the league, and the difference in value isn't huge, although LaValliere ranks 5th.

In 1990 the Gold Gloves went to Benito Santiago and Sandy Alomar Junior, and I don't see either one as being a good selection or close to a good selection. The young Benito Santiago was a good defensive catcher; he won the Gold Glove Award in 1989, and my system agrees with that selection. Santiago had a good .710 Defensive Winning Percentage in 1990, but caught just 98 games. Again, the award should have gone to Scioscia, and I would rate Scioscia, Mike LaValliere and three others all ahead of Santiago. Scioscia never won a Gold Glove Award, but I have him as deserving of three.

That award is good, however, compared to the American League Award, which went to Sandy Alomar Jr. Alomar was a rookie that year, and for some reason everybody loved him, but the data doesn't know why. He led the league in errors at catcher, 14, and had the lowest fielding percentage of any catcher save one. He had 11 Passed Balls, third in the league, and a very low assists total. He threw out 34% of base stealers, not a notable number. Indians pitchers, who had been 5th in the league in ERA in 1989 with Andy Allanson catching, dropped to 13th in a 14-team league with Alomar, and their strikeout/walk ratio deteriorated.

As to who should have won that Award—Lance Parrish or the Angels, probably, or Tony Pena of Boston. We use eight "Winning Percentage Indicators" to evaluate a team's catchers. Boston (Pena) is not only ahead of Cleveland (Alomar) in all eight categories, but far ahead of them in all eight. Anaheim (Parrish) is ahead of them in seven categories, losing Passed Balls. I have Alomar that season as the 12th-best defensive catcher in a 14-team league.

I said there were nine serious disagreements, and I've discussed five—Torre in 1965, Fosse in 1971, LaValliere in 1987, and both leagues in 1990. Tom Pagnozzi won the National League Award in 1994 over Joe Girardi, Kirt Manwaring, Benito Santiago and Brad Ausmus, all of whom my system thinks would have been better choices (in that order.) Mike Lieberthal won the NL Award in 1999; I have him as the 9th best catcher in

the league, behind a forgettable list of Dominicans headed up by Tony Eusebio, who I like to think of as Tony UCBO. Joe Mauer won the American League Award in 2009, when I have him 9th in the league, and Matt Wieters won in 2011, when I have him 5th in the league.

When I say that Johnny Bassler deserved the American League Gold Glove in 1923, that doesn't mean absolutely that he would have won it (although he would have. The MVP voters loved Bassler; we have to assume that the Gold Glove voters would have as well.) But sometimes, some years, there would have been Joe Torre-, Sandy Alomar-type situations in which the voting would not have run on the same track as the analysis.

But matching the awards to the extent that we do gives us more confidence in our guesses as to who the Award winners would have been. In the Gold Glove era (1957-2014) there isn't any case in which the Win Shares system loves a catcher, but the Gold Glove voters ignore him; the closest there is to such a situation is Mike Scioscia, with his three deserved Gold Gloves, none awarded.

XVII. Why 3 to 1 is the right ratio for Win Shares

People who are hidebound by traditional ways of thinking—which is 99% of the human race—are always pestering me about why there are three Win Shares for every win.

Because three is the right ratio. One to one doesn't work, and ten to one doesn't work. Three to one works.

Suppose we used a 1-to-1 ratio. The 2005 Cardinals, as a team, would have 23 Win Shares and Loss Shares to be distributed among their 8 fielding positions and among 20 players. That's one Win Share *or Loss Share* per player, or 3 per fielding position. An everyday shortstop would have a won-lost record of 2-1 or perhaps 1-2; almost all of the regulars would be 1-1, some part-time player would be 1-0 or 0-1, and most of the part-time players would be 0-0.

You have no level of articulation there, no distinction, no descriptive power. Even the player's entire record for a season, offense and defense, would be based on eight or nine Win Shares. Almost every player would have a won-lost record of 4-4 or 4-5 or 5-4, something like that. Almost every player would look about the same. The system would have no power to distinguish levels of ability which are perfectly easy to see in other analytical approaches.

When we create three Win Shares for each win, we are able to see meaningful levels of distinction. 5 and 4 expanded 3/1 could be 14 and 13, or 15 and 13, or 16 and 13, or 14 and 12, 15 and 12, 16 and 12, 14 and 11, 15 and 11, 16 and 11; any of these would reduce to 5-4 on a one-to-one scale. It's unworkable. 16 and 11 is meaningfully different from 14 and 13; it will not do to compress them down to the same level.

Well, then—says the super-conventional thinker, who is still afraid of his father and still somewhat wary of his 4th grade teacher—why not use a 10 to 1 ratio?

But that has the opposite problem: that it creates distinctions between players which are entirely artificial, distinctions which have no basis in fact. WAR distinguishes players on tenths of a win—one player is at 2.7, another at 2.6—but is that a real distinction, or a pretend distinction?

Well, what is one-tenth of a Win? It's one run; basically, one-tenth of a win is one run. When you say that one player is at 2.7 WAR and another player is at 2.6, what you are really saying is that Player A was one run better, over the course of the season, than Player B.

Do you honestly think we can measure that accurately? Let me tell you: We can't. It's a pretend distinction; it's not real.

It is a question of getting the right level of granularity—the level that makes the smallest distinctions that we can actually make. Let us suppose that we say that one player is 16 and 11 (16-11, 16 wins) and another player is 15-11. Are we always right in that, in saying that the 16-11 player was better than the 15-11 player?

No, we're not always right in those distinctions—but we have a reasonable chance of being right. We're going to be right quite a bit more often than we're going to be wrong. If we used 10 "shares" for each win, then the player who is 15-11 would be about 50-37, which would be equivalent to 2.4 WAR. 50-37 on a 10/1 ratio is the same as 5.0-3.7 on a 1/1 ratio; the only difference is the introduction of that ugly decimal point in there. And when we say that one player is 50-37 and the other is 49-37, we have no real basis for saying that; we're just talking to hear our heads rattle.

15 and 11, 16 and 11...this is a won-lost record that makes intuitive sense to a baseball fan, because it is on the same scale as a pitcher's won-lost record for a season. 5.0 vs. 3.7 (or 50-37) doesn't make ANY intuitive sense, and it isn't a real distinction anyway. The ratio that works is three to one.

In calculating Win Shares, we carry forward a large number of decimal points. We carry these forward from one stage of the calculation to another because constantly rounding them off would, of course, introduce another element of error into the calculations. I said that the 2005 St. Louis Cardinals had 69 Win Shares and Loss Shares attributable to defense, but it is actually 69.36.

But what is one-tenth of a Win Share, in fact? One Win Share is about three runs, in general, so one-tenth of a Win Share is roughly one-third of one run. It's one PLAY, one defensive PLAY over the course of a season. The difference between 69.4 Win Shares and 69.3 Win Shares is one defensive play over the course of the season.

And what then is one one-hundredth of a Win Share, the difference between 69.36 Win Shares and 69.37? It is *one-tenth* of one play. It is less than one pitch. Of course we cannot measure player performance, over the course of a season, that accurately; of course these are not real distinctions between players. They are mere statistical artifacts, occupying space because it is not yet appropriate to round them off and be done with them. But I would not want anyone to mistake those for real distinctions. The difference between 2.7 WAR and 2.6 WAR is nothing; it's not a real distinction that we can actually measure. But the difference between 8.1 Win Shares and 8.0 would be one-third of that.

XVIII. Assigning Defensive Responsibility to Fielding Positions

The St. Louis Cardinals in 2005 have 69 Win Shares and Loss Shares to be distributed among their fielders. Our next task is to assign those to defensive *positions*—to catchers, first basemen, etc.

I am calling this "Defensive Responsibility" because that is easy, but that isn't actually exactly what it is; it is more like "Defensive Opportunity." This is a simple and straightforward process. We assign those to positions:

16% to catchers

8% to first basemen

14% to second basemen

12% to third basemen

16% to shortstops

34% to outfielders

We're working with traditional fielding stats here. Traditional fielding stats define all outfielders as "outfielder", rather than left fielder, center fielder or right fielder. The 34% for outfielders can be seen as 9% for left fielders, 10% for right fielders, 15% for center fielders. The Cardinals in 2005 have 69 (69.36) Win Shares and Loss Shares to be attributed to defense (oh, have I mentioned that?) 16% of those go to catchers, so St. Louis catchers in 2005 have 11.10 Win Shares and Loss Shares, for their fielding.

The numbers above apply from 1935 to the present. Up to 1919, the percentage is actually 12% for second basemen, 14% for third basemen, and from 1920 to 1934 the percentage is 13% for second basemen and third basemen.

XIX. First Basemen and Pitchers

We ignore the Fielding Performance of the Pitcher because it is a subset of his performance as a pitcher. Suppose that a pitcher saved 20 runs a year by his fielding—which would be phenomenal and probably impossible, but let us suppose. That means that his Runs Allowed drop by 20, his ERA drops by a run, more or less. We already give him credit for those things; we already give him credit for not allowing runs. It would not be appropriate, in a won-lost accounting, to then give him credit for saving those runs *again*.

At this point a certain number of you, who are chronic know-it-alls because your mommy told you when you were in the second grade what a smart boy you were and you never got over it, are rushing to the comments section to inform the rest of us that the importance of fielding at first base is very much underrated.

Yeah yeah. . .we got it. The first baseman is involved in a huge number of plays; the first baseman can save plays for other fielders, a good first baseman can field a bunt the same as a third baseman can, a good first baseman can make a very important defensive contribution, etc., etc. I know. We all know.

If you make dollhouse sized replica of the White House, it is very likely that the plumbing will not work and the windows will not open. Statistical models are not absolutely accurate images of the underlying reality; rather, statistical models are simplifications of underlying realities which are vastly more complicated than the statistical imitation of them. This is true of all statistical analysis—statistical analysis of the economy, for example, or of the crime rate. A great deal gets left out.

But the fact is that most first basemen—80% of them or more—are limited defensive players who play first base because they lack the speed and the arm to play some other position. They can catch the ball, and that's about it. Every shortstop in the majors could play first base if he had to. Almost no first basemen can play shortstop.

A striking thing about high school baseball, if you ever see a high school baseball game, is that high school first basemen very often run down foul pop ups that major league first basemen would never get to. High school first basemen sometimes throw better than major league first basemen. It is almost the only thing you see in which the high school players can outperform the major leaguers. Why is that?

First basemen, in general, most of the time, make very limited or no defensive contribution to their team, and are not supposed to; they are playing first base because they can hit, and you have to put them some place. Sometimes models must take what is generally true to be an absolute. We're doing the best we can with it.

XX. Relationships between Positions

In 1971 the Kansas City Royals' regular center fielder was Amos Otis, an All Star, and their regular catcher was Ed Kirkpatrick; actually Kirkpatrick had been the regular catcher in 1970 and was the regular in early 1971, when my story takes place. In late April Otis had a small injury that kept him out of the lineup for a few days, so the Royals took their catcher, Ed Kirkpatrick, and put him in center field for the series. This was perceived as very odd, because a catcher does not normally move to center field, but Kirkpatrick played well in center field, and the Royals swept a three-game series against Cleveland. Actually, in the spirit of telling the story straight, Otis returned for the third game and hit a three-run homer, which helped, but Kirkpatrick, playing left in that game, also homered.

That sticks with me, 44 years later, because it was so odd. Suppose that, to start with, we just count the number of players playing each position. Since 1900 (1900 to 2014) there have been 9,387 players who played at least one game at catcher in a season; not 9,387 different players, that is counting Yogi Berra 19 times, since he played a game at catcher in 19 seasons. This is the chart for the nine positions:

	Catcher	First Base	Second	Third	Short	Outfield
Catcher	9387					
First Base		11686				
Second			10877			
Third				12006		
Short					9733	
Outfield						23329

That's treating "outfield" as one defensive position, obviously; I am working from traditional fielding statistics. I would very much prefer to have counts treating the three outfield positions as three positions, but. . . this is what I've got.

OK, we can see immediately that fewer players play a game at the most difficult defensive positions, catcher and shortstop, than at the other positions. It is surprising that more players have played a game in a season at third base than at first base. The reason that happens is that third base has "interactive relationships" with four positions (first, second, short and the outfield), whereas first base has serious interactive relationships only with two positions (third base and outfield.) Anyway, what I am trying to get to here is the relationship between positions. What position is most closely allied to catcher?

Of the 9,387 players who have played a game at catcher, 1,518 have also played a game at first base—more than any other "position matches" for catcher, although actually it is still a low number. These are the #2 positions for players at each position:

	Catcher	First Base	Second	Third	Short	Outfield
Catcher	9387	1518				
First Base		11686				4843
Second			10877	5868		
Third			5868	12006		
Short			5327		9733	
Outfield		4843				23329

Outfield and first base are position matches for one another, and second and third are position matches for one another. Catcher and first base are a one-way match, and shortstop with second base is a one-way match. Over one-half of players who play a game at second base in a season will also play a game at third base, and over one-half of players who play a game at shortstop will also play a game at second base. (Just short of one-half of second basemen will play a game at shortstop.) This chart fills out the data; of the 9,387 players who have played catcher in a season, 275 have also played a game at second base, and 131 have played a game at shortstop:

	Catcher	First Base	Second	Third	Short	Outfield
Catcher	9387	1518	275	664	131	921
First Base	1518	11686	1870	3140	1208	4843
Second	275	1870	10877	5868	5327	2636
Third	664	3140	5868	12006	5012	3483
Short	131	1208	5327	5012	9733	1708
Outfield	921	4843	2636	3483	1708	23329

Let's convert those to percentages. 16% of players who play a game at catcher in a season will also play a game at first base:

	Catcher	First Base	Second	Third	Short	Outfield
Catcher	100%	16%	3%	7%	1%	10%
First Base	13%	100%	16%	27%	10%	41%
Second	3%	17%	100%	54%	49%	24%
Third	6%	26%	49%	100%	42%	29%
Short	1%	12%	55%	51%	100%	18%
Outfield	4%	21%	11%	15%	7%	100%

Shortstop and catcher are the "least connected" positions, with only 1% of catchers playing a game at shortstop, and only 1% of shortstops playing a game at catcher. The lowest connection rates are 1. Catcher and Shortstop, 2. Catcher and Second Base, 3. Catcher and Third Base, and 4. Catcher and Outfield. Finally, we can figure a "multi-use percentage" for each fielding percentage, which is as follows:

	Catcher	First Base	Second	Third	Short	Outfield
Catcher	**100%**	16%	3%	7%	1%	10%
First Base	13%	**100%**	16%	27%	10%	41%
Second	3%	17%	**100%**	54%	49%	24%
Third	6%	26%	49%	**100%**	42%	29%
Short	1%	12%	55%	51%	**100%**	18%
Outfield	4%	21%	11%	15%	7%	**100%**
Multi Use Ratio	**26%**	**93%**	**134%**	**154%**	**110%**	**122%**

We can see, then, how unique the catching position is, that catchers simply do not play other positions. When I initially designed the Defensive Spectrum in the 1970s (in a letter to Dallas Adams), I didn't make catching a part of the spectrum, for this exact reason: that catching does not really interact with the rest of the spectrum.

OK, I was going to extend this by looking at players who play at least 10 games at multiple positions, but I sense I have done enough of this for now. I'd better let you go.

Range and Positioning Accounting Change: Shallow vs. Deep

The Range and Positioning System is the foundation of our statistical study of defense in baseball. The idea that you can better measure a defender's abilities by comparing the outs he is able to convert compared to similar plays by other defenders at his position rather than by using traditional statistics like fielding percentage revolutionized our understanding of fielding.

As simple as the idea of measuring a player's out conversion rate relative to his peers is, it is very complicated to execute. Beyond the intricacies of recording all the data you need to evaluate a player's Plays Saved—such as locations and velocities of every ball in play—there are many choices in the accounting that do not have a clear correct answer. For example, we group balls in play into buckets of similar balls in play based on their locations and velocities. To do that, we had to decide exactly how big each bucket should be. The smaller the buckets we chose, the more precise each comparison became. However, the smaller the buckets, the fewer balls in play actually fall into each bucket, which can create noise because of small sample sizes even when applied to multiple years of data. There are pros and cons to many of the decisions you have to make to create a sophisticated system like Range and Positioning.

One such decision was our conversion from Plays Saved to Range and Positioning Runs Saved for outfielders. As published in *The Fielding Bible—Volume II*, this process was broken into two parts. First, we estimated how many bases a batter would take on average based on similar balls in play. For example, on a bloop hit that falls between the second baseman and the right fielder, the batter will end up with a single if the hit falls in safely. The average number of bases of a hit in

that bucket would then be 1.00. In contrast, a deep hit to right-center would go for a double, so the average number of bases of similar hits would be 2.00. (In reality, most hits in play have a chance to go for singles, doubles, triples, or even inside-the-park homers, and we account for this probabilistically. However, we've used a simplified example here.)

The second step of our process applied a run value multiplier to the number of bases that each play was worth. For example, the bases-to-runs multiplier for right fielders was 0.58, meaning each base saved or cost translated into 0.58 runs saved/cost. In the example of the shallow hit above, the play was worth one base or 0.58 runs. In the deep hit example, the play was worth 2.0 * 0.58 = 1.16 runs.

For the most part, the two-part calculation of plays to bases and then bases to runs closely approximates the true run value changes of balls in play. However, this two-step process led to some slight inaccuracies. By converting to bases and then to runs, we were essentially saying that saving a double is twice as valuable as saving a single. In terms of run value, this isn't exactly true. The net result was that we were giving a little too much credit for extra-base-saving plays and too little credit for single-saving plays.

In order to improve the accuracy of the Range and Positioning System, we decided to cut out the middle man on flyballs. Rather than using the intermediary step of bases, we're now converting Plays Saved numbers directly into runs. We're translating each play to runs based on the similar plays in each bucket. Not only are we accounting for the correct run values of singles, doubles, and other hits, but we're also accounting for the difference in a flyout's value to different locations on the field. That is important because, as an example, deep flyouts are easier for baserunners to tag and advance on than shallow flyouts, so the run impact of deep and shallow flyouts can be somewhat different.

The difference between an out (-0.30) and a single (0.43) is 0.73, while the difference between an out and a double (0.75) is 1.05. As such, a double-saving play is 44 percent more valuable than a single-saving play, not the full 100 percent difference from our previous calculation (.58 vs. 1.16). Under our new calculation, the single-saving play is correctly valued at 0.73 runs while the double-saving play is worth 1.05 runs.

Whose Runs Saved Totals Were Most Affected?

Baseball Info Solutions implemented this change for team clients after the 2013 season, and all of the Runs Saved totals for outfielders from 2009-2014 in this book reflect the change. We reran Range and Positioning Runs Saved back to 2009 because that is when we began timing flyballs and line drives, which are required for our modern system of ball-in-play bucketing.

Looking back on the five years prior to the implementation, there are some players who are especially strong or weak on either deep or shallow plays. That is often the case when an outfielder positions himself deeper or shallower than the average fielder at his position, or if he excels going back or coming in on flies and line drives. Though most players had small inaccuracies in both directions that more or less evened out, the inaccuracies didn't even out for everybody.

First, let's look at the players who saw the greatest increase in Defensive Runs Saved per season between 2009 and 2013 because of the change:

Biggest DRS Gainers from the New Range and Positioning Method, 2009-13

Player	Pos	Old DRS	New DRS	Seasons	Avg. Change Per Season
Adam Jones	CF	-28	-11	5	3.4
Matt Kemp	CF	-67	-54	5	2.6
Nyjer Morgan	LF	8	15	3	2.3
Hunter Pence	RF	1	11	5	2.0
Willie Harris	CF	-13	-9	3	1.7
Alfonso Soriano	LF	-41	-33	5	1.6
Jose Bautista	RF	2	9	5	1.4
Jayson Werth	RF	-8	-1	5	1.4
Nate McLouth	CF	-24	-17	5	1.4
Nick Swisher	RF	-11	-4	5	1.4

As you can see, even in the extreme cases, players received only incremental adjustments to their DRS totals. The biggest gainer is Adam Jones, who rose from among the worst center fielders in the game to slightly below average. The list is overwhelmingly occupied by below-average defensive players. The players most affected by the change are those that tend to play more shallowly than the average defenders at their positions. Even though we were under-rewarding those players for their strength in turning shallow-hit balls into outs and over-penalizing them for allowing hits on balls over their heads, the fact is that deep balls that fall in for hits are much more damaging because they tend to turn into doubles and triples, which create more runs than shallow singles do.

It is important to note that 91 percent of outfielders changed by a total of three Runs Saved or fewer and 97 percent of outfielders changed by five Runs Saved or fewer over the five-year period. In other words, only three percent of outfielders changed by more than one run per year. The major differences really were for exceptional cases only.

Here are the players who saw the greatest decrease in Defensive Runs Saved:

Biggest DRS Decliners from the New Range and Positioning Method, 2009-13

Player	Pos	Old DRS	New DRS	Seasons	Avg. Change Per Season
Justin Upton	RF	17	-1	5	-3.6
Jason Heyward	RF	62	51	4	-2.8
Jacoby Ellsbury	CF	23	10	5	-2.6
Andre Ethier	RF	-13	-23	5	-2.0
Coco Crisp	CF	19	9	5	-2.0
Bobby Abreu	RF	-15	-22	4	-1.8
Corey Hart	RF	0	-7	4	-1.8
Dexter Fowler	CF	-26	-34	5	-1.6
Carlos Gomez	CF	66	58	5	-1.6

The biggest decliner list is headlined by two recent members of the Braves' outfield, Jason Heyward and Justin Upton. For Heyward, this change simply decreases the value ascribed to his elite right field defense slightly. In fact, Heyward finished first among all right fielders with 26 Runs Saved in 2014 using the new accounting method. In contrast, Upton's defense is now valued as simply average.

The common thread within this list is that it mimics quite closely the leaderboard of the top defenders on deep balls. It includes home run robbing maestro Carlos Gomez, who not surprisingly sees a decline thanks to his incredible ability to make plays on balls near (or beyond) the wall. Half of the players on this list are among the top 25 outfielders in deep ball Plays Saved, with the pair of former Atlanta corner outfielders topping both lists. While they remain among the best defenders in the game on balls in the deepest part of the yard, they do not receive as much credit for that excellence in the revised DRS calculation.

Overall DRS Leaders and Trailers

While some players do see their defensive value receive a moderate positive or negative adjustment, on the whole, the DRS calculation remains fairly similar. This fact is reflected in the overall leaderboards at each outfield position, which remain nearly identical to how they looked before the change.

Left Field

For the most part, the left field leaders stayed the same. Alex Gordon and Brett Gardner, who were well clear of the field before the change, only saw one Run Saved change between them. Further down the list, Carl Crawford overtook Starling Marte (who appears almost entirely on the strength of his 2013 season) and is now tied with Gerardo Parra for the third spot on the list. The left field trailers list, on the other hand, remains nearly exactly the same after the adjustment. The only difference comes in the form of Jonny Gomes' three-run gain, which allows him to barely overtake Carlos Quentin for the last slot.

Most DRS Before and After the New Range and Positioning Method, LF, 2009-13

Rank	New Method		Old Method	
	Player	DRS	Player	DRS
1	Alex Gordon	64	Alex Gordon	65
2	Brett Gardner	49	Brett Gardner	49
3	Gerardo Parra	27	Gerardo Parra	27
4	Carl Crawford	27	Starling Marte	26
5	Starling Marte	23	Carl Crawford	22

Least DRS Before and After the New Range and Positioning Method, LF, 2009-13

Rank	New Method		Old Method	
	Player	DRS	Player	DRS
1	Raul Ibanez	-53	Raul Ibanez	-54
2	Alfonso Soriano	-33	Alfonso Soriano	-41
3	Logan Morrison	-32	Logan Morrison	-34
4	Delmon Young	-30	Delmon Young	-27
5	Jonny Gomes	-26	Carlos Quentin	-26

Center Field

Carlos Gomez's drop (discussed in relation to the biggest decliner list) allows Michael Bourn to inch past him as the best glove in center between 2009 and 2013. Chris Young and Craig Gentry barely fall off the leaderboard in favor of Peter Bourjos and Franklin Gutierrez, who were sixth and seventh on the list by the old method. Despite Matt Kemp's gain, he remains by far the center fielder who cost his team the most with the glove during this period, while Adam Jones' improved numbers through the new method remove him from the list of trailers.

Most DRS Before and After the New Range and Positioning Method, CF, 2009-13

	New Method		Old Method	
Rank	Player	DRS	Player	DRS
1	Michael Bourn	63	Carlos Gomez	66
2	Carlos Gomez	58	Michael Bourn	65
3	Austin Jackson	48	Austin Jackson	50
4	Peter Bourjos	32	Chris Young	36
5	Franklin Gutierrez	30	Craig Gentry	34

Most DRS Before and After the New Range and Positioning Method, RF, 2009-13

	New Method		Old Method	
Rank	Player	DRS	Player	DRS
1	Jason Heyward	51	Jason Heyward	62
2	Gerardo Parra	41	Gerardo Parra	45
3	Josh Reddick	37	Josh Reddick	41
4	Jay Bruce	36	Jay Bruce	33
5	Ben Zobrist	32	Ben Zobrist	28

Least DRS Before and After the New Range and Positioning Method, CF, 2009-13

	New Method		Old Method	
Rank	Player	DRS	Player	DRS
1	Matt Kemp	-54	Matt Kemp	-67
2	Dexter Fowler	-34	B.J. Upton	-29
3	B.J. Upton	-27	Adam Jones	-28
4	Michael Saunders	-22	Dexter Fowler	-26
5	Jordan Schafer	-19	Nate McLouth	-24

Least DRS Before and After the New Range and Positioning Method, RF, 2009-13

	New Method		Old Method	
Rank	Player	DRS	Player	DRS
1	Michael Cuddyer	-44	Michael Cuddyer	-49
2	Jose Guillen	-28	Magglio Ordonez	-29
3	Nick Markakis	-27	Lucas Duda	-27
4	Magglio Ordonez	-26	Jose Guillen	-26
5	Lucas Duda	-24	Nick Markakis	-24

Right Field

Finally, the right field leaders retain the same group in the same order. Heyward received one of the largest downward adjustments of any defender but maintains a 10-run lead over Gerardo Parra. Jay Bruce nearly overtakes Josh Reddick, as the former benefits from the new accounting while the latter sees a four-run drop. Meanwhile, the trailers list sees some shuffling among the four similarly-valued defenders after Michael Cuddyer, but retains the same composition. Jose Guillen and Nick Markakis both receive negative adjustments, dropping them below Lucas Duda and Magglio Ordonez, who both see three-run gains thanks to the new calculation.

Overall, this slight adjustment to DRS improves the precision of the statistic for outfielders, especially those who are significantly better or worse than average on balls over their heads. However, a review of the updated leaderboard shows convincingly that the change does not result in the statistic straying far from the baseline it has produced in the past, making it simply a slightly improved version of the already trusted Runs Saved calculation.

Is Andrelton Simmons Worth 40 Runs?

In 2013, Andrelton Simmons set a new standard of excellence with his defensive play. His total of 41 Defensive Runs Saved was the most that we have ever recorded for a player in a single season going back to 2003. Of those 41 Defensive Runs Saved, his Range and Positioning Runs Saved component, a measure of his ability to turn batted balls into outs, accounted for 37. Using the rule of thumb that 10 runs is worth approximately one win in the standings, that total would suggest that Simmons was worth nearly four wins based on his defensive range alone.

Given that defensive metrics do not have the same reputation for reliability that offensive and pitching metrics have, and that defense does not garner the same attention as those other facets of the game, four wins might seem like an awful lot for a player to contribute with his defense. Therefore, we decided to undertake a study to see if it could plausibly be verified that a player—in this case Simmons—could in fact be worth that much on defense.

For this study, we wanted to keep things as simple as possible. In our calculation of a player's Plays Saved, we account for the direction the ball is hit, how hard the ball is hit, and who the primary fielder on the play is. For this study, we stripped all those specifics out.

Simmons plays shortstop for the Atlanta Braves, so we decided to simply look at all groundballs hit to the left side of the infield against the Braves in 2013 regardless of how hard the ball was hit or who fielded it. There were

1,072 of them. Of those, the Braves turned 829 of them into outs (77.3 percent of all groundballs). By comparison, the league as a whole only turned 72.5 percent of groundballs on the left side into outs. At that league average rate, the Braves would have only been expected to successfully make 777 plays given their 1,072 groundballs. That means that the Braves made an amazing 52 more plays than the average team would have on grounders to the left side, the best of any team by a wide margin.

To express those 52 plays above average in terms of runs, we used a run value of 0.75 to do the conversion. This run value accounts for the difference in the run expectancy between the play being made and the play not being made. It also assumes that if the play had not been made, it would have resulted in a single or a one-base error, which is worth about +0.45 runs to the offense using the change in run expectancy from the run matrix. An out, on the other hand, lowers the offense's run expectancy by about 0.30 runs. The difference, 0.45 - (-0.30) = +0.75, is the run value we use for the run value of an infield groundout. The Braves were approximately 52 * 0.75 = 39 runs better than average on groundballs to the left side of the infield.

That 39 runs is very similar to the the 37 Range and Positioning Runs Saved that we calculated Simmons to be worth. Of course, that 39 runs represents plays made by all Braves players—shortstops and third basemen primarily, pitchers and second basemen to a much lesser extent (we ignored bunts, so catchers may have been involved in only a small handful of these plays). However, Simmons played the overwhelming majority of innings at shortstop for the Braves, and Chris Johnson played the large majority of innings at third base. According to our Range and Positioning Runs Saved System, Johnson cost the Braves six runs in 2013, which was actually an improvement over what he had done in prior seasons. Therefore, if we can agree that Johnson had a negative impact on the Braves' left-side defense, or at the very most a neutral impact, then it does not seem like that much of a leap to imagine Simmons being worth the 37 runs that our Range and Positioning Runs Saved metric says he was.

This is not to say that this is necessarily an accurate way of evaluating an individual player's defensive abilities. The distribution of groundballs between shortstops and third basemen can vary from team to team, as can the nature (speed, location, etc.) of those groundball opportunities. However, when we consider this Braves team specifically, we know that they recorded a well-above-average number of outs on groundballs to the left side of the infield despite below average contributions at third base, making Simmons' case even stronger.

Finally, our Defensive Runs Saved also evaluates each middle infielder's performance on double plays and Good Fielding Plays/Defensive Misplays. We credited Simmons with an additional two runs in each category (which seems perfectly reasonable), bumping his 37 Range and Positioning Runs Saved to 41 Defensive Runs Saved. While the Range and Positioning and Defensive Runs Saved Systems are far more sophisticated and accurate measures of defensive contributions than our simple analysis here, this independently verifies that our estimate that Simmons saved the Braves 41 runs in 2013 is perfectly reasonable.

Infield Good Throw Rate

An infielder needs to be able to do two things in order to get an out on a groundball hit to him: he needs to come up with the ball, and he needs to get the ball down to first base. When evaluating the defensive skills of an infielder, people primarily focus on his ability to field the ball. But the throw to first is a crucial part of the play as well, so we created a new way to evaluate each infielder's accuracy on throws to first base.

We measure each infielder's throwing accuracy by calculating his Infielder Good Throw Rate. In order to know what percentage of his throws were good throws, we have to figure out how many of his throws were bad throws. There are three types of plays that we classify as bad throws. First, and least surprising, all throwing errors are considered to be errant throws. Second, plays on which the fielder is not charged with an error but is assessed a throwing Defensive Misplay by a BIS Video Scout are also added to this category. Finally, any throw that requires a Good Fielding Play on behalf of the first baseman is also considered an errant throw. While the first baseman's scoop or other difficult catch preserved the out on such plays, we still want to recognize that the infielder did not make a good throw. All throws that do not meet one of these three descriptions are considered to be good throws.

In order to calculate a player's Infielder Good Throw Rate, we simply divide the fielder's number of good throws to first by his total attempts, which include the good throws plus their throwing errors, bad throw Defensive Misplays, and first baseman Good Fielding Plays.

Let's take a look at the leaders and trailers at each position.

Second Base

While several standouts at the keystone position appear among the leaders in Good Throw Rate, the player that tops the list may actually be something of a surprise. Earlier in his career, Brian Roberts rated very well in Defensive Runs Saved, but injuries have hurt his overall defensive numbers and have prevented him from playing regularly. He has barely played a full season's worth of games in the past three years, and while he has been below average in Runs Saved, he has been remarkably steady in his ability to complete his throws to first. Roberts has not failed to complete a play on which he throws to first in the last three seasons, with his five errant throws all being saved by GFPs from the first baseman on the receiving end. Among players who have appeared in more than half of their team's games over the past three seasons, sure-handed Rockies second-sacker DJ LeMahieu's Infielder Good Throw Rate sets the bar. Meanwhile, Matt Carpenter's place on this list is especially impressive, as the vast majority of his pro career has been spent at third base. Not only did he not have trouble making the unfamiliar throws from second base, but his strong arm transitioned seamlessly from the hot corner, making him a key contributor to St. Louis' pennant-winning 2013 club.

Best Infielder Good Throw Rates, 2012-14

Second Basemen, Minimum 300 Throws

Fielder	Throws to First	Throwing Errors	Bad Throw DMs	First Base GFPs	Good Throw Rate
B. Roberts	408	0	0	5	0.988
D. Descalso	302	0	1	4	0.987
M. Carpenter	314	0	0	5	0.984
D. LeMahieu	767	0	2	11	0.983
M. Scutaro	525	1	1	7	0.983

Meanwhile, the trailers at the position feature a number of fielders who have taken heat for their defensive shortcomings. One much-maligned second baseman stands out from the rest as by far the least reliable thrower over the past three seasons. While his premium offense at the position was once good enough to overcome his below-par glovework, Dan Uggla's bat has degraded to the point where he may no longer be able to function as a contributing member of a contending ball club. Uggla ranks last among all second basemen in Infielder Good Throw Rate.

Worst Infielder Good Throw Rates, 2012-14

Second Basemen, Minimum 300 Throws

Fielder	Throws to First	Throwing Errors	Bad Throw DMs	First Base GFPs	Good Throw Rate
D. Uggla	813	6	5	41	0.936
S. Gennett	369	2	4	12	0.951
D. Murphy	906	3	10	25	0.958
J. Schoop	301	0	2	10	0.960
E. Sogard	445	1	1	16	0.960

Shortstop

On the left side of the diamond, Jordy Mercer and Pete Kozma set the pace. While Mercer was considered the more offensive option in contrast to Clint Barmes' slick glovework in Pittsburgh, Mercer's solid defense (and an injury to Barmes) has allowed him to feature full-time at the position. Meanwhile, although this metric presents another piece of evidence praising Kozma's defense, he simply didn't provide enough with the bat to figure into the mix in St. Louis once Jhonny Peralta was signed. Two players on the list will also find fewer opportunities to make throws from the shortstop position going forward, as both Stephen Drew and Asdrubal Cabrera will both presumably be taking their strong throwing skills over to second base for their 2015 teams.

Best Infielder Good Throw Rates, 2012-14

Shortstops, Minimum 300 Throws

Fielder	Throws to First	Throwing Errors	Bad Throw DMs	First Base GFPs	Good Throw Rate
J. Mercer	548	2	1	12	0.973
P. Kozma	384	1	3	9	0.966
S. Drew	500	2	3	14	0.962
A. Simmons	855	5	6	29	0.953
A. Cabrera	814	8	7	25	0.951

Among the trailers at the position, a trio of big names stand out. The Escobars are the two trailers who have more or less played shortstop full time over the last three seasons. Yunel's precipitous fall from very solid defender to the worst shortstop in baseball per DRS in 2014 was a surprise, though his fielding ability may just be declining to match his throwing skills, which were an issue even before this season. In contrast, Alcides has been a close-to neutral defender over the last three seasons and would likely be above average with a more accurate arm. Finally, Hanley Ramirez is another big bat with defensive woes, and injuries have both limited his playing time and potentially impacted his defense over the past three years. Now in Boston, he will likely end up in the outfield.

Worst Infielder Good Throw Rates, 2012-14

Shortstops, Minimum 300 Throws

Fielder	Throws to First	Throwing Errors	Bad Throw DMs	First Base GFPs	Good Throw Rate
C. Pennington	377	4	2	31	0.902
J. Villar	305	8	6	15	0.905
H. Ramirez	478	9	7	26	0.912
A. Escobar	1,004	13	14	60	0.913
Y. Escobar	890	6	8	60	0.917

Third Base

The hot corner is the home of some of the game's biggest arms, but the collection here features some intriguing and possibly unexpected names. While the budding star remains a relative unknown outside the Pacific Northwest, Kyle Seager blows away the competition by this metric. He is followed by a fellow West Coast third baseman in Juan Uribe. While Uribe has long been a solid defender, the 32 runs he has saved the last two seasons reflect a defensive Renaissance for the veteran. On a perennial contender that has dealt with some defensive woes elsewhere, Uribe has served as a consistent performer and defensive stabilizer.

Best Infielder Good Throw Rates, 2012-14

Third Basemen, Minimum 300 Throws

Fielder	Throws to First	Throwing Errors	Bad Throw DMs	First Base GFPs	Good Throw Rate
K. Seager	697	4	3	20	0.961
J. Uribe	424	4	1	15	0.953
M. Carpenter	324	2	5	15	0.932
M. Prado	355	5	1	19	0.930
P. Sandoval	569	12	4	24	0.930

The bottom five features a number of very interesting names. Pedro Alvarez's throwing performance has been the worst in baseball over the last three years, matching his reputation as a shaky defender with huge offensive potential. His erratic arm has compelled his switch to first base for the Pirates in 2015. Meanwhile, Ryan Zimmerman's shoulder problems will likely force him to join Alvarez at first base next season. His well-publicized throwing issues resulted in his seeing time in the outfield last season.

The bottom five is rounded out by three young stars in Manny Machado, Nolan Arenado, and Brett Lawrie. Machado and Arenado, in particular, are somewhat surprising, as the two defenders combined to save 65 runs in 2013, alone. It's possible that their unbelievable range results in their fielding more balls on a dive or with their momentum going away from first base, resulting in more off-balance and off-target throws.

Worst Infielder Good Throw Rates, 2012-14

Third Basemen, Minimum 300 Throws

Fielder	Throws to First	Throwing Errors	Bad Throw DMs	First Base GFPs	Good Throw Rate
P. Alvarez	718	31	8	61	0.861
R. Zimmerman	456	22	3	34	0.871
B. Lawrie	462	5	4	48	0.877
N. Arenado	490	11	5	41	0.884
M. Machado	515	9	4	40	0.897

Outfielder Throwing Arms

Outfield Arm Runs Saved, one of the components of the Defensive Runs Saved system, evaluates each outfielder's ability to limit the advancement of opposing baserunners. We specifically evaluate three sets of circumstances for potential advancement: single to the outfield with a runner on first base (second unoccupied), single to the outfield with a runner on second base, and a double to the outfield with a runner on first base. Based on the location, trajectory (grounder, line drive, flyball), and velocity of the ball in play, we estimate the likelihood that the runner would hold up, advance, or be thrown out. We compare the outcome of the play to the runner's expectation and translate to runs to credit/penalize the outfielder. Lastly, we award credit for "miscellaneous kills" in other baserunner advancement situations.

The columns in the charts are "Opps", "Extra Bases", "Pct", "Kills" and "Runs Saved". Opps is the number of opportunities to take an extra base. Extra bases are those extra bases taken. Pct is Extra Bases divided by Opps. Kills are any runner thrown out without a relay man (i.e. no other assist). Let's take a look at some of the more interesting results:

- To no surprise, left fielder Alex Gordon for the Kansas City Royals, has had the best throwing arm in baseball over the last three years. Over that span he has saved the Royals 24 runs with his arm and recorded 32 Kills. Only one other left fielder (Yoenis Cespedes) has saved double-digit runs since 2012.

Add in his superb range, and Gordon has won the Fielding Bible Award three years in a row and leads all outfielders in total Defensive Runs Saved with 67.

- The best right field arm of the last three years belongs to Jose Bautista of the Toronto Blue Jays. He has saved 20 runs with 25 kills. Unlike Gordon, however, Bautista's range is pretty average. In that same time frame he has made three less plays than an average right fielder.
- The best center field arm in 2014 was Leonys Martin of the Texas Rangers. Martin's one year total of 12 runs saved was the best single-season mark among center fielders in the last three years.
- Since we started tracking this data in 2003, Jeff Francoeur has the most Outfield Arm Runs Saved with 53. He also leads all outfielders with 78 Kills.

Outfield Arm Runs Saved, 2003-14

Player	Kills	Outfield Arm Runs Saved
Jeff Francoeur	78	53
Adam Jones	50	41
Jose Bautista	60	41
Alex Gordon	46	38
Shane Victorino	55	37

- Richard Hidalgo still holds the record for the most Runs Saved in a single season with 17 in 2003. He also had 19 Kills that year, tying him with Alfonso Soriano in 2007 for the most we've recorded for a single season. Yoenis Cespedes's legendary 2014 season, capped by several incredible throws in June, is now tied for second on the single-season list with 14 Runs Saved.
- With players such as Colby Rasmus (2012-2014), Rajai Davis (2012), Melky Cabrera (2014) and Jose Bautista (2012-2014), the Toronto Blue Jays had the best throwing outfield in baseball over the last three years with 43 Runs Saved. The Kansas City Royals were second with 34 Runs Saved.

Best Team Outfield Arms, 2012-14

Team	Outfield Arm Runs Saved
Toronto Blue Jays	43
Kansas City Royals	34
Arizona Diamondbacks	24
Boston Red Sox	17
Philadelphia Phillies	16

Worst Team Outfield Arms, 2012-14

Team	Outfield Arm Runs Saved
Detroit Tigers	-25
San Diego Padres	-25
Chicago Cubs	-22
St. Louis Cardinals	-21
Colorado Rockies	-20

Left Fielders - 3-Year Throwing

Player	Opps	Extra Bases	Pct	Kills	Runs Saved
Alex Gordon	433	125	.289	32	24
Yoenis Cespedes	208	59	.284	22	20
Domonic Brown	235	67	.285	11	8
Melky Cabrera	237	80	.338	19	8
Michael Brantley	212	72	.340	16	7
Daniel Nava	139	37	.266	6	6
Bryce Harper	151	52	.344	10	5
Dayan Viciedo	246	93	.378	16	5
Martin Prado	101	26	.257	5	4
Rajai Davis	231	79	.342	12	3
Dustin Ackley	102	29	.284	2	2
Jason Kubel	177	73	.412	16	2
Josh Hamilton	106	34	.321	4	1
David Murphy	166	58	.349	10	1
Ryan Braun	179	64	.358	5	1
J.D. Martinez	184	72	.391	8	1
Matt Joyce	101	42	.416	5	1
Starling Marte	205	70	.341	8	0
Jonny Gomes	144	52	.361	4	0
Eric Young	131	51	.389	6	-1
Ryan Ludwick	149	42	.282	0	-2
Alejandro De Aza	159	59	.371	5	-2
Michael Morse	95	37	.389	1	-2
Seth Smith	124	49	.395	5	-2
Carlos Gonzalez	278	114	.410	16	-2
Alfonso Soriano	245	107	.437	15	-2
Nate McLouth	156	54	.346	4	-3
Khris Davis	111	45	.405	1	-4
Carl Crawford	161	60	.373	1	-5
Justin Upton	175	68	.389	3	-6
Josh Willingham	242	97	.401	7	-6
Christian Yelich	155	64	.413	2	-8
Raul Ibanez	168	69	.411	2	-9
Carlos Quentin	119	53	.445	1	-9
Matt Holliday	338	133	.393	9	-12
MLB Totals	12484	4486	.359	524	

Left Fielders - 2013 Throwing

Player	Tm	Opps	Extra Bases	Pct	Kills	Runs Saved
Alex Gordon	KC	142	48	.338	13	6
Vernon Wells	NYY	60	12	.200	5	4
Domonic Brown	Phi	119	29	.244	5	4
Jonny Gomes	Bos	77	21	.273	4	4
Michael Brantley	Cle	119	38	.319	10	4
Bryce Harper	Was	78	27	.346	7	4
Dayan Viciedo	CWS	93	33	.355	9	4
Carlos Gonzalez	Col	102	37	.363	11	4
Kelly Johnson	TB	44	10	.227	3	3
Yoenis Cespedes	Oak	60	21	.350	5	3
David Murphy	Tex	98	33	.337	6	2
Ryan Braun	Mil	55	19	.345	2	2
Jason Kubel	2 tms	50	23	.460	6	2
Gregor Blanco	SF	44	13	.295	3	1
Oswaldo Arcia	Min	52	17	.327	2	1
Andy Dirks	Det	80	31	.388	6	1
J.B. Shuck	LAA	86	34	.395	7	1
Chris Heisey	Cin	35	10	.286	1	0
Melky Cabrera	Tor	58	19	.328	2	0
Alfonso Soriano	2 tms	122	53	.434	7	0
Starling Marte	Pit	94	28	.298	2	-1
Alejandro De Aza	CWS	47	15	.319	1	-1
Lucas Duda	NYM	61	20	.328	1	-1
Nate McLouth	Bal	100	35	.350	4	-1
Andres Torres	SF	38	14	.368	1	-1
Josh Willingham	Min	77	29	.377	2	-1
Eric Young	2 tms	70	28	.400	3	-1
Daniel Nava	Bos	49	20	.408	1	-1
Justin Upton	Atl	63	22	.349	0	-3
Carl Crawford	LAD	71	26	.366	0	-3
Christian Yelich	Mia	39	17	.436	0	-3
Raul Ibanez	Sea	96	39	.406	2	-5
Carlos Quentin	SD	52	24	.462	0	-5
Juan Pierre	Mia	53	28	.528	1	-5
Matt Holliday	StL	91	39	.429	1	-7
MLB Totals		4165	1461	.351	185	

Left Fielders - 2014 Throwing

Player	Tm	Opps	Extra Bases	Pct	Kills	Runs Saved
Yoenis Cespedes	2 tms	104	25	.240	14	14
Alex Gordon	KC	129	27	.209	5	9
Melky Cabrera	Tor	107	38	.355	11	6
Domonic Brown	Phi	102	34	.333	4	3
Michael Brantley	Cle	93	34	.366	6	3
Dustin Ackley	Sea	89	25	.281	2	2
Chris Young	2 tms	54	16	.296	3	2
Brandon Guyer	TB	35	8	.229	0	1
Robbie Grossman	Hou	57	18	.316	0	1
Bryce Harper	Was	68	23	.338	3	1
Matt Joyce	TB	55	20	.364	3	1
Starling Marte	Pit	76	28	.368	4	1
Josh Hamilton	LAA	57	17	.298	1	0
Nelson Cruz	Bal	50	18	.360	1	0
J.D. Martinez	Det	66	25	.379	1	0
Eric Young	NYM	55	21	.382	3	0
Josh Willingham	Min	46	18	.391	2	0
Ryan Ludwick	Cin	55	18	.327	0	-1
Carl Crawford	LAD	69	25	.362	1	-1
Brett Gardner	NYY	111	43	.387	3	-1
Michael Morse	SF	49	19	.388	1	-1
Alejandro De Aza	2 tms	110	43	.391	4	-1
Dayan Viciedo	CWS	46	18	.391	1	-1
David Lough	Bal	34	16	.471	3	-1
Chris Coghlan	ChC	92	39	.424	4	-2
Seth Smith	SD	59	26	.441	1	-2
Rajai Davis	Det	86	39	.453	5	-2
Shin-Soo Choo	Tex	66	31	.470	2	-2
Corey Dickerson	Col	99	36	.364	0	-3
Justin Upton	Atl	112	46	.411	3	-3
Khris Davis	Mil	88	37	.420	1	-3
Jonny Gomes	2 tms	41	19	.463	0	-3
Matt Holliday	StL	123	50	.407	3	-4
Carlos Gonzalez	Col	36	19	.528	0	-4
Christian Yelich	Mia	116	47	.405	2	-5
MLB Totals		4181	1520	.364	160	

Left Fielders - 2012 Throwing

Player	Tm	Opps	Extra Bases	Pct	Kills	Runs Saved
Alex Gordon	KC	162	50	.309	14	9
Daniel Nava	Bos	57	13	.228	4	5
Martin Prado	Atl	76	19	.250	5	5
Rajai Davis	Tor	102	28	.275	6	5
Yoenis Cespedes	Oak	44	13	.295	3	3
Melky Cabrera	SF	72	23	.319	6	2
Casper Wells	Sea	34	11	.324	3	2
Dayan Viciedo	CWS	107	42	.393	6	2
Jason Kubel	Ari	94	37	.394	10	2
Ryan Ludwick	Cin	72	15	.208	0	1
Desmond Jennings	TB	68	17	.250	1	1
Mark Trumbo	LAA	45	15	.333	4	1
Josh Hamilton	Tex	42	15	.357	3	1
J.D. Martinez	Hou	82	33	.402	6	1
Seth Smith	Oak	34	14	.412	3	1
Juan Pierre	Phi	79	22	.278	1	0
Jason Bay	NYM	38	12	.316	2	0
Shelley Duncan	Cle	44	15	.341	1	0
Shane Victorino	LAD	34	12	.353	1	0
Johnny Damon	Cle	40	15	.375	1	0
Matt Holliday	StL	124	44	.355	5	-1
Ryan Braun	Mil	124	45	.363	3	-1
David Murphy	Tex	68	25	.368	4	-1
Quintin Berry	Det	31	12	.387	1	-1
Logan Morrison	Mia	65	27	.415	4	-1
Michael Morse	Was	36	15	.417	0	-1
Alfonso Soriano	ChC	117	51	.436	8	-1
Nate McLouth	2 tms	41	15	.366	0	-2
Carlos Gonzalez	Col	140	58	.414	5	-2
Carlos Quentin	SD	50	19	.380	0	-3
Andy Dirks	Det	53	22	.415	0	-3
Raul Ibanez	NYY	55	23	.418	0	-3
Josh Willingham	Min	119	50	.420	3	-5
Vernon Wells	LAA	42	19	.452	0	-5
Alex Presley	Pit	47	26	.553	1	-6
MLB Totals		4138	1505	.364	179	

Center Fielders - 3-Year Throwing

Player	Opps	Extra Bases	Pct	Kills	Runs Saved
Leonys Martin	244	114	.467	19	18
Juan Lagares	163	66	.405	17	17
Adam Jones	391	195	.499	13	10
Carlos Gomez	333	183	.550	16	8
Matt Kemp	144	70	.486	9	7
Colby Rasmus	299	145	.485	5	6
Marcell Ozuna	156	82	.526	9	3
Michael Bourn	313	165	.527	10	3
Craig Gentry	118	69	.585	10	3
Drew Stubbs	211	108	.512	7	2
Jarrod Dyson	194	108	.557	11	2
Shin-Soo Choo	114	60	.526	4	1
A.J. Pollock	164	95	.579	8	1
B.J. Upton	286	171	.598	15	1
Peter Bourjos	148	72	.486	1	0
Lorenzo Cain	163	93	.571	9	0
Michael Saunders	143	75	.524	3	-1
Brett Gardner	127	74	.583	4	-1
Adam Eaton	176	104	.591	8	-2
Michael Brantley	139	86	.619	4	-2
Austin Jackson	289	159	.550	8	-3
Angel Pagan	221	124	.561	7	-3
Curtis Granderson	118	74	.627	3	-3
Jacoby Ellsbury	271	151	.557	6	-4
Alejandro De Aza	170	97	.571	3	-4
Denard Span	334	195	.584	11	-4
Desmond Jennings	207	121	.585	0	-4
Chris Young	121	71	.587	1	-4
Jon Jay	267	141	.528	6	-5
Ben Revere	199	118	.593	5	-6
Cameron Maybin	173	100	.578	3	-7
Andrew McCutchen	325	200	.615	9	-7
Coco Crisp	212	137	.646	3	-10
Mike Trout	255	154	.604	4	-11
Dexter Fowler	282	172	.610	5	-12
MLB Totals	11873	6596	.556	412	

Center Fielders - 2013 Throwing

Player	Tm	Opps	Extra Bases	Pct	Kills	Runs Saved
Juan Lagares	NYM	78	33	.423	12	11
Adam Jones	Bal	140	67	.479	6	7
Leonys Martin	Tex	93	46	.495	8	6
Carlos Gomez	Mil	127	63	.496	7	6
Lorenzo Cain	KC	61	31	.508	6	4
Brandon Barnes	Hou	99	61	.616	5	4
Andrew McCutchen	Pit	120	68	.567	6	3
Matt Kemp	LAD	56	23	.411	2	2
Colby Rasmus	Tor	101	50	.495	1	2
Austin Jackson	Det	93	48	.516	4	2
Aaron Hicks	Min	74	42	.568	5	2
Shin-Soo Choo	Cin	114	60	.526	4	1
Andre Ethier	LAD	52	29	.558	4	1
A.J. Pollock	Ari	81	47	.580	4	1
Justin Ruggiano	Mia	52	23	.442	1	0
Craig Gentry	Tex	41	20	.488	2	0
Jacoby Ellsbury	Bos	103	51	.495	1	0
Gregor Blanco	SF	60	31	.517	1	0
B.J. Upton	Atl	88	49	.557	3	0
Jarrod Dyson	KC	59	33	.559	3	0
Michael Bourn	Cle	114	65	.570	2	0
Ben Revere	Phi	55	32	.582	2	0
Michael Saunders	Sea	67	36	.537	1	-1
Will Venable	SD	35	19	.543	0	-1
Alexi Amarista	SD	60	34	.567	1	-1
Angel Pagan	SF	51	29	.569	2	-1
Brett Gardner	NYY	104	60	.577	3	-1
Desmond Jennings	TB	104	57	.548	0	-2
Mike Trout	LAA	83	46	.554	0	-3
David DeJesus	3 tms	52	36	.692	1	-3
Dexter Fowler	Col	77	46	.597	0	-4
Denard Span	Was	108	65	.602	3	-4
Alejandro De Aza	CWS	75	47	.627	1	-4
Coco Crisp	Oak	73	46	.630	1	-4
Jon Jay	StL	129	79	.612	4	-5
MLB Totals		4041	2256	.558	142	

Center Fielders - 2014 Throwing

Player	Tm	Opps	Extra Bases	Pct	Kills	Runs Saved
Leonys Martin	Tex	134	58	.433	10	12
Juan Lagares	NYM	85	33	.388	5	6
Adam Jones	Bal	115	55	.478	5	4
Jackie Bradley Jr.	Bos	83	43	.518	8	4
Billy Hamilton	Cin	101	54	.535	6	4
B.J. Upton	Atl	101	56	.554	6	3
Jon Jay	StL	55	17	.309	2	2
Danny Santana	Min	64	32	.500	4	2
Marcell Ozuna	Mia	126	65	.516	6	2
Sam Fuld	2 tms	54	26	.481	3	1
Jarrod Dyson	KC	62	31	.500	3	1
Gregor Blanco	SF	49	25	.510	2	1
Ender Inciarte	Ari	73	39	.534	4	1
Drew Stubbs	Col	86	46	.535	4	1
Michael Bourn	Cle	92	50	.543	5	1
Peter Bourjos	StL	75	30	.400	0	0
Colby Rasmus	Tor	84	45	.536	2	0
Angel Pagan	SF	57	31	.544	2	0
A.J. Pollock	Ari	66	39	.591	4	0
Charlie Blackmon	Col	39	21	.538	1	-1
Denard Span	Was	117	65	.556	4	-1
Jacoby Ellsbury	NYY	98	55	.561	3	-1
Carlos Gomez	Mil	104	63	.606	3	-1
Andre Ethier	LAD	45	28	.622	0	-1
James Jones	Sea	38	21	.553	1	-2
Adam Eaton	CWS	136	81	.596	5	-2
Desmond Jennings	TB	90	54	.600	0	-2
Cameron Maybin	SD	61	34	.557	1	-3
Lorenzo Cain	KC	72	44	.611	2	-3
Dexter Fowler	Hou	91	54	.593	2	-4
Austin Jackson	2 tms	101	61	.604	2	-4
Coco Crisp	Oak	77	51	.662	0	-5
Ben Revere	Phi	105	63	.600	1	-6
Mike Trout	LAA	116	72	.621	3	-6
Andrew McCutchen	Pit	97	70	.722	1	-7
MLB Totals		4042	2204	.545	149	

Center Fielders - 2012 Throwing

Player	Tm	Opps	Extra Bases	Pct	Kills	Runs Saved
Colby Rasmus	Tor	114	50	.439	2	4
Matt Kemp	LAD	69	38	.551	6	4
Bryce Harper	Was	60	31	.517	3	3
Carlos Gomez	Mil	102	57	.559	6	3
Shane Victorino	2 tms	82	46	.561	5	3
Craig Gentry	Tex	41	24	.585	4	3
Peter Bourjos	LAA	41	18	.439	1	2
Drew Stubbs	Cin	96	44	.458	3	2
Michael Bourn	Atl	107	50	.467	3	2
Yoenis Cespedes	Oak	35	17	.486	2	2
Andres Torres	NYM	72	41	.569	4	1
Denard Span	Min	109	65	.596	4	1
Jarrod Dyson	KC	73	44	.603	5	1
Michael Saunders	Sea	72	37	.514	2	0
Chris Young	Ari	60	31	.517	1	0
John Mayberry	Phi	49	28	.571	1	0
Justin Ruggiano	Mia	43	25	.581	0	0
Michael Brantley	Cle	114	68	.596	3	0
Jordan Schafer	Hou	60	36	.600	3	0
Austin Jackson	Det	95	50	.526	2	-1
Adam Jones	Bal	136	73	.537	2	-1
Alejandro De Aza	CWS	89	49	.551	2	-1
Justin Maxwell	Hou	43	24	.558	1	-1
Coco Crisp	Oak	62	40	.645	2	-1
Curtis Granderson	NYY	92	60	.652	3	-1
Jon Jay	StL	83	45	.542	0	-2
Angel Pagan	SF	113	64	.566	3	-2
Emilio Bonifacio	Mia	41	24	.585	0	-2
Mike Trout	LAA	56	36	.643	1	-2
B.J. Upton	TB	97	66	.680	6	-2
Andrew McCutchen	Pit	108	62	.574	2	-3
Cameron Maybin	SD	101	60	.594	2	-3
Jacoby Ellsbury	Bos	70	45	.643	2	-3
Josh Hamilton	Tex	56	37	.661	2	-3
Dexter Fowler	Col	114	72	.632	3	-4
MLB Totals		3790	2136	.564	121	

Right Fielders - 3-Year Throwing

Player	Opps	Extra Bases	Pct	Kills	Runs Saved
Jose Bautista	248	100	.403	25	20
Gerardo Parra	212	82	.387	22	13
Jeff Francoeur	184	73	.397	14	11
Josh Reddick	257	124	.482	23	11
Marlon Byrd	247	111	.449	14	7
Torii Hunter	338	156	.462	18	7
Chris Denorfia	135	52	.385	9	6
Yasiel Puig	119	50	.420	10	5
Nori Aoki	265	121	.457	16	5
Jay Bruce	332	146	.440	15	4
Shane Victorino	100	43	.430	8	3
Nick Markakis	334	154	.461	10	3
Michael Cuddyer	190	94	.495	10	1
Travis Snider	103	53	.515	7	1
Nelson Cruz	220	96	.436	5	0
Giancarlo Stanton	338	151	.447	16	0
Kole Calhoun	130	70	.538	9	0
Cody Ross	108	64	.593	7	0
Ichiro Suzuki	263	115	.437	5	-1
Carlos Beltran	218	108	.495	13	-1
Shin-Soo Choo	187	94	.503	5	-1
Nick Swisher	108	58	.537	4	-1
Jayson Werth	275	122	.444	10	-2
Ryan Braun	99	49	.495	4	-2
Andre Ethier	149	74	.497	5	-3
Hunter Pence	368	187	.508	17	-3
Alex Rios	382	195	.510	13	-3
Nate Schierholtz	181	98	.541	8	-3
Wil Myers	112	50	.446	1	-4
Matt Joyce	93	48	.516	1	-4
David Murphy	97	51	.526	3	-4
Justin Upton	150	84	.560	5	-4
Jason Heyward	298	151	.507	13	-5
Curtis Granderson	114	65	.570	2	-9
Will Venable	173	101	.584	3	-10
MLB Totals	12225	5980	.489	579	

Right Fielders - 2013 Throwing

Player	Tm	Opps	Extra Bases	Pct	Kills	Runs Saved
Gerardo Parra	Ari	107	33	.308	14	10
Jose Bautista	Tor	88	27	.307	8	9
Nori Aoki	Mil	98	34	.347	7	5
Jay Bruce	Cin	116	47	.405	7	4
Shane Victorino	Bos	81	33	.407	8	4
Chris Parmelee	Min	61	26	.426	5	4
Chris Denorfia	SD	47	16	.340	3	3
Jeff Francoeur	2 tms	38	13	.342	3	3
Marlon Byrd	2 tms	114	50	.439	8	3
Josh Reddick	Oak	88	45	.511	8	3
Alex Rios	2 tms	115	52	.452	5	2
David Lough	KC	67	31	.463	3	2
Andre Ethier	LAD	49	19	.388	2	1
Ichiro Suzuki	NYY	92	38	.413	2	1
Yasiel Puig	LAD	59	27	.458	4	1
Travis Snider	Pit	39	22	.564	4	1
Torii Hunter	Det	128	61	.477	5	0
Drew Stubbs	Cle	83	40	.482	2	0
Nick Markakis	Bal	120	60	.500	4	0
John Mayberry	Phi	40	20	.500	2	0
Delmon Young	2 tms	48	25	.521	4	0
Daniel Nava	Bos	40	21	.525	2	0
Josh Hamilton	LAA	80	37	.463	2	-1
Matt Joyce	TB	36	18	.500	1	-1
Nelson Cruz	Tex	93	40	.430	0	-2
Jayson Werth	Was	105	46	.438	2	-2
Wil Myers	TB	50	22	.440	0	-2
Michael Morse	2 tms	40	18	.450	0	-2
Giancarlo Stanton	Mia	108	53	.491	5	-2
Jason Heyward	Atl	58	29	.500	1	-3
Will Venable	SD	68	37	.544	2	-3
Carlos Beltran	StL	99	54	.545	4	-3
Nate Schierholtz	ChC	85	47	.553	4	-3
Michael Cuddyer	Col	104	59	.567	4	-3
Hunter Pence	SF	143	69	.483	2	-6
MLB Totals		4172	1986	.476	190	

Right Fielders - 2014 Throwing

Player	Tm	Opps	Extra Bases	Pct	Kills	Runs Saved
Jose Bautista	Tor	99	44	.444	8	5
Yasiel Puig	LAD	60	23	.383	6	4
Marlon Byrd	Phi	132	60	.455	6	4
Nick Markakis	Bal	132	56	.424	5	3
Daniel Nava	Bos	59	28	.475	5	3
Chris Denorfia	2 tms	40	15	.375	3	2
Oswaldo Arcia	Min	101	45	.446	5	2
Gerardo Parra	2 tms	94	44	.468	6	2
Josh Reddick	Oak	67	32	.478	4	2
Gregory Polanco	Pit	55	30	.545	5	2
Jayson Werth	Was	116	50	.431	5	1
Jason Heyward	Atl	127	57	.449	5	1
Allen Craig	2 tms	51	24	.471	3	1
Kole Calhoun	LAA	75	40	.533	6	1
Nate Schierholtz	2 tms	56	33	.589	4	1
Giancarlo Stanton	Mia	132	54	.409	6	0
Michael Saunders	Sea	42	19	.452	1	0
Nori Aoki	KC	85	41	.482	4	0
Hunter Pence	SF	108	57	.528	7	0
Oscar Taveras	StL	36	19	.528	2	0
Matt Kemp	LAD	45	28	.622	4	0
Jay Bruce	Cin	95	43	.453	3	-1
Avisail Garcia	CWS	40	19	.475	1	-1
Charlie Blackmon	Col	54	26	.481	1	-1
Dayan Viciedo	CWS	61	30	.492	2	-1
George Springer	Hou	79	39	.494	3	-1
Kevin Kiermaier	TB	44	26	.591	3	-1
Wil Myers	TB	62	28	.452	1	-2
Torii Hunter	Det	112	53	.473	3	-2
Ryan Braun	Mil	99	49	.495	4	-2
Ichiro Suzuki	NYY	68	36	.529	1	-2
David Murphy	Cle	85	43	.506	3	-3
Will Venable	SD	36	23	.639	0	-3
Alex Rios	Tex	120	62	.517	3	-4
Curtis Granderson	NYM	106	60	.566	2	-8
MLB Totals		4048	1976	.488	202	

Right Fielders - 2012 Throwing

Player	Tm	Opps	Extra Bases	Pct	Kills	Runs Saved
Torii Hunter	LAA	98	42	.429	10	9
Jeff Francoeur	KC	143	59	.413	11	8
Josh Reddick	Oak	102	47	.461	11	6
Jose Bautista	Tor	61	29	.475	9	6
Brian Bogusevic	Hou	73	31	.425	4	4
Michael Cuddyer	Col	57	24	.421	4	3
Carlos Beltran	StL	98	42	.429	8	3
Hunter Pence	2 tms	117	61	.521	8	3
Ben Zobrist	TB	38	16	.421	4	2
Giancarlo Stanton	Mia	98	44	.449	5	2
Nelson Cruz	Tex	121	55	.455	5	2
Bryce Harper	Was	27	14	.519	4	2
Chris Denorfia	SD	48	21	.438	3	1
Jay Bruce	Cin	121	56	.463	5	1
Ichiro Suzuki	2 tms	103	41	.398	2	0
Nick Markakis	Bal	82	38	.463	1	0
Nori Aoki	Mil	82	46	.561	5	0
Jose Tabata	Pit	42	24	.571	2	0
Cody Ross	Bos	60	39	.650	4	0
Gregor Blanco	SF	23	10	.435	2	-1
Nate Schierholtz	2 tms	40	18	.450	0	-1
Ben Revere	Min	69	32	.464	3	-1
Jayson Werth	Was	54	26	.481	3	-1
Shin-Soo Choo	Cle	173	86	.497	4	-1
Alex Rios	CWS	147	81	.551	5	-1
Brennan Boesch	Det	77	43	.558	2	-1
Garrett Jones	Pit	50	27	.540	1	-2
Matt Joyce	TB	48	26	.542	0	-2
Nick Swisher	NYY	77	42	.545	3	-2
Justin Upton	Ari	123	67	.545	4	-3
Jason Heyward	Atl	113	65	.575	7	-3
Andre Ethier	LAD	90	49	.544	2	-4
Lucas Duda	NYM	65	38	.585	2	-4
Will Venable	SD	69	41	.594	1	-4
David DeJesus	ChC	83	51	.614	2	-4
MLB Totals		4005	2018	.504	187	

Groundball Double Plays and Pivots

A pitcher's best friend is a successful double play. Which infielders are the best at turning double plays or executing double plays?

For each double play opportunity, we compare similar grounders based on handedness (right or left-handed batter), location, and velocity, then we estimate the likelihood that an average infield would turn the double play. We then compare the expectation to the outcome of the play and apply the run value difference between a double play and a fielder's choice (0.58 runs).

The columns in the charts are defined as follows:

GDPs: How many times the player was involved in a groundball double play, either starting the double play or as the pivot man.

GDP Opps: How many times the player was involved in a fielding play on a groundball in a double play situation (man on first with less than two outs). This includes double plays, force outs, errors, etc.

Pivots: How many times the player made the double play pivot (for second basemen: 6-4-3 double play or 5-4-3 double play or 1-4-3 or 3-4-3 or 2-4-3).

Pivot Opps: How many times the player accepted a force out at second in a situation that could have been a double play (for second basemen: 6-4, 5-4, 1-4 or 3-4).

Overall, the difference between the best and worst infielders on double play opportunities is relatively small, usually ranging only 6 to 10 runs in a given season. Let's take a look at some of the more interesting results:

The Chicago White Sox and Baltimore Orioles middle infield duos have stood out over the past three years. The White Sox duo of Gordon Beckham and Alexei Ramirez both had the highest Double Play Runs Saved total over the past three years with five and seven, respectively. Both have been in the top 10 for each of the past three years. If Beckham wasn't traded to the Angels during the 2014 season and transitioned to third base, he more than likely would have been among the top five for three consecutive years.

J.J. Hardy tied with Alexei Ramirez for the most Double Play Runs Saved among shortstops over the past three years. Hardy's job has been a little bit more difficult due to the revolving door at second base for the Orioles. Robert Andino held the position in 2012 while Ryan Flaherty and Brian Roberts split time at the keystone position in 2013. All three were above average double play partners for Hardy. Flaherty in particular, ranked first among second basemen in both double play percentage and pivot percentage in 2013. Rookie Jonathan Schoop came on to the scene in late 2013 but really made his presence known in 2014 with his superb defense. He ranked first among all middle infielders with five Double Play Runs Saved, one of the highest totals in recent history.

When *The Fielding Bible—Volume III* came out, Troy Tulowitzki had a league-leading eight Double Play Runs Saved from 2009-2011. The Rockies were having problems trying to find a counter part for Tulo as they tried fourteen different players at second base during that timeframe. Now, Tulowitzki is still an above average shortstop on double plays while the Rockies finally found a suitable double play partner in DJ LeMahieu.

Second Basemen - 3-Year GDPs & Pivots

Player	GDP Opps	GDP	GDP Pct	Rank	Pivot Opps	Pivots	Pivot Pct	Rank	Runs Saved
Gordon Beckham	334	238	.713	4	234	166	.709	5	5
Jose Altuve	450	299	.664	13	284	185	.651	16	3
Danny Espinosa	203	143	.704	5	132	100	.758	2	3
Dustin Ackley	153	112	.732	1	92	69	.750	3	3
Ian Kinsler	380	257	.676	9	244	166	.680	10	2
Omar Infante	355	232	.654	16	214	132	.617	21	2
Darwin Barney	289	193	.668	12	180	124	.689	9	2
Dan Uggla	283	190	.671	10	197	130	.660	14	2
Matt Carpenter	138	96	.696	6	88	61	.693	7	2
Chris Getz	101	73	.723	3	70	54	.771	1	2
Dustin Pedroia	412	283	.687	7	250	173	.692	8	1
DJ LeMahieu	272	179	.658	14	180	122	.678	11	1
Robinson Cano	439	279	.636	19	290	177	.610	23	0
Neil Walker	392	247	.630	21	281	173	.616	22	0
Howie Kendrick	340	218	.641	17	206	130	.631	18	0
Mark Ellis	228	144	.632	20	157	98	.624	19	0
Donovan Solano	205	140	.683	8	125	82	.656	15	0
Dee Gordon	121	81	.669	11	78	50	.641	17	0
Emilio Bonifacio	109	79	.725	2	68	50	.735	4	0
Kelly Johnson	174	108	.621	25	109	73	.670	12	-1
Brian Roberts	138	82	.594	32	91	53	.582	29	-1
Jemile Weeks	99	60	.606	29	66	41	.621	20	-1
Jason Kipnis	381	243	.638	18	214	126	.589	27	-2
Brian Dozier	299	196	.656	15	181	121	.669	13	-2
Ben Zobrist	193	120	.622	24	131	92	.702	6	-2
Scooter Gennett	165	99	.600	31	114	67	.588	28	-2
Logan Forsythe	123	75	.610	28	86	49	.570	32	-2
Rickie Weeks	253	156	.617	26	181	110	.608	24	-3
Daniel Murphy	368	231	.628	22	224	133	.594	26	-4
Brandon Phillips	342	214	.626	23	234	131	.560	33	-4
Aaron Hill	324	199	.614	27	217	130	.599	25	-4
Chase Utley	286	162	.566	35	197	108	.548	35	-4
Marco Scutaro	218	131	.601	30	142	81	.570	31	-4
Eric Sogard	197	113	.574	34	133	76	.571	30	-4
Jedd Gyorko	174	101	.580	33	111	61	.550	34	-5
MLB Totals	13507	8795	.651		8764	5645	.644		

Second Basemen - 2014 GDPs & Pivots

Player	Tm	GDP Opps	GDP	GDP Pct	Rank	Pivot Opps	Pivots	Pivot Pct	Rank	Runs Saved
Jonathan Schoop	Bal	114	89	.781	2	79	63	.797	2	5
Jose Altuve	Hou	162	109	.673	17	114	75	.658	20	2
Robinson Cano	Sea	142	98	.690	14	100	67	.670	14	2
Neil Walker	Pit	127	89	.701	11	88	58	.659	19	2
Howie Kendrick	LAA	118	82	.695	13	72	50	.694	11	2
Gordon Beckham	2 tms	99	71	.717	10	68	48	.706	9	2
Kolten Wong	StL	87	65	.747	4	59	45	.763	5	2
Danny Espinosa	Was	75	54	.720	9	48	41	.854	1	2
Joe Panik	SF	61	48	.787	1	41	31	.756	6	2
Brandon Hicks	SF	65	47	.723	8	47	36	.766	4	2
DJ LeMahieu	Col	138	96	.696	12	96	67	.698	10	1
Rougned Odor	Tex	88	64	.727	6	53	36	.679	13	1
Tommy La Stella	Atl	74	50	.676	16	46	29	.630	22	1
Ryan Goins	Tor	35	26	.743	5	26	20	.769	3	1
Asdrubal Cabrera	Was	32	24	.750	3	24	18	.750	7	1
Brian Dozier	Min	140	94	.671	18	80	55	.688	12	0
Dee Gordon	LAD	120	80	.667	19	78	50	.641	21	0
Brandon Phillips	Cin	99	63	.636	23	71	41	.577	27	0
Aaron Hill	Ari	93	60	.645	22	60	40	.667	15	0
Donovan Solano	Mia	75	49	.653	21	58	36	.621	23	0
Darwin Barney	2 tms	40	29	.725	7	27	18	.667	15	0
Munenori Kawasaki	Tor	41	26	.634	24	24	16	.667	15	0
Logan Forsythe	TB	31	21	.677	15	21	12	.571	28	0
Ian Kinsler	Det	150	95	.633	25	88	53	.602	25	-1
Omar Infante	KC	104	63	.606	30	63	33	.524	33	-1
Rickie Weeks	Mil	49	30	.612	28	39	23	.590	26	-1
Ben Zobrist	TB	44	27	.614	27	27	20	.741	8	-1
Dustin Pedroia	Bos	140	92	.657	20	86	57	.663	18	-2
Chase Utley	Phi	135	77	.570	32	89	49	.551	30	-2
Jason Kipnis	Cle	96	60	.625	26	56	30	.536	31	-2
Scooter Gennett	Mil	101	59	.584	31	69	39	.565	29	-2
Brian Roberts	NYY	64	32	.500	34	39	19	.487	35	-2
Daniel Murphy	NYM	132	80	.606	29	82	50	.610	24	-3
Jedd Gyorko	SD	88	49	.557	33	58	31	.534	32	-3
Eric Sogard	Oak	92	45	.489	35	63	31	.492	34	-3
MLB Totals		4438	2914	.657		2905	1875	.645		

Second Basemen - 2013 GDPs & Pivots

Player	Tm	GDP Opps	GDP	GDP Pct	Rank	Pivot Opps	Pivots	Pivot Pct	Rank	Runs Saved
Jose Altuve	Hou	156	110	.705	6	87	61	.701	8	3
Matt Carpenter	StL	135	94	.696	9	85	59	.694	9	2
Ian Kinsler	Tex	115	82	.713	5	77	57	.740	3	2
Dan Uggla	Atl	108	73	.676	14	79	50	.633	23	2
Ryan Flaherty	Bal	66	51	.773	1	45	35	.778	1	2
Omar Infante	Det	105	71	.676	13	62	40	.645	19	1
Gordon Beckham	CWS	91	65	.714	3	68	47	.691	12	1
DJ LeMahieu	Col	81	53	.654	17	51	35	.686	13	1
Anthony Rendon	Was	67	47	.701	8	39	25	.641	21	1
Brian Roberts	Bal	60	41	.683	12	43	29	.674	15	1
Chris Getz	KC	54	37	.685	11	36	27	.750	2	1
Elliot Johnson	2 tms	40	25	.625	26	27	19	.704	6	1
Dustin Pedroia	Bos	141	97	.688	10	78	54	.692	10	0
Daniel Murphy	NYM	130	86	.662	16	82	50	.610	28	0
Darwin Barney	ChC	110	73	.664	15	67	47	.701	7	0
Mark Ellis	LAD	111	70	.631	25	78	51	.654	17	0
Donovan Solano	Mia	91	64	.703	7	47	31	.660	16	0
Emilio Bonifacio	2 tms	75	54	.720	2	49	36	.735	4	0
Scooter Gennett	Mil	64	40	.625	26	45	28	.622	25	0
Josh Rutledge	Col	52	34	.654	18	26	16	.615	27	0
Derek Dietrich	Mia	42	30	.714	3	31	22	.710	5	0
Jason Kipnis	Cle	138	88	.638	23	79	45	.570	30	-1
Ben Zobrist	TB	107	66	.617	30	72	49	.681	14	-1
Eric Sogard	Oak	100	64	.640	22	66	41	.621	26	-1
Howie Kendrick	LAA	100	62	.620	29	59	38	.644	20	-1
Marco Scutaro	SF	96	62	.646	20	64	41	.641	22	-1
Chase Utley	Phi	96	55	.573	33	67	37	.552	34	-1
Rickie Weeks	Mil	82	52	.634	24	59	37	.627	24	-1
Brian Dozier	Min	159	102	.642	21	101	66	.653	18	-2
Robinson Cano	NYY	152	87	.572	34	98	53	.541	35	-2
Neil Walker	Pit	148	83	.561	35	103	60	.583	29	-2
Nick Franklin	Sea	97	63	.649	19	65	45	.692	10	-2
Jedd Gyorko	SD	86	52	.605	32	53	30	.566	32	-2
Aaron Hill	Ari	77	47	.610	31	56	31	.554	33	-2
Brandon Phillips	Cin	130	81	.623	28	90	51	.567	31	-3
MLB Totals		4564	2986	.654		2970	1926	.648		

Second Basemen - 2012 GDPs & Pivots

Player	Tm	GDP Opps	GDP	GDP Pct	Rank	Pivot Opps	Pivots	Pivot Pct	Rank	Runs Saved
Dustin Pedroia	Bos	131	94	.718	8	86	62	.721	11	3
Gordon Beckham	CWS	144	102	.708	9	98	71	.724	10	2
Omar Infante	2 tms	146	98	.671	13	89	59	.663	18	2
Darwin Barney	ChC	139	91	.655	16	86	59	.686	14	2
Dustin Ackley	Sea	110	81	.736	5	64	48	.750	5	2
Alexi Casilla	Min	100	73	.730	6	56	42	.750	5	2
Robert Andino	Bal	85	62	.729	7	55	40	.727	9	2
Jamey Carroll	Min	56	44	.786	2	34	27	.794	3	2
Freddy Galvis	Phi	35	28	.800	1	24	21	.875	1	2
Jason Kipnis	Cle	147	95	.646	19	79	51	.646	21	1
Ian Kinsler	Tex	115	80	.696	10	79	56	.709	13	1
Ryan Roberts	2 tms	47	36	.766	4	33	26	.788	4	1
Chris Getz	KC	45	35	.778	3	32	26	.813	2	1
Dan Uggla	Atl	146	98	.671	13	98	66	.673	17	0
Robinson Cano	NYY	145	94	.648	17	92	57	.620	24	0
Neil Walker	Pit	117	75	.641	22	90	55	.611	25	0
Danny Espinosa	Was	95	63	.663	15	62	42	.677	15	0
Mark Ellis	LAD	86	54	.628	24	56	31	.554	31	0
Ryan Theriot	SF	71	46	.648	18	47	31	.660	19	0
Daniel Descalso	StL	70	42	.600	31	43	27	.628	23	0
Ramon Santiago	Det	46	31	.674	12	23	17	.739	8	0
Skip Schumaker	StL	48	31	.646	20	35	23	.657	20	0
Ben Zobrist	TB	42	27	.643	21	32	23	.719	12	0
Donovan Solano	Mia	39	27	.692	11	20	15	.750	5	0
Kelly Johnson	Tor	158	100	.633	23	102	69	.676	16	-1
Rickie Weeks	Mil	122	74	.607	28	83	50	.602	27	-1
Howie Kendrick	LAA	122	74	.607	28	75	42	.560	30	-1
Brandon Phillips	Cin	113	70	.619	25	73	39	.534	34	-1
Daniel Murphy	NYM	106	65	.613	27	60	33	.550	32	-1
Jemile Weeks	Oak	96	59	.615	26	65	41	.631	22	-1
Chase Utley	Phi	55	30	.545	35	41	22	.537	33	-1
DJ LeMahieu	Col	53	30	.566	34	33	20	.606	26	-1
Aaron Hill	Ari	154	92	.597	32	101	59	.584	29	-2
Jose Altuve	Hou	132	80	.606	30	83	49	.590	28	-2
Logan Forsythe	SD	65	35	.538	36	48	25	.521	35	-2
Marco Scutaro	2 tms	121	69	.570	33	77	40	.519	36	-3
MLB Totals		4505	2895	.643		2889	1844	.638		

Shortstops - 3-Year GDPs & Pivots

Player	GDP Opps	GDP	GDP Pct	Rank	Pivot Opps	Pivots	Pivot Pct	Rank	Runs Saved
Alexei Ramirez	441	311	.705	4	232	148	.638	14	7
J.J. Hardy	448	310	.692	7	249	164	.659	7	7
Andrelton Simmons	312	217	.696	6	174	112	.644	12	6
Elvis Andrus	416	282	.678	11	236	148	.627	16	4
Brendan Ryan	237	178	.751	2	136	93	.684	3	4
Ian Desmond	357	247	.692	8	210	134	.638	13	3
Brandon Crawford	361	238	.659	16	202	123	.609	20	3
Jose Reyes	339	219	.646	21	203	121	.596	24	3
Pete Kozma	152	115	.757	1	87	61	.701	2	3
Jhonny Peralta	341	227	.666	15	199	122	.613	18	2
Cliff Pennington	140	103	.736	3	77	55	.714	1	2
Marwin Gonzalez	139	97	.698	5	75	51	.680	4	2
Asdrubal Cabrera	326	212	.650	17	206	137	.665	6	1
Troy Tulowitzki	271	182	.672	13	151	99	.656	8	1
Clint Barmes	212	146	.689	9	102	69	.676	5	1
Mike Aviles	181	122	.674	12	116	71	.612	19	1
Alcides Escobar	443	276	.623	26	251	154	.614	17	0
Starlin Castro	381	239	.627	25	220	128	.582	28	0
Erick Aybar	367	234	.638	22	218	131	.601	21	0
Pedro Florimon	216	147	.681	10	124	80	.645	11	0
Jordy Mercer	206	131	.636	23	108	64	.593	25	0
Hanley Ramirez	201	125	.622	27	114	64	.561	29	0
Ruben Tejada	278	180	.647	20	172	111	.645	10	-1
Jonathan Villar	128	83	.648	19	67	40	.597	23	-1
Jimmy Rollins	376	230	.612	29	194	108	.557	30	-2
Adeiny Hechavarria	291	189	.649	18	167	109	.653	9	-2
Jean Segura	300	185	.617	28	155	91	.587	26	-2
Stephen Drew	233	156	.670	14	139	83	.597	22	-2
Didi Gregorius	154	93	.604	31	89	49	.551	31	-2
Zack Cozart	355	224	.631	24	191	120	.628	15	-3
Derek Jeter	204	114	.559	33	115	60	.522	34	-3
Yunel Escobar	389	236	.607	30	235	125	.532	33	-4
Brad Miller	133	76	.571	32	75	37	.493	35	-4
Jed Lowrie	285	159	.558	34	157	84	.535	32	-5
Everth Cabrera	265	142	.536	35	151	88	.583	27	-7
MLB Totals	13428	8680	.646		7590	4618	.608		

Shortstops - 2014 GDPs & Pivots

Player	Tm	GDP Opps	GDP	GDP Pct	Rank	Pivot Opps	Pivots	Pivot Pct	Rank	Runs Saved
J.J. Hardy	Bal	124	92	.742	3	68	45	.662	11	4
Alexei Ramirez	CWS	163	120	.736	4	87	60	.690	5	3
Andrelton Simmons	Atl	130	97	.746	2	72	54	.750	1	3
Brandon Crawford	SF	121	86	.711	7	63	40	.635	14	3
Jhonny Peralta	StL	136	95	.699	9	70	42	.600	19	2
Starlin Castro	ChC	94	71	.755	1	48	35	.729	3	2
Eugenio Suarez	Det	63	44	.698	10	38	25	.658	12	2
Elvis Andrus	Tex	129	93	.721	6	76	56	.737	2	1
Ian Desmond	Was	126	84	.667	14	72	40	.556	24	1
Erick Aybar	LAA	106	74	.698	11	60	40	.667	7	1
Jordy Mercer	Pit	115	74	.643	16	64	37	.578	22	1
Jose Reyes	Tor	106	68	.642	17	59	34	.576	23	1
Troy Tulowitzki	Col	90	62	.689	12	46	33	.717	4	1
Hanley Ramirez	LAD	72	49	.681	13	45	30	.667	7	1
Andrew Romine	Det	73	46	.630	18	44	26	.591	20	0
Chris Owings	Ari	55	40	.727	5	30	20	.667	7	0
Marwin Gonzalez	Hou	57	40	.702	8	30	20	.667	7	0
Alcides Escobar	KC	146	91	.623	19	82	55	.671	6	-1
Zack Cozart	Cin	113	67	.593	24	55	34	.618	16	-1
Asdrubal Cabrera	2 tms	81	54	.667	14	44	28	.636	13	-1
Jonathan Villar	Hou	78	47	.603	22	38	20	.526	28	-1
Didi Gregorius	Ari	65	38	.585	25	36	19	.528	27	-1
Adeiny Hechavarria	Mia	148	91	.615	21	79	50	.633	15	-2
Ruben Tejada	NYM	120	74	.617	20	73	44	.603	18	-2
Jed Lowrie	Oak	119	66	.555	28	68	41	.603	17	-2
Jimmy Rollins	Phi	122	66	.541	29	65	34	.523	29	-2
Eduardo Escobar	Min	91	54	.593	23	60	33	.550	25	-2
Brad Miller	Sea	82	46	.561	27	48	25	.521	30	-2
Derek Jeter	NYY	81	41	.506	35	47	21	.447	34	-2
Alexi Amarista	SD	62	32	.516	33	36	18	.500	31	-2
Josh Rutledge	Col	58	31	.534	31	32	15	.469	32	-2
Jean Segura	Mil	140	80	.571	26	75	41	.547	26	-3
Xander Bogaerts	Bos	98	53	.541	30	48	22	.458	33	-3
Yunel Escobar	TB	83	44	.530	32	53	23	.434	35	-3
Everth Cabrera	SD	97	50	.515	34	55	32	.582	21	-4
MLB Totals		4327	2810	.649		2401	1472	.613		

Shortstops - 2013 GDPs & Pivots

Player	Tm	GDP Opps	GDP	GDP Pct	Rank	Pivot Opps	Pivots	Pivot Pct	Rank	Runs Saved
J.J. Hardy	Bal	153	108	.706	4	86	56	.651	11	3
Elvis Andrus	Tex	153	104	.680	9	86	49	.570	24	2
Alexei Ramirez	CWS	142	99	.697	7	70	45	.643	13	2
Pete Kozma	StL	131	98	.748	1	76	54	.711	3	2
Andrelton Simmons	Atl	146	90	.616	23	82	44	.537	30	2
Jose Reyes	Tor	71	49	.690	8	35	23	.657	9	2
Jimmy Rollins	Phi	142	95	.669	13	67	43	.642	14	1
Ian Desmond	Was	133	95	.714	3	78	56	.718	2	1
Alcides Escobar	KC	147	92	.626	21	88	49	.557	26	1
Jean Segura	Mil	133	90	.677	12	65	42	.646	12	1
Jose Iglesias	2 tms	64	45	.703	5	34	24	.706	4	1
Ruben Tejada	NYM	54	36	.667	14	31	23	.742	1	1
Pedro Florimon	Min	152	103	.678	10	88	59	.670	7	0
Yunel Escobar	TB	145	89	.614	26	89	50	.562	25	0
Adeiny Hechavarria	Mia	127	86	.677	11	83	55	.663	8	0
Troy Tulowitzki	Col	132	86	.652	17	79	48	.608	19	0
Starlin Castro	ChC	125	75	.600	28	77	42	.545	29	0
Asdrubal Cabrera	Cle	109	65	.596	30	69	45	.652	10	0
Everth Cabrera	SD	99	60	.606	27	59	37	.627	15	0
Clint Barmes	Pit	85	56	.659	16	42	25	.595	21	0
Jhonny Peralta	Det	88	55	.625	22	56	33	.589	22	0
Ronny Cedeno	2 tms	63	41	.651	18	40	25	.625	16	0
Jonathan Villar	Hou	50	36	.720	2	29	20	.690	5	0
Brandon Crawford	SF	125	77	.616	24	67	37	.552	28	-1
Stephen Drew	Bos	117	76	.650	19	75	45	.600	20	-1
Brendan Ryan	2 tms	87	61	.701	6	41	25	.610	18	-1
Jordy Mercer	Pit	83	53	.639	20	42	26	.619	17	-1
Didi Gregorius	Ari	83	51	.614	25	49	28	.571	23	-1
Hanley Ramirez	LAD	75	44	.587	32	39	18	.462	33	-1
Eduardo Nunez	NYY	56	31	.554	34	36	20	.556	27	-1
Zack Cozart	Cin	133	88	.662	15	77	53	.688	6	-2
Erick Aybar	LAA	140	79	.564	33	86	43	.500	32	-2
Omar Quintanilla	NYM	70	42	.600	28	39	20	.513	31	-2
Brad Miller	Sea	51	30	.588	31	27	12	.444	35	-2
Jed Lowrie	Oak	97	51	.526	35	51	23	.451	34	-3
MLB Totals		4615	2978	.645		2606	1580	.606		

Shortstops - 2012 GDPs & Pivots

Player	Tm	GDP Opps	GDP	GDP Pct	Rank	Pivot Opps	Pivots	Pivot Pct	Rank	Runs Saved
Brendan Ryan	Sea	139	108	.777	3	88	63	.716	5	4
Asdrubal Cabrera	Cle	136	93	.684	11	93	64	.688	8	2
Alexei Ramirez	CWS	136	92	.676	12	75	43	.573	24	2
Mike Aviles	Bos	124	88	.710	6	79	49	.620	16	2
Brian Dozier	Min	86	66	.767	4	53	41	.774	2	2
Elvis Andrus	Tex	134	85	.634	20	74	43	.581	23	1
Erick Aybar	LAA	121	81	.669	14	72	48	.667	9	1
Clint Barmes	Pit	111	79	.712	5	50	38	.760	3	1
Brandon Crawford	SF	115	75	.652	16	72	46	.639	13	1
Ian Desmond	Was	98	68	.694	9	60	38	.633	14	1
Cliff Pennington	Oak	82	58	.707	7	45	28	.622	15	1
Andrelton Simmons	Atl	36	30	.833	1	20	14	.700	6	1
Ben Zobrist	TB	29	24	.828	2	13	11	.846	1	1
J.J. Hardy	Bal	171	110	.643	18	95	63	.663	10	0
Jose Reyes	Mia	162	102	.630	24	109	64	.587	20	0
Alcides Escobar	KC	150	93	.620	25	81	50	.617	17	0
Jhonny Peralta	Det	117	77	.658	15	73	47	.644	12	0
Rafael Furcal	StL	114	72	.632	23	67	40	.597	18	0
Ruben Tejada	NYM	104	70	.673	13	68	44	.647	11	0
Zack Cozart	Cin	109	69	.633	22	59	33	.559	25	0
Elliot Johnson	TB	71	45	.634	21	41	24	.585	22	0
Jed Lowrie	Hou	69	42	.609	28	38	20	.526	31	0
Troy Tulowitzki	Col	49	34	.694	9	26	18	.692	7	0
Hanley Ramirez	LAD	54	32	.593	30	30	16	.533	28	0
John McDonald	Ari	44	31	.705	8	24	18	.750	4	0
Yunel Escobar	Tor	161	103	.640	19	93	52	.559	26	-1
Jimmy Rollins	Phi	112	69	.616	26	62	31	.500	34	-1
Derek Jeter	NYY	109	67	.615	27	58	34	.586	21	-1
Stephen Drew	2 tms	62	40	.645	17	30	16	.533	28	-1
Paul Janish	Atl	60	36	.600	29	29	15	.517	32	-1
Josh Rutledge	Col	53	30	.566	32	32	19	.594	19	-1
Starlin Castro	ChC	162	93	.574	31	95	51	.537	27	-2
Willie Bloomquist	Ari	57	29	.509	34	36	19	.528	30	-2
Dee Gordon	LAD	75	39	.520	33	49	24	.490	35	-3
Everth Cabrera	SD	69	32	.464	35	37	19	.514	33	-3
MLB Totals		4486	2892	.645		2583	1566	.606		

Fielding Bunts

Bunts are one of the toughest aspects of defensive play to evaluate. Hitters bunt for different reasons, teams use different bunt coverages, and fielders have many different options depending on the developing play. Additionally, there are countless different outcomes to accommodate, especially in sacrifice situations.

We compare similar bunted balls based on the fielder, situation (sacrifice/non-sacrifice), location, and velocity. For each bunt we estimate the difficulty of the play and calculate the run expectation, which we compare to the play's outcome to credit/penalize the fielder.

The following pages present bunt fielding charts with a breakdown of the bunt outcomes. Here is a brief description of each column:

Sacrifice Bunts

Attempts: A sacrifice bunt attempt is defined by the situation. If the bunt came with at least one runner on base and less than two outs, we consider it a sacrifice attempt.

Sac Hits: A sacrifice hit is any bunt where the batter is credited with a sacrifice and fielded by the player in question.

Hits: A hit is any bunt hit in a sacrifice situation.

Sac Hit Average: (Sac Hits + Hits) / Attempts. For the fielder, a lower sac hit average is better.

Bunt Hits

Attempts: A bunt hit attempt is defined as any bunt with no runners on base OR two outs.

Bunt Hits: A bunt hit is any hit (non-sacrifice situation).

Bunt Hit Average: Bunt Hits / Attempts. As with sacrifice hits, a lower Bunt Hit Average is better.

The best defensive player fielding bunts over the last three years is Anthony Rendon, third baseman for the Washington Nationals. He totaled seven Bunt Runs Saved, six of which occurred in the 2014 season. Rendon fielded 32 bunt attempts in a little over a year and half, 20 of those in sacrifice situations. Of the 20, 14 went down as sacrifice bunts for the batter, however, the batter never reached safely on a single. Batters have made 12 Bunt Hit Attempts against Rendon over his career and were only successful 25 percent of the time, the lowest bunt success rate against any third baseman since 2012.

On the opposite side of the spectrum is third basemen Mike Moustakas of the Kansas City Royals. He has cost the Royals seven runs on bunts from 2012-2014, which is tied for the worst among third basemen. Moustakas fielded 40 bunt attempts, 29 in sacrifice situations. Of the 29, only 11 went down as sacrifice bunts, however the batter reached safely an astounding 15 times, the most against any third baseman, first baseman or catcher. Moustakas has also allowed the second highest success rate on Bunt Hits (9-for-11) among third basemen. If teams need to advance a runner or start a spark in a game, laying down a bunt against Moustakas seems like a useful strategy.

Miguel Montero, is an absolute beast when it comes to fielding bunt hit attempts. He has fielded more bunt hit attempts than any other catcher over the last six years (39), and he has thrown out a league-leading 32 of them. Note to opposing hitters: if you're going to lay down a bunt against the revamped Chicago Cubs this year, push it far away from Montero. Likewise, Matt Wieters has thrown out 18 of the 21 bunt hit attempts he fielded, including a perfect 5-for-5 over the past three seasons.

Yonder Alonso and Brandon Belt were the best first basemen handling bunts over the last three years, each with four runs saved on bunts. In contrast, Anthony Rizzo of the Chicago Cubs and Freddie Freeman of the Atlanta Braves have cost their teams the most Bunt Runs Saved, each with four. Freddie Freeman turned more sacrifice bunts into hits than any other player over the three-year period of 2012-2014. It would be beneficial to both the Braves and Cubs if Freeman and Rizzo can improve on their bunt defense for the upcoming season.

Catchers - 3-Year Bunt Defense

	SAC BUNTS				BUNT HITS			
Player	Attempts	Sac Hits	Hits	Sac Hit Average	Attempts	Bunt Hits	Bunt Hit Average	Runs Saved
Yadier Molina	45	22	0	.489	8	1	.125	6
Devin Mesoraco	33	21	0	.636	1	0	.000	3
Josh Thole	10	4	0	.400	0	0		2
Jeff Mathis	15	8	0	.533	4	0	.000	2
Wilson Ramos	13	8	0	.615	9	2	.222	2
Carlos Ruiz	47	30	0	.638	12	2	.167	2
Welington Castillo	20	12	1	.650	6	0	.000	1
Miguel Montero	41	25	2	.659	16	3	.188	1
Kurt Suzuki	22	14	1	.682	15	5	.333	1
Salvador Perez	9	5	2	.778	4	0	.000	1
Yan Gomes	9	2	1	.333	2	1	.500	0
Mike Zunino	5	2	0	.400	6	2	.333	0
Ryan Hanigan	14	8	0	.571	7	3	.429	0
Jose Lobaton	9	6	0	.667	3	0	.000	0
Dioner Navarro	10	7	0	.700	2	0	.000	0
Carlos Santana	7	5	0	.714	2	0	.000	0
A.J. Pierzynski	11	7	1	.727	3	0	.000	0
Buster Posey	30	21	1	.733	1	1	1.000	0
Nick Hundley	22	18	0	.818	11	3	.273	0
Tyler Flowers	7	6	0	.857	6	2	.333	0
Chris Stewart	9	8	0	.889	4	2	.500	0
Matt Wieters	15	4	5	.600	5	0	.000	-1
Chris Iannetta	12	8	0	.667	4	2	.500	-1
Jose Molina	9	4	2	.667	3	0	.000	-1
Derek Norris	12	7	1	.667	3	2	.667	-1
Alex Avila	7	4	1	.714	9	5	.556	-1
Jonathan Lucroy	25	15	3	.720	5	2	.400	-1
J.P. Arencibia	9	5	2	.778	3	1	.333	-1
John Buck	22	19	1	.909	6	0	.000	-1
A.J. Ellis	26	17	0	.654	9	4	.444	-2
Russell Martin	31	21	3	.774	9	6	.667	-2
Wilin Rosario	31	23	1	.774	7	2	.286	-2
Jason Castro	16	14	0	.875	7	2	.286	-2
Brian McCann	30	28	1	.967	3	1	.333	-2
Jarrod Saltalamacchia	20	12	2	.700	4	2	.500	-4
MLB Totals	1083	677	64	.684	338	86	.254	

Catchers - 2014 Bunt Defense

		SAC BUNTS				BUNT HITS			
Player	Team	Attempts	Sac Hits	Hits	Sac Hit Average	Attempts	Bunt Hits	Bunt Hit Average	Runs Saved
Devin Mesoraco	Cin	10	6	0	.600	1	0	.000	2
Yadier Molina	StL	7	2	0	.286	1	1	1.000	1
Hank Conger	LAA	3	0	1	.333	6	0	.000	1
Wilin Rosario	Col	9	5	0	.556	2	1	.500	1
Yasmani Grandal	SD	9	5	0	.556	1	0	.000	1
Caleb Joseph	Bal	7	3	1	.571	2	0	.000	1
Wilson Ramos	Was	3	2	0	.667	3	0	.000	1
Salvador Perez	KC	3	2	0	.667	3	0	.000	1
Miguel Montero	Ari	8	6	0	.750	6	3	.500	1
Alex Avila	Det	1	0	0	.000	2	1	.500	0
Yan Gomes	Cle	3	1	0	.333	0	0		0
Mike Zunino	Sea	3	1	0	.333	3	1	.333	0
A.J. Ellis	LAD	6	3	0	.500	2	0	.000	0
Ryan Hanigan	TB	4	2	0	.500	3	2	.667	0
A.J. Pierzynski	2 tms	2	1	0	.500	0	0		0
Jose Molina	TB	4	2	0	.500	1	0	.000	0
Kurt Suzuki	Min	2	1	0	.500	4	3	.750	0
Jonathan Lucroy	Mil	10	5	1	.600	2	1	.500	0
Derek Norris	Oak	5	3	0	.600	2	1	.500	0
Robinson Chirinos	Tex	3	1	1	.667	2	0	.000	0
Evan Gattis	Atl	7	5	0	.714	4	2	.500	0
Welington Castillo	ChC	11	7	1	.727	3	0	.000	0
Russell Martin	Pit	11	8	0	.727	6	4	.667	0
Rene Rivera	SD	12	10	1	.917	0	0		0
Jason Castro	Hou	2	2	0	1.000	3	1	.333	0
Jose Lobaton	Was	5	5	0	1.000	0	0		0
Brian McCann	NYY	5	5	0	1.000	0	0		0
Chris Iannetta	LAA	5	3	0	.600	1	0	.000	-1
Carlos Ruiz	Phi	18	13	0	.722	5	1	.200	-1
Nick Hundley	2 tms	7	6	0	.857	4	2	.500	-1
Buster Posey	SF	10	9	0	.900	0	0		-1
Tyler Flowers	CWS	1	1	0	1.000	4	2	.500	-1
Travis d'Arnaud	NYM	8	4	1	.625	2	0	.000	-2
Jarrod Saltalamacchia	Mia	12	8	0	.667	1	0	.000	-3
Dioner Navarro	Tor	1	0	0	.000	2	0	.000	
MLB Totals		313	200	13	.681	114	32	.281	

Catchers - 2013 Bunt Defense

Player	Team	SAC BUNTS Attempts	Sac Hits	Hits	Sac Hit Average	BUNT HITS Attempts	Bunt Hits	Bunt Hit Average	Runs Saved
Carlos Ruiz	Phi	16	7	0	.438	3	0	.000	2
Buster Posey	SF	12	7	0	.583	0	0		2
Jeff Mathis	Mia	5	2	0	.400	0	0		1
Yadier Molina	StL	17	8	0	.471	2	0	.000	1
Welington Castillo	ChC	9	5	0	.556	3	0	.000	1
Rob Brantly	Mia	12	7	0	.583	0	0		1
Devin Mesoraco	Cin	18	12	0	.667	0	0		1
Kurt Suzuki	2 tms	10	6	1	.700	4	1	.250	1
Wilson Ramos	Was	7	5	0	.714	3	1	.333	1
A.J. Pierzynski	Tex	5	4	0	.800	1	0	.000	1
Tyler Flowers	CWS	6	5	0	.833	1	0	.000	1
John Buck	2 tms	4	4	0	1.000	1	0	.000	1
Jose Lobaton	TB	0	0	0		2	0	.000	0
Yan Gomes	Cle	6	1	1	.333	2	1	.500	0
Matt Wieters	Bal	12	3	3	.500	3	0	.000	0
Hank Conger	LAA	6	3	0	.500	0	0		0
Ryan Hanigan	Cin	4	2	0	.500	2	0	.000	0
Miguel Montero	Ari	15	8	1	.600	5	0	.000	0
Chris Iannetta	LAA	6	4	0	.667	3	2	.667	0
Carlos Santana	Cle	3	2	0	.667	2	0	.000	0
Alex Avila	Det	4	2	1	.750	4	2	.500	0
Chris Stewart	NYY	4	3	0	.750	3	1	.333	0
Wilin Rosario	Col	6	5	0	.833	3	1	.333	0
Salvador Perez	KC	5	3	2	1.000	1	0	.000	0
Derek Norris	Oak	5	2	1	.600	0	0		-1
Jose Molina	TB	5	2	2	.800	1	0	.000	-1
Jonathan Lucroy	Mil	12	8	2	.833	2	1	.500	-1
A.J. Ellis	LAD	8	7	0	.875	3	3	1.000	-1
Brian McCann	Atl	13	11	1	.923	2	0	.000	-1
Nick Hundley	SD	9	9	0	1.000	4	1	.250	-1
Joe Mauer	Min	2	1	1	1.000	1	1	1.000	-1
J.P. Arencibia	Tor	5	3	2	1.000	3	1	.333	-1
Jarrod Saltalamacchia	Bos	3	0	2	.667	2	1	.500	-2
Russell Martin	Pit	14	9	2	.786	2	2	1.000	-2
Jason Castro	Hou	9	8	0	.889	2	1	.500	-2
MLB Totals		396	239	31	.682	104	28	.269	

Catchers - 2012 Bunt Defense

Player	Team	SAC BUNTS Attempts	Sac Hits	Hits	Sac Hit Average	BUNT HITS Attempts	Bunt Hits	Bunt Hit Average	Runs Saved
Yadier Molina	StL	21	12	0	.571	5	0	.000	4
Josh Thole	NYM	10	4	0	.400	0	0		2
Chris Snyder	Hou	8	4	0	.500	1	0	.000	2
Carlos Ruiz	Phi	13	10	0	.769	4	1	.250	1
Jarrod Saltalamacchia	Bos	5	4	0	.800	1	1	1.000	1
Salvador Perez	KC	1	0	0	.000	0	0		0
Joe Mauer	Min	4	1	0	.250	1	0	.000	0
Jeff Mathis	Tor	4	2	0	.500	2	0	.000	0
J.P. Arencibia	Tor	4	2	0	.500	0	0		0
Miguel Olivo	Sea	8	3	2	.625	4	1	.250	0
Carlos Santana	Cle	3	2	0	.667	0	0		0
Jonathan Lucroy	Mil	3	2	0	.667	1	0	.000	0
Miguel Montero	Ari	18	11	1	.667	5	0	.000	0
Ryan Hanigan	Cin	6	4	0	.667	2	1	.500	0
Mike Napoli	Tex	3	2	0	.667	1	0	.000	0
Kurt Suzuki	2 tms	10	7	0	.700	7	1	.143	0
Jesus Flores	Was	7	5	0	.714	3	1	.333	0
Jason Castro	Hou	5	4	0	.800	2	0	.000	0
Russell Martin	NYY	6	4	1	.833	1	0	.000	0
Lou Marson	Cle	1	1	0	1.000	0	0		0
Martin Maldonado	Mil	4	4	0	1.000	1	0	.000	0
Chris Iannetta	LAA	1	1	0	1.000	0	0		0
A.J. Ellis	LAD	12	7	0	.583	4	1	.250	-1
Michael McKenry	Pit	8	6	0	.750	3	2	.667	-1
Kelly Shoppach	2 tms	4	3	0	.750	1	1	1.000	-1
A.J. Pierzynski	CWS	4	2	1	.750	2	0	.000	-1
Buster Posey	SF	8	5	1	.750	1	1	1.000	-1
Brian McCann	Atl	12	12	0	1.000	1	1	1.000	-1
Alex Avila	Det	2	2	0	1.000	3	2	.667	-1
Matt Wieters	Bal	3	1	2	1.000	2	0	.000	-1
Rod Barajas	Pit	8	5	1	.750	2	0	.000	-2
Geovany Soto	2 tms	8	6	1	.875	4	0	.000	-2
John Buck	Mia	17	14	1	.882	3	0	.000	-2
Wilin Rosario	Col	16	13	1	.875	2	0	.000	-3
Jose Molina	TB	0	0	0		1	0	.000	
MLB Totals		374	238	20	.690	120	26	.217	

First Basemen - 3-Year Bunt Defense

Player	SAC BUNTS				BUNT HITS			Runs Saved
	Attempts	Sac Hits	Hits	Sac Hit Average	Attempts	Bunt Hits	Bunt Hit Average	
Yonder Alonso	38	25	0	.658	8	5	.625	4
Brandon Belt	42	28	2	.714	5	4	.800	4
Adrian Gonzalez	38	24	0	.632	6	2	.333	3
Adam LaRoche	44	36	0	.818	9	2	.222	3
Brandon Moss	5	2	1	.600	4	1	.250	1
Matt Adams	20	14	1	.750	7	4	.571	1
James Loney	28	19	2	.750	4	1	.250	1
Eric Hosmer	22	15	2	.773	4	2	.500	1
Mark Trumbo	9	6	1	.778	2	0	.000	1
Mike Napoli	15	11	1	.800	3	1	.333	1
Allen Craig	15	11	1	.800	3	1	.333	1
Adam Lind	10	6	2	.800	1	0	.000	1
Albert Pujols	11	9	1	.909	2	2	1.000	1
Garrett Jones	15	13	1	.933	6	1	.167	1
Mark Teixeira	15	14	0	.933	3	2	.667	1
Mitch Moreland	8	2	3	.625	4	2	.500	0
Lyle Overbay	18	11	2	.722	2	1	.500	0
Ike Davis	35	24	3	.771	7	2	.286	0
Paul Konerko	9	4	3	.778	1	0	.000	0
Lucas Duda	18	14	1	.833	1	0	.000	0
Logan Morrison	8	6	1	.875	2	0	.000	0
Mark Reynolds	11	9	1	.909	2	0	.000	0
Ryan Howard	23	19	2	.913	9	6	.667	0
Justin Morneau	18	14	3	.944	10	4	.400	0
Edwin Encarnacion	7	4	2	.857	3	2	.667	-1
Chris Davis	10	6	3	.900	7	1	.143	-1
Nick Swisher	11	7	3	.909	5	4	.800	-1
Justin Smoak	16	14	2	1.000	5	2	.400	-1
Gaby Sanchez	20	14	2	.800	6	3	.500	-2
Carlos Pena	6	5	1	1.000	0	0		-2
Paul Goldschmidt	32	25	2	.844	3	3	1.000	-3
Joey Votto	34	26	3	.853	4	3	.750	-3
Prince Fielder	9	7	2	1.000	3	2	.667	-3
Anthony Rizzo	26	19	2	.808	3	2	.667	-4
Freddie Freeman	41	33	5	.927	5	4	.800	-4
MLB Totals	1009	740	85	.818	218	96	.440	

First Basemen - 2014 Bunt Defense

Player	Team	SAC BUNTS				BUNT HITS			Runs Saved
		Attempts	Sac Hits	Hits	Sac Hit Average	Attempts	Bunt Hits	Bunt Hit Average	
Yonder Alonso	SD	16	9	0	.563	2	1	.500	2
Adrian Gonzalez	LAD	13	10	0	.769	3	0	.000	2
Jon Singleton	Hou	7	4	0	.571	2	1	.500	1
Brandon Belt	SF	8	4	1	.625	0	0		1
Carlos Santana	Cle	6	4	0	.667	3	2	.667	1
James Loney	TB	8	5	1	.750	3	0	.000	1
Matt Adams	StL	10	8	0	.800	5	2	.400	1
Brandon Moss	Oak	0	0	0		1	1	1.000	0
Steve Pearce	Bal	1	0	0	.000	0	0		0
Brayan Pena	Cin	2	1	0	.500	0	0		0
Lyle Overbay	Mil	9	6	0	.667	0	0		0
Eric Hosmer	KC	3	2	0	.667	1	1	1.000	0
Mike Napoli	Bos	10	6	1	.700	2	1	.500	0
Chris Davis	Bal	4	2	1	.750	3	0	.000	0
Jose Abreu	CWS	9	6	1	.778	1	1	1.000	0
Lucas Duda	NYM	10	7	1	.800	1	0	.000	0
Gaby Sanchez	Pit	6	5	0	.833	5	2	.400	0
Ike Davis	2 tms	12	10	0	.833	3	1	.333	0
Joey Votto	Cin	6	5	0	.833	0	0		0
Mark Teixeira	NYY	9	8	0	.889	0	0		0
Adam LaRoche	Was	10	9	0	.900	3	0	.000	0
Ryan Howard	Phi	9	9	0	1.000	2	2	1.000	0
Justin Morneau	Col	9	8	1	1.000	4	1	.250	0
Miguel Cabrera	Det	3	2	1	1.000	2	0	.000	0
Joe Mauer	Min	4	3	1	1.000	1	0	.000	0
Edwin Encarnacion	Tor	2	2	0	1.000	1	1	1.000	0
Justin Smoak	Sea	5	4	1	1.000	2	0	.000	0
Mark Reynolds	Mil	8	8	0	1.000	1	0	.000	0
Garrett Jones	Mia	4	4	0	1.000	4	1	.250	0
Nick Swisher	Cle	2	2	0	1.000	2	2	1.000	0
Albert Pujols	LAA	4	4	0	1.000	2	2	1.000	0
Logan Morrison	Sea	1	1	0	1.000	1	0	.000	0
Anthony Rizzo	ChC	8	7	0	.875	0	0		-1
Paul Goldschmidt	Ari	12	11	0	.917	1	1	1.000	-1
Freddie Freeman	Atl	24	22	2	1.000	2	1	.500	-2
MLB Totals		342	257	24	.822	79	28	.354	

138

First Basemen - 2013 Bunt Defense

Player	Team	SAC BUNTS Attempts	Sac Hits	Hits	Sac Hit Average	BUNT HITS Attempts	Bunt Hits	Bunt Hit Average	Runs Saved
Chris Carter	Hou	2	1	0	.500	2	0	.000	1
Edwin Encarnacion	Tor	2	1	0	.500	1	0	.000	1
Brandon Moss	Oak	4	1	1	.500	2	0	.000	1
Mitch Moreland	Tex	2	1	0	.500	3	1	.333	1
Matt Adams	StL	8	5	0	.625	1	1	1.000	1
Allen Craig	StL	4	3	0	.750	1	0	.000	1
Garrett Jones	Pit	4	3	0	.750	1	0	.000	1
Brandon Belt	SF	16	12	0	.750	4	3	.750	1
James Loney	TB	8	5	1	.750	0	0		1
Justin Morneau	2 tms	5	4	0	.800	2	1	.500	1
Ike Davis	NYM	5	4	0	.800	3	1	.333	1
Adam LaRoche	Was	16	13	0	.813	1	0	.000	1
Mark Trumbo	LAA	6	4	1	.833	2	0	.000	1
Todd Helton	Col	11	10	0	.909	1	0	.000	1
Mike Napoli	Bos	5	5	0	1.000	1	0	.000	1
Adam Dunn	CWS	2	1	0	.500	0	0		0
Juan Francisco	Mil	2	1	0	.500	2	2	1.000	0
Yonder Alonso	SD	9	6	0	.667	3	3	1.000	0
Lyle Overbay	NYY	7	3	2	.714	2	1	.500	0
Paul Goldschmidt	Ari	13	9	1	.769	1	1	1.000	0
Adam Lind	Tor	6	3	2	.833	0	0		0
Logan Morrison	Mia	6	4	1	.833	1	0	.000	0
Ryan Howard	Phi	9	7	1	.889	5	3	.600	0
Paul Konerko	CWS	5	4	1	1.000	0	0		0
Eric Hosmer	KC	2	2	0	1.000	2	1	.500	0
Mark Reynolds	2 tms	1	0	1	1.000	1	0	.000	0
Justin Smoak	Sea	3	3	0	1.000	1	1	1.000	0
Adrian Gonzalez	LAD	16	10	0	.625	1	1	1.000	-1
Freddie Freeman	Atl	10	6	2	.800	1	1	1.000	-1
Nick Swisher	Cle	8	5	2	.875	2	2	1.000	-1
Joey Votto	Cin	17	15	1	.941	2	2	1.000	-1
Prince Fielder	Det	4	3	1	1.000	2	1	.500	-1
Chris Davis	Bal	4	2	2	1.000	4	1	.250	-1
Gaby Sanchez	Pit	10	8	1	.900	0	0		-2
Anthony Rizzo	ChC	13	9	2	.846	2	1	.500	-3
MLB Totals		308	224	27	.815	74	38	.514	

First Basemen - 2012 Bunt Defense

Player	Team	SAC BUNTS Attempts	Sac Hits	Hits	Sac Hit Average	BUNT HITS Attempts	Bunt Hits	Bunt Hit Average	Runs Saved
Adrian Gonzalez	2 tms	9	4	0	.444	2	1	.500	2
Brandon Belt	SF	18	12	1	.722	1	1	1.000	2
Yonder Alonso	SD	13	10	0	.769	3	1	.333	2
Adam LaRoche	Was	18	14	0	.778	5	2	.400	2
Chris Carter	Oak	1	0	0	.000	1	0	.000	1
Casey McGehee	2 tms	6	4	0	.667	0	0		1
Eric Hosmer	KC	17	11	2	.765	1	0	.000	1
Allen Craig	StL	9	7	0	.778	1	1	1.000	1
Todd Helton	Col	10	9	0	.900	2	1	.500	1
Mark Teixeira	NYY	6	6	0	1.000	3	2	.667	1
Bryan LaHair	ChC	2	2	0	1.000	2	0	.000	1
Paul Konerko	CWS	2	0	1	.500	0	0		0
Gaby Sanchez	2 tms	4	1	1	.500	1	1	1.000	0
Mark Reynolds	Bal	2	1	0	.500	0	0		0
Corey Hart	Mil	12	7	0	.583	0	0		0
Mitch Moreland	Tex	5	1	2	.600	0	0		0
Anthony Rizzo	ChC	5	3	0	.600	1	1	1.000	0
Ryan Howard	Phi	5	3	1	.800	2	1	.500	0
Casey Kotchman	Cle	6	3	2	.833	1	0	.000	0
Carlos Lee	2 tms	11	10	0	.909	4	1	.250	0
Ty Wigginton	Phi	6	6	0	1.000	1	1	1.000	0
Albert Pujols	LAA	4	3	1	1.000	0	0		0
Garrett Jones	Pit	7	6	1	1.000	1	0	.000	0
Ike Davis	NYM	18	10	3	.722	1	0	.000	-1
James Loney	2 tms	12	9	0	.750	1	1	1.000	-1
Freddie Freeman	Atl	7	5	1	.857	2	2	1.000	-1
Carlos Pena	TB	5	4	1	1.000	0	0		-1
Justin Smoak	Sea	8	7	1	1.000	2	1	.500	-1
Justin Morneau	Min	4	2	2	1.000	4	2	.500	-1
Prince Fielder	Det	4	4	0	1.000	1	1	1.000	-1
Joey Votto	Cin	11	6	2	.727	2	1	.500	-2
Paul Goldschmidt	Ari	7	5	1	.857	1	1	1.000	-2
Edwin Encarnacion	Tor	3	1	2	1.000	1	1	1.000	-2
Brett Wallace	Hou	9	7	2	1.000	0	0		-2
Adam Lind	Tor	1	1	0	1.000	1	0	.000	
MLB Totals		359	259	34	.816	65	30	.462	

Third Basemen - 3-Year Bunt Defense

Player	SAC BUNTS				BUNT HITS			Runs Saved
	Attempts	Sac Hits	Hits	Sac Hit Average	Attempts	Bunt Hits	Bunt Hit Average	
Anthony Rendon	20	14	0	.700	12	3	.250	7
Adrian Beltre	19	12	2	.737	12	5	.417	5
Ryan Zimmerman	36	29	2	.861	14	5	.357	5
Manny Machado	23	14	3	.739	10	4	.400	3
Nolan Arenado	17	11	3	.824	15	6	.400	2
Matt Carpenter	26	19	3	.846	18	8	.444	2
Luis Valbuena	27	20	3	.852	8	4	.500	2
David Wright	29	23	3	.897	20	9	.450	2
Evan Longoria	19	7	5	.632	12	9	.750	1
Miguel Cabrera	18	10	3	.722	18	11	.611	1
Chris Johnson	38	28	2	.789	22	17	.773	1
Juan Uribe	21	16	2	.857	5	3	.600	1
Matt Dominguez	13	10	2	.923	16	7	.438	1
Aramis Ramirez	29	16	6	.759	19	11	.579	0
Alberto Callaspo	20	14	2	.800	4	4	1.000	0
David Freese	16	9	4	.813	22	13	.591	0
Josh Donaldson	28	20	3	.821	9	6	.667	0
Will Middlebrooks	8	5	2	.875	12	7	.583	0
Cody Asche	11	10	0	.909	6	2	.333	0
Nick Castellanos	10	6	4	1.000	5	2	.400	0
Eric Chavez	8	4	2	.750	3	2	.667	-1
Brett Lawrie	23	12	6	.783	12	9	.750	-1
Chris Nelson	5	3	1	.800	5	4	.800	-1
Trevor Plouffe	17	8	7	.882	14	6	.429	-1
Todd Frazier	19	15	2	.895	18	9	.500	-1
Kyle Seager	24	15	7	.917	21	10	.476	-1
Conor Gillaspie	20	13	6	.950	8	6	.750	-1
Lonnie Chisenhall	9	6	3	1.000	16	13	.813	-1
Chase Headley	35	23	7	.857	13	8	.615	-2
Juan Francisco	9	5	3	.889	6	3	.500	-2
Casey McGehee	24	16	6	.917	8	6	.750	-3
Martin Prado	17	12	5	1.000	4	3	.750	-4
Pablo Sandoval	34	21	6	.794	15	15	1.000	-6
Pedro Alvarez	44	26	11	.841	25	16	.640	-7
Mike Moustakas	29	11	15	.897	11	9	.818	-7
MLB Totals	1116	735	203	.841	659	401	.608	

Third Basemen - 2014 Bunt Defense

Player	Team	SAC BUNTS				BUNT HITS			Runs Saved
		Attempts	Sac Hits	Hits	Sac Hit Average	Attempts	Bunt Hits	Bunt Hit Average	
Anthony Rendon	Was	17	11	0	.647	10	3	.300	6
Manny Machado	Bal	6	4	0	.667	3	1	.333	2
Adrian Beltre	Tex	9	5	1	.667	4	3	.750	1
Chris Johnson	Atl	18	14	0	.778	9	8	.889	1
David Wright	NYM	5	4	0	.800	7	2	.286	1
Juan Uribe	LAD	6	4	1	.833	2	1	.500	1
Matt Carpenter	StL	18	13	3	.889	15	7	.467	1
Conor Gillaspie	CWS	11	8	2	.909	5	4	.800	1
Todd Frazier	Cin	7	6	1	1.000	8	1	.125	1
Will Middlebrooks	Bos	1	1	0	1.000	4	1	.250	1
Josh Harrison	Pit	4	4	0	1.000	3	2	.667	1
Evan Longoria	TB	11	4	3	.636	4	4	1.000	0
Justin Turner	LAD	3	2	0	.667	3	3	1.000	0
Brett Lawrie	Tor	7	4	2	.857	2	1	.500	0
Cody Asche	Phi	9	8	0	.889	5	2	.400	0
Chase Headley	2 tms	10	8	1	.900	4	3	.750	0
Mike Olt	ChC	3	3	0	1.000	2	2	1.000	0
Matt Dominguez	Hou	7	5	2	1.000	5	3	.600	0
Nick Castellanos	Det	10	6	4	1.000	5	2	.400	0
Kyle Seager	Sea	6	4	2	1.000	5	0	.000	0
Nolan Arenado	Col	6	5	1	1.000	6	3	.500	0
Juan Francisco	Tor	3	0	2	.667	2	2	1.000	-1
Luis Valbuena	ChC	12	7	2	.750	4	3	.750	-1
Aramis Ramirez	Mil	5	2	2	.800	8	4	.500	-1
Yangervis Solarte	2 tms	9	7	1	.889	2	1	.500	-1
Casey McGehee	Mia	19	14	3	.895	7	5	.714	-1
Josh Donaldson	Oak	10	8	2	1.000	5	4	.800	-1
Danny Valencia	2 tms	2	1	1	1.000	1	1	1.000	-1
Trevor Plouffe	Min	4	1	3	1.000	5	2	.400	-1
Pablo Sandoval	SF	8	8	0	1.000	9	9	1.000	-1
David Freese	LAA	6	3	2	.833	8	7	.875	-2
Mike Moustakas	KC	8	5	3	1.000	5	5	1.000	-2
Martin Prado	2 tms	9	6	3	1.000	0	0		-2
Lonnie Chisenhall	Cle	7	4	3	1.000	9	8	.889	-2
Pedro Alvarez	Pit	14	9	4	.929	9	5	.556	-4
MLB Totals		366	248	69	.866	225	136	.604	

Third Basemen - 2013 Bunt Defense

| Player | Team | SAC BUNTS | | | | BUNT HITS | | | Runs Saved |
		Attempts	Sac Hits	Hits	Sac Hit Average	Attempts	Bunt Hits	Bunt Hit Average	
Nolan Arenado	Col	11	6	2	.727	9	3	.333	2
Ryan Zimmerman	Was	16	12	2	.875	7	2	.286	2
Luis Valbuena	ChC	10	10	0	1.000	3	1	.333	2
Evan Longoria	TB	7	2	2	.571	6	4	.667	1
David Freese	StL	5	3	0	.600	5	3	.600	1
Matt Dominguez	Hou	3	2	0	.667	8	3	.375	1
Josh Donaldson	Oak	10	7	0	.700	4	2	.500	1
Miguel Cabrera	Det	7	5	1	.857	4	3	.750	1
Kyle Seager	Sea	7	5	1	.857	11	6	.545	1
Adrian Beltre	Tex	5	4	1	1.000	5	2	.400	1
Lonnie Chisenhall	Cle	2	2	0	1.000	5	3	.600	1
David Wright	NYM	9	9	0	1.000	5	3	.600	1
Chris Nelson	3 tms	0	0	0		2	2	1.000	0
Michael Young	2 tms	3	2	0	.667	5	4	.800	0
Chris Johnson	Atl	11	7	1	.727	6	6	1.000	0
Placido Polanco	Mia	8	5	1	.750	2	1	.500	0
Manny Machado	Bal	9	5	2	.778	5	2	.400	0
Trevor Plouffe	Min	6	2	3	.833	8	3	.375	0
Mike Moustakas	KC	8	4	3	.875	2	1	.500	0
Juan Uribe	LAD	10	9	0	.900	1	1	1.000	0
Will Middlebrooks	Bos	2	2	0	1.000	3	2	.667	0
Ed Lucas	Mia	7	6	1	1.000	3	1	.333	0
Conor Gillaspie	CWS	5	4	1	1.000	3	2	.667	0
Cody Asche	Phi	2	2	0	1.000	1	0	.000	0
Yuniesky Betancourt	Mil	5	2	1	.600	2	1	.500	-1
Brett Lawrie	Tor	8	3	2	.625	3	3	1.000	-1
Aramis Ramirez	Mil	10	4	3	.700	4	2	.500	-1
Todd Frazier	Cin	8	5	1	.750	8	6	.750	-1
Pedro Alvarez	Pit	10	5	3	.800	4	3	.750	-1
Alberto Callaspo	2 tms	11	7	2	.818	1	1	1.000	-1
Eric Chavez	Ari	6	3	2	.833	0	0		-1
Chase Headley	SD	12	6	4	.833	3	2	.667	-2
Mark Reynolds	2 tms	6	4	1	.833	4	4	1.000	-2
Pablo Sandoval	SF	13	10	1	.846	2	2	1.000	-2
Martin Prado	Ari	7	5	2	1.000	2	2	1.000	-2
MLB Totals		364	246	60	.841	196	118	.602	

Third Basemen - 2012 Bunt Defense

| Player | Team | SAC BUNTS | | | | BUNT HITS | | | Runs Saved |
		Attempts	Sac Hits	Hits	Sac Hit Average	Attempts	Bunt Hits	Bunt Hit Average	
Adrian Beltre	Tex	5	3	0	.600	3	0	.000	3
Brandon Inge	2 tms	11	9	0	.818	3	2	.667	3
Ryan Zimmerman	Was	17	14	0	.824	6	2	.333	3
Aramis Ramirez	Mil	14	10	1	.786	7	5	.714	2
Placido Polanco	Phi	7	6	0	.857	3	0	.000	2
Ian Stewart	ChC	6	4	0	.667	3	3	1.000	1
Manny Machado	Bal	8	5	1	.750	2	1	.500	1
Chipper Jones	Atl	9	6	1	.778	3	1	.333	1
Alberto Callaspo	LAA	9	7	0	.778	3	3	1.000	1
Luis Valbuena	ChC	5	3	1	.800	1	0	.000	1
David Freese	StL	5	3	2	1.000	9	3	.333	1
Kevin Frandsen	Phi	1	1	0	1.000	1	0	.000	1
Jordan Pacheco	Col	7	7	0	1.000	4	3	.750	1
Wilson Betemit	Bal	2	2	0	1.000	5	2	.400	1
Scott Rolen	Cin	0	0	0		1	0	.000	0
Ryan Roberts	2 tms	4	0	1	.250	3	2	.667	0
Eric Chavez	NYY	2	1	0	.500	1	0	.000	0
Miguel Cabrera	Det	11	5	2	.636	14	8	.571	0
Josh Donaldson	Oak	8	5	1	.750	0	0		0
Kevin Youkilis	2 tms	5	3	1	.800	8	4	.500	0
Jack Hannahan	Cle	5	3	1	.800	4	2	.500	0
Chase Headley	SD	13	9	2	.846	6	3	.500	0
Trevor Plouffe	Min	7	5	1	.857	1	1	1.000	0
David Wright	NYM	15	10	3	.867	8	4	.500	0
Brett Lawrie	Tor	8	5	2	.875	7	5	.714	0
Chris Johnson	2 tms	9	7	1	.889	7	3	.429	0
Hanley Ramirez	2 tms	3	2	1	1.000	7	4	.571	0
Will Middlebrooks	Bos	5	2	2	.800	5	4	.800	-1
Chris Nelson	Col	5	3	1	.800	3	2	.667	-1
Todd Frazier	Cin	4	4	0	1.000	2	2	1.000	-1
Pedro Alvarez	Pit	20	12	4	.800	12	8	.667	-2
Kyle Seager	Sea	11	6	4	.909	5	4	.800	-2
Alex Rodriguez	NYY	5	3	2	1.000	3	3	1.000	-2
Pablo Sandoval	SF	13	3	5	.615	4	4	1.000	-3
Mike Moustakas	KC	13	2	9	.846	4	3	.750	-5
MLB Totals		386	241	74	.816	238	147	.618	

141

Descriptive Defense Information

Over the years, Baseball Info Solutions has put a lot of effort into better understanding and measuring the defensive contributions of players. In 2013, we began collecting Descriptive Defense Information, which greatly expanded the defensive data we can examine.

The idea behind Descriptive Defense Information is to better characterize a fielder's involvement in a play. This begins with the direction of his movement toward a ball that has been put in play. We then record how the fielder approaches the point of contact with the ball, be it standing in wait, jogging, sprinting, diving, sliding, or jumping. Next is his fielding method, which is the orientation of his glove and body as he fields the ball. He can either forehand, backhand, barehand, or reach over the shoulder to receive a fielded ball. Finally, we describe any throw he makes, which can be with feet planted, on the move, from the ground, or while jumping. We even track when a fielder makes a glove flip.

The detailed nature of the Descriptive Defense Information allows for many avenues of research. Here are a few examples.

Slides and Dives

No matter how good an outfielder's range is, he will have balls hit to the edge of it that demand a decision on how to approach the play. Descriptive Defense Information revealed some interesting player tendencies on those edge-of-range plays. Two possibilities for those balls are dives and slides, and while dives are more typically used on side-to-side plays and slides are more typically used on charging plays, some players showed clear preferences for one play over the other.

Most Slides and Dives, OF

2013-14, Minimum 300 Opportunities

Player	Pos	Opps	Dives	Slides	Total
A. Gordon	LF	1,181	40	15	55
A. McCutchen	CF	993	12	26	38
D. Brown	LF	808	26	12	38
J. Ellsbury	CF	1,140	12	24	36
G. Parra	RF	865	20	15	35

There are many players in baseball who either dove or slid frequently over the last two seasons. For example, Yasiel Puig has 22 dives and 0 slides. Ichiro Suzuki has 20 slides and 1 dive. But the leaders of dives plus slides all used both fielding approaches at least 12 times over the two seasons.

Alex Gordon ran away from the field with 55 slides plus dives. His 40 dives would have been enough for first place for the total leaderboard, and then he added 15 slides to his total. Beyond Gordon, Andrew McCutchen and Jacoby Ellsbury both slid more often than they dove, and Domonic Brown and Gerardo Parra both dove more often than they slid.

Fewest Slides and Dives, OF

2013-14, Minimum 300 Opportunities

Player	Pos	Opps	Dives	Slides	Total
A. Jackson	CF	1,077	1	0	1
A. Jones	CF	1,186	2	0	2
A. Dirks	LF	369	2	0	2
M. Saunders	CF	315	2	1	3
A. De Aza	CF	485	3	0	3

It's difficult to fathom that any outfielder could play full time and yet almost never slide or dive, but Austin Jackson and Adam Jones combined for just three slides plus dives despite each having more than 1,000 total opportunities. To put them in perspective, the next lowest total of slides and dives for a player with 1,000 opportunities is eight, courtesy of Carlos Gomez. Andy Dirks, Michael Saunders, and Alejando De Aza round out the list of qualifiers with fewer than five slides and dives, but none of those three players enjoyed extensive playing time at their positions during the last two years.

Getting in Front of the Ball

Everyone with a bit of Little League experience has been told to get in front of the ball, but that criticism likely disappears for most players once they reach the majors. Professionals at the highest level have earned the benefit of the doubt regarding how they approach and field a grounder. Still, getting in front of the ball never ceases to be good advice.

Highest Rate of Backhands, SS

2013-14, Minimum 300 Opportunities

Player	Opps	Backhand%	Backhand Out%	Forehand Out%
E. Suarez	334	27.5%	72.8%	81.1%
J. Peralta	1,073	23.7%	74.4%	87.1%
C. Owings	311	23.5%	76.7%	85.7%
E. Andrus	1,186	22.7%	68.0%	81.9%
J. Reyes	953	21.6%	61.7%	81.2%
J. Hardy	1,199	21.5%	66.7%	79.7%
E. Cabrera	863	21.1%	72.0%	86.0%
H. Ramirez	732	21.0%	72.1%	86.8%
B. Crawford	1,258	20.9%	72.2%	86.2%
Z. Cozart	1,238	20.5%	73.6%	85.8%
MLB Avg.		*19.2%*	*69.9%*	*83.0%*

Over the last two seasons, 10 shortstops with at least 300 opportunities backhanded 20.5 percent or more of the balls hit to them. The list ranges from Zack Cozart, who saved the Reds 23 runs over the last two seasons, to Jose Reyes, who cost the Blue Jays 20 runs.

Whether their high rate of backhands reflected their initial positioning, their defensive style, or some other factors, those shortstops were more effective with their backhands, converting backhand plays into outs 70.5 percent of the time, a little better than the 69.9 percent MLB average.

Interestingly, the increased reliance on backhands did not cause these players to suffer on their forehanded plays. In fact, these 10 players turned 84.2 percent of plays that they forehanded into outs, greater than the 83.0 percent league average. So while the mantra of getting in front of the ball is most likely helpful to players making their way to the majors, the players who are already there do quite well even if they rely more heavily on their backhand.

The New King of Jump Throws

For more than a decade, Derek Jeter owned the jump throw. Now that Jeter is retired, an heir to his throne has emerged.

Most Jump Throws, SS

2013-14, Minimum 300 Opportunities

Player	Opps	Jump Throws	Out%
T. Tulowitzki	964	25	76.0%
J. Lowrie	952	23	73.9%
E. Andrus	1,186	20	60.0%
I. Desmond	1,375	18	50.0%
A. Escobar	1,325	18	50.0%
Y. Escobar	1,093	18	38.9%

While 15 shortstops have attempted 10 or more jump throws between 2013 and 2014, only three have used the throwing method 20 or more times. Meanwhile, among the leaders, Troy Tulowitzki, Jed Lowrie, and Elvis Andrus are also the most effective with the maneuver. Tulowitzki and Lowrie are neck-and-neck at the top of the list, but Tulowitzki edges Lowrie in both attempts and successes. As such, he is the New King of Jump Throws.

The better question is whether, for shortstops other than Tulowitzki and Lowrie, jump throws are even a good idea. There is a selection bias in that fielders only attempt jump throws in situations where there will likely be a close play at first base, but jump throws were successful just 57.4 percent of the time since 2013. Compare that to a 81.5 percent success rate while on the move and a 71.7 percent success rate from the ground—two situations that also imply a close play at the base.

Moving Forward

This handful of examples just scratches the surface of the potential of Descriptive Defense Information. As we continue to collect and analyze the data, we will have the chance to evaluate and predict the effects of player positioning, style, and choice. In combination with some of our other data such as fielder positioning, batter pull tendencies, and defensive shifts, we can build toward a truly sophisticated understanding of the effects of every detail of player defense on his chances of success.

Scout's Defensive Rating

The bulk of our data collection and analysis at BIS is focused on objective measurements, things like the hang time of flyballs and the location on the field where a ball touches down. In 2013, we added a new collection item that takes a different approach. We call them "Play Difficulty Grades."

Here's how they work: BIS Video Scouts watch every single ball in play and assign primary responsibility to one fielder. Then, they assign a 1-5 rating of the difficulty of each play, from a "1" representing a routine play that every fielder is expected to make, to a "5" representing a play that the fielder had zero chance at making.

Here are some of the guidelines we give our Video Scouts when grading these plays:

1 - Easy, routine, obvious error if missed, player has time to slowly jog to or camp under a fly ball, generous hops right to an infielder.

2 - Slightly more difficult, could be a very hard hit ball, takes some effort to reach the ball and make the play, more difficult hops for infielders. You could see how somebody could possibly misplay the ball.

3 - Nice play, had to do everything right to make the play but nothing was exceptional about it. A 50/50 play; it could go either way.

4 - Very difficult play, unlikely out, definite web gem quality if made, even though the play is unlikely it can conceivably be made by somebody.

5 - Impossible play, no one can conceivably make it. If a play is made, you cannot assign it a 5.

You've likely already realized this, but there's some inevitable gray area between categories. That comes with the territory when you're collecting subjective observations. However, we have all of our Video Scouts operating out of our home office, and we encourage them to ask questions so that everyone is on the same page and our data is as consistent as possible.

Naturally, Play Difficulty Grades for each category vary somewhat by position. Here's a look at the breakdown for all shortstop plays from last season:

Shortstop Plays, 2014

Grade	Plays	Made Plays	Pct
1	11,157	10,890	98%
2	3,140	2,756	88%
3	1,724	1,150	67%
4	2,628	365	14%
5	3,156	0	0%

Scout's Defensive Rating

Of course, the data becomes a lot more valuable when you can learn something from it and apply it in everyday evaluations. We've developed a simple rating system that we call Scout's Defensive Rating (SDR) based solely on the Play Difficulty Grades data. Let's say a shortstop is faced with a "2", a somewhat difficult play that he is still expected to make. As it turns out, shortstops have converted 88 percent of plays rated a "2". If, in this case, the shortstop makes the play successfully, he has made a play that 12 percent of fielders did not make (1 - .88 = .12), so we credit him with .12 "plays". If he fails to make the play for whatever reason, he is penalized -.88. If we add up every play for a particular fielder, we have a player rating based on subjective grades assigned to every play over the entire season. Calculated this way, each fielder's SDR corresponds to a number of plays that he has made above or below average.

Let's take a look at the top-rated players of the 2014 season according to SDR.

Fielder	Pos	Total Plays	Rating
N. Arenado	3B	389	25.3
A. Simmons	SS	549	17.4
J. Donaldson	3B	506	17.3
D. Pedroia	2B	504	17.3
J. Heyward	RF	413	15.3

This list is populated by players that objective defensive rating systems, including our own Defensive Runs Saved, have also generally considered strong defenders. Nolan Arenado is third in baseball with 46 Runs Saved since the start of 2013 despite missing time because of some time lost to the DL and to the minor leagues. Andrelton Simmons is first in baseball with 69 Runs Saved over the same time period, and Dustin Pedroia leads all second basemen with 32 Runs Saved in that time. Josh Donaldson is tied with Pedroia over the last two seasons and led all third basemen with 20 Runs Saved in 2014.

With only the top five, you can't quite tell how impressive Jason Heyward's 15.3 Scout's Defensive Rating really is. However, he, Alex Gordon, and Jacoby Ellsbury are the only three outfielders in the top 25 of all players.

Outfielders, it would seem, have a very different distribution of plays. While shortstops had roughly an even distribution of plays rated 2-5, center fielders (for example) have far more 5's than 2-4. In other words, outfielders have many plays which are guaranteed outs or guaranteed hits, and there are far fewer plays for individual outfielders to distinguish themselves from each other.

Center Field Plays, 2014

Grade	Plays	Made Plays	Pct
1	9,692	9,662	100%
2	1,965	1,899	97%
3	692	478	69%
4	1,643	253	15%
5	5,286	0	0%

The decline from Heyward and Gordon at 15.3 and 14.5 SDR, respectively, to the rest of the field of outfielders is pretty dramatic. Here is the top five:.

Fielder	Pos	Total Plays	Rating
J. Heyward	RF	413	15.3
A. Gordon	LF	381	14.5
J. Ellsbury	CF	421	9.4
K. Kiermaier	RF	155	7.0
B. Hamilton	CF	380	7.0

Here is a summary of the top and bottom players at each position:

Pos	Top Fielder	Rating	Bottom Fielder	Rating
P	H. Alvarez	4.1	J. Familia	-4.1
C	R. Martin	2.4	J. Saltalamacchia	-3.6
1B	Y. Alonso	11.0	J. Singleton	-10.2
2B	D. Pedroia	17.3	D. Murphy	-11.0
3B	N. Arenado	25.3	N. Castellanos	-18.3
SS	A. Simmons	17.4	H. Ramirez	-15.6
LF	A. Gordon	14.5	Y. Cespedes	-8.5
CF	J. Ellsbury	9.4	B. Upton	-12.2
RF	J. Heyward	15.3	D. Viciedo	-6.7

Nick Castellanos, at -18.3 plays, rates as the worst fielder by this rating. Similarly, his -30 Runs Saved was worst in baseball.

Comparison to Objective Ratings

In addition to the standalone ratings presented above, the Scout's Defensive Rating system can provide interesting insights when compared with objective defensive metrics. Before we dig into a few examples, however, we should highlight the caveats that come with such comparisons.

Of course, SDR only evaluates fielders on their ability to convert batted balls into outs. Other aspects of defensive play, such as limiting opposing baserunners on stolen base attempts or base hits, turning double plays, blocking pitches in the dirt, or scooping low throws, are not included in this rating but are accounted for in Defensive Runs Saved, for example. Additionally, fielders are not credited for good pre-pitch positioning in SDR, but current objective systems do credit fielders for making plays outside of a normal fielder's range due to good positioning or instincts.

Additionally, Defensive Runs Saved translates a fielder's performance into the common currency of runs, while Scout's Defensive Rating does not have that luxury. A player preventing (or allowing) many extra-base hits may be insufficiently credited (or penalized) for his play.

Lastly, the Play Difficulty Grade is assigned to one primary fielder per play. However, on many plays there are multiple fielders who could have made the play. This could help or hurt a fielder, depending on who is playing around him and how they collaborate on balls hit between them. By contrast, most objective metrics, including Defensive Runs Saved, can assign a penalty to multiple fielders on a play if the situation calls for it.

For the large majority of players, the Scout's Defensive Rating validates the Range and Positioning

System. Here are a few examples:

Billy Hamilton and Kevin Kiermaier—Hamilton finished second in the NL Rookie of the Year vote, and his speed was a major asset for him defensively. He finished in the top five among center fielders by both Defensive Runs Saved and Scout's Defensive Rating.

Kiermaier never stood a chance in the Rookie of the Year vote with players like Jose Abreu and Masahiro Tanaka in the mix, but he was impressive with his bat and as advertised with the glove in 2014. Kiermaier saved the Rays a combined 14 runs split between center and right field in little more than half a season in the majors. He combined for 7.9 SDR at the two positions.

Adam Jones and Matt Kemp—Adam Jones secured his third consecutive Gold Glove Award in 2014, and between he and Matt Kemp, they have six total in their careers. However, our subjective SDR can't justify the hardware, with the duo sitting in the bottom 10 of center fielders. When both the subjective and objective assessments concur, we have to wonder if their offensive production is artificially boosting their Gold Glove chances.

Zack Cozart—The light-hitting Zack Cozart rarely receives the attention his quality defensive play deserves, but both our objective and subjective ratings agree that Cozart was excellent at shortstop in 2014. He finished second to Andrelton Simmons in both measures.

Rickie Weeks—The Brewers did a nice job of limiting Rickie Weeks' defensive exposure in 2014 by deploying him in a platoon with the left-handed hitting Scooter Gennett. However, in just 449.1 innings, Weeks found his way to the bottom three in DRS and SDR among second basemen.

In a few other cases, however, the SDR disagrees with objective metrics for one reason or another:

Wilin Rosario—Catchers do not have to make nearly as many fielding plays on batted balls as other defensive players. Rosario's excellent rating in this instance is a result of mostly just four difficult plays he converted.

In each case, Rosario demonstrated nice athleticism such that you would expect him to be a good defender. However, catcher DRS is made up of a variety of components that capture a catcher's ability to control the running game, block pitches in the dirt, and draw extra strike calls. Rosario is particularly poor in the latter two skills, and that is what is generally responsible for his poor DRS totals each season.

Robinson Cano—It's quite possible Robinson Cano simply had a down defensive year in his first in Seattle. After all, he had saved an average of 10 runs per season over the previous four with the Yankees before he was neutral in 2014 with the Mariners. Still, his -6.8 SDR is dramatically lower than even his neutral DRS total.

It's possible that discrepancy illustrates a key difference between objective and subjective measurements of defense, which is that fielders who make plays look easy or difficult can unconsciously make us believe those plays are easy or difficult. In Cano's case, all of his movement appears so effortless, he frequently makes challenging plays appear routine. The Play Difficulty Grades data supports that theory, as well. 67 percent of Cano's opportunities in 2014 were graded as 1s, much higher than the 55 overall percent of all second basemen. In some ways, Cano is the opposite of a player like Brandon Phillips, who frequently dives or flourishes on plays many fielders would field routinely, and in fact Phillips has had much better SDR totals than DRS totals dating back to 2013.

Yoenis Cespedes—Analogous to Wilin Rosario's discrepancy, Cespedes has disparate SDR and DRS totals because of a skill set that is not dominated by his defensive range. In Cespedes' case, his range is actually well below average, which explains his poor -8.5 SDR total, second worst among all outfielders. However, Cespedes has one of the best throwing arms in baseball. He threw out 14 baserunners in 2014 without the use of a relay man. All told, the contributions Cespedes made with his arm and his decision-making more than made up for his limited range and resulted in 11 Runs Saved, the third highest of any left fielder.

12-Year Register and Defensive Scouting Reports

In previous *Fielding Bibles*, we had two separate sections that provided insight into each player's defensive abilities. The first was a statistical Register detailing how each player had performed according to various Baseball Info Solutions advanced analytics. The second was a section dedicated to Defensive Scouting Reports describing the visual evaluations of BIS Video Scouts. For *The Fielding Bible—Volume IV*, we have combined those two sections to form the most comprehensive, in-depth summary of a player's defensive abilities available anywhere.

The 12-Year Register

This section of the book is grouped by position, and it includes tables with 12 years of data for every position player that spent 200 innings in the field and every pitcher that spent 50 innings on the mound in 2014. If a player logged more than 200 innings at multiple positions, he will show up at all those positions. The tables are organized into three main categories: basic data, position-specific evaluations, and each player's Runs Saved totals broken down by component.

The Basic section is the same for every position. We have games played, innings, total chances (abbreviated as TC), errors, and fielding percentage. Since Good Fielding Plays (GFP) and Defensive Misplays (DM) have become critical pieces to our evaluations, we also add these totals to the Basic section.

The Runs Saved columns are the final group of columns for all positions. These are the most important columns in the entire table. If you want to know who was good and who was bad, look here. Every applicable Runs Saved component for each position is displayed, followed by a player's Total Runs Saved and his ranking among other regulars at that position. Each component of Runs Saved has its own chapter in the Methodology section of this book beginning on page 319 which provides a complete explanation of the data. They are:

- Range and Positioning Runs Saved (R/P), which measures how a fielder combines his range with his initial positioning to convert batted balls into outs.
- Bunt Runs Saved (Bunt), which evaluates a corner infielder's or catcher's skill in converting bunts to outs.
- Double Play Runs Saved (GDP), which judges an infielder's ability to start and turn double plays.
- Outfield Arm Runs Saved (Throws), which assesses the run prevention ability of an outfielder's throwing arm.
- Adjusted Earned Runs Saved (Adj ER), which measures a catcher's pitcher handling ability behind the plate.
- Pitcher Stolen Base Runs Saved (SB), which evaluates the ability of a pitcher to control the running game.
- Catcher Stolen Base Runs Saved (SB), which evaluates the ability of a catcher to control the running game.
- Strike Zone Runs Saved (SZ), which measures a catcher's ability to get extra strikes called.
- Good Play/Misplay Runs Saved (GFP/DME), which measures the run impact of good plays and misplays that are not accounted for in other components of Runs Saved.

In this book we introduce several new metrics and techniques that have never been seen before. The data tables associated with each player include a mix of these new analytics with the old systems that were introduced in *Volumes I-III*. There are also terminology changes to various metrics and column headers that have been made. Because of the name change of the Plus/Minus System to Range and Positioning that was discussed in the Defensive Runs Saved section on page 11, anything that had been labeled as *Plus/Minus* is now called *Range and Positioning*. Also, columns that had been labeled as *+/-* (for pitchers), *Basic* (for outfielders), and *Total* (for infielders) in the register in *Volume III* are now called *Plays Saved*, and columns that had been labeled *Enhanced* are now called *Bases Saved*. The hope is that the information conveyed is more straight forward and more easily understandable.

For the position-specific sections of the register tables, we provide the following information:

Category	Position	Abbreviation	Explanation
Bunts	C, 1B, 3B	Opp	The number of opportunities he had to field a bunt
	C, 1B, 3B	Sac Hits	Any bunt in a sacrifice situation where the batter is credited with a sacrifice
	C, 1B, 3B	Bunt Hits	Hits in either sacrifice or non-sacrifice bunt situations
Pitcher Handling	C	W	Wins
	C	L	Losses
	C	Pct	Winning Percentage
	C	CERA	Catcher ERA
	C	Extra Strikes	The number of strikes called above or below average while he was catching
	C	Pitch Block	Catcher blocks of pitches in the dirt
Stolen Bases	C	SB	Stolen Bases
	C	CCS	Catcher Caught Stealings
	C	PCS	Pitcher Caught Stealings
	C	CPO	Catcher Pickoffs
	C	CS%	Caught Stealing Percent
	C	SB Saved	Stolen Bases Saved
GDP	Infield	Opp	Double play opportunities
	Infield	GDP	The number of successfully turned double plays
	Infield	Pct	Double play success rate
Range and Positioning	Infield, Outfield	Outs Made	Outs made
	Infield	To His Right	Plays Saved on balls hit to the right of where the average player at his position would start
	Infield	Straight On	Plays Saved on balls hit straight at where the average player at his position would start
	Infield	To His Left	Plays Saved on balls hit to the left of where the average player at his position would start
	Infield	GB	Plays Saved on groundballs
	Infield	Air	Plays Saved on balls hit in the air
	Outfield	Shallow	Plays Saved on balls hit shallow in the outfield
	Outfield	Medium	Plays Saved on balls hit to medium depth in the outfield
	Outfield	Deep	Plays Saved on balls hit deep in the outfield
	Infield, Outfield	Plays Saved	Total Plays Saved relative to the average player at his position
	1B, 3B, Outfield	Based Saved	Total Bases Saved relative to the average player at his position

Defensive Scouting Reports

The Defensive Scouting Reports associated with each player are also bigger and better than ever. No one watches more baseball than the BIS Video Scouts, which uniquely qualifies them to provide a visual evaluation of the strengths and weaknesses of each player's defensive game. Therefore, as with past volumes, the Video Scouts were invited to share their thoughts on the defensive skills of nearly 300 players. The Video Scouts who evaluated the players and wrote preliminary reports are: Joe Brehm, Dan Edwards, Dan Foehrenbach, Josh Hofer, Andy Houk, Andy Johnson, Ryan Klimek, Keanan Lamb, Spencer Moody, Kevin Morrissey, Chris Mosch, Jon Presser, Tucker Stobbe, Josh Tuchman, Zeke Turrentine and Ezra Wise. The reports went through a rigorous review process by John Dewan, Ben Jedlovec, Joe Rosales, Scott Spratt, and John Vrecsics to produce the Defensive Scouting Reports that appear in this book.

Scout's Defensive Rating

To accompany the data tables and scouting reports, we have also provided each player's Scout's Defensive Rating for the past two seasons on a separate line between the two (except for pitchers and catchers). The rating is based on the Play Difficulty Grades as determined by BIS Video Scouts. It is a subjective evaluation of a player's ability to convert batted balls into outs, and provides an interesting comparison to the objectively calculated metrics in the data tables. For more details on the Play Difficulty Grades and how they are used to calculate the Scout's Defensive Rating, see page 145 of this book.

Catchers Register and Scouting Reports

Year	Fielding Bible Award Winner	Runner Up	Third Place
2006	Ivan Rodriguez	Yadier Molina	Miguel Olivo
2007	Yadier Molina	Russell Martin	Joe Mauer
2008	Yadier Molina	Jason Kendall	Jose Molina
2009	Yadier Molina	Gerald Laird	Joe Mauer
2010	Yadier Molina	Carlos Ruiz	Kurt Suzuki
2011	Matt Wieters	Yadier Molina	Carlos Ruiz
2012	Yadier Molina	Matt Wieters	Ryan Hanigan
2013	Yadier Molina	Russell Martin	Salvador Perez
2014	Jonathan Lucroy	Russell Martin	Yadier Molina

Catchers

Alex Avila

	BASIC							BUNTS			PITCHER HANDLING						STOLEN BASES						RUNS SAVED						
Year	Team	G	Inn	TC	E	Pct	GFP	DM	Opps	Sac Hits	Bunt Hits	W	L	Pct	CERA	Extra Strikes	Pitch Block	SB	CCS	PCS	CPO	CS%	SB Saved	Adj ER	SB	Bunt	GFP/ DME	SZ	Total	Rank
2009	Det	25	153.1	108	0	1.000	0	4	2	1	1	8	9	.471	5.52	-	53	11	4	0	0	.27	0	-1	0	-1	-1	-	-3	-
2010	Det	98	756.2	594	4	.993	15	33	4	2	2	41	43	.488	4.47	42	253	43	20	0	0	.32	-2	-2	-2	-2	-2	5	-3	20
2011	Det	133	1157.0	1018	5	.995	20	59	11	6	2	78	52	.600	3.88	27	462	85	26	14	0	.23	-2	3	-2	0	-3	3	1	14
2012	Det	113	937.2	960	6	.994	9	34	5	2	2	60	47	.561	3.61	8	405	79	28	6	0	.26	3	3	2	-1	0	1	5	11
2013	Det	98	836.2	850	6	.993	7	33	8	2	3	61	35	.635	3.38	26	399	73	11	4	0	.13	-9	3	-7	0	-1	3	-2	19
2014	Det	122	1017.2	940	5	.995	7	32	3	0	1	67	49	.578	3.95	-24	571	71	26	10	0	.27	4	-1	2	0	4	-3	2	16
		589	4859.0	4470	26	.994	58	195	33	13	11	315	235	.573	3.90	79	2143	362	115	34	0	.24	-7	5	-7	-4	-3	9	0	-

At age 27, Avila should be close to peaking and better than ever behind the plate. Avila has a better than average pop time (1.91 seconds), but that has not always translated into results thanks to a pitching staff that hasn't controlled runners well. Avila is an extremely good pitch blocker. His pitch framing was a specialty the past few seasons, especially stealing strikes in the bottom of the zone, though he took a step back in 2014 in that department. The average arm and advanced blocking make Avila a valuable catcher, but the pitch framing is something to keep in mind going forward.

John Baker

	BASIC							BUNTS			PITCHER HANDLING						STOLEN BASES						RUNS SAVED						
Year	Team	G	Inn	TC	E	Pct	GFP	DM	Opps	Sac Hits	Bunt Hits	W	L	Pct	CERA	Extra Strikes	Pitch Block	SB	CCS	PCS	CPO	CS%	SB Saved	Adj ER	SB	Bunt	GFP/ DME	SZ	Total	Rank
2008	Fla	59	496.0	428	4	.991	4	14	6	3	1	27	27	.500	4.23	-	154	40	6	2	0	.13	-4	-1	-3	0	1	-	-3	22
2009	Fla	105	864.0	796	6	.992	9	31	10	3	2	54	45	.545	4.43	-	248	79	18	2	0	.19	-7	-3	-5	-1	-1	-	-10	33
2010	Fla	21	178.0	163	2	.988	3	5	1	1	0	10	10	.500	4.04	-1	55	22	5	1	0	.19	-2	0	-2	0	0	0	-2	-
2011	Fla	1	3.0	2	0	1.000	0	0				0	0		3.00	0	-	0	0	0	0		0	0	0	0	0	0	0	-
2012	SD	56	460.1	395	4	.990	3	21	5	2	1	24	28	.462	3.95	26	218	49	5	4	0	.09	-2	2	-2	0	-2	3	1	-
2013	SD	14	106.0	90	0	1.000	4	9	2	1	0	7	5	.583	3.74	3	47	8	5	0	0	.38	-2	0	-2	0	0	0	2	-
2014	ChC	55	463.0	469	2	.996	0	27	2	1	0	24	27	.471	3.40	-11	285	50	7	2	0	.12	-4	2	-3	0	-2	-1	-4	-
		311	2570.1	2343	18	.992	23	107	26	11	4	146	142	.507	4.06	17	1007	248	46	11	0	.16	-17	0	-13	-1	-4	2	-16	-

Christian Bethancourt

	BASIC							BUNTS			PITCHER HANDLING						STOLEN BASES						RUNS SAVED						
Year	Team	G	Inn	TC	E	Pct	GFP	DM	Opps	Sac Hits	Bunt Hits	W	L	Pct	CERA	Extra Strikes	Pitch Block	SB	CCS	PCS	CPO	CS%	SB Saved	Adj ER	SB	Bunt	GFP/ DME	SZ	Total	Rank
2014	Atl	31	260.1	234	3	.987	2	9	7	5	0	13	16	.448	3.70	-18	131	10	3	2	0	.23	1	-1	0	-1	0	-2	-4	-

Drew Butera

	BASIC							BUNTS			PITCHER HANDLING						STOLEN BASES						RUNS SAVED						
Year	Team	G	Inn	TC	E	Pct	GFP	DM	Opps	Sac Hits	Bunt Hits	W	L	Pct	CERA	Extra Strikes	Pitch Block	SB	CCS	PCS	CPO	CS%	SB Saved	Adj ER	SB	Bunt	GFP/ DME	SZ	Total	Rank
2010	Min	47	394.2	332	5	.985	4	15	1	0	0	22	22	.500	4.10	8	135	21	14	2	0	.40	6	-1	4	0	0	1	4	-
2011	Min	93	670.2	461	5	.989	8	26	8	3	0	27	48	.360	4.95	-71	272	48	20	2	2	.29	3	-6	3	2	-1	-8	-10	25
2012	Min	41	298.2	258	1	.996	6	15	2	0	0	15	17	.469	4.04	-20	148	23	4	3	0	.15	1	1	0	1	-1	-2	-1	-
2013	2 tms	4	15.0	6	0	1.000	0	0				1	0	1.000	3.60	-1	6	0	0	0	0		0	0	0	0	0	0	0	-
2014	LAD	57	445.1	464	0	1.000	7	15	3	1	0	28	20	.583	3.38	30	264	23	9	2	2	.28	2	-1	2	0	0	4	5	-
		242	1824.1	1521	11	.993	25	71	14	4	0	93	107	.465	4.22	-54	825	115	47	9	4	.29	12	-7	9	3	-2	-5	-2	-

Curt Casali

	BASIC							BUNTS			PITCHER HANDLING						STOLEN BASES						RUNS SAVED						
Year	Team	G	Inn	TC	E	Pct	GFP	DM	Opps	Sac Hits	Bunt Hits	W	L	Pct	CERA	Extra Strikes	Pitch Block	SB	CCS	PCS	CPO	CS%	SB Saved	Adj ER	SB	Bunt	GFP/ DME	SZ	Total	Rank
2014	TB	29	207.1	224	1	.996	1	14	1	0	0	13	9	.591	2.52	3	140	13	2	2	1	.13	-1	1	0		-1	0	0	-

Welington Castillo

	BASIC							BUNTS			PITCHER HANDLING						STOLEN BASES						RUNS SAVED						
Year	Team	G	Inn	TC	E	Pct	GFP	DM	Opps	Sac Hits	Bunt Hits	W	L	Pct	CERA	Extra Strikes	Pitch Block	SB	CCS	PCS	CPO	CS%	SB Saved	Adj ER	SB	Bunt	GFP/ DME	SZ	Total	Rank
2010	ChC	5	44.0	36	0	1.000	1	4				2	3	.400	4.30	-5	17	3	2	0	0	.40	1	0	1		-1	-1	-1	-
2011	ChC	4	31.2	20	2	.900	0	2				0	4	.000	5.97	-4	21	1	2	0	0	.67	1	0	0		0	0	0	-
2012	ChC	49	413.2	376	7	.981	4	19				10	36	.217	4.83	-39	245	33	7	4	1	.18	0	0	0	1	-5		-4	-
2013	ChC	111	956.0	825	10	.988	19	88	12	5	0	42	65	.393	4.02	-95	631	67	21	7	4	.24	4	4	4	1	5	-11	3	12
2014	ChC	106	916.1	883	6	.993	10	48	14	7	1	44	59	.427	4.21	-73	605	57	26	2	4	.31	7	-6	6	0	1	-9	-8	28
		275	2361.2	2140	25	.988	34	111	26	12	1	98	167	.370	4.27	-216	1519	161	58	13	9	.26	13	-2	11	1	6	-26	-10	-

Castillo may be one of the most contradictory catchers defensively. Castillo's control of the running game is excellent, as he threw out 26 baserunners attempting to steal in 2014 thanks to a fast pop time. He also successfully picked off four baserunners. However, Castillo struggled mightily with pitch framing, costing his pitchers 73 strikes over the course of the season and finishing with -9 Strike Zone Runs Saved. His pitch blocking skills are outstanding, thanks to some significant progress in that department before the 2013 season. However, Castillo does not receive high marks for his handling of the Cubs' pitching staff. At the same time, Castillo has shown that he is not afraid to pounce on a ball

Catchers

in front of the plate, leading all catchers with 93 assists despite playing the 16th-most innings. When you add all this together, you realize that his weaknesses slightly outweigh his strengths, but with some helpful coaching on pitch framing, Castillo could be an above average contributor at the position.

Jason Castro

		BASIC							BUNTS			PITCHER HANDLING						STOLEN BASES						RUNS SAVED						
Year	Team	G	Inn	TC	E	Pct	GFP	DM	Opps	Sac Hits	Bunt Hits	W	L	Pct	CERA	Extra Strikes	Pitch Block	SB	CCS	PCS	CPO	CS%	SB Saved	Adj ER	SB	Bunt	GFP/DME	SZ	Total	Rank
2010	Hou	67	509.1	485	2	.996	6	27	6	4	2	23	34	.404	3.92	18	222	31	17	1	0	.35	3	0	2	-1	-3	2	0	
2012	Hou	79	646.2	571	13	.989	7	41	7	4	0	27	46	.370	4.34	-62	353	57	12	1	0	.17	-1	3	-1	0	-5	-7	-8	28
2013	Hou	98	827.1	679	5	.993	8	35	11	8	1	32	63	.337	4.84	-34	486	58	17	2	0	.23	0	0	0	-2	1	-4	-5	20
2014	Hou	114	971.0	826	4	.995	4	39	5	2	1	46	64	.418	4.16	31	634	81	21	2	0	.21	-1	-3	-2	0	3	4	2	16
		358	2954.1	2561	17	.993	25	142	29	18	4	128	207	.382	4.35	-47	1695	227	67	6	0	.23	1	0	-1	-3	-2	-5	-11	

With a pitching staff full of younger talent, Castro has been the "old guy" gaining the trust of his pitchers. He has done this through raising their confidence in his pitch calling as well as through his improved pitch framing over the last three seasons, which was a focus of his work with the Astros' coaching staff this past year. The improvement was very noticeable and was evident in his numbers. It should also be noted that he also shaved a few milliseconds off his pop time, allowing him to get a few more runners out on the base paths. He also shows a quick reaction time to pop ups in and out of fair territory, and if there is a play to be made, he will make every effort to get to it. In addition, he also is up quickly out of his crouch on bunt grounders and will usually get an out if he fields the ball. Nonetheless, while he has made great improvements, he still has many more to make. Though the pitcher's delivery time directly affects if he will have an opportunity to record outs on stolen bases, his arm is the second biggest factor. So, though he makes the plays close on a number of occasions, if he wants to reduce the stolen bases against him, he needs to improve his throws even further. On top of this, he needs to improve his handling of pitches in the dirt to become a better than average defender behind the plate.

Francisco Cervelli

		BASIC							BUNTS			PITCHER HANDLING						STOLEN BASES						RUNS SAVED						
Year	Team	G	Inn	TC	E	Pct	GFP	DM	Opps	Sac Hits	Bunt Hits	W	L	Pct	CERA	Extra Strikes	Pitch Block	SB	CCS	PCS	CPO	CS%	SB Saved	Adj ER	SB	Bunt	GFP/DME	SZ	Total	Rank
2008	NYY	3	13.2	11	0	1.000	0	0				0	1	.000	7.90	-	7	1	0	0	0	.00	0	0	0		0	-	0	-
2009	NYY	40	241.1	222	1	.995	4	6	2	1	0	17	8	.680	3.43	-	61	13	8	2	0	.38	3	1	2	0	2	-	5	-
2010	NYY	90	724.0	637	13	.980	9	39	7	3	1	44	36	.550	4.34	33	270	55	8	1	1	.13	-6	3	-4	1	-3	4	1	17
2011	NYY	41	316.1	302	6	.980	5	13				25	10	.714	3.50	26	155	24	4	0	0	.14	-5	1	-3		1	3	2	-
2012	NYY	3	5.0	8	0	1.000	0	1				0	0	-	0.00	1	2	0	0	0	0	-	0	0	0	0	0	0	0	-
2013	NYY	17	138.0	131	4	.969	0	2	1	0	0	10	6	.625	3.13	4	53	2	1	1	0	.33	0	1	0	0	0	0	1	-
2014	NYY	42	348.0	356	1	.997	1	14	5	0	2	18	21	.462	3.88	27	191	18	5	1	0	.22	-1	0	-1	-1	1	3	2	-
		236	1786.1	1667	25	.985	19	75	15	4	3	114	82	.582	3.78	91	739	113	26	5	1	.19	-9	6	-6	0	1	10	11	-

Robinson Chirinos

		BASIC							BUNTS			PITCHER HANDLING						STOLEN BASES						RUNS SAVED						
Year	Team	G	Inn	TC	E	Pct	GFP	DM	Opps	Sac Hits	Bunt Hits	W	L	Pct	CERA	Extra Strikes	Pitch Block	SB	CCS	PCS	CPO	CS%	SB Saved	Adj ER	SB	Bunt	GFP/DME	SZ	Total	Rank
2011	TB	19	132.0	123	0	1.000	1	3				8	7	.533	4.43	-18	64	21	2	0	0	.09	-1	0	-1		1	-2	-2	-
2013	Tex	3	27.0	22	0	1.000	0	0				3	0	1.000	3.67	-2	7	0	0	0	0	-	0	0	0		0	0	0	-
2014	Tex	91	784.0	634	4	.994	9	28	5	1	1	36	52	.409	4.59	-37	359	44	25	4	3	.36	5	-1	5	0	1	-4	1	19
		113	943.0	779	4	.995	10	31	5	1	1	47	59	.443	4.54	-57	430	65	27	4	3	.29	4	-1	4	0	2	-6	-1	-

Robinson Chirinos has the build and body of a catcher. His main strength behind the plate is throwing out runners and controlling the running game. His pop time is above average, but it's his raw arm strength that is truly elite and overcomes mediocre footwork. As a result, Chirinos nabbed 25 runners and picked another three off. On the other hand, he is not a good pitch framer and loses extra strikes. His ability to control the running game is valuable, but he will need to improve his framing to take the next step in his catching game.

Catchers

Hank Conger

		BASIC						BUNTS			PITCHER HANDLING						STOLEN BASES						RUNS SAVED						
Year	Team	G	Inn	TC	E	Pct	GFP	DM	Opps	Sac Hits	Bunt Hits	W	L	Pct	CERA	Extra Strikes	Pitch Block	SB	CCS	PCS	CPO	CS%	SB Saved	Adj ER	SB	Bunt	GFP/DME	SZ	Total	Rank
2010	LAA	10	80.0	69	3	.957	1	1				7	2	.778	1.91	-2	22	7	1	1	0	.13	-1	0	-1		0	0	-1	-
2011	LAA	56	450.0	355	6	.983	7	20	5	3	0	24	24	.500	3.84	17	233	53	10	2	1	.16	-5	-1	-3	0	2	2	0	-
2012	LAA	7	55.0	53	1	.981	0	2	1	0	0	2	4	.333	4.75	3	19	6	2	0	0	.25	0	0	0	0	0	0	0	-
2013	LAA	71	535.0	517	7	.986	6	43	6	3	0	33	27	.550	3.67	80	320	47	13	2	0	.22	-1	2	-1	0	-2	9	8	8
2014	LAA	79	637.1	643	7	.989	3	34	9	0	1	42	28	.600	3.35	131	340	57	14	4	0	.20	-2	3	-2	1	-1	16	17	3
		223	1757.1	1637	24	.985	17	100	21	6	1	108	85	.560	3.55	229	934	170	40	9	1	.19	-9	4	-7	1	-1	27	24	-

If the pitcher paints, than the catcher is the canvas. Hank Conger was arguably the best canvas in the majors this year. Games where he was behind the plate usually lacked the ominous glares between pitcher and home plate umpire due to Conger's elite framing abilities. How elite? Conger's 131 extra strikes were good for second most in the majors, behind only Mike Zunino who needed nearly 500 more innings behind the dish to reach his mark of 133. The two catchers tied to lead the league with 16 Strike Zone Runs Saved. While Conger was one of the best at receiving pitches, he was also adept at giving away bases. Conger often looked relatively sluggish coming out of his crouch on stolen base attempts. His poor pop time, averaging 2.02 seconds to second base, is among the slowest in baseball. Baserunners were taking advantage of this inadequacy, reaching first with their sights on second. As a result, Conger averaged the second-highest rate of stolen base attempts. An improvement in this deficient area, combined with his potency for stealing strikes, would have Conger challenging for the top spot for Defensive Runs Saved.

Carlos Corporan

		BASIC						BUNTS			PITCHER HANDLING						STOLEN BASES						RUNS SAVED						
Year	Team	G	Inn	TC	E	Pct	GFP	DM	Opps	Sac Hits	Bunt Hits	W	L	Pct	CERA	Extra Strikes	Pitch Block	SB	CCS	PCS	CPO	CS%	SB Saved	Adj ER	SB	Bunt	GFP/DME	SZ	Total	Rank
2009	Mil	1	2.0	3	0	1.000	0	0				0	0	-	0.00		1	0	0	0	0		0	0	0			0	0	-
2011	Hou	50	411.1	407	6	.985	5	20	4	4	0	14	32	.304	4.00	44	245	43	9	0	0	.17	-2	1	-1	-1	2	5	6	-
2012	Hou	24	185.2	189	2	.989	4	12	4	3	0	6	16	.273	4.85	41	117	14	5	2	1	.26	0	0	0	0	1	5	6	-
2013	Hou	57	449.2	379	6	.984	5	17	5	1	1	15	36	.294	4.80	40	212	31	10	0	1	.24	-1	0	-1	0	3	5	7	-
2014	Hou	54	431.2	387	3	.992	3	25	4	2	1	23	25	.479	4.07	24	280	25	6	1	0	.19	-1	0	-1	0	0	3	2	-
		186	1480.1	1365	17	.988	17	74	17	10	2	58	109	.347	4.37	149	855	113	30	3	2	.21	-4	1	-3	-1	6	18	21	-

Tony Cruz

		BASIC						BUNTS			PITCHER HANDLING						STOLEN BASES						RUNS SAVED						
Year	Team	G	Inn	TC	E	Pct	GFP	DM	Opps	Sac Hits	Bunt Hits	W	L	Pct	CERA	Extra Strikes	Pitch Block	SB	CCS	PCS	CPO	CS%	SB Saved	Adj ER	SB	Bunt	GFP/DME	SZ	Total	Rank
2011	StL	20	99.0	96	0	1.000	1	8	3	3	0	5	3	.625	3.00	1	52	2	2	0	0	.50	0	0	0	-1	-1	0	-2	-
2012	StL	47	293.1	280	2	.993	3	9	6	2	2	12	16	.429	4.14	7	147	18	8	0	0	.31	-1	-1	-1	-1	1	1	-1	-
2013	StL	44	267.0	249	1	.996	2	7	2	1	0	14	14	.500	4.11	-8	129	12	6	0	0	.33	-1	-1	-1	0	1	-1	-2	-
2014	StL	47	325.0	291	1	.997	1	12	5	2	1	19	16	.543	4.07	-40	144	18	5	1	0	.22	-2	-1	-2	0	-1	-5	-9	-
		158	984.1	916	4	.996	7	36	16	8	3	50	49	.505	4.00	-40	472	50	21	1	0	.30	-4	-3	-4	-2	0	-5	-14	-

Travis d'Arnaud

		BASIC						BUNTS			PITCHER HANDLING						STOLEN BASES						RUNS SAVED						
Year	Team	G	Inn	TC	E	Pct	GFP	DM	Opps	Sac Hits	Bunt Hits	W	L	Pct	CERA	Extra Strikes	Pitch Block	SB	CCS	PCS	CPO	CS%	SB Saved	Adj ER	SB	Bunt	GFP/DME	SZ	Total	Rank
2013	NYM	30	258.1	224	0	1.000	3	14	3	1	0	11	19	.367	4.11	22	96	19	5	0	0	.21	0	-1	0	0	-1	3	1	-
2014	NYM	105	909.0	876	9	.990	10	46	10	4	1	47	56	.456	3.68	56	383	58	9	5	0	.13	-5	-5	-4	-2	-4	7	-8	28
		135	1167.1	1100	9	.992	13	60	13	5	1	58	75	.436	3.78	78	479	77	14	5	0	.15	-5	-6	-4	-2	-5	10	-7	-

You wouldn't know it from his defensive numbers, but d'Arnaud has good hands, quick feet, and showed flashes of an above average arm as he came through the minor leagues. The one area where d'Arnaud has excelled early in his career is in pitch framing. Oddly enough, his great strength also magnifies his greatest weaknesses. d'Arnaud was tied for last in the league with 12 passed balls and rated as one of the worst catchers at blocking balls in the dirt. d'Arnaud is often times caught trying to prematurely move his glove back toward the strike zone to frame a pitch on the corner, which often leads to passed balls. He also commits too often to backhanding low pitches, believing he can pull them up to the knees. However, when the ball does hit the dirt, he is not in position to drop down and block it, which leads to more wild pitches. d'Arnaud's throwing also deteriorated as the season wore on. His pop times were still around league average, but the ball didn't appear to have the same zip and his accuracy noticeably waned in the second half. d'Arnaud did have surgery to remove bone chips after the 2014 season, so Mets fans will have to hope that was a major factor in his throwing struggles last season.

A.J. Ellis

		BASIC							BUNTS			PITCHER HANDLING						STOLEN BASES						RUNS SAVED						
Year	Team	G	Inn	TC	E	Pct	GFP	DM	Opps	Sac Hits	Bunt Hits	W	L	Pct	CERA	Extra Strikes	Pitch Block	SB	CCS	PCS	CPO	CS%	SB Saved	Adj ER	SB	Bunt	GFP/DME	SZ	Total	Rank
2008	LAD	3	10.0	8	0	1.000	1	0				0	1	.000	4.50	-	7	0	0	0	0	.	0	0	0		0	-	0	-
2009	LAD	7	27.2	38	0	1.000	0	1				1	1	.500	3.25	-	15	0	0	0	0	.00	0	0	0		0	-	0	-
2010	LAD	43	308.2	286	1	.997	1	16	2	2	0	14	20	.412	4.14	-33	95	26	8	2	0	.24	-1	0	0	0	-2	-4	-6	-
2011	LAD	29	221.2	178	0	1.000	0	10	1	0	0	14	11	.560	3.61	-18	75	11	2	2	0	.15	-1	0	-1	0	-1	-2	-4	-
2012	LAD	131	1151.0	1100	6	.995	10	44	16	7	1	67	61	.523	3.30	-68	463	74	28	8	1	.27	3	2	2	-1	-1	-8	-6	25
2013	LAD	113	972.1	931	3	.997	8	43	11	7	3	60	49	.550	3.05	-39	424	35	24	4	0	.41	7	1	4	-1	-3	-5	-4	25
2014	LAD	92	773.2	809	4	.995	8	34	8	3	0	58	31	.652	3.23	-62	420	48	13	3	1	.21	-2	0	-2	0	3	-7	-6	27
		418	3465.0	3350	14	.996	28	148	38	19	4	214	174	.552	3.31	-220	1499	195	75	19	2	.28	6	3	3	-2	-4	-26	-26	-

After nine years in pro ball, Ellis finally became a regular in 2012, thanks in part to his patience at the plate, but also due to his defense and rapport with his pitchers. Ellis will have a plan for every at-bat of each game he catches, and is always a threat to shut down the other club's running game. Ellis has never shown an advanced knack for pitch framing and consequently loses a fair amount of measurable defensive value, but it's his hard work and reliability that his pitchers love him for. He has never had much of an arm, but has steadily got his footwork down and has a quick release that helps slow would-be base thieves. Since the beginning of 2012 Ellis is tied for third in baseball with 65 runners hosed. Ellis isn't quite an elite, all-around catcher, but what he does do well he excels at, and the Dodgers have been better off for having him around.

Tyler Flowers

		BASIC							BUNTS			PITCHER HANDLING						STOLEN BASES						RUNS SAVED						
Year	Team	G	Inn	TC	E	Pct	GFP	DM	Opps	Sac Hits	Bunt Hits	W	L	Pct	CERA	Extra Strikes	Pitch Block	SB	CCS	PCS	CPO	CS%	SB Saved	Adj ER	SB	Bunt	GFP/DME	SZ	Total	Rank
2009	CWS	6	27.0	20	0	1.000	0	1				1	2	.333	5.67	-	11	2	0	0	0	.00	0	0	0		0	-	0	-
2010	CWS	7	31.2	31	0	1.000	0	3				2	1	.667	4.26	0	11	2	1	0	0	.33	0	0	0		0	0	0	-
2011	CWS	31	256.2	260	2	.992	1	10				16	12	.571	3.96	38	120	25	6	2	0	.19	1	1	1		1	4	7	-
2012	CWS	49	360.2	355	2	.994	0	14	1	0	0	18	22	.450	4.04	39	189	28	12	2	0	.30	5	0	4		1	5	10	-
2013	CWS	84	687.2	686	4	.994	2	26	7	5	0	28	49	.364	3.86	-3	260	52	13	3	0	.20	1	3	0	1	-3	0	1	16
2014	CWS	124	1052.0	941	8	.991	5	56	5	1	2	61	59	.508	3.97	69	000	62	22	4	0	.26	2	5	1	-1	-2	8	11	6
		301	2415.2	2293	16	.993	8	110	13	6	2	126	145	.465	3.97	143	1251	171	54	11	0	.24	9	9	6	0	-3	17	29	-

The first aspect that most will notice about Flowers' game is his pitch framing and the distinct low target that he gives to each and every pitcher that he works with on the staff. Flowers will set up with a target consistently below the strike zone in hopes of establishing the lower part of the zone. It reminds the pitchers to keep the ball down and allows Flowers to steal strikes on balls that are out of the zone. This works for Flowers in terms of the lower half of the strike zone, but he has trouble convincing the umpire of the high strike. His position is so distinct at the lower part of the zone that it's often too loud of a movement for Flowers when he tries to frame a high strike for the umpire. In addition to his receiving, he handles potential base stealers well thanks to a good release and quick footwork. A surprise of Flowers' game was the handling of his pitchers and how well they seemed to pitch to him. It was a tumultuous year for White Sox starting pitching, but with Flowers starting, they compiled a winning record and an ERA under 4.00.

Evan Gattis

		BASIC							BUNTS			PITCHER HANDLING						STOLEN BASES						RUNS SAVED						
Year	Team	G	Inn	TC	E	Pct	GFP	DM	Opps	Sac Hits	Bunt Hits	W	L	Pct	CERA	Extra Strikes	Pitch Block	SB	CCS	PCS	CPO	CS%	SB Saved	Adj ER	SB	Bunt	GFP/DME	SZ	Total	Rank
2013	Atl	42	349.2	307	2	.993	3	15	3	2	0	23	15	.605	2.99	26	139	16	8	0	0	.33	2	2	1	1	0	3	7	-
2014	Atl	93	799.0	777	5	.994	7	56	11	5	2	42	47	.472	3.30	19	453	53	13	0	0	.20	-2	2	-2	0	-3	2	-1	22
		135	1148.2	1084	7	.994	10	71	14	7	2	65	62	.512	3.20	45	592	69	21	0	0	.23	0	4	-1	1	-3	5	6	-

Attempting to fill Brian McCann's shoes as the Braves' regular catcher, Evan Gattis produced a relatively neutral defensive performance in 2014; however, he did display a few noteworthy attributes. His deficiencies were centered on the advancement of baserunners. Gattis gave runners on first a couple of options for advancing to second. The stolen base attempt was a good option, considering his poor 20 percent caught stealing rate and an average pop time of 1.93 seconds. Gattis also had runners advancing due to his difficulty with blocking wild pitches. In fact, his 48 wild pitch misplays was the third-most in baseball, leading to a Catcher Block Rate of 89 percent, which also ranked 32nd among 35 regulars. Although Gattis would occasionally cede ground to opposing baserunners, he was able to somewhat compensate with his proficiency for calling games behind the plate. He routinely offered the right signs to help his pitcher log quick innings. He was also able to aid his pitching staff by plucking a handful of extra strikes for the second straight year. Ultimately, Gattis should be considered an average defensive catcher, which is an accomplishment considering his

Catchers

atrocious performance in left field the previous year. Hopefully Houston's short porch in left will minimize the damage if he sees significant innings in left.

Chris Gimenez

		BASIC							BUNTS			PITCHER HANDLING						STOLEN BASES						RUNS SAVED						
Year	Team	G	Inn	TC	E	Pct	GFP	DM	Opps	Sac Hits	Bunt Hits	W	L	Pct	CERA	Extra Strikes	Pitch Block	SB	CCS	PCS	CPO	CS%	SB Saved	Adj ER	SB	Bunt	GFP/ DME	SZ	Total	Rank
2009	Cle	8	56.0	40	0	1.000	0	1				5	1	.833	4.18	-	15	4	1	0	0	.20	0	0	0		0	-	0	-
2010	Cle	24	168.2	124	1	.992	4	9	2	2	0	4	15	.211	4.54	5	65	23	9	2	0	.28	-1	0	-1	0	0	1	0	-
2011	Sea	20	152.0	120	0	1.000	4	7				4	13	.235	4.91	-3	53	14	6	0	0	.30	2	-1	1		1	0	1	-
2012	TB	39	266.0	277	3	.989	1	10	3	1	1	21	10	.677	3.21	-11	138	20	5	0	0	.20	1	0	1	0	1	-1	1	-
2013	TB	1	1.0	1	0	1.000	0	0				0	0	-	9.00	0	1	0	0	0	0	-	0	0	0		0	0	0	-
2014	2 tms	28	225.0	218	2	.991	1	19	1	1	0	11	15	.423	4.28	24	122	11	1	1	1	.08	-2	0	-1	0	-2	3	0	-
		120	868.2	780	6	.992	10	46	6	4	1	45	54	.455	4.11	15	394	72	22	3	1	.23	0	-1	0	0	0	3	2	

Yan Gomes

		BASIC							BUNTS			PITCHER HANDLING						STOLEN BASES						RUNS SAVED						
Year	Team	G	Inn	TC	E	Pct	GFP	DM	Opps	Sac Hits	Bunt Hits	W	L	Pct	CERA	Extra Strikes	Pitch Block	SB	CCS	PCS	CPO	CS%	SB Saved	Adj ER	SB	Bunt	GFP/ DME	SZ	Total	Rank
2012	Tor	9	49.1	35	0	1.000	0	4				2	3	.400	5.29	3	27	0	0	0	0	-	0	0	0		0	0	0	-
2013	Cle	85	710.0	731	3	.996	15	30	8	1	2	49	30	.620	3.56	81	273	29	18	2	4	.38	8	4	7	0	0	10	21	3
2014	Cle	126	1082.0	1139	14	.988	10	36	3	1	0	58	63	.479	3.70	50	636	66	27	4	1	.29	3	-5	2	0	5	6	8	8
		220	1841.1	1905	17	.991	25	70	11	2	2	109	96	.532	3.69	134	936	95	45	6	5	.32	11	-1	9	0	5	16	29	

Coming off the 2013 season where he finished third in Runs Saved among catchers, expectations were very high for Yan Gomes. Though the numbers regressed slightly back toward average, Gomes still showed all of the skills of a top flight defensive catcher. He had the fastest average pop time amongn regulars in 2014 and has very quick reactions behind the plate, which allows him to get to most balls hit in his area as well as throw out runners.

The drastic change from 2013 was his number of errors. After only committing 3 in 85 games in 2013, Gomes had 14 errors (second-most among catchers) in 126 games, including 12 on throws, often on stolen base attempts. He still has positive Stolen Base Runs Saved (+2) and Strike Zone Runs Saved (+6) that keep him tied for eighth in Defensive Runs Saved among everyday catchers with eight. Despite his throwing issues in 2014, Gomes is still a very young catcher with all of the tools to be a strong defender for many years.

Tuffy Gosewisch

		BASIC							BUNTS			PITCHER HANDLING						STOLEN BASES						RUNS SAVED						
Year	Team	G	Inn	TC	E	Pct	GFP	DM	Opps	Sac Hits	Bunt Hits	W	L	Pct	CERA	Extra Strikes	Pitch Block	SB	CCS	PCS	CPO	CS%	SB Saved	Adj ER	SB	Bunt	GFP/ DME	SZ	Total	Rank
2013	Ari	13	107.2	90	1	.989	1	2				5	6	.455	2.93	6	59					.33	0	0	0		1	1	2	-
2014	Ari	35	282.1	260	1	.996	6	9	7	4	1	11	20	.355	3.89	-9	137	11	7	1	0	.39	2	0	1	-1	1	-1	0	-
		48	390.0	350	2	.994	7	11	7	4	1	16	26	.381	3.62	-3	196	15	9	1	0	.38	2	0	1	-1	2	0	2	-

Yasmani Grandal

		BASIC							BUNTS			PITCHER HANDLING						STOLEN BASES						RUNS SAVED						
Year	Team	G	Inn	TC	E	Pct	GFP	DM	Opps	Sac Hits	Bunt Hits	W	L	Pct	CERA	Extra Strikes	Pitch Block	SB	CCS	PCS	CPO	CS%	SB Saved	Adj ER	SB	Bunt	GFP/ DME	SZ	Total	Rank
2012	SD	55	461.1	429	5	.988	9	12	9	3	2	31	21	.596	4.00	99	306	44	11	2	2	.20	-1	0	0	-1	4	12	15	-
2013	SD	26	231.0	208	2	.990	3	7	3	3	0	14	12	.538	3.78	30	109	11	1	0	0	.08	-2	0	-1	0	1	4	4	-
2014	SD	76	607.2	561	4	.993	7	37	10	5	0	32	35	.478	3.35	38	311	49	6	1	1	.11	-6	0	-4	1	-3	5	-1	22
		157	1300.0	1198	11	.991	19	56	22	11	2	77	68	.531	3.66	167	726	104	18	3	3	.15	-9	0	-5	0	2	21	18	-

Though Grandal has yet to see regular time behind the dish at the major league level, there are indications that he could be an asset at the position. Grandal has proven to be an excellent pitch framer. His 21 Strike Zone Runs Saved in 1300 career innings would put him among the best catchers in baseball in that regard if given regular playing time. Granted, it is a limited sample, but our research has shown pitch framing to be a very consistent skill, even in small samples. There are weaknesses in Grandal's defense, however. Despite a league average pop time, Grandal has trouble controlling the running game. Furthermore, Grandal posted the third-worst pitch block rate among players with at least 200 opportunities. Overall though, having only turned 26 years old this past November, Yasmani Grandal does still have a bright future behind the plate.

Catchers

Ryan Hanigan

	BASIC							BUNTS			PITCHER HANDLING						STOLEN BASES						RUNS SAVED						
Year	Team	G	Inn	TC	E	Pct	GFP	DM	Opps	Sac Hits	Bunt Hits	W	L	Pct	CERA	Extra Strikes	Pitch Block	SB	CCS	PCS	CPO	CS%	SB Saved	Adj ER	SB	Bunt	GFP/ DME	SZ	Total	Rank
2007	Cin	3	20.0	16	0	1.000	0	0			0	2	0	1.000	4.05	-	9	1	0	0	0	.00	0	0	0		0	-	0	-
2008	Cin	30	229.1	206	1	.995	2	7	4	3	0	14	11	.560	4.16	-	80	15	8	0	0	.35	-1	1	-1	0	0	-	0	-
2009	Cin	88	670.1	539	1	.998	10	24	12	6	1	34	38	.472	4.27	-	183	28	19	2	2	.40	2	0	2	0	0	-	2	16
2010	Cin	68	525.2	461	4	.991	2	10	3	3	0	38	20	.655	3.36	48	132	28	12	1	0	.30	0	5	0	0	1	6	12	-
2011	Cin	89	687.1	574	4	.993	8	23	4	3	0	38	35	.521	3.97	76	209	34	13	5	0	.28	-1	4	-1	0	-1	9	11	6
2012	Cin	110	877.0	833	4	.995	13	21	8	4	1	61	37	.622	3.04	110	310	34	26	6	1	.43	8	1	6	0	3	13	23	2
2013	Cin	72	589.2	572	1	.998	7	22	6	2	0	39	27	.591	3.40	9	181	18	12	3	0	.40	4	1	2	0	-2	1	2	18
2014	TB	79	603.2	573	1	.998	5	23	7	2	2	33	33	.500	3.50	1	374	30	6	2	0	.17	0	2	-1	0	3	0	4	15
		539	4203.0	3774	16	.996	47	130	44	23	4	259	201	.563	3.61	244	1478	188	96	19	3	.34	11	14	7	0	4	29	54	-

Ryan Hanigan had a solid first season as the backstop for the Tampa Bay Rays in 2014. Although his defensive numbers in 2013 and 2014 weren't quite on par with what we have seen from him in the past, he still possesses the skill set to get back to the upper echelon of defensive catchers. The biggest reason for this decline is he moved from one of the top catchers in pitch framing and controlling the running game down to league average. Part of this might be explained by learning a new staff and the Tampa Bay pitchers' relative struggles with holding runners as compared to their Cincinnati counterparts. Hanigan still posts above average pop times, and teams still respect his arm enough that their stolen base attempts against him given the number of opportunities they had was one of the lowest percentages in the majors. Hanigan also ranks among the league leaders in his ability to block balls in the dirt, as his Catcher Block Rate was sixth among the 36 catchers with at least 300 opportunities.

Bryan Holaday

	BASIC							BUNTS			PITCHER HANDLING						STOLEN BASES						RUNS SAVED						
Year	Team	G	Inn	TC	E	Pct	GFP	DM	Opps	Sac Hits	Bunt Hits	W	L	Pct	CERA	Extra Strikes	Pitch Block	SB	CCS	PCS	CPO	CS%	SB Saved	Adj ER	SB	Bunt	GFP/ DME	SZ	Total	Rank
2012	Det	6	37.0	27	0	1.000	1	1				1	2	.333	4.14	-3	23	3	0	1	0	.00	0	0	0		0	0	0	-
2013	Det	14	84.0	78	2	.974	1	3	1	0	0	3	5	.375	5.14	-12	56	12	1	0	0	.08	-1	0	-1	0	0	-1	-2	-
2014	Det	58	395.1	363	7	.981	4	18	3	1	1	21	21	.500	4.17	-39	205	33	13	1	1	.28	-1	-1	0	-1	-1	-5	-8	-
		78	516.1	468	9	.981	6	22	4	1	1	25	28	.472	4.32	-54	284	48	14	2	1	.23	-2	-1	-1	-1	-1	-6	-10	-

Nick Hundley

	BASIC							BUNTS			PITCHER HANDLING						STOLEN BASES						RUNS SAVED						
Year	Team	G	Inn	TC	E	Pct	GFP	DM	Opps	Sac Hits	Bunt Hits	W	L	Pct	CERA	Extra Strikes	Pitch Block	SB	CCS	PCS	CPO	CS%	SB Saved	Adj ER	SB	Bunt	GFP/ DME	SZ	Total	Rank
2008	SD	59	486.1	402	4	.990	10	18	8	3	0	21	34	.382	4.76	-	166	42	13	1	0	.24	3	-1	2	-1	1	-	1	-
2009	SD	74	643.1	556	6	.989	8	36	14	7	2	38	33	.535	4.00	-	214	56	10	4	0	.15	-4	5	-3	-1	-4	-	-3	19
2010	SD	76	659.2	664	4	.994	8	17	5	1	1	37	36	.507	3.72	-27	164	41	11	6	0	.21	-1	-5	-1	0	-1	-3	-10	30
2011	SD	76	654.1	567	6	.989	10	22	9	4	2	30	43	.411	3.53	-53	258	57	24	8	1	.30	3	-1	2	0	2	-6	-3	18
2012	SD	56	492.0	478	4	.992	7	25	9	3	0	20	36	.357	4.12	-79	237	54	19	6	1	.26	5	-1	3	2	1	-9	-4	-
2013	SD	112	928.0	802	10	.988	13	36	13	9	1	44	58	.431	4.26	-60	425	81	25	3	0	.24	2	-6	1	-1	1	-7	-12	29
2014	2 tms	63	508.0	468	2	.996	5	14	11	6	2	30	24	.556	3.49	4	238	31	5	0	1	.14	-5	-1	-3	-1	2	0	-3	24
		516	4371.2	3937	36	.991	66	168	69	33	8	220	264	.455	3.98	-215	1702	362	107	28	3	.23	2	-10	1	-2	2	-25	-34	-

Chris Iannetta

	BASIC							BUNTS			PITCHER HANDLING						STOLEN BASES						RUNS SAVED						
Year	Team	G	Inn	TC	E	Pct	GFP	DM	Opps	Sac Hits	Bunt Hits	W	L	Pct	CERA	Extra Strikes	Pitch Block	SB	CCS	PCS	CPO	CS%	SB Saved	Adj ER	SB	Bunt	GFP/ DME	SZ	Total	Rank
2006	Col	21	191.2	147	0	1.000	2	10	1	1	0	12	8	.600	6.10	-	44	18	3	0	0	.14	-1	-1	-1	0	-1	-	-3	-
2007	Col	60	496.2	329	1	.997	7	7	4	2	0	31	23	.574	4.71	-	151	33	8	2	1	.20	-1	-2	0	0	2	-	0	14
2008	Col	100	837.0	657	0	1.000	9	34	10	6	0	46	50	.479	4.61	-	246	41	8	4	1	.16	-2	2	-1	1	-2	-	0	18
2009	Col	89	763.2	606	5	.992	13	29	13	8	0	46	41	.529	4.21	-	252	50	15	3	1	.23	1	1	1	1	1	4	12	-
2010	Col	52	443.0	411	6	.985	5	21	12	8	1	23	26	.469	4.63	-32	180	35	6	4	1	.15	-4	-1	-2	1	-2	-4	-8	-
2011	Col	105	943.2	817	2	.998	10	41	9	6	0	51	54	.486	4.22	-68	417	70	26	4	1	.27	4	3	1	-1	-8	-1	14	-
2012	LAA	78	623.0	532	2	.996	7	23	1	1	0	41	30	.577	3.90	-53	309	46	13	3	0	.22	-1	-1	0	2	-6	-6	25	-
2013	LAA	113	921.2	781	5	.994	17	45	9	4	2	45	57	.441	4.58	-116	475	84	15	5	5	.15	-8	-4	-4	0	0	-14	-22	35
2014	LAA	104	835.1	782	2	.997	12	44	6	3	0	56	36	.609	3.74	-54	411	49	12	9	3	.20	-1	-4	0	-1	-3	-6	-14	30
		722	6055.2	5062	23	.995	82	254	65	39	3	351	325	.519	4.36	-323	2485	426	106	34	13	.20	-13	-6	-5	3	-4	-38	-50	-

Iannetta is a veteran catcher that only committed two errors in 2014. That is about the only positive aspect of his defensive game, though. He does not move well behind the plate and racked up 40 misplays on wild pitches, which was seventh-most in baseball. Among catchers with at least 300 block attempts, his block rate of 90.4 percent was sixth-worst. After allowing the second-most stolen bases in 2013 (84, for an 85 percent baserunner success rate), Iannetta improved slightly in 2014 (80 percent success rate).

Recent research has found that Iannetta has consistently lost a significant number of strikes with poor framing. In 2014 he lost 54 strikes, leading to -6 Strike Zone Runs Saved. That was actually an improvement over his 2013 season, when

Catchers

he lost over a strike per game (116 strikes lost in 113 games). Going into his age-32 season, Iannetta still leaves much to be desired defensively.

John Jaso

	BASIC							BUNTS			PITCHER HANDLING						STOLEN BASES						RUNS SAVED						
Year	Team	G	Inn	TC	E	Pct	GFP	DM	Opps	Sac Hits	Bunt Hits	W	L	Pct	CERA	Extra Strikes	Pitch Block	SB	CCS	PCS	CPO	CS%	SB Saved	Adj ER	SB	Bunt	GFP/ DME	SZ	Total	Rank
2008	TB	3	16.0	12	0	1.000	0	1				1	0	1.000	4.50	-	9	0	0	0	0	-	-	0	0	0	-	0	-	
2010	TB	96	719.0	646	5	.992	5	28	4	0	1	43	37	.538	3.87	-35	290	41	9	3	0	.18	-3	-1	-2	0	0	-4	-7	26
2011	TB	82	603.1	509	4	.992	6	30	5	3	2	39	28	.582	3.37	-78	240	50	8	2	0	.14	-4	2	-3	-1	-1	-9	-12	31
2012	Sea	43	343.1	278	0	1.000	0	22	1	0	0	20	19	.513	3.41	-23	114	27	6	1	0	.18	0	2	0	0	-3	-3	-4	
2013	Oak	48	364.1	284	3	.989	2	20	2	2	0	24	18	.571	3.66	-39	111	28	2	2	0	.07	-3	0	-2	0	-2	-5	-9	
2014	Oak	54	391.0	349	1	.997	0	22	2	0	1	27	20	.574	3.31	-25	182	32	4	0	0	.11	-4	1	-3	0	-1	-3	-6	
		326	2437.0	2078	13	.994	13	123	14	5	4	154	122	.558	3.56	-200	946	178	29	8	0	.14	-14	4	-10	-1	-7	-24	-38	

Caleb Joseph

	BASIC							BUNTS			PITCHER HANDLING						STOLEN BASES						RUNS SAVED						
Year	Team	G	Inn	TC	E	Pct	GFP	DM	Opps	Sac Hits	Bunt Hits	W	L	Pct	CERA	Extra Strikes	Pitch Block	SB	CCS	PCS	CPO	CS%	SB Saved	Adj ER	SB	Bunt	GFP/ DME	SZ	Total	Rank
2014	Bal	78	672.2	585	4	.993	8	25	9	3	1	47	30	.610	3.01	41	252	34	21	2	0	.38	7	4	5	1	-1	5	14	5

Never considered more than a fringe prospect in his days as a minor leaguer, Joseph provided much needed relief for the Orioles following the loss of organizational centerpiece Matt Wieters to a torn UCL early in the season. Joseph emerged as one of the best in baseball at neutralizing the opponent's running game as evidenced by his 38 percent success rate throwing out would-be base stealers. He owes this high success rate to a plus arm and a consistently quick release which both play up thanks to excellent footwork. As soon as Joseph sees a runner in motion, he gets his feet into an optimal throwing position. By the time he catches the ball, his shoulders are already perpendicular to the pitcher with his toes facing the first base dugout. This subtle time-saving mechanism is one of the reasons Joseph is able to consistently produce 1.9-second pop times to second base. The well-rounded Joseph also sports an above average block rate of 91.4 percent and was able to gain 41 extra strikes for his pitchers over the course of 672.2 innings caught. Joseph possesses above average quickness for a catcher, which allows him to pounce on bunts and softly hit grounders in front of the plate. While Joseph does not meet the offensive requirements traditionally associated with an everyday catcher, he could eventually find himself playing such a role thanks to the industry's heightened understanding of pitch receiving ability and the monumental impact an excellent receiving catcher can have on team run prevention.

Erik Kratz

	BASIC							BUNTS			PITCHER HANDLING						STOLEN BASES						RUNS SAVED						
Year	Team	G	Inn	TC	E	Pct	GFP	DM	Opps	Sac Hits	Bunt Hits	W	L	Pct	CERA	Extra Strikes	Pitch Block	SB	CCS	PCS	CPO	CS%	SB Saved	Adj ER	SB	Bunt	GFP/ DME	SZ	Total	Rank
2010	Pit	9	77.1	65	0	1.000	0	3	1	1	0	4	4	.500	4.42	8	28	3	4	0	0	.57	2	0	2	0	0	1	3	-
2011	Phi	1	10.0	10	0	1.000	1	0	1	0	0	0	1	.000	3.60	-1	2	1	0	0	0	.00	0	0	0	0	0	0	0	-
2012	Phi	41	343.1	366	1	.997	6	8	11	5	0	23	15	.605	3.43	31	116	18	12	3	1	.40	4	1	3	1	1	4	10	-
2013	Phi	60	478.1	441	1	.998	6	22	6	3	0	22	32	.407	4.61	18	212	33	6	3	1	.15	-3	-1	-2	0	-1	2	-2	-
2014	2 tms	36	225.0	198	0	1.000	0	5				11	12	.478	4.28	22	99	18	6	0	0	.25	1	0	1	0	1	2	4	-
		147	1134.0	1080	2	.998	13	38	19	9	0	60	64	.484	4.17	78	457	73	28	6	2	.28	4	0	4	1	1	9	15	-

Gerald Laird

	BASIC							BUNTS			PITCHER HANDLING						STOLEN BASES						RUNS SAVED						
Year	Team	G	Inn	TC	E	Pct	GFP	DM	Opps	Sac Hits	Bunt Hits	W	L	Pct	CERA	Extra Strikes	Pitch Block	SB	CCS	PCS	CPO	CS%	SB Saved	Adj ER	SB	Bunt	GFP/ DME	SZ	Total	Rank
2003	Tex	16	111.0	74	1	.986	-	-	1	1	0	5	7	.417	5.76	-	-	4	3	0	0	.43	0	0	0	0	-	0	-	
2004	Tex	49	397.0	299	5	.983	8	12	3	1	0	23	23	.500	4.40	-	120	17	12	2	0	.41	3	2	2	0	0	-	4	-
2005	Tex	13	99.0	69	3	.957	0	4	1	1	0	5	6	.455	5.00	-	19	8	3	0	0	.27	-1	0	-1	0	0	-	-1	-
2006	Tex	71	578.1	427	5	.988	2	18	4	1	1	31	34	.477	4.39	-	108	25	19	2	1	.43	5	0	4	0	-1	-	3	9
2007	Tex	119	987.1	762	12	.984	15	30	8	2	1	53	61	.465	4.78	-	414	59	39	0	1	.40	9	0	7	1	3	-	11	3
2008	Tex	81	753.0	566	8	.986	2	29	2	2	0	43	43	.500	5.21	-	258	53	20	1	0	.27	2	5	1	0	-2	-	4	7
2009	Det	135	1090.1	925	3	.997	14	36	9	5	0	65	58	.528	4.23	-	374	59	40	2	2	.40	9	-2	7	0	0	-	5	7
2010	Det	87	670.2	573	5	.991	6	34	8	3	2	39	37	.513	4.11	-43	218	58	24	6	0	.29	-2	2	-2	-1	-3	-5	-9	26
2011	StL	31	213.0	197	3	.985	1	10	7	4	0	13	9	.591	3.51	-5	102	16	3	1	0	.16	-1	0	-1	-1	-1	-1	-4	-
2012	Det	56	429.0	419	4	.990	4	16	2	1	0	26	23	.531	4.01	-46	188	42	7	3	1	.14	-5	-2	-3	0	0	-5	-10	-
2013	Atl	40	294.1	257	0	1.000	5	19	5	3	0	13	20	.394	3.94	-40	113	16	7	2	1	.30	1	-2	1	1	-2	-5	-7	-
2014	Atl	48	377.2	369	2	.995	6	19	1	0	0	23	19	.548	3.34	-56	214	30	10	1	0	.25	1	0	1	0	-1	-7	-7	-
		753	6000.2	4937	51	.990	63	227	51	24	5	339	340	.499	4.39	-190	2128	387	187	20	6	.33	19	3	16	0	-7	-23	-11	-

Catchers

Jose Lobaton

	BASIC							BUNTS			PITCHER HANDLING						STOLEN BASES						RUNS SAVED						
Year Team	G	Inn	TC	E	Pct	GFP	DM	Opps	Sac Hits	Bunt Hits	W	L	Pct	CERA	Extra Strikes	Pitch Block	SB	CCS	PCS	CPO	CS%	SB Saved	Adj ER	SB	Bunt	GFP/DME	SZ	Total	Rank
2009 SD	6	44.0	55	1	.982	1	1	1	1	0	0	5	.000	5.32	-	15	2	1	0	0	.33	0	0	0	0	0	-	0	-
2011 TB	14	88.0	94	1	.989	0	2				5	4	.556	2.45	14	46	7	2	1	0	.22	0	0	0	0	1	2	3	-
2012 TB	66	467.0	480	4	.992	5	20	5	1	0	27	23	.540	3.24	13	225	42	7	1	0	.14	-2	-1	-1	0	-1	2	-1	-
2013 TB	96	713.2	686	3	.996	3	31	2	0	0	46	30	.605	3.73	12	405	63	9	1	1	.13	-4	-1	-3	0	1	1	-2	20
2014 Was	64	538.2	545	2	.996	5	15	5	5	0	38	20	.655	2.86	6	292	27	11	2	0	.29	2	1	1	0	3	1	6	14
	246	1851.1	1860	11	.994	14	69	13	7	0	116	82	.586	3.33	45	983	141	30	5	1	.18	-4	-1	-3	0	4	6	6	-

José Lobaton played 64 games and 538.2 innings behind the plate for the Nationals in 2014, and he may have had the best defensive season of his career. A bit of a late bloomer as he just finished his age-29 season, he's good at stealing a few extra strikes for his pitchers each season. Lobaton is not all that good at controlling the running game thanks to a below average pop time of 1.99, but he did improve in that regard in 2014. That led to a +1 Stolen Base Runs Saved for Lobaton, the first time in his career he was above average in that metric. Lobaton also had fewer Defensive Misplays and Errors in 2014 than he'd had in the past, and ultimately graded out to a solid +6 Defensive Runs Saved (DRS). That was good enough for 14th-best among all catchers, and a marked improvement over his -1 DRS in 2012 and -2 in 2013. All in all, it was a very successful first season in Washington for José Lobaton.

Jonathan Lucroy

	BASIC							BUNTS			PITCHER HANDLING						STOLEN BASES						RUNS SAVED						
Year Team	G	Inn	TC	E	Pct	GFP	DM	Opps	Sac Hits	Bunt Hits	W	L	Pct	CERA	Extra Strikes	Pitch Block	SB	CCS	PCS	CPO	CS%	SB Saved	Adj ER	SB	Bunt	GFP/DME	SZ	Total	Rank
2010 Mil	75	655.0	663	5	.992	4	37	6	5	0	36	38	.486	4.40	162	521	37	15	2	0	.29	3	-1	2	0	2	19	22	2
2011 Mil	132	1043.2	1046	7	.993	10	65	7	2	1	68	46	.596	3.63	195	647	77	21	9	0	.21	-5	-1	0	0	0	23	19	3
2012 Mil	88	717.1	755	7	.991	10	31	4	2	0	41	39	.513	4.25	123	514	70	16	3	0	.19	-2	-2	-2	0	5	15	16	3
2013 Mil	126	1074.0	921	8	.991	13	38	14	8	3	56	66	.459	4.06	121	558	80	21	1	1	.21	-3	-5	-2	-1	4	14	10	5
2014 Mil	136	1182.1	1082	4	.996	11	33	12	5	2	64	69	.481	3.62	114	804	83	24	5	2	.22	-1	1	-1	0	11	14	25	1
	557	4672.1	4467	31	.993	48	204	43	22	6	265	258	.507	3.93	715	3044	347	97	20	3	.22	-8	-7	-7	-1	22	85	92	-

Winner of the 2014 Fielding Bible Award for catchers, Jonathan Lucroy solidified himself as one of the top receivers in the game He has an uncanny ability to anticipate and react to plays unfolding. Coupled with his well-above average mobility for a catcher, his range is unrivaled in the game at his position. He tremendously improved his coordination in blocking pitches in the dirt, consistently squaring his shoulders and sliding his feet to prevent wild pitches. In 2014, Lucroy had just 31 Wild Pitches Misplays while blocking over 800 balls in the dirt–nearly 100 more than the next best catcher. Lucroy's best asset, however, has always been his receiving work, claiming hundreds of extra strikes for his pitching staff over his career. Lucroy is the best in the business when it comes to framing, including a record-setting 23 runs saved with this skill in 2011. Entering the prime of his career, Lucroy aims to be a steadying force behind the plate with many great years to come.

Martin Maldonado

	BASIC							BUNTS			PITCHER HANDLING						STOLEN BASES						RUNS SAVED						
Year Team	G	Inn	TC	E	Pct	GFP	DM	Opps	Sac Hits	Bunt Hits	W	L	Pct	CERA	Extra Strikes	Pitch Block	SB	CCS	PCS	CPO	CS%	SB Saved	Adj ER	SB	Bunt	GFP/DME	SZ	Total	Rank
2011 Mil	3	3.0	4	0	1.000	0	0				0	0	-	0.00	-	1	0	0	0	0	-	0	0	0	0	0	0	0	-
2012 Mil	69	537.1	576	6	.990	5	26	5	4	0	34	24	.586	3.89	58	412	32	12	3	3	.27	0	1	1	0	2	7	11	7
2013 Mil	47	366.2	317	1	.997	7	16	8	4	0	18	22	.450	3.17	43	209	19	8	0	2	.30	0	2	1	1	1	5	10	-
2014 Mil	42	274.1	278	6	.978	4	13	3	2	0	18	11	.621	3.77	31	168	13	5	1	2	.28	1	0	1	1	0	4	6	-
	161	1181.1	1175	13	.989	16	55	16	10	0	70	57	.551	3.63	132	791	64	25	4	7	.28	1	3	3	2	3	16	27	-

Russell Martin

	BASIC							BUNTS			PITCHER HANDLING						STOLEN BASES						RUNS SAVED						
Year Team	G	Inn	TC	E	Pct	GFP	DM	Opps	Sac Hits	Bunt Hits	W	L	Pct	CERA	Extra Strikes	Pitch Block	SB	CCS	PCS	CPO	CS%	SB Saved	Adj ER	SB	Bunt	GFP/DME	SZ	Total	Rank
2006 LAD	117	1015.0	856	6	.993	6	34	15	8	1	71	43	.623	3.93	-	216	71	25	7	0	.26	1	2	0	0	-2	-	0	14
2007 LAD	145	1254.0	1164	14	.988	25	35	27	14	2	78	65	.545	3.95	-	386	82	33	8	4	.29	7	4	7	1	6	-	18	1
2008 LAD	149	1238.0	1118	11	.990	15	37	13	7	0	76	62	.551	3.63	-	418	70	17	6	1	.20	-2	-2	-1	-1	4	-	0	19
2009 LAD	137	1201.0	1133	7	.994	19	58	19	7	0	78	55	.586	3.37	-	483	74	25	8	2	.25	0	4	1	2	1	-	8	4
2010 LAD	93	791.1	750	10	.987	19	29	11	7	1	47	42	.528	4.03	81	342	43	19	8	4	.31	3	0	4	-2	3	10	15	3
2011 NYY	125	1044.1	972	10	.990	18	51	7	3	2	67	51	.568	3.70	115	618	95	35	5	0	.27	3	0	2	-1	3	14	18	1
2012 NYY	128	1045.0	991	6	.994	11	43	7	4	1	67	49	.578	4.05	75	534	63	16	4	3	.20	-1	-5	0	0	0	9	4	17
2013 Pit	120	1051.1	990	2	.998	19	52	16	9	4	67	50	.573	3.15	58	630	53	29	7	3	.35	12	5	6	-2	2	7	21	2
2014 Pit	107	940.2	880	5	.994	10	45	17	8	0	63	43	.594	3.29	64	591	59	28	9	0	.32	9	3	6	0	2	8	19	2
	1121	9580.2	8854	71	.992	142	384	132	67	15	614	460	.572	3.67	393	4218	610	227	62	17	.27	31	11	28	-3	19	48	103	-

Martin's 2014 season was spectacular, but by no means is this something new. There is no doubt that Martin is an elite defensive catcher, and should be in consideration for the best at the position. Alongside his cannon of an arm and one of

Catchers

the best average pop times in the business, Martin does a great job of calling the game behind the dish. Martin is an excellent pitch framer who uses his veteran catching experience to control the game from a pitching perspective. What stands out about Martin is his veteran leadership; constantly visiting with his own pitchers to calm them down and help them pitch to their strengths. His incredible season landed him just behind Jonathan Lucroy in the Fielding Bible Award voting, and if we had a better understanding of pitch framing before his career began, the well-rounded Martin would have been challenging Yadier Molina annually for the hardware.

Jeff Mathis

		BASIC						BUNTS			PITCHER HANDLING						STOLEN BASES						RUNS SAVED						
Year Team	G	Inn	TC	E	Pct	GFP	DM	Opps	Sac Hits	Bunt Hits	W	L	Pct	CERA	Extra Strikes	Pitch Block	SB	CCS	PCS	CPO	CS%	SB Saved	Adj ER	SB	Bunt	GFP/DME	SZ	Total	Rank
2005 LAA	3	5.0	4	0	1.000	0	0				0	0	-	0.00	-	2	0	0	0	0	-	0	0	0		0	-	0	-
2006 LAA	20	133.0	101	3	.970	0	6	1	0	0	4	10	.286	5.82	-	58	12	2	1	0	.14	-1	-1	-1		0		-2	-
2007 LAA	57	467.0	429	4	.991	12	24	4	0	0	34	18	.654	3.89	-	261	40	8	0	7	.17	-4	0	1	0	-1		0	-
2008 LAA	94	793.1	694	13	.981	12	17	11	6	1	58	32	.644	3.66	-	395	57	16	4	3	.22	-4	3	-1	0	5		7	4
2009 LAA	79	657.0	572	7	.988	13	24	12	5	2	46	32	.590	3.99	-	340	52	17	1	1	.25	0	4	0	0	3	-	7	1
2010 LAA	67	553.2	476	7	.985	21	37	7	2	2	29	33	.468	3.67	47	317	43	7	4	3	.14	-4	2	-1	0	0	6	7	6
2011 LAA	91	698.0	568	3	.995	12	28	12	5	2	45	34	.570	3.25	38	405	48	12	6	1	.20	0	3	1	-1	3	5	11	5
2012 Tor	66	532.2	472	2	.996	11	21	6	2	0	26	33	.441	4.39	28	281	29	13	7	3	.31	3	0	3	0	1	3	7	9
2013 Mia	73	615.0	551	1	.998	10	27	5	2	0	35	35	.500	3.15	32	253	30	13	2	0	.30	3	3	2	1	0	4	10	8
2014 Mia	62	473.2	429	1	.998	4	18	8	4	0	19	33	.365	3.99	35	313	33	12	4	2	.27	1	1	1	1	1	4	8	
	612	4928.1	4296	41	.990	96	202	66	26	7	296	260	.532	3.77	180	2625	344	100	29	20	.23	-6	15	5	1	12	22	55	

Brian McCann

		BASIC						BUNTS			PITCHER HANDLING						STOLEN BASES						RUNS SAVED						
Year Team	G	Inn	TC	E	Pct	GFP	DM	Opps	Sac Hits	Bunt Hits	W	L	Pct	CERA	Extra Strikes	Pitch Block	SB	CCS	PCS	CPO	CS%	SB Saved	Adj ER	SB	Bunt	GFP/DME	SZ	Total	Rank
2005 Atl	57	449.1	334	3	.991	4	8	10	6	0	33	16	.673	3.91	-	72	22	5	0	1	.19	-2	-1	-1	1	0		-1	-
2006 Atl	124	1016.1	826	9	.989	2	26	8	2	1	62	56	.525	4.41	-	234	70	20	1	0	.22	-1	2	-1	0	0		1	19
2007 Atl	132	1139.0	973	13	.987	10	37	22	11	2	70	60	.538	3.89	-	288	70	17	2	0	.20	-3	1	-2	0	-2		-3	24
2008 Atl	138	1143.1	958	9	.991	11	38	26	17	2	61	71	.462	4.25	-	300	93	21	6	2	.18	-1	7	0	2	-1		8	5
2009 Atl	127	1078.2	994	12	.988	14	39	14	7	0	69	55	.556	3.65	-	297	76	21	3	1	.22	0	-4	0	1	-2		-5	25
2010 Atl	136	1109.2	1050	14	.987	14	36	16	11	0	74	55	.574	3.70	25	339	84	31	5	0	.27	5	-6	4	1	1	3	3	15
2011 Atl	126	1083.0	1061	5	.995	8	48	23	11	3	60	58	.508	3.61	108	463	104	22	7	0	.17	-4	-2	-3	2	-1	13	9	6
2012 Atl	114	994.2	898	2	.998	5	34	13	12	1	68	45	.602	3.35	90	407	76	17	7	0	.18	-1	3	-1	-1	1	11	13	8
2013 Atl	92	806.1	767	4	.995	2	17	15	11	1	60	31	.659	2.98	46	454	47	13	2	0	.22	0	2	-1	-1	1	5	6	15
2014 NYY	108	889.0	923	2	.998	6	34	5	5	0	57	44	.564	3.76	47	454	49	22	7	1	.31	3	0	2	0	0	6	8	8
	1154	9709.1	8784	73	.992	76	317	152	93	8	614	491	.556	3.76	316	3100	691	189	40	5	.21	-4	2	-3	5	-3	38	39	

Brian McCann continues to plug along as one of the steadiest catchers in baseball, consistently ranking above average at the position in Runs Saved. McCann has never been flashy, but his footwork has come a long ways since he allowed 104 stolen bases in 2011. His arm strength is not amazing, but his release and quick transfer are sufficient to control the running game as long as opposing runners aren't stealing off his pitching staff. McCann's one above average skill is his pitch framing, where he has saved his pitching staff five or more runs each of the last four seasons.

Michael McKenry

		BASIC						BUNTS			PITCHER HANDLING						STOLEN BASES						RUNS SAVED						
Year Team	G	Inn	TC	E	Pct	GFP	DM	Opps	Sac Hits	Bunt Hits	W	L	Pct	CERA	Extra Strikes	Pitch Block	SB	CCS	PCS	CPO	CS%	SB Saved	Adj ER	SB	Bunt	GFP/DME	SZ	Total	Rank
2010 Col	2	9.0	6	0	1.000	0	0				0	1	.000	6.00	0	7	0	0	0	0	-	0	0	0		0	0	0	
2011 Pit	58	485.0	388	5	.987	6	20	2	1	0	26	28	.481	3.73	-17	199	39	10	3	0	.20	0	0	0	0	1	-2	-1	
2012 Pit	81	607.1	539	3	.994	8	24	11	6	2	32	32	.500	4.10	-35	342	61	10	3	0	.14	-1	-1	-2	-1	3	-4	-5	23
2013 Pit	31	253.1	228	2	.991	6	18	9	3	1	18	9	.667	3.23	-25	116	35	3	3	0	.08	-6	1	-5	0	-2	-3	-9	
2014 Col	50	406.0	342	6	.982	6	20	3	2	0	20	25	.444	4.19	-34	289	34	5	3	0	.13	-3	2	-2	0	1	-4	-3	
	222	1760.2	1503	16	.989	26	82	25	12	3	96	95	.503	3.91	-111	953	169	28	12	0	.14	-12	2	-9	-1	3	-13	-18	

Devin Mesoraco

		BASIC						BUNTS			PITCHER HANDLING						STOLEN BASES						RUNS SAVED						
Year Team	G	Inn	TC	E	Pct	GFP	DM	Opps	Sac Hits	Bunt Hits	W	L	Pct	CERA	Extra Strikes	Pitch Block	SB	CCS	PCS	CPO	CS%	SB Saved	Adj ER	SB	Bunt	GFP/DME	SZ	Total	Rank
2011 Cin	16	122.1	112	3	.973	4	7				7	6	.538	4.78	-2	32	8	2	1	0	.20	-1	0	-1		-1	0	-2	
2012 Cin	53	420.2	393	1	.997	10	15	5	3	0	24	24	.500	4.19	18	167	39	9	1	0	.19	-4	-2	-3	0	1	2	-2	
2013 Cin	97	782.0	728	5	.993	11	27	18	12	0	46	38	.548	3.40	-30	355	45	13	5	0	.22	-2	-1	-2	1	1	-4	-5	25
2014 Cin	109	936.2	890	3	.997	7	29	11	6	0	51	53	.490	3.62	-55	446	51	16	2	0	.24	-3	1	-3	2	2	-7	-5	26
	275	2261.2	2123	12	.994	32	78	34	21	0	128	121	.514	3.71	-69	1000	143	40	9	0	.22	-10	-2	-9	3	3	-9	-14	

Behind the dish, Mesoraco has a big frame and looks like he could be a great catcher; however that hasn't been the case as of yet. He showcases a slightly below average pop time, though he shaved a few hundredths of a second off in 2014. Furthermore, he struggles to successfully frame pitches as he lacks the subtlety to move a pitch back over the plate without an umpire noticing. In fact, Mesoraco usually takes the easy way out and doesn't devote any effort to frame the

Catchers

pitch in the first place. When he does try, his stabbing motion with the glove is ineffective and yields unnecessary passed balls. Nevertheless, on sac bunt or bunt attempts in general, Mesoraco is up quick and charging the ball to try and get at least one out. He also does very well tracking down foul balls whether they are right behind him or down either line. Therefore, while he may not be the best option behind the dish, he has made efforts to get better and will always have a strong bat that will get him in the lineup.

Jose Molina

	BASIC							BUNTS			PITCHER HANDLING						STOLEN BASES						RUNS SAVED						
Year Team	G	Inn	TC	E	Pct	GFP	DM	Opps	Sac Hits	Bunt Hits	W	L	Pct	CERA	Extra Strikes	Pitch Block	SB	CCS	PCS	CPO	CS%	SB Saved	Adj ER	SB	Bunt	GFP/ DME	SZ	Total	Rank
2003 Ana	53	332.0	239	1	.996	-	-	2	2	0	17	22	.436	4.07	-	-	18	6	1	1	.25	-2	1	-1	0	-	-	0	-
2004 Ana	70	524.1	481	3	.994	7	20	2	0	1	34	23	.596	4.31	-	84	23	19	3	5	.45	5	1	6	0	-2	-	5	5
2005 LAA	65	480.1	452	3	.993	5	21	3	2	0	33	20	.623	3.65	-	98	19	18	2	3	.49	8	0	7	0	-1	-	6	-
2006 LAA	76	603.1	560	8	.986	12	36	2	1	0	38	33	.535	3.98	-	206	27	19	1	4	.41	5	1	5	0	-5	-	1	6
2007 2 tms	69	492.1	470	4	.991	8	20	3	2	0	31	22	.585	4.61	-	157	31	12	1	1	.28	0	0	1	-1	-1	-	-1	14
2008 NYY	97	737.0	689	3	.996	6	29	7	3	1	43	38	.531	3.69	-	197	42	32	1	1	.43	11	5	8	0	-3	-	10	2
2009 NYY	49	356.2	388	1	.997	8	18	2	2	0	24	18	.571	3.31	-	105	23	5	4	2	.18	-2	3	-1	0	-1	-	1	-
2010 Tor	56	444.2	456	2	.996	6	26	1	0	0	29	22	.569	3.72	60	163	19	13	2	2	.41	3	3	3		-2	7	11	-
2011 Tor	48	399.0	367	1	.997	5	21				26	18	.591	4.38	47	108	24	12	0	2	.33	0	1	1		-4	6	4	-
2012 TB	102	709.2	702	4	.994	7	32	1	0	0	41	39	.513	3.22	111	265	39	15	4	1	.28	6	-1	4		-2	13	14	5
2013 TB	96	749.1	712	4	.994	8	33	6	2	2	46	41	.529	3.74	87	239	56	17	6	2	.23	1	1	2	-1	-3	10	9	12
2014 TB	80	628.1	691	2	.997	2	32	5	2	0	31	39	.443	3.77	54	248	38	12	2	0	.24	0	-2	0	0	-3	6	1	19
	861	6457.0	6207	36	.994	74	288	34	16	4	393	335	.540	3.84	359	1870	359	180	27	24	.33	36	13	35	-2	-27	42	61	

Jose Molina is still playing baseball at 39 years of age, and it's not because of his bat. The light-hitting catcher is well-known in sabermetric circles as a player who derives most of his value from his ability to frame pitches. A large body at 6'0", 250 pounds, Molina is very quiet and fluid with his movement behind the plate, using the least amount of motion possible when receiving the ball. Since stealing 111 strikes in 2011, though, Molina has seen his extra strikes fall to 87 in 2013 and 54 in 2014. Still, Molina saved six runs in 2014 simply by catching balls and making them look like strikes.

Outside of his pitch-framing abilities, Molina does not have much to offer as a defender. Among catchers with 200 or more blocks in 2014, Molina was the sixth-worst at blocking balls in the dirt, with a Catcher Block Rate of 89.9 percent. Molina's age and size prevents him from reaching tougher balls in the dirt as well as pop-ups behind the plate that might not give other catchers much trouble. Given these weaknesses and a growing emphasis among catchers on framing pitches, it seems unlikely that Molina's trademark skill will keep him in baseball for much longer.

Yadier Molina

	BASIC							BUNTS			PITCHER HANDLING						STOLEN BASES						RUNS SAVED						
Year Team	G	Inn	TC	E	Pct	GFP	DM	Opps	Sac Hits	Bunt Hits	W	L	Pct	CERA	Extra Strikes	Pitch Block	SB	CCS	PCS	CPO	CS%	SB Saved	Adj ER	SB	Bunt	GFP/ DME	SZ	Total	Rank
2004 StL	51	344.0	274	2	.993	4	12	2	1	1	24	15	.615	3.64	-	83	9	8	0	1	.47	3	1	2	-1	0	-	2	-
2005 StL	114	959.1	757	7	.991	14	25	14	8	1	73	38	.658	3.39	-	239	14	17	8	9	.55	7	3	9	0	1	-	13	3
2006 StL	127	1037.1	817	4	.995	13	21	12	8	2	61	57	.517	4.53	-	431	37	26	3	7	.41	6	1	7	-1	-6	-	13	1
2007 StL	107	861.1	651	6	.991	7	28	9	5	0	46	55	.455	4.33	-	408	23	23	4	2	.50	10	6	8	1	0	-	15	2
2008 StL	119	1002.0	733	10	.986	21	40	10	4	2	61	53	.535	4.22	-	377	34	16	2	7	.32	4	-2	6	0	0	-	4	7
2009 StL	138	1176.2	971	5	.995	19	37	21	10	3	79	57	.581	3.48	-	564	32	16	6	8	.33	1	0	4	0	5	-	9	3
2010 StL	135	1138.0	979	5	.995	14	27	19	10	3	72	58	.554	3.23	52	567	35	28	5	3	.44	6	6	6	1	7	6	26	1
2011 StL	138	1150.0	929	5	.995	11	48	20	13	1	72	60	.545	3.91	65	657	46	15	4	2	.25	-1	-6	0	-1	4	8	5	13
2012 StL	136	1161.1	1053	3	.997	15	38	26	12	0	76	57	.571	3.60	94	554	38	32	3	3	.46	11	3	8	4	3	11	29	1
2013 StL	132	1115.1	1043	4	.996	8	21	19	8	0	82	46	.641	3.16	114	543	26	19	1	0	.42	4	6	2	1	7	14	30	1
2014 StL	107	931.2	868	2	.998	9	22	8	2	0	60	46	.566	3.19	-53	382	23	20	1	3	.47	6	4	5	1	3	-6	7	12
	1304	10877.0	9075	53	.994	135	319	160	81	14	706	542	.566	3.69	272	4806	317	220	37	45	.41	57	22	57	5	36	33	153	-

Since his 2004 debut, Molina has been the preeminent defensive catcher in all of baseball and shows no signs of slowing down. In spite of any lingering problems associated with his 2014 thumb injury, Molina threw out a league-leading 47 percent of would-be base stealers among catchers with at least 30 stolen base attempts against them. He successfully blocked pitches in the dirt at a 94.8 percent clip, which was good enough to place fourth among regular backstops. Historically, Molina has been one of the best receivers in the game, though in 2014 he managed to lose 53 strikes over 931 innings caught. This minor slip, combined with the missed time due to injury, allowed Jonathan Lucroy to nab the Fielding Bible Award from Molina's perpetual grasp. At 32 years of age and counting, it is not clear how long Molina will be able to sustain this level of defensive excellence, as the seemingly endless barrage of bumps and bruises tend to catch up with backstops as they enter their early to mid-thirties.

Catchers

Miguel Montero

	BASIC							BUNTS			PITCHER HANDLING						STOLEN BASES						RUNS SAVED						
Year Team	G	Inn	TC	E	Pct	GFP	DM	Opps	Sac Hits	Bunt Hits	W	L	Pct	CERA	Extra Strikes	Pitch Block	SB	CCS	PCS	CPO	CS%	SB Saved	Adj ER	SB	Bunt	GFP/DME	SZ	Total	Rank
2006 Ari	5	40.0	40	0	1.000	0	1	2	1	0	1	3	.250	4.73	-	11	3	1	0	0	.25	0	0	0	0	0	-	0	-
2007 Ari	73	510.2	376	6	.984	10	17	7	3	0	26	31	.456	4.81	-	142	35	9	1	0	.20	-5	-3	-4	2	-1	-	-6	27
2008 Ari	53	404.2	379	4	.989	4	23	8	4	2	17	28	.378	4.58	-	121	27	6	1	0	.18	-3	-2	-2	-1	-3	-	-8	-
2009 Ari	111	924.2	802	9	.989	10	49	13	5	3	48	53	.475	4.11	-	338	67	18	5	0	.21	-1	7	-1	-1	-3	-	2	14
2010 Ari	79	658.1	522	2	.996	9	31	12	3	1	30	45	.400	4.29	80	226	47	16	5	1	.25	0	1	1	1	-2	9	10	6
2011 Ari	134	1169.1	997	11	.989	21	35	25	9	3	82	49	.626	3.60	103	356	48	28	4	2	.37	3	3	3	0	1	12	19	4
2012 Ari	139	1190.0	1095	9	.992	15	44	23	11	1	67	69	.493	3.87	61	508	44	23	9	1	.34	4	0	2	0	0	7	9	12
2013 Ari	112	1006.2	898	5	.994	17	54	20	8	1	54	57	.486	4.02	60	540	31	9	6	4	.23	-1	-4	1	0	-3	4	-2	20
2014 Ari	131	1152.0	1115	13	.988	13	50	14	6	3	53	77	.408	4.34	127	510	64	20	6	1	.24	-5	-1	-4	1	-1	15	10	7
	837	7056.1	6224	59	.991	99	304	124	50	14	378	412	.478	4.11	407	2752	366	130	37	9	.26	-9	1	-4	2	-12	47	34	-

Miguel Montero has quietly remained a very consistent defensive catcher over the past five years. He possesses a couple of really great defensive tools, with his most impressive being his pitch framing ability. From 2012-14 he has saved the Diamondbacks 26 runs with his pitch framing ability. He was particularly successful at this in 2014 when he was able to get 127 extra strikes called and save the D'Backs 15 runs, third-best in all of baseball. This is something that often goes unnoticed but has proved to be very valuable. He is also one of the best at handling balls in the dirt, recording a whopping 1,558 over the past three years, placing him fourth amongst all catchers for that time period. Montero's offense has taken a bit of a dip over the past few years, but he still has the receiving skills to be an effective starter for many teams.

JR Murphy

	BASIC							BUNTS			PITCHER HANDLING						STOLEN BASES						RUNS SAVED						
Year Team	G	Inn	TC	E	Pct	GFP	DM	Opps	Sac Hits	Bunt Hits	W	L	Pct	CERA	Extra Strikes	Pitch Block	SB	CCS	PCS	CPO	CS%	SB Saved	Adj ER	SB	Bunt	GFP/DME	SZ	Total	Rank
2013 NYY	15	70.2	72	0	1.000	0	5				4	2	.667	2.55	8	11	3	3	0	0	.50	0	0	1		-1	1	1	-
2014 NYY	30	201.0	180	1	.994	1	6	2	1	0	9	12	.429	3.40	4	104	10	2	0	0	.17	-1	1	-1	0	0	1	1	-
	45	271.2	252	1	.996	1	11	2	1	0	13	14	.481	3.18	12	137	13	5	0	0	.28	0	1	0	0	-1	2	2	-

Dioner Navarro

	BASIC							BUNTS			PITCHER HANDLING						STOLEN BASES						RUNS SAVED						
Year Team	G	Inn	TC	E	Pct	GFP	DM	Opps	Sac Hits	Bunt Hits	W	L	Pct	CERA	Extra Strikes	Pitch Block	SB	CCS	PCS	CPO	CS%	SB Saved	Adj ER	SB	Bunt	GFP/DME	SZ	Total	Rank
2004 NYY	4	13.0	9	0	1.000	0	0				1	0	1.000	1.38	-	8	0	0	0	0			0	0		0	-	0	-
2005 LAD	50	435.2	367	2	.995	6	8	14	10	0	24	25	.490	4.34	-	41	33	8	1	0	.20	-1	0	-1	0	0	-	-1	-
2006 2 tms	78	653.2	524	8	.985	3	33	7	1	2	28	47	.373	4.89	-	172	48	18	2	0	.27	-2	0	-1	-1	-4	-	-6	31
2007 TB	112	956.1	895	14	.984	12	39	10	2	2	47	63	.427	5.50	-	367	71	24	6	0	.25	-4	0	-3	0	1	-	-2	21
2008 TB	117	1011.1	897	5	.994	10	33	7	2	1	70	43	.619	3.90	-	279	45	25	3	0	.36	6	-5	4	0	0	-	-1	22
2009 TB	113	921.1	784	5	.994	8	39	5	2	0	56	49	.533	4.23	-	313	61	19	3	1	.24	0	0	0	-1	0	-	-1	22
2010 TB	46	331.0	296	4	.986	4	10	1	0	0	25	11	.694	2.91	-1	106	19	7	5	0	.27	0	3	0	0	1	0	4	-
2011 LAD	54	428.0	455	7	.985	14	20	4	2	0	22	24	.478	3.43	-9	165	41	10	4	5	.20	-3	1	0	0	-1	0	0	-
2012 Cin	21	155.1	141	1	.993	1	4	2	1	0	12	4	.750	2.78	7	48	5	1	0	0	.17	0	0	0	0	1	1	1	-
2013 ChC	55	470.0	466	5	.989	8	30	7	6	0	23	30	.434	4.02	11	193	37	11	2	1	.23	1	1	1	0	-2	1	1	-
2014 Tor	112	907.1	820	3	.996	7	32	3	0	0	57	45	.559	3.86	-142	427	58	11	4	0	.16	-1	0	-1		4	-17	-14	30
	762	6283.0	5654	54	.990	73	248	60	26	5	365	341	.517	4.21	-134	2119	418	134	30	7	.24	-4	0	-1	-2	0	-16	-19	-

After spending much of the previous four seasons in a backup role, Navarro started over half the Blue Jays games behind the dish, where he was one of the worst defensive catchers in the league. Much of his struggles defensively are derived from his lack of mobility. At 5 foot 9 and 205 pounds, he often relies on his wider frame to block balls in the dirt, rather than moving his feet. As the pitch is delivered, his eyes and head don't track the ball well when the ball is down in the zone. With a particularly low pitch, his knees commit too early, not allowing him to move laterally, allowing an overabundance of wild pitches. In his younger years as a regular starter, Navarro featured an average arm and footwork that kept would-be base stealers at bay, but it reached a new low in 2014. But the worst part about his 2014 defense was the 142 strikes that Navarro turned into balls with poor receiving skills. Navarro will continue to have value as a switch-hitting catcher, but his years as a starting backstop are likely numbered as his already slow feet diminish even further.

Adrian Nieto

	BASIC							BUNTS			PITCHER HANDLING						STOLEN BASES						RUNS SAVED						
Year Team	G	Inn	TC	E	Pct	GFP	DM	Opps	Sac Hits	Bunt Hits	W	L	Pct	CERA	Extra Strikes	Pitch Block	SB	CCS	PCS	CPO	CS%	SB Saved	Adj ER	SB	Bunt	GFP/DME	SZ	Total	Rank
2014 CWS	46	299.2	216	1	.995	4	24	5	2	1	6	26	.188	5.38	-37	189	25	3	1	0	.11	-3	-1	-2	0	-3	-4	-10	-

Catchers

Wil Nieves

	BASIC								BUNTS			PITCHER HANDLING						STOLEN BASES						RUNS SAVED						
										Sac	Bunt					Extra	Pitch						SB	Adj			GFP/			
Year	Team	G	Inn	TC	E	Pct	GFP	DM	Opps	Hits	Hits	W	L	Pct	CERA	Strikes	Block	SB	CCS	PCS	CPO	CS%	Saved	ER	SB	Bunt	DME	SZ	Total	Rank
2005	NYY	3	9.0	11	0	1.000	0	0				0	0	-	4.00	-	-	0	0	0	0		0	0	0		0	-	0	-
2006	NYY	6	19.0	16	0	1.000	0	1				0	1	.000	4.74	-	6	2	1	0	0	.33	0	0	0		0	-	0	-
2007	NYY	25	169.0	119	2	.983	2	5	2	0	1	12	9	.571	4.37	-	52	21	6	0	0	.22	-1	1	-1	0	1	-	1	-
2008	Was	61	449.2	393	3	.992	7	15	6	4	0	18	28	.391	4.60	-	166	39	9	1	1	.19	0	0	1	0	0	-	1	-
2009	Was	71	553.2	427	6	.986	6	23	12	6	1	27	38	.415	5.06	-	249	34	13	0	0	.28	2	-1	1	-1	1	-	0	-
2010	Was	51	395.0	315	5	.984	3	14	8	7	0	18	25	.419	4.01	22	149	31	7	3	1	.18	-2	1	-1	-1	0	3	2	-
2011	Mil	17	129.0	118	1	.992	3	5	4	3	0	7	9	.438	3.84	2	77	7	2	1	0	.22	0	0	0	0	0	0	0	-
2012	2 tms	24	174.0	152	2	.987	2	10	3	2	1	10	9	.526	4.40	2	71	17	1	2	1	.06	-2	0	-2	0	0	0	-2	-
2013	Ari	47	380.2	339	2	.994	2	32	6	2	0	22	18	.550	3.92	-4	195	13	2	3	0	.13	-2	0	-2	1	-4	0	-5	-
2014	Phi	34	293.0	273	1	.996	4	7	7	3	1	19	15	.559	3.50	0	149	23	8	2	0	.26	1	1	1	1	1	0	4	-
		339	2572.0	2163	22	.990	29	112	48	27	4	133	152	.467	4.31	22	1114	187	49	12	3	.21	-4	2	-3	0	-1	3	1	-

Derek Norris

	BASIC								BUNTS			PITCHER HANDLING						STOLEN BASES						RUNS SAVED						
										Sac	Bunt					Extra	Pitch						SB	Adj			GFP/			
Year	Team	G	Inn	TC	E	Pct	GFP	DM	Opps	Hits	Hits	W	L	Pct	CERA	Strikes	Block	SB	CCS	PCS	CPO	CS%	Saved	ER	SB	Bunt	DME	SZ	Total	Rank
2012	Oak	58	496.2	462	5	.989	4	17	3	2	1	36	17	.679	3.10	37	140	34	6	6	1	.15	0	2	0	0	0	4	6	-
2013	Oak	91	663.0	595	3	.995	7	25	5	2	1	38	33	.535	3.65	19	245	35	7	5	1	.17	-2	-1	-1	-1	0	2	-1	23
2014	Oak	114	870.1	794	6	.992	9	34	7	3	1	53	40	.570	3.13	1	392	60	8	4	0	.12	-5	1	-4	0	0	0	-3	24
		263	2030.0	1851	14	.992	20	76	15	7	3	127	90	.585	3.29	57	777	129	21	15	2	.14	-7	2	-5	-1	0	6	2	-

Derek Norris has worked hard to become a serviceable defensive catcher. He'll likely never be mistaken for Yadier Molina behind the dish, but Norris has nonetheless demonstrated a sufficient level of defensive proficiency that justifies the presence of his bat in the lineup on a consistent basis. The most glaring weakness in Norris's defensive game is his inability to consistently throw out base stealers, who enjoyed an 88 percent success rate with him behind the plate. Though his average pop time around the major league average, his footwork can get a bit sloppy at times, leading to inaccurate throws. Norris demonstrates noisy pre-reception glove movements and tendency to catch balls aggressively, limiting his ability to garner extra strikes for his pitching staff. This could be improved with time, however.

Brayan Pena

	BASIC								BUNTS			PITCHER HANDLING						STOLEN BASES						RUNS SAVED						
										Sac	Bunt					Extra	Pitch						SB	Adj			GFP/			
Year	Team	G	Inn	TC	E	Pct	GFP	DM	Opps	Hits	Hits	W	L	Pct	CERA	Strikes	Block	SB	CCS	PCS	CPO	CS%	Saved	ER	SB	Bunt	DME	SZ	Total	Rank
2005	Atl	15	81.0	51	0	1.000	1	4	2	1	1	2	5	.286	6.33	-	18	8	1	1	0	.11	-1	0	-1	-1	0	-	-2	-
2006	Atl	15	71.0	32	0	1.000	0	0	2	1	1	2	3	.400	4.31	-	25	3	0	0	0	.00	-1	0	0	0	1	-	1	-
2007	Atl	10	59.1	54	0	1.000	1	2				0	5	.000	6.07	-	38	4	2	2	0	.33	0	0	0		0	-	0	-
2009	KC	30	213.2	175	0	1.000	3	16	1	1	0	9	15	.375	5.56	-	82	17	4	5	0	.19	-1	0	-1	0	-2	-	-3	-
2010	KC	47	337.1	296	3	.990	3	13	5	0	0	13	22	.371	4.75	21	111	29	11	1	0	.28	1	0	0	1	-1	3	3	-
2011	KC	69	537.0	444	2	.995	14	22	7	2	2	22	35	.386	4.49	9	215	48	16	11	0	.25	2	-1	2	-1	3	1	4	12
2012	KC	52	417.2	366	4	.989	8	8	4	2	1	20	26	.435	4.22	-10	153	52	10	6	0	.16	-1	0	-1	-1	1	-1	-2	-
2013	Det	64	520.0	558	5	.995	6	22	6	2	3	26	29	.473	3.76	19	236	42	9	4	0	.18	-4	0	-3	-1	1	2	-1	-
2014	Cin	46	377.1	383	2	.995	1	10	6	4	0	21	23	.477	2.86	21	92	16	10	2	0	.38	1	2	0	0	-1	2	3	-
		348	2614.1	2359	14	.994	37	97	33	13	8	115	163	.414	4.28	60	970	219	63	32	0	.22	-4	1	-4	-3	2	7	3	-

Roberto Perez

	BASIC								BUNTS			PITCHER HANDLING						STOLEN BASES						RUNS SAVED						
										Sac	Bunt					Extra	Pitch						SB	Adj			GFP/			
Year	Team	G	Inn	TC	E	Pct	GFP	DM	Opps	Hits	Hits	W	L	Pct	CERA	Strikes	Block	SB	CCS	PCS	CPO	CS%	Saved	ER	SB	Bunt	DME	SZ	Total	Rank
2014	Cle	29	232.1	244	3	.988	2	7				17	8	.680	2.60	2	184	14	7	1	1	.33	2	1	2		2	0	5	-

Salvador Perez

	BASIC								BUNTS			PITCHER HANDLING						STOLEN BASES						RUNS SAVED						
										Sac	Bunt					Extra	Pitch						SB	Adj			GFP/			
Year	Team	G	Inn	TC	E	Pct	GFP	DM	Opps	Hits	Hits	W	L	Pct	CERA	Strikes	Block	SB	CCS	PCS	CPO	CS%	Saved	ER	SB	Bunt	DME	SZ	Total	Rank
2011	KC	39	338.2	314	3	.990	10	21	4	2	0	19	20	.487	4.23	-28	187	26	5	2	3	.16	0	-1	1	0	1	-3	-2	-
2012	KC	74	653.2	579	4	.993	13	30	1	0	0	33	41	.446	4.35	-23	374	25	15	3	5	.38	1	7	0	2	-3	7	12	-
2013	KC	137	1115.1	1008	7	.993	13	47	6	3	2	67	59	.532	3.36	-11	690	46	23	2	1	.33	6	4	4	0	4	-1	11	7
2014	KC	146	1248.2	1118	9	.992	13	51	6	2	0	83	60	.580	3.24	-31	707	57	23	2	5	.29	3	5	4	1	1	-4	7	12
		396	3356.1	3019	23	.992	49	149	17	7	2	202	180	.529	3.60	-93	1958	154	66	9	14	.30	16	9	16	1	8	-11	23	-

Salvador Perez has a 6'3, 240 pound frame with a strong build and is a natural athlete. Perez demonstrates quick feet and fast reflexes behind the dish and has developed into one of the leagues finest defensive catchers. Perez's above average arm and quick release has kept would-be base stealers in check. He also demonstrates an advanced ability to contain wild pitches and balls in the dirt all while posting an average pop time of 1.90 seconds. The one area where Perez could improve is in pitch framing. Because Perez is so aggressive with pickoff throws (and often successful!), he often distracts the umpire from calling a strike on a pitch in the zone. Long term, Perez projects to be one of the game's best for years to come, assuming he remains healthy, his elite level ability should keep him in the top percentile for catchers.

A.J. Pierzynski

		BASIC							BUNTS			PITCHER HANDLING						STOLEN BASES						RUNS SAVED						
Year	Team	G	Inn	TC	E	Pct	GFP	DM	Opps	Sac Hits	Bunt Hits	W	L	Pct	CERA	Extra Strikes	Pitch Block	SB	CCS	PCS	CPO	CS%	SB Saved	Adj ER	SB	Bunt	GFP/ DME	SZ	Total	Rank
2003	Min	135	1165.2	895	6	.993	-	-	8	3	0	75	56	.573	4.15	-	-	46	17	3	0	.27	-2	6	-1	1	-	-	6	4
2004	SF	118	1022.0	754	1	.999	9	40	13	7	1	65	52	.556	4.30	-	200	51	11	4	0	.18	-5	2	-3	0	-1	-	-2	16
2005	CWS	128	1117.2	852	1	.999	6	30	8	3	1	77	47	.621	3.74	-	109	79	20	3	1	.20	-1	-5	0	1	1	-	-3	11
2006	CWS	132	1125.0	860	3	.997	1	47	4	1	0	74	52	.587	4.47	-	231	90	21	4	0	.19	-2	5	-2	0	-5	-	-2	27
2007	CWS	130	1058.0	844	2	.998	11	35	4	4	0	54	62	.466	4.41	-	234	62	12	8	0	.16	1	7	0	0	-4	-	3	9
2008	CWS	131	1134.1	976	9	.991	7	35	6	2	0	67	60	.528	4.23	-	269	96	11	10	0	.10	-4	-5	-3	1	-1	-	-8	34
2009	CWS	131	1104.0	934	5	.995	5	47	5	3	0	63	61	.508	4.10	-	314	99	20	10	1	.17	1	1	1	0	-5	-	-3	25
2010	CWS	127	1092.2	931	5	.995	5	47	12	3	2	68	55	.553	3.95	-24	356	75	16	11	2	.18	2	4	2	0	-4	-3	-1	21
2011	CWS	120	1008.0	886	4	.995	7	48	12	6	4	54	58	.482	4.04	44	405	94	14	10	0	.13	-4	-2	-3	-1	-2	5	-3	20
2012	CWS	126	1071.1	976	6	.994	5	68	6	2	0	66	55	.545	4.06	-61	450	76	19	8	1	.20	4	2	2	-1	-6	-7	-10	29
2013	Tex	119	1005.0	959	2	.998	8	49	6	4	0	61	50	.550	3.61	-27	501	49	17	7	0	.26	0	-2	0	1	0	-3	-4	25
2014	2 tms	87	721.0	658	5	.992	3	28	2	1	0	34	46	.425	4.13	-41	303	50	9	2	0	.15	-6	-4	-5	0	0	-5	-14	30
		1484	12624.2	10525	49	.995	67	474	86	39	9	758	654	.537	4.10	-109	3372	867	187	80	5	.18	-16	9	-12	2	-27	-13	-41	-

When looking at the catching position, Pierzynski's ability to "show-up" consistently and remain healthy throughout the season has been one of his saving graces during the later years of his career. Entering his age-38 season, Pierzynski has remained durable, and prior to the 2014 season, he had appeared in no fewer than 118 games in a season since 2002. Pierzynski is developing more cons than pros as the years go by, displaying a poor ability to handle pitches in the dirt and struggling to throw out runners. His footwork and ability to control wild pitches has become a cause of concern, as Pierzynski was charged with 28 Defensive Misplays throughout the 2014 season, 26 of which were wild pitch misplays. Furthermore, recent research has also confirmed A.J.'s poor pitch framing skills. Love him or hate him (and most choose the latter), Pierzynski's ability to stay healthy and offensive contributions will surely earn him a role on a club, even if it's a small one.

Josmil Pinto

		BASIC							BUNTS			PITCHER HANDLING						STOLEN BASES						RUNS SAVED						
Year	Team	G	Inn	TC	E	Pct	GFP	DM	Opps	Sac Hits	Bunt Hits	W	L	Pct	CERA	Extra Strikes	Pitch Block	SB	CCS	PCS	CPO	CS%	SB Saved	Adj ER	SB	Bunt	GFP/ DME	SZ	Total	Rank
2013	Min	20	159.1	118	2	.983	3	9				6	12	.333	5.54	-26	62	6	2	3	0	.25	0	-1	0		0	-3	-4	-
2014	Min	25	226.0	186	5	.973	1	12	2	1	1	10	15	.400	4.74	-33	107	20	0	0	0	.00	-4	0	-3	0	-1	-4	-8	-
		45	385.1	304	7	.977	4	21	2	1	1	16	27	.372	5.07	-59	169	26	2	3	0	.07	-4	-1	-3	0	-1	-7	-12	-

Buster Posey

		BASIC							BUNTS			PITCHER HANDLING						STOLEN BASES						RUNS SAVED						
Year	Team	G	Inn	TC	E	Pct	GFP	DM	Opps	Sac Hits	Bunt Hits	W	L	Pct	CERA	Extra Strikes	Pitch Block	SB	CCS	PCS	CPO	CS%	SB Saved	Adj ER	SB	Bunt	GFP/ DME	SZ	Total	Rank
2009	SF	7	40.0	36	0	1.000	0	2				1	3	.250	3.60	-	13	1	1	0	0	.50		0	0		0	-	0	-
2010	SF	76	662.0	662	6	.991	8	23	3	2	0	46	29	.613	3.18	15	250	39	18	5	0	.32	6	1	4	1	2	2	10	6
2011	SF	41	361.0	359	2	.994	1	13	1	1	0	23	18	.561	3.34	21	133	27	11	4	0	.29	3	0	2	0	0	3	5	-
2012	SF	114	973.0	932	8	.991	13	32	9	5	2	63	48	.568	3.50	122	348	87	31	7	2	.26	-2	-2	2	-1	3	14	16	4
2013	SF	121	1031.0	967	7	.993	10	37	12	7	0	56	63	.471	3.84	76	400	63	17	10	1	.21	-2	5	-1	2	1	9	16	4
2014	SF	111	929.1	843	5	.994	11	33	10	9	0	60	49	.550	3.39	94	365	59	17	8	1	.22	-2	0	-2	-1	0	11	8	8
		470	3996.1	3799	28	.993	43	140	35	24	2	249	210	.542	3.50	328	1509	276	95	34	4	.26	8	4	5	1	6	39	55	-

Despite a better than average pop time, Buster Posey has been susceptible to the stolen base over his career, allowing 74 percent of basestealers to succeed. Posey remained one of the best in the game at blocking balls in the dirt with a 93 percent catcher block rate. He is also superb at preventing wild pitches and limiting passed balls. His relationships with his pitching staff are a big part of the Giants' World Series titles. His bread and butter is his ability to call a game and get the extra strikes when needed, putting him in the upper echelon of catchers defensively. Posey, who is now 27 years old, started a small number of games for the Giants at first base, giving him some time to rest his legs for the long-run.

Only a few catchers in history have single-handedly changed the way the position is played, from Roger Bresnahan to Johnny Bench. Buster Posey has one-upped them both, as his violent collision with Scott Cousins in 2011 led to an actual rule change, certainly a rarity in baseball. The rule change has generated more than its share of controversy, but there's no doubt the catching position is safer than it was before.

Catchers

Wilson Ramos

	BASIC							BUNTS			PITCHER HANDLING						STOLEN BASES						RUNS SAVED						
Year Team	G	Inn	TC	E	Pct	GFP	DM	Opps	Sac Hits	Bunt Hits	W	L	Pct	CERA	Extra Strikes	Pitch Block	SB	CCS	PCS	CPO	CS%	SB Saved	Adj ER	SB	Bunt	GFP/DME	SZ	Total	Rank
2010 2 tms	22	192.1	147	0	1.000	8	5	3	2	0	9	12	.429	3.70	13	78	10	1	0	0	.09	0	0	0	0	1	2	3	-
2011 Was	108	951.2	744	5	.993	6	42	14	8	1	54	52	.509	3.73	110	386	48	19	4	0	.28	2	-2	1	-1	0	13	11	8
2012 Was	24	216.2	204	1	.995	0	14	6	1	1	15	9	.625	3.07	-2	117	19	3	1	0	.14	-1	0	0	0	-2	0	-2	-
2013 Was	77	667.2	636	8	.987	3	24	10	5	1	48	29	.623	3.28	31	275	34	11	3	0	.24	4	3	2	1	0	4	10	8
2014 Was	87	775.0	685	5	.993	8	23	6	2	0	49	38	.563	3.10	-7	295	30	16	2	3	.35	4	-2	4	1	0	-1	2	16
	318	2803.1	2416	19	.992	25	108	39	18	3	175	140	.556	3.39	145	1151	141	50	10	3	.26	9	-1	6	1	0	18	24	

Plagued with injuries the last few seasons, Ramos has had a hard time staying on the field. When he has been able to play, though, he has handled his duties as a catcher very well. On the defensive front, though his pitch framing wasn't as effective in 2014 as it has been in the past, Ramos does well to get extra strikes called. He also wastes no effort on pop outs and bunt grounders, pouncing on them both to try and make the out. On stolen base attempts, he no more than receives the ball and then it is gone again. Thus, while he did allow a few more stolen bases, he also caught 16 runners stealing in 2014 and picked another three off. Moreover, if Ramos can stay healthy he should return to being one of the better catchers in the game.

Anthony Recker

	BASIC							BUNTS			PITCHER HANDLING						STOLEN BASES						RUNS SAVED						
Year Team	G	Inn	TC	E	Pct	GFP	DM	Opps	Sac Hits	Bunt Hits	W	L	Pct	CERA	Extra Strikes	Pitch Block	SB	CCS	PCS	CPO	CS%	SB Saved	Adj ER	SB	Bunt	GFP/DME	SZ	Total	Rank
2011 Oak	5	42.0	46	1	.978	1	3				1	4	.200	8.36	-8	27	5	0	0	0	.00	0	0	0	0	0	-1	-1	-
2012 2 tms	17	111.2	93	1	.989	2	3	1	0	1	5	7	.417	3.06	-16	42	7	6	1	0	.46	1	0	1	-1	0	-2	-2	-
2013 NYM	38	323.1	309	3	.990	6	12	8	1	1	20	14	.588	3.28	-18	133	27	6	1	0	.18	-2	2	-2	0	2	-2	0	-
2014 NYM	52	412.2	411	5	.988	4	18	6	4	0	24	19	.558	3.10	-51	173	17	9	1	0	.35	4	2	2	1	0	-6	-1	-
	112	889.2	859	10	.988	13	36	15	5	2	50	44	.532	3.41	-93	375	56	21	3	0	.27	3	4	1	0	2	-11	-4	

Rene Rivera

	BASIC							BUNTS			PITCHER HANDLING						STOLEN BASES						RUNS SAVED						
Year Team	G	Inn	TC	E	Pct	GFP	DM	Opps	Sac Hits	Bunt Hits	W	L	Pct	CERA	Extra Strikes	Pitch Block	SB	CCS	PCS	CPO	CS%	SB Saved	Adj ER	SB	Bunt	GFP/DME	SZ	Total	Rank
2004 Sea	2	3.0	4	0	-	0	0				0	0	-	0.00	-	-	0	0	0	0	-	0	0	0		0	-	0	-
2005 Sea	15	111.0	76	3	.961	1	5	2	1	0	4	8	.333	4.38	-	20	4	1	1	0	.20	0	0	0	0	-1	-	-1	-
2006 Sea	35	266.0	237	3	.987	2	9	3	2	1	14	16	.467	3.62	-	65	15	5	4	0	.25	0	2	0	-1	-1	-	0	-
2011 Min	44	299.1	250	3	.988	4	9	4	2	0	14	21	.400	3.91	10	126	15	6	4	0	.29	0	2	0	1	1	1	5	-
2013 SD	21	180.0	198	0	1.000	2	4	1	1	0	10	11	.476	3.00	37	76	7	9	0	0	.56	6	1	4	0	0	4	9	-
2014 SD	89	734.0	754	8	.989	5	33	12	10	1	43	42	.506	3.10	74	464	58	29	4	1	.33	8	0	6	0	0	9	15	4
	206	1593.1	1519	17	.989	14	60	22	16	2	85	98	.464	3.41	121	751	99	50	13	1	.34	14	5	10	0	-1	14	28	

For the first time in Rivera's long career in professional baseball, he managed to stick at the big league level for an extended period of time, and he did not disappoint. Rivera had by far his best defensive season of his career, outplaying Yasmani Grandal while splitting time with him. His average pop time to second was an astounding 1.88 seconds compared to the league average of 1.98. It is one of the best aspects of Rivera's game, if not the best, helping him hose a league-leading 29 potential base stealers on the year. Furthermore, Rivera rates as one of the better pitcher framers in baseball. San Diego's catching depth was an unexpected strength by the end of the year, ultimately sending Rivera to ply his craft in Tampa.

Wilin Rosario

	BASIC							BUNTS			PITCHER HANDLING						STOLEN BASES						RUNS SAVED						
Year Team	G	Inn	TC	E	Pct	GFP	DM	Opps	Sac Hits	Bunt Hits	W	L	Pct	CERA	Extra Strikes	Pitch Block	SB	CCS	PCS	CPO	CS%	SB Saved	Adj ER	SB	Bunt	GFP/DME	SZ	Total	Rank
2011 Col	14	123.0	104	1	.990	1	14				3	11	.214	4.83	3	68	3	5	0	0	.63	2	0	1		-3	0	-2	-
2012 Col	105	878.0	785	13	.983	8	71	18	13	1	38	62	.380	5.01	-97	503	64	24	6	0	.27	5	4	3	-3	-10	-12	-18	33
2013 Col	106	910.1	718	9	.987	6	46	9	5	1	46	57	.447	4.31	-76	475	53	16	3	1	.23	-2	2	-2	0	-4	-9	-13	31
2014 Col	96	824.0	646	7	.989	11	51	11	5	1	35	59	.372	5.20	-42	473	37	6	1	2	.14	-1	-5	0	1	-5	-5	-14	30
	321	2735.1	2253	30	.987	26	182	38	23	3	122	189	.392	4.83	-212	1518	157	51	10	3	.25	4	1	2	-2	-22	-26	-47	

Wilin Rosario has been a project for the Colorado Rockies as a catcher who may never turn the corner. From a pitch blocking standpoint, he is often not able to get into the correct position, which has resulted in a staggering 44 Defensive Misplays on balls in the dirt that allowed runners to advance unnecessarily. This is the third consecutive season that he has allowed dozens of strikes to go as balls. He positions his glove awkwardly which makes it difficult to keep his glove steady in the strike zone. Further, Rosario rests his catching arm on the outside of his left leg, which has formed bad habits and makes him unprepared for the pitch. In addition, he will consistently lose strikes due to the ball breaking

Catchers

his wrist strength and it carrying his glove out of the strike zone. While he is still is young (25 years old), a move to first or DH is likely in the cards at some point.

David Ross

	BASIC								BUNTS			PITCHER HANDLING						STOLEN BASES						RUNS SAVED						
Year	Team	G	Inn	TC	E	Pct	GFP	DM	Opps	Sac Hits	Bunt Hits	W	L	Pct	CERA	Extra Strikes	Pitch Block	SB	CCS	PCS	CPO	CS%	SB Saved	Adj ER	SB	Bunt	GFP/ DME	SZ	Total	Rank
2003	LA	38	314.0	289	4	.986	-	-	2	2	0	16	19	.457	4.59	-	-	29	13	3	0	.31	4	-3	3	-1	-	-	-1	-
2004	LA	67	451.2	379	3	.992	4	19	7	3	0	25	26	.490	4.24	-	68	27	11	1	2	.29	-1	-1	0	1	-1	-	-1	-
2005	2 tms	42	304.0	237	3	.987	0	10	10	8	0	14	19	.424	4.14	-	40	6	7	2	0	.54	3	1	2	0	-2	-	1	-
2006	Cin	75	620.2	521	8	.985	2	22	12	10	1	34	39	.466	4.26	-	96	17	12	2	1	.41	2	2	2	1	-4	-	1	14
2007	Cin	108	837.1	717	5	.993	10	31	14	5	2	38	60	.388	4.57	-	182	36	23	2	1	.39	6	2	5	-1	-3	-	3	12
2008	2 tms	54	399.2	378	3	.992	7	17	7	4	0	16	27	.372	5.11	-	128	26	10	0	0	.28	1	-1	1	1	-1	-	0	-
2009	Atl	52	354.0	352	1	.997	4	8	4	2	0	16	20	.444	3.43	-	77	21	16	3	0	.43	6	1	4	1	0	-	6	-
2010	Atl	57	328.2	302	4	.987	3	12	5	2	1	17	16	.515	3.15	24	89	18	7	1	0	.28	1	1	1	0	0	3	5	-
2011	Atl	49	378.2	372	3	.992	3	15	7	7	0	28	14	.667	3.11	57	133	22	10	1	1	.31	3	1	3	0	-1	7	10	-
2012	Atl	54	421.2	395	2	.995	3	17	5	1	0	26	21	.553	3.56	54	140	19	14	1	1	.42	5	-1	4	0	-2	6	7	-
2013	Bos	36	286.0	302	1	.997	4	10	2	0	1	18	15	.545	3.12	23	103	19	10	3	0	.34	3	1	2	0	1	3	7	-
2014	Bos	50	418.1	415	7	.983	2	17	2	0	1	22	25	.468	4.04	7	180	32	8	1	0	.20	-1	-2	-1	-1	-1	1	-4	-
		682	5114.2	4659	44	.991	44	178	77	44	7	270	301	.473	4.04	165	1236	272	141	20	6	.34	33	1	26	1	-14	20	34	-

Carlos Ruiz

	BASIC							BUNTS			PITCHER HANDLING						STOLEN BASES						RUNS SAVED						
Year	Team	G	Inn	TC	E	Pct	GFP	DM	Opps	Sac Hits	Bunt Hits	W	L	Pct	CERA	Extra Strikes	Pitch Block	SB	CCS	PCS	CPO	CS%	SB Saved	Adj ER	SB	Bunt	GFP/ DME	SZ	Total	Rank
2006	Phi	24	176.1	161	3	.981	1	9	4	3	0	9	9	.500	4.13	-	52	11	2	1	1	.15	-1	0	0	-1	-1	-	-2	-
2007	Phi	111	912.2	744	2	.997	16	25	16	10	0	58	42	.580	4.59	-	270	57	19	7	4	.25	1	3	2	1	2	-	8	6
2008	Phi	110	828.0	686	5	.993	11	24	20	11	1	55	37	.598	3.85	-	310	65	14	6	2	.18	-3	0	-1	1	2	-	2	7
2009	Phi	107	882.1	759	3	.996	13	20	8	4	0	57	43	.570	4.00	-	271	61	15	8	0	.20	0	4	0	1	7	-	12	1
2010	Phi	118	974.1	880	6	.993	7	15	12	6	2	70	39	.642	3.33	-51	275	50	18	2	1	.26	2	5	2	-1	3	-6	3	17
2011	Phi	128	1051.0	1022	4	.996	15	16	19	10	1	70	43	.619	3.06	-77	351	77	18	5	1	.19	-3	-4	-2	1	6	-9	-8	25
2012	Phi	106	856.1	935	6	.994	15	17	17	10	1	45	50	.474	4.12	8	318	64	21	12	2	.25	-4	-4	1	1	5	1	4	15
2013	Phi	86	745.0	704	3	.996	9	31	19	7	0	39	44	.470	4.14	-18	355	63	12	9	1	.16	-2	0	-2	2	2	-2	0	17
2014	Phi	109	960.0	925	5	.995	9	37	23	13	1	47	57	.452	3.68	-52	480	74	21	7	0	.22	3	4	2	-1	2	-6	1	19
		899	7386.0	6816	37	.995	96	194	138	74	6	450	364	.553	3.82	-190	2682	522	140	57	12	.21	-2	8	2	4	28	-22	20	-

Ruiz has been a consistent, impact catcher in Philadelphia for going on a decade now. Ruiz is aging (he will be turning 36 during the 2015 season) and is terribly slow and rather bulky (5-foot-10, 205 pounds), but is still quick enough behind the plate to be an exceptional pitch blocker. His arm isn't a "wow" factor in terms of pop time (he has averaged 1.99 seconds to second base since 2012), but also is not yet a liability, thanks to his above average accuracy. Ruiz is a below average pitch framer and, thanks to lacking that asset, he should see his defensive value begin to wane as he continues to age and lose mobility behind the plate. However, if his hands and plus release don't show signs of any wear-and-tear, he may yet finish out the last two years of his contract still being a serviceable catcher in the big leagues.

Jarrod Saltalamacchia

	BASIC							BUNTS			PITCHER HANDLING						STOLEN BASES						RUNS SAVED						
Year	Team	G	Inn	TC	E	Pct	GFP	DM	Opps	Sac Hits	Bunt Hits	W	L	Pct	CERA	Extra Strikes	Pitch Block	SB	CCS	PCS	CPO	CS%	SB Saved	Adj ER	SB	Bunt	GFP/ DME	SZ	Total	Rank
2007	2 tms	47	372.2	285	3	.989	7	23	3	2	0	19	23	.452	4.76	-	139	37	6	2	0	.14	-3	-1	-2	0	-1	-	-4	-
2008	Tex	54	464.1	371	9	.976	5	21	4	0	2	26	26	.500	5.14	-	146	40	7	2	0	.15	-6	0	-5	-1	-2	-	-8	-
2009	Tex	83	714.0	537	7	.987	4	27	6	2	1	46	36	.561	4.08	-	231	61	17	2	0	.22	-1	5	-1	0	0	-	4	12
2010	2 tms	7	52.2	49	1	.980	0	0	1	1	0	1	5	.167	4.27	0	11	6	1	0	0	.14	0	0	0	0	-1	0	-1	-
2011	Bos	101	856.0	740	6	.992	9	50	10	3	2	47	49	.490	4.62	92	274	83	28	9	0	.25	-4	-2	-4	-1	-8	11	4	10
2012	Bos	104	852.0	763	7	.991	9	32	6	4	1	37	58	.389	4.85	73	339	80	15	3	0	.16	-4	-4	-3	1	2	9	5	15
2013	Bos	119	1004.0	960	6	.994	6	38	5	0	3	70	41	.631	3.86	19	468	89	21	3	0	.19	-4	-2	-4	-2	1	2	-5	23
2014	Mia	107	922.2	801	15	.981	2	42	13	8	0	54	49	.524	3.59	-131	377	72	15	2	0	.17	-3	3	-3	-3	-3	-16	-22	35
		622	5238.1	4506	54	.988	42	233	48	20	9	300	287	.511	4.31	53	1985	468	110	23	0	.19	-16	-1	-14	-6	-12	6	-27	-

After a couple of solid seasons behind the plate in Boston, Jarrod Saltalamacchia has taken a step backward with his defense. A good pitch-framer in his days with the Red Sox, Saltalamacchia lost 131 strikes with his framing in 2014, costing the Marlins 16 runs with his glove alone. Much of this can likely be attributed to working with an entirely new pitching staff, but his Strike Zone Runs Saved has declined in four consecutive seasons. Moreover, since saving four runs on stolen bases in 2011, Saltalamacchia has not thrown out more than 19 percent of runners in a single season, losing a combined 10 runs on stolen bases from 2012 to 2014. Standing at 6'4", 235 pounds, Saltalamacchia is not the most nimble or flexible backstop, a fact that exacerbated itself in the last two seasons. Saltalamacchia lost a combined five runs on bunt attempts in 2013 and 2014. Saltalamacchia's defensive numbers should improve in 2015, if only because he will have more experience with the Marlins' pitching staff. However, his lack of athleticism limits his ability to make tough plays and plays in the dirt, which in turn limits his upside on defense.

Catchers

Hector Sanchez

	BASIC							BUNTS			PITCHER HANDLING						STOLEN BASES						RUNS SAVED						
Year Team	G	Inn	TC	E	Pct	GFP	DM	Opps	Sac Hits	Bunt Hits	W	L	Pct	CERA	Extra Strikes	Pitch Block	SB	CCS	PCS	CPO	CS%	SB Saved	Adj ER	SB	Bunt	GFP/DME	SZ	Total	Rank
2011 SF	11	63.0	54	0	1.000	0	3	1	1	0	3	3	.500	5.29	-5	43	10	2	2	0	.17	-1	0	-1	0	0	-1	-2	-
2012 SF	56	441.0	383	7	.982	7	27	6	3	0	30	18	.625	4.00	-20	224	40	11	1	0	.22	0	1	0	0	-1	-2	-2	-
2013 SF	33	220.1	226	1	.996	3	17	4	2	0	15	9	.625	4.17	13	118	21	5	1	0	.19	0	0	0	0	-2	2	0	-
2014 SF	45	317.2	292	3	.990	0	18	3	2	0	18	15	.545	3.68	11	193	31	9	5	0	.23	0	1	0	0	-1	1	1	-
	145	1042.0	955	11	.988	10	65	14	8	0	66	45	.595	4.02	-1	578	102	27	9	0	.21	-1	2	-1	0	-4	0	-3	-

Geovany Soto

	BASIC							BUNTS			PITCHER HANDLING						STOLEN BASES						RUNS SAVED						
Year Team	G	Inn	TC	E	Pct	GFP	DM	Opps	Sac Hits	Bunt Hits	W	L	Pct	CERA	Extra Strikes	Pitch Block	SB	CCS	PCS	CPO	CS%	SB Saved	Adj ER	SB	Bunt	GFP/DME	SZ	Total	Rank
2006 ChC	7	55.0	71	1	.986	1	2				2	5	.286	5.24	-	19	5	0	0	0	.00	-1	0	0		0	-	0	-
2007 ChC	16	122.0	119	0	1.000	1	3				10	3	.769	3.61	-	39	10	4	0	0	.29	0	0	0		1	-	1	-
2008 ChC	136	1150.1	1071	5	.995	10	33	6	1	1	80	51	.611	3.80	-	370	69	18	7	0	.21	-6	3	-4	-1	1	-	-1	22
2009 ChC	96	811.0	775	5	.994	6	29	15	10	0	41	51	.446	4.00	-	265	59	23	0	0	.28	1	-1	-1	0	-1	-	-1	19
2010 ChC	104	847.1	811	4	.995	6	31	4	3	0	49	48	.505	4.29	45	324	74	18	3	0	.20	-6	1	-4	0	1	5	3	15
2011 ChC	122	1041.2	994	13	.987	13	36	20	13	0	49	70	.412	4.31	72	371	85	30	6	0	.26	2	-2	1	1	-1	9	8	8
2012 2 tms	96	806.2	759	8	.989	3	32	12	6	1	52	40	.565	4.17	52	302	65	13	8	0	.17	-1	0	-2	-2	-2	6	0	21
2013 Tex	53	431.1	424	2	.995	7	19	5	3	0	27	22	.551	3.67	13	184	24	10	0	0	.29	2	0	1	1	0	2	4	-
2014 2 tms	24	204.2	213	3	.986	1	12	3	3	0	9	15	.375	3.78	5	77	13	8	2	0	.38	2	0	1	0	0		1	-
	654	5470.0	5237	41	.992	48	197	65	39	2	319	305	.511	4.06	187	1951	404	124	26	0	.23	-6	1	-6	-1	-1	22	15	-

Chris Stewart

	BASIC							BUNTS			PITCHER HANDLING						STOLEN BASES						RUNS SAVED						
Year Team	G	Inn	TC	E	Pct	GFP	DM	Opps	Sac Hits	Bunt Hits	W	L	Pct	CERA	Extra Strikes	Pitch Block	SB	CCS	PCS	CPO	CS%	SB Saved	Adj ER	SB	Bunt	GFP/DME	SZ	Total	Rank
2006 CWS	5	15.0	19	0	1.000	0	0				1	0	1.000	4.80	-	1	1	2	0	0	.67	1	0	1		0	-	1	-
2007 Tex	17	105.1	106	2	.981	0	10				5	6	.455	4.96	-	28	8	4	0	0	.33	0	0	0		-2	-	-2	-
2008 NYY	1	8.0	8	0	1.000	0	2				0	1	.000	6.75	-	3	1	0	0	0	.00	0	0	0		0		0	-
2010 SD	1	1.0	1	0	1.000	0	0				0	0	.000	0.00	0		0	0	0	0	-		0	0		0		0	-
2011 SF	63	460.1	485	7	.986	9	21	6	5	0	27	24	.529	2.70	92	205	34	19	3	2	.36	7	3	6	1	0	11	21	-
2012 NYY	54	395.1	408	4	.990	2	12	3	2	1	28	18	.609	3.41	67	220	27	7	1	0	.21	0	2	0	0	1	8	11	-
2013 NYY	108	844.1	798	2	.997	10	34	7	3	1	51	46	.526	4.05	96	528	37	17	0	1	.31	2	-5	2	0	2	11	10	5
2014 Pit	46	351.0	340	3	.991	5	19	3	3	0	16	21	.432	3.79	34	191	30	7	2	3	.19	-1	-1	1	0	-1	4	3	-
	295	2180.1	2165	18	.992	26	98	19	13	2	128	116	.525	3.67	289	1176	130	56	6	6	.20	10	1	10	1	0	34	44	-

Kurt Suzuki

	BASIC							BUNTS			PITCHER HANDLING						STOLEN BASES						RUNS SAVED						
Year Team	G	Inn	TC	E	Pct	GFP	DM	Opps	Sac Hits	Bunt Hits	W	L	Pct	CERA	Extra Strikes	Pitch Block	SB	CCS	PCS	CPO	CS%	SB Saved	Adj ER	SB	Bunt	GFP/DME	SZ	Total	Rank
2007 Oak	66	539.0	465	2	.996	4	20	6	4	2	27	34	.443	5.31	-	261	29	7	0	0	.19	0	-7	0	-1	0	-	-8	30
2008 Oak	141	1215.0	986	6	.994	18	21	3	0	0	64	72	.471	3.86	-	425	55	16	16	0	.23	3	3	2	0	6	-	11	3
2009 Oak	135	1173.1	996	5	.995	27	39	6	5	0	61	71	.462	4.24	-	507	81	17	10	0	.17	-3	1	-2	0	5	-	4	7
2010 Oak	123	1058.1	868	8	.991	17	32	8	2	1	65	56	.537	3.29	-2	389	66	10	9	0	.13	-3	6	-2	1	3	0	8	9
2011 Oak	129	1132.1	976	7	.993	20	48	8	3	2	55	72	.433	3.78	-64	471	98	23	15	1	.19	0	-4	0	1	0	-8	-10	25
2012 2 tms	117	1014.0	881	5	.994	14	34	17	7	1	64	49	.566	3.51	-117	464	65	20	8	1	.24	4	-4	4	0	3	-14	-11	30
2013 2 tms	93	748.0	662	5	.991	14	16	14	6	2	41	41	.500	3.87	-40	358	57	4	4	0	.07	-7	-3	-6	1	5	-5	-8	28
2014 Min	119	1017.2	780	4	.995	6	35	6	1	3	52	63	.452	4.52	-127	461	64	11	10	0	.15	-6	0	-5	0	3	-15	-17	34
	923	7897.2	6614	43	.993	120	245	68	28	11	429	458	.484	3.97	-350	3336	515	108	72	2	.17	-12	-8	-8	1	26	-42	-31	-

Early in his career (2008-10), Kurt Suzuki consistently ranked in the top ten in Defensive Runs Saved. However, from 2011 through 2014 he has ranked in the bottom ten, bottoming out as the second-worst catcher in baseball in 2014 according to Runs Saved. Most of this is due to the inclusion of Strike Zone Runs Saved, where he was a daunting 15 runs below average. Suzuki has consistently been in the red zone with -117, -40, and -127 extra strikes called for the past three years. In his favor, his quick reflexes behind the plate are paired with his excellent ability to block balls in the dirt year after year. Suzuki's leadership has further enchanted enough teams that he has never had a shortage of potential suitors.

Josh Thole

	BASIC							BUNTS			PITCHER HANDLING						STOLEN BASES						RUNS SAVED						
Year Team	G	Inn	TC	E	Pct	GFP	DM	Opps	Sac Hits	Bunt Hits	W	L	Pct	CERA	Extra Strikes	Pitch Block	SB	CCS	PCS	CPO	CS%	SB Saved	Adj ER	SB	Bunt	GFP/DME	SZ	Total	Rank
2009 NYM	16	127.1	76	1	.987	0	6				7	8	.467	4.24	-	24	4	1	1	0	.20	0	0	0		-1	-	-1	-
2010 NYM	61	467.1	373	3	.992	6	17	14	6	3	21	30	.412	3.56	24	118	14	8	3	0	.36	1	-1	0	0	0	3	2	-
2011 NYM	102	793.1	703	2	.997	9	31	16	13	0	45	46	.495	4.23	1	284	65	14	3	0	.18	-6	-1	-4	0	-1	0	-6	20
2012 NYM	100	798.1	746	6	.992	11	26	10	4	0	44	46	.489	3.77	71	264	57	13	4	1	.19	-1	4	-1	2	-3	8	10	5
2013 Tor	39	288.1	268	2	.993	1	12				17	17	.500	4.46	3	102	22	4	4	1	.15	-1	-1	0	0	-2	0	-3	-
2014 Tor	53	356.2	307	1	.997	2	13				17	24	.415	3.94	15	139	22	1	3	0	.04	-4	0	-3	0	-2	2	-3	-
	371	2831.1	2473	15	.994	29	105	40	23	3	151	171	.469	3.98	114	931	184	41	18	2	.18	-11	1	-8	2	-9	13	-1	-

Catchers

Christian Vazquez

	BASIC								BUNTS			PITCHER HANDLING						STOLEN BASES						RUNS SAVED						
Year	Team	G	Inn	TC	E	Pct	GFP	DM	Opps	Sac Hits	Bunt Hits	W	L	Pct	CERA	Extra Strikes	Pitch Block	SB	CCS	PCS	CPO	CS%	SB Saved	Adj ER	SB	Bunt	GFP/ DME	SZ	Total	Rank
2014	Bos	54	458.1	375	5	.987	10	18	4	0	0	23	27	.460	3.71	75	199	14	15	0	3	.52	6	2	5	0	-2	9	14	-

With Vazquez, the most obvious tool that sticks out is his cannon of an arm. The Boston rookie routinely reels off sub-1.9 second pop times and can drop down even quicker when needed with help from incredibly quick transfers from his glove to his throwing hand. Vazquez finished his first season with an average pop time of 1.84 seconds—the third-best average among backstops with at least 10 attempts—and boasts an otherworldly season-best time of 1.66 seconds, which he used to gun down Mike Trout during a steal attempt in mid-August. Vazquez' ability to control the running game launched him to the top of the Stolen Base Runs Saved leaderboard in 2014 despite playing in fewer games than his peers.

While Vazquez' arm frequently leaves jaws on the floor, his more subtle but equally impressive skill is his receiving. Similar to his mentor, Jose Molina, Vazquez is extremely quiet setting up behind the plate and will frequently steal strikes with his ability to massage pitches off the plate back into the zone. Seeing Vazquez atop the Strike Zone Runs Saved leaderboard after just over a third of a major league season only confirms what the eye test suggests. During his first taste of the majors, Vazquez has flaunted tools behind the plate that rival those of his Puerto Rican catching brethren. With some extra seasoning and experience handling major league pitchers, he should quickly evolve into one of the top defensive catchers in the game.

Mike Zunino

	BASIC								BUNTS			PITCHER HANDLING						STOLEN BASES						RUNS SAVED						
Year	Team	G	Inn	TC	E	Pct	GFP	DM	Opps	Sac Hits	Bunt Hits	W	L	Pct	CERA	Extra Strikes	Pitch Block	SB	CCS	PCS	CPO	CS%	SB Saved	Adj ER	SB	Bunt	GFP/ DME	SZ	Total	Rank
2013	Sea	50	429.2	387	2	.995	2	31	5	1	1	25	23	.521	4.13	46	278	28	4	2	0	.13	-3	1	-3	0	-3	5	0	-
2014	Sea	130	1121.0	1099	5	.995	5	64	6	1	1	68	57	.544	3.18	133	685	71	25	3	0	.26	2	-4	1	0	-5	16	8	8
		180	1550.2	1486	7	.995	7	95	11	2	2	93	80	.538	3.44	179	963	99	29	5	0	.23	-1	-3	-2	0	-8	21	8	-

As a defensive catcher, Mike Zunino makes his bones as a pitch framer. Zunino led the majors by earning 133 extra strikes for Mariners pitchers in 2014. Zunino excels in getting strike calls at the bottom of the zone, which is important with the heavy changeup/split finger use of many on the Mariners staff. Zunino has also impressed with his arm in 2014, nailing 26 percent of would be basestealers. Zunino possesses a strong arm and quick feet, which leads to quicker than average pop times. If he struggles at all with his throwing, it is with his accuracy. When Zunino tries to rush too much, his ball tends to tail into the runner. Zunino is also a mixed bag when it comes to blocking balls in the dirt. Thanks in part to the difficulty of catching the Mariners staff, Zunino was last in the league with 62 wild pitches against, but was also third in the majors with 685 succesful blocks. Zunino is athletic enough that he should continue to improve his blocking abilities. If he can continue to develop the rest of his skills, the young catcher should find himself on some Fielding Bible Award ballots in the years ahead.

First Basemen Register and Scouting Reports

Year	Fielding Bible Award Winner	Runner Up	Third Place
2006	Albert Pujols	Mark Teixeira	Doug Mientkiewicz
2007	Albert Pujols	Casey Kotchman	Kevin Youkilis
2008	Albert Pujols	Mark Teixeira	Casey Kotchman
2009	Albert Pujols	Kevin Youkilis	Adrian Gonzalez
2010	Daric Barton	Albert Pujols	Ike Davis
2011	Albert Pujols	Adrian Gonzalez	James Loney
2012	Mark Teixeira	Adrian Gonzalez	Albert Pujols
2013	Paul Goldschmidt	Anthony Rizzo	Adrian Gonzalez
2014	Adrian Gonzalez	Anthony Rizzo	Justin Morneau

First Basemen

Jose Abreu

	BASIC							BUNTS			GDP			RANGE AND POSITIONING								RUNS SAVED					
Year Team	G	Inn	TC	E	Pct	GFP	DM	Opp	Sac Hits	Bunt Hits	Opp GDP		Pct	Outs Made	To His Right	Straight On	To His Left	GB	Air	Plays Saved	Bases Saved	R/P	Bunt	GDP	GFP/DME	Total	Rank
2014 CWS	109	957.1	1045	6	.994	30	21	10	6	2	13	4	.308	143	0	-7	-1	-8	-1	-9	-9	-6	0	0	-4	-10	35

Scout's Defensive Rating: -5 plays saved in 2014

Abreu's first season defensively was one of the worst by any first baseman in baseball in 2014. He is simply a big bulky guy built to hit for power and not to be a game changer on defense. He is very slow with his initial first step, which really limits his lateral range, causing many balls to skip by him down the line or in the hole.

Abreu also struggles with handling tough throws at first base. He had nine defensive misplays in 2014 in which he failed to catch the throw from another infielder, which was tied for the most in the major leagues with Ryan Howard. The best part about his defensive game is his throwing arm. When he is required and able to make a throw, it is almost always strong and on target. Unfortunately, it's only a matter of time before Abreu will need to transition to DH.

Matt Adams

	BASIC							BUNTS			GDP			RANGE AND POSITIONING								RUNS SAVED					
Year Team	G	Inn	TC	E	Pct	GFP	DM	Opp	Sac Hits	Bunt Hits	Opp GDP		Pct	Outs Made	To His Right	Straight On	To His Left	GB	Air	Plays Saved	Bases Saved	R/P	Bunt	GDP	GFP/DME	Total	Rank
2012 StL	24	194.2	225	3	.987	11	3	3	1	2	4	1	.250	40	0	+2	0	+2	0	+2	+2	2	-1	0	0	1	-
2013 StL	74	597.2	650	2	.997	28	18	9	5	1	4	2	.500	115	-3	+1	-1	-3	+2	-1	0	-1	1	0	-2	-2	22
2014 StL	133	1163.0	1204	9	.993	51	17	15	8	2	9	4	.444	188	+3	0	+4	+7	+2	+9	+10	7	1	0	0	8	4
	231	1955.1	2079	14	.993	90	38	27	14	5	17	7	.412	343	0	+3	+3	+6	+4	+10	+12	8	1	0	-2	7	-

Scout's Defensive Rating: 1 plays saved in 2013, 3 plays saved in 2014

Weighing in at 260 pounds, Matthew "Big City" Adams is large even for a first baseman. As a minor leaguer, various talent evaluators noted that, due to his hefty frame and seeming lack of mobility, Adams projected to be, at best, "good enough" defensively to justify the presence of his bat in the lineup on an everyday basis. Adams looks like a guy who should be a defensive liability, yet both traditional and advanced defensive metrics indicate that he is in fact one of the best ten or so defensive first basemen in the Majors.

Adams performed exceptionally on defense in 2014, posting eight Defensive Runs Saved and 25 Net GFP-DME. Adams' soft hands also served him well in 2014 as he accumulated 25 Good Fielding Plays scooping difficult throws in the dirt from infielders. Despite not exactly passing the traditional eye test for athleticism, Adams moves well for his size. He displayed a penchant for laying out to corral balls toward the outermost reaches of his range as evidenced by a 42 percent conversion rate on diving plays – ninth best among major league regulars at first. Adams profiles as a player whose defensive ability will likely not age well; however, he has proven doubters wrong at every stage of his baseball career. The Cardinals are hoping the trend of exceeding expectations continues for the foreseeable future.

Yonder Alonso

	BASIC							BUNTS			GDP			RANGE AND POSITIONING								RUNS SAVED					
Year Team	G	Inn	TC	E	Pct	GFP	DM	Opp	Sac Hits	Bunt Hits	Opp GDP		Pct	Outs Made	To His Right	Straight On	To His Left	GB	Air	Plays Saved	Bases Saved	R/P	Bunt	GDP	GFP/DME	Total	Rank
2010 Cin	6	30.0	30	2	.933	1	1				1	1	1.000	11	+1	0	0	0	0	0	+1	1		0	1	2	-
2011 Cin	3	13.0	11	0	1.000	0	1	1	1	0	1	0	.000	2	0	0	0	0	0	0	0	0	0	0	0	0	-
2012 SD	149	1276.1	1377	12	.991	72	20	16	10	1	13	6	.462	244	-1	+7	-2	+3	-2	+1	-3	-2	2	0	2	2	12
2013 SD	92	771.0	822	3	.996	45	16	12	6	3	15	5	.333	140	+4	+4	+3	+11	+3	+11	+10	4	0	0	-1	7	5
2014 SD	77	628.2	613	2	.997	44	5	18	9	1	9	2	.222	89	+1	+3	+1	+5	+2	+7	+6	4	2	0	3	9	3
	327	2719.0	2853	19	.993	162	43	47	26	5	39	14	.359	486	+5	+14	+2	+19	0	+19	+14	11	4	0	5	20	-

Scout's Defensive Rating: 8 plays saved in 2013, 11 plays saved in 2014

Yonder Alonso is slowly becoming one of the better defensive first basemen in Major League Baseball. From 2012 to 2014, he totaled 18 Defensive Runs Saved, which ranks him fifth among first basemen behind 2014 Fielding Bible Award winner Adrian Gonzalez, Anthony Rizzo (the man the Padres traded so Alonso could get playing time), Joey Votto and Mark Teixeira. For 2014, Alonso finished tied for second in Defensive Runs Saved with nine, and finished fifth in the Fielding Bible Awards balloting.

First Basemen

Alonso continues to make his presence known on the diamond, such as being one of the best at turning bunts into outs or as the player who strives to limit his Defensive Misplays. From 2012 to 2014, Alonso tied for the lead among first basemen with four Bunt Runs Saved. For the 2014 season, Alonso amassed only five Defensive Misplays; no other first baseman with as many Good Fielding Plays as Alonso (44) has fewer than 12 Misplays. Given his youth, Alonso should remain an above average defender at first for many years ahead.

Jeff Baker

		BASIC							BUNTS			GDP			RANGE AND POSITIONING								RUNS SAVED					
Year	Team	G	Inn	TC	E	Pct	GFP	DM	Opp	Sac Hits	Bunt Hits	Opp	GDP	Pct	Outs Made	To His Right	Straight On	To His Left	GB	Air	Plays Saved	Bases Saved	R/P	Bunt	GDP	GFP/DME	Total	Rank
2006	Col	1	3.0	4	0	1.000	0	0				-	-	-	0	0	0	0	0	0	0	0	0		-	0	0	-
2007	Col	20	96.2	125	3	.976	4	0				-	-	-	18	0	-1	+1	0	-1	-1	-1	-1			0	-1	-
2008	Col	22	128.2	148	0	1.000	2	5	1	1	0	-	-	-	25	+1	-2	0	-1	0	-1	-2	-1	0	-	-1	-2	-
2009	2 tms	3	10.0	11	0	1.000	0	0				0	0	-	0	-1	0	0	-1	0	-1	-1	-1		0	0	-1	-
2010	ChC	4	20.1	20	0	1.000	1	0				0	0	-	3	0	-1	0	0	0	0	0	0		0	0	0	-
2011	ChC	19	126.0	121	0	1.000	2	2	1	1	0	0	0	-	19	0	+1	+1	+1	0	+1	+1	1	0	0	0	1	-
2012	ChC	20	156.2	152	2	.987	7	5				2	0	.000	13	-3	-1	-1	-5	-1	-6	-6	-5	0	-1		-6	-
2013	Tex	21	114.0	112	0	1.000	3	3	1	1	0	1	0	.000	13	0	+1	0	+1	0	+1	+1	1	0	0	-1	0	-
2014	Mia	43	257.2	280	2	.993	12	4	2	2	0	3	1	.333	29	0	-2	-1	-3	-1	-4	-5	-4	0	0	1	-3	-
		153	913.0	973	7	.993	31	19	5	5	0	6	1	.167	120	-3	-5	0	-8	-3	-11	-13	-10	0	0	-2	-12	-

Scout's Defensive Rating: 1 plays saved in 2013, -2 plays saved in 2014

Brandon Belt

		BASIC							BUNTS			GDP			RANGE AND POSITIONING								RUNS SAVED					
Year	Team	G	Inn	TC	E	Pct	GFP	DM	Opp	Sac Hits	Bunt Hits	Opp	GDP	Pct	Outs Made	To His Right	Straight On	To His Left	GB	Air	Plays Saved	Bases Saved	R/P	Bunt	GDP	GFP/DME	Total	Rank
2011	SF	31	203.0	214	2	.995	9	3	1	0	0	1	1	1.000	32	0	0	+1	+2	0	+2	+1	1	0	0	0	1	-
2012	SF	139	976.1	994	8	.992	36	14	19	12	2	12	8	.667	156	+3	+2	-3	+2	+2	+4	+4	3	2	1	-1	5	8
2013	SF	143	1174.1	1162	8	.993	49	27	20	12	3	15	4	.267	204	+2	+6	+2	+10	-1	+9	+9	7	1	0	-4	4	11
2014	SF	59	487.2	558	4	.993	16	7	8	4	1	4	1	.250	96	0	+1	+2	+3	+1	+4	+4	2	1	0	0	3	13
		372	2841.1	2928	21	.993	110	51	48	28	6	32	14	.438	488	+5	+9	+2	+17	+2	+19	+18	13	4	1	-5	13	-

Scout's Defensive Rating: -1 plays saved in 2013, 0 plays saved in 2014

The high praise on Belt early on in his career was largely due to his offensive production rather than his defensive abilities at first base. Despite the question marks, however, Belt is nothing short of average when it comes to defense. He's athletic and displays some quickness, but he's not going to light up the highlight reels on a nightly basis. He has struggled to come up big on difficult plays in his direction and experienced some difficulty handling tough throws from infielders. BIS Video Scouts weren't impressed with his play either, giving Belt a +0 Scouts Defensive Rating. However Belt's inability to make the big play does not imply that he isn't a reliable defender. Belt will consistently make routine plays, as he is mobile for a player his size and covers his zone well. In the prime of his career, Belt isn't likely to make any tremendous strides forward yet could remain an average or better first baseman for several years.

Billy Butler

		BASIC							BUNTS			GDP			RANGE AND POSITIONING								RUNS SAVED					
Year	Team	G	Inn	TC	E	Pct	GFP	DM	Opp	Sac Hits	Bunt Hits	Opp	GDP	Pct	Outs Made	To His Right	Straight On	To His Left	GB	Air	Plays Saved	Bases Saved	R/P	Bunt	GDP	GFP/DME	Total	Rank
2007	KC	13	83.0	89	2	.978	5	2				-	-	-	20	+1	+2	0	+3	0	+3	+3	2		-	-1	1	-
2008	KC	34	260.0	244	2	.992	9	6	1	0	0	-	-	-	37	-5	+1	+1	-4	0	-4	-4	-3	0	-	0	-3	-
2009	KC	145	1248.0	1243	10	.992	51	34	7	3	2	16	5	.313	243	0	-8	+2	-7	0	-7	-7	-5	0	0	-3	-8	33
2010	KC	127	1102.1	1104	6	.995	33	21	7	6	1	14	5	.357	206	+2	0	-2	0	-2	-2	-2	-2	0	0	-3	-5	27
2011	KC	11	94.2	94	0	1.000	1	1	1	0	0	2	0	.000	12	-1	-2	-1	-3	+1	-2	-2	-2	0	0	0	-2	-
2012	KC	20	165.2	165	3	.982	7	5	1	1	0	2	1	.500	25	-1	-1	+1	-2	-2	-4	-3	-2	0	0	-1	-3	-
2013	KC	7	53.0	56	0	1.000	1	2	1	0	0	0	0	-	9	0	0	+1	0	0	0	0	0	0	0	0	0	-
2014	KC	37	310.0	298	2	.993	9	5	1	1	0	3	1	.333	48	-2	-1	-1	-4	0	-4	-4	-3	0	0	0	-3	-
		394	3316.2	3293	25	.992	116	76	19	11	3	37	12	.324	600	-6	-9	+1	-17	-3	-20	-19	-15	0	0	-8	-23	-

Scout's Defensive Rating: -1 plays saved in 2013, -1 plays saved in 2014

First Basemen

Miguel Cabrera

	BASIC								BUNTS			GDP			RANGE AND POSITIONING								RUNS SAVED					
Year	Team	G	Inn	TC	E	Pct	GFP	DM	Opp	Sac Hits	Bunt Hits	Opp	GDP	Pct	Outs Made	To His Right	Straight On	To His Left	GB	Air	Plays Saved	Bases Saved	R/P	Bunt	GDP	GFP/ DME	Total	Rank
2008	Det	143	1204.0	1199	9	.992	38	24	3	1	1	-	-	-	219	-4	-5	+3	-7	-1	-8	-6	-4	0	-	-3	-7	30
2009	Det	153	1315.0	1327	7	.995	68	26	10	5	3	26	8	.308	280	+1	-4	+4	+1	-1	0	+2	1	-1	0	-1	-1	21
2010	Det	148	1285.1	1327	13	.990	52	17	13	6	3	22	8	.364	243	-9	+4	0	-4	+1	-3	-4	-3	-1	0	1	-3	25
2011	Det	152	1322.0	1379	13	.991	52	15	11	5	4	23	13	.565	217	-7	0	0	-6	-2	-8	-6	-4	-1	1	2	-2	24
2012	Det	2	3.0	4	0	1.000	0	1				0	0	-	0	0	0	0	0	0	0	0	0	0	0	0	-
2014	Det	126	1083.1	1081	5	.995	39	20	5	2	1	20	12	.600	208	0	-6	+2	-4	+2	-2	-2	-2	0	1	0	-1	21
		724	6212.2	6317	47	.993	249	103	42	19	12	91	41	.451	1167	-19	-11	+9	-20	-1	-21	-16	-12	-3	2	-1	-14	

Scout's Defensive Rating: 0 plays saved in 2014

Miguel Cabrera moved back to first base full time for the 2014 season after two rough seasons at the hot corner. However, for a player of his size at 240 pounds, he is more nimble and quick on defense than one would expect. Cabrera's average defense at first base represents a massive upgrade over his -18 Runs Saved at third base during the 2013 season. Limited range and arm strength are the primary reasons that Cabrera is better off at first base than third base. However, Cabrera thinks like a first baseman with much better range, causing him to stray off the base after a grounder far enough in the hole that he can't get back for the throw from the second baseman. Cabrera has quick hands and will catch or scoop up anything close to him; this includes grounders and throws from infielders. His arm is fine for a first baseman, but it was exploited at third base. Even at 31 years old Cabrera is still a fine enough defensive first baseman, though a move to designated hitter is likely in the cards in a couple of years.

Mike Carp

	BASIC								BUNTS			GDP			RANGE AND POSITIONING								RUNS SAVED					
Year	Team	G	Inn	TC	E	Pct	GFP	DM	Opp	Sac Hits	Bunt Hits	Opp	GDP	Pct	Outs Made	To His Right	Straight On	To His Left	GB	Air	Plays Saved	Bases Saved	R/P	Bunt	GDP	GFP/ DME	Total	Rank
2009	Sea	16	127.1	130	0	1.000	6	1	1	0	1	4	2	.500	36	0	+1	+1	+2	0	+2	+2	1	0	0	1	2	-
2010	Sea	9	66.0	69	0	1.000	3	0				0	0	-	10	0	0	0	+1	0	+1	+1	1	0	0	1	1	-
2011	Sea	34	263.2	269	2	.993	13	7	3	1	0	3	1	.333	47	+2	-2	0	-1	-1	-2	-2	-1	0	0	-1	-1	-
2012	Sea	23	199.2	201	0	1.000	8	4				4	0	.000	35	0	-1	+1	+1	0	+1	+1	1	0	0	1	1	-
2013	Bos	29	202.0	202	2	.990	5	1				3	1	.333	32	+1	-1	-1	0	-1	-1	-2	-1	0	0	-1	-1	-
2014	2 tms	32	209.0	199	2	.990	13	4				3	3	1.000	35	+1	-2	0	-1	0	-1	-2	-1	0	0	-1	-1	-
		143	1067.2	1070	6	.994	48	17	4	1	1	17	7	.412	195	+4	-5	+1	+2	-2	0	-2	0	0	0	1	1	

Scout's Defensive Rating: 0 plays saved in 2013, 0 plays saved in 2014

Allen Craig

	BASIC								BUNTS			GDP			RANGE AND POSITIONING								RUNS SAVED					
Year	Team	G	Inn	TC	E	Pct	GFP	DM	Opp	Sac Hits	Bunt Hits	Opp	GDP	Pct	Outs Made	To His Right	Straight On	To His Left	GB	Air	Plays Saved	Bases Saved	R/P	Bunt	GDP	GFP/ DME	Total	Rank
2010	StL	5	17.0	17	0	1.000	1	0				1	1	1.000	4	0	0	-1	-1	0	-1	-1	0	0	0	0	0	-
2011	StL	2	4.0	6	0	1.000	0	0				0	0	-	0	0	0	0	0	0	0	0	0	0	0	0	0	-
2012	StL	91	773.2	805	4	.995	24	10	10	7	1	2	0	.000	124	-2	-4	0	-6	-2	-8	-6	-5	1	0	1	-3	25
2013	StL	95	775.2	838	1	.999	54	9	5	3	0	8	5	.625	138	-3	-4	+2	-5	+2	-3	-3	-2	1	0	0	-1	20
2014	2 tms	41	334.0	354	0	1.000	20	7	3	1	1	5	1	.200	63	0	-2	+3	+1	0	+1	+1	1	-1	0	0	0	-
		234	1904.1	2020	5	.998	99	26	18	11	2	16	7	.438	329	-5	-10	+4	-11	0	-11	-9	-6	1	0	1	-4	

Scout's Defensive Rating: 8 plays saved in 2013, 2 plays saved in 2014

Allen Craig's Scouting Report can be found on page 282.

C.J. Cron

	BASIC								BUNTS			GDP			RANGE AND POSITIONING								RUNS SAVED					
Year	Team	G	Inn	TC	E	Pct	GFP	DM	Opp	Sac Hits	Bunt Hits	Opp	GDP	Pct	Outs Made	To His Right	Straight On	To His Left	GB	Air	Plays Saved	Bases Saved	R/P	Bunt	GDP	GFP/ DME	Total	Rank
2014	LAA	36	251.0	234	1	.996	6	12	1	0	0	1	1	1.000	32	0	-1	-4	-5	0	-5	-5	-4	0	0	-1	-5	-

Scout's Defensive Rating: -3 plays saved in 2014

First Basemen

Chris Davis

Year	Team	G	Inn	TC	E	Pct	GFP	DM	Opp	Sac Hits	Bunt Hits	Opp	GDP	Pct	Outs Made	To His Right	Straight On	To His Left	GB	Air	Plays Saved	Bases Saved	R/P	Bunt	GDP	GFP/ DME	Total	Rank
2008	Tex	51	404.0	393	1	.997	22	10	3	2	0	-	-	-	78	-2	0	-2	-3	+1	-2	-3	-2	0	-	1	-1	18
2009	Tex	100	825.1	895	3	.997	55	18	2	1	1	8	3	.375	166	-2	-3	0	-5	-1	-6	-6	-4	0	0	1	-3	27
2010	Tex	41	298.2	293	2	.993	17	4	2	2	0	4	0	.000	50	+1	0	0	+1	+1	+2	+2	2	0	0	1	3	-
2011	2 tms	31	221.2	240	0	1.000	7	5	2	0	0	2	1	.500	34	0	-2	-2	-3	0	-3	-4	-3	1	0	0	-2	-
2012	Bal	38	343.0	374	4	.989	25	13	2	2	0	3	3	1.000	53	0	-1	0	0	0	0	0	0	0	0	-4	-4	-
2013	Bal	155	1377.2	1420	6	.996	70	24	8	2	3	12	4	.333	204	-1	-2	+1	-2	-2	-4	-8	-6	-1	0	0	-7	29
2014	Bal	115	942.2	965	4	.996	61	14	7	2	1	13	3	.231	143	+7	+3	-2	+9	+2	+11	+9	6	0	0	2	8	5
		531	4413.0	4580	20	.996	257	88	26	11	5	42	14	.333	728	+3	-5	-5	-3	+1	-2	-10	-7	0	0	1	-6	-

Scout's Defensive Rating: -5 plays saved in 2013, 4 plays saved in 2014

Chris Davis quietly put together the best defensive season of his career in 2014. Though out of place in his early days at the hot corner, Davis has always had the physical tools to be an excellent first basemen. He's a huge target, standing at 6'3" and weighing in at 230 pounds. Davis is a right handed first baseman and was excellent this season at using his backhand on balls that were hit in the hole between first and second. He showed tremendous athleticism while laying out for these balls that even left-handed first baseman would have struggled to get to. Adding to his above average range, Davis was able to notch 31 Good Fielding Plays that were due to his handling a difficult throw to record an out. His net GFP-DME of plus 43 ranked second at the first base position. If Davis can combine his 2013 hitting and his 2014 fielding, there is no question he would only enhance his MVP candidacy.

Ike Davis

Year	Team	G	Inn	TC	E	Pct	GFP	DM	Opp	Sac Hits	Bunt Hits	Opp	GDP	Pct	Outs Made	To His Right	Straight On	To His Left	GB	Air	Plays Saved	Bases Saved	R/P	Bunt	GDP	GFP/ DME	Total	Rank
2010	NYM	146	1263.0	1353	9	.993	44	16	28	16	3	16	11	.688	228	+5	+7	+3	+15	+2	+17	+16	11	1	1	0	13	2
2011	NYM	36	317.0	322	1	.997	8	12	4	4	0	5	0	.000	70	+2	+1	-1	+1	0	+1	+2	2	0	0	-1	1	-
2012	NYM	148	1222.1	1236	8	.994	43	14	19	10	3	16	7	.438	203	-1	0	-2	-3	0	-3	-4	-3	-1	0	1	-3	24
2013	NYM	96	781.0	852	9	.989	36	16	8	4	1	7	2	.286	139	+1	-2	0	-1	+2	+1	+1	1	1	0	-1	1	15
2014	2 tms	124	861.0	1022	9	.991	43	21	15	10	1	10	3	.300	119	-4	+1	+1	-2	-2	-4	-3	-2	0	0	-2	-4	25
		550	4444.1	4785	36	.992	174	79	74	44	8	54	23	.426	759	+3	+7	+1	+10	+2	+12	+12	9	1	1	-3	8	-

Scout's Defensive Rating: 0 plays saved in 2013, -2 plays saved in 2014

Ike Davis burst onto the scene as a rookie with the Mets in 2010, displaying great range and soft hands at first base to finish second in Defensive Runs Saved (DRS) and third in the Fielding Bible Award voting. However, a devastating ankle injury cut his 2011 season short, and his defense has never recovered. In 2014, Davis was ineffective again, and a midseason trade to Pittsburgh didn't help him fare any better. Davis had a career-worst 21 Defensive Misplays in 861 innings for the Mets and Pirates, struggling with everything from bad throws to subpar range to botched catches on line drives off the bat and on throws from his infielders. The BIS Video Scouts rated Davis below average as well according to the Scout's Defensive Rating, and frankly it's just tough to watch him play the field these days after seeing how well he performed as a rookie. Watching Davis play first base is reminiscent of former Angels first baseman Kendrys Morales, who had been a terrific defensive player himself before a similar ankle injury left him unable to play the position anymore. If Davis does not show marked improvement in 2015, he might be best suited playing for an American League team with an open designated hitter spot sooner rather than later.

Lucas Duda

Year	Team	G	Inn	TC	E	Pct	GFP	DM	Opp	Sac Hits	Bunt Hits	Opp	GDP	Pct	Outs Made	To His Right	Straight On	To His Left	GB	Air	Plays Saved	Bases Saved	R/P	Bunt	GDP	GFP/ DME	Total	Rank
2011	NYM	43	323.1	367	2	.995	15	8	6	3	1	4	2	.500	69	-1	+1	-1	-1	0	-1	-1	0	1	0	-1	0	-
2012	NYM	6	32.0	25	1	.960	1	0	2	2	0	0	0	-	6	0	0	0	+1	0	+1	+1	1	0	0	1	2	-
2013	NYM	34	280.0	255	0	1.000	23	3	6	5	0	5	3	.600	37	-2	+1	+1	-1	-1	-2	-2	-2	0	0	1	-1	-
2014	NYM	146	1225.0	1197	7	.994	64	23	11	7	1	16	8	.500	178	0	+4	-1	+3	+2	+5	+4	3	0	0	2	5	11
		229	1860.1	1844	10	.995	103	34	25	17	2	25	13	.520	290	-3	+6	-1	+2	+1	+3	+2	2	1	0	3	6	-

Scout's Defensive Rating: 1 plays saved in 2013, 2 plays saved in 2014

Lucas Duda spent 2014 primarily as a first baseman after spending almost every previous season splitting time between first and the outfield. Despite his struggles in the outfield, Duda proved to be a solid first baseman, totaling five Defen-

First Basemen

sive Runs Saved. Duda is not flashy but quietly effective. He has very soft hands and is very good at handling balls in the dirt around first. He recorded 38 Good Fielding Plays where he handled a difficult throw at first to record an out, which was only two off the major league lead. Now that Duda has put away the outfield glove for good, he should settle in as an average or better first baseman.

Edwin Encarnacion

		BASIC						BUNTS			GDP		RANGE AND POSITIONING								RUNS SAVED					
Year	Team	G	Inn	TC	E	Pct	GFP	DM	Opp	Sac Hits	Bunt Hits	Opp GDP	Pct	Outs Made	To His Right	Straight On	To His Left	GB	Air	Plays Saved	Bases Saved	R/P	Bunt	GDP	GFP/ DME	Total	Rank
2006	Cin	2	9.0	9	0	1.000	0	0	-	-	-	-	-	2	0	0	0	0	0	0	-	0	-	-	0	0	-
2011	Tor	25	190.0	205	4	.980	8	4	2	1	0	0	0	-	24	0	-1	0	-1	-1	-2	-2	-1	-1	0	-1	-3	-
2012	Tor	68	583.1	637	3	.995	35	9	4	1	3	5	2	.400	88	-2	-3	-1	-6	+2	-4	-2	-2	-2	0	3	-1	21
2013	Tor	79	698.2	739	6	.992	43	18	3	1	0	6	1	.167	115	-3	-5	-3	-10	0	-10	-9	-6	1	-1	-2	-8	31
2014	Tor	80	694.1	666	8	.988	34	13	3	2	1	2	1	.500	87	0	-4	-1	-4	-1	-5	-5	-4	0	0	-1	-5	31
		254	2175.1	2256	21	.991	120	44	12	5	4	13	4	.308	316	-5	-13	-5	-21	0	-21	-18	-13	-2	-1	-1	-17	-

Scout's Defensive Rating: -3 plays saved in 2013, 1 plays saved in 2014

The man affectionately known as "E5" finally played his way off of third base with his erratic fielding and moved across the diamond to first base for the Toronto Blue Jays. At 6'1", 230 lbs, Encarnacion has a big, muscular frame that hinders his range. As a former third baseman, Encarnacion has a strong arm, but he struggles with his accuracy. Encarnacion has pretty good hands when he gets to the ball, and handles hard hit balls at him very well. Encarnacion is a bit of a mixed bag when it comes to handling poor throws in the dirt. His hands allow him to pick some tough low throws, but his footwork around the bag is subpar, which causes him to miss throws that other first baseman routinely handle. Overall Encarnacion is never going to be even an average first baseman, but he can handle it well enough that it should remain an option for getting his bat in the lineup for the next few years before forcing a permanent move to DH.

Prince Fielder

		BASIC						BUNTS			GDP		RANGE AND POSITIONING								RUNS SAVED					
Year	Team	G	Inn	TC	E	Pct	GFP	DM	Opp	Sac Hits	Bunt Hits	Opp GDP	Pct	Outs Made	To His Right	Straight On	To His Left	GB	Air	Plays Saved	Bases Saved	R/P	Bunt	GDP	GFP/ DME	Total	Rank
2005	Mil	7	34.0	30	0	1.000	2	0	1	1	0	-	-	-	6				0	0	0	0	0	0	-	0	0	-
2006	Mil	152	1319.1	1358	11	.992	28	34	37	20	8	-	-	-	241	0	-6	-8	-15	-2	-17	-18	-13	-3	-	-6	-22	35
2007	Mil	153	1338.0	1276	14	.989	43	30	19	10	4	-	-	-	252	-4	-8	-4	-16	+1	-15	-15	-11	-3	-	-1	-15	34
2008	Mil	155	1383.2	1475	17	.988	54	30	26	15	2	-	-	-	257	-1	-4	-7	-12	-1	-13	-12	-9	1	-	-4	-12	34
2009	Mil	162	1431.0	1460	7	.995	64	23	16	9	4	12	6	.500	260	0	-4	-1	-5	+2	-3	-2	-1	-1	0	2	0	20
2010	Mil	160	1411.0	1341	4	.997	46	22	16	7	3	16	4	.250	231	+4	-9	-7	-13	-6	-19	-20	-14	0	0	-3	-17	35
2011	Mil	159	1394.2	1431	15	.989	48	27	12	7	1	17	7	.412	234	-3	-4	-2	-10	0	-10	-10	-7	0	0	-3	-10	32
2012	Det	159	1392.1	1372	11	.992	67	30	5	4	1	12	7	.583	259	0	-4	+4	0	-3	-3	-3	-2	-1	1	-2	-4	26
2013	Det	151	1323.2	1254	6	.995	54	17	6	3	2	7	4	.571	225	-5	-10	+1	-13	-3	-16	-18	-13	-1	0	1	-13	35
2014	Tex	39	345.1	351	4	.989	15	8	1	0	1	0	0	-	56	0	0	+2	+1	0	+1	+1	1	-1	0	-2	-2	-
		1297	11373.1	11348	89	.992	421	221	139	76	26	64	28	.438	2021	-9	-49	-22	-83	-12	-95	-97	-69	-9	1	-18	-95	-

Scout's Defensive Rating: -3 plays saved in 2013, 0 plays saved in 2014

The bad news was that, after years of being the MLB iron man, Prince Fielder missed the majority of 2014 with a herniated disc. The good news was that it kept Fielder from taking his annual spot among the worst defensive first basemen in the league. Due to his size, Fielder has very limited range, as his Plays Saved year-in and year-out continues to demonstrate. Fielder has a below average arm in terms of both accuracy and strength. Fielder continues to struggle handling balls in the dirt and is perennially among the leaders in potential outs lost due to failing to handle throws from other infielders. Texas has another option at first in Mitch Moreland, and while he is not an elite defensive option himself, the Rangers would probably be better off having Fielder transition more towards the DH role and letting Moreland get some more innings in the field.

Todd Frazier

		BASIC						BUNTS			GDP		RANGE AND POSITIONING								RUNS SAVED					
Year	Team	G	Inn	TC	E	Pct	GFP	DM	Opp	Sac Hits	Bunt Hits	Opp GDP	Pct	Outs Made	To His Right	Straight On	To His Left	GB	Air	Plays Saved	Bases Saved	R/P	Bunt	GDP	GFP/ DME	Total	Rank
2011	Cin	1	9.0	11	0	1.000	0	0	-	-	-	0	0	-	1	0	0	0	0	-1	-1	-1	0	0	0	0	0	-
2012	Cin	39	318.1	338	2	.994	15	11	2	2	0	4	3	.750	61	-2	-6	-2	-10	+3	-7	-8	-6	0	0	0	-6	-
2014	Cin	43	335.0	330	5	.985	16	5	5	2	0	4	3	.750	50	0	-1	-1	-1	0	-1	-1	-1	1	0	1	1	-
		83	662.1	679	7	.990	31	16	7	4	0	8	6	.750	112	-2	-7	-3	-11	+2	-9	-10	-7	1	0	1	-5	-

Scout's Defensive Rating: 1 plays saved in 2014

First Basemen

Todd Frazier's Scouting Report can be found on page 211.

Freddie Freeman

	BASIC							BUNTS			GDP			RANGE AND POSITIONING								RUNS SAVED					
Year	Team	G	Inn	TC	E	Pct	GFP	DM	Opp	Sac Hits	Bunt Hits	Opp	GDP	Pct	Outs Made	To His Right	Straight On	To His Left	GB	Air	Plays Saved	Bases Saved	R/P	Bunt	GDP	GFP/DME	Total	Rank
2010	Atl	12	39.0	41	0	1.000	4	0				0	0	-	8	0	+1	0	0	0	0	0	0		0	0	0	-
2011	Atl	156	1370.1	1415	6	.996	70	24	15	10	3	8	1	.125	226	-3	-3	0	-6	+1	-5	-5	-3	0	0	1	-2	22
2012	Atl	146	1289.1	1380	12	.991	77	15	9	5	3	16	7	.438	225	0	+1	-3	-2	+3	+1	0	1	-1	0	3	3	10
2013	Atl	147	1290.2	1345	10	.993	90	20	11	6	3	32	15	.469	231	+8	+2	-1	+10	-2	+8	+7	6	-1	0	2	7	6
2014	Atl	162	1449.0	1392	5	.996	57	20	26	22	3	17	13	.765	236	-2	0	-7	-9	-3	-12	-13	-9	-2	1	3	-7	33
		623	5438.1	5574	33	.994	298	79	61	43	12	73	36	.493	926	+3	+1	-11	-7	-1	-8	-11	-5	-4	1	9	1	

Scout's Defensive Rating: 2 plays saved in 2013, 7 plays saved in 2014

Freddie Freeman is an interesting case considering his Defensive Runs Saved dropoff in 2014. Freeman's biggest deficiency in the field is his range, as his large, 6'5" frame limits his quickness. He is much more comfortable covering the hole on his backhand than taking away hits down the line, but those hits down the line turn into doubles and triples. One area where Freeman excels is his ability to handle poor throws from other fielders. He leads the majors in Good Fielding Plays on scoops since he became a regular in 2011, but he took a step back in that department in 2014. Despite his Defensive Misplays on handling throws remaining constant, he only had 24 GFPs for handling difficult throws in 2014, down from 50 in 2013. Another area where Freeman shines is using his size to reach into the stands or dugout to catch foul balls. Freeman has 14 GFPs in those situations over the past four seasons, six more than the nearest challenger. Freeman also has a strong and accurate throwing arm and is aggressive in using it to go after lead runners. Freeman tied for the lead in 2014 among first basemen by starting 13 double plays. Finally, he has struggled handling bunts compared to other first basemen across the league. Overall, Freeman should settle in as an average defensive first baseman whose good hands and strong arm make up for his lack of range.

Nate Freiman

	BASIC							BUNTS			GDP			RANGE AND POSITIONING								RUNS SAVED					
Year	Team	G	Inn	TC	E	Pct	GFP	DM	Opp	Sac Hits	Bunt Hits	Opp	GDP	Pct	Outs Made	To His Right	Straight On	To His Left	GB	Air	Plays Saved	Bases Saved	R/P	Bunt	GDP	GFP/DME	Total	Rank
2013	Oak	59	357.2	310	1	.997	20	11	4	2	1	1	0	.000	52	-2	+2	-1	-1	-1	-2	-3	-2	0	0	-1	-3	-
2014	Oak	33	217.1	221	3	.986	7	2	2	2	0	3	1	.333	38	0	+1	-1	+1	+1	+2	+2	1	0	0	0	1	-
		92	575.0	531	4	.992	27	13	6	4	1	4	1	.250	90	-2	+3	-2	0	0	0	-1	-1	0	0	-1	-2	-

Scout's Defensive Rating: -1 plays saved in 2013, -1 plays saved in 2014

Paul Goldschmidt

	BASIC							BUNTS			GDP			RANGE AND POSITIONING								RUNS SAVED					
Year	Team	G	Inn	TC	E	Pct	GFP	DM	Opp	Sac Hits	Bunt Hits	Opp	GDP	Pct	Outs Made	To His Right	Straight On	To His Left	GB	Air	Plays Saved	Bases Saved	R/P	Bunt	GDP	GFP/DME	Total	Rank
2011	Ari	43	368.0	373	0	1.000	29	7	2	0	2	6	2	.333	60	-2	-1	-1	-4	-2	-6	-6	-5	-1	0	3	-3	-
2012	Ari	139	1205.1	1306	5	.995	67	14	8	5	2	16	7	.438	232	+2	+1	+1	+4	-2	+2	+1	1	-2	0	2	1	14
2013	Ari	159	1446.0	1598	5	.997	113	18	14	9	2	18	9	.500	293	+9	+1	+1	+10	+3	+13	+15	11	0	0	2	13	2
2014	Ari	109	966.1	1021	7	.993	54	15	13	11	1	12	7	.583	173	0	+1	+3	+4	-1	+3	+4	3	-1	0	-1	1	17
		450	3985.2	4298	19	.996	263	50	37	25	7	52	25	.481	758	+9	+2	+4	+14	-2	+12	+14	10	-4	0	6	12	-

Scout's Defensive Rating: 16 plays saved in 2013, -2 plays saved in 2014

At 6'3 and 245lbs, the Texas State University product turned the heads of many with his dominating presence at the plate, but its his defensive contributions that make Goldschmidt an elite level talent. What stands out most about his defensive play at first base is Goldschmidt's ability to get a quick first step. He anticipates the ball and handles tough hops exceptionally well. Much of this might be credited to how far he positions himself from the bag, as he see's the ball off the bat well and always finds a way to get in position to make a play. Goldschmidt rated well in multiple defensive metrics in 2013 and ultimately won his first career Fielding Bible Award and Gold Glove. Goldschmidt appeared in a little over a hundred games in 2014 after a rogue fastball fractured his left hand in August and sidelined him for the remainder of the season. Before his injury, Goldschmidt was making an impact on defense yet again, achieving a +32 Net GFP-DME, earning most of his Good Fielding Plays on his ability to handle difficult throws from infielders.

First Basemen

Adrian Gonzalez

Year	Team	G	Inn	TC	E	Pct	GFP	DM	Opp	Sac Hits	Bunt Hits	Opp	GDP	Pct	Outs Made	To His Right	Straight On	To His Left	GB	Air	Plays Saved	Bases Saved	R/P	Bunt	GDP	GFP/DME	Total	Rank
				BASIC						**BUNTS**			**GDP**			**RANGE AND POSITIONING**								**RUNS SAVED**				
2004	Tex	11	89.0	100	1	.990	1	2	1	0	0	-	-	-	15	0	+1	0	+1	0	+1	+1	1	0	-	-1	0	-
2005	Tex	10	71.0	93	2	.978	2	1	1	1	0	-	-	-	15	+1	-1	-1	-1	0	-1	-1	-1	0	-	0	-1	-
2006	SD	155	1341.0	1365	7	.995	47	22	23	15	3	-	-	-	286	-2	+4	0	+1	-1	0	0	0	0	-	3	3	14
2007	SD	161	1462.2	1620	10	.994	39	31	26	14	1	-	-	-	284	0	-5	0	-5	-1	-6	-7	-5	2	-	-5	-8	29
2008	SD	161	1417.1	1442	6	.996	53	21	26	14	1	-	-	-	282	-1	-7	-1	-8	+2	-6	-6	-4	3	-	1	0	16
2009	SD	156	1359.2	1367	7	.995	69	19	25	13	1	23	9	.391	303	+1	-1	+8	+7	+2	+9	+12	9	2	0	4	15	2
2010	SD	159	1397.1	1459	8	.995	58	29	30	18	4	24	9	.375	266	-6	0	+3	-2	-2	-4	-5	-4	0	0	0	-4	26
2011	Bos	156	1352.2	1351	4	.997	56	16	14	8	1	18	8	.444	279	+2	-2	+7	+7	+1	+8	+9	7	3	0	2	12	1
2012	2 tms	151	1246.0	1404	3	.998	65	15	11	4	1	23	10	.435	267	+1	+6	+8	+15	-1	+14	+15	11	2	0	3	16	2
2013	LAD	151	1291.0	1389	11	.992	69	19	17	10	1	15	6	.400	212	+1	+5	+5	+11	+3	+14	+15	11	-1	0	1	11	3
2014	LAD	157	1325.1	1442	6	.996	57	20	16	10	0	21	13	.619	231	+1	+2	+5	+3	+3	+6	+8	6	2	1	2	11	1
		1428	12353.0	13032	65	.995	516	195	190	107	13	124	55	.444	2440	-2	+2	+29	+29	+6	+35	+41	31	13	1	10	55	-

Scout's Defensive Rating: -2 plays saved in 2013, 3 plays saved in 2014

Although he captured his first Fielding Bible Award in 2014, Gonzalez has been one of the top first baseman for the last several years. With a range that allows him to snag balls down the line or further off first toward second, Gonzalez does very well with keeping the ball in the infield. Even more so, he does well at charging bunt grounders, fielding them, and using his strong arm and quick release to ensure at least one out is recorded. In addition, his good instincts when fielding often helps the team take down a lead runner. He does so well, that in the last five seasons he has the most Defensive Runs Saved by any first baseman with 46. Nonetheless, every player has something he needs to work on from year to year, and that something for Gonzalez is receiving balls from other fielders. It is easily the biggest thing he struggles with from year to year, and as a first baseman it is something that could help save even more runs from scoring.

Yasmani Grandal

Year	Team	G	Inn	TC	E	Pct	GFP	DM	Opp	Sac Hits	Bunt Hits	Opp	GDP	Pct	Outs Made	To His Right	Straight On	To His Left	GB	Air	Plays Saved	Bases Saved	R/P	Bunt	GDP	GFP/DME	Total	Rank
				BASIC						**BUNTS**			**GDP**			**RANGE AND POSITIONING**								**RUNS SAVED**				
2013	SD	1	5.0	4	0	1.000	0	0				0	0	-	0	0	0	0	0	0	0	0	0	0	0	0	0	-
2014	SD	37	291.0	260	3	.988	18	6	5	4	0	4	1	.250	41	0	-2	-2	-3	-2	-5	-6	-4	0	0	0	-4	-
		38	296.0	264	3	.989	18	6	5	4	0	4	1	.250	41	0	-2	-2	-3	-2	-5	-6	-4	0	0	0	-4	

Scout's Defensive Rating: -3 plays saved in 2014

Yasmani Grandal's Scouting Report can be found on page 157.

Jesus Guzman

Year	Team	G	Inn	TC	E	Pct	GFP	DM	Opp	Sac Hits	Bunt Hits	Opp	GDP	Pct	Outs Made	To His Right	Straight On	To His Left	GB	Air	Plays Saved	Bases Saved	R/P	Bunt	GDP	GFP/DME	Total	Rank
				BASIC						**BUNTS**			**GDP**			**RANGE AND POSITIONING**								**RUNS SAVED**				
2009	SF	3	14.0	10	0	1.000	1	2				0	0	-	3	0	0	0	0	0	0	0	0	0	0	0	0	-
2011	SD	53	434.0	419	4	.990	15	11	7	4	1	5	2	.400	73	+1	+3	-1	+3	-2	+1	+1	1	0	0	-1	0	15
2012	SD	19	123.2	128	0	1.000	3	1	1	1	0	0	0	-	23	0	0	+1	+1	0	+1	+1	1	0	0	0	1	-
2013	SD	38	280.1	298	3	.990	27	6	5	2	2	3	1	.333	39	+1	-1	0	+1	0	+1	+2	2	0	0	1	3	-
2014	Hou	52	310.2	326	2	.994	17	5	3	1	2	3	2	.667	37	+3	0	+1	+3	-1	+2	+3	2	-1	0	0	1	-
		165	1162.2	1181	9	.992	63	25	16	8	5	11	5	.455	175	+5	+2	+1	+8	-3	+5	+7	6	-1	0	0	5	

Scout's Defensive Rating: -1 plays saved in 2013, 1 plays saved in 2014

Eric Hosmer

Year	Team	G	Inn	TC	E	Pct	GFP	DM	Opp	Sac Hits	Bunt Hits	Opp	GDP	Pct	Outs Made	To His Right	Straight On	To His Left	GB	Air	Plays Saved	Bases Saved	R/P	Bunt	GDP	GFP/DME	Total	Rank
				BASIC						**BUNTS**			**GDP**			**RANGE AND POSITIONING**								**RUNS SAVED**				
2011	KC	127	1135.2	1182	8	.993	69	26	13	6	3	17	3	.176	197	-5	-3	-1	-9	0	-9	-11	-8	-1	-1	0	-10	33
2012	KC	148	1277.0	1295	9	.993	74	22	18	11	2	19	6	.316	227	-6	0	-2	-8	+1	-7	-10	-7	1	0	1	-5	33
2013	KC	158	1372.1	1335	8	.994	88	25	4	2	1	21	11	.524	247	0	+1	+1	+1	+3	+4	+4	3	0	1	-1	3	13
2014	KC	130	1121.2	1141	10	.991	64	18	4	2	1	10	5	.500	189	0	+1	-2	0	+1	+1	-1	-1	0	0	4	3	14
		563	4906.2	4953	35	.993	295	91	39	21	7	67	25	.373	860	-11	-1	-4	-16	+5	-11	-18	-13	0	0	4	-9	

Scout's Defensive Rating: 7 plays saved in 2013, 3 plays saved in 2014

First Basemen

Statistically, Hosmer has finished in the middle of the pack defensively among qualified first basemen in 2014. An area of concern for Hosmer's defense that seems to have recurred from previous seasons is groundballs to his left side. He will often have groundballs hit the heel of his glove or pop out when attempting to field them. On diving attempts to this side, he has had issues with completing the whole play. He's solid at the position with great range and athleticism, so it seems like he has the ability to continue to improve. He has a veteran presence in the way he handles throws from other infielders. He will often prevent bad throws from becoming errors with his good picking ability and a solid vertical leap that allows infielders to feel confidence with him in making any play. He is fine at fielding groundballs that aren't to his left and was part of the reason the Royals finished the season with the best ranked defense in baseball. At 25 years of age, Hosmer still has the potential to continue to make strides as a first baseman.

Ryan Howard

	BASIC							BUNTS			GDP			RANGE AND POSITIONING								RUNS SAVED					
Year Team	G	Inn	TC	E	Pct	GFP	DM	Opp	Sac Hits	Bunt Hits	Opp	GDP	Pct	Outs Made	To His Right	Straight On	To His Left	GB	Air	Plays Saved	Bases Saved	R/P	Bunt	GDP	GFP/ DME	Total	Rank
2004 Phi	8	60.2	65	0	1.000	0	1	-	-	-	-	-	-	9	+1	+1	0	+2	0	+2	+2	1		-	0	1	-
2005 Phi	84	706.1	752	5	.993	19	20	5	5	0	-	-	-	149	+15	+6	-2	+19	0	+19	+16	12	0	-	-1	11	3
2006 Phi	159	1412.0	1478	14	.991	34	33	20	13	2	-	-	-	257	-5	+2	-3	-6	-3	-9	-9	-7	0	-	-2	-9	30
2007 Phi	140	1241.0	1306	12	.991	39	27	24	15	0	-	-	-	240	-2	-2	-3	-8	0	-8	-5	-4	1	-	-1	-4	24
2008 Phi	159	1402.2	1528	19	.988	64	37	13	8	1	-	-	-	309	+1	-10	+5	-4	+2	-2	0	0	1	-	-5	-4	25
2009 Phi	156	1388.1	1409	14	.990	61	22	21	12	4	11	3	.273	301	-2	+3	-3	-3	0	-3	-1	-1	-1	0	-2	-4	29
2010 Phi	139	1229.0	1339	14	.990	51	27	19	12	3	9	4	.444	204	-8	-4	-7	-19	+1	-18	-15	-11	-1	0	-1	-13	34
2011 Phi	149	1309.0	1361	9	.993	58	24	28	19	3	12	7	.583	233	-8	-10	+1	-16	-2	-18	-17	-12	1	0	-2	-13	35
2012 Phi	67	589.2	530	5	.991	20	17	7	3	2	6	0	.000	75	-2	-1	0	-3	+1	-2	-2	-2	0	-1	-3	-6	34
2013 Phi	76	650.0	661	1	.998	34	16	14	7	4	4	1	.250	105	+1	+2	-1	+2	-2	0	0	0	0	0	-1	-1	19
2014 Phi	141	1256.1	1313	9	.993	49	32	11	9	2	16	5	.313	176	-4	-1	+1	-5	-1	-6	-7	-5	0	0	-5	-10	34
	1278	11245.0	11742	102	.991	429	256	162	103	21	58	20	.345	2058	-13	-14	-12	-41	-4	-45	-38	-29	1	-1	-23	-52	-

Scout's Defensive Rating: -6 plays saved in 2013, -8 plays saved in 2014

If nothing else, Ryan Howard is a consistent first basemen. In four of the five years from 2010-14, Howard ranked 34th or 35th in Defensive Runs Saved among regulars. No one has ever confused him with being overly athletic, with his 6'4" and 250-pound frame that lacks quickness and foot speed. His large size limits his range on ground balls not hit directly at him, but does provide a large target for infielder throws to first. However, he is also among the league leaders in Defensive Misplays for failing to handle throws that could have been outs. Already with limited range and a questionable glove, Howard's arm also hinders him defensively. His burdensome contract with the Phillies will keep him in the National League and prevent him from playing the position he is most suited for in the American League as a designated hitter.

Travis Ishikawa

	BASIC							BUNTS			GDP			RANGE AND POSITIONING								RUNS SAVED					
Year Team	G	Inn	TC	E	Pct	GFP	DM	Opp	Sac Hits	Bunt Hits	Opp	GDP	Pct	Outs Made	To His Right	Straight On	To His Left	GB	Air	Plays Saved	Bases Saved	R/P	Bunt	GDP	GFP/ DME	Total	Rank
2006 SF	10	55.0	58	0	1.000	3	0	2	2	0	-	-	-	16	0	0	-1	-1	0	-1	-1	-1	0	-	0	-1	-
2008 SF	29	213.1	184	3	.984	4	1	2	2	0	-	-	-	51	+3	+1	-1	+3	0	+3	+4	3	0	-	0	3	-
2009 SF	113	817.1	803	3	.996	25	13	13	8	1	17	8	.471	164	+5	+5	+3	+12	0	+12	+12	9	0	1	0	10	5
2010 SF	73	305.2	285	0	1.000	13	4	6	4	0	5	0	.000	49	+4	+1	-2	+3	-1	+2	+2	2	0	0	0	2	-
2012 Mil	43	277.0	288	2	.993	10	2	2	2	0	1	0	.000	51	+1	+2	0	+4	0	+4	+4	3	0	0	2	5	-
2013 2 tms	5	34.0	27	0	1.000	0	1				1	0	.000	3	0	0	0	0	-1	-1	-1	-1	0	0	0	-1	-
2014 2 tms	42	207.0	236	1	.996	5	2	1	0	0	5	4	.800	35	-1	-1	+1	-1	0	-1	-1	0	0	0	0	0	-
	315	1909.1	1881	9	.995	60	23	26	18	1	29	12	.414	369	+12	+8	0	+20	-2	+18	+19	15	0	1	2	18	-

Scout's Defensive Rating: -2 plays saved in 2013, -1 plays saved in 2014

Kelly Johnson

	BASIC							BUNTS			GDP			RANGE AND POSITIONING								RUNS SAVED					
Year Team	G	Inn	TC	E	Pct	GFP	DM	Opp	Sac Hits	Bunt Hits	Opp	GDP	Pct	Outs Made	To His Right	Straight On	To His Left	GB	Air	Plays Saved	Bases Saved	R/P	Bunt	GDP	GFP/ DME	Total	Rank
2013 TB	3	18.0	21	0	1.000	1	0				0	0	-	2	0	-1	0	-1	0	-1	-1	0		0	0	0	-
2014 2 tms	32	245.2	246	4	.984	5	5	1	0	0	3	0	.000	50	+3	-1	0	+2	+1	+3	+3	2	0	0	-2	0	-
	35	263.2	267	4	.985	6	5	1	0	0	3	0	.000	52	+3	-2	0	+1	+1	+2	+2	2	0	0	-2	0	-

Scout's Defensive Rating: 0 plays saved in 2013, 2 plays saved in 2014

First Basemen

Garrett Jones

		BASIC							BUNTS			GDP			RANGE AND POSITIONING								RUNS SAVED					
Year	Team	G	Inn	TC	E	Pct	GFP	DM	Opp	Sac Hits	Bunt Hits	Opp	GDP	Pct	Outs Made	To His Right	Straight On	To His Left	GB	Air	Plays Saved	Bases Saved	R/P	Bunt	GDP	GFP/ DME	Total	Rank
2007	Min	8	63.0	61	0	1.000	1	1	-	-	-	-	-	-	12	0	-2	0	-2	0	-2	-2	-1	-	0	-1	-1	-
2009	Pit	30	255.2	284	1	.996	10	4	2	2	0	4	2	.500	61	0	-1	+1	0	+1	+1	+2	1	0	0	-1	0	-
2010	Pit	112	924.2	990	9	.991	48	27	7	3	4	13	4	.308	191	-5	-2	-1	-8	+3	-5	-5	-4	-2	-1	-6	-13	33
2011	Pit	34	260.1	277	3	.989	11	11	2	0	2	1	0	.000	38	0	-2	0	-1	+1	0	0	-1	-1	0	-3	-5	-
2012	Pit	72	529.2	553	5	.991	23	13	8	6	1	2	0	.000	86	-1	+1	-3	-3	-1	-4	-5	-3	0	0	-2	-5	29
2013	Pit	83	618.0	729	6	.992	35	11	5	3	0	4	2	.500	92	-5	-1	0	-6	+1	-5	-5	-3	1	0	1	-1	21
2014	Mia	129	1080.1	1110	13	.988	53	25	8	4	1	10	3	.300	194	-4	+4	-2	-2	+1	-1	-3	-2	0	0	-3	-5	30
		468	3731.2	4004	37	.991	181	92	32	18	8	34	11	.324	674	-15	-3	-5	-22	+6	-16	-18	-13	-2	-1	-14	-30	-

Scout's Defensive Rating: -6 plays saved in 2013, -4 plays saved in 2014

Jones had another rough year in the field in 2014. His range is limited by the fact he often couldn't make a play unless he could get his entire body in front of the ball. Thus, over the course of the season, he slid more than any other first baseman and ranked second in conversion rate when diving for balls among first basemen with at least 200 opportunities. On top of his limited range, he made more Misplays and Errors than any other first baseman other than Ryan Howard. Most notably, his inability to throw accurately caused him just over half of his 13 errors, which was the most by any first baseman in 2014. The two biggest eye sores were his inability to keep the ball in the infield and poor receiving skills. While he's not likely to make any great improvements at this point in his career, he could help himself by making smarter decisions when he has the opportunity to throw.

Marc Krauss

		BASIC							BUNTS			GDP			RANGE AND POSITIONING								RUNS SAVED					
Year	Team	G	Inn	TC	E	Pct	GFP	DM	Opp	Sac Hits	Bunt Hits	Opp	GDP	Pct	Outs Made	To His Right	Straight On	To His Left	GB	Air	Plays Saved	Bases Saved	R/P	Bunt	GDP	GFP/ DME	Total	Rank
2013	Hou	2	4.0	2	0	1.000	0	0				0	0	-	0	0	0	0	0	0	0	0	0		0	0	0	-
2014	Hou	33	237.2	291	4	.986	16	4				2	0	.000	34	0	0	0	0	-1	-1	-1	0		0	-1	-1	-
		35	241.2	293	4	.986	16	4				2	0	.000	34	0	0	0	0	-1	-1	-1	0		0	-1	-1	-

Scout's Defensive Rating: 0 plays saved in 2014

Adam LaRoche

		BASIC							BUNTS			GDP			RANGE AND POSITIONING								RUNS SAVED					
Year	Team	G	Inn	TC	E	Pct	GFP	DM	Opp	Sac Hits	Bunt Hits	Opp	GDP	Pct	Outs Made	To His Right	Straight On	To His Left	GB	Air	Plays Saved	Bases Saved	R/P	Bunt	GDP	GFP/ DME	Total	Rank
2004	Atl	98	720.0	784	5	.994	17	9	8	6	0	-	-	-	123	+2	-2	+1	+1	0	+1	+1	1	0	-	1	2	17
2005	Atl	125	1019.1	1154	7	.994	28	27	11	7	2	-	-	-	232	0	-15	-3	-18	0	-18	-17	-12	-1	-	0	-13	34
2006	Atl	142	1153.1	1218	6	.996	31	26	24	16	4	-	-	-	243	-10	-1	-3	-14	-1	-15	-14	-10	0	-	-1	-11	32
2007	Pit	151	1301.1	1383	6	.996	31	16	20	9	5	-	-	-	269	-4	+6	+1	+3	-1	+2	+3	2	0	-	0	2	11
2008	Pit	129	1135.2	1219	8	.993	39	14	23	10	5	-	-	-	206	0	-1	-6	-7	+2	-5	-8	-6	1	-	0	-5	28
2009	3 tms	148	1308.1	1435	2	.999	55	24	18	9	2	22	8	.364	279	+1	+4	-3	0	-1	-1	-5	-4	1	0	1	-2	26
2010	Ari	146	1239.2	1272	11	.991	55	22	17	10	1	19	12	.632	258	+5	+1	+1	+8	+1	+9	+8	5	0	1	1	7	3
2011	Was	43	375.0	412	0	1.000	17	5	4	4	0	9	3	.333	86	+2	+2	+3	+6	+1	+7	+7	5	0	0	0	5	-
2012	Was	153	1323.1	1366	7	.994	49	15	23	14	2	12	5	.417	246	+1	0	+3	+4	+1	+5	+5	3	2	1	2	8	5
2013	Was	149	1272.0	1251	11	.991	70	21	17	13	0	11	5	.455	219	-4	-1	0	-5	0	-5	-3	-2	1	0	2	1	17
2014	Was	136	1200.0	1200	7	.994	47	22	13	9	0	16	8	.500	205	-4	-2	+2	-4	+1	-3	-3	-2	0	1	1	0	20
		1420	12048.0	12694	69	.995	439	201	178	107	21	89	41	.461	2366	-11	-9	-4	-26	+3	-23	-26	-20	4	3	7	-6	-

Scout's Defensive Rating: 1 plays saved in 2013, -3 plays saved in 2014

Though it took him a while to settle into the position, Adam LaRoche possesses the calmest defensive approach in baseball. He has the ability of making every out made seem effortless, which makes for some of the most aesthetically pleasing defensive play at first base. LaRoche picks baseballs out of the dirt with a subtle flip of the glove, redeeming his fellow infielders and denying would-be baserunners. In 2014, LaRoche tied for eighth among first basemen in Good Fielding Plays of this sort, handling 31 bad throws to record outs or prevent runners from advancing. Unfortunately, this subtype made up almost two-thirds of LaRoche's GFPs, as other aspects of this journeyman veteran's defensive game were less impressive. LaRoche's range has declined since his defensive peak in 2010-12. His fielding troubles were also evident in the 13 Defensive Misplays and Errors on groundballs through his position, which was tied for most among regulars at first base in 2014. This downtrend in range also hindered his ability to make difficult plays. All in all, the poetic putouts somewhat counteracted the mediocre range and leaves LaRoche an average first sacker heading into the second half of his 30's.

First Basemen

Adam Lind

Year	Team	G	Inn	TC	E	Pct	GFP	DM	Opp	Sac Hits	Bunt Hits	Opp	GDP	Pct	Outs Made	To His Right	Straight On	To His Left	GB	Air	Plays Saved	Bases Saved	R/P	Bunt	GDP	GFP/DME	Total	Rank
																										BASIC / BUNTS / GDP / RANGE AND POSITIONING / RUNS SAVED			
2010	Tor	11	76.0	79	0	1.000	4	2				3	0	.000	14	0	+1	0	+1	0	+1	+1	1		0	-1	0	
2011	Tor	109	965.1	1020	4	.996	48	18	4	2	1	13	4	.308	161	-2	-1	0	-3	0	-3	-3	-2	0	-1	-2	-5	28
2012	Tor	61	500.1	587	5	.991	21	7	2	1	0	9	1	.111	86	-1	-1	+2	0	+1	+1	+3	2		-1	0	1	13
2013	Tor	76	620.0	637	7	.989	33	5	6	3	2	10	4	.400	102	-2	-7	-1	-10	-2	-12	-11	-8	0	0	1	-7	30
2014	Tor	47	368.1	383	3	.992	20	9	3	2	0	6	4	.667	44	-3	-3	0	-6	-1	-7	-6	-5	1	0	1	-3	
		304	2530.0	2706	19	.993	126	41	15	8	3	41	13	.317	407	-8	-11	+1	-18	-2	-20	-16	-12	1	-2	-1	-14	

Scout's Defensive Rating: -5 plays saved in 2013, -1 plays saved in 2014

James Loney

Year	Team	G	Inn	TC	E	Pct	GFP	DM	Opp	Sac Hits	Bunt Hits	Opp	GDP	Pct	Outs Made	To His Right	Straight On	To His Left	GB	Air	Plays Saved	Bases Saved	R/P	Bunt	GDP	GFP/DME	Total	Rank
2006	LAD	39	228.2	228	1	.996	5	2	2	1	0	-	-	-	36	-2	+3	+3	+4	-1	+3	+5	4	0	-	0	4	-
2007	LAD	93	774.2	795	9	.989	33	16	11	7	1	-	-	-	159	+5	-1	-1	+2	0	+2	+2	1	0	-	1	2	12
2008	LAD	158	1362.2	1498	13	.991	69	17	21	12	1	-	-	-	248	+2	-6	+2	-2	0	-2	-1	-1	1	-	1	1	13
2009	LAD	155	1341.0	1361	7	.995	70	18	17	10	2	18	10	.556	254	-4	-1	+5	0	+2	+2	+4	3	-1	1	2	5	9
2010	LAD	160	1338.2	1368	4	.997	66	16	16	10	1	14	10	.714	226	0	+3	-2	+2	-1	+1	-1	-1	1	1	3	4	12
2011	LAD	150	1203.2	1208	5	.996	71	21	14	5	5	16	9	.563	237	+2	+5	+1	+7	+2	+9	+9	7	0	1	3	11	2
2012	2 tms	133	982.1	995	6	.994	54	15	13	9	1	17	6	.353	176	+7	+5	-3	+9	-1	+8	+8	6	-1	1	0	6	7
2013	TB	154	1277.2	1308	7	.995	68	15	8	5	1	27	15	.556	187	+1	-1	0	0	0	0	-1	-1	1	1	3	4	12
2014	TB	152	1334.0	1178	9	.992	70	14	11	5	1	17	5	.294	161	-4	0	-1	-5	-2	-7	-6	-5	1	0	3	-1	23
		1194	9843.1	9939	61	.994	506	134	113	64	13	109	55	.505	1684	+7	+7	+4	+17	-1	+16	+19	13	2	5	16	36	

Scout's Defensive Rating: -2 plays saved in 2013, 1 plays saved in 2014

One of the league's better defensive first basemen, James Loney is beginning to see some of his defensive prowess fade. Typically a plus defender to his right, Loney has lost a bit of his first step in that direction. In comparison to the average first baseman, Loney made four fewer plays to his right in 2014. Loney also lost some of his double play ability in 2014 – albeit in a small sample – turning two only 29 percent of the time that he had the opportunity to do so. Not much of an athlete, Loney's most valuable tool his his glove. Among first basemen in 2014, Loney was second in Good Fielding Plays for recording an out or preventing additional advancement on a difficult or wild throw, doing so a combined 42 times. Only Anthony Rizzo was better in this category, at 43. Loney is also not afraid to head into the stands to catch a foul pop up.

Victor Martinez

Year	Team	G	Inn	TC	E	Pct	GFP	DM	Opp	Sac Hits	Bunt Hits	Opp	GDP	Pct	Outs Made	To His Right	Straight On	To His Left	GB	Air	Plays Saved	Bases Saved	R/P	Bunt	GDP	GFP/DME	Total	Rank
2006	Cle	22	166.1	154	0	1.000	5	4	1	0	1	-	-	-	25	-1	-1	0	-2	0	-2	-2	-1	0	-	0	-1	-
2007	Cle	30	221.0	201	1	.995	8	3	2	0	1	-	-	-	49	0	+2	+1	+3	0	+3	+3	2	-1	-	-1	0	-
2008	Cle	10	82.0	87	1	.989	2	1	1	0	1	-	-	-	17	0	0	0	0	0	0	0	0	-1	-	-1	-2	-
2009	2 tms	70	575.0	531	9	.994	13	6	8	4	1	5	1	.200	93	-2	+1	-2	-2	-2	-4	-4	-3	1	0	0	-2	25
2010	Bos	14	106.0	111	2	.982	11	2	4	3	0	0	0	-	27	+3	+1	-1	+4	-1	+3	+2	2	1	0	0	3	-
2011	Det	6	52.0	48	0	1.000	1	0	0	0	0	0	0	-	12	+1	0	0	+1	0	+1	+1	1	0	0	0	1	-
2013	Det	11	97.0	99	0	1.000	9	2	0	0	0	0	0	-	23	+1	0	0	+1	+1	+2	+2	2	0	0	0	2	-
2014	Det	35	284.1	270	3	.989	8	3	1	0	0	4	1	.250	32	-3	-2	0	-6	-1	-7	-7	-5	0	0	1	-4	-
		198	1583.2	1501	10	.993	57	21	17	7	4	9	2	.222	278	-1	+1	-2	-1	-3	-4	-5	-2	0	0	-1	-3	-

Scout's Defensive Rating: 0 plays saved in 2013, -4 plays saved in 2014

Joe Mauer

Year	Team	G	Inn	TC	E	Pct	GFP	DM	Opp	Sac Hits	Bunt Hits	Opp	GDP	Pct	Outs Made	To His Right	Straight On	To His Left	GB	Air	Plays Saved	Bases Saved	R/P	Bunt	GDP	GFP/DME	Total	Rank
2011	Min	18	141.0	170	1	.994	10	6	2	0	1	3	0	.000	35	+1	+2	+1	+4	0	+4	+5	3	0	0	-2	1	-
2012	Min	30	260.1	284	2	.993	12	4	2	1	0	2	0	.000	40	0	-2	+1	-2	-3	-5	-4	-2	1	0	0	-1	-
2013	Min	8	70.0	82	1	.988	1	1				1	0	.000	12	0	-1	+1	0	0	0	+1	1	0	0	0	1	-
2014	Min	100	851.0	915	3	.997	37	10	5	3	1	10	2	.200	148	+2	+5	-1	+6	0	+6	+5	4	0	-1	1	4	12
		156	1322.1	1451	7	.995	60	21	9	4	2	16	2	.125	235	+3	+4	+2	+8	-3	+5	+7	6	1	-1	-1	5	-

Scout's Defensive Rating: 0 plays saved in 2013, 4 plays saved in 2014

After many seasons of average or better defense behind the plate, the 2014 season marked a fresh start for Joe Mauer's career, switching to first base on a full-time basis. For most players, the change from catcher to first base is necessitated

First Basemen

out of ability, but Mauer's was predicated out of a need to avoid the type of injuries usually incurred behind the dish. Translating his skills as a catcher over to first base was a quick process. Mauer's athletic ability is well above average compared to the typical rigid first basemen. His 6'5" frame stands as a big target for infielder throws as well as a large blockade for would-be base hits down the first base line. Mauer has adapted his skill-set to a new position perfectly, routinely picking balls out of the dirt, corralling errant throws, making strong throws of his own in double-play and relay situations, and taking charge on infield pop-ups. He still struggles, at times, with hard hit balls, but as the season progressed he seemed to become more comfortable with even the toughest grounders. Mauer's tools should allow him to continue to be one of the better first basemen in all of baseball.

Tommy Medica

		BASIC						BUNTS			GDP			RANGE AND POSITIONING								RUNS SAVED					
Year Team	G	Inn	TC	E	Pct	GFP	DM	Opp	Sac Hits	Bunt Hits	Opp	GDP	Pct	Outs Made	To His Right	Straight On	To His Left	GB	Air	Plays Saved	Bases Saved	R/P	Bunt	GDP	GFP/ DME	Total	Rank
2013 SD	19	164.0	166	0	1.000	9	2	2	1	1	0	0	-	30	+1	-2	+1	0	+1	+1	+1	1	0	0	0	1	-
2014 SD	46	316.0	319	1	.997	19	7	6	3	1	4	1	.250	51	0	+3	+2	+5	0	+5	+5	4	0	0	0	4	-
	65	480.0	485	1	.998	28	9	8	4	2	4	1	.250	81	+1	+1	+3	+5	+1	+6	+6	5	0	0	0	5	-

Scout's Defensive Rating: -1 plays saved in 2013, 2 plays saved in 2014

Kendrys Morales

		BASIC						BUNTS			GDP			RANGE AND POSITIONING								RUNS SAVED					
Year Team	G	Inn	TC	E	Pct	GFP	DM	Opp	Sac Hits	Bunt Hits	Opp	GDP	Pct	Outs Made	To His Right	Straight On	To His Left	GB	Air	Plays Saved	Bases Saved	R/P	Bunt	GDP	GFP/ DME	Total	Rank
2006 LAA	56	453.2	465	5	.989	8	6	8	4	2	-	-	-	119	+4	+4	+2	+10	+1	+11	+11	8	0	-	0	8	4
2007 LAA	19	121.0	128	0	1.000	2	2	-	-	-	-	-	-	26	+2	-1	+1	+1	-1	0	+1	1	-	-	0	1	-
2008 LAA	6	41.0	33	0	1.000	0	1	-	-	-	-	-	-	9	-1	0	-1	-1	0	-1	-1	-1	-	-	0	-1	-
2009 LAA	152	1279.0	1368	8	.994	64	21	11	6	3	28	16	.571	298	+4	+4	+3	+10	-2	+8	+9	7	0	1	0	8	6
2010 LAA	51	448.2	462	2	.996	18	1	4	1	2	5	2	.400	81	-3	0	+1	-1	0	-1	0	0	0	0	1	1	19
2012 LAA	28	241.0	213	1	.995	7	5	1	1	0	6	2	.333	44	+1	0	+1	+1	-1	0	+1	0	0	0	-1	-1	-
2013 Sea	31	274.1	307	1	.997	14	3	1	1	0	0	0	-	44	-1	0	-1	-3	0	-3	-4	-3	0	0	1	-2	-
2014 2 tms	27	209.2	229	1	.996	6	5	3	2	0	0	0	-	24	-1	+1	0	0	0	0	-2	-1	0	0	0	-1	-
	370	3068.1	3205	18	.994	119	44	28	15	7	39	20	.513	645	+5	+8	+6	+17	-3	+14	+15	11	0	1	1	13	-

Scout's Defensive Rating: -2 plays saved in 2013, 0 plays saved in 2014

Justin Morneau

		BASIC						BUNTS			GDP			RANGE AND POSITIONING								RUNS SAVED					
Year Team	G	Inn	TC	E	Pct	GFP	DM	Opp	Sac Hits	Bunt Hits	Opp	GDP	Pct	Outs Made	To His Right	Straight On	To His Left	GB	Air	Plays Saved	Bases Saved	R/P	Bunt	GDP	GFP/ DME	Total	Rank
2003 Min	7	34.2	34	1	.971	-	-	1	0	0	-	-	-	9	-1	-1	0	-2	0	-2	-3	-2	0	-	-	-2	-
2004 Min	61	538.1	567	3	.995	22	15	2	1	1	-	-	-	90	-2	+1	-2	-2	-1	-3	-3	-2	0	-	1	-1	23
2005 Min	138	1166.1	1290	8	.994	41	18	11	4	1	-	-	-	246	-2	+7	+6	+11	0	+11	+13	9	1	-	-1	9	5
2006 Min	153	1346.1	1415	8	.994	38	24	12	8	0	-	-	-	254	+1	-1	-1	0	+1	+1	+1	1	2	-	-1	2	17
2007 Min	143	1259.1	1296	5	.996	52	16	9	8	1	-	-	-	274	-6	+2	+1	-3	+3	0	0	0	-1	-	1	0	16
2008 Min	155	1363.2	1409	4	.997	70	25	5	4	1	-	-	-	239	+1	-3	0	-2	0	-2	-1	-1	0	-	-1	-2	20
2009 Min	123	1071.2	1045	3	.997	50	13	7	5	1	11	3	.273	198	-1	+2	+2	+3	+1	+4	+3	2	1	-1	0	2	13
2010 Min	77	688.1	734	1	.999	28	6	3	3	0	14	10	.714	128	-1	+4	+3	+6	0	+6	+7	5	0	1	1	7	3
2011 Min	56	479.1	485	1	.998	21	9	2	2	0	7	4	.571	81	-3	-1	+2	-2	+1	-1	-2	-2	0	0	-1	-3	25
2012 Min	99	879.2	957	6	.994	30	12	8	2	4	10	4	.400	143	-1	0	0	-1	0	-1	+2	1	-1	0	0	0	17
2013 2 tms	137	1189.1	1326	4	.997	75	13	7	4	1	16	6	.375	214	+1	-2	+4	+3	-2	+1	+3	2	1	0	2	5	10
2014 Col	131	1105.2	1260	4	.997	57	14	13	8	2	9	6	.667	192	0	+3	+3	+6	+1	+7	+5	4	0	1	3	8	6
	1280	11122.2	11818	48	.996	484	165	80	49	12	67	33	.493	2068	-14	+11	+18	+17	+4	+21	+25	17	3	1	4	25	-

Scout's Defensive Rating: 6 plays saved in 2013, 4 plays saved in 2014

Justin Morneau, who in 2014 finished his first full season in the National League with the Colorado Rockies, had one of the best seasons of his career defensively. He saved eight runs, which ranked him sixth among first basemen. Morneau was nearly mistake-free at first base, fielding hard grounders with ease as well as showcasing extraordinary scooping ability. He had 34 Good Fielding Plays of handling difficult throws to record an out or prevent an advancement, which ranked him in the top ten among all first basemen. Morneau finished third among Major League first basemen in the 2014 Fielding Bible balloting, behind Adrian Gonzalez and Anthony Rizzo. In an infield that has Nolan Arenado (second in 2014 balloting among third basemen), Troy Tulowitzki (fifth among shortstops) and DJ LeMahieu (third among second basemen), Morneau serves as the veteran leader of the Rockies' defensive core of players.

First Basemen

Logan Morrison

	BASIC							BUNTS			GDP			RANGE AND POSITIONING								RUNS SAVED					
Year	Team	G	Inn	TC	E	Pct	GFP	DM	Opp	Sac Hits	Bunt Hits	Opp	GDP	Pct	Outs Made	To His Right	Straight On	To His Left	GB	Air	Plays Saved	Bases Saved	R/P	Bunt	GDP	GFP/DME	Total	Rank
2011	Fla	1	8.0	6	0	1.000	0	0				0	0	-	0	0	0	0	0	0	0	0	0			0	0	-
2012	Mia	21	155.2	175	1	.994	4	1	1	1	0	5	3	.600	41	+3	+1	+1	+6	-1	+5	+5	4	0	0	0	4	-
2013	Mia	79	691.2	749	3	.996	25	18	7	4	1	10	6	.600	111	-2	-1	-4	-6	+4	-2	-3	-2	0	1	-3	-4	26
2014	Sea	79	661.1	688	3	.996	21	9	2	1	0	8	0	.000	100	-2	-1	+2	0	+2	+2	+2	1	0	-1	0	0	18
		180	1516.2	1618	7	.996	50	28	10	6	1	23	9	.391	252	-1	-1	-1	0	+5	+5	+4	3	0	0	-3	0	-

Scout's Defensive Rating: -2 plays saved in 2013, -3 plays saved in 2014

After splitting time between the outfield and first base to start his career, Logan Morrison made the move to predominantly play first base beginning in 2013. The good news is that first base is his better defensive position. However, arguably the best thing you can say about his first base defense is that he isn't the liability he proved to be in the outfield. After a season with a whopping -22 Defensive Runs Saved in left field in 2011, Morrison has played to 0 Defensive Runs Saved at first base in just over 1500 innings in the three years since. Morrison is a pretty good athlete for such a big man, but knee issues and the lack of a quick first step still limits his range. Morrison has decent hands, but has difficulty with well hit balls. Morrison's footwork has improved as he is getting more time at first, and his hands and size allow him to be an asset receiving throws at first. Morrison does have a pretty decent arm for first base, but he is hesitant to show it. He is much more likely to just get the sure out at first instead of trying to throw out the lead runner. Morrison appears to be penciled in as the everyday first baseman for the Mariners in 2015, and we will see if the increased comfort level that comes along with additional playing time helps his defense, but the Mariners probably shouldn't expect anything above average from Morrison.

Michael Morse

	BASIC							BUNTS			GDP			RANGE AND POSITIONING								RUNS SAVED					
Year	Team	G	Inn	TC	E	Pct	GFP	DM	Opp	Sac Hits	Bunt Hits	Opp	GDP	Pct	Outs Made	To His Right	Straight On	To His Left	GB	Air	Plays Saved	Bases Saved	R/P	Bunt	GDP	GFP/DME	Total	Rank
2006	Sea	2	10.0	11	0	1.000	1	0				-	-	-	1	0	0	0	0	0	0	0	0	-		0	0	-
2007	Sea	5	28.0	36	0	1.000	0	0				-	-	-	10	0	0	0	0	0	0	0	0		-	0	0	-
2009	Was	11	46.0	52	0	1.000	2	0	1	1	0	0	0		14	+1	0	+1	+2	0	+2	+2	1	0	0	0	1	-
2010	Was	19	60.0	63	0	1.000	0	1				1	0	.000	13	-1	+1	0	+1	0	+1	0	1	0	0	0	1	-
2011	Was	85	723.1	793	6	.992	35	10	12	9	2	11	5	.455	134	-1	-5	-2	-8	+1	-7	-9	-7	-1	0	1	-7	31
2012	Was	1	5.0	9	0	1.000	2	0				0	0	-	2	0	+1	0	+1	0	+1	+1	0	0	0	0	0	-
2013	Was	7	51.0	62	0	1.000	1	2				2	2	1.000	11	0	+1	+1	+2	0	+2	+2	1	0	0	-1	0	-
2014	SF	43	336.1	334	3	.991	10	8	4	4	0	4	3	.750	56	+4	-2	-1	+2	0	+2	+1	1	0	0	-1	0	-
		173	1259.2	1360	9	.993	51	21	17	14	2	18	10	.556	241	+3	-4	-1	0	+1	+1	-3	-3	-1	0	-1	-5	-

Scout's Defensive Rating: 0 plays saved in 2013, -3 plays saved in 2014

Michael Morse's Scouting Report can be found on page 252.

Brandon Moss

	BASIC							BUNTS			GDP			RANGE AND POSITIONING								RUNS SAVED					
Year	Team	G	Inn	TC	E	Pct	GFP	DM	Opp	Sac Hits	Bunt Hits	Opp	GDP	Pct	Outs Made	To His Right	Straight On	To His Left	GB	Air	Plays Saved	Bases Saved	R/P	Bunt	GDP	GFP/DME	Total	Rank
2008	Bos	2	13.0	10	0	1.000	0	1				-	-	-	4	0	0	0	+1	0	+1	+1	1		-	0	1	-
2012	Oak	55	443.1	439	8	.982	28	8	2	1	0	4	3	.750	78	-1	-1	-2	-4	0	-4	-4	-3	0	0	-1	-4	-
2013	Oak	111	801.2	717	7	.990	50	15	6	1	1	10	2	.200	123	-1	-3	-5	-9	-6	-15	-16	-12	1	-1	0	-12	34
2014	Oak	67	487.1	513	5	.990	18	13	1	0	1	3	2	.667	69	-1	0	-4	-5	0	-5	-7	-5	0	0	1	-4	28
		235	1745.1	1679	20	.988	96	37	9	2	2	17	7	.412	274	-3	-4	-11	-17	-6	-23	-26	-19	1	-1	0	-19	-

Scout's Defensive Rating: -6 plays saved in 2013, -1 plays saved in 2014

Brandon Moss's Scouting Report can be found on page 286.

First Basemen

Mike Napoli

		BASIC							BUNTS			GDP			RANGE AND POSITIONING								RUNS SAVED					
Year	Team	G	Inn	TC	E	Pct	GFP	DM	Opp	Sac Hits	Bunt Hits	Opp	GDP	Pct	Outs Made	To His Right	Straight On	To His Left	GB	Air	Plays Saved	Bases Saved	R/P	Bunt	GDP	GFP/ DME	Total	Rank
2010	LAA	70	586.1	552	6	.989	30	10	1	1	0	4	2	.500	117	+3	0	-1	+1	-1	0	0	0	0	0	0	0	20
2011	Tex	35	246.1	243	1	.996	9	7				2	1	.500	34	+1	0	-2	0	-1	-1	-1	-1		0	-1	-2	-
2012	Tex	28	207.2	192	3	.984	11	4				1	1	1.000	33	0	0	-1	0	0	0	-1	0		0	0	0	-
2013	Bos	131	1097.1	1070	6	.994	53	12	6	5	0	13	5	.385	183	-2	+5	+6	+9	+1	+10	+12	9	1	0	0	10	4
2014	Bos	110	959.1	983	8	.992	48	12	12	6	2	11	5	.455	152	+4	-3	+6	+8	0	+8	+10	7	0	0	0	7	7
		374	3097.0	3040	24	.992	151	45	19	12	2	31	14	.452	519	+6	+2	+8	+18	-1	+17	+20	15	1	0	-1	15	

Scout's Defensive Rating: 5 plays saved in 2013, 1 plays saved in 2014

After seven years of poor defensive play as a catcher, Mike Napoli has found a home at first base. His quick reactions and smooth glove work have ranked him among the top defenders at the position. In 2014, Napoli finished seventh in Runs Saved (+7). This was the second straight year he finished in the top ten in that category.

His catching background has translated to an exceptional ability to pick throws from other infielders out of the dirt. This season he managed to catch 25 errant throws for outs while only misplaying eight. He did miss significant time with multiple injuries in 2014, but he is also only going into his age-33 season and should be able to continue his exceptional defense as long as he stays healthy.

Lyle Overbay

		BASIC							BUNTS			GDP			RANGE AND POSITIONING								RUNS SAVED					
Year	Team	G	Inn	TC	E	Pct	GFP	DM	Opp	Sac Hits	Bunt Hits	Opp	GDP	Pct	Outs Made	To His Right	Straight On	To His Left	GB	Air	Plays Saved	Bases Saved	R/P	Bunt	GDP	GFP/ DME	Total	Rank
2003	Ari	75	604.0	703	2	.997	-	-	9	5	1	-	-	-	154	0	+4	+4	+8	-1	+7	+9	7	0	-	-	7	6
2004	Mil	158	1360.1	1434	11	.992	26	25	28	13	4	-	-	-	246	+2	-2	-9	-9	0	-9	-14	-10	1	-	-3	-12	35
2005	Mil	154	1265.0	1240	10	.992	37	19	23	15	1	-	-	-	247	+2	+6	-3	+5	0	+5	+4	3	1	-	1	5	11
2006	Tor	145	1233.0	1459	9	.994	41	22	4	0	2	-	-	-	305	+3	+3	-1	+5	+2	+7	+7	5	-1	-	0	4	10
2007	Tor	119	972.1	1166	5	.996	41	17	4	2	0	-	-	-	218	+3	+5	+4	+12	-1	+11	+13	9	1	-	1	11	3
2008	Tor	156	1354.2	1476	5	.997	38	21	9	3	3	-	-	-	324	+7	+7	-1	+13	0	+13	+11	8	-1	-	-1	6	8
2009	Tor	130	1055.1	1132	5	.998	38	16	6	2	2	26	10	.385	230	+1	+2	+6	+8	+2	+10	+10	7	-2	0	1	6	8
2010	Tor	153	1320.2	1416	6	.996	41	14	6	3	0	24	11	.458	237	+3	+2	+1	+7	0	+7	+8	6	-1	1	-1	5	10
2011	2 tms	109	917.0	994	8	.992	34	13	11	7	0	18	9	.500	145	-7	-1	-2	-9	+2	-7	-7	-5	1	0	-1	-5	29
2012	2 tms	23	196.1	205	1	.995	8	1	2	2	0	3	2	.667	34	-1	+1	+1	+2	0	+2	+2	1	0	0	0	1	-
2013	NYY	130	1031.0	1004	4	.996	43	13	9	3	3	13	7	.538	161	0	+1	+1	+2	+1	+3	+3	3	0	0	2	5	9
2014	Mil	83	590.1	592	5	.992	21	11	9	6	0	10	3	.300	77	-3	+1	-1	-3	0	-3	-3	-2	0	0	1	-1	21
		1435	11900.0	12821	68	.995	368	172	120	61	16	94	42	.447	2378	+10	+29	-1	+41	+5	+46	+43	32	-1	1	0	32	

Scout's Defensive Rating: -8 plays saved in 2013, -4 plays saved in 2014

Steve Pearce

		BASIC							BUNTS			GDP			RANGE AND POSITIONING								RUNS SAVED					
Year	Team	G	Inn	TC	E	Pct	GFP	DM	Opp	Sac Hits	Bunt Hits	Opp	GDP	Pct	Outs Made	To His Right	Straight On	To His Left	GB	Air	Plays Saved	Bases Saved	R/P	Bunt	GDP	GFP/ DME	Total	Rank
2007	Pit	2	9.0	12	0	1.000	0	0				-	-	-	2	0	0	0	0	0	0	0	0		-	0	0	-
2009	Pit	42	362.0	392	2	.995	19	5	9	4	3	7	1	.143	83	+5	+2	0	+7	0	+7	+6	4	-1	0	0	3	-
2010	Pit	11	75.2	86	1	.988	6	3	2	1	0	1	0	.000	13	+1	+1	0	+2	-1	+1	+1	1	0	0	0	1	-
2011	Pit	16	83.0	91	1	.989	5	0	2	2	0	3	1	.333	14	-1	+1	0	0	0	0	0	0	0	0	1	1	-
2012	2 tms	19	123.1	134	1	.993	4	4	3	2	1	0	0	-	18	0	0	+1	+1	+1	0	0	0	-1	0	0	-1	-
2013	Bal	3	26.0	23	0	1.000	1	2				0	0	-	3	0	0	0	0	0	0	0	0	0	0	-1	-1	-
2014	Bal	51	415.2	437	1	.998	29	5	1	0	0	1	1	1.000	81	+2	+2	+2	+7	+1	+8	+9	6	0	0	3	9	2
		144	1094.2	1175	6	.995	64	19	17	9	4	12	3	.250	214	+7	+6	+3	+15	+1	+16	+16	11	-2	0	3	12	

Scout's Defensive Rating: 0 plays saved in 2013, 6 plays saved in 2014

Pearce played 415 innings at first base, 231 innings in left field, and 40 innings in right field. Not only was he a versatile defender, he was a great defender, with a combined 18 Defensive Runs Saved (DRS) at the three positions. Pearce had nine DRS at first base, tied with San Diego's Yonder Alonso for the second-most in all of baseball. Adrian Gonzalez, the 2014 Fielding Bible Award winner, was the only first baseman that saved more runs than Pearce, and Gonzalez played over 900 more innings at first base than Pearce did. Pearce showed above average range at all three positions, and what was most impressive was his sure-handedness. Pearce had 36 Good Fielding Plays (GFP) and only nine Defensive Misplays and Errors (DME) at the three positions combined. In fact, a dropped throw from an infielder at first base in July was actually his only error of the season, and that was something of an anomaly as Pearce had 15 GFP for handling difficult throws at first base. When third baseman Manny Machado went down with a season-ending

First Basemen

injury, Pearce's defensive excellence enabled Showalter to move primary first baseman Chris Davis to the hot corner, and when Davis was suspended in September, Pearce was even more valuable as the undisputed starting first baseman down the stretch. He responded with six GFPs and zero DMEs in the month of September, helping the Orioles to a division title.

Brayan Pena

	BASIC							BUNTS			GDP			RANGE AND POSITIONING								RUNS SAVED					
Year Team	G	Inn	TC	E	Pct	GFP	DM	Opp	Sac Hits	Bunt Hits	Opp	GDP	Pct	Outs Made	To His Right	Straight On	To His Left	GB	Air	Plays Saved	Bases Saved	R/P	Bunt	GDP	GFP/ DME	Total	Rank
2012 KC	3	8.2	8	0	1.000	2	0				0	0	-	1	0	0	0	0	0	0	0	0		0	0	0	-
2013 Det	1	1.0	1	0	1.000	0	0				0	0	-	1	0	0	0	0	0	0	0	0		0	0	0	-
2014 Cin	53	396.2	389	1	.997	28	11	2	1	0	1	1	1.000	64	-3	+2	+2	+1	+1	+2	+1	1	0	0	-1	0	18
	57	406.1	398	1	.997	30	11	2	1	0	1	1	1.000	66	-3	+2	+2	+1	+1	+2	+1	1	0	0	-1	0	-

Scout's Defensive Rating: 0 plays saved in 2013, 8 plays saved in 2014

Buster Posey

	BASIC							BUNTS			GDP			RANGE AND POSITIONING								RUNS SAVED					
Year Team	G	Inn	TC	E	Pct	GFP	DM	Opp	Sac Hits	Bunt Hits	Opp	GDP	Pct	Outs Made	To His Right	Straight On	To His Left	GB	Air	Plays Saved	Bases Saved	R/P	Bunt	GDP	GFP/ DME	Total	Rank
2010 SF	30	248.0	214	1	.995	16	5	3	0	0	6	2	.333	37	-5	+1	-1	-5	0	-5	-5	-4	0	0	0	-4	-
2011 SF	2	18.0	18	0	1.000	0	1				1	1	1.000	3	0	0	0	+1	0	+1	+1	0		0	0	0	-
2012 SF	29	216.0	212	2	.991	6	4	2	2	0	1	1	1.000	28	+1	0	0	+1	-1	0	0	1	-1	0	-1	-1	-
2013 SF	21	138.2	145	2	.986	6	3	1	1	0	0	0	-	20	-1	0	+1	0	0	0	-1	0	0	0	0	0	-
2014 SF	35	261.0	269	1	.996	11	5	3	3	0	5	0	.000	44	0	+1	-1	+1	+1	+2	+2	2	0	0	0	2	-
	117	881.2	858	6	.993	39	18	9	6	0	13	4	.308	132	-5	+2	-1	-2	0	-2	-3	-1	-1	0	-1	-3	-

Scout's Defensive Rating: -2 plays saved in 2013, 1 plays saved in 2014

Buster Posey's Scouting Report can be found on page 165.

Albert Pujols

	BASIC							BUNTS			GDP			RANGE AND POSITIONING								RUNS SAVED					
Year Team	G	Inn	TC	E	Pct	GFP	DM	Opp	Sac Hits	Bunt Hits	Opp	GDP	Pct	Outs Made	To His Right	Straight On	To His Left	GB	Air	Plays Saved	Bases Saved	R/P	Bunt	GDP	GFP/ DME	Total	Rank
2003 StL	62	369.2	374	1	.997	-	-	2	2	0	-	-	-	76	+3	-1	+3	+5	+1	+6	+7	5	0	-	-	5	-
2004 StL	150	1338.2	1582	10	.994	51	19	10	7	0	-	-	-	300	-1	+1	+6	+6	-1	+5	+8	6	1	-	0	7	4
2005 StL	158	1358.2	1707	14	.992	67	21	17	3	4	-	-	-	304	+6	0	+3	+9	0	+9	+10	7	2	-	4	13	2
2006 StL	143	1244.1	1463	6	.996	45	22	26	16	5	-	-	-	287	+19	+5	+3	+26	+2	+28	+25	18	-1	-	0	17	1
2007 StL	154	1324.2	1457	8	.995	68	23	17	9	1	-	-	-	334	+12	+14	+6	+33	+1	+34	+37	27	0	-	4	31	1
2008 StL	144	1215.0	1438	6	.996	62	16	10	4	2	-	-	-	303	+9	+8	+4	+20	+1	+21	+20	15	0	-	3	18	2
2009 StL	159	1376.2	1671	13	.992	97	16	15	7	1	32	13	.406	364	+12	+5	-3	+14	+1	+15	+14	10	1	0	6	17	1
2010 StL	157	1380.2	1619	4	.998	93	18	12	7	2	25	17	.680	283	-2	-4	+5	-1	+4	+3	+2	1	-1	1	5	6	8
2011 StL	146	1260.1	1430	11	.992	67	18	16	8	4	21	11	.524	271	0	+5	+2	+7	+3	+10	+10	7	0	1	2	10	3
2012 LAA	120	1021.0	1117	7	.994	56	15	4	3	1	16	6	.375	209	+2	+2	+3	+6	+3	+9	+8	6	0	0	2	8	4
2013 LAA	34	302.0	297	3	.990	16	5	3	2	0	3	0	.000	51	-1	0	+1	0	0	0	0	0	1	0	0	1	-
2014 LAA	116	1017.0	963	3	.997	51	13	6	4	2	14	7	.500	143	+3	+2	0	+5	+2	+7	+7	5	0	0	1	6	9
	1543	13209.1	15118	86	.994	673	186	138	72	22	111	54	.486	2925	+62	+37	+33	+130	+17	+147	+148	107	3	2	27	139	-

Scout's Defensive Rating: 3 plays saved in 2013, 7 plays saved in 2014

At 6'3", 230 pounds, Albert Pujols is a prototypical first baseman. Placed there in 2004 after an elbow injury, Pujols has excelled at the position, winning five Fielding Bible Awards and two Gold Gloves in a six-year period from 2006 to 2011. However, at 34 years of age, Pujols is beginning to see some of his innings in the field replaced by innings on the bench as a designated hitter. This is primarily because of Pujols' durability; while he no longer has the athleticism to be an elite defender, Pujols remains one of the better first basemen in the league. Known for his low, crouching stance, Pujols makes up for subpar foot speed with instinct and a quick first step in all directions. Moreover, Pujols' glove is a model of consistency; if he gets to a ball, Pujols often makes a play. Pujols' 32 percent conversion rate on Difficult Plays (plays graded a 4 in difficulty by BIS Video Scouts) ranked fifth among first basemen with 20 or more opportunities in 2014. Pujols last won a Fielding Bible Award in 2011, but the numbers and the scouts agree that Pujols remains an above average first sacker.

First Basemen

Mark Reynolds

	BASIC							BUNTS			GDP			RANGE AND POSITIONING								RUNS SAVED					
Year	Team	G	Inn	TC	E	Pct	GFP	DM	Opp	Sac Hits	Bunt Hits	Opp	GDP	Pct	Outs Made	To His Right	Straight On	To His Left	GB	Air	Plays Saved	Bases Saved	R/P	Bunt	GDP	GFP/DME	Total	Rank
2008	Ari	1	2.0	2	1	.500	0	0				-	-	-	0	0	0	-1	-1	0	-1	-1	-1		0	0	-1	-
2009	Ari	28	218.0	202	5	.975	14	8				2	1	.500	30	-2	-3	-1	-6	0	-6	-6	-4		0	-2	-6	-
2010	Ari	5	9.0	8	0	1.000	0	0				0	0		2	-1	0	0	-1	0	-1	-1	-1		0	0	-1	-
2011	Bal	44	375.2	392	5	.987	31	8	2	1	0	3	1	.333	64	-2	0	-1	-3	0	-3	-2	-2	0	0	1	-1	-
2012	Bal	108	957.0	971	5	.995	71	13	2	1	0	11	7	.636	136	-3	-2	-2	-8	-1	-9	-8	-6	0	0	4	-2	22
2013	2 tms	65	500.0	526	4	.992	34	9	2	0	1	5	3	.600	99	-2	-4	-1	-6	+1	-5	-6	-4	0	0	-1	-5	27
2014	Mil	91	658.0	689	3	.996	42	12	9	8	0	9	4	.444	114	0	+2	0	+2	-1	+1	+3	3	0	0	-1	2	15
		342	2719.2	2790	23	.992	192	50	15	10	1	30	16	.533	445	-10	-7	-6	-23	-1	-24	-21	-15	0	0	1	-14	-

Scout's Defensive Rating: 6 plays saved in 2013, 2 plays saved in 2014

Anthony Rizzo

	BASIC							BUNTS			GDP			RANGE AND POSITIONING								RUNS SAVED					
Year	Team	G	Inn	TC	E	Pct	GFP	DM	Opp	Sac Hits	Bunt Hits	Opp	GDP	Pct	Outs Made	To His Right	Straight On	To His Left	GB	Air	Plays Saved	Bases Saved	R/P	Bunt	GDP	GFP/DME	Total	Rank
2011	SD	45	341.2	344	2	.994	13	6	5	4	0	5	1	.200	61	+1	-1	+2	+3	-1	+2	+2	2	0	0	0	2	-
2012	ChC	85	730.2	735	4	.995	24	9	6	3	1	11	6	.545	115	+3	+1	-1	+3	+2	+5	+3	3	0	1	0	4	9
2013	ChC	159	1415.0	1441	5	.997	73	18	15	9	3	19	7	.368	252	+9	+10	0	+19	+5	+24	+22	16	-3	0	3	16	1
2014	ChC	140	1259.0	1311	9	.993	63	20	8	7	0	15	9	.600	211	+3	+5	+1	+9	0	+9	+7	6	-1	0	1	6	8
		429	3746.1	3831	20	.995	173	53	34	23	4	50	23	.460	639	+16	+15	+2	+34	+6	+40	+34	27	-4	1	4	28	-

Scout's Defensive Rating: 4 plays saved in 2013, -2 plays saved in 2014

In his first two full seasons in the majors, Anthony Rizzo has proven to be one of the best defensive first basemen in the majors. He put up back-to-back seasons finishing second in Fielding Bible Award voting at the position. Rizzo has soft hands and handles hard hit balls very well. His soft hands also help him excel at scooping poor throws in the dirt. Rizzo led all first basemen in 2014 with 40 Good Fielding Plays on handling difficult throws. Rizzo also has surprising range for a man his size, though he's been better with his forehand in the hole than making plays down the line on his backhand. If there is one area where Rizzo can improve it is in his handling of bunts. Rizzo usually gets the sure out on sacrifice bunts and soft grounders, but unlike other top defensive first basemen, he is not very aggressive in cutting down the lead runner. Overall, Rizzo is going to be a top first baseman in baseball for many years to come, one capable not only of leading the league in home runs but picking up some defensive honors as well.

Adam Rosales

	BASIC							BUNTS			GDP			RANGE AND POSITIONING								RUNS SAVED					
Year	Team	G	Inn	TC	E	Pct	GFP	DM	Opp	Sac Hits	Bunt Hits	Opp	GDP	Pct	Outs Made	To His Right	Straight On	To His Left	GB	Air	Plays Saved	Bases Saved	R/P	Bunt	GDP	GFP/DME	Total	Rank
2009	Cin	11	84.2	79	0	1.000	5	2	3	1	0	1	0	.000	21	0	-1	+1	-1	-1	-2	-1	-1	1	0	0	0	-
2010	Oak	7	38.0	35	0	1.000	3	0	1	0	1	0	0		6	+1	0	0	+1	0	+1	+1	1	0	0	0	1	-
2011	Oak	5	38.0	38	0	1.000	0	1				2	0	.000	6	-1	0	0	-1	+1	0	0	0	0	0	0	0	-
2012	Oak	7	33.0	33	0	1.000	2	0				0	0		9	0	0	0	0	0	0	0	0	0	0	0	0	-
2013	Tex	4	7.2	5	0	1.000	1	1				0	0		1	0	0	0	0	0	0	0	0	0	0	0	0	-
2014	Tex	32	252.0	238	1	.996	24	5	4	2	0	4	3	.750	51	-1	-1	+4	+1	+1	+2	+4	2	1	0	2	5	-
		66	453.1	428	1	.998	35	9	8	3	1	7	3	.429	94	-1	-2	+5	0	+1	+1	+4	2	2	0	2	6	-

Scout's Defensive Rating: 0 plays saved in 2013, 3 plays saved in 2014

Gaby Sanchez

	BASIC							BUNTS			GDP			RANGE AND POSITIONING								RUNS SAVED					
Year	Team	G	Inn	TC	E	Pct	GFP	DM	Opp	Sac Hits	Bunt Hits	Opp	GDP	Pct	Outs Made	To His Right	Straight On	To His Left	GB	Air	Plays Saved	Bases Saved	R/P	Bunt	GDP	GFP/DME	Total	Rank
2008	Fla	3	11.0	14	0	1.000	1	1				-	-	-	1	-1	+1	0	0	0	0	0	0	-	0	0	0	-
2009	Fla	1	8.0	12	0	1.000	0	0				0	0		1	0	0	0	0	0	0	0	0	0	0	0	0	-
2010	Fla	149	1253.1	1196	11	.991	64	18	11	5	2	11	5	.455	226	0	-11	+2	-9	-3	-12	-11	-8	0	0	-2	-10	30
2011	Fla	153	1354.0	1368	5	.996	50	24	19	13	2	17	5	.294	260	+2	+5	-1	+5	+2	+7	+7	5	0	0	0	5	8
2012	2 tms	95	697.1	769	3	.996	35	12	5	1	2	10	5	.500	151	+6	0	+1	+8	+1	+9	+12	8	0	0	-2	6	6
2013	Pit	113	652.1	757	3	.996	44	19	10	8	1	7	3	.429	107	+2	+1	-5	-2	+1	-1	-1	-1	-2	0	-1	-3	23
2014	Pit	96	515.2	595	3	.995	23	11	11	5	2	10	4	.400	82	-3	+3	-4	-3	+1	-2	-3	-2	0	0	-1	-3	24
		610	4491.2	4711	25	.995	217	83	56	32	9	55	22	.400	828	+6	-1	-7	-1	+2	+1	+4	2	-2	0	-5	-5	-

Scout's Defensive Rating: -1 plays saved in 2013, -1 plays saved in 2014

First Basemen

Carlos Santana

Year	Team	G	Inn	TC	E	Pct	GFP	DM	Opp	Sac Hits	Bunt Hits	Opp GDP	GDP	Pct	Outs Made	To His Right	Straight On	To His Left	GB	Air	Plays Saved	Bases Saved	R/P	Bunt	GDP	GFP/DME	Total	Rank
2011	Cle	66	565.0	669	4	.994	37	13	5	1	2	11	5	.455	119	-3	0	+1	-2	-1	-3	-2	-1	1	0	-1	-1	19
2012	Cle	21	162.2	175	2	.989	12	1	1	1	0	1	1	1.000	30	-1	0	+1	+1	0	+1	+1	1	0	0	0	1	-
2013	Cle	29	215.0	195	1	.995	15	7	1	1	0	0	0	-	40	0	-2	-1	-3	+2	-1	-1	-1	0	0	1	0	-
2014	Cle	94	851.0	911	5	.995	50	17	9	4	2	14	6	.429	137	-3	-5	+1	-7	0	-7	-7	-5	1	0	0	-4	28
		210	1793.2	1950	12	.994	114	38	16	7	4	26	12	.462	326	-7	-7	+2	-11	+1	-10	-9	-6	2	0	0	-4	-

Scout's Defensive Rating: 3 plays saved in 2013, 6 plays saved in 2014

It seems to be that Carlos Santana is currently searching for a home defensively. The Indians planned to move Santana out from behind the plate, and they hoped that he could help fill a void at third base. That proved to be a disaster, however. It seemed that Santana was rushing plays, whether it was issues with the throw or charging the ball on slower grounders, which led to seven defensive misplays and six errors in 225 innings. When it fell apart, Santana switched over to his old friend, first base. Though Santana may never be a great first baseman, he has a larger frame which can translate well to first base if he continues to work at it. If he can't stick at first, he may find himself in a designated hitter role earlier than anticipated in his career.

Jon Singleton

Year	Team	G	Inn	TC	E	Pct	GFP	DM	Opp	Sac Hits	Bunt Hits	Opp GDP	GDP	Pct	Outs Made	To His Right	Straight On	To His Left	GB	Air	Plays Saved	Bases Saved	R/P	Bunt	GDP	GFP/DME	Total	Rank
2014	Hou	91	770.2	840	11	.987	39	19	9	4	1	8	1	.125	99	+1	-1	-7	-7	-1	-8	-8	-5	1	0	-1	-5	32

Scout's Defensive Rating: -10 plays saved in 2014

Singleton's first season in the major leagues was a defensive struggle. He ended up costing the Astros five runs and really struggled on balls hit down the line. He has a large frame (6'2", 255 lbs), which really prohibits him from moving very swiftly in either direction. Singleton is also a work in progress when it comes to handling throws in the dirt or wide of the bag. He had seven Defensive Misplays on handling wild throws this year over the 91 games that he appeared in. Singleton has some clear deficiencies in his defensive game, but he is still young and has plenty of time to smooth out some of the rough edges.

Justin Smoak

Year	Team	G	Inn	TC	E	Pct	GFP	DM	Opp	Sac Hits	Bunt Hits	Opp GDP	GDP	Pct	Outs Made	To His Right	Straight On	To His Left	GB	Air	Plays Saved	Bases Saved	R/P	Bunt	GDP	GFP/DME	Total	Rank
2010	2 tms	94	807.2	833	5	.994	37	14	10	4	3	7	1	.143	157	+1	-4	+2	0	-2	-2	-3	-2	-1	0	1	-2	23
2011	Sea	108	926.2	950	7	.993	36	11	5	1	2	13	5	.385	162	0	0	-1	-1	-3	-4	-2	-1	-1	0	1	-1	19
2012	Sea	131	1155.2	1168	4	.997	43	15	10	7	2	18	8	.444	181	-2	-2	+1	-2	+1	-1	-1	-1	-1	0	2	0	18
2013	Sea	125	1084.1	1101	5	.995	39	11	4	3	1	14	3	.214	159	-9	0	+2	-7	-1	-8	-7	-6	0	-1	-1	-8	31
2014	Sea	79	608.0	620	2	.997	23	7	7	4	1	9	2	.222	87	-1	-1	0	-1	-2	-3	-4	-3	0	-1	0	-4	26
		537	4582.1	4672	23	.995	178	58	36	19	9	61	19	.311	746	-11	-7	+4	-11	-7	-18	-17	-13	-3	-2	3	-15	-

Scout's Defensive Rating: -3 plays saved in 2013, 2 plays saved in 2014

For his tall muscular body, Justin Smoak has been consistently just below average throughout his career. His range and ability to make difficult plays where he has to dive leave a lot to be desired, but he handles the routine plays and is above average at fielding throws from infielders. He is tall enough to get the high throws to first without coming off the base, and he has the vision and coordination to make a lot of scoops on throws in the dirt. Smoak's arm is average, which is good enough for him to turn the double plays he is supposed to make as a first baseman. Smoak's lack of mobility is what makes him a below average defender.

First Basemen

Nick Swisher

Year	Team	G	Inn	TC	E	Pct	GFP	DM	Opp	Sac Hits	Bunt Hits	Opp	GDP	Pct	Outs Made	To His Right	Straight On	To His Left	GB	Air	Plays Saved	Bases Saved	R/P	Bunt	GDP	GFP/ DME	Total	Rank
2004	Oak	3	18.0	19	0	1.000	0	0	-	-	-	-	-	-	1				0		0	0	0		-	0	0	-
2005	Oak	21	119.0	119	0	1.000	3	1	3	1	1	-	-	-	25	+1	-1	0	+1	0	+1	+1	1	0	-	0	1	-
2006	Oak	90	700.0	712	5	.993	17	12	6	2	1	-	-	-	148	+3	-2	0	0	-2	-2	-1	-1	0	-	1	0	20
2007	Oak	44	346.2	419	3	.993	16	10	2	1	0	-	-	-	89	+4	+1	-5	+1	0	+1	-1	-1	0	-	-1	-2	-
2008	CWS	71	462.0	481	2	.996	32	3	3	0	1	-	-	-	79	-7	-1	+1	-7	+1	-6	-5	-4	0	-	3	-1	19
2009	NYY	20	104.0	95	1	.989	4	1	1	0	0	1	0	.000	19	0	-1	0	0	0	0	0	0	0	0	0	0	-
2010	NYY	6	21.0	21	0	1.000	3	0				0	0	-	4	0	+1	-1	0	0	0	0	0		0	0	0	-
2011	NYY	11	44.0	31	0	1.000	5	0				0	0	-	4	0	0	-1	-1	0	-1	-3	-2		0	0	-2	-
2012	NYY	41	259.0	276	3	.989	21	3	2	0	1	2	1	.500	63	+3	+1	0	+4	0	+4	+4	3	0	0	2	5	-
2013	Cle	112	910.1	908	8	.991	60	15	10	5	4	18	10	.556	174	+2	0	+1	+4	+2	+6	+6	5	-1	1	1	6	8
2014	Cle	52	459.0	448	9	.980	19	9	4	2	2	7	3	.429	64	-1	-4	0	-4	-2	-6	-6	-4	0	0	0	-4	27
		471	3443.0	3529	31	.991	180	54	31	11	10	28	14	.500	670	+5	-6	-5	-2	-1	-3	-5	-3	-1	1	6	3	-

Scout's Defensive Rating: 6 plays saved in 2013, -10 plays saved in 2014

An above average glove man at first base in prior years, Nick Swisher's defensive play in 2014 leaves much to be desired. He stabs at groundballs with the leather in a way resembling barehanded fishing–blindly grasping and often fruitless. Grounders seem to have a way of trickling past him and through the infield dirt. He was tied for 13th among first basemen with eight Defensive Misplays and Errors on groundballs. That may not seem too significant, but his defensive ineptitude becomes more apparent when considering his relatively light workload at first base. Swisher compiled these groundball DMEs at a faster rate than any other regular first baseman in the majors. A broader look into Swisher's statistics shows that his poor defensive play transcends this specific subtype. When focusing on the rate of DMEs committed in general, it is found again that he led his position. Furthermore, Swisher's Good Fielding Plays were too few to compensate for his miscues. Among first basemen, he ranked second-worst among regulars in Net GFP-DME. A full workload at his 2014 pace would have Swisher competing for worst defensive first baseman in the majors. Cleveland might be well-served by increasing his appearances at designated hitter.

Mark Teixeira

Year	Team	G	Inn	TC	E	Pct	GFP	DM	Opp	Sac Hits	Bunt Hits	Opp	GDP	Pct	Outs Made	To His Right	Straight On	To His Left	GB	Air	Plays Saved	Bases Saved	R/P	Bunt	GDP	GFP/ DME	Total	Rank
2003	Tex	116	932.2	1006	4	.996	-	-	13	6	6	-	-	-	208	+11	+16	+2	+29	+2	+31	+29	21	-2	-	-	19	1
2004	Tex	142	1223.0	1317	10	.992	37	18	13	8	2	-	-	-	320	0	-1	+5	+4	-1	+3	+7	5	0	-	0	5	9
2005	Tex	155	1358.0	1482	3	.998	66	23	10	6	0	-	-	-	337	+8	+2	+3	+13	+1	+14	+17	12	1	-	0	13	1
2006	Tex	159	1399.0	1572	4	.997	55	17	6	1	1	-	-	-	307	0	+2	+3	+5	-1	+4	+2	1	1	-	6	8	5
2007	2 tms	128	1098.0	1190	5	.996	50	15	14	13	1	-	-	-	228	-2	-2	+2	-3	+1	-2	-4	-3	0	-	3	0	19
2008	2 tms	153	1335.0	1498	5	.997	93	17	10	9	0	-	-	-	312	+5	+11	+7	+23	+1	+24	+23	17	0	-	4	21	1
2009	NYY	152	1303.2	1275	4	.997	78	26	5	1	1	13	3	.231	249	+4	-1	0	+3	-2	+1	0	0	0	-1	3	2	14
2010	NYY	149	1291.2	1310	3	.998	79	18	11	7	2	26	11	.423	289	+4	0	+1	+5	+1	+6	+6	5	0	0	1	6	6
2011	NYY	147	1274.0	1306	4	.997	79	25	12	6	3	15	4	.267	249	+9	-1	+1	+9	-1	+8	+6	4	0	-1	0	3	12
2012	NYY	119	1032.0	1056	1	.999	69	13	9	6	2	20	10	.500	210	+10	+3	+2	+15	+1	+16	+17	12	1	1	3	17	1
2013	NYY	14	121.1	108	0	1.000	2	3				2	2	1.000	21	0	0	0	-1	0	-1	0	0	0	0	0	0	-
2014	NYY	117	1021.1	987	6	.994	44	15	9	8	0	8	4	.500	141	0	+2	-2	+1	-1	0	+1	1	0	0	1	2	16
		1551	13389.2	14107	49	.997	652	190	112	71	18	84	34	.405	2871	+49	+31	+24	+103	+1	+104	+104	75	1	-1	21	96	-

Scout's Defensive Rating: -1 plays saved in 2013, 2 plays saved in 2014

Once viewed as the best defensive first baseman in the league, former Fielding Bible Award winner Mark Teixeira has lost that recognition with his aging and injuries. Back, groin, lat, wrist, and finger are just a few of the injuries Teixeira has endured in 2014 as he hit his mid-30s. His range, which used to be a strength to both sides but especially to the left, has now deteriorated to league average levels. He's been hurt by the combination of slow reactions and poor footwork when anticipating a grounder. On the positive side, one area that Teixeira seems to always be strong in is his picking ability. He can scoop out balls that seem they are destined for an error in the score sheet. The glove is still a plus, as he handled many difficult grounders well. There is optimism for Teixeira to be at full health in 2015 and if that means he can get himself in better position to make plays, he could rebound defensively. All caveats aside, he's never posted a below average defensive season at the position, though age and injuries may change that soon.

First Basemen

Mark Trumbo

	BASIC							BUNTS			GDP			RANGE AND POSITIONING								RUNS SAVED					
Year	Team	G	Inn	TC	E	Pct	GFP	DM	Opp	Sac Hits	Bunt Hits	Opp	GDP	Pct	Outs Made	To His Right	Straight On	To His Left	GB	Air	Plays Saved	Bases Saved	R/P	Bunt	GDP	GFP/ DME	Total	Rank
2010	LAA	6	33.0	42	0	1.000	1	0	1	1	0	0	0	-	7	+1	0	0	+2	0	+2	+2	1	0	0	0	1	-
2011	LAA	149	1257.1	1384	10	.993	48	19	9	6	2	18	14	.778	273	+6	+3	0	+10	0	+10	+10	7	0	2	0	9	4
2012	LAA	21	159.0	150	0	1.000	2	1				0	0	-	21	0	0	+1	+1	-2	-1	-1	0			0	0	-
2013	LAA	123	1030.2	1002	8	.992	59	30	8	4	1	20	9	.450	204	+4	+3	0	+7	-3	+4	+4	3	1	0	-2	2	14
2014	Ari	43	377.0	384	3	.992	14	5	3	2	0	2	0	.000	53	-1	+1	0	-1	0	-1	-1	-1	0	0	0	-1	-
		342	2857.0	2962	21	.993	124	55	21	13	3	40	23	.575	558	+10	+7	+1	+19	-5	+14	+14	10	1	2	-2	11	-

Scout's Defensive Rating: -9 plays saved in 2013, 0 plays saved in 2014

Mark Trumbo's Scouting Report can be found on page 255.

Stephen Vogt

	BASIC							BUNTS			GDP			RANGE AND POSITIONING								RUNS SAVED					
Year	Team	G	Inn	TC	E	Pct	GFP	DM	Opp	Sac Hits	Bunt Hits	Opp	GDP	Pct	Outs Made	To His Right	Straight On	To His Left	GB	Air	Plays Saved	Bases Saved	R/P	Bunt	GDP	GFP/ DME	Total	Rank
2014	Oak	47	346.2	364	2	.995	20	11	3	2	1	3	2	.667	50	0	+1	+1	+2	0	+2	+2	1	-1	0	-1	-1	-

Scout's Defensive Rating: 3 plays saved in 2014

Joey Votto

	BASIC							BUNTS			GDP			RANGE AND POSITIONING								RUNS SAVED					
Year	Team	G	Inn	TC	E	Pct	GFP	DM	Opp	Sac Hits	Bunt Hits	Opp	GDP	Pct	Outs Made	To His Right	Straight On	To His Left	GB	Air	Plays Saved	Bases Saved	R/P	Bunt	GDP	GFP/ DME	Total	Rank
2007	Cin	17	137.0	118	0	1.000	9	1	2	1	1	-	-	-	26	+2	-4	+1	-1	+1	0	0	0	0	-	1	1	-
2008	Cin	144	1223.2	1197	11	.991	57	33	27	16	5	-	-	-	282	+6	+4	+7	+17	+1	+18	+18	13	-2	-	-4	7	6
2009	Cin	130	1097.0	1071	10	.991	55	23	13	5	2	18	4	.222	222	0	+5	-5	-1	+1	0	0	0	0	-1	-1	-2	22
2010	Cin	148	1283.0	1265	5	.996	75	19	17	14	0	14	9	.643	237	+5	-2	-2	+1	+2	+3	-1	-1	0	1	4	4	12
2011	Cin	160	1427.2	1520	6	.996	61	28	22	14	3	21	5	.238	285	+11	+4	0	+15	+1	+16	+14	10	-1	-1	-1	7	5
2012	Cin	109	969.0	972	6	.994	59	20	13	8	3	17	5	.204	205	+2	+7	-2	+7	+2	+9	+9	6	-2	0	5	9	3
2013	Cin	161	1430.2	1413	14	.990	73	22	19	15	3	16	5	.313	235	+5	+7	-4	+8	+2	+10	+9	7	-1	-1	1	6	7
2014	Cin	61	539.0	569	7	.988	23	9	6	5	0	5	1	.200	93	+5	+1	-2	+4	+1	+5	+6	4	0	0	1	5	10
		930	8107.0	8125	59	.993	412	155	119	76	17	91	29	.319	1585	+36	+22	-7	+50	+11	+61	+55	39	-6	-2	6	37	-

Scout's Defensive Rating: -1 plays saved in 2013, -2 plays saved in 2014

Votto, a 2011 Gold Glove winner, is such an offensive juggernaut that his defense is often overlooked. The former high school catcher now shows just average arm strength, but can gobble up tough hops and make accurate throws back to the bag all day. Very solid to his right, though not so hot toward the line, Votto has twice led his position in assists. The 31-year old is 6-foot-2, 220 pounds and has had leg problems in the past, so how he returns in 2015 will be an interesting case to keep an eye on.

The 2010 NL MVP has been in the top ten at first base by Runs Saved each year since 2011, including 2014 which only saw him get 61 games in at first base before a quad problem shut him down. Although he's third in total Runs Saved over the last three seasons, Votto isn't quite an elite glove, but is far from hurting his team's defense and should continue to be an asset to the Reds at first base even as he ages.

Second Basemen Register and Scouting Reports

Year	Fielding Bible Award Winner	Runner Up	Third Place
2006	Orlando Hudson	Mark Ellis	Chase Utley
2007	Aaron Hill	Orlando Hudson	Brandon Phillips
2008	Brandon Phillips	Mark Ellis	Chase Utley
2009	Aaron Hill	Dustin Pedroia	Chase Utley
2010	Chase Utley	Orlando Hudson	Mark Ellis
2011	Dustin Pedroia	Ben Zobrist	Brandon Phillips
2012	Darwin Barney	Dustin Pedroia	Robinson Cano
2013	Dustin Pedroia	Darwin Barney	Mark Ellis
2014	Dustin Pedroia	Ian Kinsler	DJ LeMahieu

Second Basemen

Arismendy Alcantara

Year Team	G	Inn	TC	E	Pct	GFP	DM	Opps	GDP	Pct	Outs Made	To His Right	Straight On	To His Left	GB	Air	Plays Saved	R/P	GDP	GFP/DME	Total	Rank
	BASIC							GDP			RANGE AND POSITIONING							RUNS SAVED				
2014 ChC	25	208.2	95	1	.989	7	4	15	9	.600	58	+4	+2	-1	+5	0	+5	4	0	0	4	-

Scout's Defensive Rating: 4 plays saved in 2014

Jose Altuve

Year Team	G	Inn	TC	E	Pct	GFP	DM	Opps	GDP	Pct	Outs Made	To His Right	Straight On	To His Left	GB	Air	Plays Saved	R/P	GDP	GFP/DME	Total	Rank
	BASIC							GDP			RANGE AND POSITIONING							RUNS SAVED				
2011 Hou	55	460.2	217	2	.991	22	5	37	26	.703	142	-1	0	+3	+2	-1	+1	0	1	1	2	16
2012 Hou	147	1226.2	677	11	.984	59	33	132	80	.606	398	0	-1	-19	-20	+1	-19	-14	-2	-2	-18	35
2013 Hou	145	1261.2	675	9	.987	60	13	156	110	.705	343	+4	-8	-7	-11	+2	-9	-7	3	1	-3	25
2014 Hou	156	1362.1	737	10	.986	68	29	162	109	.673	299	-6	-7	+1	-11	-2	-13	-10	2	1	-7	29
	503	4311.1	2306	32	.986	209	80	487	325	.667	1182	-3	-16	-22	-40	0	-40	-31	4	1	-26	-

Scout's Defensive Rating: 11 plays saved in 2013, 0 plays saved in 2014

Jose Altuve is one of the best pivot men in the majors. He is fairly close to being the quintessential second stop on a pitcher's best friend: sure handed to get the out at second, lightning-quick relay for the out at first, and no regard for extremities with sliding baserunners at his feet. In 2014, Altuve led the league in two different pivot-related Good Fielding Play categories with nine double plays despite an aggressive slide and 11 quick double play pivots. Otherwise, watching Altuve field his position at second is simply disappointing at times. He possesses an amazing quickness, but he fails to execute the play relatively often. In 2014, Altuve led his position with 16 Defensive Misplays and Errors of on groundballs that he reached. He also finished in the bottom ten in Range and Positioning Runs for the third straight year. His propensity for completing the double play only marginally makes up for his consistently poor execution on balls he reaches, leaving him below average overall.

Mike Aviles

Year Team	G	Inn	TC	E	Pct	GFP	DM	Opps	GDP	Pct	Outs Made	To His Right	Straight On	To His Left	GB	Air	Plays Saved	R/P	GDP	GFP/DME	Total	Rank
	BASIC							GDP			RANGE AND POSITIONING							RUNS SAVED				
2008 KC	28	114.1	59	0	1.000	5	3	12	5	.417	42	-3	+2	0	-1	0	-1	-1	0	0	-1	-
2010 KC	87	755.2	452	11	.976	24	21	81	41	.506	273	+1	-9	+7	-1	-2	-3	-3	-3	-2	-8	29
2011 2 tms	27	191.2	113	3	.973	8	11	26	14	.538	67	-1	0	+2	+1	+1	+2	2	-1	-1	0	-
2012 Bos	2	10.0	4	0	1.000	1	0	0	0	-	2	0	0	0	0	0	0	0	0	0	0	-
2013 Cle	12	94.0	45	1	.978	3	1	7	5	.714	33	0	-1	+1	0	0	0	0	0	0	0	-
2014 Cle	33	266.1	139	1	.993	13	7	31	21	.677	81	-2	0	+7	+4	+1	+5	4	0	0	4	-
	189	1432.0	812	16	.980	54	43	157	86	.548	498	-5	-8	+17	+3	0	+3	2	-4	-3	-5	-

Scout's Defensive Rating: 0 plays saved in 2013, 1 plays saved in 2014

Javier Baez

Year Team	G	Inn	TC	E	Pct	GFP	DM	Opps	GDP	Pct	Outs Made	To His Right	Straight On	To His Left	GB	Air	Plays Saved	R/P	GDP	GFP/DME	Total	Rank
	BASIC							GDP			RANGE AND POSITIONING							RUNS SAVED				
2014 ChC	25	210.0	116	5	.957	7	4	25	19	.760	52	0	-3	0	-2	0	-2	-2	1	-1	-2	-

Scout's Defensive Rating: -1 plays saved in 2014

Darwin Barney

Year Team	G	Inn	TC	E	Pct	GFP	DM	Opps	GDP	Pct	Outs Made	To His Right	Straight On	To His Left	GB	Air	Plays Saved	R/P	GDP	GFP/DME	Total	Rank
	BASIC							GDP			RANGE AND POSITIONING							RUNS SAVED				
2010 ChC	10	54.1	32	2	.938	4	0	9	5	.556	14	-1	+1	0	0	0	0	0	0	1	1	-
2011 ChC	135	1110.1	619	12	.981	47	30	100	56	.560	369	-2	0	+4	+2	+3	+5	4	-2	0	2	14
2012 ChC	155	1270.1	731	2	.997	68	26	139	91	.655	446	+8	-4	+18	+21	+8	+29	22	2	4	28	1
2013 ChC	141	1237.1	603	4	.993	53	25	110	73	.664	344	+8	+4	+2	+15	0	+15	11	0	0	11	3
2014 2 tms	79	565.0	255	4	.984	28	5	40	29	.725	158	+4	+3	+2	+9	+3	+12	9	0	1	10	4
	520	4237.1	2240	24	.989	200	86	398	254	.638	1331	+17	+4	+26	+47	+14	+61	46	0	6	52	-

Scout's Defensive Rating: 3 plays saved in 2013, 7 plays saved in 2014

Second Basemen

Darwin Barney is one of the quietest defensive wizards in baseball at second base. He received his first Fielding Bible Award in 2012 and finished fourth in the balloting in 2014 despite playing just 565 innings. In his first full season of 2011, one of Barney's weaknesses had been converting double plays, particularly when he was the lead man, converting just 56 percent of double plays. After gaining familiarity with former middle infield partner Starlin Castro, Barney improved dramatically at converting double plays, all the way up to a respectable 73 percent in 2014. Barney's ability to cover a lot of ground and to make difficult plays, complemented by his strong arm, have helped him save 49 runs over the past three years, the most in baseball at the position. On top of his great range, he rarely makes mistakes, highlighted by his 2012 errorless streak that fell three outs shy of setting the major league record. If Barney could hit enough to stay in the lineup every day, he'd be a perennial Fielding Bible Award candidate.

Gordon Beckham

		BASIC							GDP			RANGE AND POSITIONING							RUNS SAVED				
Year	Team	G	Inn	TC	E	Pct	GFP	DM	Opps	GDP	Pct	Outs Made	To His Right	Straight On	To His Left	GB	Air	Plays Saved	R/P	GDP	GFP/ DME	Total	Rank
2010	CWS	126	1111.1	632	12	.981	49	25	135	93	.689	369	-8	-4	+3	-9	+1	-8	-7	1	2	-4	25
2011	CWS	149	1307.2	723	8	.989	64	26	130	80	.615	461	-8	+2	+14	+8	+1	+9	6	0	-1	5	10
2012	CWS	149	1308.2	698	7	.990	67	21	144	102	.708	404	-9	+1	+2	-6	-6	-12	-9	2	1	-6	30
2013	CWS	103	884.1	479	12	.975	40	17	91	65	.714	274	-3	-1	+2	-2	0	-2	-2	1	-2	-3	24
2014	2 tms	105	914.2	534	10	.981	46	13	99	71	.717	282	-1	-7	+4	-4	+1	-3	-2	2	3	3	14
		632	5526.2	3066	49	.984	266	102	599	411	.686	1790	-29	-9	+25	-13	-3	-16	-14	6	3	-5	-

Scout's Defensive Rating: 0 plays saved in 2013, 10 plays saved in 2014

Gordon Beckham is an interesting case. To start, what he does well: the double play. As the lead man, his quick feeds can turn one out into two; as the pivot man, he secures the out at second and fires an accurate relay to first despite having his footing unfixed by the occasional take-out slide. Beckham actually tied for fourth among second basemen in Good Fielding Plays of this subtype, compiling six pivot assists despite aggressive slides. He and double-play-partner Alexei Ramirez developed quite a profitable relationship in the middle infield for the White Sox. The duo's rapport helped to produce Beckham's five GDP Runs Saved over the past three years, tied for first among all second baseman during that span.

As for the interesting, we'll take a look at Beckham's range. To the eye, Beckham has above average range, reaching groundballs that might elude the average second baseman with rather impressive speed and solids hands and arm strength. This is reflected by a remarkable Scout's Defensive Rating of 10 plays above average, fourth among second basemen. The only three second basemen ahead of him (Pedroia, Kinsler, and LeMahieu) were atop the Defensive Runs Saved leaderboards, while Gordon's numbers have never been that high. The discrepancy is a matter of poor positioning and instincts. Gordon plays shallower than almost every other second baseman, costing him a valuable fraction of a second before a hot grounder rushes by him. Though his athleticism is as good as it gets at second base, Beckham's lack of instincts have kept him from stepping ahead of the pack.

Emilio Bonifacio

		BASIC							GDP			RANGE AND POSITIONING							RUNS SAVED				
Year	Team	G	Inn	TC	E	Pct	GFP	DM	Opps	GDP	Pct	Outs Made	To His Right	Straight On	To His Left	GB	Air	Plays Saved	R/P	GDP	GFP/ DME	Total	Rank
2007	Ari	6	46.0	25	1	.960	1	3	8	6	.750	13	+1	0	-1	+1	0	+1	1	1	-1	1	-
2008	Was	37	325.0	167	7	.958	10	13	46	22	.478	100	-1	-2	+2	-1	+3	+2	2	0	-2	0	-
2009	Fla	7	38.0	19	0	1.000	3	4	5	5	1.000	12	+1	0	+1	+1	0	+1	1	0	0	1	-
2010	Fla	5	27.1	17	1	.941	2	1	3	3	1.000	15	0	0	0	0	0	0	0	0	1	1	-
2011	Fla	5	28.0	12	0	1.000	1	1	2	1	.500	8	-1	0	0	-1	+1	0	0	0	0	0	-
2012	Mia	15	122.2	62	3	.952	6	1	8	7	.875	45	-1	0	-1	-2	+1	-1	-1	0	0	-1	-
2013	2 tms	90	710.2	381	10	.974	31	16	75	54	.720	217	+5	-5	+6	+5	+5	+10	9	0	1	10	5
2014	2 tms	31	227.1	112	3	.973	7	6	26	18	.692	45	0	0	0	0	-1	-1	-1	0	-2	-3	-
		196	1525.0	795	25	.969	61	45	173	116	.671	455	+4	-7	+7	+3	+9	+12	11	1	-3	9	-

Scout's Defensive Rating: -5 plays saved in 2013, -3 plays saved in 2014

Emilio Bonifacio's Scouting Report can be found on page 260.

Second Basemen

Asdrubal Cabrera

		BASIC							GDP			RANGE AND POSITIONING							RUNS SAVED				
Year	Team	G	Inn	TC	E	Pct	GFP	DM	Opps	GDP	Pct	Outs Made	To His Right	Straight On	To His Left	GB	Air	Plays Saved	R/P	GDP	GFP/ DME	Total	Rank
2007	Cle	40	321.0	190	1	.995	19	9	42	26	.619	122	+4	0	+1	+4	0	+4	3	2	0	5	-
2008	Cle	94	776.2	486	3	.994	31	9	112	79	.705	315	+12	+1	-6	+6	-2	+4	3	7	1	11	7
2009	Cle	28	244.0	142	1	.993	7	4	36	30	.833	75	0	-1	-6	-7	-1	-8	-6	1	1	-4	-
2014	Was	48	432.0	206	1	.995	21	7	32	24	.750	117	-3	-3	-5	-12	-3	-15	-11	1	0	-10	32
		210	1773.2	1024	6	.994	78	29	222	159	.716	629	+13	-3	-16	-9	-6	-15	-11	11	2	2	-

Scout's Defensive Rating: 3 plays saved in 2014

Asdrubal Cabrera's Scouting Report can be found on page 224.

Alberto Callaspo

		BASIC							GDP			RANGE AND POSITIONING							RUNS SAVED				
Year	Team	G	Inn	TC	E	Pct	GFP	DM	Opps	GDP	Pct	Outs Made	To His Right	Straight On	To His Left	GB	Air	Plays Saved	R/P	GDP	GFP/ DME	Total	Rank
2006	Ari	3	26.0	19	1	.947	2	0	3	1	.333	14	-1	0	0	0	0	0	0	0	0	0	-
2007	Ari	10	41.0	16	0	1.000	1	1	6	4	.667	14	0	+1	+1	+1	0	+1	1	0	-1	0	-
2008	KC	46	365.2	193	0	1.000	9	2	44	32	.727	128	0	+4	-7	-3	-2	-5	-4	3	1	0	-
2009	KC	146	1240.0	629	17	.973	33	19	151	97	.642	399	+1	-4	-9	-12	-7	-19	-14	-2	0	-16	35
2010	2 tms	12	101.0	50	1	.980	2	6	14	8	.571	28	+1	0	-2	-2	0	-2	-1	0	0	-1	-
2013	Oak	33	247.2	98	3	.969	13	7	18	8	.444	47	-1	-3	-1	-4	-5	-9	-7	-1	0	-8	-
2014	Oak	46	347.1	184	4	.978	10	11	39	24	.615	91	+2	-1	-5	-4	+1	-3	-2	0	-1	-3	-
		296	2368.2	1189	26	.978	70	46	275	174	.633	721	+2	-3	-23	-24	-13	-37	-27	0	-1	-28	-

Scout's Defensive Rating: -3 plays saved in 2013, 1 plays saved in 2014

Robinson Cano

		BASIC							GDP			RANGE AND POSITIONING							RUNS SAVED				
Year	Team	G	Inn	TC	E	Pct	GFP	DM	Opps	GDP	Pct	Outs Made	To His Right	Straight On	To His Left	GB	Air	Plays Saved	R/P	GDP	GFP/ DME	Total	Rank
2005	NYY	131	1142.2	666	17	.974	40	19	152	70	.461	441	-16	-2	-15	-33	+6	-27	-21	-2	1	-22	34
2006	NYY	118	1009.0	572	9	.984	24	25	137	69	.504	387	-2	-3	-1	-5	+1	-4	-3	0	-1	-4	24
2007	NYY	159	1408.2	830	13	.984	47	25	187	122	.652	530	+6	+2	+9	+16	+1	+17	13	9	1	23	1
2008	NYY	159	1376.2	800	13	.984	69	29	178	88	.494	530	-6	+1	-8	-13	-4	-17	-13	0	1	-12	33
2009	NYY	161	1399.2	744	12	.984	60	39	153	91	.595	485	+1	-1	+8	+8	0	+8	6	-3	0	0	18
2010	NYY	158	1393.1	776	3	.996	45	29	171	113	.661	451	+3	+1	+11	+16	+6	+22	17	2	-1	18	1
2011	NYY	157	1340.0	777	10	.987	68	40	139	96	.691	454	+11	-5	-3	+3	0	+3	2	2	-2	2	15
2012	NYY	154	1343.1	726	6	.992	70	27	145	94	.648	453	+21	-1	+5	+24	-2	+22	17	0	-2	15	2
2013	NYY	153	1350.1	657	6	.991	65	20	152	87	.572	356	+7	+1	-1	+8	0	+8	6	-2	2	6	11
2014	Sea	150	1304.0	697	9	.987	44	25	142	98	.690	353	-1	-6	+3	-4	0	-4	-3	2	1	0	18
		1500	13067.2	7245	98	.986	532	278	1556	928	.596	4440	+24	-13	+8	+20	+8	+28	21	8	-3	26	-

Scout's Defensive Rating: 8 plays saved in 2013, -7 plays saved in 2014

Despite some dramatic inconsistencies in his early years, Robinson settled in as a consistently above average second baseman before moving to Seattle. As recently as 2012, Cano placed third in the voting for the Fielding Bible Award at second base. However, Cano did improve defensively in one key aspect in his first season in Seattle, and that was on double plays. On double plays Cano was involved in, the Mariners converted 69.0 percent of their double play opportunities, compared to a league average of 65.9 percent. We wrote about Cano's underappreciated double play abilities in *Volume III*, and he rebounded to that level his first year in Seattle. It's a testament to Cano's natural ability that a down year for him defensively was merely league average overall, but as he enters his age-32 season in 2015, it's fair to wonder if Cano's days as an elite defender are behind him for good.

Derek Dietrich

		BASIC							GDP			RANGE AND POSITIONING							RUNS SAVED				
Year	Team	G	Inn	TC	E	Pct	GFP	DM	Opps	GDP	Pct	Outs Made	To His Right	Straight On	To His Left	GB	Air	Plays Saved	R/P	GDP	GFP/ DME	Total	Rank
2013	Mia	57	502.1	258	2	.992	23	19	42	30	.714	148	-7	-1	0	-8	0	-8	-7	0	1	-6	29
2014	Mia	44	358.2	202	10	.950	21	7	39	24	.615	118	-5	-5	+5	-5	-3	-8	-6	-1	-1	-8	-
		101	861.0	460	12	.974	44	26	81	54	.667	266	-12	-6	+5	-13	-3	-16	-13	-1	0	-14	-

Scout's Defensive Rating: -4 plays saved in 2013, -7 plays saved in 2014

Second Basemen

Brian Dozier

Year	Team	BASIC							GDP			RANGE AND POSITIONING							RUNS SAVED				
		G	Inn	TC	E	Pct	GFP	DM	Opps	GDP	Pct	Outs Made	To His Right	Straight On	To His Left	GB	Air	Plays Saved	R/P	GDP	GFP/ DME	Total	Rank
2013	Min	146	1255.1	734	6	.992	88	29	159	102	.642	440	+5	+8	0	+13	+1	+14	11	-2	0	9	8
2014	Min	156	1361.0	751	15	.980	74	33	140	94	.671	424	+5	+6	-16	-6	0	-6	-4	0	4	0	19
		302	2616.1	1485	21	.986	162	62	299	196	.656	864	+10	+14	-16	+7	+1	+8	7	-2	4	9	-

Scout's Defensive Rating: 11 plays saved in 2013, 4 plays saved in 2014

Brian Dozier had an interesting year on defense in 2014, as the hard hitting second baseman put forth an inconsistent and somewhat confounding display with the leather. Dozier excelled at some defensive aspects and failed miserably at others. Dozier topped all second basemen in 2014 with 74 Good Fielding Plays. While he demonstrated an ability to make spectacular plays, he also struggled to avoid mistakes, seeing his error total jump from 6 to 15. While Dozier is a positive defender moving to his right and coming straight on, Dozier made 16 fewer plays than the average second basemen going to his left. A former shortstop, Dozier possesses an above average arm for a second baseman but is unable to maximize its utility given the shorter throwing distances associated with the second base position. Dozier's 2013 season was much more successful on the defensive front, however, so it would not be totally unreasonable to expect a rebound or at least some defensive progression that falls more in line with his overall body of work.

Stephen Drew

Year	Team	BASIC							GDP			RANGE AND POSITIONING							RUNS SAVED				
		G	Inn	TC	E	Pct	GFP	DM	Opps	GDP	Pct	Outs Made	To His Right	Straight On	To His Left	GB	Air	Plays Saved	R/P	GDP	GFP/ DME	Total	Rank
2014	NYY	34	274.0	136	4	.971	15	6	28	15	.536	72	-2	-3	+4	0	+3	+3	2	-1	-1	0	-

Scout's Defensive Rating: 4 plays saved in 2014

Mark Ellis

Year	Team	BASIC							GDP			RANGE AND POSITIONING							RUNS SAVED				
		G	Inn	TC	E	Pct	GFP	DM	Opps	GDP	Pct	Outs Made	To His Right	Straight On	To His Left	GB	Air	Plays Saved	R/P	GDP	GFP/ DME	Total	Rank
2003	Oak	153	1297.2	793	14	.982	-	-	174	87	.500	535	-1	+1	+16	+17	+6	+23	17	0	-	17	3
2005	Oak	115	972.0	543	6	.989	19	20	134	74	.552	373	+2	+1	+5	+9	+2	+11	8	2	-2	8	11
2006	Oak	123	1070.0	632	2	.997	17	24	152	89	.586	390	-3	+8	+5	+10	+3	+13	10	4	1	15	5
2007	Oak	150	1322.0	806	5	.994	40	31	177	95	.537	560	0	+5	+11	+16	+3	+19	14	2	-3	13	6
2008	Oak	115	1011.2	568	4	.993	29	18	131	81	.618	373	+9	+7	+5	+22	+3	+25	19	5	-1	23	2
2009	Oak	105	906.2	487	5	.990	32	10	91	59	.648	335	+3	+3	-3	+3	-3	0	0	0	2	2	14
2010	Oak	116	986.1	549	3	.995	31	16	107	74	.692	335	+1	+3	+3	+7	+1	+8	6	1	1	8	6
2011	2 tms	123	1054.2	636	3	.995	46	13	129	84	.651	383	+6	+6	0	+13	+6	+19	13	1	3	17	3
2012	LAD	110	910.1	488	3	.994	25	10	86	54	.628	290	+3	+5	0	+7	+4	+11	8	0	2	10	7
2013	LAD	119	950.0	533	6	.989	49	10	111	70	.631	307	+4	+5	-2	+9	+5	+14	10	0	2	12	2
2014	StL	50	392.1	193	0	1.000	16	3	31	20	.645	114	+1	+4	+1	+6	0	+6	5	0	2	7	-
		1279	10873.2	6228	51	.992	304	155	1323	787	.595	3995	+25	+48	+41	+119	+30	+149	110	15	7	132	-

Scout's Defensive Rating: 1 plays saved in 2013, 2 plays saved in 2014

Danny Espinosa

Year	Team	BASIC							GDP			RANGE AND POSITIONING							RUNS SAVED				
		G	Inn	TC	E	Pct	GFP	DM	Opps	GDP	Pct	Outs Made	To His Right	Straight On	To His Left	GB	Air	Plays Saved	R/P	GDP	GFP/ DME	Total	Rank
2010	Was	25	211.1	131	0	1.000	14	3	25	20	.800	70	-3	-1	+6	+2	+1	+3	2	1	1	4	-
2011	Was	158	1393.0	784	14	.982	65	33	136	89	.654	481	+6	+2	+2	+10	-2	+8	6	0	0	6	9
2012	Was	126	1069.2	528	6	.989	48	18	95	63	.663	325	+8	+4	-8	+4	0	+4	3	0	0	3	17
2013	Was	43	371.2	217	2	.991	16	8	33	26	.788	120	+2	+2	-5	-1	+3	+2	2	1	0	3	-
2014	Was	89	710.1	392	4	.990	34	13	75	54	.720	225	+5	+4	-13	-3	0	-3	-3	2	0	-1	21
		441	3756.0	2052	26	.987	177	75	364	252	.692	1221	+18	+11	-18	+12	+2	+14	10	4	1	15	-

Scout's Defensive Rating: 2 plays saved in 2013, -6 plays saved in 2014

Espinosa has struggled to find consistent playing time over the past two seasons, but when he has it has been at second base. Espinosa has always shown a great ability to field balls to his right and straight on throughout his career. Playing shortstop throughout his minor league career and at times during his major league career, there is no questioning his arm. Espinosa has one of the strongest arms of any second baseman in the league. This has allowed him to make plays on balls deep in the hole where other fielders don't always have the arm strength to complete the play. He is great at turning double plays due to his experience at both middle infield positions. He has experience being both the lead man

Second Basemen

and the pivot man, and he has no fear of hanging around the bag and making the tough throws with runners trying to take him out.

Ryan Flaherty

		BASIC							GDP			RANGE AND POSITIONING							RUNS SAVED				
Year	Team	G	Inn	TC	E	Pct	GFP	DM	Opps	GDP	Pct	Outs Made	To His Right	Straight On	To His Left	GB	Air	Plays Saved	R/P	GDP	GFP/ DME	Total	Rank
2012	Bal	28	172.1	93	1	.989	7	2	24	11	.458	51	+2	+1	0	+3	+1	+4	3	-1	-1	1	-
2013	Bal	65	515.0	283	2	.993	29	12	66	51	.773	154	+1	+2	-2	+1	-1	0	0	2	1	3	15
2014	Bal	30	258.2	140	2	.986	6	3	23	15	.652	75	0	0	+3	+3	+1	+4	3	0	0	3	-
		123	946.0	516	5	.990	42	17	113	77	.681	280	+3	+3	+1	+7	+1	+8	6	1	0	7	-

Scout's Defensive Rating: -2 plays saved in 2013, 1 plays saved in 2014

Logan Forsythe

		BASIC							GDP			RANGE AND POSITIONING							RUNS SAVED				
Year	Team	G	Inn	TC	E	Pct	GFP	DM	Opps	GDP	Pct	Outs Made	To His Right	Straight On	To His Left	GB	Air	Plays Saved	R/P	GDP	GFP/ DME	Total	Rank
2011	SD	23	147.1	84	4	.952	13	2	17	12	.706	35	-2	0	+1	-1	+1	0	1	0	0	1	-
2012	SD	81	647.0	365	12	.967	21	16	65	35	.538	208	-3	-2	-5	-11	0	-11	-8	-2	-1	-11	31
2013	SD	34	282.1	160	2	.988	12	7	27	19	.704	100	+1	+2	0	+3	+1	+4	3	0	-1	2	-
2014	TB	74	553.0	233	2	.991	16	3	31	21	.677	127	-3	-2	+5	0	+1	+1	1	0	1	2	15
		212	1629.2	842	20	.976	62	28	140	87	.621	470	-7	-2	+1	-9	+4	-5	-3	-2	-1	-6	-

Scout's Defensive Rating: 3 plays saved in 2013, 4 plays saved in 2014

Logan Forsythe spent time at all four infield positions plus left field in 2014, which is not unusual for him. He has played most regularly at second base, but he doesn't excel in any aspect of defensive play. His hands are great, but he has trouble transitioning the ball from his glove. His arm is also below average, so second is probably the best fit. Forsythe has decent range, and his ability to play the whole infield and even corner outfield is valuable off the bench. Forsythe has the ability to make plays that other second baseman wouldn't make, but he also lacks the quickness and arm strength to turn double plays that other fielders would make.

Scooter Gennett

		BASIC							GDP			RANGE AND POSITIONING							RUNS SAVED				
Year	Team	G	Inn	TC	E	Pct	GFP	DM	Opps	GDP	Pct	Outs Made	To His Right	Straight On	To His Left	GB	Air	Plays Saved	R/P	GDP	GFP/ DME	Total	Rank
2013	Mil	59	487.2	264	5	.981	23	20	64	40	.625	121	-1	-3	+4	-1	+3	+2	2	0	0	2	16
2014	Mil	119	966.0	479	9	.981	32	18	101	59	.584	237	+3	-4	-3	-3	0	-3	-3	-2	0	-5	26
		178	1453.2	743	14	.981	55	38	165	99	.600	358	+2	-7	+1	-4	+3	-1	-1	-2	0	-3	-

Scout's Defensive Rating: -3 plays saved in 2013, -10 plays saved in 2014

Scooter Gennett entered the 2014 season looking to challenge Rickie Weeks for the Brewers' second base job, one that he eventually won because of a terrific offensive season. However, his defense didn't stack up with the numbers he put up at the plate. He showed inconsistencies that come with youth and struggled to finish plays. He'd often get to the hard hit ball, and then throw it away or have issues on the transfer. The athletic ability isn't in question for Gennett, who has the range for the position; it's the question if he can put it all together. He needs to take a more aggressive approach on groundballs and attack them with a demeanor that every ball is his. Gennett has the tools to be a good defensive second baseman but needs to make 2015 a year in which he makes it a point to finish each play. The talent that Gennett has displayed on certain plays suggests that he can improve and reverse his fortunes defensively.

Ryan Goins

		BASIC							GDP			RANGE AND POSITIONING							RUNS SAVED				
Year	Team	G	Inn	TC	E	Pct	GFP	DM	Opps	GDP	Pct	Outs Made	To His Right	Straight On	To His Left	GB	Air	Plays Saved	R/P	GDP	GFP/ DME	Total	Rank
2013	Tor	32	262.1	148	1	.993	21	1	28	27	.964	84	+3	+1	+3	+7	+4	+11	8	2	2	12	-
2014	Tor	57	396.0	204	1	.995	15	4	35	26	.743	106	+3	-3	0	0	+1	+1	1	1	1	3	13
		89	658.1	352	2	.994	36	5	63	53	.841	190	+6	-2	+3	+7	+5	+12	9	3	3	15	-

Scout's Defensive Rating: 4 plays saved in 2013, 1 plays saved in 2014

Second Basemen

Ryan Goins has bounced back and forth between the Toronto Blue Jays and their Triple-A affiliate for the past two seasons, spending a bit more time in Triple-A. The reason he has not been able to stay in the majors is more of an offensive issue than defensive. Goins is only 26 years old and has the build of an average second baseman at 5'10" and 185 pounds. Goins has experience at both sides up the middle, as he logged 86 innings at shortstop to go along with nearly 400 at second base, but his arm strength is subpar for the left side of the infield. His range has played well in very limited time in the majors, but if given a chance he could be a defensive stalwart at second.

Dee Gordon

| | | BASIC | | | | | | | GDP | | | RANGE AND POSITIONING | | | | | | Plays | RUNS SAVED | | GFP/ | | |
Year	Team	G	Inn	TC	E	Pct	GFP	DM	Opps	GDP	Pct	Outs Made	To His Right	Straight On	To His Left	GB	Air	Saved	R/P	GDP	DME	Total	Rank
2013	LAD	3	3.2	4	0	1.000	0	0	1	1	1.000	4	+1	0	0	+1	0	+1	1	0	0	1	-
2014	LAD	144	1240.1	643	12	.981	62	34	120	80	.667	368	-1	+5	-7	-3	-2	-5	-3	0	-2	-5	26
		147	1244.0	647	12	.981	62	34	121	81	.669	372	0	+5	-7	-2	-2	-4	-2	0	-2	-4	-

Scout's Defensive Rating: 0 plays saved in 2013, 9 plays saved in 2014

Breaking into the big leagues, Gordon's elite speed was utilized at shortstop where, despite his excellent range, he could not overcome his lack of arm strength. In his first full year at second base, he started 139 games and his freak athleticism made him one of the most unique defenders at his position. That athleticism allows him to get to balls most second basemen would have no shot at ranging towards, often times causing wild throws but also creating the potential for highlight reel-quality plays. BIS Video Scouts were much more impressed than Defensive Runs Saved, but the primary difference of opinion is related to his pre-pitch positioning. While most second baseman move several steps left or right depending on the batter, Gordon remains relatively stationary, costing him a step or two. On a hard-hit grounder, it's difficult to make up for the lost step or two even with Gordon's range. New to the position, Gordon should be able to improve those instincts and his athleticism could make him an above average second baseman.

Jedd Gyorko

| | | BASIC | | | | | | | GDP | | | RANGE AND POSITIONING | | | | | | Plays | RUNS SAVED | | GFP/ | | |
Year	Team	G	Inn	TC	E	Pct	GFP	DM	Opps	GDP	Pct	Outs Made	To His Right	Straight On	To His Left	GB	Air	Saved	R/P	GDP	DME	Total	Rank
2013	SD	117	1008.0	502	4	.992	48	20	86	52	.605	308	+1	+6	-4	+3	-1	+2	1	-2	0	-1	21
2014	SD	109	951.1	477	11	.977	35	12	88	49	.557	263	-7	+7	-2	-2	-6	-8	-6	-3	0	-9	30
		226	1959.1	979	15	.985	83	32	174	101	.580	571	-6	+13	-6	+1	-7	-6	-5	-5	0	-10	-

Scout's Defensive Rating: 8 plays saved in 2013, 2 plays saved in 2014

Jedd Gyorko's first two defensive seasons at second base have been a struggle. He isn't blessed with the best speed in the world and has a hard time getting to balls in either direction when he has to cover ground. He has good hands when he has time to make the play, but he doesn't have a quick glove-to-throwing hand transfer. This really hurts him around the bag, as he doesn't turn double plays very well. With time Gyorko's defense at second can improve. Throughout 2014 he showed flashes of what the Padres hope he can be at second base. However, if he isn't hitting, it will be hard to keep him in the lineup with his current defensive skills.

Brandon Hicks

| | | BASIC | | | | | | | GDP | | | RANGE AND POSITIONING | | | | | | Plays | RUNS SAVED | | GFP/ | | |
Year	Team	G	Inn	TC	E	Pct	GFP	DM	Opps	GDP	Pct	Outs Made	To His Right	Straight On	To His Left	GB	Air	Saved	R/P	GDP	DME	Total	Rank
2010	Atl	1	1.0	0	0	-	0	0	0	0	-	0	0	0	0	0	0	0	0	0		0	-
2012	Oak	1	9.0	4	0	1.000	0	1	0	0	-	3	0	0	0	0	0	0	0	0		0	-
2014	SF	61	530.0	292	5	.983	28	14	65	47	.723	150	+5	0	-4	+1	0	+1	1	2	2	5	10
		63	540.0	296	5	.983	28	15	65	47	.723	153	+5	0	-4	+1	0	+1	1	2	2	5	-

Scout's Defensive Rating: -1 plays saved in 2014

After years of bouncing around the minors and the diamond, Brandon Hicks got the opportunity to start at second base for the Giants in 2014. After spending a lot of time on the left side of the infield coming up through the minors, the strength of Hicks' defensive game at second is his strong and accurate arm. His arm strength allows him to make more plays going up the middle than most second baseman in the league. His arm also made him one of the best in the league

Second Basemen

at turning double plays, with his .766 pivot percentage ranking fourth-best among regulars at the position. Where Hicks struggles at times was with his overall range. At 6'2", 215 lbs, Hicks is big for second base, and he doesn't possess the same quickness as others at the position. Hicks does possess soft hands though, and makes most of the plays on balls he reaches.

Aaron Hill

		BASIC							GDP			RANGE AND POSITIONING							RUNS SAVED				
												Outs Made	To His Right	Straight On	To His Left	GB	Air	Plays Saved	R/P	GDP	GFP/ DME	Total	Rank
Year	Team	G	Inn	TC	E	Pct	GFP	DM	Opps	GDP	Pct												
2005	Tor	22	177.2	111	1	.991	9	6	34	14	.412	78	0	+1	+2	+3	-2	+1	1	-1	0	0	-
2006	Tor	112	914.1	526	7	.987	34	19	132	86	.652	355	+15	+3	+11	+28	-3	+25	19	6	1	26	1
2007	Tor	160	1410.0	818	14	.983	76	26	193	110	.570	575	+7	+9	+7	+23	-1	+22	17	4	1	22	2
2008	Tor	55	479.0	238	1	.996	17	8	50	25	.500	164	-2	+2	0	0	-2	-2	-2	0	1	-1	-
2009	Tor	156	1372.0	798	7	.991	65	31	181	116	.641	480	+8	+5	+10	+23	-3	+20	15	-2	0	13	4
2010	Tor	137	1188.0	629	10	.984	45	26	141	86	.610	362	+4	-7	+8	+5	-5	0	0	-2	0	-2	21
2011	2 tms	137	1198.1	635	7	.989	40	21	130	80	.615	380	+2	-3	+6	+5	-1	+4	2	0	-2	0	20
2012	Ari	153	1336.2	757	6	.992	75	19	154	92	.597	483	-4	+4	+1	+1	-3	-2	-2	-2	2	-2	25
2013	Ari	84	741.0	384	2	.995	33	11	77	47	.610	212	-5	-1	-3	-9	-1	-10	-8	-2	1	-9	31
2014	Ari	116	1020.2	569	7	.988	57	19	93	60	.645	322	-2	+2	-11	-12	0	-12	-9	0	2	-7	28
		1132	9837.2	5465	62	.989	451	186	1185	716	.604	3411	+23	+15	+31	+67	-21	+46	33	1	6	40	-

Scout's Defensive Rating: -3 plays saved in 2013, -4 plays saved in 2014

Hill, a two-time Fielding Bible Award winner, has always been a great defender at second base. However, as he has aged, he has been more vulnerable to injury and has missed significant playing time the last couple seasons because of it. He has also lost a step or two off of his speed, causing his overall range to slip dramatically. While ranging to his left was once his best movement, he has steadily gotten worse every year, bottoming out in 2014. On any ball hit to his left, he had to hope the ball wasn't hit too hard or too soft or he would have no chance to make a play. He was significantly better on balls hit to his right or straight at him, as his first step on such balls in play was much more natural. In addition, though he will have a bad throw here and there, he continues to show a very strong and accurate arm, best displayed on tough balls hit up the middle. Unfortunately, a worn-down Hill is no longer an asset in the field.

Omar Infante

		BASIC							GDP			RANGE AND POSITIONING							RUNS SAVED				
												Outs Made	To His Right	Straight On	To His Left	GB	Air	Plays Saved	R/P	GDP	GFP/ DME	Total	Rank
Year	Team	G	Inn	TC	E	Pct	GFP	DM	Opps	GDP	Pct												
2003	Det	2	13.0	6	0	1.000	-	-	2	2	1.000	3				0	0	0	0	0	-	0	-
2004	Det	105	874.2	499	12	.976	16	20	124	71	.573	270	-6	-5	+3	-8	-1	-9	-7	3	-1	-5	28
2005	Det	69	591.2	343	4	.988	10	8	88	47	.534	190	-5	-2	0	-6	-1	-7	-5	1	-1	-5	23
2006	Det	37	307.1	177	4	.977	3	3	41	26	.634	110	+4	-1	+2	+5	0	+5	4	2	0	6	-
2007	Det	20	124.1	69	1	.986	3	2	15	6	.400	44	-1	0	+2	+1	0	+1	1	0	0	1	-
2008	Atl	10	74.0	33	0	1.000	2	0	13	6	.462	19	+1	+1	0	+2	0	+2	2	0	0	2	-
2009	Atl	30	199.0	106	2	.981	6	2	15	11	.733	72	+1	+3	-6	-3	-2	-5	-4	0	-1	-5	-
2010	Atl	65	555.2	312	7	.978	19	14	57	41	.719	198	+1	+1	0	+2	+2	+4	3	1	-2	2	13
2011	Fla	146	1283.1	734	8	.989	54	28	111	72	.649	505	0	+4	+1	+6	0	+6	4	0	1	5	11
2012	2 tms	144	1246.1	702	17	.976	69	24	146	98	.671	448	+2	0	+8	+8	0	+8	6	2	-2	6	12
2013	Det	118	1025.1	509	10	.980	40	29	105	71	.676	323	-2	+3	+2	+3	-7	-4	-3	1	-3	-5	27
2014	KC	134	1170.0	502	11	.978	29	18	104	63	.606	282	0	-1	0	-1	+5	+4	3	-1	-1	1	17
		880	7464.2	3992	76	.981	251	148	821	514	.626	2464	-5	+3	+12	+9	-4	+5	4	9	-10	3	-

Scout's Defensive Rating: -8 plays saved in 2013, -6 plays saved in 2014

After years of playing all around the diamond, Omar Infante has found a home at second base in recent years. His range has declined a bit as he advances in age, but he still covers enough ground to be effective at second base. Infante struggles a bit with his backhand, often times trying to circle around balls up the middle. Infante has good arm strength for second base, but a shoulder injury in 2014 caused him to throw from a lower angle and lose some strength and accuracy. One area where Infante does excel is his ability to get rid of the ball quickly and accurately while making plays on the move, especially throwing on the run in short right field. Infante doesn't have great footwork around second base, which causes some issues when trying to turn the double play. He has the ability to continue producing around league average defense for the next couple of seasons, but there is a possibility that his age and the miles on his legs start to catch up with him and he starts slipping down the defensive ranks.

Second Basemen

Munenori Kawasaki

		BASIC							GDP			RANGE AND POSITIONING						Plays	RUNS SAVED		GFP/		
Year	Team	G	Inn	TC	E	Pct	GFP	DM	Opps	GDP	Pct	Outs Made	To His Right	Straight On	To His Left	GB	Air	Saved	R/P	GDP	DME	Total	Rank
2012	Sea	10	39.2	19	0	1.000	1	0	4	3	.750	14	0	0	-1	0	0	0	-1	0	0	-1	-
2013	Tor	18	126.0	72	1	.986	7	2	8	6	.750	49	-4	+2	0	-2	+3	+1	1	0	0	1	-
2014	Tor	64	444.2	222	5	.977	20	7	41	26	.634	120	+3	-5	0	-3	-1	-4	-3	0	0	-3	24
		92	610.1	313	6	.981	28	9	53	35	.660	183	-1	-3	-1	-5	+2	-3	-3	0	0	-3	-

Scout's Defensive Rating: 3 plays saved in 2013, 3 plays saved in 2014

A true utility infielder, Kawasaki logged time at second base, shortstop, and third base during the 2014 season. In 2014 he spent most of his time at second base, where Kawasaki showed flashes of brilliance yet still managed to under-achieve overall. Kawasaki is extremely athletic, and has become a fan favorite in Toronto because of the energy and bounce that he plays with. His athleticism and ability to throw off balance can create some highlight reel plays (his visual appeal is confirmed by his Scout's Defensive Rating), but it also gets in the way of his ability at times by compli-cating routine groundballs. He has only been in Major League Baseball for three years, but being on the wrong side of 30 does not leave much hope that he is going to improve much over the rest of his career.

Howie Kendrick

		BASIC							GDP			RANGE AND POSITIONING						Plays	RUNS SAVED		GFP/		
Year	Team	G	Inn	TC	E	Pct	GFP	DM	Opps	GDP	Pct	Outs Made	To His Right	Straight On	To His Left	GB	Air	Saved	R/P	GDP	DME	Total	Rank
2006	LAA	28	220.0	115	0	1.000	6	4	33	23	.697	75	-4	+2	+4	+2	+1	+3	2	2	0	4	-
2007	LAA	86	751.1	409	9	.978	22	18	91	49	.538	275	-2	0	+9	+7	0	+7	5	1	0	6	10
2008	LAA	92	776.0	446	4	.991	28	7	99	61	.616	308	-13	-4	+13	-5	+1	-4	-3	3	3	3	14
2009	LAA	95	805.2	431	4	.991	35	16	98	69	.704	293	-7	-1	+13	+4	+1	+5	4	1	0	5	10
2010	LAA	143	1251.0	634	9	.986	47	29	116	70	.603	381	-12	-4	+11	-5	0	-5	-4	-2	1	-5	27
2011	LAA	108	937.2	483	4	.992	35	16	89	59	.663	311	+6	+7	+9	+21	-7	+14	11	0	-1	10	5
2012	LAA	143	1242.0	659	14	.979	47	22	122	74	.607	414	+1	-5	+5	+1	-5	-4	-2	-4	1	1	21
2013	LAA	118	1043.1	553	10	.982	50	24	100	62	.620	304	-8	-3	+11	0	0	0	0	-1	-2	-3	23
2014	LAA	154	1386.0	684	11	.984	46	21	118	82	.695	410	-1	-2	+5	+2	+4	+6	4	2	1	7	7
		967	8413.0	4414	65	.985	316	157	866	549	.634	2771	-40	-10	+80	+27	-5	+22	17	5	6	28	-

Scout's Defensive Rating: 2 plays saved in 2013, -4 plays saved in 2014

Kendrick has enjoyed a successful defensive career, spending the majority of his time at second base and posting con-sistently above average defensive numbers. Kendrick continues to display good range and a natural feel for the second base position, particularly on grounders in the hole. Consistency on defense has been the summary of Kendrick's career thus far, though his defensive misplay and error totals have slowly crept up over time. Kendrick will enter his age 32 season in 2015 and has shown no signs of slowing down.

Ian Kinsler

		BASIC							GDP			RANGE AND POSITIONING						Plays	RUNS SAVED		GFP/		
Year	Team	G	Inn	TC	E	Pct	GFP	DM	Opps	GDP	Pct	Outs Made	To His Right	Straight On	To His Left	GB	Air	Saved	R/P	GDP	DME	Total	Rank
2006	Tex	119	1032.0	658	18	.973	28	31	153	86	.562	424	-3	+1	-8	-10	+6	-4	-3	3	-3	-3	22
2007	Tex	130	1136.2	736	17	.977	43	26	163	88	.540	459	+7	-4	+1	+4	+3	+7	5	2	-3	4	11
2008	Tex	121	1064.0	700	18	.974	38	15	201	113	.562	412	-1	+2	-15	-13	-2	-15	-11	4	-2	-9	30
2009	Tex	144	1258.0	711	11	.985	63	22	125	89	.712	495	+6	-1	+10	+16	+7	+23	17	3	2	22	1
2010	Tex	103	905.1	475	7	.985	38	15	110	67	.609	294	-2	0	+4	+2	+10	+12	9	-1	0	8	5
2011	Tex	144	1269.0	677	11	.984	54	27	142	102	.718	425	+9	+2	+1	+12	+6	+18	14	3	0	17	2
2012	Tex	144	1265.0	607	18	.970	41	31	115	80	.696	373	0	-4	+4	0	+1	+1	0	1	0	1	20
2013	Tex	124	1095.1	595	13	.978	44	21	115	82	.713	328	+3	-1	+1	+3	+7	+10	8	2	1	11	4
2014	Det	160	1414.0	766	9	.988	50	24	150	95	.633	479	+7	+12	+2	+20	+10	+30	23	-1	-2	20	1
		1189	10439.1	5925	122	.979	399	212	1274	802	.630	3689	+26	+7	0	+34	+48	+82	62	16	-7	71	-

Scout's Defensive Rating: -6 plays saved in 2013, 14 plays saved in 2014

At 6'0" and 200 pounds, Ian Kinsler has a great build for his position. As the 2014 Fielding Bible Award runner-up for second basemen, Kinsler has many of the tools that make excellent second basemen. His range is amongst the best in all of baseball, his arm is excellent, and quite frankly it is difficult to find a flaw in his game. He gets a great first step on the ball off the bat, which, combined with his length, makes for some excellent plays. He's historically been excel-lent at starting and turning two with Elvis Andrus in Texas, but instability at the Tigers' shortstop position made it tough for Kinsler to acclimate right away. Kinsler has an uncanny ability to find himself in the right spot to nab liners,

Second Basemen

and he chases down shallow pop-ups all over the diamond. Though Kinsler has yet to bring home a Fielding Bible Award despite leading the league in Runs Saved twice, he'll be ready in case Dustin Pedroia stumbles.

Jason Kipnis

		BASIC							GDP			RANGE AND POSITIONING							RUNS SAVED				
Year	Team	G	Inn	TC	E	Pct	GFP	DM	Opps	GDP	Pct	Outs Made	To His Right	Straight On	To His Left	GB	Air	Plays Saved	R/P	GDP	GFP/ DME	Total	Rank
2011	Cle	36	305.0	164	6	.963	11	10	29	13	.448	110	-1	+1	-1	-1	-1	-2	-2	-1	-1	-4	-
2012	Cle	146	1293.1	686	6	.991	32	38	147	95	.646	410	+5	+4	-2	+7	-1	+6	4	1	-2	3	16
2013	Cle	147	1292.1	649	12	.982	40	28	138	88	.638	386	+4	+2	-5	+2	-1	+1	1	-1	-1	-1	21
2014	Cle	123	1075.0	534	6	.989	34	27	96	60	.625	311	-2	+2	-5	-5	-3	-8	-6	-2	-3	-11	33
		452	3965.2	2033	30	.985	117	103	410	256	.624	1217	+6	+9	-13	+3	-6	-3	-3	-3	-7	-13	-

Scout's Defensive Rating: -9 plays saved in 2013, 2 plays saved in 2014

Jason Kipnis had a down year offensively and defensively in 2014. He was hampered with injuries during the year, which contributed to his reduced performance. Kipnis' poor defensive play seemed to fit into a troubling trend for his team, as the Cleveland Indians were the third-worst team defensively in the majors with -56 Defensive Runs Saved. Kipnis single-handedly accounted for 11 of these 56 runs below average. In 2014, Kipnis ranked in the top 10 in Defensive Misplays among second basemen with 27. Kipnis' arm strength is not on par with other second basemen, which costs him when trying to turn a quick double play, evidenced by the fact that he ranked among the league leaders in Defensive Misplays and Errors on double plays. Kipnis is known for his offensive talent, which helps him to be an acceptable choice at second base even with his defensive shortcomings. He makes all of the routine plays, but doesn't have the skill to make the more difficult plays. With the offseason to get healthy, hopefully Kipnis will rebound back to league average in the field and let his bat carry his value.

Tommy La Stella

		BASIC							GDP			RANGE AND POSITIONING							RUNS SAVED				
Year	Team	G	Inn	TC	E	Pct	GFP	DM	Opps	GDP	Pct	Outs Made	To His Right	Straight On	To His Left	GB	Air	Plays Saved	R/P	GDP	GFP/ DME	Total	Rank
2014	Atl	88	721.2	368	6	.984	35	13	74	50	.676	203	-1	-6	0	-7	-1	-8	-7	1	2	-4	25

Scout's Defensive Rating: -8 plays saved in 2014

La Stella appeared in 88 games for the Braves in 2014, committing six errors, but proving to be a reliable defender. Early reports on La Stella project him to be an average defender with a so-so glove who will provide solid infield depth. While he hasn't been shown much love early on in his career, La Stella will consistently make the routine plays and displays a natural feel for the second base position. La Stella isn't particularly quick, but more often than not, he finds himself in a position to make a play on any ball in his zone. This can be credited to his ability to anticipate the ball coming off the bat and getting a good jump early. La Stella accumulated a Net GFP-DME of 16, with ground ball outs making up a majority of his Good Fielding Plays. He won't be lighting up the highlight reels, but he's a reliable defender that will make the routine play consistently and will provide infield depth.

DJ LeMahieu

		BASIC							GDP			RANGE AND POSITIONING							RUNS SAVED				
Year	Team	G	Inn	TC	E	Pct	GFP	DM	Opps	GDP	Pct	Outs Made	To His Right	Straight On	To His Left	GB	Air	Plays Saved	R/P	GDP	GFP/ DME	Total	Rank
2011	ChC	15	77.2	38	0	1.000	3	1	8	5	.625	23	+1	0	-1	+1	-1	0	0	0	1	1	-
2012	Col	67	509.0	311	2	.994	21	9	53	30	.566	208	+7	+2	0	+9	+2	+11	8	-1	1	8	9
2013	Col	90	750.0	442	3	.993	45	10	81	53	.654	275	0	0	+4	+3	+6	+9	7	1	2	10	7
2014	Col	144	1179.2	676	6	.991	69	24	138	96	.696	388	+8	+4	+4	+17	+3	+20	15	1	0	16	3
		316	2516.1	1467	11	.993	138	44	280	184	.657	894	+16	+6	+7	+30	+10	+40	30	1	4	35	-

Scout's Defensive Rating: 8 plays saved in 2013, 12 plays saved in 2014

DJ LeMahieu has quietly turned himself into one of the best defensive second baseman in baseball, helping him to finish in third place in the 2014 Fielding Bible Awards balloting. Since being acquired by the Rockies, his playing time has increased each year for the last three years, as has his Defensive Runs Saved totals. LeMahieu's 69 Good Fielding Plays were the third most for any second baseman in 2014, just five shy of the major league lead.

Second Basemen

One of LeMahieu's strengths is hanging tough around the bag on double plays. He is excellent at completing the double play and making an accurate throw with a runner taking him out in the process. His arm strength is another very strong asset. LeMahieu has the arm to play third base, which has really helped him at second. His strong arm allows him to utilize his range to make plays deep in the hole and up the middle and still get the out. Provided a continued opportunity for regular play, LeMahieu will surely be in the mix for the Fielding Bible Award at second base in the years ahead.

Daniel Murphy

		BASIC							GDP			RANGE AND POSITIONING							RUNS SAVED				
Year	Team	G	Inn	TC	E	Pct	GFP	DM	Opps	GDP	Pct	Outs Made	To His Right	Straight On	To His Left	GB	Air	Plays Saved	R/P	GDP	GFP/DME	Total	Rank
2011	NYM	24	168.1	93	2	.978	6	5	8	4	.500	64	0	0	0	0	-2	-2	-1	0	0	-1	-
2012	NYM	138	1127.2	568	15	.974	43	29	106	65	.613	344	-8	-6	-1	-15	+5	-10	-8	-1	-2	-11	31
2013	NYM	150	1334.1	670	16	.976	53	34	130	86	.662	386	-16	-1	+6	-10	-3	-13	-10	0	-3	-13	33
2014	NYM	126	1140.1	571	15	.974	42	21	132	80	.606	323	-13	-6	+13	-6	-2	-8	-6	-3	-1	-10	31
		438	3770.2	1902	48	.975	144	89	376	235	.625	1117	-37	-13	+18	-31	-2	-33	-25	-4	-6	-35	-

Scout's Defensive Rating: -5 plays saved in 2013, -11 plays saved in 2014

It took Murphy a few years to find a home in the field, and while Murphy has played well enough at second to keep his bat in the lineup, he still rates by almost any metric as one of the worst fielding second baseman in baseball. In 2014, he was fourth-worst in Defensive Runs Saved and worst in Scout's Defensive Rating out of anyone to play the keystone. Murphy plays a very deep second base to help compensate for his lack of range. This positioning allows him to get to more balls, but often times he is fielding the ball too deep to complete the play. This is especially true on balls up the middle with the longer throw necessary to get the out. Furthermore, he doesn't move from side-to-side from batter to batter. Murphy's deep defensive positioning also causes him to rush on softer hit balls, which leads to more Defensive Misplays on routine grounders. Murphy' has subpar footwork around the bag which doesn't allow him to convert double play pivots at a high percentage.

Rougned Odor

		BASIC							GDP			RANGE AND POSITIONING							RUNS SAVED				
Year	Team	G	Inn	TC	E	Pct	GFP	DM	Opps	GDP	Pct	Outs Made	To His Right	Straight On	To His Left	GB	Air	Plays Saved	R/P	GDP	GFP/DME	Total	Rank
2014	Tex	110	933.0	478	9	.981	42	27	88	64	.727	265	-12	+1	-2	-14	-2	-16	-12	1	0	-11	34

Scout's Defensive Rating: -6 plays saved in 2014

Rougned Odor endured a trying 2014 season on defense. His 42 Good Fielding Plays indicate he is not a stranger to making flashy plays, yet his greater body of work suggests his range and overall run prevention abilities are severely limited at this early stage in his career. While Odor appears to be at least a competent defender on balls hit straight on and to his left, he struggles mightily up the middle. Odor's demonstrated inability to cover ground to his right is characterized by a deficiency at both reaching balls in that vicinity and failing to cleanly field balls he does reach. Furthermore, when he does field the ball cleanly, it is no guarantee that he'll get the ball to first base accurately: his 95.3 percent Good Throw Rate ranked as the worst among regulars at second base. He possesses a solid average for a second baseman, yet his throw velocity and accuracy tend to suffer when his momentum is carrying him the other direction. Odor would likely benefit from some creative defensive positioning designed to compensate for his severe deficiencies moving to his right. Furthermore, at 20 years old, Odor was the youngest player to appear in an American League game in 2014 and has yet to reach his physical peak. Therefore, it is fairly reasonable to expect improvement for Odor moving forward if he is to settle in a second base long term.

Joe Panik

		BASIC							GDP			RANGE AND POSITIONING							RUNS SAVED				
Year	Team	G	Inn	TC	E	Pct	GFP	DM	Opps	GDP	Pct	Outs Made	To His Right	Straight On	To His Left	GB	Air	Plays Saved	R/P	GDP	GFP/DME	Total	Rank
2014	SF	70	579.0	323	8	.975	21	6	61	48	.787	175	-1	+5	-5	-1	-4	-5	-3	2	0	-1	21

Scout's Defensive Rating: 4 plays saved in 2014

Second Basemen

For a team in dire need of an everyday second baseman, Joe Panik turned out to be a big factor in the Giants' World Series victory in 2014. Going into his age-24 season, Panik has already shown quick reflexes and a strong glove that prove he is very capable to continue filling that role. He did commit eight errors, but two were on throws and four were on receiving throws from other fielders. His ability to field the ball is strong and those types of errors should lessen with experience. More importantly, he made up for his 14 total errors and misplays with 21 GFPs in only 70 games.

Panik reads the ball well, has good speed and range, and transitions from fielding to throwing quickly, which are all factors in both his ability to make the plays on balls hit to him as well as his very high double-play conversion rate (78.7%). He is still very young, so expect his numbers to improve with experience as well.

Dustin Pedroia

		BASIC							GDP			RANGE AND POSITIONING							RUNS SAVED				
Year	Team	G	Inn	TC	E	Pct	GFP	DM	Opps	GDP	Pct	Outs Made	To His Right	Straight On	To His Left	GB	Air	Plays Saved	R/P	GDP	GFP/DME	Total	Rank
2006	Bos	27	172.0	121	3	.975	5	6	28	15	.536	82	-1	0	-2	-2	+1	-1	-1	0	0	-1	-
2007	Bos	137	1141.1	625	6	.990	68	18	126	71	.563	417	-1	+3	-5	-4	-1	-5	-4	2	4	2	15
2008	Bos	157	1376.1	733	6	.992	66	25	176	90	.511	477	+1	+4	+9	+13	+2	+15	11	1	1	13	5
2009	Bos	154	1346.2	663	6	.991	50	11	112	80	.714	458	-3	+5	+7	+10	+4	+14	11	2	1	14	3
2010	Bos	75	667.1	352	3	.991	32	4	69	50	.725	200	+1	+4	-1	+5	-3	+2	1	1	1	3	12
2011	Bos	159	1392.1	722	7	.990	66	15	131	82	.626	452	+8	+6	+12	+25	-5	+20	16	-1	3	18	1
2012	Bos	139	1216.0	625	5	.992	56	15	131	94	.718	346	-5	+2	+11	+8	-2	+6	5	3	3	11	6
2013	Bos	160	1398.0	688	5	.993	89	18	141	97	.688	385	+2	+4	+12	+18	-1	+17	13	0	2	15	1
2014	Bos	135	1187.1	654	2	.997	70	20	140	92	.657	361	-3	+14	+13	+25	-1	+24	19	-2	0	17	2
		1143	9897.1	5183	43	.992	502	132	1054	671	.637	3178	-1	+42	+56	+98	-6	+92	71	6	15	92	-

Scout's Defensive Rating: 20 plays saved in 2013, 17 plays saved in 2014

The 2014 campaign may have been a down year at the plate for Dustin Pedroia, but the scrappy second baseman enjoyed perhaps his best season defensively for the Red Sox. The Arizona State product accumulated a career high in Plays Made and tallied his second-highest single-season Defensive Runs Saved total.

If Pedroia's first step is at all hampered by the notorious hop he takes before pitches, the effect is discreet. He gets to balls that few other infielders can with help from his speed, efficient routes, and a willingness to lay out for anything remotely within reach. Pedroia leaves his feet often, perhaps even too much at times; you'll often see him sprawled out on a play he could have probably made standing up. Pedroia compensates by being incredibly quick back up to his feet, which you'll see time and time again on his trademark diving backhand snag on grounders up the middle.

The Red Sox cycled through a collection of double play partners for Pedroia this past season, which may explain why he has graded out as slightly below average in GDP Runs Saved for just the second time in his career. However, his quick hands still led to eight quick double play pivot GFPs, which were tied for the second-most in the big leagues. Nonetheless, Pedroia was second-best at his position in Defensive Runs Saved with 17 and brought home his second consecutive Fielding Bible Award.

Brandon Phillips

		BASIC							GDP			RANGE AND POSITIONING							RUNS SAVED				
Year	Team	G	Inn	TC	E	Pct	GFP	DM	Opps	GDP	Pct	Outs Made	To His Right	Straight On	To His Left	GB	Air	Plays Saved	R/P	GDP	GFP/DME	Total	Rank
2003	Cle	109	925.1	572	11	.981	-	-	144	73	.507	345	+8	+4	-5	+7	-1	+6	5	0	-	5	14
2004	Cle	6	56.2	37	1	.973	5	2	10	4	.400	16	0	-1	+1	0	0	0	0	0	0	0	-
2005	Cle	2	18.0	9	0	1.000	0	0	2	2	1.000	6	0	0	0	0	0	0	0	0	0	0	-
2006	Cin	142	1216.1	681	16	.977	41	29	170	76	.447	403	+1	-5	-2	-5	+1	-4	-3	-3	-1	-7	27
2007	Cin	156	1371.0	782	8	.990	76	35	198	101	.510	491	+3	+7	-2	+8	+3	+11	8	1	0	9	8
2008	Cin	140	1237.2	706	7	.990	66	27	183	80	.437	429	+17	+4	0	+21	-4	+17	13	-3	3	13	4
2009	Cin	151	1332.1	725	9	.988	65	29	150	101	.673	444	+5	+1	-6	0	-1	-1	-1	0	3	2	15
2010	Cin	152	1311.0	703	3	.996	63	19	138	89	.645	424	+9	+5	-4	+9	0	+9	7	-1	5	11	4
2011	Cin	148	1324.0	721	6	.992	57	28	153	94	.614	423	+6	+2	+5	+13	-2	+11	8	-1	0	7	7
2012	Cin	146	1251.0	637	5	.992	57	26	113	70	.619	411	+14	-1	-1	+12	+1	+13	10	-1	2	11	4
2013	Cin	151	1347.0	715	9	.987	73	28	130	81	.623	408	+1	+8	-3	+6	0	+6	5	-3	-1	1	17
2014	Cin	121	1054.1	525	2	.996	46	22	99	63	.636	296	+11	+3	-6	+8	-1	+7	5	0	1	6	8
		1424	12444.2	6813	77	.989	549	245	1490	834	.560	4096	+75	+27	-23	+79	-4	+75	57	-11	12	58	-

Scout's Defensive Rating: 14 plays saved in 2013, 8 plays saved in 2014

Second Basemen

Phillips will likely go down as the smoothest defensive second baseman of this era. He has the rare ability to make routine or easy plays seem difficult and difficult plays seems routine and easy. According to BIS Video Scouts, Phillips only converted 87 percent of plays identified as "easy" and 62 percent identified as "moderate", both below average. In contrast, he converted 30 percent of plays identified as difficult, which was second-highest among all qualified second baseman. Phillips is still among the elite second baseman in MLB even though his range and speed have declined with his age. His arm is slightly above average, but his glove work and concentration on balls that he actually tries for is elite. He has quick hands and has mastered turning the double play in a variety of ways (barehanded grabs, glove flips, etc). If second basemen were judged based on their Web Gems, Brandon Phillips would be king; in the real world, however, Phillips is merely one of the better defensive second basemen of the past decade.

Nick Punto

		BASIC							GDP			RANGE AND POSITIONING							RUNS SAVED				
Year	Team	G	Inn	TC	E	Pct	GFP	DM	Opps	GDP	Pct	Outs Made	To His Right	Straight On	To His Left	GB	Air	Plays Saved	R/P	GDP	GFP/ DME	Total	Rank
2003	Phi	16	83.0	65	1	.985	-	-	17	5	.294	38	-1	0	+2	+1	+1	+2	2	-1	-	1	-
2004	Min	19	111.1	55	1	.982	3	5	19	10	.526	35	+2	+2	-2	+2	0	+2	2	0	0	2	-
2005	Min	73	564.1	331	7	.979	17	7	70	42	.600	226	-3	+1	+14	+12	0	+12	9	2	0	11	9
2006	Min	17	114.2	73	2	.973	3	9	18	9	.500	50	-2	+1	0	-1	+1	0	0	0	-1	-1	-
2007	Min	25	172.1	112	3	.973	13	3	26	9	.346	73	+1	-2	-2	-3	+2	-1	-1	-1	0	-2	-
2008	Min	26	215.2	135	2	.985	9	5	30	16	.533	88	-1	-2	+4	+2	-1	+1	1	0	0	1	-
2009	Min	63	510.1	269	0	1.000	29	5	51	33	.647	180	-8	0	+7	-1	0	-1	-1	0	3	2	15
2010	Min	12	77.0	47	3	.936	3	2	6	5	.833	35	0	+1	-1	0	+1	+1	1	0	0	1	-
2011	StL	45	243.0	151	2	.987	9	6	34	24	.706	95	0	0	+3	+3	+1	+4	3	0	1	4	-
2012	2 tms	26	156.1	88	1	.989	7	0	26	15	.577	54	+1	0	+1	+2	+2	+4	3	0	1	4	-
2013	LAD	33	186.2	89	1	.989	10	5	23	16	.696	40	-1	-1	0	-1	0	-1	-1	0	0	-1	-
2014	Oak	52	363.2	225	6	.973	11	3	51	39	.765	109	-2	0	+3	+1	0	+1	0	1	0	1	-
		407	2798.1	1640	29	.982	114	50	371	223	.601	1023	-14	0	+29	+17	+7	+24	18	1	4	23	

Scout's Defensive Rating: 0 plays saved in 2013, -3 plays saved in 2014

Anthony Rendon

		BASIC							GDP			RANGE AND POSITIONING							RUNS SAVED				
Year	Team	G	Inn	TC	E	Pct	GFP	DM	Opps	GDP	Pct	Outs Made	To His Right	Straight On	To His Left	GB	Air	Plays Saved	R/P	GDP	GFP/ DME	Total	Rank
2013	Was	82	714.1	369	9	.976	36	16	67	47	.701	223	-7	-2	+3	-6	-1	-7	-5	1	-1	-5	28
2014	Was	28	215.1	103	0	1.000	11	1	8	5	.625	59	-2	+2	+3	+4	+1	+5	3	0	1	4	-
		110	929.2	472	9	.981	47	17	75	52	.693	282	-9	0	+6	-2	0	-2	-2	1	0	-1	

Scout's Defensive Rating: 7 plays saved in 2013, 3 plays saved in 2014

Anthony Rendon's Scouting Report can be found on page 218.

Brian Roberts

		BASIC							GDP			RANGE AND POSITIONING							RUNS SAVED				
Year	Team	G	Inn	TC	E	Pct	GFP	DM	Opps	GDP	Pct	Outs Made	To His Right	Straight On	To His Left	GB	Air	Plays Saved	R/P	GDP	GFP/ DME	Total	Rank
2003	Bal	107	925.0	529	7	.987	-	-	120	63	.525	353	-3	+3	+13	+12	+4	+16	12	1	-	13	5
2004	Bal	150	1322.1	669	8	.988	28	40	167	89	.533	448	-1	-4	+3	-2	0	-2	-2	2	-3	-3	21
2005	Bal	141	1208.0	659	8	.988	35	20	152	84	.553	453	+8	+2	+6	+16	+2	+18	14	2	-1	15	8
2006	Bal	137	1167.2	598	9	.985	31	20	156	85	.545	397	-4	+8	+4	+8	-1	+7	5	2	1	8	11
2007	Bal	154	1329.2	742	7	.991	56	24	205	101	.493	488	+1	+3	-2	+1	-1	0	0	0	0	0	19
2008	Bal	154	1320.0	738	8	.989	57	29	211	105	.498	474	+13	+2	-15	-1	-3	-4	-3	0	3	0	18
2009	Bal	158	1340.2	692	11	.984	38	21	144	99	.688	435	-5	-4	+1	-7	-3	-10	-8	0	0	-8	29
2010	Bal	59	498.1	235	3	.987	14	7	49	37	.755	137	+1	+3	-8	-3	0	-3	-3	1	0	-2	22
2011	Bal	39	347.0	191	3	.984	17	5	37	23	.622	122	0	-2	+2	0	0	0	0	0	1	1	-
2012	Bal	17	149.0	79	1	.987	3	3	14	9	.643	44	-4	-3	-1	-8	0	-8	-6	0	0	-6	-
2013	Bal	60	540.1	301	1	.997	19	10	60	41	.683	153	-2	+2	+1	+1	-3	-2	-1	1	0	0	20
2014	NYY	91	774.2	384	10	.974	29	12	64	32	.500	189	-3	-1	+10	+6	+3	+9	7	-2	-2	3	11
		1267	10922.2	5817	76	.987	327	191	1379	768	.557	3693	+1	+9	+14	+23	-2	+21	15	7	-1	21	

Scout's Defensive Rating: 1 plays saved in 2013, -4 plays saved in 2014

Roberts had an up-and-down swan song season, but he ended with his best Defensive Runs Saved (DRS) performance since 2006, saving three runs in 91 games after finishing with no better than one DRS in any season over the previous seven years. Roberts had 29 Good Fielding Plays (GFP) in 774.2 innings, a respectable number for a player who played more innings and games than he had in five years. Roberts especially excelled at defending balls hit to his left where he saved 10 plays, his highest total on balls to his left in 11 years. However, Roberts made 4 of his 10 errors in July, and he

Second Basemen

had one of the worst double play conversion percentages in baseball, both of which may have contributed to the Yankees' decision to move on from him at the July 31 non-waiver trade deadline. All in all, Roberts put forth a very respectable final performance and retires tied for 21st in DRS among all second basemen in the DRS era.

Carlos Sanchez

Year	Team	G	Inn	TC	E	Pct	GFP	DM	Opps	GDP	Pct	Outs Made	To His Right	Straight On	To His Left	GB	Air	Plays Saved	R/P	GDP	GFP/ DME	Total	Rank
2014	CWS	27	232.2	122	1	.992	16	5	23	16	.696	60	-1	-2	-1	-4	0	-4	-3	1	1	-1	-

Scout's Defensive Rating: 3 plays saved in 2014

Jonathan Schoop

Year	Team	G	Inn	TC	E	Pct	GFP	DM	Opps	GDP	Pct	Outs Made	To His Right	Straight On	To His Left	GB	Air	Plays Saved	R/P	GDP	GFP/ DME	Total	Rank
2013	Bal	4	36.0	21	1	.952	1	0	6	4	.667	10	0	0	-2	-2	0	-2	-2	0	1	-1	-
2014	Bal	123	1010.2	551	7	.987	37	17	114	89	.781	277	+1	-1	+5	+4	+2	+6	5	5	0	10	5
		127	1046.2	572	8	.986	38	17	120	93	.775	287	+1	-1	+3	+2	+2	+4	3	5	1	9	-

Scout's Defensive Rating: -1 plays saved in 2013, -3 plays saved in 2014

A 23-year-old, Schoop established himself in the Baltimore infield in 2014 as a reliable second baseman with limited range, but a strong arm and solid foot work. Schoop, who played in Curacao as a youngster with names like Simmons, Profar and Bogaerts, has played short for a large part of his pro career, but the presence of Machado and Hardy on the left side at Camden Yards pushed him to the right side, at least for now. His slow foot speed and strong arm could see him move to third or right field in the future. His agility and first step, while not a detriment, aren't anything flashy either. Schoop can move to either side well, but fails to come up with the challenging plays more often than not. He has worked to improve on his turn of double plays but is otherwise a talented defender looking to settle in at his best position, second base.

Marcus Semien

Year	Team	G	Inn	TC	E	Pct	GFP	DM	Opps	GDP	Pct	Outs Made	To His Right	Straight On	To His Left	GB	Air	Plays Saved	R/P	GDP	GFP/ DME	Total	Rank
2013	CWS	3	13.0	8	0	1.000	1	2	1	0	.000	8	+1	-1	-1	0	0	0	0	0	0	0	-
2014	CWS	26	223.2	133	4	.970	5	4	29	23	.793	57	-7	-2	+7	-2	-1	-3	-2	1	0	-1	-
		29	236.2	141	4	.972	6	6	30	23	.767	65	-6	-3	+6	-2	-1	-3	-2	1	0	-1	-

Scout's Defensive Rating: 0 plays saved in 2013, -4 plays saved in 2014

Eric Sogard

Year	Team	G	Inn	TC	E	Pct	GFP	DM	Opps	GDP	Pct	Outs Made	To His Right	Straight On	To His Left	GB	Air	Plays Saved	R/P	GDP	GFP/ DME	Total	Rank
2010	Oak	3	15.0	9	0	1.000	0	1	4	4	1.000	4	0	0	0	0	0	0	0	0	0	0	-
2011	Oak	3	27.0	15	1	.933	4	1	2	2	1.000	10	0	+1	0	+1	0	+1	1	0	0	1	-
2012	Oak	6	49.1	27	0	1.000	1	1	5	4	.800	16	+1	0	0	+1	0	+1	1	0	1	2	-
2013	Oak	113	865.0	472	7	.985	49	8	100	64	.640	259	+5	-4	0	+1	+3	+4	3	-1	3	5	12
2014	Oak	102	721.0	406	5	.988	34	14	92	45	.489	222	+5	+4	0	+9	0	+9	7	-3	1	5	9
		227	1677.1	929	13	.986	88	25	203	119	.586	511	+11	+1	0	+12	+3	+15	12	-4	5	13	-

Scout's Defensive Rating: 3 plays saved in 2013, 8 plays saved in 2014

The elected 2014 Face of Major League Baseball isn't just a popular cult hero of the Oakland Athletics. As it turns out, Eric Sogard is a pretty good defender, too. Playing mostly second base but filling in at shortstop on occasion, Sogard uses excellent reaction skills to get a quick first step on grounders and hard hit balls. He also has superb tracking abilities that get him to difficult pop ups in-between outfielders and down the foul line. Getting to the ball isn't usually the problem, it's getting the ball to first base that is sometimes problematic. His one weakness is an erratic arm that sometimes lacks accuracy and velocity, though he has a quick release that makes up for some of the shortfalls. He could be an above average shortstop if not for the arm inconsistencies. Regardless, Sogard is among the better second basemen

Second Basemen

in the game despite limited playing time. Defense will not be the issue for Sogard holding down a role as an everyday regular, as his hitting will need to improve to keep him in the lineup.

Donovan Solano

	BASIC							GDP			RANGE AND POSITIONING							RUNS SAVED				
Year Team	G	Inn	TC	E	Pct	GFP	DM	Opps	GDP	Pct	Outs Made	To His Right	Straight On	To His Left	GB	Air	Plays Saved	R/P	GFP/ GDP	DME	Total	Rank
2012 Mia	58	488.2	256	2	.992	14	10	39	27	.692	172	+1	0	-1	+1	+3	+4	3	0	-2	1	19
2013 Mia	93	806.1	464	8	.983	40	14	91	64	.703	288	+1	+5	-2	+4	0	+4	3	0	1	4	14
2014 Mia	73	576.0	352	1	.997	18	12	75	49	.653	202	-6	+2	+3	-1	+2	+1	1	0	-2	-1	20
	224	1871.0	1072	11	.990	72	36	205	140	.683	662	-4	+7	0	+4	+5	+9	7	0	-3	4	

Scout's Defensive Rating: -2 plays saved in 2013, 4 plays saved in 2014

The diminutive 5-foot-9 Colombian has yet to play a full major league season but impressed enough in 95 games in the field in 2013 to be named the Marlins defensive player of the year by Wilson. Thanks to not often showing much promise at the plate, the former Cardinal farmhand projects a bit of a utility aura, and has played MLB innings at third, short and left, in addition to second. Fairly average across the board, he doesn't make many throwing errors (just three so far in his career), and shows normal range and average ability as a double play pivot man. After posting 40 GFPs in 2013, he wasn't as flashy in 2014, seeing that number more than cut in half (down to 18), while his DMs stayed relatively static (14 to 12) despite playing time differences.

Steve Tolleson

	BASIC							GDP			RANGE AND POSITIONING							RUNS SAVED				
Year Team	G	Inn	TC	E	Pct	GFP	DM	Opps	GDP	Pct	Outs Made	To His Right	Straight On	To His Left	GB	Air	Plays Saved	R/P	GFP/ GDP	DME	Total	Rank
2010 Oak	4	21.0	10	1	.900	0	0	3	2	.667	3	-1	0	0	-1	0	-1	0	0	0	0	-
2012 Bal	4	19.0	13	0	1.000	0	2	6	2	.333	4	0	+1	-1	0	0	0	0	0	0	0	-
2014 Tor	55	252.1	136	5	.963	10	6	29	13	.448	69	+2	+1	-4	-1	+3	+2	2	-1	0	1	-
	63	292.1	159	6	.962	10	8	38	17	.447	76	+1	+2	-5	-2	+3	+1	2	-1	0	1	

Scout's Defensive Rating: 0 plays saved in 2014

Dan Uggla

	BASIC							GDP			RANGE AND POSITIONING							RUNS SAVED				
Year Team	G	Inn	TC	E	Pct	GFP	DM	Opps	GDP	Pct	Outs Made	To His Right	Straight On	To His Left	GB	Air	Plays Saved	R/P	GFP/ GDP	DME	Total	Rank
2006 Fla	151	1304.1	752	15	.980	26	43	206	107	.519	486	-6	+3	+5	+2	-2	0	0	1	-4	-3	21
2007 Fla	158	1383.2	736	11	.985	30	40	196	102	.520	438	-7	+4	-15	-18	-1	-19	-14	1	-2	-15	34
2008 Fla	144	1272.2	700	13	.981	62	27	154	74	.481	464	+9	-5	0	+3	+1	+4	3	-1	2	4	11
2009 Fla	158	1401.1	706	16	.977	52	35	143	91	.636	469	+1	-4	-12	-16	+3	-13	-10	-2	0	-12	33
2010 Fla	158	1392.1	745	18	.976	50	21	131	83	.634	429	-2	+1	-6	-8	-1	-9	-7	-1	0	-8	30
2011 Atl	159	1431.2	749	15	.980	45	38	140	82	.586	437	-3	+1	-12	-11	-5	-16	-12	-1	-2	-15	35
2012 Atl	152	1348.1	741	12	.984	45	28	146	98	.671	445	+1	+1	-2	+1	+3	+4	3	0	1	4	15
2013 Atl	133	1161.2	595	14	.976	37	30	108	73	.676	317	-7	+1	-10	-16	-4	-20	-15	2	-6	-19	35
2014 2 tms	39	333.0	187	11	.941	13	5	29	19	.655	103	0	-3	+1	-1	-1	-2	-1	0	-1	-2	-
	1252	11029.0	5911	125	.979	360	267	1253	729	.582	3588	-14	+1	-51	-64	-7	-71	-53	-1	-12	-66	

Scout's Defensive Rating: -12 plays saved in 2013, -3 plays saved in 2014

Chase Utley

	BASIC							GDP			RANGE AND POSITIONING							RUNS SAVED				
Year Team	G	Inn	TC	E	Pct	GFP	DM	Opps	GDP	Pct	Outs Made	To His Right	Straight On	To His Left	GB	Air	Plays Saved	R/P	GFP/ GDP	DME	Total	Rank
2003 Phi	37	302.0	175	3	.983	-	-	47	29	.617	105	+6	0	-6	0	-1	-1	-1	2		1	-
2004 Phi	50	410.1	227	4	.982	17	7	54	26	.481	136	+6	-3	+2	+4	+3	+7	5	0	2	7	-
2005 Phi	135	1195.1	687	15	.978	45	17	144	64	.444	456	+20	+1	+3	+23	+3	+26	20	-2	2	20	3
2006 Phi	156	1367.1	800	18	.978	47	29	194	106	.546	474	+6	-1	+9	+14	+2	+16	12	3	3	18	2
2007 Phi	132	1167.0	671	10	.985	46	27	172	80	.465	407	+17	0	+4	+21	+1	+22	17	-2	3	18	3
2008 Phi	159	1395.2	816	13	.984	57	35	204	96	.471	513	+8	+6	+32	+46	0	+46	35	-2	-3	30	1
2009 Phi	155	1357.0	774	12	.984	42	25	131	92	.702	482	+10	+7	-6	+12	0	+12	11	1	0	12	6
2010 Phi	114	1007.0	586	11	.981	49	9	106	81	.764	368	+12	+2	-7	+7	+8	+15	11	3	3	17	2
2011 Phi	100	887.2	488	5	.990	28	18	86	50	.581	313	+5	+5	+1	+11	0	+11	8	-1	0	7	7
2012 Phi	81	720.1	372	7	.981	20	13	55	30	.545	234	-1	+4	+4	+6	+7	+13	10	-1	0	9	8
2013 Phi	125	1071.0	581	17	.971	42	22	96	55	.573	342	-3	+6	-6	-3	0	-3	-3	-1	0	-4	26
2014 Phi	147	1321.2	726	11	.985	42	33	135	77	.570	396	+3	+6	-1	+8	0	+8	6	-2	-1	3	12
	1391	12202.1	6903	126	.982	435	235	1424	786	.552	4226	+89	+33	+29	+149	+25	+174	131	-2	9	138	

Scout's Defensive Rating: -8 plays saved in 2013, -4 plays saved in 2014

Second Basemen

Once an elite defender for the Phillies, Chase Utley is beginning to enter the twilight of his baseball career. The diminutive, 6'1", 200-pound second baseman has battled injuries since 2010; his 147 games played in 2014 were his most since 2009. In his heyday, Utley was an outstanding defender on plays to his right and left, often because of his intuitive positioning. While Utley no longer has the foot speed to range to either side for more difficult plays, he remains reliable on the plays he does reach. One facet of Utley's defense that has not changed is his sure-handedness; when he gets to a ball, Utley is one of the best in the majors at making a play.

Neil Walker

		BASIC							GDP			RANGE AND POSITIONING							RUNS SAVED				
Year	Team	G	Inn	TC	E	Pct	GFP	DM	Opps	GDP	Pct	Outs Made	To His Right	Straight On	To His Left	GB	Air	Plays Saved	R/P	GDP	GFP/DME	Total	Rank
2010	Pit	105	894.2	463	7	.985	27	12	83	62	.747	268	-3	-3	-13	-19	+4	-15	-11	2	0	-9	31
2011	Pit	159	1382.1	781	6	.992	58	31	172	106	.616	438	+20	0	-18	+2	-10	-8	-6	-1	4	-3	25
2012	Pit	125	1068.2	604	9	.985	54	17	117	75	.641	340	+8	+5	-14	0	-4	-4	-3	0	-1	-4	27
2013	Pit	132	1144.0	660	7	.989	74	18	148	83	.561	327	+20	-5	-4	+11	-1	+10	8	-2	3	9	9
2014	Pit	135	1175.2	632	5	.992	35	19	127	89	.701	313	+12	-5	-9	-2	-4	-6	-5	2	1	-2	23
		656	5665.1	3140	34	.989	248	97	647	415	.641	1686	+57	-8	-58	-8	-15	-23	-17	1	7	-9	

Scout's Defensive Rating: 2 plays saved in 2013, -8 plays saved in 2014

Neil Walker is larger than the prototypical second baseman. Drafted as a catcher, Walker made the difficult transition to second base and has found a home there. Injuries have limited Walker's defensive contributions; in fact, he's only played more than 135 games once in his five-year major league career. Walker is able to backhand balls up the middle well and get off a strong throw across his body. On balls to his glove side, he'll often react different and try to time them perfectly. It isn't a smooth movement but one that is more rigid and loud. He needs to display better footwork and get around the baseball instead of playing it to his side. History tells us that Walker has and may always struggle to his glove side, but if he's able to handle groundballs at him better. He can continue to be serviceable at second, and that's all the Pirates want from the offense-minded second sacker.

Rickie Weeks

		BASIC							GDP			RANGE AND POSITIONING							RUNS SAVED				
Year	Team	G	Inn	TC	E	Pct	GFP	DM	Opps	GDP	Pct	Outs Made	To His Right	Straight On	To His Left	GB	Air	Plays Saved	R/P	GDP	GFP/DME	Total	Rank
2003	Mil	4	21.0	3	1	.667	-	-	1			1	-1					0	0			0	-
2005	Mil	95	837.1	432	21	.951	25	38	109	52	.477	273	-3	-9	+4	-8	-3	-11	-8	-1	-1	-10	31
2006	Mil	92	794.0	460	22	.952	19	34	141	65	.461	265	-1	-8	-2	-10	-3	-13	-10	-2	-2	-14	32
2007	Mil	115	984.0	531	13	.976	38	33	129	67	.519	301	-1	-5	-5	-12	-5	-17	-13	1	2	-10	32
2008	Mil	120	1056.0	604	15	.975	36	44	163	75	.460	356	+3	-7	+4	+1	+1	+2	2	-2	-4	-4	24
2009	Mil	35	303.2	167	6	.964	11	4	35	21	.600	98	+5	0	+3	+9	+1	+10	8	-1	0	7	-
2010	Mil	159	1389.1	736	15	.980	44	38	131	92	.702	407	+4	+3	-13	-6	-7	-13	-10	1	-5	-14	34
2011	Mil	115	974.0	481	15	.969	31	25	93	63	.677	263	+2	-3	+4	+3	-7	-4	-3	1	-3	-5	26
2012	Mil	152	1344.1	626	16	.974	46	33	122	74	.607	350	-13	+4	-15	-24	-10	-34	-26	-1	-3	-30	36
2013	Mil	95	815.2	407	10	.975	26	20	82	52	.634	213	-7	-1	-4	-12	-6	-18	-14	-1	0	-15	34
2014	Mil	62	449.1	225	7	.969	8	12	49	30	.612	103	0	-4	-7	-11	-8	-19	-15	-1	-1	-17	35
		1044	8968.2	4672	141	.970	284	281	1055	591	.560	2630	-12	-30	-31	-70	-47	-117	-89	-6	-17	-112	-

Scout's Defensive Rating: -12 plays saved in 2013, -9 plays saved in 2014

Weeks had been the Brewers' starting second baseman for nearly nine years despite never showing anything near league average defense at the spot. Weeks was finally supplanted in 2014, playing the fewest innings he's seen in a full, non-injury plagued year in his ten year career. He struggles to both sides, often bobbles grounders that should be routine and easy, and doesn't have the most accurate of arms. He has above average speed, but has never had the instincts to turn that into decent range. In addition to his woes in the field, when offered the chance to get more playing time this past summer by learning left field, he declined. Once he lost his starting role, his trade value was severely limited by his bottom-of-the-barrel defense.

Second Basemen

Kolten Wong

	BASIC							GDP			RANGE AND POSITIONING							RUNS SAVED				
Year Team	G	Inn	TC	E	Pct	GFP	DM	Opps	GDP	Pct	Outs Made	To His Right	Straight On	To His Left	GB	Air	Plays Saved	R/P	GDP	GFP/ DME	Total	Rank
2013 StL	18	111.0	65	0	1.000	2	0	11	8	.727	36	-1	+1	+1	+1	-1	0	0	0	0	0	-
2014 StL	107	887.0	481	12	.975	30	20	87	65	.747	251	+7	-4	+3	+6	+3	+9	7	2	0	9	6
	125	998.0	546	12	.978	32	20	98	73	.745	287	+6	-3	+4	+7	+2	+9	7	2	0	9	-

Scout's Defensive Rating: 2 plays saved in 2013, -1 plays saved in 2014

In his first full season as a starting second baseman for the Cardinals, Kolten Wong made good on the Cardinals' decision to place him there and move Matt Carpenter back to third base. What Wong lacks in size–he's 5'9", 185-pounds–he makes up for with speed, agility, and a solid first step on plays to his left and right. Wong was also adept in turning double plays; working alongside Jhonny Peralta, Wong converted double plays on 74.7 percent of opportunities in 2014, saving the Cardinals two runs with his double play prowess.Despite all the statistics which seemingly point to Wong having a stellar season at the keystone–Wong's nine Runs Saved in 2014 were sixth in the league among second basemen–he only managed a Scout's Defensive Rating of -0.9 on the season. Wong was especially prone to weakness on balls hit in front of him, and he often failed to make a play after getting his glove on the ball. If Wong can tighten up these miscues, look for him to be an above average second baseman for seasons to come.

Ben Zobrist

	BASIC							GDP			RANGE AND POSITIONING							RUNS SAVED				
Year Team	G	Inn	TC	E	Pct	GFP	DM	Opps	GDP	Pct	Outs Made	To His Right	Straight On	To His Left	GB	Air	Plays Saved	R/P	GDP	GFP/ DME	Total	Rank
2008 TB	8	41.0	22	0	1.000	2	1	8	3	.375	11	+1	0	+1	+2	0	+2	2	0	0	2	-
2009 TB	91	714.2	372	4	.989	19	7	68	41	.603	253	+8	+4	+8	+20	+3	+23	17	0	-1	16	2
2010 TB	55	371.0	193	3	.984	18	6	42	25	.595	105	+3	-1	+4	+6	0	+6	4	-1	0	3	-
2011 TB	131	1058.1	535	6	.989	39	22	98	65	.663	301	+14	0	-2	+12	+7	+19	14	1	-1	14	4
2012 TB	58	408.1	186	6	.968	12	7	42	27	.643	93	0	+1	-3	-2	-2	-4	-3	0	-2	-5	28
2013 TB	125	1017.1	554	4	.993	45	14	107	66	.617	292	+4	+8	-1	+10	-2	+8	6	-1	2	7	10
2014 TB	79	625.0	296	6	.980	11	8	44	27	.614	173	+4	+2	-2	+5	+2	+7	5	-1	-3	1	16
	547	4235.2	2158	29	.987	146	65	409	254	.621	1228	+34	+14	+5	+53	+8	+61	45	-2	-5	38	-

Scout's Defensive Rating: 9 plays saved in 2013, 0 plays saved in 2014

Had we started the Multi-Position Fielding Bible Award before Zobrist emerged with the Rays, Zobrist would already have plenty of defensive hardware to his credit. As a switch-hitting super utility player, his flexibility means he doesn't always know from one game to another where he may start. The 2014 season was no different for him, as he played a total of five different positions, playing more than 100 innings at four of them. Furthermore, Zobrist excels almost everywhere he plays. As it is in the infield, Zobrist's range to his right in the outfield is very good. Coupled with average to above average speed, Zobrist made playing left field look relatively easy for a guy who doesn't play there very often. On the infield, Zobrist is very good at charging choppers and softly hit groundballs and utilizing his strong arm to get outs in the closest of plays, whether he plays shortstop or second. His range isn't quite good enough to be an asset at shortstop, but he can fill in there on occasion.

Third Basemen Register and Scouting Reports

Year	Fielding Bible Award Winner	Runner Up	Third Place
2006	Adrian Beltre	Scott Rolen	Joe Crede
2007	Pedro Feliz	Scott Rolen	Ryan Zimmerman
2008	Adrian Beltre	Evan Longoria	Scott Rolen
2009	Ryan Zimmerman	Adrian Beltre	Chone Figgins
2010	Evan Longoria	Ryan Zimmerman	Adrian Beltre
2011	Adrian Beltre	Evan Longoria	Pablo Sandoval
2012	Adrian Beltre	Mike Moustakas	Brett Lawrie
2013	Manny Machado	Nolan Arenado	Evan Longoria
2014	Josh Donaldson	Nolan Arenado	Juan Uribe

Third Basemen

Pedro Alvarez

Year	Team	G	Inn	TC	E	Pct	GFP	DM	Opp	Sac Hits	Bunt Hits	Opp	GDP	Pct	Outs Made	To His Right	Straight On	To His Left	GB	Air	Plays Saved	Bases Saved	R/P	Bunt	GDP	GFP/DME	Total	Rank
2010	Pit	94	814.2	276	17	.938	35	19	11	7	4	19	13	.684	228	+1	-9	-4	-12	-1	-13	-14	-10	0	0	-1	-11	29
2011	Pit	66	549.0	214	14	.935	24	17	11	4	5	22	10	.455	167	0	-3	-3	-6	0	-6	-9	-6	-1	-1	-1	-9	29
2012	Pit	145	1273.0	364	27	.926	46	32	32	12	12	34	22	.647	289	-1	-5	+5	-1	0	-1	-2	-2	-2	0	-1	-5	28
2013	Pit	150	1328.1	458	27	.941	65	36	14	5	6	42	21	.500	360	+1	-2	+6	+5	+1	+6	+8	6	-1	-1	-1	3	13
2014	Pit	99	823.1	327	25	.924	36	21	23	9	9	26	14	.538	205	-8	+2	+9	+2	+1	+3	+3	2	-4	-1	-2	-5	25
		554	4788.1	1639	110	.933	206	123	91	37	36	143	80	.559	1249	-7	-17	+13	-12	+1	-11	-14	-10	-8	-3	-6	-27	-

Scout's Defensive Rating: 0 plays saved in 2013, -16 plays saved in 2014

At 6'3", 235 pounds, Pedro Alvarez lacks the athleticism and range to be a successful third baseman. Effort is not an issue, as he never hesitates to dive for balls that he isn't quick enough to reach on his feet. He is good at making plays to his left, and clearly prefers to be moving on his approach to the ball, as the easier plays that he misses are generally hit straight at him. Where things really break down for him, though, is his throwing. Alvarez was the worst in baseball in 2014 with 42 throwing-related DMEs. At times, he is slow to transfer the ball to his throwing hand, which allows runners to occasionally beat out otherwise routine plays. More often, because of his lack of athleticism and range, he will force the throw without setting his feet, resulting in wild throws off the mark.

The BIS Video Scouts rated Alvarez as the second-worst third baseman in baseball in 2014 according to the Scout's Defensive Rating. However, his Range and Positioning numbers are less damning (though still below average), as the Pirates have done a great job positioning him in the best spots to make plays, compensating for his lack of range. Long term, however, it appears that the Pirates have realized that Alvarez is unsuited to third base, and will be transitioning him over to first base for the 2015 season.

Nolan Arenado

Year	Team	G	Inn	TC	E	Pct	GFP	DM	Opp	Sac Hits	Bunt Hits	Opp	GDP	Pct	Outs Made	To His Right	Straight On	To His Left	GB	Air	Plays Saved	Bases Saved	R/P	Bunt	GDP	GFP/DME	Total	Rank
2013	Col	130	1110.0	411	11	.973	76	24	20	6	5	30	19	.633	343	+6	+21	+5	+32	+4	+36	+36	27	2	0	1	30	2
2014	Col	111	967.0	365	15	.959	64	18	12	5	4	35	24	.686	301	-1	+8	+6	+13	+5	+18	+18	13	0	1	2	16	3
		241	2077.0	776	26	.966	140	42	32	11	9	65	43	.662	644	+5	+29	+11	+45	+9	+54	+54	40	2	1	3	46	-

Scout's Defensive Rating: 19 plays saved in 2013, 25 plays saved in 2014

Arenado has the distinction of finishing runner-up in Fielding Bible Award voting in his first two major league seasons. Arenado gets a quick first-step on batted balls in his zone. While he lacks pure speed, his natural instincts and ability to get an early jump on contact more than make up for it. Arenado displays an advanced ability to react and make even the toughest plays at the hot corner look simple, all while displaying good range and a strong throwing arm. Arenado's Scout's Defensive Rating in 2013 of +19 was the best among third basemen. He then improved upon that mark in 2014, finishing with a +25 Scout's Defensive Rating, good enough for league's best at all defensive positions. His claim to fame is his tendency to charge groundballs, earning him the nickname "Sharknado" from his teammates. Based on his first two years in the majors, it would be a surprise if Arenado isn't able to land a couple of Fielding Bible Awards before the decade is out.

Cody Asche

Year	Team	G	Inn	TC	E	Pct	GFP	DM	Opp	Sac Hits	Bunt Hits	Opp	GDP	Pct	Outs Made	To His Right	Straight On	To His Left	GB	Air	Plays Saved	Bases Saved	R/P	Bunt	GDP	GFP/DME	Total	Rank
2013	Phi	44	383.2	121	5	.959	23	8	3	2	0	2	2	1.000	97	0	-3	-6	-10	-1	-11	-11	-8	0	0	1	-7	28
2014	Phi	112	924.2	281	16	.943	30	21	14	8	2	23	12	.522	216	-4	-1	+1	-5	+3	-2	-2	-2	0	0	-1	-3	23
		156	1308.1	402	21	.948	53	29	17	10	2	25	14	.560	313	-4	-4	-5	-15	+2	-13	-13	-10	0	0	0	-10	-

Scout's Defensive Rating: 2 plays saved in 2013, -7 plays saved in 2014

Cody Asche's first two seasons at third base have been uninspiring, to say the least. There are questions about Asche's ability to stick at third, and with Maikel Franco's arrival to the majors, those questions are only going to get louder. Asche does not have great speed, and his first step is not quite good enough to compensate for it. Roughly 1,300

Third Basemen

innings into his major league career, Asche is 15 plays below average on ground balls. Asche has just enough arm to play at third, and it's generally pretty steady; on the season, Asche had only five bad throw misplays and errors. In addition, Philadelphia's coaches have lauded his improvement at the position. With Franco likely seeing more time in the majors in 2015, however, a move to the outfield may soon be in the cards for Asche, if he sticks in the majors at all.

Mike Aviles

								BASIC	BUNTS			GDP			RANGE AND POSITIONING								RUNS SAVED					
Year	Team	G	Inn	TC	E	Pct	GFP	DM	Opp	Sac Hits	Bunt Hits	Opp	GDP	Pct	Outs Made	To His Right	Straight On	To His Left	GB	Air	Plays Saved	Bases Saved	R/P	Bunt	GDP	GFP/ DME	Total	Rank
2008	KC	7	29.2	6	0	1.000	1	0				-	-	-	5	-2	-1	+2	-1	0	-1	-1	-1		0		-1	-
2009	KC	2	10.0	0	0	-	0	0				0	0		0	0	0	0	0	0	0	0	0		0		0	-
2010	KC	5	35.0	4	1	.750	0	0				0	0	-	2	-1	0	0	-1	0	-1	-1	-1		0	0	-1	-
2011	2 tms	46	347.2	106	8	.925	11	8	9	4	4	12	4	.333	87	-2	+1	0	-1	0	-1	-2	0	0	0	0	0	-
2012	Bos	1	8.1	3	0	1.000	0	1				0	0		3	-1	0	+1	0	0	0	-1	-1		0	0	-1	-
2013	Cle	56	375.2	95	3	.968	5	5	10	4	3	10	6	.600	74	0	-3	-3	-6	+1	-5	-5	-4	0	0	-1	-5	-
2014	Cle	36	256.2	77	7	.909	5	5	3	2	0	7	1	.143	54	0	+1	-1	0	+1	+1	+1	0	1	-1	1	1	-
		153	1063.0	291	19	.935	22	19	22	10	7	29	11	.379	225	-6	-2	-1	-9	+2	-7	-9	-7	1	-1	0	-7	-

Scout's Defensive Rating: 1 plays saved in 2013, -5 plays saved in 2014

Adrian Beltre

								BASIC	BUNTS			GDP			RANGE AND POSITIONING								RUNS SAVED					
Year	Team	G	Inn	TC	E	Pct	GFP	DM	Opp	Sac Hits	Bunt Hits	Opp	GDP	Pct	Outs Made	To His Right	Straight On	To His Left	GB	Air	Plays Saved	Bases Saved	R/P	Bunt	GDP	GFP/ DME	Total	Rank
2003	LA	157	1346.0	439	19	.957	-	-	15	3	2	-	-	-	350	+13	+11	+2	+26	-1	+25	+30	23	2	-	-	25	2
2004	LA	155	1340.1	452	10	.978	35	39	34	18	9	-	-	-	381	+10	+18	+1	+30	-1	+29	+30	23	-1	-	0	22	2
2005	Sea	155	1325.2	425	14	.967	38	34	18	4	6	-	-	-	364	+5	-3	+5	+7	+1	+8	+11	8	0	-	0	8	9
2006	Sea	155	1358.0	474	15	.968	54	27	16	8	4	-	-	-	404	+23	-7	+8	+23	-2	+21	+24	18	1	-	0	19	4
2007	Sea	147	1279.1	426	18	.958	45	26	10	5	3	-	-	-	370	+3	-2	+4	+4	+3	+7	+7	5	-1	-	0	4	13
2008	Sea	139	1208.1	386	14	.964	62	15	13	6	4	-	-	-	328	+6	+3	+21	+30	+1	+31	+32	24	1	-	2	27	1
2009	Sea	111	988.1	341	14	.959	45	21	11	4	2	19	13	.684	302	+9	+1	+11	+21	+1	+22	+26	20	1	0	-1	20	3
2010	Bos	154	1342.2	442	19	.957	46	30	18	7	4	42	27	.643	362	+2	+9	+16	+27	-4	+23	+22	17	2	1	0	20	1
2011	Tex	112	980.1	312	11	.965	35	21	9	4	2	30	19	.633	251	+5	+5	+7	+17	-2	+15	+15	12	0	0	-1	11	4
2012	Tex	129	1125.1	312	8	.974	41	20	8	3	0	22	16	.727	241	+6	+3	+3	+12	0	+12	+12	9	3	1	0	13	4
2013	Tex	146	1289.2	339	14	.959	33	20	10	4	3	36	22	.611	266	-3	-3	-2	-8	0	-8	-10	-7	1	0	1	-5	24
2014	Tex	136	1171.1	362	12	.967	50	31	13	5	4	24	16	.667	250	+5	+5	-1	+8	-2	+6	+8	6	1	1	1	9	8
		1696	14755.1	4710	168	.964	484	284	175	71	43	173	113	.653	3869	+84	+40	+75	+197	-10	+187	+207	158	10	3	2	173	

Scout's Defensive Rating: -4 plays saved in 2013, 8 plays saved in 2014

Now in his 17th big league season, the 5-foot-11, 220-pound Beltre is still topping charts and grabbing eyes nationwide for his play at the hot corner. Quick reflexes and a lightning fast arm have allowed him to age gracefully at the demanding position. Perhaps his trademark play is his charging of short choppers and bunts, but he's also more than capable of flashy plays from the coaches' box and moving to his left. His whirling-yet-graceful throws from one foot are appearing with less frequency than in the past, and his range is now shrinking – thanks in part to eroding hamstrings – but his vacuum-like glove hasn't yet shown the same kind of fade. The 35-year old Beltre has been as consistent as they come, in a good way. The four-time Fielding Bible Award winner has probably past his defensive prime, but Beltre has several good years left before he hangs them up.

Xander Bogaerts

								BASIC	BUNTS			GDP			RANGE AND POSITIONING								RUNS SAVED					
Year	Team	G	Inn	TC	E	Pct	GFP	DM	Opp	Sac Hits	Bunt Hits	Opp	GDP	Pct	Outs Made	To His Right	Straight On	To His Left	GB	Air	Plays Saved	Bases Saved	R/P	Bunt	GDP	GFP/ DME	Total	Rank
2013	Bos	9	57.1	18	0	1.000	2	3	1	1	0	2	1	.500	10	0	-3	0	-3	-1	-4	-4	-3	0	0	0	-3	-
2014	Bos	44	385.1	111	10	.910	20	7	6	3	1	8	2	.250	70	-3	-7	-2	-13	+1	-12	-11	-8	1	-1	1	-7	-
		53	442.2	129	10	.922	22	10	7	4	1	10	3	.300	80	-3	-10	-2	-16	0	-16	-15	-11	1	-1	1	-10	-

Scout's Defensive Rating: -1 plays saved in 2013, 2 plays saved in 2014

Xander Bogaerts's Scouting Report can be found on page 224.

Third Basemen

Matt Carpenter

								BUNTS			GDP			RANGE AND POSITIONING								RUNS SAVED					
Year Team	G	Inn	TC	E	Pct	GFP	DM	Opp	Sac Hits	Bunt Hits	Opp	GDP	Pct	Outs Made	To His Right	Straight On	To His Left	GB	Air	Plays Saved	Bases Saved	R/P	Bunt	GDP	GFP/DME	Total	Rank
2011 StL	5	39.0	13	0	1.000	2	3	2	1	1	0	0	-	12	-1	0	0	-1	0	-1	-1	-1	0	0	0	-1	-
2012 StL	33	217.2	60	3	.950	7	1	3	1	0	6	3	.500	46	+1	-1	+3	+3	0	+3	+3	2	0	0	0	2	-
2013 StL	42	253.0	72	3	.958	17	4	8	5	1	12	8	.667	55	+1	-1	0	0	0	0	-1	-1	1	0	1	1	-
2014 StL	156	1371.0	394	16	.959	34	26	33	13	10	33	22	.667	298	-7	+1	+1	-5	+1	-4	-3	-2	1	1	-2	-2	21
	236	1880.2	539	22	.959	60	34	46	20	12	51	33	.647	411	-6	-1	+4	-3	+1	-2	-2	-2	2	1	-1	0	-

Scout's Defensive Rating: 2 plays saved in 2013, -2 plays saved in 2014

A year after impressing baseball analysts with a surprising performance at second base, Matt Carpenter had a solid, if not spectacular, season at his natural position of third base. Pushed there by the full-time arrival of Kolten Wong, the 6'3", 215-pound Carpenter was average to slightly above average in nearly every facet of his game, with the exception of balls hit to his right. Carpenter usually makes up for a lack of foot speed with a good first read.

Although it occasionally looks as if Carpenter is throwing change-ups to first base, his arm plays well enough at third base. Coupled with sure hands and decent athleticism, Carpenter has been slightly above average when fielding bunts and turning double plays. In his last two seasons combined at third base, Carpenter has saved two runs on bunts; moreover, Carpenter turned double plays on 68.9 percent of all his opportunities in 2013 and 2014. If nothing else, Carpenter offers potential versatility for the Cardinals, with considerable experience at second and third and cameo appearances at first base, left field and right field.

Nick Castellanos

								BUNTS			GDP			RANGE AND POSITIONING								RUNS SAVED					
Year Team	G	Inn	TC	E	Pct	GFP	DM	Opp	Sac Hits	Bunt Hits	Opp	GDP	Pct	Outs Made	To His Right	Straight On	To His Left	GB	Air	Plays Saved	Bases Saved	R/P	Bunt	GDP	GFP/DME	Total	Rank
2014 Det	145	1229.0	302	15	.950	30	24	15	6	6	29	10	.345	237	-19	-10	-2	-32	-5	-37	-39	-29	0	-2	1	-30	35

Scout's Defensive Rating: -18 plays saved in 2014

The stars aligned favorably for Castellanos at the outset of the 2014 season. The Tigers traded Prince Fielder to the Rangers, which allowed the defensively challenged Miguel Cabrera to slide across the diamond to first base, thus freeing up a spot for the young Castellanos at his "natural" position of third base. The organization hoped Castellanos would prove to be a defensive upgrade over the lumbering, heavy-footed Cabrera, yet all Castellanos has been able to muster thus far in the majors is a similarly dreadful performance with the leather.

Castellanos possesses an above average arm and performs reasonably well on balls in play that do not warrant excessive movement; however, the young third baseman struggles with almost every other facet of the position as evidenced by the fact that he made 37 plays fewer than average with his range and positioning—last among all major league third basemen. Below average foot speed, quickness and agility severely limit both his lateral range and his ability to successfully field balls in play that he must charge. Castellanos has converted only 45 percent of balls hit to his left into outs and has struggled when required to sprint, converting on only 25 percent of such plays. Castellanos, with an appalling -30 Defensive Runs "Saved" in 2014, does not appear to be the Tigers' long-term solution at third base. Realistically, he possesses the defensive profile of a first baseman; however, he has not yet demonstrated the offensive thump required to carry the position and the Tigers already have a guy named Cabrera occupying that role. Perhaps the Tigers will give Castellanos another shot in left field, the position he played primarily in 2013 while with Triple-A Toledo; however, there is no reason to believe he would be able to man the position at an acceptable level given his below average speed and athleticism.

Third Basemen

Lonnie Chisenhall

		BASIC							BUNTS			GDP			RANGE AND POSITIONING								RUNS SAVED					
Year	Team	G	Inn	TC	E	Pct	GFP	DM	Opp	Sac Hits	Bunt Hits	Opp	GDP	Pct	Outs Made	To His Right	Straight On	To His Left	GB	Air	Plays Saved	Bases Saved	R/P	Bunt	GDP	GFP/ DME	Total	Rank
2011	Cle	58	461.0	168	10	.940	12	10	7	3	1	14	6	.429	138	-3	+4	+2	+4	0	+4	+4	4	1	0	0	5	9
2012	Cle	30	255.0	76	6	.921	3	6	2	0	2	9	6	.667	62	-2	-4	-1	-7	0	-7	-6	-5	0	0	1	-4	-
2013	Cle	88	697.0	198	9	.955	24	13	7	2	3	24	17	.708	162	0	-3	-3	-7	+3	-4	-4	-3	1	1	2	1	15
2014	Cle	114	973.2	260	18	.931	29	18	16	4	11	16	5	.313	195	-4	-3	-5	-12	0	-12	-16	-12	-2	-1	1	-14	34
		290	2386.2	702	43	.939	68	47	32	9	17	63	34	.540	557	-9	-6	-7	-22	+3	-19	-22	-16	0	0	4	-12	-

Scout's Defensive Rating: -6 plays saved in 2013, -12 plays saved in 2014

Despite his offensive breakout, Chisenhall had his worst defensive season in 2014. Chisenhall struggled with his throwing mightily, recording 10 throwing errors in under 1,000 innings. . His arm strength is not awful, but his accuracy is extremely suspect. It was such a rough year for him at third base that he actually netted seven more Defensive Misplays and Errors on the season (36) than Good Fielding Plays (29), one of the lower totals in baseball. On top of his throwing issues, Chisenhall has subpar range despite his willingness to layout for balls hit in his direction. Although he is still a young player, he has to improve his throwing ability and range so the Indians do not have to lose his bat.

Matt Dominguez

		BASIC							BUNTS			GDP			RANGE AND POSITIONING								RUNS SAVED					
Year	Team	G	Inn	TC	E	Pct	GFP	DM	Opp	Sac Hits	Bunt Hits	Opp	GDP	Pct	Outs Made	To His Right	Straight On	To His Left	GB	Air	Plays Saved	Bases Saved	R/P	Bunt	GDP	GFP/ DME	Total	Rank
2011	Fla	16	122.0	29	2	.931	2	6				2	1	.500	25	+1	-1	-1	-1	-2	-3	-4	-3		0	0	-3	-
2012	Hou	31	245.2	78	1	.987	5	4	6	3	1	8	4	.500	59	-2	0	+2	0	0	0	-1	-1	0	0	1	0	-
2013	Hou	149	1312.1	431	16	.963	52	28	11	2	3	37	21	.568	325	-15	+13	+15	+13	-4	+9	+7	6	1	-1	2	8	6
2014	Hou	153	1302.2	398	11	.972	40	23	12	5	5	26	15	.577	239	-9	+5	+3	-2	-3	-5	-7	-6	0	0	2	-4	24
		349	2982.2	936	30	.968	99	61	29	10	9	73	41	.562	648	-25	+17	+19	+10	-9	+1	-5	-4	1	-1	5	1	-

Scout's Defensive Rating: -5 plays saved in 2013, -1 plays saved in 2014

Matt Dominguez will occasionally flash the leather in a way reminiscent of his pedigree as a touted defensive prospect, a way that reminds us of why he was drafted in the first round. A sharp groundball to his left takes a funny hop just before reaching him as he leaves his feet, fully extended; he adjusts mid-air, picks the ball clean, and throws a dart across the diamond from one knee. Dominguez will occasionally make these plays; however, they've been far too rare for him to be considered anything more than an average defensive third baseman. Far too many grounders down the line have gotten past him for costly extra-base hits. The 15 groundball misplays and errors ranked tied for sixth-most among third basemen. His below average lateral range and defensive miscues meant he was a below average third baseman in 2014.. Nevertheless, Dominguez has shown potential in glimpses; hopefully the young third baseman will continue to develop and realize that potential.

Josh Donaldson

		BASIC							BUNTS			GDP			RANGE AND POSITIONING								RUNS SAVED					
Year	Team	G	Inn	TC	E	Pct	GFP	DM	Opp	Sac Hits	Bunt Hits	Opp	GDP	Pct	Outs Made	To His Right	Straight On	To His Left	GB	Air	Plays Saved	Bases Saved	R/P	Bunt	GDP	GFP/ DME	Total	Rank
2012	Oak	71	633.2	217	12	.945	28	12	8	5	1	17	12	.706	170	-2	+8	+3	+9	-2	+7	+6	4	0	0	0	4	10
2013	Oak	155	1373.0	414	16	.961	63	37	14	7	2	34	20	.588	320	+8	+2	+1	+11	+1	+12	+13	10	1	0	1	12	4
2014	Oak	150	1320.2	482	23	.952	77	23	15	8	6	50	35	.700	365	+8	+5	0	+12	+4	+16	+20	15	-1	1	5	20	1
		376	3327.1	1113	51	.954	168	72	37	20	9	101	67	.663	855	+14	+15	+4	+32	+3	+35	+39	29	0	1	6	36	-

Scout's Defensive Rating: 14 plays saved in 2013, 17 plays saved in 2014

Though Kyle Seager beat out Donaldson for the Gold Glove, Fielding Bible Award voters recognized Donaldson's excellence in the field, and BIS Video Scouts and Defensive Runs Saved each concur. . The converted catcher is best described as an aggressive third baseman, leading to many Web Gem highlights. A key aspect of his success is his ability to read the ball off the bat exceptionally well, which plays a large role in his 36 Good Fielding Plays in 2014. Despite 23 errors on the season, Donaldson still makes more plays than anyone else. Of his 23 charged errors, 17 were the result of a bad throw, so there is room for improvement on that front. For more discussion of Donaldson's defense, see the Donaldson and Seager comparison on page 87.

Third Basemen

Eduardo Escobar

	BASIC							BUNTS			GDP			RANGE AND POSITIONING								RUNS SAVED					
Year	Team	G	Inn	TC	E	Pct	GFP	DM	Opp	Sac Hits	Bunt Hits	Opp	GDP	Pct	Outs Made	To His Right	Straight On	To His Left	GB	Air	Plays Saved	Bases Saved	R/P	Bunt	GDP	GFP/ DME	Total	Rank
2012	2 tms	25	152.1	37	1	.973	5	5				6	3	.500	33	+1	+2	+1	+3	0	+3	+5	4		0	-1	3	-
2013	Min	23	135.1	24	2	.917	3	4				4	3	.750	21	-3	-2	0	-6	-1	-7	-6	-5		0	0	-5	-
2014	Min	25	200.0	54	3	.944	13	3	2	1	1	6	4	.667	37	-1	-1	0	-3	-1	-4	-3	-2	0	0	1	-1	-
		73	487.2	115	6	.948	21	12	2	1	1	16	10	.625	91	-3	-1	+1	-6	-2	-8	-4	-3	0	0	0	-3	-

Scout's Defensive Rating: -3 plays saved in 2013, 0 plays saved in 2014

Eduardo Escobar's Scouting Report can be found on page 227.

Ryan Flaherty

	BASIC							BUNTS			GDP			RANGE AND POSITIONING								RUNS SAVED					
Year	Team	G	Inn	TC	E	Pct	GFP	DM	Opp	Sac Hits	Bunt Hits	Opp	GDP	Pct	Outs Made	To His Right	Straight On	To His Left	GB	Air	Plays Saved	Bases Saved	R/P	Bunt	GDP	GFP/ DME	Total	Rank
2012	Bal	17	80.0	17	1	.941	2	0	1	0	1	1	1	1.000	14	+1	-2	-1	-2	0	-2	-2	-1	0	0	0	-1	-
2013	Bal	7	34.0	12	0	1.000	1	0	1	0	1	1	1	1.000	10	+1	0	0	+1	0	+1	+1	1	-1	0	0	0	-
2014	Bal	43	255.1	78	5	.936	7	1	3	2	1	8	6	.750	57	+1	+1	+1	+3	+1	+4	+4	3	0	1	0	4	-
		67	369.1	107	6	.944	10	1	5	2	3	10	8	.800	81	+3	-1	0	+2	+1	+3	+3	3	-1	1	0	3	-

Scout's Defensive Rating: 0 plays saved in 2013, -2 plays saved in 2014

Juan Francisco

	BASIC							BUNTS			GDP			RANGE AND POSITIONING								RUNS SAVED					
Year	Team	G	Inn	TC	E	Pct	GFP	DM	Opp	Sac Hits	Bunt Hits	Opp	GDP	Pct	Outs Made	To His Right	Straight On	To His Left	GB	Air	Plays Saved	Bases Saved	R/P	Bunt	GDP	GFP/ DME	Total	Rank
2009	Cin	4	30.0	10	1	.900	1	0				2	2	1.000	9	0	0	+1	+1	0	+1	+1	1		0	0	1	-
2010	Cin	12	74.2	12	1	.917	1	2				3	3	1.000	11	-1	0	0	0	0	0	+1	0		0	0	0	-
2011	Cin	24	186.2	52	2	.962	3	6	2	1	1	4	2	.500	43	-1	+3	0	+2	0	+2	+2	2	0	0	-2	0	-
2012	Atl	49	363.1	93	6	.935	6	5	4	1	1	11	8	.727	73	+1	0	-1	+1	+1	+2	+2	1	0	0	0	1	-
2013	2 tms	34	255.2	91	7	.923	11	7	6	4	1	10	6	.600	73	-2	0	+2	-1	-1	-2	-3	-2	-1	0	-1	-4	-
2014	Tor	74	482.2	134	9	.933	10	8	5	0	4	17	8	.471	89	-2	-6	-2	-10	+2	-8	-8	-7	-1	0	1	-7	29
		197	1393.0	392	26	.934	32	28	17	6	7	45	28	.622	298	-5	-3	0	-7	+2	-5	-5	-5	-2	0	-2	-9	-

Scout's Defensive Rating: -4 plays saved in 2013, -6 plays saved in 2014

The 2014 season was not a memorable one for Juan Francisco, defensively and offensively. He was a defensive liability in 74 games at the hot corner. Francisco's 240-plus pounds makes him a slightly bigger version of Juan Uribe, but without the quick reactions and cannon arm that make Uribe a great third baseman. He is not quick on his feet, making him exceptionally slow to reach slow grounders or choppers straight on. His reaction time to his left and right is subpar, and he also makes numerous poor decisions on throws, allowing baserunners to take extra bases and inevitably costing the team runs. Despite his caveats, Francisco's arm is fairly accurate making the throw across the diamond. If Francisco finds regular playing time it will be because his bat compensates for his subpar glove at the hot corner.

Todd Frazier

	BASIC							BUNTS			GDP			RANGE AND POSITIONING								RUNS SAVED					
Year	Team	G	Inn	TC	E	Pct	GFP	DM	Opp	Sac Hits	Bunt Hits	Opp	GDP	Pct	Outs Made	To His Right	Straight On	To His Left	GB	Air	Plays Saved	Bases Saved	R/P	Bunt	GDP	GFP/ DME	Total	Rank
2011	Cin	27	207.2	64	2	.969	7	3	3	1	1	4	1	.250	48	+1	+1	+2	+3	-1	+2	+2	1	0	0	0	1	-
2012	Cin	73	589.2	155	5	.968	9	9	6	4	2	10	3	.300	124	0	+3	+4	+7	+1	+8	+8	6	-1	-1	-1	3	12
2013	Cin	147	1256.2	337	10	.970	32	23	16	5	7	32	20	.625	259	-1	+8	+1	+7	-2	+6	+6	5	-1	0	1	5	10
2014	Cin	124	1046.2	298	9	.970	20	19	15	6	2	17	12	.706	241	0	+5	+3	+8	+3	+11	+8	6	1	0	0	7	11
		371	3100.2	854	26	.970	68	54	40	16	12	63	36	.571	672	0	+17	+10	+25	+1	+26	+24	18	-1	-1	0	16	-

Scout's Defensive Rating: -2 plays saved in 2013, 3 plays saved in 2014

Though he'll rarely dazzle you with his glove, Frazier has settled in as a solid third baseman, perhaps even slightly above average. He struggles with the harder hit balls, and tries to compensate for it by diving a lot, but more often than not comes up empty. However, if he is able to snag a ball on a dive, especially on balls hit to his left, he is able to jump back up quickly and get off a strong throw. On balls hit to his right, though he may be able to get to the ball, his throws are often too short or overthrown resulting in Defensive Misplays or Errors. While his baseball instincts on throwing decisions leave something to be desired, Frazier does charge choppers and grounders very well. In addition to his third base play, he can be used to spell Joey Votto at first base on occasion.

Third Basemen

David Freese

	BASIC							BUNTS			GDP			RANGE AND POSITIONING								RUNS SAVED					
Year	Team	G	Inn	TC	E	Pct	GFP	DM	Opp	Sac Hits	Bunt Hits	Opp	GDP	Pct	Outs Made	To His Right	Straight On	To His Left	GB	Air	Plays Saved	Bases Saved	R/P	Bunt	GDP	GFP/ DME	Total	Rank
2009	StL	7	41.1	11	0	1.000	1	0				1	1	1.000	9	-1	0	-1	-1	0	-1	-1	-1	0	0		-1	
2010	StL	66	557.0	179	9	.950	22	9	8	5	0	19	16	.842	144	-3	-4	+1	-6	-2	-8	-8	-6	1	1	-1	-5	23
2011	StL	88	674.0	204	12	.941	24	14	8	5	3	24	19	.792	170	-3	+2	0	-1	0	-1	-2	-2	0	1	1	0	17
2012	StL	134	1153.2	354	18	.949	27	24	14	3	5	38	22	.579	295	+14	-9	-7	-2	+1	-1	+1	+1	1	0	0	2	15
2013	StL	132	1050.2	256	11	.957	33	17	10	3	3	25	17	.680	208	-5	-10	-4	-18	-2	-20	-22	-17	1	1	1	-14	33
2014	LAA	122	959.1	237	8	.966	22	17	14	3	9	17	13	.765	180	+5	-9	-5	-9	-2	-11	-11	-9	-2	0	2	-9	30
		549	4436.0	1241	58	.953	129	81	54	19	20	124	88	.710	1006	+7	-30	-16	-37	-5	-42	-43	-34	1	3	3	-27	

Scout's Defensive Rating: -5 plays saved in 2013, -7 plays saved in 2014

David Freese is a poor defensive third baseman as evidenced by his -9 Defensive Runs Saved. He is adept at fielding balls hit to his right (+5 plays above average) but he struggles with fielding balls hit straight on (-10) and with balls hit to his left (-5). Freese is a capable fielder when he is not required to move drastically from his setup position; however, when he is required to sprint, he sports an out conversion rate of only 31 percent, the third-lowest mark among regulars at third base. Freese possesses both above average arm strength and accuracy which combine to inform his above average .929 Good Throw Rate. Freese is able to field balls within a very narrow range of territory and was only able to convert on 7 percent of plays rated "difficult" by BIS's Video Scouts, ranking last among third basemen with at least 100 opportunities during the 2014 season. Freese's defense is undeniably poor but as long as he continues to provide above average performance with the stick, his presence at the position will remain justified.

Conor Gillaspie

	BASIC							BUNTS			GDP			RANGE AND POSITIONING								RUNS SAVED					
Year	Team	G	Inn	TC	E	Pct	GFP	DM	Opp	Sac Hits	Bunt Hits	Opp	GDP	Pct	Outs Made	To His Right	Straight On	To His Left	GB	Air	Plays Saved	Bases Saved	R/P	Bunt	GDP	GFP/ DME	Total	Rank
2008	SF	2	4.0	1	0	1.000	1	0	-	-	-	-	-	-	0	0	0	0				0				-	0	-
2011	SF	4	22.0	3	0	1.000	1	0	0	0		0	0	-	2	0	0	0	0	-1	-1	-1	-1	0	0		-1	-
2012	SF	5	45.0	14	2	.857	1	2	4	1	3	0	0	-	10	-3	+1	0	-2	-1	-3	-2	-2	-2	0	1	-3	-
2013	CWS	113	940.0	280	16	.943	41	18	8	4	3	21	12	.571	228	-2	-2	+1	-3	-3	-6	-9	-7	0	0	3	-4	22
2014	CWS	127	1063.2	307	12	.961	37	19	16	8	6	30	20	.667	221	-5	-9	-3	-17	-4	-21	-20	-16	1	0	3	-12	32
		251	2074.2	605	30	.950	81	39	28	13	12	51	32	.627	461	-10	-10	-2	-22	-9	-31	-32	-26	-1	0	7	-20	

Scout's Defensive Rating: 1 plays saved in 2013, -1 plays saved in 2014

Gillaspie needs to remember to keep his footwork sharp at all times, as it can often become lazy and have him in an incorrect position to make a play. Balls that often ate up Gillaspie defensively were sharp groundballs that he couldn't corral right at him. In many cases he didn't look comfortable in his positioning and reacted awkwardly on these attempts. He was repeatedly handcuffed by hard groundballs when he wasn't in the proper position. He can handle a tough hop and has soft hands to field tough plays, but he is very immobile. It's tough to imagine Gillaspie improving to be more than a below average third baseman going forward.

Josh Harrison

	BASIC							BUNTS			GDP			RANGE AND POSITIONING								RUNS SAVED					
Year	Team	G	Inn	TC	E	Pct	GFP	DM	Opp	Sac Hits	Bunt Hits	Opp	GDP	Pct	Outs Made	To His Right	Straight On	To His Left	GB	Air	Plays Saved	Bases Saved	R/P	Bunt	GDP	GFP/ DME	Total	Rank
2011	Pit	50	363.1	137	6	.956	15	7	5	3	0	9	6	.667	110	+7	+1	-2	+6	+1	+7	+7	6	1	0	0	7	-
2012	Pit	14	74.1	22	1	.955	4	1	2	1	1	2	1	.500	16	+1	+1	0	+1	0	+1	+2	1	0	0	0	1	-
2013	Pit	7	31.0	13	1	.923	2	1				1	0	.000	10	+1	-1	0	0	0	0	0	0	0	0	0	0	-
2014	Pit	72	518.2	183	3	.984	32	10	7	4	2	15	10	.667	129	+5	-2	+5	+8	0	+8	+9	6	1	0	1	8	10
		143	987.1	355	11	.969	53	19	14	8	3	27	17	.630	265	+14	-1	+3	+15	+1	+16	+18	13	2	0	1	16	

Scout's Defensive Rating: -1 plays saved in 2013, 10 plays saved in 2014

Harrison may have had a breakout year offensively in 2014, but it was his defensive abilities and versatility that allowed him to become an everyday player for the Pirates. With Pedro Alvarez continuing to rack up errors at third base, Harrison did most of his work as a fill-in there (72 games) with very capable results. He showed very quick reactions and strong range. That led to his finishing tied for ninth in Runs Saved (+8) among third basemen despite the limited playing time at the position.

Third Basemen

With injuries to multiple outfielders, Harrison also split 50 games between right and left field. His reads on the ball from the outfield are not as good as they are in the infield, but his above average speed allows him to maintain about league average range in both corners. He also wields a strong arm that is very capable of making throws from both third base and right field. Additionally, Harrison has filled in capably at both middle infield positions over the years, proving himself to be a true super-utility player. With Alvarez likely moving over to first base, however, Harrison will be given the opportunity to establish himself full-time at his best position: third base.

Chase Headley

	BASIC							BUNTS			GDP			RANGE AND POSITIONING								RUNS SAVED					
Year Team	G	Inn	TC	E	Pct	GFP	DM	Opp	Sac Hits	Bunt Hits	Opp	GDP	Pct	Outs Made	To His Right	Straight On	To His Left	GB	Air	Plays Saved	Bases Saved	R/P	Bunt	GDP	GFP/DME	Total	Rank
2007 SD	5	38.1	6	1	.833	1	0	-	-	-	-	-	-	5	0	-2	0	-2	-1	-3	-3	-2		-	0	-2	-
2008 SD	7	55.0	13	1	.923	2	0	-	-	-	-	-	-	11	+1	0	0	+1	0	+1	+1	1		-	0	1	-
2009 SD	28	225.2	54	5	.907	7	2	2	0	1	3	1	.333	46	-2	+3	-1	0	0	0	0	0	0	0	0	0	-
2010 SD	158	1407.2	388	13	.966	35	9	16	9	3	35	19	.543	330	0	+9	+9	+18	+1	+19	+18	14	1	-1	2	16	3
2011 SD	107	895.1	272	11	.960	33	14	9	7	2	15	10	.667	211	-6	+1	+4	-1	+2	+1	0	-1	-1	0	2	0	15
2012 SD	159	1397.0	425	10	.976	45	29	19	9	5	28	11	.393	335	+8	-5	-1	+3	-1	+2	+2	1	0	-2	-2	-3	24
2013 SD	140	1235.0	346	11	.968	41	10	15	6	6	19	13	.684	279	+17	0	-11	+5	+1	+6	+8	6	-2	0	1	5	9
2014 2 tms	127	1082.2	319	8	.975	30	13	14	8	4	22	13	.591	234	+11	+6	-1	+16	+1	+17	+19	14	0	0	-1	13	4
	731	6336.2	1823	60	.967	194	77	75	39	21	122	67	.549	1451	+29	+12	-1	+40	+3	+43	+45	33	-2	-3	2	30	-

Scout's Defensive Rating: 5 plays saved in 2013, 5 plays saved in 2014

Headley enjoyed a strong defensive season in 2014, resembling his 2010 self when he first moved back to his natural position of third base. His lateral movement to each side is the reason Headley separated himself from the pack. While he has become a strong fielder to his backhand over the years, but he also improved his play in the hold. He'll never amaze you with his range, but his first step allows him to make the difficult play. He's light on his feet and every diving play he makes seems to be timed perfectly. He has soft hands on groundballs, which, combined with his footwork, makes every play appear to be possible for him to make.

Brock Holt

	BASIC							BUNTS			GDP			RANGE AND POSITIONING								RUNS SAVED					
Year Team	G	Inn	TC	E	Pct	GFP	DM	Opp	Sac Hits	Bunt Hits	Opp	GDP	Pct	Outs Made	To His Right	Straight On	To His Left	GB	Air	Plays Saved	Bases Saved	R/P	Bunt	GDP	GFP/DME	Total	Rank
2013 Bos	20	151.2	41	2	.951	8	4	4	1	3	3	2	.667	25	-2	-2	0	-4	0	-4	-4	-3	-1	0	-1	-5	-
2014 Bos	39	327.0	109	6	.945	18	10	5	3	1	9	3	.333	72	-2	-1	0	-3	0	-3	-5	-4	0	-1	1	-4	-
	59	478.2	150	8	.947	26	14	9	4	4	12	5	.417	97	-4	-3	0	-7	0	-7	-9	-7	-1	-1	0	-9	-

Scout's Defensive Rating: 0 plays saved in 2013, -3 plays saved in 2014

The 26-year old Holt first showed off his chops at third base this season, turning in a few games of hit-but-mostly-miss defense at the hot corner, sprinkling in gems here and there to keep his spot long enough to rack up more than 300 innings there. His average size and speed have allowed him to spend time in various positions around the park. Though he settled in right field, he earned 70 innings at first base, 175 between second and short, and nearly another 120 in left and center fields. During those excursions, he absolutely provided value through his sheer competence and versatility at each stop, never being a serious threat to the team's defense wherever they put him, but also not impressing enough to ever scream out that he'd found a place to stick. Though his primary tool on defense is that versatility, he's managed to shine a bit in right field. Despite limited time (just over 260 innings played), Holt was fourth in right field DRS in 2014 among players with at least 200 innings at the position. Holt's arm hasn't been particularly impressive from the outfield, but he's been able to cover considerable ground, and has shown the ability to make the flashy, lay-out plays when he gets the chance. At the end of the day, he's not a starter at any one position, but he won't hurt you with his glove, and he provides a lot of value through his unique versatility.

Third Basemen

Chris Johnson

Year	Team	G	Inn	TC	E	Pct	GFP	DM	Opp	Sac Hits	Bunt Hits	Opp	GDP	Pct	Outs Made	To His Right	Straight On	To His Left	GB	Air	Plays Saved	Bases Saved	R/P	Bunt	GDP	GFP/ DME	Total	Rank
		BASIC							**BUNTS**			**GDP**			**RANGE AND POSITIONING**								**RUNS SAVED**					
2009	Hou	7	48.0	7	0	1.000	0	0				1	0	.000	7	-1	0	0	-1		-1	-2	-2	0	0		-2	
2010	Hou	90	790.0	195	18	.908	13	6	8	5	1	20	11	.550	153	0	-10	-8	-18	-1	-19	-19	-15	0	0	0	-15	35
2011	Hou	101	841.1	237	15	.937	18	13	9	6	2	23	14	.609	184	-3	-5	-7	-14	-2	-16	-18	-14	1	0	2	-11	32
2012	2 tms	127	1069.1	315	19	.940	24	21	16	7	4	26	14	.538	252	-6	-4	-2	-12	-1	-13	-12	-10	0	-1	0	-11	32
2013	Atl	125	1020.0	286	14	.951	30	13	17	7	7	24	11	.458	228	+1	-7	-2	-8	+1	-7	-8	-6	0	-1	0	-7	27
2014	Atl	150	1317.2	271	6	.978	24	23	27	14	8	26	14	.538	213	-1	-7	-6	-14	+1	-13	-13	-10	1	-1	-3	-13	33
		600	5086.1	1311	72	.945	109	76	77	39	22	120	64	.533	1037	-10	-33	-25	-67	-2	-69	-72	-57	2	-3	-1	-59	

Scout's Defensive Rating: -2 plays saved in 2013, -3 plays saved in 2014

There are few baseball luxuries better than getting to play third base next to Andrelton Simmons. Having Simmons patrolling shortstop can feel like having an extra man on the field at times, which is good for the Braves, because starting third baseman Chris Johnson could use all the help he can get. Johnson was the worst defensive third baseman in the National League in 2014, the sixth time in his six major league seasons that he finished with a negative DRS total. Since arriving in Atlanta, Johnson has improved on balls to his right in large part because he can cheat towards the third base line knowing that Simmons covers so much ground in the hole. To his credit, Johnson isn't completely a lost cause at the hot corner, as he does handle bunts very well. He also had a career-low six errors, but his career-high 23 Defensive Misplays negate that progress. The bottom line is that Johnson has not made the necessary improvements to be a legitimate starting-caliber third baseman. With three more guaranteed years on his contract, Johnson had better regain his 2013 offensive form if he has any shot at living up to his contract.

Kelly Johnson

Year	Team	G	Inn	TC	E	Pct	GFP	DM	Opp	Sac Hits	Bunt Hits	Opp	GDP	Pct	Outs Made	To His Right	Straight On	To His Left	GB	Air	Plays Saved	Bases Saved	R/P	Bunt	GDP	GFP/ DME	Total	Rank
		BASIC							**BUNTS**			**GDP**			**RANGE AND POSITIONING**								**RUNS SAVED**					
2013	TB	16	118.0	45	1	.978	4	2	1	1	0	4	2	.500	34	+2	-2	0	0	0	0	0	1	0	0	0	1	-
2014	3 tms	60	369.0	96	6	.938	5	6	3	0	3	7	3	.429	64	+4	+1	-3	+3	-1	+2	+4	4	-2	0	0	2	-
		76	487.0	141	7	.950	9	8	4	1	3	11	5	.455	98	+6	-1	-3	+3	-1	+2	+4	5	-2	0	0	3	-

Scout's Defensive Rating: 0 plays saved in 2013, -7 plays saved in 2014

Jake Lamb

Year	Team	G	Inn	TC	E	Pct	GFP	DM	Opp	Sac Hits	Bunt Hits	Opp	GDP	Pct	Outs Made	To His Right	Straight On	To His Left	GB	Air	Plays Saved	Bases Saved	R/P	Bunt	GDP	GFP/ DME	Total	Rank
		BASIC							**BUNTS**			**GDP**			**RANGE AND POSITIONING**								**RUNS SAVED**					
2014	Ari	34	289.1	76	1	.987	10	6	7	3	2	7	4	.571	61	+1	-1	0	0	0	0	0	0	0	0	0	0	-

Scout's Defensive Rating: 1 plays saved in 2014

Brett Lawrie

Year	Team	G	Inn	TC	E	Pct	GFP	DM	Opp	Sac Hits	Bunt Hits	Opp	GDP	Pct	Outs Made	To His Right	Straight On	To His Left	GB	Air	Plays Saved	Bases Saved	R/P	Bunt	GDP	GFP/ DME	Total	Rank
		BASIC							**BUNTS**			**GDP**			**RANGE AND POSITIONING**								**RUNS SAVED**					
2011	Tor	43	380.1	164	6	.963	19	12	4	2	1	12	5	.417	133	+3	+7	+4	+15	+1	+16	+16	12	0	-1	0	11	6
2012	Tor	123	1072.0	375	17	.955	50	20	15	5	7	31	20	.645	264	+2	+15	+8	+25	+2	+27	+28	21	0	0	-1	20	1
2013	Tor	103	888.2	267	10	.963	52	14	11	3	5	20	14	.700	211	-2	+7	+1	+5	-2	+3	+5	3	-1	0	2	4	11
2014	Tor	63	403.0	126	2	.984	16	6	9	4	3	13	7	.538	87	+2	0	+1	+3	-1	+2	+1	1	0	0	-1	0	16
		332	2744.0	932	35	.962	137	52	39	14	16	76	46	.605	695	+5	+29	+14	+48	0	+48	+50	37	-1	-1	0	35	

Scout's Defensive Rating: 10 plays saved in 2013, 5 plays saved in 2014

Originally a catcher in the minor leagues, Lawrie has become a versatile infielder when he's healthy. Lawrie is a very athletic player that has shown great reflexes and reactions on plays in both directions. Lawrie also possesses great range for a third baseman, and is able to cut off a lot of balls in the hole. Lawrie is aggressive on charging balls and adept at making barehanded plays. Lawrie's quickness and athleticism also allows the Blue Jays to transition him to second base when necessary, and position him aggressively in many roles during defensive shifts. Lawrie's greatest asset might be his plus-plus arm strength. He routinely makes highlight reel throws from foul territory or after getting up from a dive down the line. His arm can sometimes be erratic, but has improved over the past couple years. Lawrie has struggled with injuries during his young career but could return to an elite defensive level if he can stay on the field.

Third Basemen

Evan Longoria

	BASIC							BUNTS			GDP			RANGE AND POSITIONING								RUNS SAVED					
Year	Team	G	Inn	TC	E	Pct	GFP	DM	Opp	Sac Hits	Bunt Hits	Opp	GDP	Pct	Outs Made	To His Right	Straight On	To His Left	GB	Air	Plays Saved	Bases Saved	R/P	Bunt	GDP	GFP/DME	Total	Rank
2008	TB	119	1045.2	328	12	.963	49	15	20	8	8	-	-	-	292	0	+5	+4	+10	-1	+9	+11	8	0	-	2	10	4
2009	TB	151	1302.2	427	13	.970	63	18	24	8	9	44	35	.795	371	+3	+5	+10	+18	+1	+19	+21	16	0	2	1	19	4
2010	TB	151	1330.2	417	14	.966	59	19	30	9	10	42	30	.714	302	+10	-1	+1	+10	-1	+9	+13	10	3	2	2	17	2
2011	TB	130	1124.2	367	14	.962	49	16	17	6	2	42	28	.667	273	+11	-3	-3	+5	+4	+9	+14	11	4	1	4	20	1
2012	TB	50	413.0	126	8	.937	19	7	3	1	1	7	4	.571	75	0	+2	-2	-1	0	-1	+1	1	0	0	0	1	-
2013	TB	147	1289.0	386	11	.972	67	21	13	2	6	38	23	.605	285	+12	-2	-1	+9	+2	+11	+14	10	1	0	1	12	4
2014	TB	155	1381.2	396	13	.967	49	22	15	4	7	33	16	.485	248	+3	-8	-6	-10	+2	-8	-7	-5	0	0	0	-5	27
		903	7887.1	2447	85	.965	355	118	122	38	43	206	136	.660	1846	+39	-2	+3	+41	+7	+48	+67	51	8	5	10	74	-

Scout's Defensive Rating: 17 plays saved in 2013, 5 plays saved in 2014

There is one word to describe Evan Longoria's defensive play in 2014: disappointing. A rock in Tampa Bay's infield, Longoria was never ranked lower than fourth since entering the league in 2008, including the 2010 Fielding Bible Award. However, he simply was not himself in 2014, noticeably frustrated as groundballs ricocheted off his glove or when coming up empty on failed dives. Longoria was, in fact, tied for sixth-most Defensive Misplays and Errors of this subtype, accumulating 15 groundballs through his position. If the defensive woes of the oft-injured Longoria was tied to some ailment, then he hid it well. He played with a fervent effort and was able to post a career-high in games started and innings; unfortunately, he also posted career-worsts with 22 total Defensive Misplays and -5 Runs Saved. Given his track record and underlying skillset, it would be a surprise if Longoria weren't able to bounce back to above-average, if not league-leading, form.

Manny Machado

	BASIC							BUNTS			GDP			RANGE AND POSITIONING								RUNS SAVED					
Year	Team	G	Inn	TC	E	Pct	GFP	DM	Opp	Sac Hits	Bunt Hits	Opp	GDP	Pct	Outs Made	To His Right	Straight On	To His Left	GB	Air	Plays Saved	Bases Saved	R/P	Bunt	GDP	GFP/DME	Total	Rank
2012	Bal	51	468.0	151	5	.967	15	6	10	5	2	2	1	.500	119	-1	+6	+2	+7	+3	+10	+8	6	1	0	0	7	5
2013	Bal	156	1390.0	484	13	.973	69	27	14	5	4	49	33	.673	355	+11	+16	+14	+40	+7	+47	+47	36	0	1	-2	35	1
2014	Bal	82	737.1	238	9	.962	34	11	9	4	1	24	15	.625	169	+2	+3	-1	+5	+2	+7	+6	4	2	0	0	6	14
		289	2595.1	873	27	.969	118	44	33	14	7	75	49	.653	643	+12	+25	+15	+52	+12	+64	+61	46	3	1	-2	48	-

Scout's Defensive Rating: 17 plays saved in 2013, 2 plays saved in 2014

When thinking of the best defensive third baseman in baseball, it is impossible to leave Machado, the 2013 Fielding Bible Award winner, out of the discussion. Already in his young career, Machado has made several unforgettable, highlight-reel plays. Whether he has his feet set or he is making his signature play of throwing on the run, no other third baseman has arm strength in the same category that he does. He has made countless plays down the line where he has to throw while fading towards the line and is still able to get the out at first where other players wouldn't even take the risk of attempting a throw. On top of his physical talents, Machado has shown the instincts to outsmart opposing baserunners and catch them straying off their bases. Provided he can stay healthy, Machado will have many more years of elite defense ahead of him during which he will no doubt challenge for more Fielding Bible Awards.

Casey McGehee

	BASIC							BUNTS			GDP			RANGE AND POSITIONING								RUNS SAVED					
Year	Team	G	Inn	TC	E	Pct	GFP	DM	Opp	Sac Hits	Bunt Hits	Opp	GDP	Pct	Outs Made	To His Right	Straight On	To His Left	GB	Air	Plays Saved	Bases Saved	R/P	Bunt	GDP	GFP/DME	Total	Rank
2008	ChC	6	41.2	16	0	1.000	1	0	-	-	-	-	-	-	16	+1	0	+1	+3	0	+3	+3	2			0	2	-
2009	Mil	71	530.1	155	13	.916	14	15	8	2	4	16	10	.625	128	-4	-2	-4	-9	-3	-12	-11	-8	-1	0	-1	-10	30
2010	Mil	153	1326.0	366	17	.954	36	20	21	11	4	40	25	.625	297	+2	-12	-4	-14	-3	-17	-17	-13	-1	0	0	-12	30
2011	Mil	147	1233.1	347	20	.942	32	20	9	5	2	22	15	.682	278	+1	-2	+3	+2	0	+2	-1	0	0	1	3	4	11
2012	2 tms	21	146.0	34	1	.971	5	7	6	2	4	2	2	1.000	28	+2	-1	0	+1	0	+1	+1	0	-2	0	-1	-3	-
2014	Mia	158	1409.2	326	7	.979	23	17	26	14	8	42	29	.690	263	+7	-3	-4	-1	-4	-5	-6	-4	-1	1	2	-2	22
		556	4687.0	1244	58	.953	111	79	70	34	22	122	81	.664	1010	+9	-20	-8	-18	-10	-28	-31	-23	-3	2	3	-21	-

Scout's Defensive Rating: -11 plays saved in 2014

Casey McGehee is 32 years old and has a heavy bulky frame. He has played multiple positions throughout previous seasons but played third base exclusively in 2014. McGehee has made some strides as a third baseman, but he remains below average in every aspect of fielding. The main weakness is range and speed. McGehee looks like a first baseman or a DH, not a third baseman. There are bigger third basemen in MLB, but they seem to have better raw instincts for

Third Basemen

diving than McGehee has at third. With the speed at which balls are hit to third, reaction time is crucial, and McGehee lacks the raw instincts to handle those balls well. McGehee will field the ball cleanly if it is hit right to him and his arm is average for a third baseman. He has trouble coming in on the ball on bunts and short choppers, and he can't transition the ball from glove to throwing hand very well either. McGehee should be moved from third base sooner rather than later.

Will Middlebrooks

	BASIC							BUNTS			GDP			RANGE AND POSITIONING								RUNS SAVED					
Year Team	G	Inn	TC	E	Pct	GFP	DM	Opp	Sac Hits	Bunt Hits	Opp	GDP	Pct	Outs Made	To His Right	Straight On	To His Left	GB	Air	Plays Saved	Bases Saved	R/P	Bunt	GDP	GFP/ DME	Total	Rank
2012 Bos	72	606.2	175	9	.949	14	14	10	2	6	18	10	.556	148	-5	+5	0	+1	+1	+2	0	0	-1	0	-2	-3	25
2013 Bos	92	797.2	218	10	.954	20	19	5	2	2	18	8	.444	160	-3	+1	-2	-4	0	-4	-7	-5	0	-1	-2	-8	29
2014 Bos	62	522.1	141	4	.972	13	8	5	1	1	13	9	.692	102	0	-4	-2	-6	-1	-7	-8	-6	1	0	0	-5	28
	226	1926.2	534	23	.957	47	41	20	5	9	49	27	.551	410	-8	+2	-4	-9	0	-9	-15	-11	0	-1	-4	-16	-

Scout's Defensive Rating: -5 plays saved in 2013, -2 plays saved in 2014

When you look at Middlebrooks, you think he has all the skills necessary to be an above average defensive third baseman, but the skills just haven't translated to on-field production yet. Middlebrooks uses his size and athleticism to make difficult plays look easy, but appears to lose concentration on easier chances and struggles with short hops. He charges balls well and capably makes barehanded plays when necessary. Middlebrooks doesn't have a strong arm at third, and he has struggled with accuracy at times, but did improve in that regard in 2014. In his limited time in the the majors, Middlebrooks has struggled to limit his Defensive Misplays to an acceptable level. Barring an improvement in that regard, Middlebrooks' bat is going to have to compensate for his below average third base defense.

Mike Moustakas

	BASIC							BUNTS			GDP			RANGE AND POSITIONING								RUNS SAVED					
Year Team	G	Inn	TC	E	Pct	GFP	DM	Opp	Sac Hits	Bunt Hits	Opp	GDP	Pct	Outs Made	To His Right	Straight On	To His Left	GB	Air	Plays Saved	Bases Saved	R/P	Bunt	GDP	GFP/ DME	Total	Rank
2011 KC	89	778.0	240	11	.954	19	15	10	2	7	16	10	.625	194	0	+6	-3	+3	+1	+4	+4	3	-2	0	0	1	14
2012 KC	149	1314.1	454	15	.967	53	21	17	2	12	41	29	.707	341	+20	-1	-3	+16	-1	+15	+20	15	-5	1	3	14	3
2013 KC	134	1129.2	340	16	.953	37	17	10	4	4	19	15	.789	257	-3	-2	-3	-8	0	-8	-4	-3	0	1	-1	-3	20
2014 KC	138	1148.2	357	19	.947	33	19	13	5	8	17	9	.529	261	+1	+3	-2	+2	+1	+3	+4	3	-2	0	-3	-2	18
	510	4370.2	1391	61	.956	142	72	50	13	31	93	63	.677	1053	+18	+6	-11	+13	+1	+14	+24	18	-9	2	-1	10	-

Scout's Defensive Rating: -3 plays saved in 2013, -4 plays saved in 2014

Despite some mediocre Defensive Runs Saved numbers the past two years, Moustakas still possesses the tools to be an above average third baseman. His first full year as a starter, 2012, he ranked third overall in Runs Saved at third base with 14 and put together a terrific all around defensive season. As was evidenced in the 2014 playoffs, Moustakas has the ability to make some amazing highlight reel plays. He reacts well to the ball off the bat and has a strong throwing arm. He doesn't have the best set of hands, but he has been able to do a solid job despite that. Moustakas is still a young player who has put together a great defensive season recently and has shown glimpses since then, as well as the tools, to be a very solid defender.

Mike Olt

	BASIC							BUNTS			GDP			RANGE AND POSITIONING								RUNS SAVED					
Year Team	G	Inn	TC	E	Pct	GFP	DM	Opp	Sac Hits	Bunt Hits	Opp	GDP	Pct	Outs Made	To His Right	Straight On	To His Left	GB	Air	Plays Saved	Bases Saved	R/P	Bunt	GDP	GFP/ DME	Total	Rank
2012 Tex	5	24.2	9	1	.889	1	0	1	1	0	0	0	-	7	0	0	0	0	0	0	+1	1	0	0	0	1	-
2014 ChC	52	395.1	99	7	.929	15	10	5	3	2	3	1	.333	76	+1	-1	0	-1	0	-1	-1	-1	0	0	0	-1	17
	57	420.0	108	8	.926	16	10	6	4	2	3	1	.333	83	+1	-1	0	-1	0	-1	0	0	0	0	0	0	-

Scout's Defensive Rating: -2 plays saved in 2014

Still relatively new to the majors, Mike Olt has all the tools to be an above average third basemen. Although he saw some action at first base, Olt would be best served at the hot corner where his plus arm can be featured. An aggressive fielder, he likes to charge weakly hit balls and isn't afraid to make a barehanded play when rushed. Perhaps his greatest weakness involves reacting to a batted ball properly, as he consistently is late to adjusting to the ball's path. He often leaves his feet unnecessarily, misjudging the ball's velocity and missing the timing of his jump. Judging solely by his

Third Basemen

defensive numbers, one would assume Olt isn't poised to be even an average big league third basemen. With a Scout's Defensive Rating in the bottom third of all players at the position, he simply needs to adjust to the speed of the game. If Olt can assimilate his skills to the majors, he could become a serviceable defender, but there is still plenty of room for growth.

Trevor Plouffe

	BASIC								BUNTS			GDP			RANGE AND POSITIONING								RUNS SAVED					
Year	Team	G	Inn	TC	E	Pct	GFP	DM	Opp	Sac Hits	Bunt Hits	Opp	GDP	Pct	Outs Made	To His Right	Straight On	To His Left	GB	Air	Plays Saved	Bases Saved	R/P	Bunt	GDP	GFP/ DME	Total	Rank
2012	Min	95	804.2	261	17	.935	34	18	8	5	2	15	11	.733	220	-11	+4	0	-7	-2	-9	-12	-9	0	0	1	-8	31
2013	Min	120	1035.2	298	13	.956	25	18	14	2	6	26	19	.731	244	+2	-6	0	-4	+1	-3	+1	1	0	1	-2	0	16
2014	Min	127	1110.2	349	14	.960	32	15	9	1	5	31	22	.710	280	-2	+9	+1	+8	0	+8	+6	5	-1	1	1	6	12
		342	2951.0	908	44	.952	91	51	31	8	13	72	52	.722	744	-11	+7	+1	-3	-1	-4	-5	-3	-1	2	0	-2	-

Scout's Defensive Rating: -7 plays saved in 2013, -6 plays saved in 2014

After struggling at several positions in the Minnesota infield since his debut, Plouffe settled into the role of everyday third baseman in 2014. He has the quick reactions and strong arm that are necessary to play the hot corner. His strong arm was especially beneficial on balls down the line, which is where Plouffe made his biggest improvement last year. Overall, he finished the year 12th among third basemen with six Runs Saved.

There are only two potential negatives regarding his defense at third base. He did commit 14 errors (11th among third basemen) and 15 misplays in 2014. However, those were balanced by his 32 GFPs. The one other question is whether he will be healthy for Spring Training after surgery to repair a broken left forearm suffered late in the season. If a healthy Plouffe can repeat his 2014 at third base, he may finally have found a home.

Martin Prado

	BASIC								BUNTS			GDP			RANGE AND POSITIONING								RUNS SAVED					
Year	Team	G	Inn	TC	E	Pct	GFP	DM	Opp	Sac Hits	Bunt Hits	Opp	GDP	Pct	Outs Made	To His Right	Straight On	To His Left	GB	Air	Plays Saved	Bases Saved	R/P	Bunt	GDP	GFP/ DME	Total	Rank
2006	Atl	8	38.0	7	1	.857	0	1	1	0	1	-	-	-	6	-2	0	-1	-2	0	-2	-2	-2	-1	-	0	-3	-
2007	Atl	9	44.0	11	0	1.000	1	1	2	1	1	-	-	-	10	0	-1	+2	+1	0	+1	+1	1	0	-	0	1	-
2008	Atl	24	158.2	56	1	.982	9	7	3	1	1	-	-	-	52	0	+2	+2	+4	0	+4	+4	3	0	-	0	3	-
2009	Atl	41	266.0	81	2	.975	12	3	3	2	1	8	5	.625	72	+2	+1	+4	+8	0	+8	+8	6	0	0	0	6	-
2010	Atl	43	369.2	118	5	.958	15	8	5	2	1	8	8	1.000	89	-4	+7	+4	+8	+1	+9	+7	5	1	1	-1	6	-
2011	Atl	41	297.0	101	5	.950	9	5	8	4	2	10	6	.600	84	-1	+5	+2	+6	-2	+4	+4	3	1	0	1	5	-
2012	Atl	25	186.1	49	1	.980	6	2	3	1	1	4	4	1.000	37	+3	+1	-1	+3	-1	+2	+2	1	0	1	0	2	-
2013	Ari	113	881.0	268	6	.978	34	14	9	5	4	24	15	.625	222	0	+2	+2	+4	+1	+5	+2	1	-2	0	1	0	16
2014	2 tms	110	942.2	290	13	.955	36	17	9	6	3	16	12	.750	219	+3	+6	+4	+12	+2	+14	+14	11	-2	1	-2	8	9
		414	3183.2	981	34	.965	122	58	43	22	15	70	50	.714	791	+1	+23	+18	+44	+1	+45	+40	29	-3	3	-1	28	-

Scout's Defensive Rating: 9 plays saved in 2013, 1 plays saved in 2014

Over the past several seasons, Martin Prado has proven to be one of the most versatile defensive players in baseball. After spending time at nearly every position on the field, Prado plays mostly third base–his primary position for most of his career. Unlike many utility players that feature varying tools at different positions, his steady hands and ability to read the ball off the bat quickly make him an adept fielder at every position. Not the fastest or most athletic player, he instead relies on his recognition skills to quickly dissect the play, react within his own abilities, and make the smart play. He transfers quickly from glove to hand, which helps an average to slightly below average throwing arm. However, he can always be counted on for an accurate throw whether stationary or on the run, ranking in the top ten in Infielder Good Throw Rate (93.4 percent). Not one to regularly appear on highlight reels making the spectacular play, Prado's steady-handed approach makes him an above average defender at the hot corner. But third base was just one position for Prado. Logging innings at second base, left field, and right field during the 2014 season, he was able to show the ability to play at least capable defense at each position. On the wrong side of 30, he'll have to rely on his instincts if he wants to remain a versatile defender, otherwise Prado will see his overall value diminish as he is relegated to playing only third base or left field.

Third Basemen

Aramis Ramirez

Year	Team	G	Inn	TC	E	Pct	GFP	DM	Opp	Sac Hits	Bunt Hits	Opp	GDP	Pct	Outs Made	To His Right	Straight On	To His Left	GB	Air	Plays Saved	Bases Saved	R/P	Bunt	GDP	GFP/DME	Total	Rank
2003	2 tms	159	1397.2	466	33	.929	-	-	18	10	5	-	-	-	377	+1	-1	-4	-4	-3	-7	-4	-3	1	-	-	-2	24
2004	ChC	144	1245.1	323	10	.969	36	29	17	9	4	-	-	-	272	+2	-9	-3	-10	-1	-11	-8	-6	1	-	1	-4	22
2005	ChC	119	1020.1	304	16	.947	26	23	13	10	3	-	-	-	257	-2	0	+3	+1	0	+1	0	0	0	-	-1	-1	22
2006	ChC	156	1353.0	375	13	.965	28	39	16	12	3	-	-	-	321	-5	+3	-5	-7	0	-7	-6	-5	0	-	-2	-7	27
2007	ChC	126	1091.1	358	10	.972	41	28	16	9	3	-	-	-	316	+4	+8	+4	+16	-2	+14	+15	11	1	-	-1	11	6
2008	ChC	147	1282.2	326	18	.945	39	21	15	8	4	-	-	-	279	-8	-2	-1	-11	-1	-12	-12	-9	1	-	-1	-9	31
2009	ChC	79	683.2	192	10	.948	20	17	15	7	3	20	10	.500	152	-3	-4	-1	-8	+1	-7	-8	-6	1	0	0	-5	22
2010	ChC	118	1003.1	262	16	.939	26	26	19	8	8	20	7	.350	203	-5	-10	0	-15	+2	-13	-13	-10	-2	-1	-2	-15	34
2011	ChC	145	1241.1	298	14	.953	38	34	21	11	5	24	12	.500	247	-7	-13	-4	-24	+3	-21	-22	-16	2	-1	-2	-17	34
2012	Mil	143	1242.1	300	7	.977	36	18	21	10	6	20	9	.450	228	+9	-3	-1	+5	-1	+4	+4	4	2	-1	-1	4	10
2013	Mil	80	657.0	155	7	.955	12	12	14	4	5	11	5	.455	99	-2	-2	-7	-11	-1	-12	-12	-9	-1	-1	-1	-12	32
2014	Mil	126	1077.0	268	10	.963	29	15	13	2	6	17	7	.412	197	-1	0	-2	-4	0	-4	-3	-2	-1	-1	-1	-5	26
		1542	13295.0	3627	164	.955	331	262	198	100	55	112	50	.446	2948	-17	-33	-21	-72	-3	-75	-69	-51	5	-5	-11	-62	-

Scout's Defensive Rating: -7 plays saved in 2013, -5 plays saved in 2014

Ramirez's biggest issues stem from his terrible arm accuracy and his inability to get his body in front of the ball, both of which he has struggled with his entire career. While many of his failures have come on bunt grounders or softly hit balls, some have also come on routine plays in which he just didn't get his glove down or tried fielding barehanded. Even though a number of plays may require a barehand because of the batter's speed, Ramirez tends to do this more than necessary. Most of the errors he has committed in his career have come from bad throws, which is a major part of why he has only been on the positive side of Defensive Runs Saved twice in his career. His throwing issues also rear their head when Ramirez feeds the pivot man on double plays. There's no sugar coating Ramirez's defense at this stage of his career.

Anthony Rendon

Year	Team	G	Inn	TC	E	Pct	GFP	DM	Opp	Sac Hits	Bunt Hits	Opp	GDP	Pct	Outs Made	To His Right	Straight On	To His Left	GB	Air	Plays Saved	Bases Saved	R/P	Bunt	GDP	GFP/DME	Total	Rank
2013	Was	15	98.0	38	5	.868	4	2	5	3	0	2	2	1.000	24	-3	-2	-1	-6	0	-6	-7	-5	1	0	-1	-5	
2014	Was	134	1148.2	356	15	.958	42	15	27	11	3	33	25	.758	255	+3	+1	-2	+2	+1	+3	+3	3	6	2	1	12	6
		149	1246.2	394	20	.949	46	17	32	14	3	35	27	.771	279	0	-1	-3	-4	+1	-3	-4	-2	7	2	0	7	-

Scout's Defensive Rating: -2 plays saved in 2013, 8 plays saved in 2014

Anthony Rendon began the season as the starting second baseman for the Nationals, but an injury to Ryan Zimmerman opened up a move to third base, and it doesn't appear that Rendon has any intention of moving off third for years to come. Rendon's reaction time and first step are excellent, which allows him to make numerous highlight-reel diving plays. Although his lateral movement and range might not be ideal at second, it is above average at third base. Rendon possesses a strong arm and has a quick release. The area where Rendon has most excelled is charging balls and in bunt defense. Rendon charges aggressively and makes strong accurate throws on the move. Only Manny Machado had as many as two Bunt Runs Saved compared to Rendon's six. Overall, Rendon saved 12 runs at third base and four more in his limited time at second, marking an improvement at both positions from 2013 when he struggled to avoid misplays and errors. Rendon appears ready to take the leap into the upper echelon of third basemen, and while his bat may get more of the credit, his defensive prowess could have him competing for Fielding Bible Awards in the years ahead.

Mark Reynolds

Year	Team	G	Inn	TC	E	Pct	GFP	DM	Opp	Sac Hits	Bunt Hits	Opp	GDP	Pct	Outs Made	To His Right	Straight On	To His Left	GB	Air	Plays Saved	Bases Saved	R/P	Bunt	GDP	GFP/DME	Total	Rank
2007	Ari	104	842.1	223	11	.951	29	18	11	7	2	-	-	-	188	-6	-5	+3	-9	-1	-10	-8	-6	2	-	-	-3	25
2008	Ari	150	1288.1	356	34	.904	46	33	16	9	5	-	-	-	293	-4	-6	-3	-13	0	-13	-11	-8	-2	-	-1	-11	33
2009	Ari	130	1125.2	347	19	.945	55	33	20	8	6	35	23	.657	294	0	-10	+4	-6	-1	-7	-6	-5	0	0	0	-5	21
2010	Ari	142	1214.0	369	18	.951	56	20	18	12	4	31	17	.548	293	-3	0	-2	-5	+3	-2	-3	-4	0	-1	-1	-4	19
2011	Bal	114	984.1	253	26	.897	29	31	12	5	7	25	16	.640	197	-7	-13	-1	-21	-1	-22	-23	-17	-3	1	-1	-20	35
2012	Bal	15	142.0	40	6	.850	3	7	2	1	1	4	2	.500	28	-5	0	-3	-7	-1	-8	-8	-6	0	0	-1	-7	
2013	2 tms	54	409.2	100	7	.930	13	11	10	4	5	6	6	1.000	62	-1	-1	-1	-4	-2	-6	-5	-4	-2	0	0	-6	25
2014	Mil	42	273.1	83	3	.964	13	4	4	2	1	13	6	.462	64	+4	+1	+1	+6	0	+6	+6	5	0	-1	0	4	
		751	6279.2	1771	124	.930	244	157	93	48	31	114	70	.614	1419	-22	-34	-2	-59	-3	-62	-58	-43	-5	-1	-3	-52	-

Scout's Defensive Rating: -4 plays saved in 2013, 5 plays saved in 2014

Third Basemen

Pablo Sandoval

Year Team	BASIC							BUNTS			GDP			RANGE AND POSITIONING								RUNS SAVED					
	G	Inn	TC	E	Pct	GFP	DM	Opp	Sac Hits	Bunt Hits	Opp	GDP	Pct	Outs Made	To His Right	Straight On	To His Left	GB	Air	Plays Saved	Bases Saved	R/P	Bunt	GDP	GFP/ DME	Total	Rank
2008 SF	12	85.0	17	0	1.000	1	2	1	1	0	-	-	-	16	+2	+1	-1	+2	-1	+1	+1	1	0	-	0	1	-
2009 SF	120	1028.0	276	11	.960	31	17	22	13	5	24	10	.417	233	0	-7	-5	-12	-1	-13	-13	-10	1	-1	-1	-11	31
2010 SF	143	1224.2	334	13	.961	44	17	7	3	3	33	20	.606	271	+4	-5	-2	-3	-1	-4	-4	-3	0	1	2	0	17
2011 SF	106	904.2	295	10	.966	42	17	8	5	0	24	11	.458	245	+11	+8	+2	+21	-1	+20	+20	15	1	0	-2	14	2
2012 SF	102	842.0	283	13	.954	36	23	17	3	9	24	10	.417	225	+2	+1	+2	+5	0	+5	+4	3	-3	-1	-4	-5	27
2013 SF	137	1152.0	301	18	.940	53	21	15	10	3	18	11	.611	227	0	-6	+1	-5	0	-5	-4	-3	-2	0	0	-5	23
2014 SF	151	1265.2	382	11	.971	60	19	17	8	9	35	22	.629	288	-2	+7	0	+5	0	+5	+6	5	-1	0	0	4	15
	771	6502.0	1888	76	.960	267	116	87	43	29	158	84	.532	1505	+17	-1	-3	+13	-4	+9	+10	8	-4	-1	-5	-2	-

Scout's Defensive Rating: 2 plays saved in 2013, 12 plays saved in 2014

It's easy to question the athleticism of Pablo Sandoval at first glance because of his large frame, but beneath the 5'11", 245 pound third baseman's thick exterior is an agile athlete. Known to many as "Kung Fu Panda", Sandoval takes on this persona in the field with his quick reaction speed and ability to be nimble while being bigger than most at the position. Sandoval possesses surprisingly good range, specifically to his glove side, where he is constantly diving for anything near him. His quick hands and willingness to lay out helped him notch 60 Good Fielding Plays in 2014, the third-highest at the position. However, Sandoval's defensive performance has historically fluctuated with his weight. When Sandoval shows up to Spring Training trim and fit, he's turned in above average defensive seasons, confirmed both visually and with the metrics. Now sitting on a hefty long-term contract, it will be up to Sandoval to keep in shape and prolong his tenure at third base.

Carlos Santana

Year Team	BASIC							BUNTS			GDP			RANGE AND POSITIONING								RUNS SAVED					
	G	Inn	TC	E	Pct	GFP	DM	Opp	Sac Hits	Bunt Hits	Opp	GDP	Pct	Outs Made	To His Right	Straight On	To His Left	GB	Air	Plays Saved	Bases Saved	R/P	Bunt	GDP	GFP/ DME	Total	Rank
2014 Cle	26	225.2	66	6	.909	11	7	4	2	0	3	1	.333	40	-6	-1	-1	-8	0	-8	-8	-6	1	0	0	-5	-

Scout's Defensive Rating: -5 plays saved in 2014

Carlos Santana's Scouting Report can be found on page 186.

Kyle Seager

Year Team	BASIC							BUNTS			GDP			RANGE AND POSITIONING								RUNS SAVED					
	G	Inn	TC	E	Pct	GFP	DM	Opp	Sac Hits	Bunt Hits	Opp	GDP	Pct	Outs Made	To His Right	Straight On	To His Left	GB	Air	Plays Saved	Bases Saved	R/P	Bunt	GDP	GFP/ DME	Total	Rank
2011 Sea	42	335.2	120	4	.967	10	6	5	2	2	8	2	.250	103	0	-3	+2	0	+2	+2	+3	2	0	0	0	2	-
2012 Sea	138	1208.2	338	13	.962	36	21	16	6	8	24	15	.625	270	+6	-11	-3	-8	-1	-9	-6	-4	-2	0	-1	-7	30
2013 Sea	160	1425.0	417	15	.964	46	24	18	5	7	41	28	.683	332	+1	-12	-1	-12	0	-12	-13	-10	1	1	0	-8	30
2014 Sea	157	1402.0	421	8	.981	44	28	11	4	2	43	29	.674	327	+12	-6	+7	+13	-1	+12	+13	10	0	1	-1	10	7
	497	4371.1	1296	40	.969	136	79	50	17	19	116	74	.638	1032	+19	-32	+5	-7	0	-7	-3	-2	-1	2	-2	-3	-

Scout's Defensive Rating: -7 plays saved in 2013, 10 plays saved in 2014

Early in his career, Seager played both shortstop and second base, but found his comfort zone at third base. Exceptional reaction time combined with quick speed and a strong and accurate arm enabled him to make more plays to his right compared to other third basemen. Seager continually has improved defensively in each year of his career. Despite winning his first Gold Glove in 2014, he finished the season in seventh place in Runs Saved at third base behind newly crowned Fielding Bible Award winner and fellow American Leaguer Josh Donaldson. For a more detailed breakdown of Seager's defense, please see the comparison to Donaldson on page 87.

Marcus Semien

Year Team	BASIC							BUNTS			GDP			RANGE AND POSITIONING								RUNS SAVED					
	G	Inn	TC	E	Pct	GFP	DM	Opp	Sac Hits	Bunt Hits	Opp	GDP	Pct	Outs Made	To His Right	Straight On	To His Left	GB	Air	Plays Saved	Bases Saved	R/P	Bunt	GDP	GFP/ DME	Total	Rank
2013 CWS	17	121.2	38	3	.921	4	1	2	1	1	2	2	1.000	30	+1	+2	-1	+2	+1	+3	+3	2	0	0	0	2	-
2014 CWS	33	279.1	96	10	.896	10	6	1	0	0	8	5	.625	65	0	-1	-1	-2	-1	-3	-3	-2	0	0	-1	-3	-
	50	401.0	134	13	.903	14	7	3	1	1	10	7	.700	95	+1	+1	-2	0	0	0	0	0	0	0	-1	-1	-

Scout's Defensive Rating: -2 plays saved in 2013, -7 plays saved in 2014

Third Basemen

Yangervis Solarte

	BASIC							BUNTS			GDP			RANGE AND POSITIONING								RUNS SAVED					
									Sac	Bunt				Outs	To His	Straight	To His			Plays	Bases				GFP/		
Year	Team	G	Inn	TC	E	Pct	GFP	DM	Opp	Hits	Hits	Opp	GDP	Pct	Made	Right	On	Left	GB	Air	Saved	Saved	R/P	Bunt	GDP	DME	Total	Rank
2014	2 tms	111	877.2	228	12	.947	31	24	11	7	2	22	14	.636	152	-1	+1	0	+1	-2	-1	-1	0	-1	0	-1	-2	19

Scout's Defensive Rating: -1 plays saved in 2014

A veteran of eight minor league seasons, Solarte saw time at four positions, but he played the majority of his innings at third base. Solarte showed some solid instincts at the hot corner but didn't necessarily stand out at any one aspect. He made his fair share of flashy plays at third base, but he also fumbled more than his fair share of easier plays. His 24 Defensive Misplays tied for fourth-most at the position despite playing less than 900 innings there. His position flexibility will likely earn him more opportunities. If he can find a way to cut down on the mistakes, he has the potential to be an average fielder at multiple positions.

Justin Turner

	BASIC							BUNTS			GDP			RANGE AND POSITIONING								RUNS SAVED					
									Sac	Bunt				Outs	To His	Straight	To His			Plays	Bases				GFP/		
Year	Team	G	Inn	TC	E	Pct	GFP	DM	Opp	Hits	Hits	Opp	GDP	Pct	Made	Right	On	Left	GB	Air	Saved	Saved	R/P	Bunt	GDP	DME	Total	Rank
2009	Bal	7	34.0	10	0	1.000	0	1				2	1	.500	10	0	+1	+1	+2	0	+2	+2	2		0	0	2	-
2010	NYM	1	2.0	2	0	1.000	0	0				1	1	1.000	2	0	-1	0	-1	0	-1	-1	-1		0	0	-1	-
2011	NYM	36	277.2	79	4	.949	8	8	5	2	2	5	3	.600	60	-1	+3	-3	-1	+1	0	-1	0	0	0	0	0	-
2012	NYM	11	57.2	13	0	1.000	4	1	1	0	1	1	1	1.000	12	0	0	+1	0	+1	0	+1	0	-1	0	0	-1	-
2013	NYM	23	127.1	31	1	.968	3	3	2	1	0	4	1	.250	24	-2	+1	-1	-1	0	-1	-1	-1	1	0	0	0	-
2014	LAD	59	406.0	127	5	.961	15	5	6	2	3	13	8	.615	102	+5	+3	+1	+8	-1	+7	+7	5	0	0	1	6	12
		137	904.2	262	10	.962	30	18	14	5	6	26	15	.577	210	+2	+7	-1	+8	0	+8	+6	5	0	0	1	6	

Scout's Defensive Rating: -1 plays saved in 2013, 2 plays saved in 2014

Turner spent time at every position in the infield in 2014, making his greatest contributions at third base. Turner is 30 years old and, at 210 pounds, you would expect his speed and range to be worse than it is. Turner's best asset is his arm, which is the main reason he fits best at third base. Although his range is good for his size, he lacks the speed for shortstop and has struggled turning double plays from either middle infield position over his career. Though he can hold down the hot corner and has experience around the infield, it's best to rely on him only in emergencies.

Juan Uribe

	BASIC							BUNTS			GDP			RANGE AND POSITIONING								RUNS SAVED					
									Sac	Bunt				Outs	To His	Straight	To His			Plays	Bases				GFP/		
Year	Team	G	Inn	TC	E	Pct	GFP	DM	Opp	Hits	Hits	Opp	GDP	Pct	Made	Right	On	Left	GB	Air	Saved	Saved	R/P	Bunt	GDP	DME	Total	Rank
2004	CWS	27	181.1	57	2	.965	3	0	3	1	2	-	-		48	0	+3	+1	+3	0	+3	+3	2	-1	-	1	2	-
2008	CWS	57	460.1	173	7	.960	18	14	8	4	4	-	-		152	+6	-7	-2	-3	0	-3	-3	-2	-1	-	-1	-4	-
2009	SF	44	323.1	99	4	.960	13	5	9	6	2	9	7	.778	80	+1	-1	0	0	0	0	+1	1	0	1	0	2	-
2010	SF	26	192.2	69	3	.957	8	4	5	4	0	3	1	.333	53	0	+1	0	0	0	0	0	1	-1	0	0	0	-
2011	LAD	59	462.2	136	3	.978	23	6	8	6	1	8	2	.250	111	+3	+3	0	+6	+1	+7	+8	5	1	0	-1	5	8
2012	LAD	46	357.0	109	4	.963	10	8	7	3	2	12	4	.333	90	+1	+4	+1	+6	0	+6	+6	5	0	-1	0	4	-
2013	LAD	123	900.1	297	5	.983	38	14	11	9	1	37	17	.459	260	+11	+10	+2	+24	+1	+25	+24	18	0	-1	-2	15	3
2014	LAD	102	874.1	281	6	.979	25	16	8	4	2	29	20	.690	233	+8	+9	+2	+20	+3	+23	+22	17	1	1	-2	17	2
		484	3752.0	1221	34	.972	138	67	59	37	14	98	51	.520	1027	+30	+22	+4	+56	+5	+61	+61	47	-1	0	-5	41	

Scout's Defensive Rating: 14 plays saved in 2013, 6 plays saved in 2014

Juan Uribe is one of the most unorthodox players in Major League Baseball. His unique style of play in some ways overshadows his abilities on the field. Despite battling injuries, Uribe has quietly put together back-to-back elite level defensive seasons. Simply put, Uribe does a great job of turning batted balls into outs. Dating back to his shortstop days, Uribe has always had good reflexes and a quick first step, but in recent seasons Uribe has improved his fitness, which has benefited his overall range greatly. Uribe is especially proficient at going to his backhand and making a strong throw across the diamond. Uribe's greatest asset is his arm. Not only does he have plus arm strength, but he is arguably the most accurate throwing infielder in baseball. He made only one throwing error in 2014 and led all third basemen in Good Throw Rate. After years of playing various positions around the diamond, Uribe has had a defensive resurgence late in his career at third base. If he can stay healthy, he should have a couple more seasons of outstanding defense left in him.

Third Basemen

Luis Valbuena

	BASIC							BUNTS			GDP			RANGE AND POSITIONING								RUNS SAVED					
Year	Team	G	Inn	TC	E	Pct	GFP	DM	Opp	Sac Hits	Bunt Hits	Opp	GDP	Pct	Outs Made	To His Right	Straight On	To His Left	GB	Air	Plays Saved	Bases Saved	R/P	Bunt	GDP	GFP/ DME	Total	Rank
2009	Cle	1	2.0	1	0	1.000	0	0						-	1	0	0	0	0			0	0		0	0	0	-
2010	Cle	9	66.2	17	2	.882	1	1						-	12	+1	-1	-1	-2	0	-2	-1	-1		0	-1	-2	-
2012	ChC	82	638.1	189	7	.963	20	11	6	3	1	19	13	.684	146	+5	-2	0	+3	+2	+5	+6	4	1	1	-1	5	9
2013	ChC	94	760.2	213	7	.967	27	11	13	10	1	13	10	.769	162	+2	0	+1	+4	+1	+5	+5	4	2	0	0	6	7
2014	ChC	124	971.0	289	9	.969	34	18	16	7	5	25	12	.480	210	-1	-2	-7	-9	-2	-11	-11	-8	-1	-1	0	-10	31
		310	2438.2	709	25	.965	82	41	35	20	7	57	35	.614	531	+7	-5	-7	-4	+1	-3	-1	-1	2	0	-2	-1	-

Scout's Defensive Rating: 5 plays saved in 2013, 2 plays saved in 2014

For most of his career, Luis Valbuena has been an average third baseman. His 2014 season, however, was a bit of a train wreck. Valbuena plays pretty deep at third base, leaving him long and difficult throws across the diamond. Of the nine errors he had this season, five of them were due to poor throws, and his Good Throw Rate to first base was .906, ranking 20th among the 29 third basemen who made at least 100 throws.

Danny Valencia

	BASIC							BUNTS			GDP			RANGE AND POSITIONING								RUNS SAVED					
Year	Team	G	Inn	TC	E	Pct	GFP	DM	Opp	Sac Hits	Bunt Hits	Opp	GDP	Pct	Outs Made	To His Right	Straight On	To His Left	GB	Air	Plays Saved	Bases Saved	R/P	Bunt	GDP	GFP/ DME	Total	Rank
2010	Min	81	709.1	223	6	.973	23	11	10	7	3	19	12	.632	193	+6	-1	+1	+5	0	+5	+4	3	0	0	0	3	14
2011	Min	147	1280.2	351	18	.949	28	26	20	8	10	34	20	.588	300	-2	-7	-5	-14	0	-14	-14	-11	-1	0	-1	-13	33
2012	2 tms	44	357.0	113	4	.965	11	4	7	4	3	11	8	.727	95	-1	0	0	-1	0	-1	-1	0	-1	1	-1	-1	-
2013	Bal	6	29.0	4	0	1.000	0	1				1	1	1.000	3	-1	0	0	0	0	0	0	0	0	0	0	0	-
2014	2 tms	66	489.1	152	4	.974	8	5	3	1	2	15	8	.533	119	-1	+1	0	-1	+1	0	-1	-1	-1	0	0	-2	20
		344	2865.1	843	32	.962	70	47	40	20	18	80	49	.613	710	+1	-7	-4	-11	+1	-10	-12	-9	-3	1	-2	-13	-

Scout's Defensive Rating: -1 plays saved in 2013, 0 plays saved in 2014

David Wright

	BASIC							BUNTS			GDP			RANGE AND POSITIONING								RUNS SAVED					
Year	Team	G	Inn	TC	E	Pct	GFP	DM	Opp	Sac Hits	Bunt Hits	Opp	GDP	Pct	Outs Made	To His Right	Straight On	To His Left	GB	Air	Plays Saved	Bases Saved	R/P	Bunt	GDP	GFP/ DME	Total	Rank
2004	NYM	69	603.2	189	11	.942	11	10	7	1	3	-	-	-	155	-2	+14	-2	+10	-3	+7	+6	5	0	-	-1	4	13
2005	NYM	160	1404.1	462	24	.948	56	38	24	11	7	-	-	-	396	-14	+2	0	-12	-2	-14	-17	-13	2	-	0	-11	32
2006	NYM	153	1365.1	414	19	.954	38	34	18	13	2	-	-	-	339	-10	-6	+9	-8	-2	-10	-11	-8	2	-	-2	-8	28
2007	NYM	159	1418.1	452	21	.954	56	26	25	13	6	-	-	-	384	-11	+9	+18	+16	0	+16	+13	10	1	-	1	12	5
2008	NYM	159	1433.1	416	16	.962	78	24	13	7	1	-	-	-	356	-2	+6	+1	+5	-2	+3	+2	2	1	-	2	5	12
2009	NYM	142	1232.0	361	18	.950	44	25	19	10	7	28	14	.500	302	-6	0	-1	-8	-1	-9	-15	-11	-1	-1	-1	-14	33
2010	NYM	155	1373.0	451	20	.956	76	28	17	7	5	43	23	.535	360	-11	0	-2	-13	-2	-15	-17	-13	0	-1	1	-13	32
2011	NYM	101	893.2	267	19	.929	31	13	13	5	4	15	6	.400	200	-4	-3	+8	+2	-4	-2	-3	-2	-1	-1	-1	-5	22
2012	NYM	155	1348.1	384	10	.974	61	22	23	10	7	26	14	.538	315	-3	+9	+12	+18	+1	+19	+19	14	0	0	2	16	2
2013	NYM	111	1003.1	330	9	.973	48	24	14	9	3	23	12	.522	264	-5	+10	+6	+11	-1	+10	+9	7	1	0	-3	5	8
2014	NYM	133	1190.0	329	15	.954	53	18	12	4	2	30	15	.500	250	-6	+14	+12	+19	+1	+20	+17	13	1	-1	0	13	5
		1497	13265.1	4055	182	.955	552	262	185	90	47	165	84	.509	3321	-74	+55	+61	+40	-15	+25	+3	4	6	-4	-2	4	-

Scout's Defensive Rating: 10 plays saved in 2013, 6 plays saved in 2014

David Wright has had a bit of resurgence in recent seasons, returning to the top of defensive leader boards after three subpar seasons from 2009-11. The main reason for this bounce back is reduced Defensive Misplays and Errors. Wright excels on reflex plays and in moving towards his left. There are a couple of reasons for this difference. First, he routinely positions himself well off the line and makes many more plays in front of the shortstop than down the line. Second, he doesn't have the prototypical third baseman's arm and can struggle with longer throws. He also likes to throw with a low arm angle, which can cause the ball to sink as it approaches first base on longer throws. Wright does throw pretty well on the move. Wright is one of the best in baseball in charging bunts and slow rollers and making a barehanded play. The fact that Wright's preferred arm slot is similar to that required to throw on the move makes it a comfortable play for him. Wright might never be among the elite defensive third basemen in the league, but he should continue to be an above average option at the hot corner for the Mets for the foreseeable future.

Shortstops Register and Scouting Reports

Year	Fielding Bible Award Winner	Runner Up	Third Place
2006	Adam Everett	Omar Vizquel	Jimmy Rollins
2007	Troy Tulowitzki	Adam Everett	John McDonald
2008	Jimmy Rollins	J.J. Hardy	Yunel Escobar
2009	Jack Wilson	Troy Tulowitzki	Elvis Andrus
2010	Troy Tulowitzki	Brendan Ryan	Alexei Ramirez
2011	Troy Tulowitzki	Brendan Ryan	Alex Gonzalez
2012	Brendan Ryan	J.J. Hardy	Elvis Andrus
2013	Andrelton Simmons	Elvis Andrus	Pedro Florimon
2014	Andrelton Simmons	Zack Cozart	J.J. Hardy

Shortstops

Alexi Amarista

Year	Team	G	Inn	TC	E	Pct	GFP	DM	Opps	GDP	Pct	Outs Made	To His Right	Straight On	To His Left	GB	Air	Plays Saved	R/P	GDP	GFP/DME	Total	Rank
2011	LAA	1	3.0	0	0	-	0	0	0	0	-	0						0		0		0	-
2012	SD	12	73.0	37	1	.973	7	4	11	7	.636	30	0	0	0	0	0	0	0	0	0	0	-
2013	SD	13	83.2	38	1	.974	7	5	9	6	.667	28	-2	-1	0	-3	0	-3	-2	0	0	-2	-
2014	SD	73	626.0	303	6	.980	36	8	62	32	.516	200	+9	-1	-2	+7	+3	+10	7	-2	2	7	7
		99	785.2	378	8	.979	50	17	82	45	.549	258	+7	-2	-2	+4	+3	+7	5	-2	2	5	-

Scout's Defensive Rating: 0 plays saved in 2013, 9 plays saved in 2014

Alexi Amarista is one of the premier defensive utility players in baseball. In 2014 he spent time at five different positions: shortstop, third base, second base, left field, and center field, posting a positive Defensive Runs Saved total at four of these positions. He does his best work on the infield, using his speed and instincts to cover ground in both directions, especially to his right. Playing both outfield and infield has really helped fine tune all his defensive skills, sharpening his ability to track down popups in the infield and charge groundballs to the outfield. Amarista is one of the few players who can bring solid defensive value to multiple positions on the field.

Elvis Andrus

Year	Team	G	Inn	TC	E	Pct	GFP	DM	Opps	GDP	Pct	Outs Made	To His Right	Straight On	To His Left	GB	Air	Plays Saved	R/P	GDP	GFP/DME	Total	Rank
2009	Tex	145	1238.0	690	22	.968	60	25	132	94	.712	472	+2	+4	+6	+12	+3	+15	11	2	2	15	3
2010	Tex	148	1291.1	659	16	.976	40	27	145	94	.648	436	-1	+2	-8	-8	+1	-7	-5	0	-3	-8	31
2011	Tex	147	1261.1	677	25	.963	54	15	148	109	.736	426	+12	+1	-12	+1	+4	+5	4	3	-1	6	11
2012	Tex	153	1333.0	663	16	.976	66	32	134	85	.634	443	+1	-3	+11	+9	+3	+12	9	1	-2	8	10
2013	Tex	146	1288.2	588	14	.976	65	25	153	104	.680	361	0	-1	+10	+9	+2	+11	8	2	1	11	4
2014	Tex	153	1309.1	626	18	.971	47	27	129	93	.721	377	-9	-1	-6	-16	0	-16	-12	1	-2	-13	33
		892	7721.2	3903	111	.972	332	151	841	579	.688	2515	+5	+2	+1	+7	+13	+20	15	9	-5	19	-

Scout's Defensive Rating: 6 plays saved in 2013, -4 plays saved in 2014

Elvis Andrus was somewhat of a mystery in the field in 2014. At times, the 6'0", 200-pound shortstop can demonstrate spectacular range, especially to his left; Andrus had a +21 on plays to his left in 2012 and 2013. In 2014, however, Andrus' range was poor in all directions, resulting in -16 Plays Made. Compare Andrus' Net GFP-DME of 2 in 2014 with his 26 and 18 in 2013 and 2012, respectively, and this looks like a simple one year drop off. Andrus' accuracy on throws explains part of the problem: among shortstops with 100 or more throws to first base in 2014, Andrus tied for 25th with a 93.5 percent Good Throw Rate while he ranked seventh in the statistic in 2013, at 95 percent.

Despite his inconsistencies, Andrus is 26 years old with a track record of great range, an outstanding arm and double play artistry. As recently as 2013, Andrus ranked fourth among all shortstops in Defensive Runs Saved with 11. While it is concerning that Andrus experiences such wide swings in defensive performance, one should consider his good to very good defensive performances from 2011 to 2013 and look to 2015 with the expectation that he will return to the top 10 among shortstops in Defensive Runs Saved.

Erick Aybar

Year	Team	G	Inn	TC	E	Pct	GFP	DM	Opps	GDP	Pct	Outs Made	To His Right	Straight On	To His Left	GB	Air	Plays Saved	R/P	GDP	GFP/DME	Total	Rank
2006	LAA	19	76.0	39	4	.897	4	0	8	6	.750	23	-3	0	+2	-1	0	-1	-1	0	0	-1	-
2007	LAA	20	79.0	41	3	.927	3	1	9	2	.222	31	-1	-1	+2	0	-1	-1	-1	-1	0	-2	-
2008	LAA	96	784.2	434	18	.959	55	17	101	60	.594	304	+6	+3	-6	+3	+5	+8	6	0	4	10	7
2009	LAA	136	1189.1	629	11	.983	60	25	145	99	.683	422	-4	+2	-2	-4	0	-4	-3	2	2	1	19
2010	LAA	135	1179.2	563	21	.963	44	36	105	64	.610	384	+6	-4	+5	+7	+3	+10	8	-2	-1	5	11
2011	LAA	142	1262.0	658	13	.980	56	30	154	107	.695	430	-4	-1	-2	-8	+1	-7	-5	2	2	-1	20
2012	LAA	139	1189.2	606	15	.975	71	26	121	81	.669	393	+7	+2	-15	-7	+5	-2	-1	1	3	3	15
2013	LAA	138	1203.0	561	15	.973	56	34	140	79	.564	350	-3	-8	0	-11	+4	-7	-5	-2	0	-7	29
2014	LAA	155	1365.0	563	10	.982	65	35	106	74	.698	367	+5	-9	-5	-9	+1	-8	-6	1	2	-3	21
		980	8328.1	4094	110	.973	414	204	889	572	.643	2704	+9	-16	-21	-30	+18	-12	-8	1	12	5	-

Scout's Defensive Rating: -7 plays saved in 2013, -3 plays saved in 2014

Shortstops

Aybar is an effective defender at shortstop, but despite his Gold Glove reputation he does not have the range to be considered among the elite in the majors at his position. Aybar lacks the arm strength to complete difficult plays even when he fields the ball cleanly while moving towards the hole. While his athleticism and versatility enable him to get to more ground balls than most shortstops, he often displays erratic footwork that reduces the velocity of his throws and slows down his ball transfer. He often displays poor judgment by making throws when it is clear that he has no play.

Overall, Aybar cost his team three runs during the 2014 season, ranking him 21st among shortstops. His flashiness ranked him in the top 10 in Good Fielding Plays at the position. Conversely, it also put him in the top 10 in Defensive Misplays and Errors among shortstops. To his credit, Aybar excels at reaching short liners heading into the outfield. His speed gives him the ability to track those balls down and make a play. Aybar should be considered an average defender at short until his skills deteriorate and require a move off the position.

Javier Baez

	BASIC							GDP			RANGE AND POSITIONING							RUNS SAVED				
Year	Team	G	Inn	TC	E	Pct	GFP	DM	Opps	GDP	Pct	Outs Made	To His Right	Straight On	To His Left	GB	Air	Plays Saved	R/P	GDP	GFP/ DME	Total	Rank
2014	ChC	30	255.0	139	5	.964	12	5	28	21	.750	82	0	-2	0	-3	-1	-4	-3	0	1	-2	-

Scout's Defensive Rating: 0 plays saved in 2014

Xander Bogaerts

	BASIC							GDP			RANGE AND POSITIONING							RUNS SAVED				
Year	Team	G	Inn	TC	E	Pct	GFP	DM	Opps	GDP	Pct	Outs Made	To His Right	Straight On	To His Left	GB	Air	Plays Saved	R/P	GDP	GFP/ DME	Total	Rank
2013	Bos	8	52.2	26	0	1.000	3	0	4	1	.250	22	+1	+2	+1	+3	-1	+2	2	0	0	2	-
2014	Bos	99	880.0	404	10	.975	32	19	98	53	.541	255	-14	+3	+3	-8	0	-8	-6	-3	0	-9	28
		107	932.2	430	10	.977	35	19	102	54	.529	277	-13	+5	+4	-5	-1	-6	-4	-3	0	-7	-

Scout's Defensive Rating: 2 plays saved in 2013, -7 plays saved in 2014

The 22-year-old mega-prospect was a full-timer for the Red Sox in 2014, earning nearly 900 innings at shortstop and another 300-plus at third base. The Aruban has plus arm strength to go along with average range, but his 6-foot-1, 210-pound frame may lose quickness as it fills in. He revealed a habit of rushing plays and pulling up too early on grounders, but overall shows a lot of promise to stick at short for his career. His arm, however, would allow more time at third, or perhaps even in right.

He did struggle early on at third, showing that aforementioned propensity to rush plays while at the hot corner. He ended up with ten errors apiece at the two positions, despite his time at shortstop more than doubling his time at third. His advanced metrics were ugly in his first full big league season, finishing 16 runs below average between third and short, but he is young and has shown the ability to learn quickly and make adjustments. It will be a race between Bogaerts' improving skills and his growing body to ultimately decide his defensive future.

Asdrubal Cabrera

	BASIC							GDP			RANGE AND POSITIONING							RUNS SAVED				
Year	Team	G	Inn	TC	E	Pct	GFP	DM	Opps	GDP	Pct	Outs Made	To His Right	Straight On	To His Left	GB	Air	Plays Saved	R/P	GDP	GFP/ DME	Total	Rank
2007	Cle	7	42.0	29	0	1.000	4	1	9	5	.556	23	0	+1	+1	+2	0	+2	2	0	0	2	-
2008	Cle	20	154.2	102	5	.951	10	6	22	16	.727	68	+1	-3	+1	-1	+2	+1	1	1	0	2	-
2009	Cle	100	870.0	440	9	.980	44	17	109	79	.725	326	-5	+1	-4	-7	+5	-2	-2	2	0	0	22
2010	Cle	95	825.1	431	12	.972	41	15	104	79	.760	256	+3	-2	-8	-8	-3	-11	-8	1	3	-4	24
2011	Cle	151	1326.2	617	15	.976	62	25	117	73	.624	395	-1	-4	+1	-4	+2	-2	-1	-1	2	0	16
2012	Cle	136	1161.1	651	19	.971	49	29	136	93	.684	370	-9	+1	-1	-9	+2	-7	-6	2	-1	-5	24
2013	Cle	129	1099.2	503	9	.982	56	24	109	65	.596	299	-13	-5	-1	-18	-3	-21	-16	0	0	-16	33
2014	2 tms	93	823.2	384	14	.964	23	11	81	54	.667	225	-9	-1	+1	-10	+4	-6	-5	-1	-1	-7	26
		731	6303.1	3157	83	.974	289	128	687	464	.675	1962	-33	-12	-10	-55	+9	-46	-35	4	3	-28	-

Scout's Defensive Rating: 0 plays saved in 2013, -4 plays saved in 2014

After spending over seven seasons as the Indians shortstop, Cabrera was traded to the Washington Nationals where he played both shortstop and second base. Unfortunately for the 6'0", 205 pound middle infielder, he had a rough go at both positions. Cabrera lacks the range to be a solid everyday shortstop and looks like he may fall into a utility role.

Shortstops

Although Cabrera has had some incredible highlight reel plays over his career, those days are largely over. Cabrera performed poorly according to BIS Video Scouts in 2014, finishing with a rating of four plays below average. While quickness and range are not on his side, his throwing accuracy is average at best.

Everth Cabrera

		BASIC							GDP			RANGE AND POSITIONING							RUNS SAVED				
Year	Team	G	Inn	TC	E	Pct	GFP	DM	Opps	GDP	Pct	Outs Made	To His Right	Straight On	To His Left	GB	Air	Plays Saved	R/P	GDP	GFP/ DME	Total	Rank
2009	SD	102	896.2	467	23	.951	48	23	92	63	.685	338	+13	-10	-13	-10	0	-10	-8	0	0	-8	30
2010	SD	61	456.0	207	7	.966	15	7	38	27	.711	145	+2	+2	-5	-2	+3	+1	0	1	0	1	-
2011	SD	2	17.0	9	0	1.000	1	2	6	0	.000	5	0	-1	0	-1	0	-1	-1	-1	0	-2	-
2012	SD	111	915.1	471	16	.966	42	28	69	32	.464	355	+6	-1	-6	-2	+2	0	0	-3	-1	-4	22
2013	SD	95	847.2	447	6	.987	56	22	99	60	.606	306	+5	0	-6	-1	-3	-4	-4	0	1	-3	24
2014	SD	90	804.0	393	13	.967	46	15	97	50	.515	256	+3	+3	0	+6	+4	+10	7	-4	0	3	12
		461	3936.2	1994	65	.967	208	97	401	232	.579	1405	+29	-7	-30	-10	+6	-4	-6	-7	0	-13	-

Scout's Defensive Rating: 3 plays saved in 2013, 12 plays saved in 2014

Despite spending much of his minor league career at second base, Cabrera was asked to fill the shortstop gap upon his promotion to the major leagues in 2009. Cabrera struggled in his first exposure to his new position, committing twenty-three errors in 102 games played. Cabrera has failed to remain on the field consistently, the result of being plagued with injuries in addition to his suspension following the Biogenesis scandal. When on the field Cabrera shows his skills and leaves many wondering just how high his ceiling could be if he could remain healthy throughout an entire season. Cabrera displays a natural feel for the shortstop position and often makes difficult plays appear simple. He anticipates balls off the bat exceptionally well, and, combined with his plus speed, possesses the ability to make a play on nearly every ball hit into his zone. Despite the injuries, Cabrera has settled in as a roughly average shortstop, but six years into his career we're wondering if ever be healthy enough to capitalize on his tools.

Starlin Castro

		BASIC							GDP			RANGE AND POSITIONING							RUNS SAVED				
Year	Team	G	Inn	TC	E	Pct	GFP	DM	Opps	GDP	Pct	Outs Made	To His Right	Straight On	To His Left	GB	Air	Plays Saved	R/P	GDP	GFP/ DME	Total	Rank
2010	ChC	123	1073.2	544	27	.950	45	40	122	77	.631	359	+3	-7	+7	+3	+3	+6	5	0	-8	-3	21
2011	ChC	158	1398.2	742	29	.961	69	56	139	78	.561	503	-7	-4	0	-11	+5	-6	-5	-2	-1	-8	29
2012	ChC	162	1402.2	758	27	.964	62	41	162	93	.574	497	+17	-10	+2	+9	+3	+12	9	-2	-4	3	14
2013	ChC	159	1418.0	676	22	.967	60	43	125	75	.600	423	+3	-7	-3	-7	+1	-6	-5	0	-3	-8	30
2014	ChC	133	1188.0	549	15	.973	41	38	94	71	.755	375	-11	+7	-2	-6	-1	-7	-6	2	-3	-7	27
		735	6481.0	3269	120	.963	277	218	642	394	.614	2157	+5	-21	+4	-12	+11	-1	-2	-2	-19	-23	-

Scout's Defensive Rating: -22 plays saved in 2013, -6 plays saved in 2014

Just looking at Starlin Castro, one might assume at least an average defensive shortstop, with good athleticism and a strong enough arm to play up the middle. However, Castro has largely underachieved defensively during his time as a professional. The physical tools are present, but often times it appears he becomes disinterested in the game, showing lapses in concentration that lead to misplays. Effort routinely is called into question, although it does seem to have improved over the years. Most damningly, Castro has made 25 percent more Defensive Misplays and Errors since 2010 than any other player in baseball, period (338 compared to Ian Desmond's 270).

As Castro struggled to convert routine plays, his Scout's Defensive Rating also reflected an inability to make more challenging plays as well. As the degree of difficulty went up, the likelihood relative to league average that the play would be made became increasingly unlikely. The lateral quickness is present, and so is an arm that featured a Good Throw Rate that sat in the middle of the pack among regular shortstops. The hand-eye coordination from ball, to glove, to throwing hand needs serious improvement if Castro is ever to be considered an average defender at the position, with an ultimate move to second base perhaps beneficial to both Castro and the Cubs.

Shortstops

Zack Cozart

	BASIC							GDP			RANGE AND POSITIONING							RUNS SAVED				
											Outs	To His	Straight	To His			Plays			GFP/		
Year	Team	G	Inn	TC	E	Pct	GFP	DM	Opps	GDP	Pct	Made	Right	On	Left	GB	Air	Saved	R/P	GDP	DME	Total	Rank
2011	Cin	11	77.1	63	0	1.000	5	1	11	7	.636	40	+2	+2	+1	+5	0	+5	4	0	0	4	-
2012	Cin	138	1163.2	567	14	.975	50	19	109	69	.633	394	-10	+5	+13	+9	+7	+16	12	0	0	12	8
2013	Cin	150	1308.0	622	14	.977	51	24	133	88	.662	392	-1	+4	+3	+5	+1	+6	5	-2	1	4	9
2014	Cin	147	1274.1	614	10	.984	54	18	113	67	.593	430	+1	+9	+12	+22	+5	+27	20	-1	0	19	2
		446	3823.1	1866	38	.980	160	62	366	231	.631	1256	-8	+20	+29	+41	+13	+54	41	-3	1	39	

Scout's Defensive Rating: -2 plays saved in 2013, 15 plays saved in 2014

While the Reds still wait for a more consistent bat out of Cozart, he continues to impress with his stellar defense, most evident in his range and strong arm. When moving to his left, he is among the best shortstops in the league in getting outs. In going to his right, his first step isn't as quick and, thus he must rely on his strong arm and quick release to have a better chance to get the outs. And while he can't make every play hit in his direction, he's aggressive in at least knocking the ball down to prevent runner advancement. Cozart was neck and neck with Andrelton Simmons for the most Defensive Runs Saved by a shortstop in 2014, ultimately finishing second. However, Cozart has quietly become Simmons' biggest challenger for the Fielding Bible Award for years to come.

Brandon Crawford

	BASIC							GDP			RANGE AND POSITIONING							RUNS SAVED				
											Outs	To His	Straight	To His			Plays			GFP/		
Year	Team	G	Inn	TC	E	Pct	GFP	DM	Opps	GDP	Pct	Made	Right	On	Left	GB	Air	Saved	R/P	GDP	DME	Total	Rank
2011	SF	65	507.1	248	7	.972	24	12	43	29	.674	181	-3	+3	+3	+3	0	+3	2	0	-1	1	15
2012	SF	139	1101.0	608	18	.970	65	36	115	75	.652	425	+1	+4	+7	+12	+1	+13	10	1	1	12	9
2013	SF	147	1226.0	588	15	.974	70	31	125	77	.616	417	0	-2	+6	+4	+1	+5	4	-1	-1	2	14
2014	SF	149	1273.0	635	21	.967	57	21	121	86	.711	428	-8	+7	+9	+10	-3	+7	5	3	0	8	6
		500	4107.1	2079	61	.971	216	100	404	267	.661	1451	-10	+12	+25	+29	-1	+28	21	3	-1	23	

Scout's Defensive Rating: -1 plays saved in 2013, 10 plays saved in 2014

Brandon Crawford is one of the ten best defensive shortstops in baseball. He excels at fielding balls in play of all speeds and difficulties. Crawford's defensive movements are effortless and fluid. Very simply, he looks good playing shortstop and possesses all of the defensive qualities scouts covet in a first division starting shortstop. Crawford's loudest tool is his arm, which really shines when he is forced to field balls deep in the 5.5 hole and when occupying the pivot position on double play attempts.

Crawford did accumulate the second-highest error total for shortstops in 2014 with 21, but is more a reflection of him having a chance to make plays that other shortstops simply would not. His already impressive defensive performance could progress even further with improved positioning. (Crawford and the Giants did make an improved effort in this regard in 2014.) The unheralded Crawford is one of the most underrated assets in the game based on his ability to play plus shortstop defense while performing at a slightly below league average level at the plate.

Ian Desmond

	BASIC							GDP			RANGE AND POSITIONING							RUNS SAVED				
											Outs	To His	Straight	To His			Plays			GFP/		
Year	Team	G	Inn	TC	E	Pct	GFP	DM	Opps	GDP	Pct	Made	Right	On	Left	GB	Air	Saved	R/P	GDP	DME	Total	Rank
2009	Was	17	136.1	84	4	.952	9	7	22	15	.682	50	-1	-1	-1	-3	+1	-2	-2	0	-1	-3	-
2010	Was	149	1208.0	637	34	.947	46	33	134	88	.657	408	+8	-1	-12	-4	+2	-2	-2	-1	-3	-6	29
2011	Was	152	1317.2	686	23	.966	48	35	140	84	.600	470	-13	+4	+1	-9	+7	-2	-2	-1	-1	-4	23
2012	Was	128	1139.1	492	15	.970	39	33	98	68	.694	337	-28	+8	+12	-8	-1	-9	-7	1	0	-6	27
2013	Was	158	1400.0	700	20	.971	67	29	133	95	.714	477	-22	+5	+10	-8	+6	-2	-2	1	-2	-3	22
2014	Was	154	1377.2	643	24	.963	41	24	126	84	.667	445	-5	+7	0	+1	+2	+3	2	1	-2	1	15
		758	6579.0	3242	120	.963	250	161	653	434	.665	2187	-61	+22	+10	-31	+17	-14	-13	1	-9	-21	

Scout's Defensive Rating: -3 plays saved in 2013, -5 plays saved in 2014

Desmond is one of the few active shortstops that brings a legitimate bat to the table, but even if he won't be contending for a Fielding Bible Award, he did take some steps forward defensively in 2014. Though he did lead the league in errors, he's come a long way in that department from the 34 errors of 2010 and has reduced his Defensive Misplays in four consecutive seasons now. Further, the Nationals were successful turning two-thirds (66.7 percent, compared to a league average of 63.8 percent) of double play opportunities involving Desmond, even with six different players getting time at second base over the course of the year. Ian Desmond may not ever get lauded for his glovework, but with his offensive profile, a slightly below average defender at shortstop will certainly play.

Stephen Drew

		BASIC							GDP			RANGE AND POSITIONING							RUNS SAVED				
Year	Team	G	Inn	TC	E	Pct	GFP	DM	Opps	GDP	Pct	Outs Made	To His Right	Straight On	To His Left	GB	Air	Plays Saved	R/P	GDP	GFP/ DME	Total	Rank
2006	Ari	56	480.1	228	5	.978	16	9	55	32	.582	161	+5	0	-5	0	+2	+2	2	0	0	2	18
2007	Ari	147	1283.1	638	17	.973	41	34	145	90	.621	434	+17	-10	-15	-7	+6	-1	-1	1	-1	-1	20
2008	Ari	151	1294.1	582	14	.976	40	23	128	78	.609	422	+6	-8	-7	-8	+3	-5	-4	1	1	-2	23
2009	Ari	132	1142.0	546	11	.980	45	14	103	69	.670	404	+14	-7	-2	+6	+4	+10	8	0	1	9	8
2010	Ari	147	1259.1	607	10	.984	35	13	120	83	.692	405	+7	+8	-11	+4	-8	-4	-3	2	1	0	16
2011	Ari	84	731.1	345	7	.980	38	11	71	46	.648	239	+1	0	-2	-1	+2	+1	1	1	1	3	12
2012	2 tms	75	658.2	282	8	.972	24	11	62	40	.645	191	+5	-1	-8	-5	-3	-8	-5	-1	-1	-7	28
2013	Bos	124	1093.1	516	8	.984	48	20	117	76	.650	302	+3	0	0	+3	-6	-3	-2	-1	1	-2	21
2014	2 tms	51	413.1	207	3	.986	17	7	54	40	.741	122	0	0	+2	+1	+2	+3	3	0	1	4	-
		967	8356.0	3951	83	.979	304	142	855	554	.648	2680	+58	-18	-48	-7	+2	-5	-1	3	4	6	

Scout's Defensive Rating: 1 plays saved in 2013, 5 plays saved in 2014

Alcides Escobar

		BASIC							GDP			RANGE AND POSITIONING							RUNS SAVED				
Year	Team	G	Inn	TC	E	Pct	GFP	DM	Opps	GDP	Pct	Outs Made	To His Right	Straight On	To His Left	GB	Air	Plays Saved	R/P	GDP	GFP/ DME	Total	Rank
2008	Mil	2	2.0	0	0	-	0	0	0			0	0	0	0	0	0	0				0	-
2009	Mil	37	300.0	159	6	.962	15	11	34	23	.676	112	-4	+2	0	-2	+2	0	0	-1	-1	-2	-
2010	Mil	138	1151.1	552	20	.964	31	19	96	66	.688	393	+6	-6	+4	+4	+4	+8	6	1	1	8	9
2011	KC	158	1387.1	745	15	.980	77	32	169	97	.574	485	+19	+5	-5	+18	-4	+14	11	-3	2	10	4
2012	KC	155	1379.2	669	19	.972	67	35	150	93	.620	424	+2	-7	-4	-9	+6	-3	-3	0	1	-2	20
2013	KC	158	1388.1	629	13	.979	71	27	147	92	.626	384	+10	-4	-1	+5	0	+5	4	1	-1	4	11
2014	KC	162	1433.2	669	16	.976	73	44	146	91	.623	417	+6	-10	0	-4	-1	-5	-4	-1	1	-4	22
		810	7042.1	3423	89	.974	334	168	742	462	.623	2215	+39	-20	-6	+12	+7	+19	14	-3	3	14	

Scout's Defensive Rating: 9 plays saved in 2013, 1 plays saved in 2014

Alcides Escobar is a feast or famine type of shortstop. He makes more highlight reel plays than any shortstop this side of Andrelton Simmons, but also misplays more easy plays than a fielder of his ability should. In 2014, Escobar had the third-most Good Fielding Plays among shortstops but also had the most Defensive Misplays at the position. Escobar has tremendous range, regularly making plays both deep in the hole and on the other side of second base. Conversely, Escobar will commonly bobble easier chances or hesitate too long to make throws, allowing runners to beat out routine grounders. Escobar possesses a plus-plus arm but struggles with accuracy. Escobar had the most misplays on bad throws in 2014, and was saved from having even more thanks to the scooping ability of Eric Hosmer at first. Escobar has the skill set and ceiling of a Fielding Bible Award winner, but he must first become steadier in the field and less prone to the valleys that go along with his exceptional peaks.

Eduardo Escobar

		BASIC							GDP			RANGE AND POSITIONING							RUNS SAVED				
Year	Team	G	Inn	TC	E	Pct	GFP	DM	Opps	GDP	Pct	Outs Made	To His Right	Straight On	To His Left	GB	Air	Plays Saved	R/P	GDP	GFP/ DME	Total	Rank
2011	CWS	3	6.0	4	0	1.000	0	0	0	0	-	3	0	0	0	+1	0	+1	1	0	0	1	-
2012	2 tms	10	59.0	37	1	.973	3	0	10	6	.600	25	+1	-1	+1	+1	0	+1	1	0	0	1	-
2013	Min	38	216.2	105	5	.952	9	3	15	10	.667	76	+4	+1	+1	+5	-1	+4	3	0	0	3	-
2014	Min	98	771.2	359	5	.986	20	20	91	54	.593	219	+5	-4	-2	-1	-3	-4	-3	-2	-1	-6	25
		149	1053.1	505	11	.978	32	23	116	70	.603	323	+10	-4	0	+6	-4	+2	2	-2	-1	-1	

Scout's Defensive Rating: -2 plays saved in 2013, -7 plays saved in 2014

During his prospect days, Eduardo Escobar was labeled a defense-first shortstop whose slick glove might one day carry him into a starting role at the big league level. However, it appears now that Escobar's defensive skills should be categorized closer to the fattest part of the shortstop bell curve. He is a prime example of the manner in which flashy tools and aesthetic excellence at the minor league level do not always translate into actual run prevention ability when compared to his major league peers. Escobar excelled moving to his right, making five plays more than average in that direction based mostly on arm strength and relative proficiency backhanding balls. On the other hand, Escobar proved to be a negative defender when forced to charge balls and when ranging to his left. Escobar possesses a plus to plus-

Shortstops

plus arm, but its utility can play down in game action due to an inability to throw from different angles. This becomes especially problematic when Escobar is faced with plays in which he lacks time to set his feet conventionally. In addition to his time at shortstop, Escobar was deployed at second base, third base, center field and left field in 2014. With limited offensive upside, he is likely better suited for a bench or utility type of role long term.

Yunel Escobar

		BASIC							GDP			RANGE AND POSITIONING							RUNS SAVED				
Year	Team	G	Inn	TC	E	Pct	GFP	DM	Opps	GDP	Pct	Outs Made	To His Right	Straight On	To His Left	GB	Air	Plays Saved	R/P	GDP	GFP/ DME	Total	Rank
2007	Atl	53	363.0	176	4	.977	13	8	29	21	.724	135	-2	+3	+1	+2	-2	0	0	1	0	1	-
2008	Atl	126	1105.2	605	16	.974	44	27	145	74	.510	439	0	+3	+19	+22	-2	+20	15	-3	-4	8	9
2009	Atl	139	1208.2	613	13	.979	52	32	130	86	.662	451	-5	+9	+14	+18	-1	+17	13	-1	-5	7	10
2010	2 tms	134	1179.1	645	18	.972	58	28	170	127	.747	414	+2	-1	+12	+14	-3	+11	8	3	-2	9	6
2011	Tor	132	1121.0	539	14	.974	35	25	121	77	.636	360	+9	0	+5	+15	-2	+13	10	0	-2	8	6
2012	Tor	143	1250.2	683	12	.982	38	20	161	103	.640	419	+4	+3	+17	+23	-1	+22	17	-1	-2	14	4
2013	TB	153	1320.0	610	7	.989	61	34	145	89	.614	372	+14	-2	-8	+5	+2	+7	5	0	-1	4	9
2014	TB	136	1183.1	451	16	.965	36	20	83	44	.530	249	-2	-8	-13	-24	+2	-22	-17	-3	-4	-24	35
		1016	8731.2	4322	100	.977	337	194	984	621	.631	2839	+20	+7	+47	+75	-7	+68	51	-4	-20	27	-

Scout's Defensive Rating: 2 plays saved in 2013, -4 plays saved in 2014

Throughout most of his career Escobar has proven himself to be a very capable defender at shortstop, rating above average every season from 2007 to 2013. His lateral range in both directions has been excellent, but he's really stood out on balls up the middle. The 2014 season proved to be a different story, however. His range deteriorated sharply, and he isn't getting to all the balls that he used to. Further, he dropped off from 61 Good Fielding Plays in 2013 to just 36 GFPs in 2014. He is still very sure handed, so there is hope for a bounce back in 2015. Nevertheless, the 38-run drop from 2012 to 2014 suggests his days as an above average defender are over.

Ryan Flaherty

		BASIC							GDP			RANGE AND POSITIONING							RUNS SAVED				
Year	Team	G	Inn	TC	E	Pct	GFP	DM	Opps	GDP	Pct	Outs Made	To His Right	Straight On	To His Left	GB	Air	Plays Saved	R/P	GDP	GFP/ DME	Total	Rank
2012	Bal	1	1.0	0	0	-	0	0	0	0	-	0	0	0	0	0	0	0	0	0		0	-
2013	Bal	9	33.0	12	0	1.000	0	1	3	3	1.000	12	0	+1	0	+1	0	+1	1	0	0	1	-
2014	Bal	29	204.1	86	3	.965	1	5	17	10	.588	48	-4	0	0	-4	-1	-5	-4	0	-1	-5	-
		39	238.1	98	3	.969	1	6	20	13	.650	60	-4	+1	0	-3	-1	-4	-3	0	-1	-4	-

Scout's Defensive Rating: 0 plays saved in 2013, 1 plays saved in 2014

Wilmer Flores

		BASIC							GDP			RANGE AND POSITIONING							RUNS SAVED				
Year	Team	G	Inn	TC	E	Pct	GFP	DM	Opps	GDP	Pct	Outs Made	To His Right	Straight On	To His Left	GB	Air	Plays Saved	R/P	GDP	GFP/ DME	Total	Rank
2014	NYM	51	443.1	193	4	.979	13	10	39	32	.821	131	-5	+7	-2	0	-2	-2	-2	1	-2	-3	-

Scout's Defensive Rating: 1 plays saved in 2014

Pedro Florimon

		BASIC							GDP			RANGE AND POSITIONING							RUNS SAVED				
Year	Team	G	Inn	TC	E	Pct	GFP	DM	Opps	GDP	Pct	Outs Made	To His Right	Straight On	To His Left	GB	Air	Plays Saved	R/P	GDP	GFP/ DME	Total	Rank
2011	Bal	4	18.2	10	1	.900	0	1	1	1	1.000	9	-1	-1	0	-1	0	-1	-1	0	0	-1	-
2012	Min	43	367.0	201	7	.965	16	7	40	25	.625	138	+12	-1	-5	+6	+5	+11	9	-1	-1	7	-
2013	Min	133	1099.2	664	18	.973	68	35	152	103	.678	436	+12	+8	-7	+13	+2	+15	12	0	0	12	3
2014	Min	31	224.2	114	2	.982	6	7	24	19	.792	78	+7	+2	-5	+5	-2	+3	2	1	0	3	-
		211	1710.0	989	28	.972	90	50	217	148	.682	661	+30	+8	-17	+23	+5	+28	22	0	-1	21	-

Scout's Defensive Rating: 0 plays saved in 2013, -1 plays saved in 2014

Shortstops

Freddy Galvis

	BASIC							GDP			RANGE AND POSITIONING							RUNS SAVED				
Year Team	G	Inn	TC	E	Pct	GFP	DM	Opps	GDP	Pct	Outs Made	To His Right	Straight On	To His Left	GB	Air	Plays Saved	R/P	GDP	GFP/DME	Total	Rank
2012 Phi	5	36.1	22	0	1.000	4	1	3	3	1.000	18	+2	+1	-1	+2	0	+2	2	0	0	2	-
2013 Phi	11	67.0	37	0	1.000	2	1	9	7	.778	23	-2	+1	-1	-2	0	-2	-2	0	0	-2	-
2014 Phi	25	200.0	112	1	.991	6	7	22	17	.773	71	-2	0	-1	-3	-1	-4	-3	0	-1	-4	-
	41	303.1	171	1	.994	12	9	34	27	.794	112	-2	+2	-3	-3	-1	-4	-3	0	-1	-4	-

Scout's Defensive Rating: 1 plays saved in 2013, -2 plays saved in 2014

Marwin Gonzalez

	BASIC							GDP			RANGE AND POSITIONING							RUNS SAVED				
Year Team	G	Inn	TC	E	Pct	GFP	DM	Opps	GDP	Pct	Outs Made	To His Right	Straight On	To His Left	GB	Air	Plays Saved	R/P	GDP	GFP/DME	Total	Rank
2012 Hou	47	347.2	173	5	.971	13	9	34	21	.618	117	-5	+2	+2	-1	+1	0	0	0	0	0	-
2013 Hou	53	450.1	228	10	.956	26	5	48	36	.750	128	+3	-4	-1	0	0	0	0	2	0	2	-
2014 Hou	71	576.2	282	6	.979	19	13	57	40	.702	141	-1	-6	+7	0	+2	+2	1	0	3	4	11
	171	1374.2	683	21	.969	58	27	139	97	.698	386	-3	-8	+10	-1	+3	+2	1	2	3	6	-

Scout's Defensive Rating: -1 plays saved in 2013, -1 plays saved in 2014

Gonzalez has bounced around the infield the past two seasons for the Astros and leaves you wondering if he is able to take the reigns at shortstop. What can be so frustrating with Gonzalez is the fact that he can wow you with a diving play up the middle but misplay a ball right to him. Of the three infield positions he played most, Gonzalez is clearly best at shortstop, ranking below average in the field at both second and third base, and he may benefit from some stability rather than bouncing around six different positions as he did in 2014. He never seemed to establish his identity with all the positional changes. At only 25, Gonzalez still has time to establish himself as an everyday shortstop.

Didi Gregorius

	BASIC							GDP			RANGE AND POSITIONING							RUNS SAVED				
Year Team	G	Inn	TC	E	Pct	GFP	DM	Opps	GDP	Pct	Outs Made	To His Right	Straight On	To His Left	GB	Air	Plays Saved	R/P	GDP	GFP/DME	Total	Rank
2012 Cin	6	46.0	18	0	1.000	2	0	6	4	.667	10	0	0	+1	0	+1	+1	1	0	0	1	-
2013 Ari	100	894.2	444	13	.971	61	19	83	51	.614	289	+11	+3	-10	+5	-1	+4	2	-1	-2	-1	18
2014 Ari	67	580.2	293	5	.983	41	19	65	38	.585	202	+2	0	-1	+2	0	+2	1	-1	0	0	16
	173	1521.1	755	18	.976	104	38	154	93	.604	501	+13	+3	-10	+7	0	+7	4	-2	-2	0	-

Scout's Defensive Rating: 6 plays saved in 2013, 7 plays saved in 2014

Though his defense was heralded throughout the minor leagues, Gregorius has yet to put it all together at the major league level. He is great at tracking balls in the hole, recording more plays made than average over the past two seasons. However, going up the middle has been a different story, where he has been below average over the same time period. Gregorius has also struggled when it comes to handling double plays, costing his teams two runs over the last three years, which ranks him in the bottom half among regular shortstops.

J.J. Hardy

	BASIC							GDP			RANGE AND POSITIONING							RUNS SAVED				
Year Team	G	Inn	TC	E	Pct	GFP	DM	Opps	GDP	Pct	Outs Made	To His Right	Straight On	To His Left	GB	Air	Plays Saved	R/P	GDP	GFP/DME	Total	Rank
2005 Mil	119	937.2	402	10	.975	14	21	78	46	.590	316	+13	0	-4	+9	+1	+10	8	0	0	8	10
2006 Mil	32	257.2	143	2	.986	4	6	39	25	.641	93	+5	0	+3	+8	-1	+7	5	1	1	7	-
2007 Mil	149	1271.2	578	13	.978	48	19	122	76	.623	443	-14	+4	+16	+6	+1	+7	5	1	3	9	9
2008 Mil	145	1268.1	647	15	.977	52	19	147	79	.537	477	-1	-1	+18	+16	+3	+19	14	-2	1	13	3
2009 Mil	112	949.1	472	8	.983	38	23	97	60	.619	351	0	-2	+8	+5	-1	+4	3	-1	0	2	16
2010 Min	100	858.1	450	11	.976	22	14	101	57	.564	308	+2	+2	-5	-2	-3	-5	-3	-1	-1	-5	25
2011 Bal	129	1133.0	620	6	.990	46	17	123	73	.593	424	+9	+7	-10	+7	+4	+11	8	-1	1	8	8
2012 Bal	158	1439.0	779	6	.992	68	25	171	110	.643	494	+7	+3	+7	+18	+1	+19	14	0	4	18	3
2013 Bal	159	1417.0	645	12	.981	47	13	153	108	.706	385	+6	+3	-6	+3	+1	+4	3	3	2	8	6
2014 Bal	141	1257.0	594	13	.978	36	13	124	92	.742	343	+5	-2	+2	+4	0	+4	3	4	3	10	4
	1244	10789.0	5330	96	.982	375	170	1155	726	.629	3634	+32	+14	+29	+74	+6	+80	60	4	14	78	-

Scout's Defensive Rating: -7 plays saved in 2013, -1 plays saved in 2014

At 6' 1" tall and with a lean athletic frame J.J. Hardy looks like a major league shortstop. Hardy is the ultimate model of consistency; while he's never finished first or second in Runs Saved, he has rated above average in 9 out of his 10

MLB seasons and saved at least eight runs in seven seasons. He's not flashy, but he uses quick hands to compensate for his lack of dazzling plays. His quick release helps his ability to convert routine plays and avoid errors and misplays, but Hardy struggles to make the harder plays that other great shortstops seem to make. Hardy has only converted 8 percent of the plays that the BIS Video Scouts have deemed "difficult" compared to the league average of 14 percent. It is worth noting that Hardy made major improvements on double plays over the last couple of years; he led the majors in quick pivot double play GFPs in 2013 with 11 (four more than Andrelton Simmons). Though he often gets overlooked from year to year, Hardy's decade of consistently good defensive performance establishes him as one of the top defensive shortstops of the era.

Adeiny Hechavarria

		BASIC						GDP			RANGE AND POSITIONING							RUNS SAVED				
Year	Team	G	Inn	TC	E	Pct	GFP	DM	Opps	GDP	Pct	Outs Made	To His Right	Straight On	To His Left	GB	Air	Plays Saved	R/P	GDP	GFP/ DME	Total	Rank
2012	Tor	17	114.0	48	2	.958	3	5	16	12	.750	30	+1	-1	+2	+1	+1	+2	2	0	0	2	-
2013	Mia	148	1297.1	613	15	.976	76	27	127	86	.677	393	-16	-3	+15	-5	+1	-4	-2	0	-1	-3	22
2014	Mia	146	1294.2	652	14	.979	88	27	148	91	.615	440	-13	-3	+8	-7	+2	-5	-4	-2	3	-3	19
		311	2706.0	1313	31	.976	167	59	291	189	.649	863	-28	-7	+25	-11	+4	-7	-4	-2	2	-4	

Scout's Defensive Rating: 11 plays saved in 2013, 10 plays saved in 2014

When it comes to players that exhibit a split between defensive metrics and the eye test, Adeiny Hechavarria is one of the most polarizing. Over the 2013-14 seasons, Hechavarria cost the Marlins six runs compared to an average shortstop according to Defensive Runs Saved; however, he finished third among shortstops over that same timeframe according to the Scout's Defensive Rating. The Cuban shortstop boasts a strong arm, quick feet, and is no stranger to making flashy, highlight-reel plays, but suboptimal positioning ultimately weighs down his defensive value. Hechavarria's raw tools and athleticism allow him to make plays and get to balls that few players can, but he tends to be positioned more up the middle than most major league shortstops. Ultimately, his below average play on balls hit toward the hole outweighed the advantage gained on balls hit up the middle since 2013. Tools-wise, there's little doubt that he is maturing into one of the most skilled shortstops in the game. However, it appears that he's not being put in the best position to reap the full benefits of his defensive talents.

Derek Jeter

		BASIC						GDP			RANGE AND POSITIONING							RUNS SAVED				
Year	Team	G	Inn	TC	E	Pct	GFP	DM	Opps	GDP	Pct	Outs Made	To His Right	Straight On	To His Left	GB	Air	Plays Saved	R/P	GDP	GFP/ DME	Total	Rank
2003	NYY	118	1033.2	444	14	.968	-	-	88	46	.523	336	-12	+3	-6	-15	+1	-14	-11	-2	-	-13	34
2004	NYY	154	1341.2	678	13	.981	28	20	146	85	.582	456	-24	+5	-5	-25	+9	-16	-12	0	-1	-13	33
2005	NYY	157	1352.2	731	15	.979	42	20	156	84	.538	526	-18	+3	-25	-39	+5	-34	-26	-2	1	-27	34
2006	NYY	150	1292.1	610	15	.975	32	15	131	75	.573	450	-10	+1	-10	-19	-3	-22	-17	-1	2	-16	33
2007	NYY	155	1318.1	607	18	.970	45	15	152	98	.645	420	-14	-6	-14	-33	-1	-34	-26	3	-1	-24	34
2008	NYY	148	1258.2	579	12	.979	35	17	106	58	.547	430	-17	+9	-1	-10	-1	-11	-8	-1	-1	-10	32
2009	NYY	150	1260.2	554	8	.986	39	16	131	74	.565	398	-3	+7	+2	+5	+1	+6	5	-3	1	3	13
2010	NYY	151	1303.2	553	6	.989	29	33	150	95	.633	373	-12	+10	-4	-6	-3	-9	-6	0	1	-5	27
2011	NYY	122	1047.1	432	12	.972	31	19	103	63	.612	290	-15	+2	-2	-14	0	-14	-11	-1	0	-12	33
2012	NYY	135	1186.1	506	10	.980	32	14	109	67	.615	343	-1	-13	-7	-21	-5	-26	-20	-1	3	-18	35
2013	NYY	13	109.2	52	2	.962	5	4	14	6	.429	29	-3	0	-3	-6	-1	-7	-5	0	0	-5	-
2014	NYY	130	1138.1	411	11	.973	25	21	81	41	.506	239	+7	-8	-12	-14	+2	-12	-9	-2	-1	-12	32
		1583	13643.1	6157	136	.978	343	194	1367	792	.579	4290	-122	+13	-87	-197	+4	-193	-146	-10	4	-152	-

Scout's Defensive Rating: -2 plays saved in 2013, -14 plays saved in 2014

There are few players whose defensive ability is discussed more often than Derek Jeter's. His supporters will argue that Jeter is solid and makes the plays that he should, while his detractors will point to the defensive metrics and how Jeter doesn't get to enough balls to be even an average defender at shortstop. In some ways both camps are correct. Jeter made very few mistakes on the balls that he gets to thanks to his sure hands and an accurate but relatively weak throwing arm. His error totals are year-in and year-out among the lowest at the position.

The pro-Jeter argument goes off the rails when they rave about his spectacular range and patented jump throws.The fact is that he fails to get to many balls that other major league shortstops do. Even the highlight reel plays that he does make in some ways only further underscore his defensive deficiencies. The jump throw from the hole looks pretty, but is often times only necessary due to his lack of range and arm strength. Most other shortstops will make the play look

Shortstops

more routine by just planting their feet and firing a strong throw to first. Jeter will retire with only one player worse than him in terms of negative career DRS (Adam Dunn) but that won't stop the debate on his defensive prowess from continuing for years to come.

Jed Lowrie

		BASIC						GDP			RANGE AND POSITIONING							RUNS SAVED				
Year	Team	G	Inn	TC	E	Pct	GFP	DM	Opps	GDP	Pct	Outs Made	To His Right	Straight On	To His Left	GB	Air	Plays Saved	R/P	GDP	GFP/ DME	Total	Rank
2008	Bos	49	386.0	155	0	1.000	9	6	35	21	.600	123	+3	+2	0	+6	+2	+8	6	0	0	6	-
2009	Bos	26	163.2	75	1	.987	7	5	21	15	.714	49	-2	+2	+1	+1	-2	-1	-1	0	0	-1	-
2010	Bos	23	176.2	73	1	.986	2	4	23	17	.739	47	-3	0	-1	-3	-1	-4	-4	0	0	-4	-
2011	Bos	49	398.0	181	10	.945	14	6	34	21	.618	120	+6	0	-6	0	-3	-3	-2	0	0	-2	-
2012	Hou	93	773.1	394	8	.980	18	12	69	42	.609	286	+21	0	-19	+2	-3	-1	-1	0	-2	-3	21
2013	Oak	119	1023.1	421	16	.962	41	14	97	51	.526	270	+8	-4	-20	-16	-6	-22	-17	-3	2	-18	34
2014	Oak	130	1146.1	503	13	.974	33	19	119	66	.555	303	+1	0	-8	-6	-2	-8	-6	-2	-2	-10	31
		489	4067.1	1802	49	.973	124	66	398	233	.585	1198	+34	0	-53	-16	-15	-31	-25	-5	-2	-32	-

Scout's Defensive Rating: -8 plays saved in 2013, -10 plays saved in 2014

In 2014, his first full season playing shortstop exclusively, Lowrie continued the sub-standard defensive production that has marked his entire career at the position. He lacks quick reactions, which causes two problems. The first is that it limits his range. The second is that he is slow in his transition from fielding to throwing, nullifying his strong throwing arm. In 2014, Lowrie did improve over his 2013 performance in most defensive categories, including Plays Made and Defensive Runs Saved. Another healthy season playing full time at shortstop could bring more improvement.

Jordy Mercer

		BASIC						GDP			RANGE AND POSITIONING							RUNS SAVED				
Year	Team	G	Inn	TC	E	Pct	GFP	DM	Opps	GDP	Pct	Outs Made	To His Right	Straight On	To His Left	GB	Air	Plays Saved	R/P	GDP	GFP/ DME	Total	Rank
2012	Pit	28	104.1	56	1	.982	7	3	8	4	.500	43	0	-1	+1	+1	0	+1	1	0	0	1	-
2013	Pit	78	594.0	315	12	.962	29	14	83	53	.639	194	-1	+1	+1	+1	-1	0	0	-1	-1	-2	20
2014	Pit	144	1222.1	609	11	.982	51	20	115	74	.643	390	+4	+4	+9	+18	-5	+13	9	1	-1	9	5
		250	1920.2	980	24	.976	87	37	206	131	.636	627	+3	+4	+11	+20	-6	+14	10	0	-2	8	-

Scout's Defensive Rating: -5 plays saved in 2013, 5 plays saved in 2014

Jordy Mercer earned the starting shortstop role for the Pirates in 2014 based largely on the offensive upgrade he could provide over incumbent Clint Barmes. While Mercer may never be the elite defensive shortstop that Barmes has proven to be over the years, Mercer really impressed defensively in his first year with the full time role. Mercer possesses a very strong arm that allows him to make plays deep in the hole. He is also very adept at making the spin pivot and throw on balls up the middle. Mercer struggled a bit with his arm accuracy during his appearances in 2013, but he showed great improvement in this area in 2014 and led all shortstops (minimum 200 throws) in Good Throw Rate. Mercer is never going to have elite range due to his larger frame, but thanks to good defensive positioning and better reads off the bat, Mercer showed greatly improved range in 2014. Mercer might not make as many highlight reel plays as some of his contemporaries, but he also doesn't make many mistakes on plays that should be made. Mercer should provide enough quality defense to remain a starting option for the Pirates for the next few seasons.

Brad Miller

		BASIC						GDP			RANGE AND POSITIONING							RUNS SAVED				
Year	Team	G	Inn	TC	E	Pct	GFP	DM	Opps	GDP	Pct	Outs Made	To His Right	Straight On	To His Left	GB	Air	Plays Saved	R/P	GDP	GFP/ DME	Total	Rank
2013	Sea	68	561.0	249	7	.972	23	19	51	30	.588	169	+3	-2	0	+1	+3	+4	3	-2	-3	-2	19
2014	Sea	107	924.0	431	18	.958	27	28	82	46	.561	271	+4	-1	-3	0	-3	-3	-2	-2	1	-3	18
		175	1485.0	680	25	.963	50	47	133	76	.571	440	+7	-3	-3	+1	0	+1	1	-4	-2	-5	-

Scout's Defensive Rating: 0 plays saved in 2013, -8 plays saved in 2014

At 6'2", Brad Miller is a little taller than your average shortstop, and it shows in his approach to balls in play. Miller has an awkward approach to fielding groundballs, and the lack of fundamentals shows in his errors and his inability to make routine plays. According to BIS Video Scouts, Miller was eight plays below average (Scout's Defensive Rating); only four shortstops had worse ratings in the major leagues. Miller has decent range and a decent arm, but his glove is well below average and his throwing motion causes him to lose outs. However, his range and arm aren't the main problems with Miller, it's his approach and glove. Miller is only 25 years old, so he has time to improve, but at such an important defensive position he needs to hurry.

Chris Owings

		BASIC						GDP			RANGE AND POSITIONING							RUNS SAVED				
											Outs Made	To His Right	Straight On	To His Left			Plays Saved			GFP/		
Year	Team	G	Inn	TC	E	Pct	GFP	DM	Opps	GDP	Pct					GB	Air		R/P	GDP	DME	Total	Rank
2013	Ari	13	93.0	50	1	.980	2	3	9	5	.556	37	-2	-2	0	-3	+2	-1	-1	0	-1	-2	-
2014	Ari	61	527.0	253	11	.957	26	7	55	40	.727	167	+1	+5	+2	+8	0	+8	6	0	-1	5	9
		74	620.0	303	12	.960	28	10	64	45	.703	204	-1	+3	+2	+5	+2	+7	5	0	-2	3	

Scout's Defensive Rating: 0 plays saved in 2013, 2 plays saved in 2014

Owings is a very slick-fielding young player that seems to have a very bright future. The biggest question is which position he will play going forward. Owings racked up 26 GFPs as a shortstop in only 61 games, but he also recorded 11 errors and 7 other misplays. Among the errors, five were on poor throws and four more were on bobbles, both of which could be improved with experience.

Owings did also shine at second base. In 21 career games and 91 total chances at the keystone, Owings has yet to commit an error. He is very effective turning double plays from both sides of the base, converting over 70 percent of his opportunities from either position. He has a strong enough arm to stay at shortstop if given the opportunity. Either way, the Diamondbacks have a very talented, young middle infielder at their disposal.

Jhonny Peralta

		BASIC						GDP			RANGE AND POSITIONING							RUNS SAVED				
											Outs Made	To His Right	Straight On	To His Left			Plays Saved			GFP/		
Year	Team	C	Inn	TC	E	Pct	GFP	DM	Opps	GDP	Pct					GB	Air		R/P	GDP	DME	Total	Rank
2003	Cle	72	624.0	334	8	.976	-	-	67	38	.567	222	+4	+2	-8	-1	+1	0	0	0	-	0	18
2004	Cle	7	55.0	27	3	.889	0	1	4	2	.500	15	0	-2	0	-2	+1	-1	-1	0	0	-1	-
2005	Cle	141	1232.1	638	19	.970	35	20	132	94	.712	465	-5	+3	-10	-12	-2	-14	-11	5	1	-5	26
2006	Cle	147	1275.1	710	16	.977	22	40	152	93	.612	535	-3	-1	-15	-13	+4	-9	-7	1	-1	-7	28
2007	Cle	152	1348.0	720	19	.974	39	33	164	95	.579	511	+12	-7	-8	-3	0	-3	-2	0	0	-2	22
2008	Cle	146	1271.1	658	14	.979	34	20	153	97	.634	469	0	-6	-2	-7	-3	-10	-8	2	1	-5	29
2009	Cle	41	334.0	189	4	.979	15	6	51	39	.765	128	+4	-2	+1	+2	+2	+4	3	1	-2	2	-
2010	Det	46	392.1	191	3	.984	15	3	38	25	.658	131	-4	+3	+3	+2	0	+2	1	0	0	1	-
2011	Det	145	1245.0	608	7	.988	26	26	125	81	.648	403	-6	+8	+9	+10	-4	+6	5	0	-3	2	13
2012	Det	149	1277.2	595	7	.988	29	17	117	77	.658	404	-10	+10	+8	+7	-7	0	0	0	-1	-1	19
2013	Det	106	935.2	438	4	.991	26	18	88	55	.625	304	-6	-1	+5	-2	+2	0	0	0	0	0	16
2014	StL	152	1325.0	621	12	.981	31	7	136	95	.699	426	+1	+10	+4	+15	+2	+17	13	2	2	17	3
		1304	11316.0	5729	116	.980	272	191	1227	791	.645	4013	-7	+17	-13	-4	-4	-8	-7	11	-3	1	

Scout's Defensive Rating: -7 plays saved in 2013, -3 plays saved in 2014

Always known as a bat-first shortstop, Peralta was one of the most puzzling defenders in 2014. Early in his career Peralta rated below average defensively, though he dramatically reduced his Errors and Defensive Misplays to improve to the level of an average shortstop in recent years. In 2014, Peralta ranked among the league leaders for shortstop Defensive Runs Saved with 17, though this is contradicted by ranking comfortably below average shortstop by the BIS Video Scouts via Scout's Defensive Rating. Making sense of it all, Peralta seemed to always be in the right place at the right time. He is buoyed by his ability to make routine plays at an above average rate, often choosing to make the right play instead of the risky one. When tasked with making more difficult plays, Peralta's numbers begin to slide quickly. He ranks near the bottom among everyday shortstops when it comes to converting Moderate and Difficult plays as well as Good Fielding Plays. This stems from his lack of arm strength, which can be hidden during routine opportunities, but is often exposed as the degree of difficulty is increased. His 6'2" frame is fairly stiff, usually upright when fielding with very little bend at the waist or knees. He is able to track the ball off the bat with above average reflexes, but his lack of mobile quickness puts him at a disadvantage to reaching balls not hit right at him. Though it feels as if he's been around forever, Peralta is now entering his mid-30s, and it's hard to imagine him replicating his 2014 success going forward.

Shortstops

Alexei Ramirez

		BASIC							GDP			RANGE AND POSITIONING							RUNS SAVED				
Year	Team	G	Inn	TC	E	Pct	GFP	DM	Opps	GDP	Pct	Outs Made	To His Right	Straight On	To His Left	GB	Air	Plays Saved	R/P	GDP	GFP/DME	Total	Rank
2008	CWS	16	53.0	24	1	.958	3	1	6	4	.667	18	-3	0	0	-2	-1	-3	-2	0	0	-2	-
2009	CWS	148	1293.2	650	20	.969	51	26	133	89	.669	453	+9	-4	+3	+7	-4	+3	2	0	0	2	17
2010	CWS	156	1376.2	768	20	.974	56	22	158	105	.665	513	+19	+4	-3	+20	+6	+26	19	1	0	20	3
2011	CWS	155	1382.0	690	16	.977	64	30	136	95	.699	473	+16	-4	-1	+11	-4	+7	5	3	2	10	5
2012	CWS	158	1392.0	673	12	.982	55	28	136	92	.676	477	+11	+2	+5	+18	-1	+17	12	2	0	14	6
2013	CWS	158	1400.2	691	22	.968	77	29	142	99	.697	473	+10	-4	-6	0	0	0	0	2	-1	1	15
2014	CWS	158	1376.2	696	15	.978	75	31	163	120	.736	436	+20	-21	-11	-12	-2	-14	-10	3	3	-4	23
		949	8274.2	4192	106	.975	381	167	874	604	.691	2843	+82	-27	-13	+42	-6	+36	26	11	4	41	-

Scout's Defensive Rating: 7 plays saved in 2013, 4 plays saved in 2014

Alexei Ramirez is the definition of smooth when it comes to shortstops. He has one of the most fluid throwing motions of any player in the league and makes most plays look effortless no matter what the degree of difficulty. One of his greatest strengths is the transfer from his glove to his throwing hand. It is extremely quick with no wasted motion. This is very evident on plays in the hole when he gets to the ball and is immediately ready to throw the ball as he plants his feet.

The arm strength has always been there for Ramirez and still is. However, as he has aged, the range has started to decline, especially in the last two years. He doesn't have the same ability to reach balls up the middle or slow rollers that he used to. He has always been a quality defensive shortstop and still possesses a great package of skills, but the best of Ramirez's glovework is likely in the past.

Hanley Ramirez

		BASIC							GDP			RANGE AND POSITIONING							RUNS SAVED				
Year	Team	G	Inn	TC	E	Pct	GFP	DM	Opps	GDP	Pct	Outs Made	To His Right	Straight On	To His Left	GB	Air	Plays Saved	R/P	GDP	GFP/DME	Total	Rank
2005	Bos	2	6.0	1	0	1.000	0	0		0	-	1				0		0	0		0	0	-
2006	Fla	154	1323.1	694	26	.963	42	36	163	103	.632	467	0	-5	+2	-3	-3	-6	-5	2	0	-3	24
2007	Fla	151	1301.2	641	24	.963	54	46	150	90	.600	462	-21	-8	-6	-34	-3	-37	-28	1	-1	-28	35
2008	Fla	150	1302.0	659	22	.967	48	25	139	79	.568	473	+10	-4	-1	+5	-2	+3	2	-1	-4	-3	24
2009	Fla	146	1259.0	580	10	.983	38	27	123	76	.618	412	+8	+1	-2	+7	-2	+5	4	-2	0	2	15
2010	Fla	140	1217.0	558	16	.971	47	35	115	77	.670	358	-14	-2	+2	-15	-5	-20	-16	-1	0	-17	34
2011	Fla	86	754.2	329	14	.957	35	19	73	42	.575	211	-21	+2	+9	-10	-3	-13	-10	-1	0	-11	32
2012	LAD	57	503.1	228	6	.974	17	12	54	32	.593	154	-7	-3	+4	-6	0	-6	-5	0	-2	-7	28
2013	LAD	76	651.0	328	13	.960	34	14	75	44	.587	231	-1	-3	+7	+4	+4	+8	6	-1	-2	3	12
2014	LAD	115	919.2	410	16	.961	36	24	72	49	.681	265	-15	+2	0	-12	-1	-13	-10	1	0	-9	30
		1077	9237.2	4428	147	.967	351	238	964	592	.614	3034	-61	-20	+15	-64	-15	-79	-62	-2	-9	-73	-

Scout's Defensive Rating: -1 plays saved in 2013, -16 plays saved in 2014

For the first time since being traded to the Dodgers in 2012, Ramirez appeared in over one-hundred games at shortstop in 2014, as he had been the constant victim of the injury bug and split 2012 between short and third. However, that didn't change the fact that he is a well-below average infielder. Dating back to his time in Miami, Ramirez has struggled to find consistency and his effort has always been an open question. Ramirez still displays quickness and raw ability to make a play on just about any ball hit into his zone, but sloppy glovework and lack of effort have led to more Defensive Misplays and errors than any other shortstop since his rookie season despite the missed time. The Red Sox are expected to convert Ramirez into a left fielder, where his inconsistency can hide while his athletic ability shines.

Jose Ramirez

		BASIC							GDP			RANGE AND POSITIONING							RUNS SAVED				
Year	Team	G	Inn	TC	E	Pct	GFP	DM	Opps	GDP	Pct	Outs Made	To His Right	Straight On	To His Left	GB	Air	Plays Saved	R/P	GDP	GFP/DME	Total	Rank
2013	Cle	2	2.0	0	0	-	0	0	0	0	-	0	0	0	0	0	0	0	0	0	0	0	-
2014	Cle	56	498.2	235	4	.983	19	13	46	29	.630	149	-2	0	+4	+2	+2	+4	3	0	1	4	-
		58	500.2	235	4	.983	19	13	46	29	.630	149	-2	0	+4	+2	+2	+4	3	0	1	4	-

Scout's Defensive Rating: 4 plays saved in 2014

Shortstops

Jose Reyes

Year	Team	G	Inn	TC	E	Pct	GFP	DM	Opps	GDP	Pct	Outs Made	To His Right	Straight On	To His Left	GB	Air	Plays Saved	R/P	GDP	GFP/DME	Total	Rank
		BASIC							**GDP**			**RANGE AND POSITIONING**							**RUNS SAVED**				
2003	NYM	69	596.1	329	9	.973	-	-	73	39	.534	248	+9	+3	-2	+9	+1	+10	8	-1	-	7	8
2004	NYM	10	72.2	46	2	.957	2	1	9	5	.556	34	0	0	+1	+1	-3	-2	-2	0	0	-2	-
2005	NYM	161	1398.1	682	18	.974	47	35	148	97	.655	481	-14	-1	+3	-13	+3	-10	-8	3	-1	-6	27
2006	NYM	149	1320.1	583	17	.971	29	36	121	68	.562	444	+2	+11	+2	+14	+2	+16	12	-1	-2	9	6
2007	NYM	160	1431.1	660	12	.982	54	29	134	82	.612	500	+5	+5	+7	+16	-3	+13	10	1	0	11	8
2008	NYM	158	1420.1	660	17	.974	51	23	149	86	.577	481	-3	+4	-1	0	-2	-2	-2	0	0	-2	20
2009	NYM	35	305.1	145	5	.966	6	5	23	11	.478	110	+5	-1	-2	+2	-2	0	0	-1	0	-1	-
2010	NYM	133	1171.1	556	15	.973	38	26	117	82	.701	371	-5	+1	-3	-7	+1	-6	-4	2	-3	-5	26
2011	NYM	124	1087.0	554	18	.968	45	21	131	84	.641	361	-18	+4	+4	-11	-7	-18	-14	0	0	-14	35
2012	Mia	160	1410.2	663	18	.973	45	35	162	102	.630	417	-21	+2	+7	-12	-6	-18	-14	0	-2	-16	34
2013	Tor	92	793.0	344	9	.974	32	12	71	49	.690	232	-6	+5	-8	-9	0	-9	-7	2	1	-4	25
2014	Tor	142	1243.2	550	19	.965	37	27	106	68	.642	330	-12	-5	-3	-20	-1	-21	-16	1	-1	-16	34
		1393	12250.1	5772	159	.972	386	250	1244	773	.621	4009	-58	+28	+5	-30	-17	-47	-37	6	-8	-39	

Scout's Defensive Rating: 0 plays saved in 2013, -5 plays saved in 2014

After changing teams twice in the last four seasons, Reyes is a shadow of his former self on defense. As a matter of fact, the 2014 season may have been the worst defensive season of his career. Though he can be speedy in the field, he really struggled to knock down balls and/or get an out on harder hit balls. Despite the fact he has a very strong arm and quick release, his arm tool could be identified as his best and worst tool. When he has to range to his right or charge in on a chopper and doesn't have a chance to set his feet, he makes very bad throws. These bad throws have followed him his entire career and usually account for the largest percentage of his Defensive Misplays and Errors year after year. On the flip side, when he is able to track down balls and position his body right, his quick release and strong arm is one of the best in the game. This helps him in starting and turning double plays, one area where he still excels. Nonetheless, Jose Reyes is a liability at short and might be more effective at second or center during the latter portion of his career.

Miguel Rojas

Year	Team	G	Inn	TC	E	Pct	GFP	DM	Opps	GDP	Pct	Outs Made	To His Right	Straight On	To His Left	GB	Air	Plays Saved	R/P	GDP	GFP/DME	Total	Rank
		BASIC							**GDP**			**RANGE AND POSITIONING**							**RUNS SAVED**				
2014	LAD	66	283.2	146	4	.973	14	3	32	25	.781	103	+4	+4	+2	+10	0	+10	8	2	1	11	-

Scout's Defensive Rating: 1 plays saved in 2014

Making his major league debut in 2014, Miguel Rojas found a niche with the Los Angeles Dodgers as a backup infielder, usually at shortstop. Despite playing limited innings, Rojas was able to put up defensive numbers comparable to or better than most everyday players. In addition to his 11 Defensive Runs Saved at shortstop (fourth in MLB), he managed to save another four runs at third base despite playing just 100 innings there. His strengths are based on two key components: glove and arm. If he gets to the ball, more often than not the glove corrals would-be base hits, making just four defensive misplays across four positions. Coupled with a strong arm and equally quick transfer from the glove, he flashes the ability to make very difficult plays to either his left or right. What Rojas lacks is foot speed. His glove, arm, and quick first step often compensate for the traditional speed found in most elite shortstops. Even if his bat can't carry him, Rojas will be valuable as a defensive whiz capable of manning any infield position.

Shortstops

Jimmy Rollins

	BASIC								GDP			RANGE AND POSITIONING							RUNS SAVED				
Year	Team	G	Inn	TC	E	Pct	GFP	DM	Opps	GDP	Pct	Outs Made	To His Right	Straight On	To His Left	GB	Air	Plays Saved	R/P	GDP	GFP/ DME	Total	Rank
2003	Phi	154	1357.2	680	14	.979	-	-	140	89	.636	511	+6	+5	0	+11	+1	+12	9	2	-	11	2
2004	Phi	154	1376.2	621	9	.986	39	20	130	82	.631	442	+2	+4	-1	+5	0	+5	4	2	3	9	6
2005	Phi	157	1356.0	631	12	.981	35	26	127	76	.598	473	+3	-2	+17	+19	+4	+23	17	0	1	18	4
2006	Phi	157	1378.0	670	11	.984	44	37	135	90	.667	500	-3	+4	+7	+8	+4	+12	9	3	0	12	5
2007	Phi	162	1441.1	717	11	.985	55	21	164	101	.616	529	+12	-6	-1	+5	+2	+7	5	1	-1	5	13
2008	Phi	132	1168.0	593	7	.988	65	26	127	69	.543	455	+2	+2	+16	+20	+3	+23	17	-2	3	18	1
2009	Phi	155	1364.2	607	6	.990	55	36	115	72	.626	469	-1	+4	-5	-2	-1	-3	-2	0	0	-2	24
2010	Phi	88	744.1	335	6	.982	29	11	71	56	.789	242	-9	+4	+5	0	+2	+2	1	2	0	3	14
2011	Phi	138	1207.0	581	7	.988	38	16	122	88	.721	426	-15	+9	-5	-12	+1	-11	-8	2	0	-6	28
2012	Phi	156	1364.0	594	13	.978	37	18	112	69	.616	407	-15	+5	+1	-9	-5	-14	-10	-1	3	-8	30
2013	Phi	153	1318.1	625	11	.982	47	21	142	95	.669	444	-34	+1	+10	-22	-1	-23	-18	1	2	-15	32
2014	Phi	131	1170.2	563	7	.988	24	14	122	66	.541	411	-19	+12	+13	+6	-1	+5	4	-2	2	4	10
		1737	15246.2	7217	114	.984	468	246	1507	953	.632	5309	-71	+42	+57	+29	+9	+38	28	8	13	49	-

Scout's Defensive Rating: -7 plays saved in 2013, 0 plays saved in 2014

After years of declining play, Jimmy Rollins had a bit of a defensive resurgence in 2014. While he did look better in 2014, much of his improved numbers had to do with a philosophical change of the Phillies. The Phillies were much more aggressive in defensive positioning under their new manager Ryne Sandberg. Previously a statue before the pitch, Rollins found himself in the right spot more often, allowing him to turn more batted balls into outs. Rollins' calling card over the years has been making plays on the balls he should, as he year after year has one of the lowest error totals for anyone at the position. He obviously has lost a step or two as he hits his mid-30s and the athleticism that made it exciting to watch him play shortstop is mostly gone. Although Rollins still has an accurate arm, he has lost something off his fastball, which makes plays deep in the hole very difficult for him. Dating back to his days alongside David Bell and Pedro Feliz on the left side of the Phillies infield, Rollins has cheated up the middle a step or two compared to an average shortstop, and that held true in 2014 as well. Rollins' sure hands and instincts should ensure he has a couple of more years at shortstop, but his declining range will continue to be more and more of a negative factor moving forward.

Andrew Romine

	BASIC								GDP			RANGE AND POSITIONING							RUNS SAVED				
Year	Team	G	Inn	TC	E	Pct	GFP	DM	Opps	GDP	Pct	Outs Made	To His Right	Straight On	To His Left	GB	Air	Plays Saved	R/P	GDP	GFP/ DME	Total	Rank
2010	LAA	4	29.0	19	2	.895	3	1	3	2	.667	9	0	0	0	0	-1	-1	-1	0	0	-1	-
2011	LAA	7	30.0	20	1	.950	2	0	3	3	1.000	15	0	-1	-1	-1	0	-1	-1	0	0	-1	-
2012	LAA	8	43.1	30	1	.967	4	0	9	6	.667	18	+1	-2	-2	-2	+1	-1	-1	0	0	-1	-
2013	LAA	17	86.2	48	1	.979	6	0	15	9	.600	32	+1	-1	-1	-1	+1	0	0	0	0	0	-
2014	Det	83	651.2	326	8	.975	22	12	73	46	.630	212	0	-4	-1	-5	0	-5	-4	0	1	-3	19
		119	840.2	443	13	.971	37	16	103	66	.641	286	+2	-8	-5	-9	+1	-8	-7	0	1	-6	

Scout's Defensive Rating: 1 plays saved in 2013, -4 plays saved in 2014

Andrew Romine, a veteran of seven minor league seasons, was acquired via trade late in spring training with the reputation of being a glove-first shortstop. Romine struggled at times handling relatively easy ground balls. Of his 20 Defensive Misplays and Errors (DME), seven were throwing related, and seven more came on ground balls that should've been converted into outs. To Romine's credit, he did not have a single DME in 20 September games at shortstop, a month in which he also had five of his 22 Good Fielding Plays. Despite that strong finish, Romine is likely not the long-term answer at shortstop and profiles better as a backup/utility infielder going forward.

Josh Rutledge

	BASIC								GDP			RANGE AND POSITIONING							RUNS SAVED				
Year	Team	G	Inn	TC	E	Pct	GFP	DM	Opps	GDP	Pct	Outs Made	To His Right	Straight On	To His Left	GB	Air	Plays Saved	R/P	GDP	GFP/ DME	Total	Rank
2012	Col	57	483.0	251	11	.956	24	13	53	30	.566	162	-2	-2	-7	-11	0	-11	-8	-1	-2	-11	31
2013	Col	14	115.1	61	1	.984	6	1	13	7	.538	39	0	+1	-1	+1	-1	0	0	0	0	0	-
2014	Col	69	515.1	232	9	.961	23	12	58	31	.534	162	-4	0	-1	-4	-5	-9	-7	-2	0	-9	29
		140	1113.2	544	21	.961	53	26	124	68	.548	363	-6	-1	-9	-14	-6	-20	-15	-3	-2	-20	

Scout's Defensive Rating: 0 plays saved in 2013, 2 plays saved in 2014

Rutledge was plugged in as an everyday shortstop in 2014 when Troy Tulowitzki went down for the season, but no one mistook him for the former Fielding Bible Award winner in the field. He looks a step slow and, while he can make

Shortstops

plays on balls that aren't too far away from him, his mistakes are on chances that good shortstops convert routinely. He'll bobble groundballs, which often times lead to extended innings. He hasn't fared much better in limited time at second base either. Hopefully for Rutledge he can find a way to turn his fortunes around and grow into a utility player. Barring another injury or a trade, he won't be able to crack the Rockies infield anytime soon.

Danny Santana

		BASIC						GDP			RANGE AND POSITIONING							RUNS SAVED				
Year Team	G	Inn	TC	E	Pct	GFP	DM	Opps	GDP	Pct	Outs Made	To His Right	Straight On	To His Left	GB	Air	Plays Saved	R/P	GDP	GFP/ DME	Total	Rank
2014 Min	34	261.2	120	2	.983	9	10	21	14	.667	72	-3	0	+1	-3	+1	-2	-1	0	0	-1	-

Scout's Defensive Rating: -4 plays saved in 2014

Danny Santana's Scouting Report can be found on page 274.

Jean Segura

		BASIC						GDP			RANGE AND POSITIONING							RUNS SAVED				
Year Team	G	Inn	TC	E	Pct	GFP	DM	Opps	GDP	Pct	Outs Made	To His Right	Straight On	To His Left	GB	Air	Plays Saved	R/P	GDP	GFP/ DME	Total	Rank
2012 2 tms	44	389.0	171	10	.942	20	9	27	15	.556	100	+1	-4	+1	-1	0	-1	-1	0	1	0	-
2013 Mil	144	1251.0	673	15	.978	94	46	133	90	.677	451	+4	-2	+2	+4	0	+4	3	1	-1	3	13
2014 Mil	144	1236.2	643	16	.975	65	36	140	80	.571	419	+20	-9	0	+11	-2	+9	7	-3	-2	2	14
	332	2876.2	1487	41	.972	179	91	300	185	.617	970	+25	-15	+3	+14	-2	+12	9	-2	-2	5	

Scout's Defensive Rating: 14 plays saved in 2013, 4 plays saved in 2014

Things did not come nearly as easily for Segura in 2014, as he struggled to regain his All-Star form while dealing with a tragic personal issue during the season that may have affected his play. While his offense took a major step back, he still played solid defense at shortstop, no matter where he was positioned in the Brewers' aggressive shifts. Segura's biggest strength was fielding balls hit into the hole, taking advantage of his strong arm and leading to a lofty number of Good Fielding Plays. Further, the BIS Video Scouts were very impressed by his play, resulting in the fourth-highest Scout's Defensive Rating at shortstop over 2013-14. However, Segura did not fare well turning double plays, ranking just 26th out of 35 in double plays converted per double play opportunity as both the lead man and as the pivot man. Though he may look better subjectively than objectively, he has the talent to remain an above average shortstop for years to come.

Andrelton Simmons

		BASIC						GDP			RANGE AND POSITIONING							RUNS SAVED				
Year Team	G	Inn	TC	E	Pct	GFP	DM	Opps	GDP	Pct	Outs Made	To His Right	Straight On	To His Left	GB	Air	Plays Saved	R/P	GDP	GFP/ DME	Total	Rank
2012 Atl	49	426.0	228	3	.987	23	7	36	30	.833	162	+7	+4	+7	+18	+2	+20	16	1	2	19	2
2013 Atl	156	1352.1	753	14	.981	76	25	146	90	.616	522	+27	+14	-2	+38	+11	+49	37	2	2	41	1
2014 Atl	146	1277.0	642	14	.978	69	14	130	97	.746	402	+29	+1	-4	+25	+3	+28	21	3	4	28	1
	351	3055.1	1623	31	.981	168	46	312	217	.696	1086	+63	+19	+1	+81	+16	+97	74	6	8	88	

Scout's Defensive Rating: 15 plays saved in 2013, 17 plays saved in 2014

For the second straight season, Andrelton Simmons captured the Fielding Bible Award at the shortstop position. At 6'2" and 195 pounds, Simmons is long, freakishly athletic, and extremely smooth. At the young age of 25, there is no question that Simmons is the best defensive shortstop in baseball. His hands are quick, transfers are flawless, and there is not another shortstop that has the arm strength he possesses. His backhand, transfer, and throw from deep in the hole between shortstop and third have become routine, making such plays look much easier than they actually are. He turns double plays well, ranges far in all directions... there's no part of his game that is deficient. His 41 Runs Saved in 2013 set a Defensive Runs Saved record for any player and any position. He is still so young that you can almost guarantee we will be seeing his name at the top of the Fielding Bible Awards for many years to come.

Shortstops

Eugenio Suarez

Year	Team	G	Inn	TC	E	Pct	GFP	DM	Opps	GDP	Pct	Outs Made	To His Right	Straight On	To His Left	GB	Air	Plays Saved	R/P	GDP	GFP/ DME	Total	Rank
2014	Det	81	622.1	312	10	.968	20	11	63	44	.698	198	0	-1	-6	-8	-1	-9	-6	2	-1	-5	24

Scout's Defensive Rating: -2 plays saved in 2014

There were few bright spots in Suarez's defensive game during his rookie season. He would intermittently reach a groundball that screamed single off the bat, pick it on a dive and throw the batter out in one fluid movement; however, his poor range usually had him jogging past as the groundball shot into the outfield. Intermittently indeed, Suarez was awarded just five Good Fielding Plays on groundball outs, good for second fewest among regulars at shortstop. The overall manner in which he fields his position is unimpressive. In fact, he converted just 7 percent of "difficult" plays compared to the league average of 14 percent. Suarez's athleticism did shine through in one area, accumulating Good Fielding Plays on six line drive outs that might have gone over the head of a lesser shortstop. Unfortunately, he may not have much opportunity to improve going forward as Jose Iglesias is expected to return to short for the Tigers.

Chris Taylor

Year	Team	G	Inn	TC	E	Pct	GFP	DM	Opps	GDP	Pct	Outs Made	To His Right	Straight On	To His Left	GB	Air	Plays Saved	R/P	GDP	GFP/ DME	Total	Rank
2014	Sea	47	365.0	184	7	.962	14	10	31	20	.645	130	+5	-1	0	+4	0	+4	3	0	1	4	-

Scout's Defensive Rating: -2 plays saved in 2014

Ruben Tejada

Year	Team	G	Inn	TC	E	Pct	GFP	DM	Opps	GDP	Pct	Outs Made	To His Right	Straight On	To His Left	GB	Air	Plays Saved	R/P	GDP	GFP/ DME	Total	Rank
2010	NYM	28	221.2	110	2	.982	11	4	28	15	.536	75	-2	-1	+4	+1	-2	-1	0	-1	0	-1	-
2011	NYM	41	353.0	181	8	.956	30	10	43	19	.442	126	-7	+1	+9	+2	+2	+4	3	-3	0	0	-
2012	NYM	112	964.2	456	12	.974	52	15	104	70	.673	291	-9	-1	+6	-2	-2	-4	-3	0	3	0	17
2013	NYM	55	499.0	257	8	.969	30	13	54	36	.667	168	-3	0	0	-3	-6	-9	-7	1	0	-6	28
2014	NYM	114	939.1	494	8	.984	42	17	120	74	.617	322	+1	+7	-1	+6	+1	+7	6	-2	-1	3	13
		350	2977.2	1498	38	.975	165	59	349	214	.613	982	-20	+8	+18	+4	-7	-3	-1	-5	2	-4	-

Scout's Defensive Rating: 0 plays saved in 2013, 7 plays saved in 2014

Ruben Tejada is a young, versatile shortstop for the Metropolitans who doesn't get a lot of attention in an infield that has such star players as David Wright, Daniel Murphy and Lucas Duda. Tejada has a strong arm and a quick release, helping him rank in the top 15 shortstops in Defensive Runs Saved in 2014. However, after three seasons partnering with Daniel Murphy, Tejada is still struggling to find a rhythm on double plays, costing the Mets five runs between the two in 2014. Tejada sometimes rushes his throws, which leads to inaccuracy. He has a smooth approach when fielding balls straight on and shows good range to his right, but mediocre range to his left. All told, Tejada rates as an average defender, which has plenty of value even if he doesn't live up to New Yorkers' lofty expectations.

Troy Tulowitzki

Year	Team	G	Inn	TC	E	Pct	GFP	DM	Opps	GDP	Pct	Outs Made	To His Right	Straight On	To His Left	GB	Air	Plays Saved	R/P	GDP	GFP/ DME	Total	Rank
2006	Col	25	220.1	118	2	.983	11	9	34	23	.676	71	-1	-2	-3	-6	+1	-5	-4	1	0	-3	-
2007	Col	155	1375.0	834	11	.987	77	45	167	108	.647	614	+24	+5	+6	+35	0	+35	27	3	1	31	1
2008	Col	101	863.1	509	8	.984	39	18	114	62	.544	355	-4	+4	+1	+1	+3	+4	3	-1	0	2	15
2009	Col	151	1294.0	657	9	.986	75	27	119	85	.714	485	+11	0	-1	+9	+2	+11	8	2	3	13	5
2010	Col	122	1065.0	610	10	.984	58	23	144	107	.743	376	+5	+4	+4	+12	+3	+15	11	4	1	16	4
2011	Col	140	1208.1	684	6	.991	67	23	146	104	.712	430	+12	+1	-2	+10	-3	+7	6	2	4	12	3
2012	Col	47	404.0	224	8	.964	19	9	49	34	.694	149	-6	+1	+1	-4	-4	-8	-6	0	0	-6	26
2013	Col	121	1029.1	570	8	.986	55	22	132	86	.652	381	-7	+14	+5	+13	-4	+9	7	0	-1	6	7
2014	Col	89	739.2	392	4	.990	45	14	90	62	.689	269	-10	+10	+7	+6	+1	+7	5	1	1	7	8
		951	8199.0	4598	66	.986	446	190	995	671	.674	3130	+24	+37	+18	+76	-1	+75	57	12	9	78	-

Scout's Defensive Rating: 10 plays saved in 2013, 11 plays saved in 2014

Shortstops

A force with the lumber and the leather, Troy Tulowitzki is one of the most complete baseball players in the majors. Here's a measure of a great defensive infielder: the number of times you'll watch a replay of a groundball that doesn't record an out. Tulowitzki is one of a few shortstops that create highlights with plays nearly made. He stretches the realm of possibility with great hands, flawless footwork, a powerful and accurate arm, and instincts that maximize the value of these physical attributes. The way he fields the ball is hypnotically fluid and results in some of the most entertaining defense displayed by a shortstop. In 2014, injury-prone Tulowitzki was sidelined by ailment yet again, logging only 88 games started and limiting the effect of this prowess on some of his defensive statistics. He was ranked 10th with 24 groundball-related Good Fielding Plays, a mark that would have certainly been inflated with a full season, as he compiled them at a per inning rate which ranked third.

One of Tulowitzki's only shortcomings in 2014–besides the health issues–was ranging to his right. Formerly his greatest strength, he has become far less effective in the hole, marked by failed dives and empty stabs. Groundballs just seemed to have a hard time reaching his webbing in that direction, evidenced by his below average out rate on backhanded plays. Nevertheless, the rest of his game was able to make up for this inadequacy. Overall, this three-time Fielding Bible Award winner remains among the best shortstops in baseball when he's on the field.

Jonathan Villar

		BASIC							GDP			RANGE AND POSITIONING							RUNS SAVED				
Year	Team	G	Inn	TC	E	Pct	GFP	DM	Opps	GDP	Pct	Outs Made	To His Right	Straight On	To His Left	GB	Air	Plays Saved	R/P	GDP	GFP/DME	Total	Rank
2013	Hou	58	499.0	252	16	.937	13	12	50	36	.720	140	+1	-2	-2	-4	+2	-2	-2	0	-3	-5	26
2014	Hou	82	678.2	351	18	.949	35	21	78	47	.603	165	0	-4	+2	-2	+1	-1	0	-1	-1	-2	17
		140	1177.2	603	34	.944	48	33	128	83	.648	305	+1	-6	0	-6	+3	-3	-2	-1	-4	-7	-

Scout's Defensive Rating: -9 plays saved in 2013, -9 plays saved in 2014

At 23 years of age, Jonathan Villar is still something of a work in progress at shortstop for the Astros. There's a lot to like about the 6'1", 205-pound Dominican, particularly in his ability to make tougher plays; among shortstops with 300 or more total opportunities in 2014, Villar ranked 12th in making plays viewed as "difficult," at 14.3 percent. But, as is often the case with younger players, Villar struggled with "routine" plays, making them 96.5 percent of the time, fourth-worst among shortstops in that category.

Despite his inconsistencies, Villar showed demonstrable improvement from 2013 to 2014. In 2013, Villar's Good Throw Rate was 86.4 percent, by far the worst in baseball among shortstops with 100 or more throws to first base. In 2014, that number improved to 93 percent, roughly in-line with Didi Gregorius and above notables such as Alcides Escobar and Erick Aybar. All told, Villar improved from 26th in Defensive Runs Saved in 2013 to 17th in 2014 among shortstops. Villar has the athleticism, hands and arm strength to play well at shortstop; he needs to improve mentally for that to happen.

Ben Zobrist

		BASIC							GDP			RANGE AND POSITIONING							RUNS SAVED				
Year	Team	G	Inn	TC	E	Pct	GFP	DM	Opps	GDP	Pct	Outs Made	To His Right	Straight On	To His Left	GB	Air	Plays Saved	R/P	GDP	GFP/DME	Total	Rank
2006	TB	52	440.2	242	9	.963	21	9	52	30	.577	173	-1	-2	-2	-5	0	-5	-4	0	2	-2	23
2007	TB	30	224.2	106	6	.943	4	9	25	14	.560	71	-2	-4	-1	-7	0	-7	-5	0	0	-5	-
2008	TB	35	293.1	136	7	.949	14	8	41	22	.537	90	0	-1	-7	-8	0	-8	-6	-1	-1	-8	-
2009	TB	13	62.0	27	2	.926	4	1	7	5	.714	16	+1	-1	+2	+2	0	+2	2	0	0	2	-
2012	TB	47	392.0	189	4	.979	9	6	29	24	.828	135	+2	0	-5	-2	-2	-4	-3	1	2	0	17
2013	TB	21	115.0	49	1	.980	7	1	8	4	.500	36	+4	0	0	+4	0	+4	3	0	0	3	-
2014	TB	31	236.1	75	2	.973	13	3	15	11	.733	54	+1	+1	-2	+1	0	+1	0	0	0	0	-
		229	1764.0	824	31	.962	72	37	177	110	.621	575	+5	-7	-15	-15	-2	-17	-13	0	3	-10	-

Scout's Defensive Rating: 1 plays saved in 2013, 3 plays saved in 2014

Ben Zobrist's Scouting Report can be found on page 205.

Left Fielders Register and Scouting Reports

Year	Fielding Bible Award Winner	Runner Up	Third Place
2006	Carl Crawford	Reed Johnson	Dave Roberts
2007	Eric Byrnes	Carl Crawford	Alfonso Soriano
2008	Carl Crawford	Willie Harris	Matt Holliday
2009	Carl Crawford	Nyjer Morgan	David DeJesus
2010	Brett Gardner	Carl Crawford	Jose Tabata
2011	Brett Gardner	Tony Gwynn Jr.	Gerardo Parra
2012	Alex Gordon	Martin Prado	Desmond Jennings
2013	Alex Gordon	Starling Marte	Carlos Gonzalez
2014	Alex Gordon	Christian Yelich	Yoenis Cespedes

Left Fielders

Dustin Ackley

Year	Team	G	Inn	TC	E	Pct	GFP	DM	Opps to Advance	Extra Bases	Pct	Kills	Outs Made	Plays Saved	Shallow	Medium	Deep	Bases Saved	R/P	Throws	GFP/ DME	Total	Rank
				BASIC					THROWING				RANGE AND POSITIONING		Plays Saved				RUNS SAVED				
2013	Sea	11	81.1	21	0	1.000	1	1	13	4	.308	0	20	+1	0	0	0	+1	0	0	0	0	-
2014	Sea	133	1130.0	252	2	.992	17	17	89	25	.281	2	247	+8	+9	+4	-5	+6	5	2	1	8	4
		144	1211.1	273	2	.993	18	18	102	29	.284	2	267	+9	+9	+4	-5	+7	5	2	1	8	-

Scout's Defensive Rating: 0 plays saved in 2013, -1 plays saved in 2014

After splitting time primarily between second base and center field in 2013, Dustin Ackley found a home for himself in left field for the Mariners in 2014. The amount of work he put in with coach Andy Van Slyke was very evident in his ability to read balls and take efficient routes. He still has some trouble going back on the ball, but his overall Plays Made was a strong +8 and he finished the season tied for fourth among left fielders with eight Runs Saved.

Ackley does not have a strong arm, but he is often able to hold runners with his accuracy and ability to catch and throw quickly. There is further improvement to be made, but Dustin Ackley has shown he has all the ability to be a very effective left fielder. And although he is unlikely to play the position again in the near future with the presence of Robinson Cano, Ackley is still very capable of playing second base as well.

Gregor Blanco

Year	Team	G	Inn	TC	E	Pct	GFP	DM	Opps to Advance	Extra Bases	Pct	Kills	Outs Made	Plays Saved	Shallow	Medium	Deep	Bases Saved	R/P	Throws	GFP/ DME	Total	Rank
				BASIC					THROWING				RANGE AND POSITIONING		Plays Saved				RUNS SAVED				
2008	Atl	77	512.2	91	2	.978	7	9	52	26	.500	2	86	0	-1	-1	+2	+3	2	-3	0	-1	19
2009	Atl	3	8.0	2	1	.500	0	0	1	0	.000	0	0	-1	-1	0	0	-1	-1	0	0	-1	-
2010	2 tms	8	21.1	2	0	1.000	0	1	3	1	.333	0	2	-2	0	-1	-2	-3	-2	0	0	-2	-
2012	SF	53	278.1	46	0	1.000	4	4	28	6	.214	1	44	+2	0	0	+1	+3	1	2	0	3	-
2013	SF	72	470.2	94	0	1.000	7	5	44	13	.295	3	90	+6	+4	+2	0	+8	5	1	0	6	4
2014	SF	64	361.0	80	1	.988	10	6	22	8	.364	1	78	+4	+1	0	+4	+10	5	-1	0	4	-
		277	1652.0	315	4	.987	28	25	150	54	.360	7	300	+9	+3	0	+5	+20	10	-1	0	9	-

Scout's Defensive Rating: 0 plays saved in 2013, 3 plays saved in 2014

Gregor Blanco's Scouting Report can be found on page 259.

Michael Brantley

Year	Team	G	Inn	TC	E	Pct	GFP	DM	Opps to Advance	Extra Bases	Pct	Kills	Outs Made	Plays Saved	Shallow	Medium	Deep	Bases Saved	R/P	Throws	GFP/ DME	Total	Rank
				BASIC					THROWING				RANGE AND POSITIONING		Plays Saved				RUNS SAVED				
2009	Cle	8	63.1	13	0	1.000	0	0	11	1	.091	0	13	0	0	0	0	+1	0	1	0	1	-
2010	Cle	7	63.0	5	0	1.000	0	0	7	0	.000	0	5	-1	+1	0	-2	-3	-1	1	0	0	-
2011	Cle	66	558.1	125	2	.984	10	8	52	14	.269	3	118	+8	+3	+5	0	+10	6	2	1	9	6
2013	Cle	151	1293.1	268	0	1.000	23	9	119	38	.319	10	257	-2	+8	-2	-8	-10	-4	4	4	4	10
2014	Cle	107	931.1	175	0	1.000	14	10	93	34	.366	6	165	-4	+2	-2	-5	-8	-4	3	2	1	17
		339	2909.1	586	2	.997	47	27	282	87	.309	19	558	+1	+14	+1	-15	-10	-3	11	7	15	-

Scout's Defensive Rating: 2 plays saved in 2013, -2 plays saved in 2014

Michael Brantley has a phenomenal build for an outfielder, standing at 6'2" and 200 pounds. He is fairly athletic, but the best aspect of his defense is his arm. History has shown that his arm plays very well in left but struggles with the longer distances from center field. His range is below average in center, with most of his difficulties occurring on flyballs that had him sprinting back on the ball. He does manage to get decent breaks on the ball in left, though, especially those that involve him coming in on the ball. On the other hand, he has struggled with Progressive Field's tall left field wall. If Brantley stays put in left, his arm should continue to make him an asset.

Left Fielders

Domonic Brown

	BASIC							THROWING				RANGE AND POSITIONING						RUNS SAVED			
Year Team	G	Inn	TC	E	Pct	GFP	DM	Opps to Advance	Extra Bases	Pct	Kills	Outs Made	Plays Saved	Plays Saved Shallow	Medium	Deep	Bases Saved	R/P	Throws	GFP/DME	Total	Rank
2012 Phi	29	141.2	34	0	1.000	4	4	14	4	.286	2	31	-2	-2	0	0	-4	-2	1	1	0	-
2013 Phi	132	1123.2	199	5	.975	26	25	119	29	.244	5	185	-12	0	-8	-4	-22	-11	4	2	-5	29
2014 Phi	127	1041.1	188	2	.989	14	19	102	34	.333	4	182	-9	0	-1	-7	-15	-8	3	-2	-7	31
	288	2306.2	421	7	.983	44	48	235	67	.285	11	398	-23	-2	-9	-11	-41	-21	8	1	-12	-

Scout's Defensive Rating: -4 plays saved in 2013, -2 plays saved in 2014

Dominic Brown is 6'5" and 230 pounds with an athletic frame. He actually has decent speed for his size, but he is simply not a good outfielder no matter where you hide him. His routes are terrible and his glove is below average too. Brown has trouble catching the ball on the run and often overruns balls that are hit in the gap. Brown's arm is adequate for right field thanks to the fact that he cheats in, but that costs him when chasing flies over his head. Brown's arm plays well in left but does not compensate for his terrible range. Even if his offensive production rebounds, his defense will always limit his upside.

Melky Cabrera

	BASIC							THROWING				RANGE AND POSITIONING						RUNS SAVED			
Year Team	G	Inn	TC	E	Pct	GFP	DM	Opps to Advance	Extra Bases	Pct	Kills	Outs Made	Plays Saved	Plays Saved Shallow	Medium	Deep	Bases Saved	R/P	Throws	GFP/DME	Total	Rank
2006 NYY	116	998.2	230	1	.996	18	17	121	44	.364	9	217	+10	+6	+4	0	+13	7	3	3	13	3
2007 NYY	18	142.0	36	0	1.000	5	2	13	3	.231	2	34	+2	+2	+1	0	+5	3	2	2	7	-
2008 NYY	8	18.0	4	0	1.000	1	0	2	1	.500	0	4	0	0	-1	+1	+1	1	0	0	1	-
2009 NYY	40	204.1	39	1	.974	3	3	17	6	.353	0	38	+2	+1	0	+1	+4	2	0	0	2	-
2010 Atl	84	481.1	86	1	.988	6	12	48	14	.292	3	82	-5	-2	0	-4	-8	-4	2	0	-2	25
2011 KC	12	63.0	15	0	1.000	0	0	10	1	.100	0	15	0	-1	+1	0	0	0	1	0	1	-
2012 SF	106	898.0	195	4	.979	21	15	72	23	.319	6	185	-2	+2	+1	-4	-7	-3	2	1	0	19
2013 Tor	77	620.2	130	1	.992	17	10	58	19	.328	2	126	-7	-1	-2	-4	-12	-6	0	2	-4	26
2014 Tor	133	1134.2	245	2	.992	27	19	107	38	.355	11	230	-10	0	-10	0	-23	-11	6	2	-3	26
	594	4560.2	980	10	.990	98	78	448	149	.333	33	931	-10	+7	-6	-10	-27	-11	16	10	15	-

Scout's Defensive Rating: 3 plays saved in 2013, 1 plays saved in 2014

Melky Cabrera has one of the best arms of any left fielder in the majors. His 11 Kills and six Outfield Arm Runs Saved were both second and third, respectively, among left fielders in 2014. These highlight reel throws can overshadow the struggles that Cabrera has with the rest of his defensive game, though. Cabrera routinely gets bad jumps and takes bad routes, playing catchable balls into hits. In 2014,Cabrera's issues with medium depth flyballs just further point to his struggles getting good reads off the bat. Cabrera still has enough speed to cover up for some of his mistakes, and he has pretty good range when he does get a good jump on the ball. Overall, though, his struggles in getting to catchable balls negate any positives he brings with his arm and athleticism.

Yoenis Cespedes

	BASIC							THROWING				RANGE AND POSITIONING						RUNS SAVED			
Year Team	G	Inn	TC	E	Pct	GFP	DM	Opps to Advance	Extra Bases	Pct	Kills	Outs Made	Plays Saved	Plays Saved Shallow	Medium	Deep	Bases Saved	R/P	Throws	GFP/DME	Total	Rank
2012 Oak	56	468.2	102	3	.971	15	13	44	13	.295	3	94	-5	-4	-4	-2	-6	-3	3	1	1	16
2013 Oak	94	801.1	200	4	.980	15	21	60	21	.350	5	187	+3	-4	+1	+6	+8	3	3	-3	3	12
2014 2 tms	125	1090.2	237	5	.979	25	21	104	25	.240	14	217	-9	-7	-2	0	-9	-7	14	4	11	3
	275	2360.2	539	12	.978	55	55	208	59	.284	22	498	-11	-15	0	+4	-7	-7	20	2	15	-

Scout's Defensive Rating: -1 plays saved in 2013, -9 plays saved in 2014

The 2014 season for Cespedes was a memorable one defensively with plays that seem to have etched themselves into many fans' memories forever. During back-to-back games in mid June, Cespedes gunned down Howie Kendrick at home and Albert Pujols at third on extra-base hits to deep left field. While he initially misplayed both these balls, his 300-foot throws more than made up for that. He led all of Major League Baseball in outfield assists with 16, 14 of which were Kills (outfield assists without the use of a cutoff man), the most in baseball. While he has always graded out poorly on shallow flyballs, it's understandable because of the trust Cespedes has (rightfully so) in his cannon of an arm. He wants to keep the play in front of him at all times and plays naturally deep. His naturally deep positioning has also helped him stay in front of the baseball and hold runners to singles. This allows Cespedes to keep the play in front of him while charging after the ball.

Left Fielders

Michael Choice

Year	Team	G	Inn	TC	E	Pct	GFP	DM	Opps to Advance	Extra Bases	Pct	Kills	Outs Made	Plays Saved	Shallow	Medium	Deep	Bases Saved	R/P	Throws	GFP/DME	Total	Rank
				BASIC					THROWING				RANGE AND POSITIONING		Plays Saved				RUNS SAVED				
2013	Oak	2	12.0	3	0	1.000	0	0				0	3	0	0	0	0	0	0	0	0	0	-
2014	Tex	41	314.0	82	3	.963	6	8	49	22	.449	2	75	-4	-3	+3	-4	-7	-4	-1	0	-5	-
		43	326.0	85	3	.965	6	8	49	22	.449	2	78	-4	-3	+3	-4	-7	-4	-1	0	-5	-

Scout's Defensive Rating: 0 plays saved in 2013, -1 plays saved in 2014

Shin-Soo Choo

Year	Team	G	Inn	TC	E	Pct	GFP	DM	Opps to Advance	Extra Bases	Pct	Kills	Outs Made	Plays Saved	Shallow	Medium	Deep	Bases Saved	R/P	Throws	GFP/DME	Total	Rank
				BASIC					THROWING				RANGE AND POSITIONING		Plays Saved				RUNS SAVED				
2006	Cle	9	77.2	15	1	.933	1	0	6	2	.333	0	14	0	0	0	0	+1	1	0	0	1	-
2007	Cle	3	32.0	11	0	1.000	1	0	4	2	.500	1	10	+1	+1	0	0	+1	1	0	0	1	-
2008	Cle	26	223.0	44	1	.977	7	5	38	14	.368	3	40	+2	+1	0	+1	+2	1	2	0	3	-
2009	Cle	20	164.0	37	0	1.000	4	3	19	9	.474	0	37	0	0	-2	+2	+3	1	-2	0	-1	-
2013	Cin	3	28.0	5	0	1.000	0	0	2	0	.000	0	4	0	0	0	0	0	0	0	0	0	-
2014	Tex	64	520.1	106	3	.972	6	14	66	31	.470	2	100	-8	-2	-4	-2	-10	-6	-2	-1	-9	33
		125	1045.0	218	5	.977	19	22	135	58	.430	6	205	-5	0	-6	+1	-3	-2	-2	-1	-5	-

Scout's Defensive Rating: 0 plays saved in 2013, -5 plays saved in 2014

Hampered by injuries this year to the point of calling it a season early, Choo's defensive numbers in left field for Texas were so bad that they rivaled his poor showing in center a year ago. Choo's arm, both its power and accuracy, is his obvious calling card. While he has shown above average range in right field in his past, he was below average as a center fielder in 2013 and not very impressive in left.

In fact, 2014 was his third straight season with horrific defensive metrics, and it was fairly clear during games how the numbers would judge him. Again, his arm saves him from moving to DH sooner than he will. He is above average at preventing runners from taking extra bases on batted balls. He has shown athleticism and good jumps in the field before, and perhaps in 2015 he will be fully healthy and show improvements.

Chris Coghlan

Year	Team	G	Inn	TC	E	Pct	GFP	DM	Opps to Advance	Extra Bases	Pct	Kills	Outs Made	Plays Saved	Shallow	Medium	Deep	Bases Saved	R/P	Throws	GFP/DME	Total	Rank
				BASIC					THROWING				RANGE AND POSITIONING		Plays Saved				RUNS SAVED				
2009	Fla	123	1039.1	217	5	.977	16	22	94	33	.351	2	210	-15	-5	-2	-8	-31	-15	-1	-3	-19	35
2010	Fla	90	770.0	168	1	.994	20	12	83	29	.349	7	160	-1	+2	+2	-6	-8	-3	3	4	4	11
2012	Mia	21	120.1	32	0	1.000	4	4	22	11	.500	0	32	-1	-1	-2	+2	+1	0	-1	0	-1	-
2013	Mia	18	146.0	44	0	1.000	3	1	17	4	.235	0	43	-3	-2	-1	0	-3	-2	0	0	-2	-
2014	ChC	101	812.2	174	4	.977	16	11	92	39	.424	4	164	-10	+1	-4	-7	-21	-10	-2	1	-11	35
		353	2888.1	635	10	.984	59	50	308	116	.377	13	609	-30	-5	-7	-19	-62	-30	-1	2	-29	-

Scout's Defensive Rating: 0 plays saved in 2013, 4 plays saved in 2014

Coghlan is a below average outfielder in every regard. He has the tendency to get a late break and take bad routes, at times forcing himself to make extreme efforts to make up for an early miscue. Furthermore, he thinks like a better defensive outfielder and plays shallow, but it only burns him with frequent extra-base hits over his head. Coghlan shows fair arm strength but is encouraged to not force a throw as his accuracy is below average. Coghlan's bat has continued to get him looks, but his glove ensures that they are brief.

Tyler Colvin

Year	Team	G	Inn	TC	E	Pct	GFP	DM	Opps to Advance	Extra Bases	Pct	Kills	Outs Made	Plays Saved	Shallow	Medium	Deep	Bases Saved	R/P	Throws	GFP/DME	Total	Rank
				BASIC					THROWING				RANGE AND POSITIONING		Plays Saved				RUNS SAVED				
2010	ChC	55	262.0	47	0	1.000	0	4	28	15	.536	0	47	0	-2	+1	+1	+2	1	-2	-1	-2	-
2011	ChC	10	43.1	10	0	1.000	0	0	3	3	1.000	0	10	+1	0	0	+2	+3	2	-1	0	1	-
2012	Col	10	52.0	6	0	1.000	1	1	12	4	.333	0	6	-1	-1	0	0	-1	-1	-1	0	-2	-
2013	Col	4	21.0				0	0	3	1	.333	0	5	0	0	0	0	0	0	0	0	0	-
2014	SF	43	292.0	52	1	.981	3	2	25	12	.480	1	49	-1	-1	-1	+1	-1	-1	-1	0	-2	-
		122	670.1	120	1	.992	4	7	71	35	.493	1	117	-1	-4	0	+4	+3	1	-5	-1	-5	-

Scout's Defensive Rating: 0 plays saved in 2013, -1 plays saved in 2014

Left Fielders

Collin Cowgill

Year	Team		BASIC							THROWING				RANGE AND POSITIONING						RUNS SAVED				
		G	Inn	TC	E	Pct	GFP	DM	Opps to Advance	Extra Bases	Pct	Kills	Outs Made	Plays Saved	Shallow	Medium	Deep	Bases Saved	R/P	Throws	GFP/DME	Total	Rank
2011	Ari	18	138.0	44	0	1.000	2	2	18	8	.444	0	43	+6	+2	+2	+3	+10	5	-1	-1	3	-
2012	Oak	16	100.1	27	0	1.000	0	2	15	4	.267	0	27	0	0	+1	-1	-1	0	0	0	0	-
2013	2 tms	32	124.1	18	1	.944	4	1	18	6	.333	0	17	+1	+1	0	0	+2	1	-1	0	0	-
2014	LAA	44	272.0	69	1	.986	5	2	19	8	.421	1	67	+3	+2	+1	-1	+4	2	0	0	2	-
		110	634.2	158	2	.987	11	7	70	26	.371	1	154	+10	+5	+4	+1	+15	8	-2	-1	5	-

Scout's Defensive Rating: 1 plays saved in 2013, 2 plays saved in 2014

Carl Crawford

Year	Team		BASIC							THROWING				RANGE AND POSITIONING						RUNS SAVED				
		G	Inn	TC	E	Pct	GFP	DM	Opps to Advance	Extra Bases	Pct	Kills	Outs Made	Plays Saved	Shallow	Medium	Deep	Bases Saved	R/P	Throws	GFP/DME	Total	Rank
2003	TB	137	1159.1	330	3	.991	-	-	134	47	.351	5	294	+9	+5	+1	+4	+14	8	2	-	10	1
2004	TB	123	1010.0	280	1	.996	14	21	107	30	.280	3	270	+14	+8	+3	+3	+22	12	3	-1	14	1
2005	TB	147	1246.2	346	2	.994	29	20	159	38	.239	3	341	+15	+6	+2	+7	+19	11	4	-3	12	2
2006	TB	148	1252.1	314	3	.990	14	28	156	60	.385	7	302	+6	+2	+2	+1	+10	6	-1	0	5	9
2007	TB	139	1186.1	293	4	.986	18	16	143	45	.315	2	286	0	+1	+1	-1	0	0	-1	-1	-2	22
2008	TB	108	920.2	237	4	.983	20	11	69	23	.333	0	231	+16	+9	+5	+3	+23	13	-1	-1	11	2
2009	TB	154	1282.2	337	4	.988	29	24	118	36	.305	5	328	+22	+22	+6	-6	+22	15	4	0	19	1
2010	TB	147	1260.1	315	2	.994	32	15	85	31	.365	3	306	+10	+9	+5	-4	+12	7	0	1	8	4
2011	Bos	127	1098.1	239	3	.987	17	19	112	35	.313	0	235	-1	+3	+8	-11	-4	-2	0	1	-1	22
2012	Bos	30	245.2	43	1	.977	3	1	21	9	.429	0	42	+2	+3	0	-1	+2	1	-1	1	1	-
2013	LAD	107	835.2	172	4	.977	12	10	71	26	.366	0	165	+6	+3	+2	+1	+11	5	-3	-2	0	18
2014	LAD	94	736.0	136	3	.978	11	13	69	25	.362	1	132	+3	-2	+4	+1	+5	3	-1	-1	1	16
		1461	12234.0	3042	34	.989	199	178	1244	405	.326	29	2932	+102	+69	+39	-3	+136	79	5	-6	78	-

Scout's Defensive Rating: 2 plays saved in 2013, -2 plays saved in 2014

Carl Crawford was once a mainstay on lists of elite defensive outfielders, winning three of the first four Fielding Bible Awards for left fielders between 2006 and 2009. Crawford is now a consistently average left fielder. Crawford's best defensive attribute is still his range. He continues to possess enough of his once elite speed to cover a lot of ground in left field. Crawford has a subpar arm in terms of both strength and accuracy, and teams aggressively challenge his arm and successfully take the extra base with great frequency. Crawford has cost his team 5 runs with his arm over the past 3 seasons, which places him 29th out of the 35 regulars in left field over that time period. Crawford is no longer among the elite left fielders in the game, but as long as his legs continue to be an asset, he should remain serviceable in the field for a few more seasons.

Nelson Cruz

Year	Team		BASIC							THROWING				RANGE AND POSITIONING						RUNS SAVED				
		G	Inn	TC	E	Pct	GFP	DM	Opps to Advance	Extra Bases	Pct	Kills	Outs Made	Plays Saved	Shallow	Medium	Deep	Bases Saved	R/P	Throws	GFP/DME	Total	Rank
2005	Mil	2	2.0	0	0	-	0	0				0										0	-
2006	Tex	1	3.0	0	0	-	0	0				0	0	0	0	0	0	0	0			0	-
2007	Tex	16	118.0	20	0	1.000	2	1	11	5	.455	1	19	+1	0	0	+1	+2	1	0	0	1	-
2009	Tex	2	17.0	8	1	.875	0	1	2	2	1.000	0	7	+1	0	0	0	+1	0	-1	0	-1	-
2010	Tex	14	88.2	22	0	1.000	1	1	8	3	.375	0	22	+1	0	0	+1	+2	1	-1	0	0	-
2011	Tex	18	135.0	31	1	.968	1	1	8	3	.375	1	29	0	+1	0	-1	0	0	1	0	1	-
2012	Tex	6	21.0	2	0	1.000	0	0				0	2	-1	0	0	-1	-2	-1	0	0	-1	-
2014	Bal	60	501.2	115	0	1.000	8	8	50	18	.360	1	113	+2	-2	+4	+1	+3	2	0	0	2	13
		119	886.1	198	2	.990	12	12	79	31	.392	3	192	+4	-1	+4	+1	+6	3	-1	0	2	-

Scout's Defensive Rating: -1 plays saved in 2014

At 6'2" and 230 pounds, Cruz has never been a nimble outfielder, and though he spent over half of the season in the designated hitter role, he made a case that he won't necessarily hurt a team by playing either corner outfield spot. Overall, Cruz's speed is not much to write home about, and at age 34 it is unlikely that Cruz is going to be able to improve his ability to track down flyballs using his legs. His arm is much like his overall outfield abilities, which is average, meaning he can be used in right as well as left. He can fill the role of playing in the outfield if needed, and he will give an honest effort as he has zero fear of laying out, but his value as a player lies with his offense more so than his defense.

Left Fielders

Khris Davis

Year	Team	G	Inn	TC	E	Pct	GFP	DM	Opps to Advance	Extra Bases	Pct	Kills	Outs Made	Plays Saved	Shallow	Medium	Deep	Bases Saved	R/P	Throws	GFP/DME	Total	Rank
2013	Mil	34	265.0	49	1	.980	3	3	23	8	.348	0	47	0	-1	0	+1	+1	0	-1	-1	-2	-
2014	Mil	134	1156.1	257	3	.988	16	12	88	37	.420	1	252	+8	-1	+5	+5	+16	8	-3	-1	4	10
		168	1421.1	306	4	.987	19	15	111	45	.405	1	299	+8	-2	+5	+6	+17	8	-4	-2	2	-

Scout's Defensive Rating: 1 plays saved in 2013, 2 plays saved in 2014

The lesser-known "Khrush Davis" established himself as a full time left fielder in 2014. Davis proved that he could play a solid left field, saving the Brewers four runs at the position in 2014. He has shown a knack for being able to use his speed to track down deep flyballs, almost always taking good routes and minimizing mistakes.

The one thing that's keeping Davis from the upper tier of left fielders is his arm. In 2014 alone, he cost the Brewers three runs with his arm and allowed opponents to take the extra base on 37 of 88 chances, a rate of 42 percent. Davis is fast and almost always gets a good break on the ball to help alleviate the arm strength issue. The arm will likely always be a problem, but it is fairly manageable if kept in left field.

Rajai Davis

Year	Team	G	Inn	TC	E	Pct	GFP	DM	Opps to Advance	Extra Bases	Pct	Kills	Outs Made	Plays Saved	Shallow	Medium	Deep	Bases Saved	R/P	Throws	GFP/DME	Total	Rank
2007	SF	7	20.2	7	0	1.000	0	1	4	1	.250	0	7	0	0	0	0	0	0	0	0	0	-
2008	SF	3	7.0	2	0	1.000	0	0	2	1	.500	0	2	0	-1	0	+1	+1	1	0	0	1	-
2010	Oak	47	320.1	59	1	.983	1	10	29	11	.379	0	56	-1	-1	-1	+1	-2	-1	-2	-3	-6	-
2011	Tor	4	36.0	5	0	1.000	0	0	1	0	.000	0	5	0	-1	0	0	0	0	0	0	0	-
2012	Tor	114	856.1	186	7	.962	18	15	102	28	.275	6	171	-8	-5	-4	+1	-11	-6	5	2	1	17
2013	Tor	57	381.1	93	2	.978	8	4	43	12	.279	1	89	+3	+2	-1	+2	+5	3	0	-1	2	-
2014	Det	99	684.0	170	4	.976	11	11	86	39	.453	5	161	-3	0	0	-3	-8	-4	-2	-1	-7	29
		331	2305.2	522	14	.973	38	41	267	92	.345	12	491	-9	-6	-6	+2	-15	-7	1	-3	-9	-

Scout's Defensive Rating: 3 plays saved in 2013, 1 plays saved in 2014

Rajai Davis's best asset is his speed; unfortunately, he has not quite figured out how to appropriately apply that talent to the outfield. Somewhat awkward routes and occasional timidity plagued this speed demon and limited his productivity in left field. On numerous occasions, a flyball to Davis's area of the field would fall just out of reach as he jogged to field the bounce or slid in a reserved attempt to make the out. Reservations were the main issue here. On the instances where Davis decided to open up the jets and leave his feet, remarkably Good Fielding Plays ensued. Poor range was not the only defensive woe experienced by Davis in 2014, as the lack of an adequate throwing arm proved to be trouble-some as well. An adeptness in getting to the ball quickly was often nullified by mediocre arm strength. Balls hit to his position resulted in extras bases at a rate that ranked fifth highest among regulars in left field despite tying for fourth in baserunner kills by gunning down five of the baserunners who decided to challenge him without the need for a cutoff man. A bolder approach would allow Davis to take better advantage of his speed and make him an asset, rather than a question mark, in left field.

Alejandro De Aza

Year	Team	G	Inn	TC	E	Pct	GFP	DM	Opps to Advance	Extra Bases	Pct	Kills	Outs Made	Plays Saved	Shallow	Medium	Deep	Bases Saved	R/P	Throws	GFP/DME	Total	Rank
2009	Fla	6	10.0	2	0	1.000	0	0	1	1	1.000	0	2	0	0	0	0	0	0	0	0	0	-
2011	CWS	4	21.0	2	0	1.000	0	0	2	0	.000	0	9	0	-1	0	0	0	0	0	0	0	-
2012	CWS	11	54.2	12	0	1.000	1	1	2	1	.500	0	12	+1	0	0	0	0	0	0	0	0	-
2013	CWS	79	426.2	102	3	.971	10	10	47	15	.319	1	97	+2	+1	+1	0	+4	2	-1	-3	-2	25
2014	2 tms	132	1035.1	236	3	.987	15	19	110	43	.391	4	229	+3	-1	+1	+3	+5	3	-1	-2	0	18
		232	1547.2	361	6	.983	26	30	162	60	.370	5	349	+6	-1	+2	+3	+9	5	-2	-5	-2	-

Scout's Defensive Rating: 2 plays saved in 2013, 0 plays saved in 2014

Though De Aza transitioned to a full-time left fielder in 2014, just two years ago he was the starting center fielder for the Chicago White Sox. In his time as a center fielder, he was less than impressive thanks to a weak arm and a high value of mistakes. Although he demonstrates good speed, he doesn't have baseball instincts. In left field, however, De

Left Fielders

Aza's range plays well and his arm is adequate though he still struggles to avoid misplays. His misplays exacerbate his throwing issues when he struggles to cleanly field a safe hit and return it quickly to the infield to prevent baserunner advancement. While he left center as one of the weakest defenders in baseball, his skillset should keep him a viable left field option for a few years.

Matt den Dekker

		BASIC						THROWING					RANGE AND POSITIONING						RUNS SAVED				
Year	Team	G	Inn	TC	E	Pct	GFP	DM	Opps to Advance	Extra Bases	Pct	Kills	Outs Made	Plays Saved	Plays Saved Shallow	Medium	Deep	Bases Saved	R/P	Throws	GFP/ DME	Total	Rank
2013	NYM	1	1.0	0	0	-	0	0					0	0	0	0	0	0	0			0	-
2014	NYM	28	222.2	42	1	.976	3	4	23	6	.261	1	40	0	+2	-1	0	0	0	0	0	0	-
		29	223.2	42	1	.976	3	4	23	6	.261	1	40	0	+2	-1	0	0	0	0	0	0	-

Scout's Defensive Rating: 0 plays saved in 2014

Corey Dickerson

		BASIC						THROWING					RANGE AND POSITIONING						RUNS SAVED				
Year	Team	G	Inn	TC	E	Pct	GFP	DM	Opps to Advance	Extra Bases	Pct	Kills	Outs Made	Plays Saved	Plays Saved Shallow	Medium	Deep	Bases Saved	R/P	Throws	GFP/ DME	Total	Rank
2013	Col	36	238.1	52	0	1.000	3	5	24	5	.208	0	52	0	-1	+2	-1	0	0	-1	0	-1	-
2014	Col	99	803.0	162	4	.975	6	12	99	36	.364	0	156	+2	0	+1	+1	+4	2	-3	-1	-2	22
		135	1041.1	214	4	.981	9	17	123	41	.333	0	208	+2	-1	+3	0	+4	2	-4	-1	-3	-

Scout's Defensive Rating: -3 plays saved in 2013, 0 plays saved in 2014

Dickerson burst onto the scene in 2014 thanks to an offensive breakout, and the Rockies slotted him in as the regular left fielder once Carlos Gonzalez landed on the disabled list. Dickerson occasionally gets poor jumps and demonstrates poor route efficiency, but his range and positioning are a net positive in the expansive outfield of Coors Field. However, he does possess a terrible arm, even for a left fielder, so a move to center or right is probably ill-conceived. Regardless, Corey Dickerson has proven he can hit in Coors Field, so the Rockies will have a decision on their hands with a crowded outfield presuming Car-Go returns to full health.

Sam Fuld

		BASIC						THROWING					RANGE AND POSITIONING						RUNS SAVED				
Year	Team	G	Inn	TC	E	Pct	GFP	DM	Opps to Advance	Extra Bases	Pct	Kills	Outs Made	Plays Saved	Plays Saved Shallow	Medium	Deep	Bases Saved	R/P	Throws	GFP/ DME	Total	Rank
2007	ChC	1	1.0	0	0	-	0	0				0									0	0	-
2009	ChC	29	79.1	26	1	.962	5	1	9	2	.222	1	24	+3	+2	0	0	+5	3	1	0	4	-
2010	ChC	8	10.0	1	0	1.000	0	1				0	1	-1	0	0	-1	-1	-1	0	0	-1	-
2011	TB	75	604.2	170	3	.982	30	16	48	14	.292	4	162	+4	+5	+2	-4	+4	3	4	3	10	4
2012	TB	14	94.0	20	0	1.000	4	2	4	2	.500	0	19	+2	+1	0	0	+3	2	0	1	3	-
2013	TB	55	204.2	44	0	1.000	9	9	22	8	.364	1	42	+1	0	+1	0	+1	1	0	1	2	-
2014	2 tms	36	224.0	65	0	1.000	5	4	20	8	.400	0	64	+3	+4	0	-1	+3	2	-1	0	1	-
		218	1217.2	326	4	.988	53	33	103	34	.330	6	312	+12	+12	+3	-6	+15	10	4	5	19	-

Scout's Defensive Rating: -1 plays saved in 2013, 3 plays saved in 2014

Sam Fuld's Scouting Report can be found on page 265.

Brett Gardner

		BASIC						THROWING					RANGE AND POSITIONING						RUNS SAVED				
Year	Team	G	Inn	TC	E	Pct	GFP	DM	Opps to Advance	Extra Bases	Pct	Kills	Outs Made	Plays Saved	Plays Saved Shallow	Medium	Deep	Bases Saved	R/P	Throws	GFP/ DME	Total	Rank
2008	NYY	17	145.1	26	0	1.000	2	2	11	2	.182	1	25	-1	0	-1	0	-2	-1	1	0	0	-
2010	NYY	123	906.0	210	1	.995	17	8	67	16	.239	8	200	+16	+4	+5	+7	+26	14	7	4	25	1
2011	NYY	149	1158.2	305	4	.987	33	19	89	27	.303	5	294	+26	+17	+6	+3	+36	21	3	-1	23	1
2012	NYY	15	85.1	15	0	1.000	3	2	9	3	.333	1	14	0	0	0	+1	+1	0	1	0	1	-
2014	NYY	126	1067.1	232	2	.991	19	15	111	43	.387	3	226	+4	+3	+1	+1	+5	3	-1	1	3	11
		430	3362.2	788	7	.991	74	46	287	91	.317	18	759	+45	+24	+11	+12	+66	37	11	4	52	-

Scout's Defensive Rating: 4 plays saved in 2014

Brett Gardner was recognized by the Fielding Bible Award panel as the best defensive left fielder in baseball in 2010 and 2011. Gardner was injured in 2012, and in 2013 he played center field (well, I might add). But in 2014, Gardner resurfaced as one of the better defensive left fielders in the major leagues. Gardner's range remains very good, even if he's lost a step. His speed enables him to avoid mistakes and make plays other left fielders can't. Gardner only has average arm strength, but is very accurate with his throws. He demonstrates good fundamentals by getting his body behind the ball every time he attempts a throw. He is quick in getting rid of the ball, a skill that helps prevent the advancement of baserunners. In left, he consistently held runners to less than a 40 percent advancement rate since 2010. Even though 2014 was a down year for Gardner in Defensive Runs Saved (+3) compared to his Fielding Bible Award winning seasons, he was still ranked in the top five in the Fielding Bible Awards balloting for left fielders. He may not return to the days of saving 20 or more runs in a season, but he is still an asset in either left or center.

Jonny Gomes

		BASIC							THROWING				RANGE AND POSITIONING						RUNS SAVED				
									Opps to Advance	Extra Bases	Pct	Kills	Outs Made	Plays Saved	Plays Saved Shallow	Medium	Deep	Bases Saved	R/P	Throws	GFP/ DME	Total	Rank
Year	Team	G	Inn	TC	E	Pct	GFP	DM															
2005	TB	14	110.0	31	0	1.000	3	2	13	2	.154	1	30	-4	-1	+1	-4	-9	-5	1	0	-4	-
2007	TB	26	186.1	44	0	1.000	1	7	22	8	.364	1	42	-7	-3	-2	-3	-10	-6	1	0	-5	-
2008	TB	9	40.0	13	0	1.000	1	0	6	5	.833	0	13	-1	0	-1	0	-2	-1	-1	0	-2	-
2009	Cin	37	253.0	50	1	.980	5	8	29	7	.241	3	46	-4	-1	0	-3	-7	-4	1	0	-3	-
2010	Cin	129	1037.0	207	4	.981	18	26	126	47	.373	4	197	-17	-7	-1	-9	-30	-15	-2	-2	-19	35
2011	2 tms	73	550.1	117	2	.983	7	8	63	16	.254	1	114	-1	-5	+1	+3	+1	-1	1	-2	-2	24
2012	Oak	39	258.2	59	2	.966	7	4	26	12	.462	0	56	-2	-1	+1	-2	0	-1	-1	0	-2	-
2013	Bos	98	634.0	120	1	.992	25	8	77	21	.273	1	113	-7	+2	-2	-7	-11	-6	4	2	0	22
2014	2 tms	84	553.0	104	4	.962	16	13	41	19	.463	0	99	-5	+1	+1	-8	-15	-6	-3	1	-8	32
		509	3622.1	745	14	.981	83	76	403	137	.340	14	710	-48	-15	-2	-33	-83	-45	1	-1	-45	

Scout's Defensive Rating: 4 plays saved in 2013, -2 plays saved in 2014

Renowned for his clubhouse presence, when given the opportunity to play, Gomes goes out and gives 110 percent. He isn't afraid to put his body on the line for a ball: between 2013 and 2014 he made 15 diving plays, usually coming up with the catch. What is more, when his dives come up short, he still often knocks the ball down and prevents runners from advancing. While he does occasionally mishandle a ball after a safe hit, he does everything in his power to keep the ball in front of him and get it back into the infield as quickly as possible. In doing so, he has allowed less than 34 percent of baserunners to take an extra base when given the opportunity. His greatest liability, however, are the extra-base hits that continue to fall in over his head. Despite his best efforts, he doesn't have the natural speed or instincts to handle a corner outfield spot well enough to justify regular playing time.

Carlos Gonzalez

		BASIC							THROWING				RANGE AND POSITIONING						RUNS SAVED				
									Opps to Advance	Extra Bases	Pct	Kills	Outs Made	Plays Saved	Plays Saved Shallow	Medium	Deep	Bases Saved	R/P	Throws	GFP/ DME	Total	Rank
Year	Team	G	Inn	TC	E	Pct	GFP	DM															
2009	Col	47	294.1	69	0	1.000	9	6	23	6	.261	2	67	+3	+2	+1	-1	+2	2	1	0	3	-
2010	Col	63	472.1	83	1	.988	10	6	37	17	.459	4	77	+2	0	0	+2	+2	1	0	2	3	13
2011	Col	61	518.0	99	1	.990	17	8	48	12	.250	4	93	-2	0	-3	+1	-2	-2	2	2	2	17
2012	Col	131	1127.2	218	4	.982	23	42	140	58	.414	5	207	-8	-5	-5	+1	-13	-7	-2	-4	-13	35
2013	Col	106	857.0	186	3	.984	31	17	102	37	.363	11	172	+4	-1	+4	+2	+5	3	4	4	11	3
2014	Col	48	386.1	69	1	.986	8	10	36	19	.528	0	67	-2	-1	0	-1	-3	-2	-4	0	-6	28
		456	3655.2	724	10	.986	98	89	386	149	.386	26	683	-3	-5	-3	+4	-9	-5	1	4	0	

Scout's Defensive Rating: 5 plays saved in 2013, -2 plays saved in 2014

It wasn't all that long ago that Carlos Gonzalez was lauded for his defense, collecting three Gold Gloves. However, the numbers highlighted some chinks in the armor even before the injury bug bit him. Gonzalez had a disastrous 42 Defensive Misplays (DM) in 1127.2 innings in 2012, the most among all MLB outfielders. While he appeared to rebound somewhat in 2013, he regressed in 2014, demonstrating diminished range and questionable approaches on balls at times. He didn't do the Rockies any favors with his arm either, as his -3 Outfield Arms Runs Saved ranked in the bottom 25 out of 116 players who played at least 500 innings in the outfield. He had a career-low three outfield assists, along with three throwing-related DMs and a throwing error to boot. As injuries have plagued him throughout the past couple of seasons, it's only fair to wonder how long Gonzalez can handle the spacious Coors Field outfield on a daily basis going forward.

Left Fielders

Alex Gordon

Year	Team	G	Inn	TC	E	Pct	GFP	DM	Opps to Advance	Extra Bases	Pct	Kills	Outs Made	Plays Saved	Shallow	Medium	Deep	Bases Saved	R/P	Throws	GFP/DME	Total	Rank
2010	KC	55	486.1	136	2	.985	17	13	69	21	.304	2	132	+3	0	+2	+1	+5	3	2	-2	3	12
2011	KC	148	1309.0	335	3	.991	31	23	126	34	.270	12	313	+5	+2	+4	-1	+10	5	13	2	20	2
2012	KC	160	1424.1	338	2	.994	46	22	162	50	.309	14	320	+8	+4	+1	+2	+14	7	9	8	24	1
2013	KC	155	1364.1	341	1	.997	48	25	142	48	.338	13	323	+7	+2	+3	+2	+8	5	6	6	17	2
2014	KC	156	1372.2	351	2	.994	44	16	129	27	.209	5	341	+18	+3	+10	+5	+29	15	9	2	26	1
		674	5956.2	1501	10	.993	186	99	628	180	.287	46	1429	+41	+11	+20	+9	+66	35	39	16	90	-

Scout's Defensive Rating: 9 plays saved in 2013, 15 plays saved in 2014

Since moving from third base and taking over left field full-time for the Royals in 2011, Alex Gordon has been the pre-eminent left fielder in all of baseball. Despite making tremendous strides in his range on medium and deep balls in play, Gordon's hallmark remains his ability to throw baserunners out and prevent them from advancing. In 2014, Gordon had only five baserunner kills, a significant drop from his 13 in 2013 and 14 in 2012; however, runners took an extra base on Gordon only 20.9 percent of the time in 2014, surely wary of testing the left fielder's arm. Gordon lapped the field twice in Net GFP - DME statistic in 2014 with 26 more Good Fielding Plays than Defensive Misplays. Gordon has earned his three Fielding Bible Awards, and barring injury he will contend for a few more.

Robbie Grossman

Year	Team	G	Inn	TC	E	Pct	GFP	DM	Opps to Advance	Extra Bases	Pct	Kills	Outs Made	Plays Saved	Shallow	Medium	Deep	Bases Saved	R/P	Throws	GFP/DME	Total	Rank
2013	Hou	45	340.1	68	2	.971	9	4	25	7	.280	1	65	0	+2	+2	-4	-2	0	0	1	1	-
2014	Hou	67	558.1	117	2	.983	6	5	57	18	.316	0	114	+5	+7	-1	-1	+2	3	1	-1	3	11
		112	898.2	185	4	.978	15	9	82	25	.305	1	179	+5	+9	+1	-5	0	3	1	0	4	-

Scout's Defensive Rating: 3 plays saved in 2013, 2 plays saved in 2014

Robbie Grossman is young and has good speed which allows him to play everywhere in the outfield. In addition to his time in left, he spent 40 innings in center and 266 innings in right. Grossman is still trying to optimize his routes, and until he settles in a set corner of the outfield, he may take another year or two to adjust (his speed isn't quite enough to be an everyday center fielder). He gets good jumps on the ball off of the bat, but his routes hurt his ability to make more plays. Grossman saved three runs in left field but offset that by costing the Astros six runs in his brief time in center. Despite spending the majority of his time in left field, his strong and accurate arm projects him to be better suited for right field, where he fared above average in 2014. Coming in on the ball and making a throw on the run really shows off his arm. He has the arm and the speed for a corner outfield position, but he should stay clear of center field on a regular basis.

Brandon Guyer

Year	Team	G	Inn	TC	E	Pct	GFP	DM	Opps to Advance	Extra Bases	Pct	Kills	Outs Made	Plays Saved	Shallow	Medium	Deep	Bases Saved	R/P	Throws	GFP/DME	Total	Rank
2011	TB	3	20.0	7	0	1.000	1	0	1	0	.000	0	7	0	+1	0	0	0	0	0	0	0	-
2012	TB	3	14.0	3	1	.667	0	0	2	1	.500	0	2	0	0	0	0	0	0	0	0	0	-
2014	TB	62	470.2	101	0	1.000	10	10	35	8	.229	0	101	+4	+2	+2	0	+4	3	1	1	5	9
		68	504.2	111	1	.991	11	10	38	9	.237	0	110	+4	+3	+2	0	+4	3	1	1	5	-

Scout's Defensive Rating: 1 plays saved in 2014

Josh Hamilton

Year	Team	G	Inn	TC	E	Pct	GFP	DM	Opps to Advance	Extra Bases	Pct	Kills	Outs Made	Plays Saved	Shallow	Medium	Deep	Bases Saved	R/P	Throws	GFP/DME	Total	Rank
2007	Cin	9	27.0	5	0	1.000	1	0	6	1	.167	0	5	0	0	0	-1	-1	-1	0	0	-1	-
2010	Tex	92	772.2	190	4	.979	14	11	71	24	.338	2	179	+10	+8	-1	+4	+13	8	0	0	8	3
2011	Tex	85	709.0	161	4	.975	19	8	65	22	.338	2	153	+5	+3	+1	0	+7	4	0	0	4	11
2012	Tex	84	481.0	102	3	.971	7	12	42	15	.357	3	96	+1	-1	+1	+1	+4	1	1	-1	1	15
2013	LAA	19	161.1	52	0	1.000	2	3	7	2	.286	0	52	+2	0	0	+2	+5	2	0	-1	1	-
2014	LAA	68	598.2	155	5	.968	10	4	57	17	.298	1	148	-3	-1	-4	+2	-3	-2	0	0	-2	23
		357	2749.2	665	16	.976	53	38	248	81	.327	8	633	+15	+9	-3	+8	+25	12	1	-2	11	-

Scout's Defensive Rating: 1 plays saved in 2013, -1 plays saved in 2014

Left Fielders

Hamilton has been shuffled around the three outfield spots over the last three injury-plagued seasons. As the injuries continue to mount and age takes its toll, Hamilton's range continues to decrease no matter which position he is playing. Hamilton's arm is still adequate and it can play at any of the three outfield spots. He is still a very aggressive fielder and makes very few mistakes for a player who takes as many chances as he does. Nevertheless, the Angels will be forced to use Hamilton in the outfield and hope that he can turn back the clock to provide a few more productive seasons in the outfield.

Bryce Harper

		BASIC							THROWING				RANGE AND POSITIONING						RUNS SAVED				
Year	Team	G	Inn	TC	E	Pct	GFP	DM	Opps to Advance	Extra Bases	Pct	Kills	Outs Made	Plays Saved	Shallow	Medium	Deep	Bases Saved	R/P	Throws	GFP/ DME	Total	Rank
2012	Was	7	58.0	14	0	1.000	2	1	5	2	.400	0	14	+2	+2	+1	-1	+3	2	0	0	2	-
2013	Was	97	800.1	166	5	.970	21	12	78	27	.346	7	150	-2	-3	+2	-1	-2	-1	4	1	4	9
2014	Was	90	737.2	159	3	.981	16	12	68	23	.338	3	147	-2	+3	+1	-6	-6	-2	1	1	0	19
		194	1596.0	339	8	.976	39	25	151	52	.344	10	311	-2	+2	+4	-8	-5	-1	5	2	6	-

Scout's Defensive Rating: -2 plays saved in 2013, 0 plays saved in 2014

After playing 139 games in his Rookie of the Year season in 2012, injuries limited Bryce Harper to 118 games in 2013, and a career-low 100 games in 2014. Perhaps even more alarming for the Nationals is that Harper's defensive performance has trended the wrong direction since his arrival. Though Harper reached the majors with the athleticism to be a defensive asset, his physical maturation and injuries have severely limited his effectiveness in the field. Throughout his career, Harper's biggest struggles have come defending deep balls, and 2014 was no exception. His arm is his biggest weapon and can play well at all three outfield positions. If Harper tones down his aggressiveness to limit injury risk in the future, it may keep him on the field but will limit his defensive upside.

Chris Heisey

		BASIC							THROWING				RANGE AND POSITIONING						RUNS SAVED				
Year	Team	G	Inn	TC	E	Pct	GFP	DM	Opps to Advance	Extra Bases	Pct	Kills	Outs Made	Plays Saved	Shallow	Medium	Deep	Bases Saved	R/P	Throws	GFP/ DME	Total	Rank
2010	Cin	38	96.2	25	0	1.000	2	1	12	1	.083	0	24	+1	0	0	+1	+1	1	0	0	1	-
2011	Cin	88	393.0	88	2	.977	3	9	29	15	.517	1	85	+3	+3	+3	-3	+1	1	-2	-1	-2	-
2012	Cin	63	355.2	89	3	.966	7	10	27	13	.481	2	83	+1	0	+1	-1	-1	0	-1	-1	-2	-
2013	Cin	69	423.0	91	0	1.000	5	5	35	10	.286	1	90	+8	+5	+2	+1	+11	6	0	-1	5	7
2014	Cin	53	315.1	76	0	1.000	6	3	24	9	.375	0	76	+9	+4	+3	+2	+13	7	-1	0	6	-
		311	1583.2	369	5	.986	23	28	127	48	.378	4	358	+22	+12	+9	0	+25	15	-4	-3	8	-

Scout's Defensive Rating: 2 plays saved in 2013, 1 plays saved in 2014

L.J. Hoes

		BASIC							THROWING				RANGE AND POSITIONING						RUNS SAVED				
Year	Team	G	Inn	TC	E	Pct	GFP	DM	Opps to Advance	Extra Bases	Pct	Kills	Outs Made	Plays Saved	Shallow	Medium	Deep	Bases Saved	R/P	Throws	GFP/ DME	Total	Rank
2012	Bal	1	1.0	0	0	-	0	0					0	0	0	0	0	0	0			0	-
2013	2 tms	3	13.2	4	0	1.000	1	0	2	0	.000	0	4	+1	+1	0	0	+1	1	0	0	1	-
2014	Hou	36	250.2	54	1	.981	9	2	27	10	.370	3	50	+3	-1	+1	+2	+6	3	3	2	8	-
		40	265.1	58	1	.983	10	2	29	10	.345	3	54	+4	0	+1	+2	+7	4	3	2	9	-

Scout's Defensive Rating: 1 plays saved in 2013, 2 plays saved in 2014

Left Fielders

Matt Holliday

		BASIC						THROWING				RANGE AND POSITIONING						RUNS SAVED				
Year	Team	G	Inn	TC	E	Pct	GFP	DM	Opps to Advance	Extra Bases	Pct	Kills	Outs Made	Plays Saved	Shallow	Medium	Deep	Bases Saved	R/P	Throws	GFP/ DME	Total	Rank
2004	Col	115	917.0	188	7	.963	10	18	110	42	.382	1	168	0	+3	-3	0	-2	-1	-6	-2	-9	31
2005	Col	123	1049.2	248	7	.972	12	15	117	40	.342	3	236	+8	+7	-1	+1	+12	7	-3	-2	2	11
2006	Col	153	1334.1	291	6	.979	12	30	138	60	.435	3	277	-3	+3	+2	-9	-12	-7	-5	0	-12	32
2007	Col	157	1383.2	306	3	.990	22	17	144	46	.319	3	296	+3	-3	+3	+4	+4	2	-1	-1	0	17
2008	Col	139	1229.1	252	3	.988	24	16	163	54	.331	3	240	+3	-3	+2	+3	+9	5	-2	1	4	9
2009	2 tms	155	1353.1	287	5	.983	18	20	124	43	.347	4	275	+4	0	+5	0	+12	5	-1	1	5	10
2010	StL	155	1341.2	272	3	.989	13	16	117	44	.376	4	261	+7	-3	-2	+12	+19	8	-1	-2	5	6
2011	StL	115	990.2	203	3	.985	10	13	97	42	.433	4	197	-4	-8	-3	+7	+1	-1	-2	1	-2	24
2012	StL	152	1312.2	235	3	.987	12	24	124	44	.355	5	226	-9	-8	-1	+1	-10	-6	-1	1	-6	32
2013	StL	136	1150.1	215	1	.995	13	20	91	39	.429	1	212	-4	-4	-2	+2	-7	-4	-7	-2	-13	34
2014	StL	150	1280.2	252	7	.972	8	23	123	50	.407	3	240	+3	-1	0	+3	+9	4	-4	-1	-1	21
		1550	13343.1	2749	48	.983	154	212	1348	504	.374	34	2628	+8	-17	0	+24	+35	12	-33	-6	-27	-

Scout's Defensive Rating: -7 plays saved in 2013, -7 plays saved in 2014

Holliday has historically gotten the most out of his limited defensive talents by playing deep enough to trade some extra-base hits for singles. However, even a conservative approach can do little to help him at this point, as his athleticism has deteriorated with age. To the eye, he looks like the worst defensive left fielder in baseball, with a disproportionate amount of Defensive Misplays and a league-worst Scout's Defensive Rating. Failed dives and missed catches outnumbered Good Fielding Plays. It is apparent especially on shallow hit balls, as he wavers between selling out or playing liners off the bounce. His skills with his glove and arm don't add much to the overall defensive package. He must focus on making smart decisions in the outfield to limit his defensive liability in the future.

Ender Inciarte

		BASIC						THROWING				RANGE AND POSITIONING						RUNS SAVED				
Year	Team	G	Inn	TC	E	Pct	GFP	DM	Opps to Advance	Extra Bases	Pct	Kills	Outs Made	Plays Saved	Shallow	Medium	Deep	Bases Saved	R/P	Throws	GFP/ DME	Total	Rank
2014	Ari	37	251.2	71	2	.972	4	3	30	6	.200	2	67	+5	+3	0	+2	+9	5	3	-1	7	-

Scout's Defensive Rating: -1 plays saved in 2014

Ender Inciarte's Scouting Report can be found on page 266.

Matt Joyce

		BASIC						THROWING				RANGE AND POSITIONING						RUNS SAVED				
Year	Team	G	Inn	TC	E	Pct	GFP	DM	Opps to Advance	Extra Bases	Pct	Kills	Outs Made	Plays Saved	Shallow	Medium	Deep	Bases Saved	R/P	Throws	GFP/ DME	Total	Rank
2008	Det	60	409.1	99	3	.970	6	7	54	15	.278	1	94	+1	+1	0	0	+4	2	1	0	3	12
2010	TB	13	75.0	16	0	1.000	1	0	6	3	.500	0	16	0	0	0	0	0	0	-1	0	-1	-
2011	TB	15	86.2	20	0	1.000	1	3	9	5	.556	0	20	+1	0	+1	0	+1	1	-1	-1	-1	-
2012	TB	33	245.1	50	0	1.000	7	4	28	9	.321	2	48	-1	0	+1	-2	-4	-1	3	2	4	-
2013	TB	58	364.2	80	0	1.000	6	6	18	13	.722	0	79	+9	+6	+4	-1	+9	6	-3	0	3	-
2014	TB	81	611.0	139	2	.986	11	5	55	20	.364	3	132	+2	+1	+4	-3	0	1	1	0	2	14
		260	1792.0	404	5	.988	32	25	170	65	.382	6	389	+12	+8	+10	-6	+10	9	0	1	10	-

Scout's Defensive Rating: 2 plays saved in 2013, 3 plays saved in 2014

Matt Joyce has proven to be a solid, if unspectacular, corner outfielder during his time in the big leagues. Joyce doesn't have great speed, but his instincts and good jumps still allow him to have decent range in the outfield. Where his lack of speed does hurt him, though, is going back on deep balls. Joyce has an accurate throwing arm, but its strength is more suited for left field rather than right. Joyce aggressively charges groundballs, and he did a good job of preventing runner advancements in 2014. Overall, Joyce is a guy a manager can be comfortable putting out there in either corner spot, and while he might not make a lot of flashy plays, he won't hurt the team either.

Left Fielders

Matt Kemp

Year	Team	G	Inn	TC	E	Pct	GFP	DM	Opps to Advance	Extra Bases	Pct	Kills	Outs Made	Plays Saved	Shallow	Medium	Deep	Bases Saved	R/P	Throws	GFP/ DME	Total	Rank
2006	LAD	11	72.1	20	1	.950	0	3	10	5	.500	0	18	0	-1	0	0	-1	-1	-1	-1	-3	-
2014	LAD	44	369.1	62	1	.984	5	4	31	12	.387	0	60	-8	-2	-3	-3	-13	-7	0	-1	-8	-
		55	441.2	82	2	.976	5	7	41	17	.415	1	78	-8	-3	-3	-3	-14	-8	-1	-2	-11	-

Scout's Defensive Rating: 0 plays saved in 2014

Matt Kemp's Scouting Report can be found on page 285.

Jason Kubel

Year	Team	G	Inn	TC	E	Pct	GFP	DM	Opps to Advance	Extra Bases	Pct	Kills	Outs Made	Plays Saved	Shallow	Medium	Deep	Bases Saved	R/P	Throws	GFP/ DME	Total	Rank
2004	Min	2	18.0	4	0	1.000	2	1	2	1	.500	0	1	-1	+1	-1	0	-2	-1	1	0	0	-
2006	Min	30	204.0	36	2	.944	5	4	21	7	.333	0	33	-2	-1	-1	0	-2	-1	0	0	-1	-
2007	Min	84	700.1	163	2	.988	9	18	69	27	.391	1	159	-4	-2	+1	-3	-7	-4	-4	0	-8	27
2008	Min	18	130.0	27	2	.926	1	4	19	5	.263	0	24	-3	-2	+1	-2	-6	-3	0	-1	-4	-
2009	Min	29	208.1	52	0	1.000	2	3	22	9	.409	1	51	+2	0	0	+2	+2	1	0	0	1	-
2010	Min	16	131.0	29	1	.966	2	2	8	6	.750	1	27	-1	0	0	-1	-1	-1	0	0	-1	-
2011	Min	9	70.0	15	0	1.000	0	2	7	3	.429	1	15	+1	0	+1	0	+1	1	-1	0	0	-
2012	Ari	124	1061.1	196	1	.995	23	13	94	37	.394	10	182	-12	-7	-4	-1	-20	-11	2	4	-5	30
2013	2 tms	56	450.0	77	1	.987	13	4	50	23	.460	6	70	-5	-4	-3	+2	-5	-3	2	2	1	17
2014	Min	36	317.2	70	0	1.000	2	6	33	13	.394	0	70	-9	-2	-2	-4	-13	-7	-2	0	-9	-
		404	3290.2	669	9	.987	59	57	325	131	.403	20	632	-34	-17	-8	-7	-53	-29	-2	5	-26	-

Scout's Defensive Rating: 2 plays saved in 2013, -3 plays saved in 2014

Junior Lake

Year	Team	G	Inn	TC	E	Pct	GFP	DM	Opps to Advance	Extra Bases	Pct	Kills	Outs Made	Plays Saved	Shallow	Medium	Deep	Bases Saved	R/P	Throws	GFP/ DME	Total	Rank
2013	ChC	32	260.1	54	0	1.000	4	10	19	5	.263	1	53	+1	+1	+3	-2	0	0	1	-2	-1	-
2014	ChC	53	375.0	97	4	.959	4	9	50	23	.460	1	91	+6	+1	+2	+3	+12	6	-2	-2	2	-
		85	635.1	151	4	.974	8	19	69	28	.406	2	144	+7	+2	+5	+1	+12	6	-1	-4	1	-

Scout's Defensive Rating: -1 plays saved in 2013, -3 plays saved in 2014

Junior Lake is still fairly new to the outfield. He played his first games away from the dirt in 2013 while in Triple-A, and since then has played the outfield exclusively at the major league level. Lake has performed like an above average left fielder thus far, which, given his relative inexperience at the position, is quite impressive and serves as a testament to his plus athleticism and above average speed. The majority of Lake's nine Defensive Misplays in 2014 were a consequence of inefficient route-running and/or getting a poor initial read on the ball, mistakes he should minimize with more experience. He does have limitations, however, as his arm did not fare well and his inexperience was glaringly apparent in brief time in center. With a large batch of shiny new prospects knocking on the door, the Cubs outfield is going to be quite crowded in 2015 and, as a result, Lake may struggle to find playing time to gain more experience.

David Lough

Year	Team	G	Inn	TC	E	Pct	GFP	DM	Opps to Advance	Extra Bases	Pct	Kills	Outs Made	Plays Saved	Shallow	Medium	Deep	Bases Saved	R/P	Throws	GFP/ DME	Total	Rank
2012	KC	1	7.0	4	0	1.000	1	0	1	0	.000	0	4	+2	+1	0	0	+2	1	0	0	1	-
2013	KC	15	83.0	29	0	1.000	3	0	6	1	.167	1	27	+5	+1	+3	+2	+9	5	0	0	5	-
2014	Bal	85	398.1	107	1	.991	11	5	34	16	.471	3	102	+8	+4	0	+4	+12	7	-1	1	7	5
		101	488.1	140	1	.993	15	5	41	17	.415	4	133	+15	+6	+3	+6	+23	13	-1	1	13	-

Scout's Defensive Rating: 1 plays saved in 2013, 2 plays saved in 2014

David Lough put forth an impressive defensive performance in 2014, tying for the sixth-best Defensive Runs Saved total among all left fielders despite only playing under 400 innings at the position. Lough is exceptional in that he is able to make plays on balls that most outfielders simply do not have a chance at. He typically does not give up on a ball until it is absolutely clear it is out of his reach, and he is adept at tracking balls down near or at the outfield wall. Lough demonstrates excellent athleticism and a solid feel for outfield play characterized by efficient route-running and getting

Left Fielders

good jumps off the bat. Lough was used primarily in a bench role in 2014, but his excellent defense and only slightly below league average bat make him a strong candidate for a starting job moving forward.

Ryan Ludwick

		BASIC							THROWING				RANGE AND POSITIONING						RUNS SAVED				
Year	Team	G	Inn	TC	E	Pct	GFP	DM	Opps to Advance	Extra Bases	Pct	Kills	Outs Made	Plays Saved	Shallow	Medium	Deep	Bases Saved	R/P	Throws	GFP/ DME	Total	Rank
2003	2 tms	17	132.0	35	0	1.000	-	-	10	3	.300	0	34	+3	+1	+1	+2	+6	4	-1	-	3	-
2005	Cle	9	59.0	17	1	.941	0	2	9	3	.333	0	16	-2	-3	+1	+1	-2	-1	0	-1	-2	-
2007	StL	49	324.0	87	0	1.000	14	5	25	9	.360	1	86	+6	+2	+2	+2	+9	5	-1	1	5	-
2008	StL	29	169.2	44	0	1.000	3	3	21	14	.667	0	42	-3	-2	-1	0	-5	-3	-4	0	-7	-
2009	StL	1	8.0	1	0	1.000	0	1	0	0		0	1	0	0	0	0	0	0	0	0	0	-
2010	StL	1	5.0	2	0	1.000	0	0				0	2	+1	0	0	+1	+3	1	0	0	1	-
2011	2 tms	117	1005.0	200	1	.995	22	17	85	36	.424	4	190	0	+3	-3	0	-4	-1	-3	1	-3	27
2012	Cin	108	929.1	192	1	.995	11	15	72	15	.208	0	191	-1	+5	+3	-9	-9	-3	1	-1	-3	27
2013	Cin	32	250.1	39	0	1.000	1	4	22	9	.409	0	39	-1	+1	0	-2	-2	-1	-2	0	-3	-
2014	Cin	92	751.2	136	0	1.000	15	8	55	18	.327	0	135	-7	0	-3	-4	-12	-6	-1	2	-5	27
		455	3634.0	753	3	.996	66	55	299	107	.358	5	736	-4	+7	0	-9	-16	-5	-11	2	-14	-

Scout's Defensive Rating: -3 plays saved in 2013, 3 plays saved in 2014

There are a few factors that severely stunt Ryan Ludwick's defensive performance in left field. His poor speed is one contributing factor. Ludwick is a veteran who's lost a step or two when he didn't have any to spare. Often times, balls hit to his position that seemed playable off the bat were quickly realized to be hits after seeing his lumbering strides across the outfield grass. His dives were less than graceful and looked more like carefully timed falls, never reaching full extension and often coming to a knee before sprawling out in his attempt to make the play. He displayed mediocre instincts for tracking, with potential flyouts often carrying overhead and bouncing off the outfield wall. However, he was able to make solid defensive plays on the balls within his limited range. His dives, while awkward, produced some relatively impressive defensive plays. This combined with a scant accumulation of miscues resulted in Ludwick's third-ranked ratio of Good Fielding Plays to Defensive Misplays and Errors. Aside from one outlier season in right in which he compiled eight baserunner kills, his arm is a below average tool as well. Ludwick isn't an ideal choice in the outfield, but he will at least be reliable.

Starling Marte

		BASIC							THROWING				RANGE AND POSITIONING						RUNS SAVED				
Year	Team	G	Inn	TC	E	Pct	GFP	DM	Opps to Advance	Extra Bases	Pct	Kills	Outs Made	Plays Saved	Shallow	Medium	Deep	Bases Saved	R/P	Throws	GFP/ DME	Total	Rank
2012	Pit	43	338.0	69	3	.957	6	4	35	14	.400	2	63	+5	0	+2	+2	+8	4	0	1	5	-
2013	Pit	124	1038.1	187	6	.968	16	11	94	28	.298	2	176	+19	+3	+4	+12	+34	17	-1	2	18	1
2014	Pit	114	943.2	160	5	.969	19	12	76	28	.368	4	151	+2	-6	-2	+9	+13	4	1	2	7	6
		281	2320.0	416	14	.966	41	27	205	70	.341	8	390	+26	-3	+4	+23	+55	25	0	5	30	

Scout's Defensive Rating: 0 plays saved in 2013, -1 plays saved in 2014

The 26-year old Pirate left fielder would probably be playing center field on most teams, but the man to his left is an MVP who won't be moved anytime soon. His range is exceptional in three directions, only lacking a bit on short flies, which he struggled with somewhat in 2014, dropping balls he should've had in the air while charging. His arm is strong for left field, intimidating runners into not taking the extra base. Though he sometimes struggles with his accuracy, that wasn't a problem in 2014, as he was charged with zero throwing errors during his time in left field (though he did have one in center field). That's probably thanks to not rushing throws as runners simply stopped trying to run on him. He has 12 assists in just over 2300 innings in left since breaking into the big leagues in 2012. Marte was one of the most exciting left fielders to watch in 2014, flashing both his range to make a few exceptional catches, as well as using the aforementioned arm to not just throw runners out, but often to prevent them from even trying to advance. Marte has settled in as one of the best left fielders in the game.

Left Fielders

J.D. Martinez

Year	Team	G	Inn	TC	E	Pct	GFP	DM	Opps to Advance	Extra Bases	Pct	Kills	Outs Made	Plays Saved	Plays Saved Shallow	Medium	Deep	Bases Saved	R/P	Throws	GFP/DME	Total	Rank
2011	Hou	51	436.1	98	1	.990	13	7	45	14	.311	4	92	-2	+3	0	-4	-4	-2	2	2	2	17
2012	Hou	100	833.0	142	2	.986	13	16	82	33	.402	6	131	-4	-3	+4	-5	-7	-4	1	1	-2	24
2013	Hou	50	377.2	69	1	.986	7	5	36	14	.389	1	65	-5	-1	-2	-2	-7	-4	0	0	-4	19
2014	Det	83	689.0	154	4	.974	9	10	66	25	.379	1	149	0	+3	+2	-5	-5	-2	0	2	0	19
		284	2336.0	463	8	.983	42	38	229	86	.376	12	437	-11	+2	+4	-16	-23	-12	3	5	-4	-

Scout's Defensive Rating: -2 plays saved in 2013, -2 plays saved in 2014

A breakout star at the plate for the Detroit Tigers in 2014, JD Martinez marginally improved upon his skills in the field. Always seeming to be a step slow, Martinez looks unnatural in the outfield where he's spent his entire career. A glaring weakness in his game is his inability to track and run efficient routes to the ball. This is most evident in deep fly balls where he seems reluctant to approach the wall and often takes an overly-conservative approach. In a big ballpark, such as the Tigers home field of Comerica Park, Martinez's lack of range is exposed even further. Both his glove and arm are barely average but they are adequate enough for left field. Perhaps a long-term move to first base is in the cards provided his bat keeps him in the majors long enough for his defense to decline.

Michael Morse

Year	Team	G	Inn	TC	E	Pct	GFP	DM	Opps to Advance	Extra Bases	Pct	Kills	Outs Made	Plays Saved	Plays Saved Shallow	Medium	Deep	Bases Saved	R/P	Throws	GFP/DME	Total	Rank
2005	Sea	8	55.0	11	0	1.000	1	2	6	2	.333	0	10	0	0	0	+1	0	0	-1	0	-1	-
2006	Sea	2	10.0	1	0	1.000	0	0	1	1	1.000	0	1	0	0	-1	0	0	0	0	0	0	-
2009	Was	2	9.2	4	0	1.000	1	0	0	0	-	0	4	0	0	0	0	+1	0	0	0	0	-
2011	Was	55	421.0	94	1	.989	7	7	37	12	.324	2	89	-4	0	-2	-2	-5	-3	1	2	0	20
2012	Was	67	493.2	84	0	1.000	4	6	36	15	.417	0	82	-4	-2	-1	-2	-3	-3	-1	-1	-5	29
2013	2 tms	19	124.1	30	0	1.000	1	2	10	3	.300	0	30	-1	0	0	-1	-1	-1	0	0	-1	-
2014	SF	84	579.0	111	2	.982	5	10	49	19	.388	1	107	-11	-7	-1	-3	-14	-9	-1	0	-10	34
		237	1692.2	335	3	.991	19	27	139	52	.374	3	323	-20	-9	-5	-7	-22	-16	-2	1	-17	-

Scout's Defensive Rating: -1 plays saved in 2013, -5 plays saved in 2014

Originally drafted as a shortstop, Morse has traveled all the way down the defensive spectrum. The numbers reflect what you would imagine them to be defensively for a man of Morse's size and stature as an aging slugger who makes his living in the batter's box. The range, or lack thereof, can be seen in his inability to reach both shallow and deep balls hit to him in left field. He is more comfortable at first base, which he occupied for 43 games while Brandon Belt was out with an injury. Still mainly stationary, Morse was able to field balls at a league average level, handling balls hit to his right side particularly well. It's tough to believe a 2015 team would employ Morse in the outfield, but he's still capable at first base.

Brandon Moss

Year	Team	G	Inn	TC	E	Pct	GFP	DM	Opps to Advance	Extra Bases	Pct	Kills	Outs Made	Plays Saved	Plays Saved Shallow	Medium	Deep	Bases Saved	R/P	Throws	GFP/DME	Total	Rank
2007	Bos	13	52.0	12	0	1.000	1	2	6	1	.167	0	11	0	-1	0	0	0	0	0	0	0	-
2008	2 tms	36	294.1	63	1	.984	2	4	25	9	.360	0	60	0	+1	0	0	-1	0	-2	0	-2	-
2009	Pit	21	170.2	48	1	.979	2	3	20	10	.500	1	46	+1	0	0	+2	+3	2	-2	-1	-1	-
2010	Pit	2	5.0	1	0	1.000	0	0	1	1	1.000	0	1	0	0	0	0	0	0	0	0	0	-
2012	Oak	11	60.1	11	0	1.000	1	0	7	1	.143	0	10	-1	-1	0	0	-1	-1	0	0	-1	-
2013	Oak	8	54.0	10	0	1.000	1	1	2	0	.000	0	10	0	0	0	0	+1	0	0	0	0	-
2014	Oak	56	377.0	79	2	.975	5	8	40	15	.375	2	75	-2	-5	+1	+1	0	-1	0	0	-1	-
		147	1013.1	224	4	.982	12	18	101	37	.366	3	213	-2	-6	+1	+3	+2	0	-4	-1	-5	-

Scout's Defensive Rating: 1 plays saved in 2013, -3 plays saved in 2014

Brandon Moss's Scouting Report can be found on page 286.

Left Fielders

Daniel Nava

		BASIC							THROWING				RANGE AND POSITIONING		Plays Saved				RUNS SAVED				
Year	Team	G	Inn	TC	E	Pct	GFP	DM	Opps to Advance	Extra Bases	Pct	Kills	Outs Made	Plays Saved	Shallow	Medium	Deep	Bases Saved	R/P	Throws	GFP/DME	Total	Rank
2010	Bos	54	380.0	67	0	1.000	10	10	34	8	.235	2	65	-6	-2	+2	-5	-9	-5	3	2	0	-
2012	Bos	76	611.1	114	2	.982	20	10	57	13	.228	4	107	-2	+4	0	-6	-5	-2	5	1	4	8
2013	Bos	63	469.1	93	1	.989	13	7	49	20	.408	1	90	-2	+2	-1	-3	-1	-1	-1	2	0	20
2014	Bos	38	273.0	59	1	.983	6	2	33	4	.121	1	57	+1	+4	-1	-2	0	0	2	2	4	-
		231	1733.2	333	4	.988	49	29	173	45	.260	8	319	-9	+8	0	-16	-15	-8	9	7	8	-

Scout's Defensive Rating: -1 plays saved in 2013, -2 plays saved in 2014

Daniel Nava's Scouting Report can be found on page 287.

Steve Pearce

		BASIC							THROWING				RANGE AND POSITIONING		Plays Saved				RUNS SAVED				
Year	Team	G	Inn	TC	E	Pct	GFP	DM	Opps to Advance	Extra Bases	Pct	Kills	Outs Made	Plays Saved	Shallow	Medium	Deep	Bases Saved	R/P	Throws	GFP/DME	Total	Rank
2008	Pit	1	4.0	1	0	1.000	0	0	0	0	-	0	1	0	0	0	0	0	0	0	0	0	-
2012	2 tms	23	147.1	32	0	1.000	4	3	16	4	.250	1	31	+1	+1	0	-1	+1	0	1	1	2	-
2013	Bal	15	107.1	21	0	1.000	3	2	10	3	.300	0	21	+1	0	+1	+1	+1	1	0	1	2	-
2014	Bal	35	231.0	65	0	1.000	6	3	14	5	.357	4	61	+5	+2	+1	+2	+8	4	2	1	7	-
		74	489.2	119	0	1.000	13	8	40	12	.300	5	114	+7	+3	+2	+2	+10	5	3	3	11	-

Scout's Defensive Rating: 0 plays saved in 2013, 1 plays saved in 2014

Steve Pearce's Scouting Report can be found on page 183.

David Peralta

		BASIC							THROWING				RANGE AND POSITIONING		Plays Saved				RUNS SAVED				
Year	Team	G	Inn	TC	E	Pct	GFP	DM	Opps to Advance	Extra Bases	Pct	Kills	Outs Made	Plays Saved	Shallow	Medium	Deep	Bases Saved	R/P	Throws	GFP/DME	Total	Rank
2014	Ari	36	260.1	40	3	.925	4	6	31	9	.290	0	36	+1	-1	0	+2	+2	1	-1	-2	-2	-

Scout's Defensive Rating: 0 plays saved in 2014

David Peralta's Scouting Report can be found on page 289.

Alex Presley

		BASIC							THROWING				RANGE AND POSITIONING		Plays Saved				RUNS SAVED				
Year	Team	G	Inn	TC	E	Pct	GFP	DM	Opps to Advance	Extra Bases	Pct	Kills	Outs Made	Plays Saved	Shallow	Medium	Deep	Bases Saved	R/P	Throws	GFP/DME	Total	Rank
2010	Pit	2	11.0	0	0	-	0	0				0	0	0	0	0	0	0	0	0	0	0	-
2011	Pit	48	406.0	74	1	.986	7	8	64	21	.328	0	71	+2	-2	0	+5	+6	3	0	-1	2	15
2012	Pit	81	607.2	141	2	.986	5	9	47	26	.553	1	138	+6	+1	-1	+5	+11	6	-6	-2	-2	22
2013	Pit	12	71.2	18	1	.944	2	1	5	3	.600	0	17	+4	0	0	+3	+7	3	0	-1	2	-
2014	Hou	43	263.1	51	0	1.000	3	2	23	12	.522	1	50	+2	+1	+1	0	+1	1	-1	0	0	-
		186	1359.2	284	4	.986	17	20	139	62	.446	2	276	+14	0	0	+13	+25	13	-7	-4	2	-

Scout's Defensive Rating: 0 plays saved in 2013, 1 plays saved in 2014

Carlos Quentin

		BASIC							THROWING				RANGE AND POSITIONING		Plays Saved				RUNS SAVED				
Year	Team	G	Inn	TC	E	Pct	GFP	DM	Opps to Advance	Extra Bases	Pct	Kills	Outs Made	Plays Saved	Shallow	Medium	Deep	Bases Saved	R/P	Throws	GFP/DME	Total	Rank
2006	Ari	2	11.0	1	0	1.000	0	1	0	0	-	0	1	0	0	0	0	0	0	0	0	0	-
2007	Ari	3	7.1	3	0	1.000	0	0	2	1	.500	0	3	0	0	0	0	0	0	0	0	0	-
2008	CWS	130	1147.0	240	7	.971	18	17	113	32	.283	2	228	-3	+2	-2	-3	-7	-4	3	0	-1	21
2009	CWS	88	753.0	165	2	.988	12	18	97	34	.351	3	158	-10	-1	-3	-6	-19	-9	0	-1	-10	27
2012	SD	69	565.0	99	3	.970	3	5	50	19	.380	0	94	-9	-8	-1	0	-10	-6	-3	-1	-10	33
2013	SD	69	556.0	107	1	.991	9	12	52	24	.462	0	105	+2	+2	+1	0	+4	2	-5	-2	-5	28
2014	SD	32	229.0	43	0	1.000	3	3	17	10	.588	1	42	-2	-1	-2	0	-3	-2	-1	0	-3	-
		393	3268.1	658	13	.980	45	56	331	120	.363	6	631	-22	-6	-7	-9	-35	-19	-6	-4	-29	-

Scout's Defensive Rating: 0 plays saved in 2013, -1 plays saved in 2014

Left Fielders

Cody Ross

Year	Team	G	Inn	TC	E	Pct	GFP	DM	Opps to Advance	Extra Bases	Pct	Kills	Outs Made	Plays Saved	Shallow	Medium	Deep	Bases Saved	R/P	Throws	GFP/DME	Total	Rank
2006	3 tms	41	214.2	41	0	1.000	4	3	12	3	.250	0	41	0	+1	0	-2	-2	-2	0	0	-2	-
2007	Fla	8	47.0	18	1	.944	2	0	8	2	.250	0	16	+1	0	+1	0	+1	1	1	0	2	-
2008	Fla	17	45.0	11	0	1.000	4	0	8	1	.125	1	10	+1	0	0	0	+1	1	1	1	3	-
2010	2 tms	23	90.1	14	1	.929	3	2	6	2	.333	2	11	0	+1	-1	0	+1	1	2	0	3	-
2011	SF	83	530.0	114	1	.991	8	10	54	18	.333	4	109	-4	+4	-3	-5	-13	-5	2	0	-3	28
2012	Bos	22	166.1	23	0	1.000	1	6	20	6	.300	1	22	-2	+2	-3	-1	-4	-2	2	0	0	-
2013	Ari	46	351.0	69	0	1.000	7	3	31	10	.323	1	68	+4	+1	0	+3	+7	4	1	0	5	-
2014	Ari	37	271.1	39	2	.949	7	3	22	10	.455	1	34	-4	-1	-1	-1	-6	-3	-1	0	-4	-
		277	1715.2	329	5	.985	36	27	161	52	.323	10	311	-4	+8	-7	-6	-15	-5	8	1	4	-

Scout's Defensive Rating: 1 plays saved in 2013, 0 plays saved in 2014

Jordan Schafer

Year	Team	G	Inn	TC	E	Pct	GFP	DM	Opps to Advance	Extra Bases	Pct	Kills	Outs Made	Plays Saved	Shallow	Medium	Deep	Bases Saved	R/P	Throws	GFP/DME	Total	Rank
2013	Atl	15	74.2	12	0	1.000	3	2	7	4	.571	0	12	+1	0	0	+1	+1	1	-1	0	0	-
2014	2 tms	49	312.2	70	1	.986	10	2	41	17	.415	1	67	-1	-3	+1	+1	+1	0	-2	1	-1	-
		64	387.1	82	1	.988	13	4	48	21	.438	1	79	0	-3	+1	+2	+2	1	-3	1	-1	-

Scout's Defensive Rating: 0 plays saved in 2013, 4 plays saved in 2014

Skip Schumaker

Year	Team	G	Inn	TC	E	Pct	GFP	DM	Opps to Advance	Extra Bases	Pct	Kills	Outs Made	Plays Saved	Shallow	Medium	Deep	Bases Saved	R/P	Throws	GFP/DME	Total	Rank
2005	StL	14	22.1	6	0	1.000	1	0	4	2	.500	0	6	-1	-1	0	-1	-1	-1	0	0	-1	-
2006	StL	13	63.0	13	0	1.000	0	0	4	0	.000	0	13	-1	-1	-1	+1	-3	-2	0	0	-2	-
2007	StL	23	122.2	21	1	.952	1	2	10	6	.600	0	20	-1	0	0	0	-1	-1	-1	0	-2	-
2008	StL	56	338.1	90	1	.989	9	3	47	14	.298	3	85	+5	+2	+2	+1	+8	4	2	1	7	-
2009	StL	39	82.1	17	1	.941	0	1	7	2	.286	0	16	-3	-2	+1	-1	-4	-2	0	0	-2	-
2010	StL	4	6.0	2	0	1.000	0	0	1	0	.000	0	2	-1	0	-1	0	-1	0	0	0	0	-
2011	StL	6	16.0	1	0	1.000	1	0				0	1	0	0	0	0	0	0	0	0	0	-
2012	StL	1	1.0	1	0	1.000	0	0				0	1	+1	+1	0	0	+1	1	0	0	1	-
2013	LAD	35	157.1	24	0	1.000	3	0	11	6	.545	0	24	+1	+1	-1	+1	+2	1	0	2	3	-
2014	Cin	33	235.2	38	0	1.000	3	3	18	5	.278	0	38	-2	-2	0	-1	-3	-2	0	-1	-3	-
		224	1044.2	213	3	.986	18	9	102	35	.343	3	206	-2	-2	0	0	-2	-2	1	2	1	-

Scout's Defensive Rating: 2 plays saved in 2013, 1 plays saved in 2014

Grady Sizemore

Year	Team	G	Inn	TC	E	Pct	GFP	DM	Opps to Advance	Extra Bases	Pct	Kills	Outs Made	Plays Saved	Shallow	Medium	Deep	Bases Saved	R/P	Throws	GFP/DME	Total	Rank
2014	2 tms	52	371.1	85	1	.988	7	8	51	18	.353	0	82	+1	+3	0	-1	+2	1	0	1	2	-

Scout's Defensive Rating: 1 plays saved in 2014

Seth Smith

Year	Team	G	Inn	TC	E	Pct	GFP	DM	Opps to Advance	Extra Bases	Pct	Kills	Outs Made	Plays Saved	Shallow	Medium	Deep	Bases Saved	R/P	Throws	GFP/DME	Total	Rank
2008	Col	8	17.2	5	0	1.000	0	0	2	1	.500	0	5	-1	0	-1	0	-1	-1	0	0	-1	-
2009	Col	86	627.1	140	1	.993	8	11	46	19	.413	1	135	+5	+1	-1	+5	+11	5	-3	-1	1	13
2010	Col	71	512.1	112	2	.982	3	8	52	18	.346	2	107	+2	-1	-1	+4	+3	2	0	-2	0	19
2011	Col	25	186.2	38	0	1.000	5	5	19	10	.526	2	34	-1	-1	0	+1	-1	-1	-1	0	-2	-
2012	Oak	57	439.1	106	1	.991	7	7	34	14	.412	3	102	0	-1	0	+1	-1	0	1	1	2	12
2013	Oak	50	382.1	102	0	1.000	7	2	31	9	.290	1	101	0	-2	+1	+2	+2	1	-1	1	1	-
2014	SD	102	740.0	160	1	.994	10	18	59	26	.441	1	157	+4	-3	0	+7	+9	4	-2	-1	2	15
		399	2905.2	663	5	.992	40	51	243	97	.399	10	641	+9	-7	-2	+20	+22	10	-6	-2	2	-

Scout's Defensive Rating: 2 plays saved in 2013, -2 plays saved in 2014

For the first four seasons of his career, Seth Smith had the unique misfortune of having to cover the expansive outfield in Coors Field. Despite having no arm to speak of, Smith acquitted himself fairly well there, ranking as high as 13th in Runs Saved among left fielders in 2009. Smith still does not have much of an arm; when Smith was in left, runners took an extra base on him 44.1 percent of the time in 2014. Smith's range largely compensates, particularly excelling on

Left Fielders

deeper balls in play. Moving on to Safeco Field, Smith will battle for playing time in yet another expansive outfield, but if given a chance Smith should be able to continue to chase down balls in the gaps.

Travis Snider

Year	Team	G	Inn	TC	E	Pct	GFP	DM	Opps to Advance	Extra Bases	Pct	Kills	Outs Made	Plays Saved	Plays Saved Shallow	Medium	Deep	Bases Saved	R/P	Throws	GFP/DME	Total	Rank
2008	Tor	13	99.0	16	0	1.000	3	3	5	2	.400	2	14	-2	0	-1	-1	-3	-2	1	0	-1	-
2009	Tor	56	435.1	91	1	.989	8	8	47	16	.340	3	87	0	0	+1	0	-1	0	2	-1	1	-
2010	Tor	53	433.2	93	3	.968	9	6	41	13	.317	1	87	+7	+2	0	+4	+11	6	-1	0	5	8
2011	Tor	44	367.0	83	3	.964	8	5	43	11	.256	2	77	-1	0	0	-1	0	0	3	0	3	-
2012	2 tms	15	115.0	27	1	.963	5	2	12	4	.333	0	26	0	+1	0	-1	0	0	0	0	0	-
2013	Pit	5	33.0	5	0	1.000	2	2	6	4	.667	0	5	0	-1	0	0	0	0	-1	0	-1	-
2014	Pit	36	226.2	46	0	1.000	6	5	34	7	.206	0	44	+5	0	+2	+3	+8	4	3	0	7	-
		222	1709.2	361	8	.978	41	31	188	57	.303	10	340	+9	+2	+2	+4	+15	8	7	-1	14	-

Scout's Defensive Rating: 0 plays saved in 2013, 2 plays saved in 2014

Mark Trumbo

Year	Team	G	Inn	TC	E	Pct	GFP	DM	Opps to Advance	Extra Bases	Pct	Kills	Outs Made	Plays Saved	Plays Saved Shallow	Medium	Deep	Bases Saved	R/P	Throws	GFP/DME	Total	Rank
2011	LAA	1	2.0	0	0	-	0	0					0	0	0	0	0	0	0			0	-
2012	LAA	66	497.1	106	0	1.000	10	8	45	15	.333	4	102	+1	-2	-3	+6	+7	2	1	2	5	7
2013	LAA	8	58.1	20	1	.950	2	2	8	4	.500	0	19	+3	+3	0	0	+3	2	-1	-1	0	-
2014	Ari	41	358.2	70	0	1.000	5	15	37	13	.351	3	65	-9	-6	-1	-2	-16	-8	1	0	-7	-
		116	916.1	196	1	.995	17	25	90	32	.356	7	186	-5	-5	-4	+4	-6	-4	1	1	-2	-

Scout's Defensive Rating: 1 plays saved in 2013, -4 plays saved in 2014

Arizona brought him in expecting him to be their everyday left fielder. However, injuries drastically curtailed his time on the field in 2014, and defensively the Diamondbacks were much better off. He does not read the ball well and has very limited closing speed. Though he did not commit an error in 2014 in left field, he did commit 15 DMs against only 5 GFPs. He also had -7 Runs Saved, which was one of the ten worst totals among left fielders.

Due to the injury of Paul Goldschmidt, Trumbo played first base almost exclusively after the beginning of August and managed average defense. He is able to read and react to balls on the ground much more effectively than flyballs. Despite his serviceable defense at first base, his time there is obviously limited by the health of Goldschmidt. Unfortunately, putting him in left field and accepting the drop in defense may continue to be the only way to keep his bat in the lineup.

Justin Upton

Year	Team	G	Inn	TC	E	Pct	GFP	DM	Opps to Advance	Extra Bases	Pct	Kills	Outs Made	Plays Saved	Plays Saved Shallow	Medium	Deep	Bases Saved	R/P	Throws	GFP/DME	Total	Rank
2013	Atl	108	839.2	178	4	.978	12	18	63	22	.349	3	174	-4	-7	0	+3	-3	-3	-3	-3	-9	31
2014	Atl	150	1319.2	284	8	.972	12	25	112	46	.411	3	270	0	-5	-5	+10	+12	4	-3	-4	-3	25
		258	2159.1	462	12	.974	24	43	175	68	.389	3	444	-4	-12	-5	+13	+9	1	-6	-7	-12	-

Scout's Defensive Rating: -4 plays saved in 2013, -7 plays saved in 2014

Upton, a former right field Fielding Bible Award winner, has struggled with the transition to left. Upton's always defended deep balls well as a result of conservative positioning, trading a handful of extra-base hits for singles which fall in front of him. While this works to his benefit on batted balls, it translates to a longer distance when throwing to keep baserunners at bay, making his arm seem weaker than it actually is. He has also begun to struggle with challenging flies and liners. In fact, of the 46 balls in plays that BIS Video Scouts graded as "difficult" plays for Upton, he only made one play compared to the league average of 14 percent. Along those lines, BIS Video Scouts rated Upton as the second-worst left fielder in baseball according to the Scout's Defensive Rating in 2014. While Upton has the athletic ability to bounce back, he is in danger of becoming a defensive liability instead of an asset on both sides of the ball.

Left Fielders

Scott Van Slyke

		BASIC							THROWING				RANGE AND POSITIONING						RUNS SAVED				
Year	Team	G	Inn	TC	E	Pct	GFP	DM	Opps to Advance	Extra Bases	Pct	Kills	Outs Made	Plays Saved	Plays Saved Shallow	Medium	Deep	Bases Saved	R/P	Throws	GFP/ DME	Total	Rank
2012	LAD	11	26.0	5	0	1.000	0	0	4	1	.250	0	5	0	0	0	0	+1	0	0	0	0	-
2013	LAD	30	211.1	42	2	.952	6	5	20	5	.250	0	40	+4	+2	0	+2	+7	4	0	-1	3	-
2014	LAD	32	221.1	46	2	.957	5	2	27	4	.148	0	44	+4	+2	0	+2	+8	4	1	-1	4	-
		73	458.2	93	4	.957	11	7	51	10	.196	0	89	+8	+4	0	+4	+16	8	1	-2	7	-

Scout's Defensive Rating: 1 plays saved in 2013, 3 plays saved in 2014

Dayan Viciedo

		BASIC							THROWING				RANGE AND POSITIONING						RUNS SAVED				
Year	Team	G	Inn	TC	E	Pct	GFP	DM	Opps to Advance	Extra Bases	Pct	Kills	Outs Made	Plays Saved	Plays Saved Shallow	Medium	Deep	Bases Saved	R/P	Throws	GFP/ DME	Total	Rank
2012	CWS	131	1093.0	248	2	.992	19	21	107	42	.393	6	234	+1	+4	-1	-2	0	0	2	0	2	12
2013	CWS	109	892.2	164	5	.970	25	18	93	33	.355	9	147	-13	-4	-2	-7	-20	-11	4	3	-4	27
2014	CWS	55	381.0	84	4	.952	6	9	46	18	.391	1	78	-6	0	-1	-5	-11	-5	-1	-1	-7	30
		295	2366.2	496	11	.978	50	48	246	93	.378	16	459	-18	0	-4	-14	-31	-16	5	2	-9	-

Scout's Defensive Rating: -7 plays saved in 2013, -6 plays saved in 2014

Dayan Viciedo's Scouting Report can be found on page 294.

Josh Willingham

		BASIC							THROWING				RANGE AND POSITIONING						RUNS SAVED				
Year	Team	G	Inn	TC	E	Pct	GFP	DM	Opps to Advance	Extra Bases	Pct	Kills	Outs Made	Plays Saved	Plays Saved Shallow	Medium	Deep	Bases Saved	R/P	Throws	GFP/ DME	Total	Rank
2004	Fla	3	21.0	6	0	1.000	0	1	1	0	.000	0	6	-1	0	0	-1	-1	-1	0	0	-1	-
2005	Fla	1	1.0	0	0	-	0	0				0										0	-
2006	Fla	132	1069.2	218	7	.968	13	18	107	33	.308	3	206	-2	+1	-2	-1	-6	-3	2	-2	-3	27
2007	Fla	137	1176.1	223	3	.987	14	16	151	40	.265	5	211	-14	-8	+2	-7	-18	-10	4	0	-6	26
2008	Fla	90	855.1	173	0	1.000	18	17	93	30	.323	7	166	+5	+3	0	+3	+8	4	4	3	11	3
2009	Was	87	691.2	172	5	.971	13	15	67	28	.418	1	165	+1	+4	+4	-6	-2	0	-1	-2	-3	22
2010	Was	108	880.1	172	1	.994	18	12	93	39	.419	5	164	0	+2	0	-2	-4	-1	2	1	2	18
2011	Oak	96	829.1	164	2	.988	14	9	80	25	.313	3	159	-6	-2	-1	-2	-6	-4	0	3	-1	23
2012	Min	119	1027.2	247	4	.984	15	21	119	50	.420	3	237	-3	-1	+1	-3	-9	-4	-5	-3	-12	34
2013	Min	72	607.2	131	1	.992	13	11	77	29	.377	2	125	-7	-2	+2	-7	-14	-7	-1	2	-6	30
2014	Min	53	439.1	106	0	1.000	10	5	46	18	.391	2	103	-6	-6	0	0	-9	-5	0	3	-2	24
		906	7599.1	1612	23	.986	128	125	834	292	.350	31	1542	-33	-9	+6	-26	-61	-31	5	5	-21	-

Scout's Defensive Rating: -1 plays saved in 2013, -3 plays saved in 2014

Christian Yelich

		BASIC							THROWING				RANGE AND POSITIONING						RUNS SAVED				
Year	Team	G	Inn	TC	E	Pct	GFP	DM	Opps to Advance	Extra Bases	Pct	Kills	Outs Made	Plays Saved	Plays Saved Shallow	Medium	Deep	Bases Saved	R/P	Throws	GFP/ DME	Total	Rank
2013	Mia	59	505.1	103	0	1.000	5	7	39	17	.436	0	103	+6	+5	-3	+3	+6	4	-3	-1	0	19
2014	Mia	138	1182.0	262	1	.996	16	19	116	47	.405	2	255	+21	+6	+6	+9	+34	19	-5	-1	13	2
		197	1687.1	365	1	.997	21	26	155	64	.413	2	358	+27	+11	+3	+12	+40	23	-8	-2	13	-

Scout's Defensive Rating: 1 plays saved in 2013, 4 plays saved in 2014

Enjoying his first full season in the big leagues, Christian Yelich staked his claim as one of the best young outfielders in the game. Primarily in left field, Yelich looked like a seasoned veteran as he displayed an excellent ability to read the ball off the bat and take efficient routes to the flight path. Not the fastest outfielder, his first reaction always seems to be quick and in the right direction with few wasted steps. As with many young outfielders, Yelich does have room for improvement. He was among the league leaders in failed diving attempts, either leaving his feet unnecessarily or allowing the ball to tip off his glove. Furthermore, Yelich's arm is terrible, even for a left fielder, and he occasionally makes poor judgments getting the ball back in. The more repetitions Yelich gets in the field as he matures will likely see his Defensive Misplays diminish and his stock as an elite outfielder rise.

Left Fielders

Chris Young

Year	Team	G	Inn	TC	E	Pct	GFP	DM	Opps to Advance	Extra Bases	Pct	Kills	Outs Made	Plays Saved	Shallow	Medium	Deep	Bases Saved	R/P	Throws	GFP/DME	Total	Rank
				BASIC					THROWING				RANGE AND POSITIONING		Plays Saved				RUNS SAVED				
2013	Oak	24	164.1	44	0	1.000	3	2	16	5	.313	0	44	-1	-1	-2	+2	0	0	-1	0	-1	-
2014	2 tms	73	497.0	115	1	.991	6	4	54	16	.296	3	108	+6	+3	+3	+1	+9	5	2	-1	6	7
		97	661.1	159	1	.994	9	6	70	21	.300	3	152	+5	+2	+1	+3	+9	5	1	-1	5	-

Scout's Defensive Rating: -1 plays saved in 2013, 2 plays saved in 2014

During his defensive peak in 2010-11, Young could chase down deep balls better than anyone in baseball. However, since his 2012 injury and subsequent playing time battles, Young has struggled to regain his once elite defense. He's always had a terrible arm, even for center field, compiling more than two kills exactly once in his center field career. While he could probably still hold his own in center as a fourth outfielder, his range would make him an above average left fielder when given playing time.

Eric Young

Year	Team	G	Inn	TC	E	Pct	GFP	DM	Opps to Advance	Extra Bases	Pct	Kills	Outs Made	Plays Saved	Shallow	Medium	Deep	Bases Saved	R/P	Throws	GFP/DME	Total	Rank
				BASIC					THROWING				RANGE AND POSITIONING		Plays Saved				RUNS SAVED				
2010	Col	10	65.0	12	1	.917	3	5	7	4	.571	0	11	0	0	0	0	0	0	-1	-1	-2	-
2011	Col	35	269.1	51	1	.980	4	5	34	15	.441	0	50	-1	0	0	-1	-1	0	-3	-1	-4	-
2012	Col	8	42.0	7	0	1.000	1	1	6	2	.333	0	7	+1	-1	+2	0	+1	1	0	0	1	-
2013	2 tms	95	790.1	189	2	.989	23	16	70	28	.400	3	180	+6	+4	+3	-1	+6	4	-1	-1	2	15
2014	NYM	73	577.1	135	1	.993	14	8	55	21	.382	3	128	+7	+2	+5	0	+6	4	0	1	5	8
		221	1744.0	394	5	.987	45	35	172	70	.407	6	376	+13	+5	+10	-2	+12	9	-5	-2	2	-

Scout's Defensive Rating: 5 plays saved in 2013, 7 plays saved in 2014

Eric Young quietly put together a great defensive year in 2014 for the Mets in left field. Being one of the fastest players in Major League Baseball helps Young cover a lot of ground. He was exceptional charging in on shallow and medium hit balls. Deep fly balls are a little more challenging, especially in the expansive Citi Field outfield. Young has the tendency to dive to make a lot of run-saving catches, but when he does not catch the ball in these situations, he gives the opposition the ability to take extra bases. Young does not have a great arm, as players took an extra base against him in 38 percent of opportunities, right about the league average for a left fielder. Young started in left field only 65 times in 2014, but played in 73 total games at the position, often being inserted as a backup or defensive replacement. However, in his limited appearances, he managed to save five runs for the Mets, which ranked him eighth among Major League left fielders for the season.

Ryan Zimmerman

Year	Team	G	Inn	TC	E	Pct	GFP	DM	Opps to Advance	Extra Bases	Pct	Kills	Outs Made	Plays Saved	Shallow	Medium	Deep	Bases Saved	R/P	Throws	GFP/DME	Total	Rank
				BASIC					THROWING				RANGE AND POSITIONING		Plays Saved				RUNS SAVED				
2014	Was	30	265.2	50	0	1.000	5	3	25	8	.320	0	48	-2	-1	-2	+1	-2	-1	-1	0	-2	-

Scout's Defensive Rating: 2 plays saved in 2014

Ryan Zimmerman was once one of the elite third basemen in the league with great range and a strong, accurate throwing arm. Between 2007-10 Zimmerman was second only to Adrian Beltre at third base with 60 Defensive Runs Saved, picking up a Gold Glove and Fielding Bible Award along the way. However, shoulder injuries have severely hindered his throwing ability in recent years. Zimmerman is still capable of flashing the skills that made him special. He made 163 GFPs between 2012 and 2013, which was 52 more than the next third baseman on the list, but he also found himself among the league leaders in throwing errors. While he is still very adept at making throws on the move or after a bare hand play, he really struggles with the routine play. After losing his position to Anthony Rendon in 2014, Zimmerman filled in adequately in left field. His athletic ability served him well in tracking down balls hit to the outfield, but teams were aggressive in challenging his suspect arm. With the departure of Adam LaRoche, it appears that Zimmerman will find a new home a first base, where he should excel. Obviously this move will help hide his arm while still allowing his glove to shine. There is no reason that, as he becomes more comfortable with the position, he won't find himself challenging for a Fielding Bible Award at first base.

Center Fielders Register and Scouting Reports

Year	Fielding Bible Award Winner	Runner Up	Third Place
2006	Carlos Beltran	Andruw Jones	Corey Patterson
2007	Andruw Jones	Carlos Beltran	Ichiro Suzuki
2008	Carlos Beltran	Carlos Gomez	Grady Sizemore
2009	Franklin Gutierrez	Carlos Gomez	Curtis Granderson
2010	Michael Bourn	Franklin Gutierrez	Chris Young
2011	Austin Jackson	Chris Young	Franklin Gutierrez
2012	Mike Trout	Michael Bourn	Denard Span
2013	Carlos Gomez	Juan Lagares	Jacoby Ellsbury
2014	Juan Lagares	Jackie Bradley Jr.	Billy Hamilton

Center Fielders

Arismendy Alcantara

		BASIC							THROWING				RANGE AND POSITIONING						RUNS SAVED				
Year	Team	G	Inn	TC	E	Pct	GFP	DM	Opps to Advance	Extra Bases	Pct	Kills	Outs Made	Plays Saved	Shallow	Medium	Deep	Bases Saved	R/P	Throws	GFP/DME	Total	Rank
2014	ChC	48	421.0	119	5	.958	10	10	49	31	.633	2	111	+4	+3	+2	-1	+8	4	-1	-1	2	-

Scout's Defensive Rating: -1 plays saved in 2014

Abraham Almonte

		BASIC							THROWING				RANGE AND POSITIONING						RUNS SAVED				
Year	Team	G	Inn	TC	E	Pct	GFP	DM	Opps to Advance	Extra Bases	Pct	Kills	Outs Made	Plays Saved	Shallow	Medium	Deep	Bases Saved	R/P	Throws	GFP/DME	Total	Rank
2013	Sea	15	111.2	22	2	.909	2	3	9	7	.778	0	19	-1	0	0	-1	-2	-1	0	0	-1	-
2014	2 tms	41	345.2	119	6	.950	7	8	37	17	.459	4	108	+6	+4	+3	-1	+9	6	4	-2	8	-
		56	457.1	141	8	.943	9	11	46	24	.522	5	127	+5	+4	+3	-2	+7	5	4	-2	7	-

Scout's Defensive Rating: 0 plays saved in 2013, 0 plays saved in 2014

Mookie Betts

		BASIC							THROWING				RANGE AND POSITIONING						RUNS SAVED				
Year	Team	G	Inn	TC	E	Pct	GFP	DM	Opps to Advance	Extra Bases	Pct	Kills	Outs Made	Plays Saved	Shallow	Medium	Deep	Bases Saved	R/P	Throws	GFP/DME	Total	Rank
2014	Bos	28	249.2	66	0	1.000	9	6	25	12	.480	1	64	0	-2	+3	-1	-1	0	1	1	2	-

Scout's Defensive Rating: 1 plays saved in 2014

Charlie Blackmon

		BASIC							THROWING				RANGE AND POSITIONING						RUNS SAVED				
Year	Team	G	Inn	TC	E	Pct	GFP	DM	Opps to Advance	Extra Bases	Pct	Kills	Outs Made	Plays Saved	Shallow	Medium	Deep	Bases Saved	R/P	Throws	GFP/DME	Total	Rank
2011	Col	2	16.0	4	0	1.000	1	1	1	1	1.000	0	4	-1	-1	-1	+1	-1	-1	0	0	-1	-
2012	Col	1	8.0	0	0	-	0	0	1	0	.000	0	0	0	0	0	0	0	0	0	0	0	-
2013	Col	25	196.2	49	3	.939	5	4	36	14	.389	0	46	-4	-1	0	-3	-7	-4	0	-1	-5	-
2014	Col	69	513.1	156	2	.987	9	3	39	21	.538	1	153	+2	+1	0	0	+3	2	-1	0	1	17
		97	734.0	209	5	.976	15	8	77	36	.468	1	203	-3	-1	-1	-2	-5	-3	-1	-1	-5	-

Scout's Defensive Rating: 0 plays saved in 2013, 2 plays saved in 2014

Charlie Blackmon is a versatile defender who can play all three outfield positions with proficiency. Blackmon is an athletic player that shows plus range in the spacious outfield of Coors Field. He gets good jumps off the bat and closes on the ball well. A former pitcher in college, Blackmon has a strong throwing arm. He does struggle with throwing accuracy at times, and can be guilty of having too little confidence in his arm, which leads to him making low percentage throws through to bases instead of just hitting the cutoff man. Blackmon is on track to be the everyday center fielder for the Rockies in 2015, but his defensive versatility should ensure he continues to find himself in the lineup one way or another.

Gregor Blanco

		BASIC							THROWING				RANGE AND POSITIONING						RUNS SAVED				
Year	Team	G	Inn	TC	E	Pct	GFP	DM	Opps to Advance	Extra Bases	Pct	Kills	Outs Made	Plays Saved	Shallow	Medium	Deep	Bases Saved	R/P	Throws	GFP/DME	Total	Rank
2008	Atl	69	494.1	132	0	1.000	10	6	53	26	.491	1	128	+1	+1	0	0	0	0	1	1	2	-
2009	Atl	9	72.0	20	0	1.000	1	2	6	1	.167	0	20	+1	0	0	0	+1	0	1	0	1	-
2010	2 tms	66	515.0	140	1	.993	9	6	53	30	.566	2	136	+4	+3	+3	-1	+7	4	0	-1	3	-
2012	SF	30	168.2	52	1	.981	5	2	20	15	.750	0	51	+2	+4	0	-2	-1	1	-1	0	0	-
2013	SF	76	550.0	144	0	1.000	11	13	60	31	.517	1	142	+13	+15	+3	-6	+11	8	0	-1	7	8
2014	SF	72	525.2	145	0	1.000	14	12	49	25	.510	2	140	-5	0	-3	-3	-17	-7	1	2	-4	25
		322	2325.2	633	2	.997	50	41	241	128	.531	6	617	+16	+23	+3	-12	+1	6	2	1	9	-

Scout's Defensive Rating: 2 plays saved in 2013, -2 plays saved in 2014

Blanco very narrowly avoided becoming something of a 21st century Merkle or Buckner when he botched handling Alex Gordon's two-out single in the ninth inning of Game 7 of the 2014 World Series. It's fortunate for him that Gordon didn't score because, as the observant onlooker knows, Blanco is a very capable fielder. Reared in the Atlanta system as a speedy, fourth outfielder-type, the 31-year-old has shown the Giants he's got the potential to be more valuable than that at times. He used the absence of Angel Pagan to his advantage in 2014, and got a majority of his defensive time in center for the second consecutive season.

Despite probably belonging in left, Blanco has shown the ability to shut down the large center field area by the bay, both to his left in Triples Alley and also charging short bloopers. While he mostly plies his trade in left and center, he also saw a large chunk of time in right field for Bruce Bochy in 2012, a testament to his versatility. His 20 DRS across all outfield positions over the last three seasons make him by no means an elite defender, but do place him in the top 20 in MLB during that time.

Emilio Bonifacio

		BASIC							THROWING				RANGE AND POSITIONING						RUNS SAVED				
Year	Team	G	Inn	TC	E	Pct	GFP	DM	Opps to Advance	Extra Bases	Pct	Kills	Outs Made	Plays Saved	Plays Saved Shallow	Medium	Deep	Bases Saved	R/P	Throws	GFP/DME	Total	Rank
2009	Fla	11	58.2	20	0	1.000	0	2	8	5	.625	0	20	-1	+1	-1	-1	-3	-1	-1	0	-2	-
2010	Fla	17	130.0	43	1	.977	8	4	15	8	.533	1	40	-1	-1	-1	+2	+1	0	1	1	2	-
2011	Fla	16	89.0	25	0	1.000	0	6	12	8	.667	0	25	-2	-2	+2	-1	-3	-2	-1	-2	-5	-
2012	Mia	51	427.1	113	1	.991	1	9	41	24	.585	0	111	-2	-3	-1	+2	+1	0	-2	-1	-3	23
2013	2 tms	15	118.0	32	0	1.000	1	2	15	6	.400	0	32	-1	0	0	-1	-3	-1	0	-1	-2	-
2014	2 tms	65	481.0	126	2	.984	6	6	39	21	.538	1	123	+2	0	-1	+3	+5	2	0	0	2	-
		175	1304.0	359	4	.989	16	29	130	72	.554	2	351	-5	-5	-2	+4	-2	-2	-3	-3	-8	-

Scout's Defensive Rating: 1 plays saved in 2013, 1 plays saved in 2014

One of the most versatile utility players in baseball, Bonifacio saw time at six different positions in 2014. Due to his solid range, particularly on deep balls, his playing time in the outfield is most often spent in center field. His arm is below average, so he does not profile as well in right field. He does not always make the best read or take the best route, but his great speed allows him to make up ground despite that.

Bonifacio's best position in the infield is second base due to his previously mentioned below average arm strength. In 2013, the majority of his innings were spent at the keystone, and he finished the season fifth in Runs Saved with 10. There have also been seasons where Bonifacio's primary position has been third base (2009) and shortstop (2011). However, at those positions his throws are more erratic and his footwork is not as smooth. He appears most comfortable making plays at second base, but he is not a liability anywhere on the field, making him a manager's best friend.

Peter Bourjos

		BASIC							THROWING				RANGE AND POSITIONING						RUNS SAVED				
Year	Team	G	Inn	TC	E	Pct	GFP	DM	Opps to Advance	Extra Bases	Pct	Kills	Outs Made	Plays Saved	Plays Saved Shallow	Medium	Deep	Bases Saved	R/P	Throws	GFP/DME	Total	Rank
2010	LAA	51	449.2	160	1	.994	22	7	41	20	.488	4	149	+8	+6	+1	+1	+8	6	3	5	14	-
2011	LAA	147	1269.1	361	4	.989	29	19	98	45	.459	4	351	+3	+3	+1	0	+10	4	3	3	10	5
2012	LAA	90	501.2	167	1	.994	13	3	41	18	.439	1	164	+9	+6	0	+3	+13	7	2	0	9	7
2013	LAA	53	415.0	120	1	.992	8	7	32	24	.750	0	117	-1	-1	-1	+1	0	0	-2	1	-1	-
2014	StL	104	649.1	196	2	.990	9	12	75	30	.400	0	193	+11	+5	+7	0	+16	9	0	-2	7	11
		445	3285.0	1004	9	.991	81	48	287	137	.477	9	974	+30	+19	+8	+5	+47	26	6	7	39	-

Scout's Defensive Rating: -3 plays saved in 2013, 3 plays saved in 2014

Bourjos has two main weapons in his defensive arsenal: his elite range in center field and his strong throwing arm. He has always been able to get great reads on flyballs, and, combined with his speed, has been able to show off some of the best range of any center fielder. Three out of the last four seasons he has registered a positive rating according to Plays Made despite only having full time status in one of those seasons.

Arm strength is the other defining attribute in Bourjos' defensive game. He has a very strong arm that runners don't even attempt to advance on, limiting his assists totals. Bourjos only has one Kill over the past three years, but runners have only taken the extra base 49 percent of the time against him, which puts him tied for fourth among all qualified center fielders over the last three years. It's hard to argue against the defensive value that he brings to a team. If he stays healthy and gets a chance to play full time, he would be a lock to finish in the top five of the voting for a Fielding Bible Award.

Center Fielders

Michael Bourn

		BASIC							THROWING				RANGE AND POSITIONING						RUNS SAVED				
Year	Team	G	Inn	TC	E	Pct	GFP	DM	Opps to Advance	Extra Bases	Pct	Kills	Outs Made	Plays Saved	Shallow	Medium	Deep	Bases Saved	R/P	Throws	GFP/DME	Total	Rank
2007	Phi	12	56.2	16	0	1.000	1	2	7	4	.571	0	16	+3	+2	0	+2	+6	3	0	0	3	-
2008	Hou	130	1009.0	305	5	.984	24	19	100	59	.590	4	291	-1	-6	+4	+2	+3	2	-2	2	2	14
2009	Hou	154	1326.0	385	3	.992	29	23	147	82	.558	7	371	+13	+6	0	+7	+21	11	3	1	15	2
2010	Hou	138	1189.1	370	3	.992	34	11	105	55	.524	5	359	+26	+9	+2	+15	+49	25	2	1	28	1
2011	2 tms	156	1359.0	376	3	.992	16	23	131	75	.573	2	367	-4	-13	-1	+10	+5	0	-3	-2	-5	25
2012	Atl	153	1340.1	388	2	.995	28	14	107	50	.467	3	384	+23	+13	+6	+5	+37	20	2	1	23	1
2013	Cle	128	1098.1	281	3	.989	26	15	114	65	.570	2	272	+3	+2	+3	-2	+5	2	0	0	2	18
2014	Cle	105	925.2	242	2	.992	18	17	92	50	.543	5	235	-6	0	+2	-8	-14	-6	1	1	-4	24
		976	8304.1	2363	21	.991	176	124	803	440	.548	28	2295	+57	+13	+16	+31	+112	57	3	4	64	-

Scout's Defensive Rating: 7 plays saved in 2013, 1 plays saved in 2014

Michael Bourn has struggled defensively since coming over from Atlanta to Cleveland. While he displays plus speed that allows him to have above average range, Bourn has failed to live up to the defensive hype, struggling to adapt to his new environment. The 2010 Fielding Bible Award winner in Houston's expansive center field adapted to Atlanta well enough to again lead the league in Runs Saved in 2012. However, Bourn declined to the level of an average center fielder in 2013 and dropped off even further in 2014, ultimately costing the Indians four runs with his efforts. Bourn's speed is ideal for a center fielder, though he's lost a step or two when it comes to chasing costly deep flyballs. His arm has never been great, but it can hold its own in center. While many believe he can rebound, his formerly above average speed is on the decline. He might benefit from moving back a step or two, trading a couple extra-base hits for less costly singles.

Jackie Bradley Jr.

		BASIC							THROWING				RANGE AND POSITIONING						RUNS SAVED				
Year	Team	G	Inn	TC	E	Pct	GFP	DM	Opps to Advance	Extra Bases	Pct	Kills	Outs Made	Plays Saved	Shallow	Medium	Deep	Bases Saved	R/P	Throws	GFP/DME	Total	Rank
2013	Bos	19	146.0	42	0	1.000	1	2	12	8	.667	0	42	0	+1	+1	-2	-2	-1	-1	0	-2	-
2014	Bos	113	949.0	307	1	.997	26	20	83	43	.518	8	293	+15	+10	+8	-3	+18	11	4	0	15	3
		132	1095.0	349	1	.997	27	22	95	51	.537	8	335	+15	+11	+9	-5	+16	10	3	0	13	-

Scout's Defensive Rating: 1 plays saved in 2013, 1 plays saved in 2014

Graceful is the word that comes to mind when watching Bradley Jr. handle center field. The 24-year old South Carolina product is easily a plus-plus defender who is near the top of the center field game already. He isn't exceptionally fast, but he has outstanding instincts that help him get almost preternatural jumps on flies hit his way. Coming in on balls is his strongest play, and he makes sprawling catches with ease. His arm is a surprisingly big plus too, and he is still working on becoming a more accurate thrower. He led all center fielders in baseball with 13 assists despite his not even having 1,000 innings played. Bradley Jr. finished the year as one of the best defenders in the league, placing him in a tie for third in MLB with 15 Runs Saved. If he can hit enough to play in Boston's overcrowded outfield, he could be the most exciting center fielder in recent times.

Michael Brantley

		BASIC							THROWING				RANGE AND POSITIONING						RUNS SAVED				
Year	Team	G	Inn	TC	E	Pct	GFP	DM	Opps to Advance	Extra Bases	Pct	Kills	Outs Made	Plays Saved	Shallow	Medium	Deep	Bases Saved	R/P	Throws	GFP/DME	Total	Rank
2009	Cle	20	166.0	47	1	.979	1	4	22	14	.636	0	46	-3	0	-1	-1	-7	-3	-1	-1	-5	-
2010	Cle	65	562.2	158	2	.987	9	8	55	34	.618	0	156	-11	0	-1	-10	-22	-11	-3	1	-13	32
2011	Cle	52	412.2	119	1	.992	3	7	40	23	.575	0	118	+2	+3	+1	-2	-1	1	-1	-1	-1	-
2012	Cle	144	1237.0	342	1	.997	16	15	114	68	.596	3	336	-4	-2	-1	-1	-7	-4	0	4	0	19
2013	Cle	1	4.0			-	0	0					0	0	0	0	0	0	0			0	-
2014	Cle	46	373.0	109	1	.991	3	1	25	18	.720	1	106	-1	+1	-2	0	-3	-1	-2	1	-2	-
		328	2755.1	775	6	.992	32	35	256	157	.613	4	762	-17	+2	-4	-14	-40	-18	-7	4	-21	-

Scout's Defensive Rating: 0 plays saved in 2014

Michael Brantley's Scouting Report can be found on page 240.

Center Fielders

Lorenzo Cain

	BASIC							THROWING				RANGE AND POSITIONING		Plays Saved				RUNS SAVED		GFP/		
Year Team	G	Inn	TC	E	Pct	GFP	DM	Opps to Advance	Extra Bases	Pct	Kills	Outs Made	Plays Saved	Shallow	Medium	Deep	Bases Saved	R/P	Throws	DME	Total	Rank
2010 Mil	38	306.1	100	2	.980	9	4	25	12	.480	2	96	+5	+2	-2	+6	+13	6	1	0	7	-
2011 KC	2	17.0	2	0	1.000	0	0				0	2	0	0	0	0	-1	0	0	0	0	-
2012 KC	50	403.0	124	4	.968	10	4	30	18	.600	1	117	+7	0	+3	+3	+14	7	-1	-2	4	-
2013 KC	92	761.1	255	1	.996	26	13	61	31	.508	6	248	+11	+2	+3	+6	+18	10	4	3	17	3
2014 KC	93	723.1	239	1	.996	16	13	72	44	.611	2	234	+19	+7	+11	0	+26	15	-3	2	14	4
	275	2211.0	720	8	.989	61	34	188	105	.559	11	697	+42	+11	+15	+15	+70	38	1	3	42	-

Scout's Defensive Rating: 3 plays saved in 2013, 2 plays saved in 2014

Cain has quietly become one of the most dependable outfielders in the game. He has deceptive speed that comes from very long strides. He seems to simply glide to balls hit deep in the gap to make even difficult plays look almost effortless. He also has very long arms that allow him to go high for balls against the wall and dive farther for balls at the limits of his wide range. Primarily a center fielder, he tied for fourth in Runs Saved (14) despite playing only part-time. Between injuries to Nori Aoki and the increased role of Jarrod Dyson, Cain saw an increased amount of time in right field as well in 2014, where he finished eighth in Runs Saved (8). Cain also exhibits an above average arm that has allowed him to rack up 15 outfield assists over the past two seasons, tied for 21st over that span. Cain's excellence in both right field and center field earned him the first ever Multi-Position Fielding Bible Award.

Coco Crisp

	BASIC							THROWING				RANGE AND POSITIONING		Plays Saved				RUNS SAVED		GFP/		
Year Team	G	Inn	TC	E	Pct	GFP	DM	Opps to Advance	Extra Bases	Pct	Kills	Outs Made	Plays Saved	Shallow	Medium	Deep	Bases Saved	R/P	Throws	DME	Total	Rank
2003 Cle	53	462.0	126	0	1.000	-	-	34	18	.529	1	112	+1	0	0	+2	+3	2	-1	-	1	16
2004 Cle	94	807.1	212	4	.981	13	19	85	48	.565	0	199	+2	-2	0	+4	+3	2	-2	-1	-1	19
2005 Cle	10	79.2	22	1	.955	0	2	5	3	.600	0	21	-1	-1	0	-1	-3	-2	0	0	-2	-
2006 Bos	103	900.2	250	1	.996	18	18	98	55	.561	1	246	-5	0	-2	-3	-7	-4	-2	0	-6	29
2007 Bos	144	1216.1	416	1	.998	26	17	108	55	.509	4	408	+18	+8	+2	+9	+26	15	-1	1	15	2
2008 Bos	114	886.0	240	2	.992	9	14	74	44	.595	1	234	-2	-3	+1	-1	-2	-1	-4	1	-4	21
2009 KC	49	412.0	123	3	.976	6	6	45	26	.578	0	120	+4	+1	0	+4	+7	4	-2	0	2	-
2010 Oak	73	625.0	186	2	.989	19	5	46	28	.609	1	183	+3	-2	+1	+4	+9	4	-1	3	6	9
2011 Oak	133	1134.1	324	1	.997	26	16	96	62	.646	1	321	-4	-5	-3	+5	+4	0	-3	2	-1	17
2012 Oak	97	840.0	251	2	.992	15	5	62	40	.645	2	245	-5	-4	-2	+1	-4	-3	-1	3	-1	22
2013 Oak	110	919.0	309	0	1.000	16	9	73	46	.630	1	307	+5	-8	+6	+7	+17	7	-4	0	3	16
2014 Oak	111	900.2	197	3	.985	14	16	77	51	.662	0	194	-15	-11	-6	+3	-20	-12	-5	-1	-18	34
	1091	9183.0	2656	20	.992	162	127	803	476	.593	12	2590	+1	-27	-3	+34	+33	12	-26	8	-6	-

Scout's Defensive Rating: 2 plays saved in 2013, -6 plays saved in 2014

Coco Crisp, who just completed his 13th season in professional baseball, was an elite defender in left or center in his younger days. His speed, which previously allowed him to close on line drives in front of him, has deteriorated to the point that those shallow liners are turning into singles or doubles in the gaps. His below average range on shallow and medium hit balls during the 2014 season was among the worst in center field, and his -18 Defensive Runs Saved ranked second-worst at the position. Crisp has well-below average arm strength and accuracy for a center fielder, failing to record one kill during the 2014 season and allowing baserunners to take an extra base 66 percent of time. This is not a recent problem either, as Crisp has cost his team runs with his arm every season but one of his center field career. Crisp could transition to left, where his speed will leave him an average or better defender for a couple more years.

Rajai Davis

	BASIC							THROWING				RANGE AND POSITIONING		Plays Saved				RUNS SAVED		GFP/		
Year Team	G	Inn	TC	E	Pct	GFP	DM	Opps to Advance	Extra Bases	Pct	Kills	Outs Made	Plays Saved	Shallow	Medium	Deep	Bases Saved	R/P	Throws	DME	Total	Rank
2007 2 tms	58	379.1	127	0	1.000	13	10	44	23	.523	2	124	-1	+2	+4	-6	-4	-2	2	-1	-1	-
2008 2 tms	88	487.2	158	1	.994	12	8	61	29	.475	2	153	+5	+2	0	+3	+7	4	1	1	6	-
2009 Oak	113	856.1	271	4	.985	23	18	80	43	.538	6	260	+4	+1	+2	+1	+9	4	3	0	7	11
2010 Oak	83	677.1	194	2	.990	7	11	55	37	.673	1	190	-3	-3	+2	-2	0	-1	-3	-2	-6	29
2011 Tor	79	652.0	178	2	.989	11	9	53	33	.623	0	174	-7	-7	+2	-2	-11	-6	-4	1	-9	32
2012 Tor	6	34.0	5	0	1.000	1	0	1	0	.000	0	5	+1	+1	0	0	+2	1	0	0	1	-
2013 Tor	16	114.0	35	0	1.000	1	2	11	5	.455	1	35	+4	+1	+2	0	+6	3	1	0	4	-
2014 Det	48	374.0	118	1	.992	7	7	36	25	.694	0	117	+2	+1	+1	0	+1	1	-3	-1	-1	-
	491	3574.2	1086	10	.991	75	65	341	195	.572	12	1058	+5	-2	+13	-6	+10	4	-3	-2	-1	-

Scout's Defensive Rating: 0 plays saved in 2013, 1 plays saved in 2014

Center Fielders

Rajai Davis's Scouting Report can be found on page 244.

Jarrod Dyson

	BASIC							THROWING				RANGE AND POSITIONING						RUNS SAVED				
Year Team	G	Inn	TC	E	Pct	GFP	DM	Opps to Advance	Extra Bases	Pct	Kills	Outs Made	Plays Saved	Plays Saved Shallow	Medium	Deep	Bases Saved	R/P	Throws	GFP/ DME	Total	Rank
2010 KC	15	129.0	52	2	.962	7	1	12	6	.500	2	48	+2	-1	+2	+1	+4	2	1	0	3	-
2011 KC	17	98.2	31	0	1.000	1	3	8	4	.500	0	31	+4	0	+3	+1	+8	4	0	0	4	-
2012 KC	88	699.0	245	6	.976	19	15	73	44	.603	5	230	+3	0	+1	+3	+8	4	1	-1	4	13
2013 KC	73	571.2	184	5	.973	14	9	59	33	.559	3	176	+9	+8	-2	+3	+12	7	0	-1	6	10
2014 KC	106	678.1	232	4	.983	14	7	62	31	.500	3	224	+13	+3	+3	+8	+23	12	1	0	13	6
	299	2176.2	744	17	.977	55	35	214	118	.551	13	709	+31	+10	+7	+16	+55	29	3	-2	30	-

Scout's Defensive Rating: 2 plays saved in 2013, 4 plays saved in 2014

On a per inning basis, Dyson is one of the best defensive center fielders in baseball. The problem is that he shares a roster with another elite defensive center fielder in Lorenzo Cain. While Cain was getting all the recognition for his outstanding defense during the 2014 postseason, the Royals would still move Cain to right field to accommodate Dyson when he would come in as a defensive substitute in the late innings. Dyson's greatest asset is his speed. He is arguably the fastest player in baseball, which contributes immensely to his excellent range, especially on deep flies. His speed also allows him to charge balls quickly to help prevent runner advancements. Dyson has an above average arm in terms of both strength and accuracy. Even with his limited innings, Dyson finished fourth in the Fielding Bible Award voting for center fielders in 2014, and if he can manage to earn every day at bats moving forward, he should continue to be on a lot of ballots for years to come.

Adam Eaton

	BASIC							THROWING				RANGE AND POSITIONING						RUNS SAVED				
Year Team	G	Inn	TC	E	Pct	GFP	DM	Opps to Advance	Extra Bases	Pct	Kills	Outs Made	Plays Saved	Plays Saved Shallow	Medium	Deep	Bases Saved	R/P	Throws	GFP/ DME	Total	Rank
2012 Ari	21	185.2	40	1	.975	6	5	15	7	.467	2	37	-1	-2	+1	+1	+1	0	1	0	1	-
2013 Ari	30	232.1	50	2	.960	5	8	25	16	.640	1	44	-2	-1	0	-1	-3	-2	-1	-1	-4	-
2014 CWS	121	1043.2	325	4	.988	29	14	136	81	.596	5	312	+12	+4	+3	+4	+20	11	-2	2	11	8
	172	1461.2	415	7	.983	40	27	176	104	.591	8	393	+9	+1	+4	+4	+18	9	-2	1	8	-

Scout's Defensive Rating: -2 plays saved in 2013, 6 plays saved in 2014

Adam Eaton is an all-out type of player, whether it be running full speed on a routine grounder to a second baseman, or running full speed and jumping towards a wall, risking injury to himself. He has become notorious for making running catches and colliding into the wall, reminding South Siders of a similar grinder-type center fielder in Aaron Rowand. At times in 2014, there were times it seemed like there was no ball that Eaton couldn't get to. Eaton saved the Sox 11 runs with his range and positioning in 2014, the fifth-highest total in baseball.

However, even with his heroics in the outfield, Eaton also has demonstrated an unwanted degree of erratic fielding. He didn't always take the most direct route towards the ball, and missed opportunities to make easier putouts, or sometimes costs his team the chance to hold a baserunner from taking an extra base. Adam Eaton's arm is one of the weaker aspects of his game. In 2014, he cost the team two runs with his arm, while baserunners advanced an extra base 60 percent of the time on balls hit to him. This represented a modest improvement from his 2013 campaign, when runners advanced 64 percent of the time. While his speed and ability to make difficult acrobatic catches are both fun to watch, his arm may keep him from becoming an elite defender.

Center Fielders

Jacoby Ellsbury

		BASIC							THROWING				RANGE AND POSITIONING						RUNS SAVED				
Year	Team	G	Inn	TC	E	Pct	GFP	DM	Opps to Advance	Extra Bases	Pct	Kills	Outs Made	Plays Saved	Shallow	Medium	Deep	Bases Saved	R/P	Throws	GFP/ DME	Total	Rank
2007	Bos	16	107.0	38	0	1.000	2	3	9	4	.444	0	38	-1	0	0	0	-2	-1	0	0	-1	-
2008	Bos	66	546.2	174	0	1.000	19	9	62	34	.548	1	171	+4	-1	+4	+1	+8	4	-2	1	3	12
2009	Bos	153	1302.2	364	2	.995	20	28	129	75	.581	1	357	-14	-9	-4	-1	-17	-11	-4	0	-15	35
2010	Bos	13	104.2	33	0	1.000	4	1	9	6	.667	0	33	+2	+1	0	+2	+5	2	-1	0	1	-
2011	Bos	154	1358.1	394	0	1.000	19	25	125	78	.624	3	388	+12	+4	+1	+6	+17	10	-2	1	9	7
2012	Bos	73	611.1	169	3	.982	9	8	70	45	.643	2	164	+4	0	+2	+3	+11	5	-3	0	2	15
2013	Bos	134	1188.1	353	3	.992	27	10	103	51	.495	1	347	+13	+8	+1	+5	+22	12	0	1	13	5
2014	NYY	141	1237.0	384	1	.997	33	14	98	55	.561	3	380	+2	+8	-5	-1	-8	-2	-1	0	-3	23
		750	6456.0	1909	9	.995	133	98	605	348	.575	11	1878	+22	+11	-1	+15	+36	19	-13	3	9	-

Scout's Defensive Rating: 1 plays saved in 2013, 9 plays saved in 2014

Touting elite speed, Ellsbury seemingly glides to every ball hit into the outfield, with fairly effective flyball routes. Tying for second in Good Fielding Plays for center fielders, he is particularly effective at reaching shallow pop ups and liners, plays that he routinely makes with flash and flair. His excellent Scout's Defensive Rating was tops among center fielders and reflects his fluidity in chasing down balls in play. He has two weaknesses: a weak arm and difficulty with balls hit to his left or right. Ellsbury has a below average arm that lacks the strength one would like to see out of their center fielder. And although very good at chasing down balls hit in front or behind him, he can sometimes misjudge the depth of balls hit into the gaps. Ellsbury will continue to man center field, where he'll be average or better for the foreseeable future.

Andre Ethier

		BASIC							THROWING				RANGE AND POSITIONING						RUNS SAVED				
Year	Team	G	Inn	TC	E	Pct	GFP	DM	Opps to Advance	Extra Bases	Pct	Kills	Outs Made	Plays Saved	Shallow	Medium	Deep	Bases Saved	R/P	Throws	GFP/ DME	Total	Rank
2012	LAD	1	9.0	4	0	1.000	1	0	3	0	.000	0	4	0	0	0	0	+1	0	1	0	1	-
2013	LAD	74	645.1	139	2	.986	9	10	52	29	.558	4	133	-4	-3	-1	0	-7	-4	1	0	-3	23
2014	LAD	68	507.0	121	1	.992	5	3	45	28	.622	0	120	-5	-3	-1	-1	-7	-4	-1	0	-5	26
		143	1161.1	264	3	.989	15	13	100	57	.570	4	257	-9	-6	-2	-1	-13	-8	1	0	-7	-

Scout's Defensive Rating: -1 plays saved in 2013, -4 plays saved in 2014

Andre Ethier has spent time at all three outfield positions over the past three years thanks to the Dodgers' oversupply of corner outfielders and lack of true center fielders. Ethier's skills don't play well in center field, as he is not very fast and lacks the range that is necessary to play the position. His deficiencies and lack of speed aren't so apparent when he plays right field, though. He has played adequately in right over the years and has proven to be skilled at playing balls hit deep. Though he probably didn't deserve the 2011 Gold Glove, he still profiles as an average corner outfielder.

Dexter Fowler

		BASIC							THROWING				RANGE AND POSITIONING						RUNS SAVED				
Year	Team	G	Inn	TC	E	Pct	GFP	DM	Opps to Advance	Extra Bases	Pct	Kills	Outs Made	Plays Saved	Shallow	Medium	Deep	Bases Saved	R/P	Throws	GFP/ DME	Total	Rank
2008	Col	9	49.2	13	0	1.000	1	1	4	4	1.000	1	12	+1	0	0	+1	+2	1	0	0	1	-
2009	Col	127	977.2	256	4	.984	13	26	117	69	.590	5	248	-8	0	-6	-2	-18	-8	-2	-3	-13	34
2010	Col	120	948.1	242	1	.996	22	6	105	63	.600	1	239	-3	-5	-3	+5	+3	0	-4	4	0	15
2011	Col	122	1072.2	323	8	.975	13	22	83	55	.663	3	309	0	-8	-2	+10	+6	2	-2	-5	-5	24
2012	Col	131	1026.0	267	6	.978	15	18	114	72	.632	3	257	-10	-10	-3	+4	-7	-6	-4	-2	-12	34
2013	Col	110	921.1	237	3	.987	11	18	77	46	.597	0	231	0	-1	-1	+1	+1	0	-4	0	-4	24
2014	Hou	111	959.0	247	5	.980	14	12	91	54	.593	2	239	-18	-4	-7	-6	-29	-15	-4	0	-19	35
		730	5954.2	1585	27	.983	89	103	591	363	.614	15	1535	-38	-28	-22	+13	-42	-26	-20	-6	-52	-

Scout's Defensive Rating: -5 plays saved in 2013, -5 plays saved in 2014

While his last season in Colorado was among his top career years defensively, Fowler struggled immensely in his first year with Houston in 2014. Although his lateral movement was still good, his range on medium to deep hit balls was declined significantly, as there were many occasions of balls being hit over his head. Furthermore, he didn't really help his cause with all of his Defensive Misplays and Errors. He is often too eager to get the ball back into the infield, fumbling around with the ball as he fields it and allowing runners to unnecessarily advance. Another issue that Fowler showed was his lack of success on diving plays. He doesn't judge where the ball will be very well, which leads to a tendency for the ball either to bounce off his glove or for him to miss it completely. Due to this, he ranks tied for first

Center Fielders

among all outfielders with 20 failed dives since 2009. Finally, Fowler's arm is the worst at the position, allowing base-runners to advance near or above 60 percent of the time compared to the league average of 55 percent. You'd expect more from a player with Fowler's speed and athleticism, but now on his third major league team in three years, he's running out of excuses.

Sam Fuld

		BASIC							THROWING				RANGE AND POSITIONING						RUNS SAVED			
Year	Team	G	Inn	TC	E	Pct	GFP	DM	Opps to Advance	Extra Bases	Pct	Kills	Outs Made	Plays Saved	Shallow	Medium	Deep	Bases Saved	R/P Throws	GFP/ DME	Total	Rank
2007	ChC	1	1.0	0	0	-	0	0				0	0	0	0	0	0	0	0		0	-
2009	ChC	26	161.2	39	0	1.000	4	5	17	11	.647	0	39	-3	0	-1	-1	-7	-3	-1	1	-3	-
2010	ChC	7	47.0	22	0	1.000	1	0	4	3	.750	0	22	+2	0	0	+1	+3	2	-1	0	1	-
2011	TB	7	37.2	14	0	1.000	1	1	2	1	.500	0	14	+1	+1	0	0	+1	0	0	0	0	-
2012	TB	6	33.0	11	0	1.000	1	0	1	0	.000	0	11	0	0	0	0	-1	0	0	0	0	-
2013	TB	29	186.1	53	1	.981	4	3	15	9	.600	0	52	-1	-1	-3	+3	+1	0	-1	0	-1	-
2014	2 tms	62	517.2	194	1	.995	17	7	54	26	.481	3	188	+3	0	+3	0	+7	3	1	1	5	12
		138	984.1	333	2	.994	28	16	93	50	.538	3	326	+2	0	-1	+3	+4	2	-2	2	2	-

Scout's Defensive Rating: 0 plays saved in 2013, 3 plays saved in 2014

Sam Fuld is the type of outfielder that fans come to love for his all-out, gritty play. The best asset of the 5'10" and 175 pound left hander is unquestionably his speed. He has above average range, and of all three outfield positions, his talent is shown mostly when he stretches his legs in center field. Throughout his career, Fuld has made numerous highlight reel catches. Fuld makes some spectacular diving grabs that have become a his signature play. He also uses his speed to cut off balls in the gap to prevent runners from further advancement. On a few instances, Fuld did have some trouble going back on balls and anticipating the wall as well as some failed dives that allow runners to advance. These are things to expect with a grinder like Fuld, whose effort knows no bounds. Unfortunately, Fuld's anemic bat will likely keep him out of the regular lineup, but when he does see semi-regular time (like he did in 600 innings in Tampa's left field in 2011), he can save double digit runs in a heartbeat.

Craig Gentry

		BASIC							THROWING				RANGE AND POSITIONING						RUNS SAVED			
Year	Team	G	Inn	TC	E	Pct	GFP	DM	Opps to Advance	Extra Bases	Pct	Kills	Outs Made	Plays Saved	Shallow	Medium	Deep	Bases Saved	R/P Throws	GFP/ DME	Total	Rank
2009	Tex	7	33.0	9	0	1.000	1	2	5	3	.600	1	8	+1	0	+1	0	+1	1	0	0	1	-
2010	Tex	7	44.0	9	0	1.000	0	0	3	1	.333	0	9	0	+1	0	0	+1	0	0	0	0	-
2011	Tex	55	313.2	104	1	.990	6	2	33	18	.545	0	103	+9	+3	+2	+4	+16	8	-1	0	7	-
2012	Tex	114	648.0	196	0	1.000	12	13	41	24	.585	4	189	+9	+3	+2	+4	+14	7	3	5	15	4
2013	Tex	71	444.2	150	1	.993	12	10	41	20	.488	2	145	+8	+2	+2	+4	+14	7	0	0	7	9
2014	Oak	50	324.2	95	0	1.000	9	3	36	25	.694	4	91	+1	-3	+2	+3	+8	3	0	1	4	-
		304	1808.0	563	2	.996	40	30	159	91	.572	11	545	+28	+6	+9	+15	+54	26	2	6	34	-

Scout's Defensive Rating: -1 plays saved in 2013, 3 plays saved in 2014

Carlos Gomez

		BASIC							THROWING				RANGE AND POSITIONING						RUNS SAVED			
Year	Team	G	Inn	TC	E	Pct	GFP	DM	Opps to Advance	Extra Bases	Pct	Kills	Outs Made	Plays Saved	Shallow	Medium	Deep	Bases Saved	R/P Throws	GFP/ DME	Total	Rank
2007	NYM	4	12.0	4	0	1.000	1	0				0	4	+1	0	0	+1	+3	2	0	0	2	-
2008	Min	151	1271.2	453	8	.982	34	32	135	73	.541	4	437	+14	-2	+5	+11	+29	16	-2	-2	12	2
2009	Min	132	848.2	301	1	.997	16	14	86	52	.605	2	298	+4	-5	+2	+8	+12	5	-3	2	4	13
2010	Mil	75	594.2	159	5	.969	13	9	70	33	.471	2	152	+3	-1	+4	0	+10	4	1	-1	4	10
2011	Mil	87	569.0	188	0	1.000	22	16	49	19	.388	3	184	+13	+8	+2	+3	+17	10	3	3	16	3
2012	Mil	128	911.1	269	5	.981	20	17	102	57	.559	6	255	-3	-6	-1	+4	0	-1	3	0	2	16
2013	Mil	145	1242.0	407	5	.988	40	18	127	63	.496	7	391	+15	-7	+2	+19	+44	19	6	7	32	1
2014	Mil	145	1269.2	367	5	.986	22	25	104	63	.606	3	355	0	-6	0	+6	+8	2	-1	0	1	17
		867	6719.0	2148	29	.986	168	131	673	360	.535	27	2076	+47	-19	+14	+52	+123	57	7	9	73	-

Scout's Defensive Rating: 7 plays saved in 2013, -3 plays saved in 2014

Gomez brings energy and explosiveness to the center field position. Harnessing that explosiveness was an issue for him in 2014. After receiving regular playing time for just the second time in his career in 2013, Gomez excelled in every facet of the game and was a no-doubt choice as the Fielding Bible Award winner. However, he was unable to reproduce his outstanding 2013 performance in the field. He robbed an astounding five home runs in 2013 but only one in 2014. Observations by the BIS Video Scouts concur, as his Scout's Defensive Rating dropped from 2nd-best to below average. Furthermore, Gomez had issues mishandling balls after base hits in 2014. His 30 DMEs were the third-highest amongst all center fielders. Eleven of these DMEs came from mishandling balls after base hits. His effort cannot be denied, as Gomez sprints to every flyball in the gap or hits that drop in front of him. Finding a healthy balance between turning on the burners and being out of control approaching balls in play remains a challenge.

He plays a very deep center field which creates a doubled edged sword for the Brewers. His deep positioning when combined with his above average speed make his glove the place where doubles go to die, but it allows a few extra shallow liners to fall in safely. Despite playing so deep, Gomez has no trouble limiting opposing baserunners thanks to his ability to cut balls off and launch them back in with a rifle arm. His energy and the fire he plays with can work against him, but given his track record we should expect it to carry him to a rebound season in 2014.

Anthony Gose

		BASIC							THROWING				RANGE AND POSITIONING		Plays Saved				RUNS SAVED		GFP/		
Year	Team	G	Inn	TC	E	Pct	GFP	DM	Opps to Advance	Extra Bases	Pct	Kills	Outs Made	Plays Saved	Shallow	Medium	Deep	Bases Saved	R/P	Throws	DME	Total	Rank
2012	Tor	22	146.1	46	0	1.000	2	2	9	4	.444	0	46	+2	-1	+1	+2	+6	3	-1	0	2	-
2013	Tor	34	269.1	75	4	.947	7	8	32	19	.594	1	68	-1	+1	+2	-3	-4	-2	2	-1	-1	-
2014	Tor	65	485.2	144	1	.993	8	8	27	12	.444	1	142	+3	-1	+3	+1	+6	3	-1	-1	1	-
		121	901.1	265	5	.981	17	18	68	35	.515	2	256	+4	-1	+6	0	+8	4	0	-2	2	-

Scout's Defensive Rating: -1 plays saved in 2013, 1 plays saved in 2014

Billy Hamilton

		BASIC							THROWING				RANGE AND POSITIONING		Plays Saved				RUNS SAVED		GFP/		
Year	Team	G	Inn	TC	E	Pct	GFP	DM	Opps to Advance	Extra Bases	Pct	Kills	Outs Made	Plays Saved	Shallow	Medium	Deep	Bases Saved	R/P	Throws	DME	Total	Rank
2013	Cin	7	45.0	16	0	1.000	0	0	1	0	.000	0	16	+1	0	+1	+1	+2	1	0	0	1	-
2014	Cin	144	1199.1	354	2	.994	33	21	101	54	.535	6	342	+9	+6	+4	0	+15	8	4	2	14	5
		151	1244.1	370	2	.995	33	21	102	54	.529	6	358	+10	+6	+5	+1	+17	9	4	2	15	-

Scout's Defensive Rating: 0 plays saved in 2013, 7 plays saved in 2014

Billy Hamilton was an error-prone shortstop until he converted to center field full time in 2013 at Triple-A. With explosive speed and elite athleticism, Hamilton has already blossomed into an elite major league center fielder. Hamilton plays shallower than most outfielders, which allows him to turn short liners into outs and have a closer throw to third base and home. Furthermore, his speed allows him to corral balls quicker than other center fielders, giving his strong arm an extra fraction of a second to make an accurate throw. Despite his shallow starting position, his raw speed and quick ability to learn the center field position allows Hamilton to take good routes on balls over his head. Billy was tied for second among center fielders in GFPs and only recorded two errors in 2014. Having already established himself as an elite defensive player in his first major league season, Hamilton should continue to get even better as he learns the nuances of the position.

Aaron Hicks

		BASIC							THROWING				RANGE AND POSITIONING		Plays Saved				RUNS SAVED		GFP/		
Year	Team	G	Inn	TC	E	Pct	GFP	DM	Opps to Advance	Extra Bases	Pct	Kills	Outs Made	Plays Saved	Shallow	Medium	Deep	Bases Saved	R/P	Throws	DME	Total	Rank
2013	Min	81	701.1	224	0	1.000	24	13	74	42	.568	5	215	-6	-2	-2	-1	-8	-5	2	5	2	19
2014	Min	57	478.2	169	2	.988	13	10	52	21	.404	2	163	-7	-4	-1	-2	-11	-6	2	1	-3	-
		138	1180.0	393	2	.995	37	23	126	63	.500	7	378	-13	-6	-3	-3	-19	-11	4	6	-1	-

Scout's Defensive Rating: 1 plays saved in 2013, -3 plays saved in 2014

Ender Inciarte

		BASIC							THROWING				RANGE AND POSITIONING		Plays Saved				RUNS SAVED		GFP/		
Year	Team	G	Inn	TC	E	Pct	GFP	DM	Opps to Advance	Extra Bases	Pct	Kills	Outs Made	Plays Saved	Shallow	Medium	Deep	Bases Saved	R/P	Throws	DME	Total	Rank
2014	Ari	76	649.1	208	2	.990	19	15	73	39	.534	4	198	+11	-1	+4	+8	+24	11	1	1	13	7

Scout's Defensive Rating: 4 plays saved in 2014

Center Fielders

In an otherwise dismal year, the Diamondbacks were able to uncover some pieces that may be able to contribute moving forward as a part of the rebuilding effort. One of those pieces was Ender Inciarte, who accumulated the majority of his playing time in center field and ranked tied for sixth among all players at the position with 13 Defensive Runs Saved. Inciarte is able to cover a great deal of outfield real estate thanks to plus to plus-plus speed and his ability to consistently get good reads off the bat.

He excels at tracking down "high leverage" balls in play nearing the outfield wall that would go for extra bases without being caught. Inciarte's above average arm strength handled center field well but really stood out in limited time in left. Inciarte is an exciting player to watch given his demonstrated willingness to slide, dive, jump and run into walls for the sake of converting balls in the air into outs. Inciarte will likely have to earn a starting job in Spring Training prior to the 2015 season; however, Inciarte has the opportunity to follow in Gerrardo Parra's footsteps as an elite defender at any outfield position if given an opportunity.

Austin Jackson

| | | BASIC | | | | | | | THROWING | | | | RANGE AND POSITIONING | | Plays Saved | | | | RUNS SAVED | | | | |
Year	Team	G	Inn	TC	E	Pct	GFP	DM	Opps to Advance	Extra Bases	Pct	Kills	Outs Made	Plays Saved	Shallow	Medium	Deep	Bases Saved	R/P	Throws	GFP/DME	Total	Rank
2010	Det	149	1256.1	398	6	.985	29	22	123	68	.553	5	385	+18	+7	0	+10	+30	16	-1	-3	12	4
2011	Det	152	1264.0	390	3	.992	20	14	104	56	.538	5	379	+20	+2	+6	+12	+40	20	2	4	26	1
2012	Det	137	1184.0	345	1	.997	13	20	95	50	.526	2	339	+6	+7	-3	+2	+8	5	-1	2	6	11
2013	Det	129	1145.2	307	2	.993	13	19	93	48	.516	4	300	+4	+4	0	+1	+4	3	2	-1	4	15
2014	2 tms	154	1326.0	388	6	.985	13	14	101	61	.604	2	378	+2	+1	-3	+5	+9	3	-4	0	-1	21
		721	6176.0	1828	18	.990	88	89	516	283	.548	18	1781	+50	+21	0	+30	+91	47	-2	2	47	-

Scout's Defensive Rating: -4 plays saved in 2013, -2 plays saved in 2014

In his first year in the major leagues, Jackson boasted a strong defensive campaign, recording 12 Defensive Runs Saved in 2010. He followed up that year with an even better performance in the field, recording 26 Defensive Runs Saved and winning a Fielding Bible Award. Since then, its been a downhill ride for Jackson, whose defensive contributions have declined every year since. Jackson is known for his speed, and he possesses a quick first step to get himself in position to make a play on balls hit into his area. His arm has never been his biggest asset, but in 2014 he allowed over 60 percent of runners to take the extra base for the first time in his career. While he doesn't have the range that he once did in Detroit's expansive outfield, he has a fresh chance in his new home in Safeco Field.

Jon Jay

| | | BASIC | | | | | | | THROWING | | | | RANGE AND POSITIONING | | Plays Saved | | | | RUNS SAVED | | | | |
Year	Team	G	Inn	TC	E	Pct	GFP	DM	Opps to Advance	Extra Bases	Pct	Kills	Outs Made	Plays Saved	Shallow	Medium	Deep	Bases Saved	R/P	Throws	GFP/DME	Total	Rank
2010	StL	27	195.0	65	0	1.000	4	7	18	9	.500	2	63	-2	+2	-1	-4	-8	-3	1	0	-2	-
2011	StL	75	570.0	174	3	.983	19	8	41	25	.610	3	167	+8	+6	+2	0	+8	5	0	0	5	10
2012	StL	116	993.1	292	0	1.000	26	22	83	45	.542	0	291	+4	+3	+2	-2	+5	3	-2	0	1	17
2013	StL	152	1285.2	340	1	.997	22	20	129	79	.612	4	335	-2	-1	+5	-5	-8	-3	-5	-2	-10	31
2014	StL	98	749.0	196	1	.995	12	8	55	17	.309	2	193	+4	+4	-1	+1	+3	4	-4	-1	-1	13
		468	3793.0	1067	5	.995	83	65	326	175	.537	11	1049	+12	+14	+7	-10	0	4	-4	-1	-1	-

Scout's Defensive Rating: 0 plays saved in 2013, 1 plays saved in 2014

Jon Jay figured to take a back seat for the Cardinals with the offseason acquisition of Peter Bourjos, especially after Jay struggled defensively in center field to the tune of a -10 Defensive Runs Saved in 2013. Instead, Jay's bat kept him in the lineup on a near everyday basis in 2014, and he also had a big bounce-back season in the field. Jay saw time at all three outfield positions in 2014 but fits best as a center fielder. While he didn't wow scouts with spectacular plays, Jay's strong defensive season was due mostly in part to cutting down on the misplays that plagued him in the past and nearly cost him his job. His pre-2013 play suggests that 2013 was the outlier, and his 2014 play suggests that he's righted the ship and will resume his above average defensive play.

Center Fielders

Desmond Jennings

		BASIC							THROWING				RANGE AND POSITIONING						RUNS SAVED				
Year	Team	G	Inn	TC	E	Pct	GFP	DM	Opps to Advance	Extra Bases	Pct	Kills	Outs Made	Plays Saved	Plays Saved Shallow	Medium	Deep	Bases Saved	R/P	Throws	GFP/ DME	Total	Rank
2010	TB	4	16.0	10	0	1.000	1	0	2	1	.500	0	10	+1	+1	0	+1	+2	1	0	0	1	-
2011	TB	8	64.0	18	0	1.000	1	0	6	1	.167	0	18	0	+1	0	-2	-2	-1	0	0	-1	-
2012	TB	21	162.0	45	0	1.000	1	0	13	10	.769	0	45	+1	+1	0	-1	+1	1	0	0	1	-
2013	TB	136	1188.2	325	3	.991	14	19	104	57	.548	0	319	-3	-3	+1	-1	-4	-2	-2	-2	-6	29
2014	TB	118	1033.1	309	0	1.000	19	9	90	54	.600	0	307	+5	+4	0	+1	+7	4	-2	2	4	14
		287	2464.0	707	3	.996	36	28	215	123	.572	0	699	+4	+4	+1	-2	+4	3	-4	0	-1	-

Scout's Defensive Rating: -5 plays saved in 2013, 5 plays saved in 2014

Jennings is able to perform at a solid defensive level thanks to plus speed and a level of athleticism that once made him the best junior college wide receiver in the nation. Jennings' arm leaves a bit to be desired; in fact, he's never completed a baserunner kill from center field. Nonetheless, he maintains a net positive defensive profile thanks to above average range and a particular ability to track down deep fly balls that would otherwise land for extra-base hits. While Jennings is solid in center, like Carl Crawford before him, he likely possesses the potential to be an excellent left fielder as he carries a track record of performing at a much higher level in that position. The Rays have some options in the outfield, and depending on how their personnel stacks up heading into the 2015 season, they may decide to shuffle up their alignment in an attempt to maximize the overall run prevention ability of their outfield defense.

Adam Jones

		BASIC							THROWING				RANGE AND POSITIONING						RUNS SAVED				
Year	Team	G	Inn	TC	E	Pct	GFP	DM	Opps to Advance	Extra Bases	Pct	Kills	Outs Made	Plays Saved	Plays Saved Shallow	Medium	Deep	Bases Saved	R/P	Throws	GFP/ DME	Total	Rank
2006	Sea	26	193.0	75	3	.960	3	3	20	10	.500	3	67	-1	-2	0	0	0	0	3	0	3	-
2007	Sea	7	34.0	11	1	.909	0	0	0	0	-	0	10	+2	0	0	+1	+3	2	0	0	2	-
2008	Bal	129	1102.0	343	3	.991	18	20	115	49	.426	4	337	+5	+3	+4	-3	+7	4	5	-3	6	8
2009	Bal	118	1005.0	363	5	.986	26	28	105	40	.381	5	349	-5	+7	-5	-7	-14	-6	10	6	10	6
2010	Bal	149	1298.1	423	7	.984	23	28	113	60	.531	10	423	-9	0	-7	-2	-22	-10	5	-1	-6	31
2011	Bal	148	1281.0	403	8	.980	24	27	141	78	.553	13	380	-7	+5	-3	-9	-21	-9	8	0	-1	18
2012	Bal	162	1458.0	454	8	.982	14	24	136	73	.537	2	439	-7	+10	-7	-11	-23	-10	-1	-2	-13	35
2013	Bal	156	1394.0	365	2	.995	18	26	140	67	.479	6	353	-8	+1	-2	-7	-16	-8	7	0	-1	21
2014	Bal	155	1368.1	387	11	.984	11	10	115	55	.478	5	374	+1	+9	-1	-7	-8	-2	4	1	3	15
		1050	9133.2	2842	43	.985	137	166	885	432	.488	48	2732	-29	+33	-21	-45	-94	-39	41	1	3	-

Scout's Defensive Rating: -8 plays saved in 2013, -3 plays saved in 2014

A four-time Gold Glove winner, Jones has been one of the most controversial players for defensive metrics. His best quality has always his arm, as he's saved 19 more runs with his arm than any other center fielder since 2003 (41 vs. Jim Edmonds' 22). Jones has also generally excelled at defending shallow flyballs, posting positive Range and Positioning numbers on shallow balls in play in five of the last seven seasons, including nine plays above average in 2014, the second best total at the position in baseball last season.

However, there are times when Jones does not get good jumps and is slow to react to deep balls in particular, and that can lead to misplays on otherwise catchable balls. As a result, Jones has allowed more extra-base hits to fall in than any other center fielder in baseball over the last three years. Even with his ability to make up for a poor initial read, Jones has struggled with flyballs bouncing off his glove, as his nine Defensive Misplays and three errors since the start of the 2013 season are only one fewer than the league leader over than span. In total, Jones plays a respectable league average center field, but that performance does not match up with his golden reputation.

James Jones

		BASIC							THROWING				RANGE AND POSITIONING						RUNS SAVED				
Year	Team	G	Inn	TC	E	Pct	GFP	DM	Opps to Advance	Extra Bases	Pct	Kills	Outs Made	Plays Saved	Plays Saved Shallow	Medium	Deep	Bases Saved	R/P	Throws	GFP/ DME	Total	Rank
2014	Sea	85	649.0	155	1	.994	10	13	38	21	.553	1	153	-8	-4	-4	0	-11	-6	-2	-1	-9	30

Scout's Defensive Rating: -1 plays saved in 2014

James Jones was inserted into the Mariners lineup in 2014 with the hopes of being a speedy spark plug that could score runs and cover ground in Safeco Field for the contending Mariners. Unfortunately, his defense became more of a prob-

Center Fielders

lem than a solution for Seattle. Jones had difficulty reading balls off the bat, but his tendency to turn one mistake into two proved more damaging. Jones may have felt the urgency to perform as a rookie, but bad ball reads soon turned into failed dives or wasted throws after retrieving the ball. Jones is still a raw player in center field and, because these mistakes are more self-inflected than a lack of talent, he should progress as a defender. If he can harness his overaggressive playing style, then he should be able to steadily improve and minimize his mistakes.

Matt Kemp

		BASIC							THROWING					RANGE AND POSITIONING							RUNS SAVED				
Year	Team	G	Inn	TC	E	Pct	GFP	DM	Opps to Advance	Extra Bases	Pct	Kills	Outs Made	Plays Saved	Plays Saved Shallow	Medium	Deep	Bases Saved	R/P	Throws	GFP/ DME	Total	Rank
2006	LAD	29	189.2	40	3	.925	3	9	21	13	.619	0	37	-2	-1	-1	0	-4	-2	0	-1	-3	-
2007	LAD	6	17.1	8	0	1.000	2	0	1	0	.000	0	8	0	0	0	0	+1	1	0	2	3	-
2008	LAD	101	825.2	220	1	.995	22	13	76	40	.526	8	209	0	+5	-2	-2	-2	-1	5	1	5	10
2009	LAD	158	1355.1	383	2	.995	48	33	114	55	.482	8	366	-6	0	-1	-4	-15	-6	7	0	1	16
2010	LAD	158	1346.0	338	5	.985	26	28	120	70	.583	3	330	-28	-4	-13	-11	-53	-26	-4	-3	-33	35
2011	LAD	159	1380.0	361	5	.985	28	23	109	59	.541	8	346	-14	-8	+1	-6	-20	-12	4	1	-7	31
2012	LAD	105	911.0	216	1	.995	20	16	69	38	.551	6	208	-13	-1	-6	-7	-32	-15	4	1	-10	32
2013	LAD	70	576.1	140	5	.964	10	8	56	23	.411	2	133	-10	-5	-2	-3	-16	-8	2	1	-5	28
2014	LAD	41	326.0	80	4	.950	6	9	19	9	.474	1	75	-11	-4	-3	-4	-20	-10	1	-2	-11	-
		827	6927.1	1786	26	.985	165	139	585	307	.525	36	1712	-84	-18	-27	-37	-161	-79	19	0	-60	-

Scout's Defensive Rating: -6 plays saved in 2013, -3 plays saved in 2014

Matt Kemp's Scouting Report can be found on page 285.

Kevin Kiermaier

		BASIC							THROWING					RANGE AND POSITIONING							RUNS SAVED				
Year	Team	G	Inn	TC	E	Pct	GFP	DM	Opps to Advance	Extra Bases	Pct	Kills	Outs Made	Plays Saved	Plays Saved Shallow	Medium	Deep	Bases Saved	R/P	Throws	GFP/ DME	Total	Rank
2013	TB	1	1.0	0	0	-	0	0														0	-
2014	TB	42	298.1	103	1	.990	9	5	28	12	.429	1	100	0	+1	0	-2	-2	-1	1	1	1	-
		43	299.1	103	1	.990	9	5	28	12	.429	1	100	0	+1	0	-2	-2	-1	1	1	1	-

Scout's Defensive Rating: 1 plays saved in 2014

Kevin Kiermaier's Scouting Report can be found on page 285.

Juan Lagares

		BASIC							THROWING					RANGE AND POSITIONING							RUNS SAVED				
Year	Team	G	Inn	TC	E	Pct	GFP	DM	Opps to Advance	Extra Bases	Pct	Kills	Outs Made	Plays Saved	Plays Saved Shallow	Medium	Deep	Bases Saved	R/P	Throws	GFP/ DME	Total	Rank
2013	NYM	108	819.2	276	5	.982	29	14	78	33	.423	12	258	+15	+12	0	+2	+19	11	11	4	26	2
2014	NYM	112	945.0	304	5	.984	25	13	85	33	.388	5	294	+22	+9	+4	+9	+40	20	6	0	26	1
		220	1764.2	580	10	.983	54	27	163	66	.405	17	552	+37	+21	+4	+11	+59	31	17	4	52	-

Scout's Defensive Rating: -1 plays saved in 2013, 6 plays saved in 2014

After struggling as a shortstop early in his minor league career, Juan Lagares made the switch to outfield and has quickly established himself as an elite defensive center fielder in MLB. Despite barely playing 800 innings in center field in his rookie season, Lagares was the runner up for the Fielding Bible Award. Lagares picked up right where he left off in 2014, almost doubling the next closest center fielder's Defensive Runs Saved. Much like Andruw Jones before him, Lagares' great jumps and closing speed on deep flyballs allows him to play a very shallow center field and cut off base hits that fall in front of other center fielders. Lagares' aggressive positioning and ability to charge the ball allows him to get to base hits quickly, which, in concert with a strong and accurate throwing arm, helped him lead all MLB center fielders with 14 assists in 2013. Although his assist total declined in 2014, this is mainly due to baserunners and coaches giving him more respect and not testing him as often. If Lagares can hit enough to stay in the lineup, his glove makes him a very valuable player and he should perennially contend for a Fielding Bible Award for years to come.

Center Fielders

Junior Lake

	BASIC								THROWING				RANGE AND POSITIONING						RUNS SAVED				
									Opps to	Extra			Outs	Plays	Plays Saved			Bases			GFP/		
Year	Team	G	Inn	TC	E	Pct	GFP	DM	Advance	Bases	Pct	Kills	Made	Saved	Shallow	Medium	Deep	Saved	R/P	Throws	DME	Total	Rank
2013	ChC	27	238.1	70	3	.957	4	11	20	9	.450	1	66	-1	+1	+1	-3	-3	-1	1	-1	-1	-
2014	ChC	36	256.2	57	3	.947	0	6	27	18	.667	0	54	-5	0	0	-4	-11	-5	-1	-1	-7	-
		63	495.0	127	6	.953	4	17	47	27	.574	1	120	-6	+1	+1	-7	-14	-6	0	-2	-8	-

Scout's Defensive Rating: -1 plays saved in 2013, -2 plays saved in 2014

Junior Lake's Scouting Report can be found on page 250.

Jake Marisnick

	BASIC								THROWING				RANGE AND POSITIONING						RUNS SAVED				
									Opps to	Extra			Outs	Plays	Plays Saved			Bases			GFP/		
Year	Team	G	Inn	TC	E	Pct	GFP	DM	Advance	Bases	Pct	Kills	Made	Saved	Shallow	Medium	Deep	Saved	R/P	Throws	DME	Total	Rank
2013	Mia	32	261.0	80	0	1.000	10	6	18	11	.611	4	75	+3	+1	-1	+2	+5	3	2	2	7	-
2014	2 tms	30	254.2	99	0	1.000	7	2	18	8	.444	3	96	+8	+3	+2	+3	+12	7	2	1	10	-
		62	515.2	179	0	1.000	17	8	36	19	.528	7	171	+11	+4	+1	+5	+17	10	4	3	17	-

Scout's Defensive Rating: 1 plays saved in 2013, 1 plays saved in 2014

Splitting time between center and right field, Marisnick has shown the ability to cover ground quickly with exceptional closing speed and timing abilities. A natural center fielder, he lacks the normal top-end speed you see from most players at the position, but he takes excellent routes from shallow-to-deep and gap-to-gap. In barely 500 innings, Marisnick managed to save 15 runs across three outfield positions, including 10 runs in center field alone. Marisnick possesses good arm strength, but his accuracy stands out. Tested often after his midseason call-up (and mid-season trade to the Astros), he tallied five baserunner kills in a relatively short amount of time. Certainly an above average athlete, Marisnick has the makings of a superb outfielder if given a chance.

Leonys Martin

	BASIC								THROWING				RANGE AND POSITIONING						RUNS SAVED				
									Opps to	Extra			Outs	Plays	Plays Saved			Bases			GFP/		
Year	Team	G	Inn	TC	E	Pct	GFP	DM	Advance	Bases	Pct	Kills	Made	Saved	Shallow	Medium	Deep	Saved	R/P	Throws	DME	Total	Rank
2011	Tex	8	19.0	7	0	1.000	1	0	1	1	1.000	0	7	-1	0	0	-1	-1	-1	0	0	-1	-
2012	Tex	14	105.0	33	0	1.000	2	2	17	10	.588	1	32	-1	-1	+1	-1	-2	-1	0	0	-1	-
2013	Tex	127	974.1	303	5	.983	25	24	93	46	.495	8	287	+10	+4	+3	+2	+16	9	6	-1	14	4
2014	Tex	152	1247.1	434	8	.982	35	31	134	58	.433	10	415	+3	+3	+4	-4	+1	1	12	3	16	2
		301	2345.2	777	13	.983	63	57	245	115	.469	19	741	+11	+6	+8	-4	+14	8	18	2	28	-

Scout's Defensive Rating: -1 plays saved in 2013, -5 plays saved in 2014

Leonys Martin possesses an elite arm which ranks as the best among all center fielders. Its supreme in-game utility is evidenced by the impressive 12 Outfield Arm Runs Saved he accumulated in 2014–first among center fielders and second-best among all outfielders, trailing only left fielder Yoenis Cespedes's mark of 14. Beyond the arm, however, Martin still leaves something to be desired on defense. Martin accumulated the most Good Fielding Plays (GFP) among center fielders in 2014 but also accumulated the highest Defensive Misplay and Error (DME) total. Martin's eight DMEs resulting from balls bouncing off of his glove and six DMEs from mishandling a ball after a safe hit indicate that Martin struggles with his concentration at times. Further, he was burned by balls over his head on multiple occasions. The concentration errors are resolvable, but Martin's arm will continue to carry his defensive value.

Center Fielders

Cameron Maybin

		BASIC							THROWING				RANGE AND POSITIONING		Plays Saved				RUNS SAVED		GFP/		
Year	Team	G	Inn	TC	E	Pct	GFP	DM	Opps to Advance	Extra Bases	Pct	Kills	Outs Made	Plays Saved	Shallow	Medium	Deep	Bases Saved	R/P	Throws	DME	Total	Rank
2007	Det	5	25.0	10	0	1.000	2	2	3	2	.667	0	10	0	0	0	0	+1	1	0	0	1	-
2008	Fla	8	63.0	23	0	1.000	1	1	3	2	.667	0	23	+1	0	+1	0	+2	1	0	0	1	-
2009	Fla	52	416.0	126	1	.992	7	13	43	28	.651	1	124	0	-5	+5	0	0	0	-3	-1	-4	-
2010	Fla	77	634.1	223	4	.982	20	13	62	38	.613	3	214	+7	+1	+3	+4	+13	7	-1	0	6	8
2011	SD	136	1173.0	349	5	.986	27	21	108	62	.574	2	342	+18	+11	+1	+7	+31	17	-2	-1	14	4
2012	SD	145	1210.1	337	3	.991	27	23	101	60	.594	2	330	+6	-4	+1	+8	+15	6	-3	4	7	8
2013	SD	14	120.1	33	0	1.000	2	7	11	6	.545	0	33	-4	-2	-2	+1	-6	-3	-1	-1	-5	-
2014	SD	86	631.0	164	2	.988	8	12	61	34	.557	1	161	+5	-2	0	+7	+14	6	-3	-1	2	16
		523	4273.0	1265	15	.988	94	92	392	232	.592	9	1237	+33	-1	+9	+27	+70	35	-13	0	22	-

Scout's Defensive Rating: -1 plays saved in 2013, -1 plays saved in 2014

It has been tough for Maybin to earn some playing time during the past two years, as injuries and a suspension have kept him off the field. Despite the ups and downs, Maybin has shown that he is capable of making most plays regardless of difficulty. His speed paired with his athleticism provide him with fantastic range, especially on deep hit balls in cavernous Petco Park. Prior to the injuries, Maybin was one of the more aggressive center fielders in the game, but he seemed to play more conservatively upon his return. For example, whereas in years past Maybin would charge in on weakly-hit balls, now he will hold up and play the ball on a bounce. Occasionally, he still shows signs of great defense by making an acrobatic catch. Regrettably for Maybin and his team, his Defensive Misplays outnumber his Good Fielding Plays. Maybin has a strong arm, but his accuracy is a problem. Runners will challenge Maybin on the basepaths, and have been successful at taking an extra base at a rate of 56 percent. At this point, it's probably best to consider Maybin an average defender in center unless he returns to full health and once again displays the aggressiveness that he displayed previously.

Andrew McCutchen

		BASIC							THROWING				RANGE AND POSITIONING		Plays Saved				RUNS SAVED		GFP/		
Year	Team	G	Inn	TC	E	Pct	GFP	DM	Opps to Advance	Extra Bases	Pct	Kills	Outs Made	Plays Saved	Shallow	Medium	Deep	Bases Saved	R/P	Throws	DME	Total	Rank
2009	Pit	108	952.2	275	2	.993	18	21	91	49	.538	2	262	+2	+15	-3	-10	-13	-3	1	1	-1	23
2010	Pit	152	1290.1	386	5	.987	36	27	133	84	.632	8	373	-6	+8	-6	-8	-18	-7	1	1	-5	27
2011	Pit	155	1353.2	430	7	.984	28	22	132	73	.553	5	414	+3	-5	-5	+9	+14	5	-3	0	2	12
2012	Pit	156	1364.0	371	1	.997	18	29	108	62	.574	2	368	-3	-6	0	+3	-1	-1	-3	-2	-6	27
2013	Pit	155	1378.0	338	6	.982	28	21	120	68	.567	6	322	0	-8	+2	+6	+10	3	3	-1	5	11
2014	Pit	146	1286.0	308	6	.981	20	19	97	70	.722	1	301	-4	-8	-2	+5	+1	-2	-7	-4	-13	32
		872	7624.2	2108	27	.987	148	139	681	406	.596	22	2040	-8	-4	-9	+5	-7	-5	-8	-5	-18	-

Scout's Defensive Rating: 3 plays saved in 2013, 4 plays saved in 2014

Like many elite hitters, Andrew McCutchen receives too much credit for his glove. Upon his arrival in Pittsburgh, McCutchen took pride in playing shallow and as a result allowed far too many extra-base hits to fall in over his head. However, the Pirates' front office and coaching staff worked with their young franchise player to move him back several steps. Now, thanks to great foot speed and steady routes, the 2012 Gold Glove winner often makes outstanding plays on balls over his head, though singles fall in front with regularity. The move was a net positive, but he still isn't anything better than an average center fielder chasing down flies. McCutchen's arm took a turn for the worse in 2014, perhaps partially as a result of the rib injury he suffered in early August. McCutchen made only one kill on the season, and runners took extra bases on him 72.2 percent of the time after doing so only 56.7 percent of the time in 2013. All told, McCutchen lost seven runs with his arm in 2014 after saving three runs with his arm in 2013. Assuming his arm rebounds to roughly average, McCutchen has the speed, first step and route-running to stick at the position for several more years.

Marcell Ozuna

		BASIC							THROWING				RANGE AND POSITIONING		Plays Saved				RUNS SAVED		GFP/		
Year	Team	G	Inn	TC	E	Pct	GFP	DM	Opps to Advance	Extra Bases	Pct	Kills	Outs Made	Plays Saved	Shallow	Medium	Deep	Bases Saved	R/P	Throws	DME	Total	Rank
2013	Mia	33	301.0	80	0	1.000	6	11	30	17	.567	3	77	-1	0	-2	0	-4	-1	1	0	0	-
2014	Mia	140	1206.0	338	5	.985	20	16	126	65	.516	6	325	+5	+3	-4	+6	+14	6	2	0	8	9
		173	1507.0	418	5	.988	26	27	156	82	.526	9	402	+4	+3	-6	+6	+10	5	3	0	8	-

Scout's Defensive Rating: 0 plays saved in 2013, -3 plays saved in 2014

Center Fielders

While he alternated between right field and center field in 2013 for the Marlins, Ozuna has solidified himself as the center fielder for Miami with above average defense in 2014. With an extremely spacious outfield, Ozuna has been able to play both the shallow and deep flyballs well. His first step is second to none on reacting to flyballs in either direction and allows him to retrieve balls that the average player can't reach. The spacious confines of Marlins Park require a center fielder who can cover ground, and Ozuna supplied that as a top ten player at his position. One area Ozuna will look to improve in 2015 is the line drives that are hit within medium range, which were the most difficult for Ozuna in 2014. Showing plus range in both directions should be an indication, however, that Ozuna can figure out those mid-range balls in center field. Besides his range, another strength of Ozuna's is his throwing arm and the accuracy that he is able to apply to each throw. He has a gift at getting his whole body into each throw, which allows him to uncork a bullet that resulted in 8 Kills in 2014. With Ozuna's young age and now-permanent position, there is no reason to believe that he won't continue to be a plus defender for years to come.

Angel Pagan

		BASIC						THROWING				RANGE AND POSITIONING						RUNS SAVED				
Year Team	G	Inn	TC	E	Pct	GFP	DM	Opps to Advance	Extra Bases	Pct	Kills	Outs Made	Plays Saved	Plays Saved Shallow	Medium	Deep	Bases Saved	R/P	Throws	GFP/ DME	Total	Rank
2006 ChC	1	3.0	1	0	1.000	1	0	0	0	-	0	1	+1	0	+1	0	+1	1	0	0	1	-
2007 ChC	34	236.0	60	0	1.000	1	8	29	13	.448	0	60	+1	+1	-1	+1	+2	1	1	0	2	-
2008 NYM	2	18.2	8	0	1.000	0	0	1	1	1.000	0	8	0	-1	+1	0	0	0	0	0	0	-
2009 NYM	61	506.1	138	2	.986	12	12	48	24	.500	3	132	+5	-2	+1	+6	+14	6	3	1	10	5
2010 NYM	94	792.1	270	4	.985	15	16	94	44	.468	4	258	+10	+3	+5	+2	+20	10	4	-2	12	5
2011 NYM	121	1045.0	317	10	.968	17	26	128	74	.578	1	302	-10	-3	-7	0	-9	-6	-1	-2	-9	32
2012 SF	151	1279.1	389	5	.987	19	28	113	64	.566	3	377	+2	+2	+3	-3	-2	0	-2	-3	-5	24
2013 SF	71	579.2	158	4	.975	10	15	51	29	.569	2	149	-8	-5	-1	-2	-13	-7	-1	-1	-9	30
2014 SF	91	775.1	213	1	.995	15	14	57	31	.544	2	209	-6	-2	-1	-2	-8	-5	0	0	-5	27
	626	5235.2	1554	26	.983	90	119	521	280	.537	15	1496	-5	-7	+1	+2	+5	0	4	-7	-3	-

Scout's Defensive Rating: -4 plays saved in 2013, -2 plays saved in 2014

Since having a couple great defensive seasons with the Mets, Angel Pagan has been a below average defensive center fielder. Pagan does not demonstrate good or even average range in any direction, primarily due to poor reads and unsteady routes. Pagan certainly has the speed to play center field, but 2014 marked the third season of the last four in which Pagan made fewer plays than average. Pagan does not have much of an arm to speak of, with a cumulative -4 Outfield Arm Runs Saved since 2011. In addition to poor routes, Pagan has a tendency to overrun plays and give up extra bases. Although Pagan was once an excellent center fielder, those days are long past.

A.J. Pollock

		BASIC						THROWING				RANGE AND POSITIONING						RUNS SAVED				
Year Team	G	Inn	TC	E	Pct	GFP	DM	Opps to Advance	Extra Bases	Pct	Kills	Outs Made	Plays Saved	Plays Saved Shallow	Medium	Deep	Bases Saved	R/P	Throws	GFP/ DME	Total	Rank
2012 Ari	14	124.0	42	0	1.000	1	3	17	9	.529	0	42	-3	-3	-2	+2	0	-1	0	0	-1	-
2013 Ari	110	915.2	248	2	.992	27	17	81	47	.580	4	238	+10	-4	+3	+11	+26	11	1	0	12	6
2014 Ari	68	576.0	160	1	.994	15	9	66	39	.591	4	151	+2	-6	0	+7	+11	4	0	4	8	10
	192	1615.2	450	3	.993	43	29	164	95	.579	8	431	+9	-13	+1	+20	+37	14	1	4	19	-

Scout's Defensive Rating: 3 plays saved in 2013, 1 plays saved in 2014

Pollock has the size, tools, and raw speed to be an above average center fielder. He takes good routes and reads the ball extremely well off the bat, allowing him to get early jumps and reach balls that other center fielders can't reach. Besides his routes, Pollock also has a lot of speed and above average range. Add that to an above average glove on dives and slides and you get a borderline elite center fielder. The only thing holding Pollock back from being truly elite is his arm. His arm strength is average, but he struggles with accuracy. If he can learn to throw with a little more accuracy, then Pollock can enter the conversation of elite outfielders in MLB.

Center Fielders

Yasiel Puig

		BASIC							THROWING				RANGE AND POSITIONING						RUNS SAVED				
Year	Team	G	Inn	TC	E	Pct	GFP	DM	Opps to Advance	Extra Bases	Pct	Kills	Outs Made	Plays Saved	Shallow	Medium	Deep	Bases Saved	R/P	Throws	GFP/ DME	Total	Rank
2013	LAD	10	55.1	12	1	.917	3	4	12	5	.417	0	11	-2	-2	-1	+1	0	-1	0	0	-1	-
2014	LAD	53	442.1	114	2	.982	9	9	42	20	.476	4	104	-7	-3	-3	-1	-8	-5	4	0	-1	-
		63	497.2	126	3	.976	12	13	54	25	.463	4	115	-9	-5	-4	0	-8	-6	4	0	-2	-

Scout's Defensive Rating: 0 plays saved in 2013, 1 plays saved in 2014

Yasiel Puig's Scouting Report can be found on page 289.

Colby Rasmus

		BASIC							THROWING				RANGE AND POSITIONING						RUNS SAVED				
Year	Team	G	Inn	TC	E	Pct	GFP	DM	Opps to Advance	Extra Bases	Pct	Kills	Outs Made	Plays Saved	Shallow	Medium	Deep	Bases Saved	R/P	Throws	GFP/ DME	Total	Rank
2009	StL	124	945.2	266	5	.981	9	16	94	41	.436	3	258	+9	+7	0	+2	+12	7	4	-2	9	7
2010	StL	134	1105.1	266	5	.981	12	16	101	49	.485	0	260	-3	+2	+2	-8	-12	-5	-1	1	-5	26
2011	2 tms	127	1092.2	312	6	.981	12	20	85	52	.612	1	302	-1	+1	+1	-4	-2	-1	-2	-1	-4	22
2012	Tor	145	1237.1	317	6	.981	21	22	114	50	.439	2	304	+5	+9	-1	-3	+5	3	4	0	7	9
2013	Tor	114	1002.2	313	4	.987	21	27	101	50	.495	1	308	+11	+8	+5	-1	+12	8	2	2	12	7
2014	Tor	87	719.1	238	1	.996	11	18	84	45	.536	2	234	-4	-2	+6	-8	-11	-5	0	-1	-6	28
		731	6103.0	1712	27	.984	86	119	579	287	.496	9	1666	+17	+25	+13	-22	+4	7	7	-1	13	-

Scout's Defensive Rating: 1 plays saved in 2013, -3 plays saved in 2014

Rasmus's center field defense has been inconsistent throughout his career, and unfortunately he had one of his weaker seasons heading into free agency. Battling injuries for portions of 2014, he never looked comfortable, often stiff when taking routes to the ball, often times looking tentative or cautious. He struggled in particular with hard hit balls over his head, either taking bad routes or failing to anticipate the wall on base hits. All too often, Rasmus seemed to lack focus, having a ball go off his glove rather than completing the catch. Instead of letting his natural athletic tendencies take over, he looked as though he were overthinking the play in front of him and not allowing his muscle memory take over. Though he doesn't throw out a ton of runners, he gets to the ball quickly and seldom allows them to take the extra base. He still possesses the natural abilities to stick in center field, and maybe without the distractions of a looming contract or nagging injuries he can regain some of his defensive prestige.

Ben Revere

		BASIC							THROWING				RANGE AND POSITIONING						RUNS SAVED				
Year	Team	G	Inn	TC	E	Pct	GFP	DM	Opps to Advance	Extra Bases	Pct	Kills	Outs Made	Plays Saved	Shallow	Medium	Deep	Bases Saved	R/P	Throws	GFP/ DME	Total	Rank
2010	Min	6	38.0	10	1	.900	0	0	4	3	.750	0	9	0	0	0	0	0	0	0	0	0	-
2011	Min	89	776.1	252	6	.976	14	16	89	56	.629	3	244	+3	0	-2	+5	+7	3	-3	-2	-2	19
2012	Min	39	309.0	89	0	1.000	10	13	39	23	.590	2	87	+1	+3	0	-2	-3	0	0	-1	-1	-
2013	Phi	87	708.0	228	2	.991	16	23	55	32	.582	2	220	0	+5	+1	-6	-9	-3	0	0	-3	22
2014	Phi	141	1199.0	329	4	.988	24	23	105	63	.600	1	323	-9	+4	-10	-3	-19	-9	-6	-2	-17	33
		362	3030.1	908	13	.986	64	75	292	177	.606	8	883	-5	+12	-11	-6	-24	-9	-9	-5	-23	-

Scout's Defensive Rating: -2 plays saved in 2013, 4 plays saved in 2014

Ben Revere is a player that has become known for some tremendous catches over his short career. However, it would be dangerous to judge his defensive abilities on those few plays. Revere has one of the weakest arms of any outfielder in baseball. This has always plagued him and continues to be a problem. Aggressive base runners will tag up not only from third, but also from first on long flyballs to center field and be able to advance successfully. Overall he cost his team six runs with his arm in 2014, but the impact is even greater than that. Having to contend with his arm strength forces Revere to have to be very aggressive and play very shallow, leading to an inordinate number of extra-base hits.

In limited playing time in right field in 2012 with Minnesota, Revere's Defensive Runs Saved was improved dramatically. He was able to use his speed to his advantage and cover a large amount of ground. His reads aren't what you want for a center fielder. He doesn't always get a great jump, but if he is playing a corner he has enough speed to make up for it. If a team is willing to stomach his arm, Revere is a great weapon off the bench and could be a solid left field option or fourth outfielder very similar to Juan Pierre.

Center Fielders

Danny Santana

				BASIC					THROWING				RANGE AND POSITIONING		Plays Saved				RUNS SAVED		GFP/		
Year	Team	G	Inn	TC	E	Pct	GFP	DM	Opps to Advance	Extra Bases	Pct	Kills	Outs Made	Plays Saved	Shallow	Medium	Deep	Bases Saved	R/P	Throws	DME	Total	Rank
2014	Min	69	535.2	176	4	.977	8	12	64	32	.500	4	167	-3	-1	0	-2	-3	-2	2	0	0	20

Scout's Defensive Rating: -3 plays saved in 2014

Santana made his Major League Debut in 2014, displaying his versatility as a fielder. Though pegged to be the future at shortstop for the Twins, Santana saw the majority of his playing time in center field. In turn, he used the opportunity to show off his overall speed and that he is willing to play where the team needs him. As a center fielder, he demonstrated good lateral movement and a good first step. When he was unable to make an out on a medium or shallow hit ball, he was able to at least knock the ball down and prevent runners from advancing more than a base. On deep flyballs, however, he wasn't as comfortable, often taking bad routes and struggling with balls hit to the wall. Also, though he has a strong arm which helped him amass five outfield assists, it was also the reason he had 6 of his 16 Defensive Misplays or Errors in center field. His arm issues also translated to his play at shortstop, as his accuracy caused him to lose a number of outs when moving to his right. However, he was especially good with balls right at him, utilizing quick glove work and sometimes a great vertical leap that saved a lot of extra bases.

Denard Span

				BASIC					THROWING				RANGE AND POSITIONING		Plays Saved				RUNS SAVED		GFP/		
Year	Team	G	Inn	TC	E	Pct	GFP	DM	Opps to Advance	Extra Bases	Pct	Kills	Outs Made	Plays Saved	Shallow	Medium	Deep	Bases Saved	R/P	Throws	DME	Total	Rank
2008	Min	19	116.2	36	1	.972	5	3	22	12	.545	1	34	-2	-1	0	0	-2	-1	1	0	0	-
2009	Min	84	587.1	181	1	.994	8	7	56	42	.750	1	179	+3	0	+1	+1	+3	2	-6	1	-3	24
2010	Min	153	1349.2	416	4	.990	27	25	136	79	.581	4	408	0	+5	-6	+2	-6	-2	-3	1	-4	21
2011	Min	67	585.1	208	1	.995	12	9	51	32	.627	0	206	+15	+6	+2	+6	+24	13	-3	-1	9	6
2012	Min	125	1073.1	349	4	.989	20	18	109	65	.596	4	339	+16	+4	+2	+10	+31	16	1	2	19	3
2013	Was	153	1300.2	384	0	1.000	33	11	108	65	.602	3	379	+7	+11	-2	-2	+8	5	-4	2	3	17
2014	Was	147	1302.2	388	4	.990	24	18	117	65	.556	4	377	+1	+3	0	-3	-4	-1	-1	0	-2	22
		748	6315.2	1962	15	.992	129	91	599	360	.601	17	1922	+40	+28	-3	+14	+54	32	-15	5	22	-

Scout's Defensive Rating: 6 plays saved in 2013, 2 plays saved in 2014

Watching Denard Span sprinting around in center field is truly a pleasure. It seems that no well-struck ball to center field is a for-sure hit when Span is churning up the outfield grass with his dynamic speed and acceleration; however, the quickness is not the most impressive aspect of his defense. Rather, it is the manner in which he utilizes his quickness. Span's superior instincts produce confident strides seemingly at the instant of contact, with routes that are so close to perfect, almost linear. In fact, Span did not receive a single Defensive Misplay or Error due to a bad route in all of 2014. Unfortunately, there's one aspect of his elite defense in Minnesota that has not translated to Washington: positioning. A good deal of deep flyballs that he's previously tracked down have started dropping just out of Span's range. Though his talent is as good as ever, Span could resurrect his top-flight defense by cheating back a step or two to limit those extra-base hits.

Drew Stubbs

				BASIC					THROWING				RANGE AND POSITIONING		Plays Saved				RUNS SAVED		GFP/		
Year	Team	G	Inn	TC	E	Pct	GFP	DM	Opps to Advance	Extra Bases	Pct	Kills	Outs Made	Plays Saved	Shallow	Medium	Deep	Bases Saved	R/P	Throws	DME	Total	Rank
2009	Cin	42	368.2	115	0	1.000	8	9	33	14	.424	1	111	+7	+3	+3	+2	+13	7	1	-1	7	-
2010	Cin	147	1229.2	392	5	.987	13	20	108	51	.472	4	380	-8	-10	-1	+3	-4	-5	0	1	-4	22
2011	Cin	157	1329.0	377	3	.992	15	26	124	66	.532	8	365	-9	-9	+5	-5	-14	-8	5	-1	-4	23
2012	Cin	135	1107.1	282	5	.982	17	14	96	44	.458	3	272	-3	-3	0	0	0	-1	2	0	1	18
2013	Cle	43	339.0	97	0	1.000	5	6	29	18	.621	0	95	-2	-1	0	-1	-3	-2	-1	0	-3	-
2014	Col	113	835.0	229	7	.969	7	12	86	46	.535	4	215	+2	0	+1	0	+3	2	1	-3	0	19
		637	5208.2	1492	20	.987	65	87	476	239	.502	20	1438	-13	-20	+8	-1	-5	-7	8	-4	-3	-

Scout's Defensive Rating: -1 plays saved in 2013, -1 plays saved in 2014

A speedy center fielder is no rarity in the majors, and Drew Stubbs offers little else to set himself apart. He is comfortable tracking down the ball once airborne, although his initial reads off the bat sometimes produced less than optimal routes. This difficulty tended to manifest itself most on deeper balls, as Stubbs's routes would occasionally bow towards the infield. Opportunities to make difficult plays often become stand-up doubles with Stubbs jogging to the

Center Fielders

outfield wall. In 2014, Stubbs indeed made few of these challenging plays, ranking tied for 33rd among 35 regular center fielders with just five Good Fielding Plays on fair flyball outs. Further, Stubbs shows substandard arm strength, though it's offset by fair arm accuracy, and has a habit of putting forth a dissonant effort that was followed by the ball skipping away and baserunner(s) advancing. Stubbs was tied for third with seven Defensive Misplays and Errors of this subtype in 2014. Overall, Stubbs is comfortable patrolling center field though he's far from spectacular.

Mike Trout

	BASIC							THROWING				RANGE AND POSITIONING						RUNS SAVED				
								Opps to Advance	Extra Bases	Pct	Kills	Outs Made	Plays Saved	Plays Saved Shallow	Medium	Deep	Bases Saved			GFP/		
Year Team	G	Inn	TC	E	Pct	GFP	DM											R/P	Throws	DME	Total	Rank
2011 LAA	13	107.2	38	1	.974	2	1	9	5	.556	0	37	+1	0	0	+1	+3	1	0	0	1	-
2012 LAA	110	885.2	268	2	.993	26	15	56	36	.643	1	264	+17	+2	+5	+10	+34	17	-2	6	21	2
2013 LAA	111	952.2	276	1	.996	14	21	83	46	.554	0	275	-7	-8	-2	+3	-6	-5	-3	-3	-11	32
2014 LAA	149	1314.0	390	3	.992	24	11	116	72	.621	3	383	-12	-11	-5	+3	-10	-8	-6	2	-12	31
	383	3260.0	972	7	.993	66	48	264	159	.602	4	959	-1	-17	-2	+17	+21	5	-11	5	-1	-

Scout's Defensive Rating: -1 plays saved in 2013, 2 plays saved in 2014

Bursting onto the scene his rookie year, Trout wowed the league with home run robberies and highlight reel catches, capturing the Fielding Bible Award for his efforts. However, Trout reported to Angels camp much bulkier in 2013 and his defense has never been the same. Trout demonstrates great speed, allowing him to move well laterally as well as track down deeper hit balls. What is more, he shows great awareness of his surroundings. He very rarely has difficulties with the wall or knowing where his fellow outfielders are in reference to his position. However, his deep positioning means that he has to pull up and play shallow liners on a hop rather than taking away the hit. What is more, his arm is among the worst in the outfield. His weak arm turns the average opposing baserunner into...well, Mike Trout…when taking the extra base. While his Range and Position numbers are at best average at this point, his arm makes him a below average center fielder. Given his weak arm, an eventual move to left field may do him some good and allow him to focus on the offensive side of his game.

B.J. Upton

	BASIC							THROWING				RANGE AND POSITIONING						RUNS SAVED				
								Opps to Advance	Extra Bases	Pct	Kills	Outs Made	Plays Saved	Plays Saved Shallow	Medium	Deep	Bases Saved			GFP/		
Year Team	G	Inn	TC	E	Pct	GFP	DM											R/P	Throws	DME	Total	Rank
2007 TB	78	664.2	217	2	.991	14	29	84	48	.571	7	204	+1	-1	+1	+1	+1	1	3	-3	1	18
2008 TB	143	1248.2	401	7	.983	32	34	121	72	.595	13	378	+3	+13	-2	-8	-10	-6	6	-3	-3	19
2009 TB	144	1228.2	385	4	.983	26	22	108	61	.565	1	376	0	+9	-1	-8	-9	-2	1	0	-1	22
2010 TB	154	1301.2	405	5	.988	20	29	97	46	.474	1	396	-7	+3	-1	-8	-22	-9	-1	-6	-16	33
2011 TB	151	1326.1	391	3	.992	26	24	114	63	.553	5	381	-4	+5	-5	-3	-12	-5	1	-1	-5	27
2012 TB	142	1254.2	303	3	.990	13	18	97	66	.680	6	290	-5	-4	-2	+1	-4	-3	-2	0	-5	25
2013 Atl	118	975.1	237	4	.983	8	12	88	49	.557	3	230	0	-1	0	+1	+3	1	0	-1	0	20
2014 Atl	139	1218.1	345	7	.980	17	27	101	56	.554	6	329	-11	-7	-3	-1	-14	-9	3	-2	-8	29
	1069	9218.1	2684	35	.987	156	195	810	461	.569	46	2584	-23	+17	-11	-27	-67	-32	11	-16	-37	-

Scout's Defensive Rating: -5 plays saved in 2013, -12 plays saved in 2014

With a high-waisted, slender frame and long limbs that produce an effortless gait, B.J. Upton possesses all of the physical characteristics talent evaluators covet when searching for a Major League-caliber center fielder. Unfortunately for Upton, winning first place in a "Looks Good in a Uniform" contest does not translate into above average run prevention capabilities. Upton possesses an above average arm and he is no stranger to the occasional highlight reel-worthy play; however, the mercurial center fielder struggles with essentially every other aspect of manning the position. Poor jumps off the bat, inefficient route running, an inability (or unwillingness in some cases) to finish plays, and trouble with simply catching the ball severely limit Upton's capacity to successfully convert balls in play into outs. Upton's league-low Scout's Defensive Rating of -12 ranks more than six points below the next-worst performer in center field. Upton has historically struggled on deep balls, but shallow liners were more troublesome for Upton in 2014. On more difficult plays, Upton often appears tentative in his approach right before the moment he must commit to diving, sliding or simply just extending his reach to catch balls one would expect an outfielder with such impressive athletic gifts to successfully reel in. The next few years will be interesting for Upton as the Braves will likely be forced to make difficult decisions regarding the playing time of their well-paid but severely underperforming center fielder.

Center Fielders

Will Venable

Year	Team	G	Inn	TC	E	Pct	GFP	DM	Opps to Advance	Extra Bases	Pct	Kills	Outs Made	Plays Saved	Shallow	Medium	Deep	Bases Saved	R/P	Throws	GFP/DME	Total	Rank
2008	SD	27	238.0	85	0	1.000	4	2	21	16	.762	1	84	+3	-1	+1	+3	+6	3	-2	0	1	-
2009	SD	16	117.0	31	0	1.000	1	2	13	8	.615	0	30	0	-1	0	0	+1	0	-1	0	-1	-
2010	SD	25	164.1	57	1	.982	4	3	14	9	.643	0	56	+3	0	0	+3	+8	4	-1	1	4	-
2011	SD	14	93.0	23	0	1.000	1	4	7	3	.429	0	22	0	-2	0	+1	+1	0	0	1	1	-
2012	SD	21	131.1	28	0	1.000	2	6	14	10	.714	0	28	-2	-3	0	+1	-1	-1	0	0	-1	-
2013	SD	80	478.1	133	1	.992	9	8	35	19	.543	0	132	+9	+5	+2	+1	+10	6	-1	-1	4	14
2014	SD	76	506.1	148	0	1.000	5	9	54	31	.574	0	146	+4	+5	+2	-3	0	2	-1	0	1	-
		259	1728.1	505	2	.996	26	34	158	96	.608	1	498	+17	+3	+5	+6	+25	14	-6	1	9	-

Scout's Defensive Rating: 3 plays saved in 2013, -3 plays saved in 2014

Throughout the years, Will Venable has been one of the more consistent outfielders in Major League Baseball. At 6'3" and 205 pounds, Venable uses his long and athletic frame to glide to the ball while making catches look very smooth. His range is above average at any outfield spot. Between all three outfield positions, including the six innings he played in left field this season, Venable finished with 10 Defensive Runs Saved. The left hander sports subpar arm strength, and it is a consistent liability especially in right. Runners advance at will given that Venable rarely throws out opposing baserunners from any position. He is on the wrong side of 30 now, so it will be interesting to see if his range begins to deteriorate, but as it stands Venable is a solid fourth outfielder best suited for left or center despite his experience in right.

Right Fielders Register and Scouting Reports

Year	Fielding Bible Award Winner	Runner Up	Third Place
2006	Ichiro Suzuki	Alex Rios	J.D. Drew
2007	Alex Rios	Austin Kearns	Jeff Francoeur
2008	Franklin Gutierrez	Nick Markakis	Denard Span
2009	Ichiro Suzuki	Hunter Pence	Ryan Sweeney
2010	Ichrio Suzuki	Jay Bruce	Jason Heyward
2011	Justin Upton	Jason Heyward	Giancarlo Stanton
2012	Jason Heyward	Josh Reddick	Torii Hunter
2013	Gerardo Parra	Shane Victorino	Jason Heyward
2014	Jason Heyward	Kevin Kiermaier	Josh Reddick

Right Fielders

Nori Aoki

Year	Team	G	Inn	TC	E	Pct	GFP	DM	Opps to Advance	Extra Bases	Pct	Kills	Outs Made	Plays Saved	Shallow	Medium	Deep	Bases Saved	R/P	Throws	GFP/DME	Total	Rank
2012	Mil	107	896.0	203	2	.990	17	8	82	46	.561	5	195	+5	+2	-4	+6	+12	5	0	1	6	10
2013	Mil	149	1288.1	301	3	.990	33	23	98	34	.347	7	289	+7	-3	+2	+8	+16	7	5	-2	10	6
2014	KC	119	937.1	216	2	.991	18	20	85	41	.482	4	209	-5	+1	-2	-5	-12	-6	0	-1	-7	28
		375	3121.2	720	7	.990	68	51	265	121	.457	16	693	+7	0	-4	+9	+16	6	5	-2	9	-

Scout's Defensive Rating: 8 plays saved in 2013, -2 plays saved in 2014

Aside from some stunning plays in the postseason, the 2014 season was a very negative one for Nori Aoki defensively. Whether it was the change from Milwaukee to Kansas City or the recurring groin injuries, Aoki's defensive performance took a massive downturn. Over the past three years, his defensive numbers show drastic changes in 2014.

He does have great speed that boosts his range above average, but he was unable to reach or unable to field many balls that were recorded as outs in previous years. Aoki does boast a surprisingly strong arm despite his small stature. He is very quick to get the ball back in after it is fielded, which makes it difficult for runners to advance on him. The looming question for Aoki is if he can come back fully healthy in 2015 and see his defensive numbers return to their previous position in the top ten among right fielders.

Oswaldo Arcia

Year	Team	G	Inn	TC	E	Pct	GFP	DM	Opps to Advance	Extra Bases	Pct	Kills	Outs Made	Plays Saved	Shallow	Medium	Deep	Bases Saved	R/P	Throws	GFP/DME	Total	Rank
2013	Min	29	236.1	57	1	.982	3	8	28	14	.500	1	54	-7	-3	-1	-3	-11	-6	1	-1	-6	-
2014	Min	100	846.2	204	5	.975	23	20	101	45	.446	5	191	-16	-7	-1	-8	-20	-12	2	1	-9	33
		129	1083.0	261	6	.977	26	28	129	59	.457	6	245	-23	-10	-2	-11	-31	-18	3	0	-15	-

Scout's Defensive Rating: -1 plays saved in 2013, -3 plays saved in 2014

Oswaldo Arcia is 23 years old and 220 pounds of muscle. Though he has split time between left and right, he has a strong and accurate arm that can play in right. The problem is that unless he gets to camp under a flyball, he doesn't get to show it off very often. Arcia takes terrible routes and his glove is so poor he will often misplay balls even after getting to them. His speed isn't terrible for his size, but it also isn't great. Arcia has some upside with his age and athleticism. With an above average arm, he might be able to learn to take better routes with time and put himself in better position to use his arm. However, he's been primarily a right fielder his entire pro career, so he's not likely to improve beyond being one of the worst corner outfielders in baseball on a per inning basis.

Brandon Barnes

Year	Team	G	Inn	TC	E	Pct	GFP	DM	Opps to Advance	Extra Bases	Pct	Kills	Outs Made	Plays Saved	Shallow	Medium	Deep	Bases Saved	R/P	Throws	GFP/DME	Total	Rank
2012	Hou	5	14.0	1	0	1.000	1	0	2	0	.000	1	0	-1	0	-1	0	-2	-1	1	0	0	-
2013	Hou	13	87.0	23	0	1.000	1	0	18	7	.389	1	22	-1	0	-1	0	-2	-1	0	0	-1	-
2014	Col	55	385.0	96	1	.990	9	6	35	18	.514	2	93	+4	-1	-1	+5	+11	5	-1	0	4	-
		73	486.0	120	1	.992	11	6	55	25	.455	4	115	+2	-1	-3	+5	+7	3	0	0	3	-

Scout's Defensive Rating: 1 plays saved in 2013, 1 plays saved in 2014

Right Fielders

Jose Bautista

Year	Team	BASIC							THROWING				RANGE AND POSITIONING						RUNS SAVED				
		G	Inn	TC	E	Pct	GFP	DM	Opps to Advance	Extra Bases	Pct	Kills	Outs Made	Plays Saved	Plays Saved Shallow	Medium	Deep	Bases Saved	R/P	Throws	GFP/ DME	Total	Rank
2004	4 tms	19	89.1	19	1	.947	1	2	10	3	.300	1	15	-1	-1	0	-1	-2	-1	0	0	-1	-
2006	Pit	25	172.2	32	0	1.000	1	2	13	4	.308	0	31	0	-2	+2	+1	+2	1	0	-1	0	-
2007	Pit	16	130.0	26	2	.923	2	1	10	5	.500	1	23	0	0	0	0	-1	-1	1	0	0	-
2009	Tor	36	286.1	72	0	1.000	7	7	33	10	.303	3	69	0	0	0	0	-3	-1	4	0	3	-
2010	Tor	113	982.2	194	3	.985	25	13	99	43	.434	11	179	-14	-3	-3	-8	-23	-12	6	4	-2	24
2011	Tor	116	1014.0	252	6	.976	21	26	97	49	.505	10	233	-8	+1	0	-8	-23	-10	3	3	-4	27
2012	Tor	90	775.2	168	2	.988	21	10	61	29	.475	9	155	-1	+7	0	-8	-10	-3	6	3	6	11
2013	Tor	109	966.0	205	5	.976	23	16	88	27	.307	8	192	+1	+8	-4	-4	-7	-2	9	-1	6	12
2014	Tor	131	1080.2	279	4	.986	36	20	99	44	.444	8	265	-3	+12	+1	-16	-20	-6	5	2	1	15
		655	5497.1	1247	23	.982	137	97	510	214	.420	51	1162	-26	+22	-4	-45	-87	-35	34	10	9	-

Scout's Defensive Rating: -2 plays saved in 2013, 5 plays saved in 2014

Jose Bautista came up to the majors with the Pittsburgh Pirates splitting time between third and the outfield, but he didn't handle either very well. He's always had a great arm, and when Toronto slotted him in at right field he found a home. He racked up double-digit baserunner kills in 2010 and 2011, and in 2013 Bautista was second among all qualified right fielders in Outfield Arm Runs Saved. The accuracy isn't always there, but the pure strength of his throws allows Bautista to throw out runners trying to score or advance at an elite rate. He has plus speed for his size, but not enough to get to some of the difficult plays that his fellow right fielders can. Bautista makes up for his declining range by taking efficient routes, and his arm should allow him to continue as an average right fielder for a couple more seasons.

Carlos Beltran

Year	Team	BASIC							THROWING				RANGE AND POSITIONING						RUNS SAVED				
		G	Inn	TC	E	Pct	GFP	DM	Opps to Advance	Extra Bases	Pct	Kills	Outs Made	Plays Saved	Plays Saved Shallow	Medium	Deep	Bases Saved	R/P	Throws	GFP/ DME	Total	Rank
2011	2 tms	134	1153.2	241	1	.996	22	26	114	56	.491	4	230	-3	-2	-4	+3	-3	-2	0	-2	-4	25
2012	StL	132	1126.2	222	2	.991	19	14	98	42	.429	8	211	+1	0	-3	+4	+4	2	3	2	7	9
2013	StL	137	1138.1	251	5	.980	14	7	99	54	.545	4	242	-4	-5	-3	+4	-4	-3	-3	-1	-7	28
2014	NYY	32	259.2	56	3	.946	0	8	21	12	.571	1	51	-2	0	-2	-1	-5	-2	-1	-2	-5	-
		435	3678.1	770	11	.986	55	55	332	164	.494	17	734	-8	-7	-12	+10	-8	-5	-1	-3	-9	-

Scout's Defensive Rating: -3 plays saved in 2013, -3 plays saved in 2014

Knee injuries have sapped Carlos Beltran of the natural ability that once made him one of the best defensive center fielders in the league, and have left him capable of playing only a slightly below average right field at best. Beltran still gets good reads off the bat, but his speed is diminished, which makes it difficult for him to get to anything that's much tougher than a routine play. He plays a deep right field, and has historically been better than average at tracking down balls that look like they will be doubles off the bat, but gives up more hits in front of him than an average right fielder. Beltran has a strong and accurate throwing arm with a quick release, but bone spurs in his elbow really affected his arm in 2014. Beltran still has enough ability to play right field, but injuries have slowed him up enough that he is no more than a part time option in the field.

Charlie Blackmon

Year	Team	BASIC							THROWING				RANGE AND POSITIONING						RUNS SAVED				
		G	Inn	TC	E	Pct	GFP	DM	Opps to Advance	Extra Bases	Pct	Kills	Outs Made	Plays Saved	Plays Saved Shallow	Medium	Deep	Bases Saved	R/P	Throws	GFP/ DME	Total	Rank
2012	Col	17	107.1	25	0	1.000	2	1	11	5	.455	1	23	+1	0	+1	0	+1	1	1	0	2	-
2013	Col	34	243.0	54	1	.981	3	5	33	15	.455	0	53	+3	-1	+2	+2	+6	3	-1	-2	0	-
2014	Col	73	573.2	134	0	1.000	8	12	54	26	.481	1	131	+1	+1	0	0	0	1	-1	0	0	18
		124	924.0	213	1	.995	13	18	98	46	.469	2	207	+5	0	+3	+2	+7	5	-1	-2	2	-

Scout's Defensive Rating: 0 plays saved in 2013, -1 plays saved in 2014

Charlie Blackmon's Scouting Report can be found on page 259.

Right Fielders

Ryan Braun

			BASIC					THROWING				RANGE AND POSITIONING		Plays Saved				RUNS SAVED		GFP/		
Year	Team	G	Inn	TC	E	Pct	GFP	DM	Opps to Advance	Extra Bases	Pct	Kills	Outs Made	Plays Saved	Shallow	Medium	Deep	Bases Saved	R/P	Throws	DME	Total	Rank
2014	Mil	134	1165.0	270	2	.993	17	21	99	49	.495	4	263	-7	-9	+1	+1	-7	-5	-2	-1	-8	29

Scout's Defensive Rating: 0 plays saved in 2014

Ryan Braun's first year in right field marked a tough transition for the outfelder, as 2014 revealed several holes in his defensive play. No longer capable of stealing 30 bases in a season, Braun's pure speed doesn't afford him the range that it once did. Furthermore, mediocre routes would sometimes have Braun meandering about the outfield, failing to make the more difficult plays. Unfortunately, the trouble for Braun did not end once the ball hit the ground. Fielding balls from the ground also proved to be somewhat of a struggle, as hits that fell in right field had a habit of bouncing off the heel of his glove–reminiscent of his stint at third base as a rookie. He collected six Defensive Misplays and Errors of this subtype, which was tied for third-most. An adequate arm is paired with modest at best accuracy, at times testing the reactions of his infield teammates and allowing baserunners to advance freely. His declining range and inability to keep baserunners at bay suggest that an aging Braun is best off in left for the foreseeable future.

Jay Bruce

			BASIC					THROWING				RANGE AND POSITIONING		Plays Saved				RUNS SAVED		GFP/		
Year	Team	G	Inn	TC	E	Pct	GFP	DM	Opps to Advance	Extra Bases	Pct	Kills	Outs Made	Plays Saved	Shallow	Medium	Deep	Bases Saved	R/P	Throws	DME	Total	Rank
2008	Cin	78	590.0	157	9	.943	15	12	57	27	.474	5	143	+1	+3	+3	-5	-4	-2	1	-1	-2	20
2009	Cin	98	810.1	213	2	.991	19	22	88	37	.420	9	200	-2	-1	+2	-3	-1	-1	5	1	5	13
2010	Cin	146	1199.1	353	3	.992	27	14	108	53	.491	5	343	+20	+6	+7	+6	+31	17	-2	1	16	1
2011	Cin	155	1371.0	320	4	.988	16	22	128	62	.484	5	306	+4	+6	+1	-3	+1	2	-2	0	0	16
2012	Cin	154	1343.1	311	6	.981	22	22	121	56	.463	5	297	+1	+7	+1	-7	-8	-2	1	0	-1	23
2013	Cin	160	1438.2	346	3	.991	37	13	116	47	.405	7	330	+10	-2	+6	+7	+18	9	4	3	16	3
2014	Cin	131	1136.1	244	5	.980	17	17	95	43	.453	3	231	-9	-4	+3	-8	-16	-8	-1	3	-6	27
		922	7889.0	1944	32	.984	153	122	713	325	.456	39	1850	+25	+15	+23	-13	+21	15	6	7	28	-

Scout's Defensive Rating: 5 plays saved in 2013, -4 plays saved in 2014

Few players are as inconsistent in the field as Jay Bruce. The 2010 Fielding Bible Award runner-up has a strong arm and the reputation to back it up; runners took an extra base on Bruce only 45 percent of the time in 2014, an impressive figure for a right fielder. In addition, Bruce has never allowed runners to take an extra base more than 49 percent of the time in a single season. On the other hand, Bruce had only three baserunner kills in 2014; his career low before the season was five. An early-season knee injury hobbled Bruce for most of the year, limiting his range on deep balls in both directions. A year after displaying above average-range on medium and deep balls, Bruce lacked the range in the same category in 2014. It's not difficult to envision Bruce's defense rebounding in 2015, but knee injuries are tricky; if Bruce's good first step does not return, his value as a defender will rely on an arm that had a career-worst year in 2014.

Marlon Byrd

			BASIC					THROWING				RANGE AND POSITIONING		Plays Saved				RUNS SAVED		GFP/		
Year	Team	G	Inn	TC	E	Pct	GFP	DM	Opps to Advance	Extra Bases	Pct	Kills	Outs Made	Plays Saved	Shallow	Medium	Deep	Bases Saved	R/P	Throws	DME	Total	Rank
2005	Was	4	34.0	10	0	1.000	1	0	2	1	.500	0	10	+1	+1	0	+1	+2	1	0	0	1	-
2006	Was	18	83.0	24	1	.958	2	1	5	2	.400	0	23	-1	-1	0	-1	-2	-1	0	0	-1	-
2007	Tex	40	304.1	84	1	.988	10	7	44	16	.364	4	78	+1	0	0	+1	0	0	5	0	5	-
2008	Tex	39	279.0	77	3	.961	8	9	45	23	.511	2	71	+4	+5	-2	+1	+6	3	-1	-2	0	-
2009	Tex	6	52.0	18	0	1.000	1	2	5	5	1.000	1	17	+3	0	+1	+1	+5	3	-1	0	2	-
2012	Bos	2	10.0	2	1	.500	0	0	1	1	1.000	0	1	0	0	0	0	0	0	0	0	0	-
2013	2 tms	138	1168.1	252	5	.980	27	14	114	50	.439	8	237	+3	-4	+1	+6	+11	4	3	1	8	10
2014	Phi	149	1337.1	341	6	.982	36	26	132	60	.455	6	330	+9	+13	0	-5	+6	6	4	-1	9	6
		396	3268.0	808	17	.979	85	59	348	158	.454	21	767	+20	+14	0	+4	+28	16	10	-2	24	-

Scout's Defensive Rating: 2 plays saved in 2013, 1 plays saved in 2014

Marlon Byrd has enjoyed a career resurgence over the past two seasons of 2013-14. Not only did his power stroke return, but he also put together two good defensive seasons as well. Byrd isn't an outstanding defender, but he does everything pretty well. He has decent speed, gets good jumps, and takes an efficient route to the ball. When he does make a misplay in the field, it is usually a hustle mistake (i.e. failed dives, failing to anticipate the wall, etc.) Although he doesn't have great arm strength, his arm has ranked among the best in the majors over the past two years. He gets to

Right Fielders

hits quickly, gets behind flyballs so he is ready to throw, has a quick release, and consistently makes good, accurate throws. Over the past two seasons Byrd is third among right fielders with 14 Kills and seven Outfield Arm Runs Saved. Byrd's fundamental soundness should ensure that even as his range decreases with age, he should continue to at least be an average right fielder for the next couple of seasons.

Lorenzo Cain

		BASIC							THROWING				RANGE AND POSITIONING						RUNS SAVED				
Year	Team	G	Inn	TC	E	Pct	GFP	DM	Opps to Advance	Extra Bases	Pct	Kills	Outs Made	Plays Saved	Shallow	Medium	Deep	Bases Saved	R/P	Throws	GFP/DME	Total	Rank
2010	Mil	1	9.0	3	0	1.000	1	0	1	1	1.000	1	2	0	0	0	0	0	0	1	0	1	-
2011	KC	4	34.2	5	0	1.000	0	1	4	1	.250	0	5	0	0	+1	0	+1	0	0	0	0	-
2012	KC	9	80.0	22	0	1.000	3	0	10	4	.400	0	22	+1	0	0	+1	+3	1	0	0	1	-
2013	KC	32	186.2	51	2	.961	2	2	18	5	.278	0	49	+8	+2	+4	+2	+13	7	0	-1	6	-
2014	KC	77	388.1	109	1	.991	7	3	35	17	.486	3	105	+9	+3	+2	+4	+16	8	0	0	8	-
		123	698.2	190	3	.984	13	6	68	28	.412	4	183	+18	+5	+7	+7	+33	16	1	-1	16	-

Scout's Defensive Rating: 1 plays saved in 2013, 2 plays saved in 2014

Lorenzo Cain's Scouting Report can be found on page 262.

Kole Calhoun

		BASIC							THROWING				RANGE AND POSITIONING						RUNS SAVED				
Year	Team	G	Inn	TC	E	Pct	GFP	DM	Opps to Advance	Extra Bases	Pct	Kills	Outs Made	Plays Saved	Shallow	Medium	Deep	Bases Saved	R/P	Throws	GFP/DME	Total	Rank
2012	LAA	14	33.0	9	0	1.000	1	1	2	1	.500	0	9	+1	0	0	+1	+2	1	0	0	1	-
2013	LAA	54	420.2	118	6	.949	10	15	53	29	.547	3	108	-2	-2	0	0	-2	-2	-1	-3	-6	-
2014	LAA	123	1036.1	240	1	.996	17	9	75	40	.533	6	230	-7	-5	-5	+3	-5	-4	1	4	1	14
		191	1490.0	367	7	.981	28	25	130	70	.538	9	347	-8	-7	-5	+4	-5	-5	0	1	-4	-

Scout's Defensive Rating: 2 plays saved in 2013, 2 plays saved in 2014

The 5'10", 200-pound Calhoun plays a relatively deep right field and defended deep balls well in 2014. In under 500 innings in right field over 2012-13, Calhoun had 11 Good Fielding Plays (GFP) and 22 Defensive Misplays and Errors (DME), many of the DMEs due to his aggressive approach on make-or-break diving attempts and his propensity to mishandle balls he's charging after they've landed safely for base hits. However, Calhoun made significant strides in 2014 and improved his GFP and DME rates.

Calhoun has the arm strength for right field, and hasn't been reckless with his throws. He has 13 outfield assists in his career and only one throwing error. He had six throwing-related DMEs in 2012 and 2013, but zero in 2014. Now getting consistent playing time, Calhoun's defensive value should stabilize as he gains more experience and confidence in his abilities. Already above average defensively in right field, there may still be room to grow for Calhoun heading into 2015.

Endy Chavez

		BASIC							THROWING				RANGE AND POSITIONING						RUNS SAVED				
Year	Team	G	Inn	TC	E	Pct	GFP	DM	Opps to Advance	Extra Bases	Pct	Kills	Outs Made	Plays Saved	Shallow	Medium	Deep	Bases Saved	R/P	Throws	GFP/DME	Total	Rank
2005	Phi	5	10.0	2	0	1.000	0	0	0	0	-	0	2	-1	-1	0	0	-1	-1	0	0	-1	-
2006	NYM	45	310.2	74	0	1.000	6	2	23	13	.565	1	71	-1	+3	0	-3	-4	-2	-1	1	-2	-
2007	NYM	24	100.0	31	0	1.000	4	2	8	6	.750	0	31	+3	+1	+1	+2	+5	3	-1	-1	1	-
2008	NYM	60	400.0	114	1	.991	13	5	42	19	.452	3	110	+7	+4	0	+3	+11	6	1	2	9	-
2009	Sea	4	23.0	6	0	1.000	0	0	1	0	.000	0	6	+1	+1	0	0	+1	0	0	0	0	-
2011	Tex	6	41.0	4	0	1.000	0	1	4	1	.250	0	4	0	0	0	0	-1	0	0	0	0	-
2012	Bal	21	146.0	37	1	.973	3	0	8	4	.500	0	36	+1	+1	-1	+2	+2	1	-1	0	0	-
2013	Sea	50	349.1	93	4	.957	11	6	30	15	.500	2	86	-2	-3	0	0	-1	-1	-1	3	1	-
2014	Sea	46	318.0	56	0	1.000	1	4	13	8	.615	1	55	-3	0	-1	-2	-5	-3	0	0	-3	-
		261	1698.0	417	6	.986	38	20	129	66	.512	7	401	+5	+6	-1	+2	+7	3	-3	5	5	-

Scout's Defensive Rating: 3 plays saved in 2013, 0 plays saved in 2014

Right Fielders

Collin Cowgill

Year Team	G	Inn	TC	E	Pct	GFP	DM	Opps to Advance	Extra Bases	Pct	Kills	Outs Made	Plays Saved	Shallow	Medium	Deep	Bases Saved	R/P	Throws	GFP/DME	Total	Rank
			BASIC						THROWING				RANGE AND POSITIONING		Plays Saved				RUNS SAVED			
2012 Oak	8	56.2	18	0	1.000	3	0	10	6	.600	2	16	+3	+2	0	+1	+5	3	2	1	6	-
2013 LAA	17	106.0	33	0	1.000	5	5	14	7	.500	2	30	+2	+2	+2	-1	+2	1	1	0	2	-
2014 LAA	49	348.1	98	2	.980	5	2	40	19	.475	0	94	+6	0	+2	+4	+12	6	0	0	6	-
	74	511.0	149	2	.987	13	7	64	32	.500	4	140	+11	+4	+4	+4	+19	10	3	1	14	-

Scout's Defensive Rating: 0 plays saved in 2013, 0 plays saved in 2014

Allen Craig

Year Team	G	Inn	TC	E	Pct	GFP	DM	Opps to Advance	Extra Bases	Pct	Kills	Outs Made	Plays Saved	Shallow	Medium	Deep	Bases Saved	R/P	Throws	GFP/DME	Total	Rank
2010 StL	30	175.2	33	0	1.000	1	5	19	4	.211	0	32	-2	-1	0	0	-2	-1	1	0	0	-
2011 StL	18	106.0	26	0	1.000	2	0	8	3	.375	0	26	+1	+1	0	0	+2	1	0	1	2	-
2012 StL	23	165.2	31	0	1.000	1	6	12	5	.417	0	31	-2	-2	+1	-1	-3	-2	-1	0	-3	-
2013 StL	22	179.2	32	0	1.000	2	1	11	8	.727	0	32	0	0	-2	+2	0	0	-1	0	-1	-
2014 2 tms	82	652.2	132	0	1.000	12	12	51	24	.471	3	129	+3	-1	+1	+3	+5	3	1	-1	3	10
	175	1279.2	254	0	1.000	18	24	101	44	.436	3	250	0	-3	0	+4	+2	1	0	0	1	-

Scout's Defensive Rating: 1 plays saved in 2013, 4 plays saved in 2014

While Allen Craig struggled mightily on offense during the 2014 season, he was able to perform at an acceptable level on defense. Playing mostly in right field, Craig's defense was not always aesthetically pleasing, but he was sure-handed and able to make plays within a reasonable distance of his initial position. He did his best work deep in the outfield, tracking down balls hit in that territory. He understands his limits as an athlete and refrains from taking unnecessary risks. Despite Craig's limited athleticism, he was able to accumulate three Defensive Runs Saved in 2014, placing him tenth among regular right fielders. Craig's sure-handedness is evidenced by a .918 success rate converting balls hit in his zone into outs–the sixth best rate among right fielders with 650 or more innings played at the position. Craig possesses a below average arm for a right fielder but is able to compensate somewhat for this shortcoming by consistently hitting cutoff men and getting balls back into the infield in an especially quick manner.

Michael Cuddyer

Year Team	G	Inn	TC	E	Pct	GFP	DM	Opps to Advance	Extra Bases	Pct	Kills	Outs Made	Plays Saved	Shallow	Medium	Deep	Bases Saved	R/P	Throws	GFP/DME	Total	Rank
2003 Min	17	139.0	25	0	1.000	-	-	7	5	.714	0	21	-1	0	+1	-1	-1	-1	-1		-2	-
2004 Min	8	49.0	13	0	1.000	1	1	4	2	.500	0	10	0	0	0	0	-1	-1	0	0	-1	-
2005 Min	20	159.0	35	0	1.000	3	1	7	3	.429	0	35	+3	+1	0	+2	+6	3	0	0	3	-
2006 Min	142	1227.1	260	5	.981	16	18	113	45	.398	7	245	-13	+4	0	-17	-28	-16	4	1	-11	34
2007 Min	140	1224.1	279	4	.986	24	15	129	50	.388	12	256	-12	+1	-3	-10	-22	-13	10	4	1	17
2008 Min	58	501.2	130	1	.992	18	14	51	21	.412	5	123	-4	+1	-2	-3	-8	-5	3	0	-2	21
2009 Min	117	991.2	206	2	.990	13	12	95	39	.411	2	199	-10	-1	-3	-7	-22	-10	0	2	-8	28
2010 Min	66	539.1	124	2	.984	10	8	41	18	.439	4	117	-10	+2	-2	-11	-24	-11	2	3	-6	26
2011 Min	77	639.1	152	4	.974	15	8	63	32	.508	3	142	-8	0	-1	-7	-19	-9	0	2	-7	32
2012 Col	74	593.1	131	3	.977	9	10	57	24	.421	4	121	-13	-8	-4	0	-17	-10	3	-1	-8	31
2013 Col	118	992.0	199	2	.990	15	19	104	59	.567	4	191	-14	-5	-3	-6	-20	-11	-3	-1	-15	35
2014 Col	35	279.1	61	0	1.000	6	6	29	11	.379	2	57	-1	+1	0	-2	-5	-2	1	0	-1	-
	872	7335.1	1615	23	.986	130	112	700	309	.441	43	1517	-83	-4	-17	-62	-161	-86	19	10	-57	-

Scout's Defensive Rating: -4 plays saved in 2013, 0 plays saved in 2014

Michael Cuddyer played three positions during an injury plagued 2014 season, and while he should predominantly see time in right field for the Mets in 2015, he likely will continue to get some innings at first base as well. Cuddyer annually finds himself at the bottom of the right field Defensive Runs Saved list in large part due to his poor Range and Positioning numbers. This is due almost entirely to his lack of speed. Cuddyer still gets decent jumps in the outfield and takes good routes to the ball, but he just doesn't have the closing speed necessary to make enough plays in the outfield. While his arm isn't what it once was, Cuddyer still possesses a strong, accurate arm that can be a weapon in the outfield. At first base, Cuddyer has average range, but flashes soft hands and is very adept at handling poor throws. Frankly, at this point in his career Cuddyer is much better suited for a first base job, as he doesn't possess the range necessary to play an every day outfield position. But the Mets are going to take their chances with him in right field and hope that Juan Lagares can help cover some of the extra ground he can't get to anymore.

Right Fielders

Chris Denorfia

Year	Team	BASIC							THROWING				RANGE AND POSITIONING		Plays Saved				RUNS SAVED				
		G	Inn	TC	E	Pct	GFP	DM	Opps to Advance	Extra Bases	Pct	Kills	Outs Made	Plays Saved	Shallow	Medium	Deep	Bases Saved	R/P	Throws	GFP/DME	Total	Rank
2005	Cin	2	16.1	9	0	1.000	1	1	2	1	.500	0	9	+1	+1	0	0	+1	1	0	0	1	-
2006	Cin	15	118.1	36	0	1.000	1	2	11	2	.182	2	34	+3	+1	+2	0	+5	3	2	0	5	-
2008	Oak	2	10.0	2	0	1.000	0	0	2	1	.500	0	2	-1	0	0	-1	-1	-1	0	0	-1	-
2009	Oak	1	2.0	0	0	-	0	0	0	0	-	0	0	0	0	0	0	0	0	0	0	0	-
2010	SD	18	116.0	24	0	1.000	2	2	6	2	.333	1	23	+2	+1	+1	0	+3	2	1	0	3	-
2011	SD	62	445.0	109	2	.982	10	9	46	23	.500	4	101	+3	+2	+3	-2	+2	2	0	1	3	9
2012	SD	79	507.1	98	1	.990	15	12	48	21	.438	3	94	0	+4	-2	-2	-3	-1	1	2	2	17
2013	SD	97	530.0	137	2	.985	15	5	47	16	.340	3	127	+9	+3	+2	+4	+10	6	3	0	9	9
2014	2 tms	76	515.0	143	1	.993	13	13	40	15	.375	3	139	+1	+5	-4	+2	0	0	2	0	2	12
		352	2260.0	558	6	.989	57	44	202	81	.401	16	529	+18	+17	+2	+1	+17	12	9	3	24	-

Scout's Defensive Rating: 6 plays saved in 2013, -2 plays saved in 2014

Chris Denorfia has been the ultimate utility outfielder over the past five years. He has the ability to play all three outfield spots effectively and has consistently put up solid defensive numbers across the board. He won't impress you with any one aspect of his defensive game. He isn't your highlight reel type of defender, but he makes all of the routine plays and then some. He always has a sense of where he is on the field and is great at reading the angles and trajectories off the bat despite bouncing around from position to position.

Avisail Garcia

Year	Team	BASIC							THROWING				RANGE AND POSITIONING		Plays Saved				RUNS SAVED				
		G	Inn	TC	E	Pct	GFP	DM	Opps to Advance	Extra Bases	Pct	Kills	Outs Made	Plays Saved	Shallow	Medium	Deep	Bases Saved	R/P	Throws	GFP/DME	Total	Rank
2012	Det	18	104.1	18	0	1.000	0	1	9	6	.667	0	18	0	0	0	-1	-1	-1	-1	0	-2	-
2013	2 tms	41	328.2	76	2	.974	3	7	38	18	.474	1	73	0	-1	-2	+2	-1	0	0	-1	-1	-
2014	CWS	46	401.0	90	2	.978	7	6	40	19	.475	1	84	-7	-1	+2	-7	-15	-7	-1	0	-8	32
		105	834.0	184	4	.978	10	14	87	43	.494	2	175	-7	-2	0	-6	-17	-8	-2	-1	-11	-

Scout's Defensive Rating: 0 plays saved in 2013, 0 plays saved in 2014

Although he made his debut in 2012, Garcia has been subject to limited playing time due to injuries as well as being blocked behind Torii Hunter while playing in Detroit. However, when given the opportunity, he displayed a need for more experience in the field. Though he dazzled with his diving and sliding grabs the last few years, he has also made plenty of mistakes. He had a number of failed dives where he either completely missed the ball or the ball bounced off his glove. Also, while he was much better at it in 2014, in 2013 he struggled to keep balls in front of him, often allowing runners to advance. In addition, he struggled to take a good route on balls over his head, and given his lack of speed he can't easily make up for one bad step. His arm, however, could be an asset if he learns to use it well and avoid mental mistakes. Garcia needs to stay healthy and get a full season under his belt before we should draw any firm conclusions about the type of right fielder he can be.

Curtis Granderson

Year	Team	BASIC							THROWING				RANGE AND POSITIONING		Plays Saved				RUNS SAVED				
		G	Inn	TC	E	Pct	GFP	DM	Opps to Advance	Extra Bases	Pct	Kills	Outs Made	Plays Saved	Shallow	Medium	Deep	Bases Saved	R/P	Throws	GFP/DME	Total	Rank
2013	NYY	14	85.0	24	0	1.000	0	1	8	5	.625	0	24	+3	+3	0	-1	+4	2	-1	0	1	-
2014	NYM	142	1177.1	271	1	.996	12	16	106	60	.566	2	265	+6	0	-2	+7	+14	6	-8	0	-2	21
		156	1262.1	295	1	.997	12	17	114	65	.570	2	289	+9	+3	-2	+6	+18	8	-9	0	-1	-

Scout's Defensive Rating: 0 plays saved in 2013, 1 plays saved in 2014

Granderson is an odd case in that his positive work running down flyballs was undone in 2014 by his severely poor performance dealing with advancing base runners. Granderson totaled -8 Outfield Arm Runs Saved in 2014, the worst total among all right fielders. Advancing baserunners had a field day against Granderson by successfully taking the extra base roughly 57 percent of the time compared to the league average of 48 percent. His arm was sufficient in his younger, center field days, but it has been challenged by the move to right field. Furthermore, Granderson is tasked with covering Citi Field's expansive right-center field gap in half of his games, thus runners were sometimes advancing based more so on the extreme distances Granderson had to throw than on the arm itself. New to the position in 2014, he

Right Fielders

could improve by creating better angles in the outfield and by fielding balls with his momentum directed toward the intended target of his throw.

Robbie Grossman

		BASIC							THROWING				RANGE AND POSITIONING						RUNS SAVED				
Year	Team	G	Inn	TC	E	Pct	GFP	DM	Opps to Advance	Extra Bases	Pct	Kills	Outs Made	Plays Saved	Plays Saved Shallow	Medium	Deep	Bases Saved	R/P	Throws	GFP/ DME	Total	Rank
2013	Hou	2	5.0	3	0	1.000	0	0				0	3	0	0	0	0	0	0	0	0	0	-
2014	Hou	32	266.2	62	1	.984	5	5	32	14	.438	3	56	+2	+3	+1	-1	+3	2	2	2	6	-
		34	271.2	65	1	.985	5	5	32	14	.438	3	59	+2	+3	+1	-1	+3	2	2	2	6	-

Scout's Defensive Rating: 0 plays saved in 2013, -2 plays saved in 2014

Robbie Grossman's Scouting Report can be found on page 247.

Jason Heyward

		BASIC							THROWING				RANGE AND POSITIONING						RUNS SAVED				
Year	Team	G	Inn	TC	E	Pct	GFP	DM	Opps to Advance	Extra Bases	Pct	Kills	Outs Made	Plays Saved	Plays Saved Shallow	Medium	Deep	Bases Saved	R/P	Throws	GFP/ DME	Total	Rank
2010	Atl	140	1196.1	246	6	.976	17	14	104	56	.538	4	236	+17	+3	-4	+18	+33	16	-5	0	11	3
2011	Atl	122	990.1	228	6	.974	12	14	86	47	.547	2	218	+14	0	+1	+13	+32	15	-2	-3	10	1
2012	Atl	154	1337.2	347	5	.986	25	18	113	65	.575	7	331	+23	+9	+7	+7	+40	21	-3	-1	17	2
2013	Atl	86	697.2	176	0	1.000	18	14	58	29	.500	1	173	+18	+4	+5	+10	+32	17	-3	-1	13	4
2014	Atl	149	1317.0	375	1	.997	33	14	127	57	.449	5	366	+22	-3	+6	+19	+50	23	1	2	26	1
		651	5539.0	1372	18	.987	105	74	488	254	.520	19	1324	+94	+13	+15	+67	+187	92	-12	-3	77	-

Scout's Defensive Rating: 0 plays saved in 2013, 15 plays saved in 2014

With basketball in his bloodlines, Jason Heyward does not really look like a baseball player at 6'5". However, he uses his long strides and athleticism to his advantage to track down balls that most fielders cannot reach. More than that, Heyward starts and finishes every play extremely well. He excels at picking up the ball off the bat and rarely takes the wrong angle toward balls. He is not afraid to dive for a ball either, demonstrating tremendous body control and maintaining his balance to avoid mistakes. He plays a bit deeper than most right fielders, which when combined with his NBA-caliber leaping ability means he rarely allows an extra-base hit over his head.

Heyward has a substandard arm for a right fielder (which isn't helped by the fact that he plays deeper than average), but his range more than compensates. Heyward has twice been recognized as the best defensive right fielder in the game, winning the 2012 and 2014 Fielding Bible Awards, and he's finished in the top three in voting twice more. His 15 Scout's Defensive Rating and 26 Defensive Runs Saved in 2014 were tops among all outfielders, and his 77 Defensive Runs Saved since 2010 are 29 more than any other right fielder in baseball.

Brock Holt

		BASIC							THROWING				RANGE AND POSITIONING						RUNS SAVED				
Year	Team	G	Inn	TC	E	Pct	GFP	DM	Opps to Advance	Extra Bases	Pct	Kills	Outs Made	Plays Saved	Plays Saved Shallow	Medium	Deep	Bases Saved	R/P	Throws	GFP/ DME	Total	Rank
2014	Bos	35	264.2	60	0	1.000	7	2	28	16	.571	0	59	+11	+2	+3	+6	+18	10	-2	2	10	-

Scout's Defensive Rating: 4 plays saved in 2014

Brock Holt's Scouting Report can be found on page 213.

Torii Hunter

		BASIC							THROWING				RANGE AND POSITIONING						RUNS SAVED				
Year	Team	G	Inn	TC	E	Pct	GFP	DM	Opps to Advance	Extra Bases	Pct	Kills	Outs Made	Plays Saved	Plays Saved Shallow	Medium	Deep	Bases Saved	R/P	Throws	GFP/ DME	Total	Rank
2010	LAA	46	410.0	110	2	.982	8	10	30	16	.533	2	106	-3	-4	+3	-2	-5	-3	0	2	-1	22
2011	LAA	136	1179.1	278	3	.989	36	23	125	68	.544	14	259	-4	-9	-1	+6	0	-2	5	4	7	2
2012	LAA	134	1112.2	258	4	.984	25	19	98	42	.429	10	240	-4	-8	-3	+7	+5	0	9	3	12	3
2013	Det	143	1236.1	235	3	.987	19	24	128	61	.477	5	223	-11	-8	-1	-2	-15	-9	0	-1	-10	33
2014	Det	128	1114.0	228	5	.978	14	15	112	53	.473	3	219	-15	-3	-6	-7	-28	-14	-2	-1	-17	35
		587	5052.1	1109	17	.985	102	91	493	240	.487	34	1047	-37	-32	-8	+2	-43	-28	12	7	-9	-

Scout's Defensive Rating: -6 plays saved in 2013, -3 plays saved in 2014

Right Fielders

We're witnessing the twilight of Hunter's career as one of the great defensive outfielders of the modern era. Once the best center fielder in baseball, nothing could stop Hunter from chasing down deep flyballs, not even outfield walls. As he lost a step or two and the Angels brought up more spry center field options, Hunter shifted to right field and excelled there. He even demonstrated arm strength in right that he'd never shown in center, and his center field range played even better in right. However, his range continued to fade with age, leaving Hunter a below average right fielder over the past two years and the worst in baseball in 2014. Furthermore, he's made fewer Good Fielding Plays each year since moving to right. While his bat seems to have some pop left, the 39-year-old is a liability in the outfield and should have his innings managed carefully.

Matt Kemp

		BASIC							THROWING				RANGE AND POSITIONING		Plays Saved				RUNS SAVED				
Year	Team	G	Inn	TC	E	Pct	GFP	DM	Opps to Advance	Extra Bases	Pct	Kills	Outs Made	Plays Saved	Shallow	Medium	Deep	Bases Saved	R/P	Throws	GFP/DME	Total	Rank
2006	LAD	10	71.2	10	1	.900	2	2	10	2	.200	1	8	0	0	0	0	0	0	2	-1	1	-
2007	LAD	88	619.2	135	4	.970	9	13	53	27	.509	1	129	0	0	+1	-1	-1	-1	-2	-1	-4	26
2008	LAD	63	478.2	105	2	.981	9	10	54	22	.407	3	98	0	+2	-3	+1	+1	1	3	0	4	-
2009	LAD	7	50.0	10	0	1.000	1	1	2	0	.000	0	10	0	0	-1	0	-1	0	0	0	0	-
2014	LAD	59	500.1	99	2	.980	4	9	45	28	.622	4	92	-3	0	-1	-2	-4	-2	0	-1	-3	23
		227	1720.1	359	9	.975	25	35	164	79	.482	9	337	-3	+2	-4	-2	-5	-2	3	-3	-2	

Scout's Defensive Rating: -3 plays saved in 2014

Matt Kemp has always left much to be desired on defense, and 2014 was no different. The Dodgers finally moved him off of center field, where balls over his head have eaten him alive for years. After he posted -11 Runs Saved in 41 games in center, he saw similar results in left (-8 Runs Saved in 44 games). In right, his -3 Runs Saved in 59 games were at least serviceable given his offensive production. He reads the ball well off the bat and his arm was always strong for a center fielder, but his two arthritic hips severely limit his range at this point in his career. He'll be best off sticking to right field.

Kevin Kiermaier

		BASIC							THROWING				RANGE AND POSITIONING		Plays Saved				RUNS SAVED				
Year	Team	G	Inn	TC	E	Pct	GFP	DM	Opps to Advance	Extra Bases	Pct	Kills	Outs Made	Plays Saved	Shallow	Medium	Deep	Bases Saved	R/P	Throws	GFP/DME	Total	Rank
2014	TB	68	526.1	145	5	.966	19	12	44	26	.591	3	137	+18	+6	+6	+6	+26	15	-1	-1	13	2

Scout's Defensive Rating: 7 plays saved in 2014

Kevin Kiermaier was a breath of fresh air for the Tampa Bay Rays in 2014. When Wil Myers went down in early May, Kiermaier took over in right and showed off his extraordinary speed and range. Whether the ball was hit deep, shallow, to his left, or to his right Kiermaier could read the ball off the bat very well and would utilize his speed to run it down. Though wild at times, his strong arm helped him gain five outfield assists and, more often than not, he prevented base-runners from advancing an extra base. He did make more Defensive Misplays than you'd like to see, but that is to be expected from a young outfielder. His biggest issue stemmed from mishandling a ball after a safe hit, in which it seemed prone to the little league mistake of not getting his glove down and having the ball zip right under it. Kiermaier will be an asset in center or a Fielding Bible Award candidate in right, depending on where the Rays decide to deploy him.

Rymer Liriano

		BASIC							THROWING				RANGE AND POSITIONING		Plays Saved				RUNS SAVED				
Year	Team	G	Inn	TC	E	Pct	GFP	DM	Opps to Advance	Extra Bases	Pct	Kills	Outs Made	Plays Saved	Shallow	Medium	Deep	Bases Saved	R/P	Throws	GFP/DME	Total	Rank
2014	SD	34	256.1	63	4	.937	7	9	35	21	.600	1	57	+2	0	-2	+5	+6	3	-3	-2	-2	-

Scout's Defensive Rating: 0 plays saved in 2014

Right Fielders

Jake Marisnick

		BASIC						THROWING				RANGE AND POSITIONING						RUNS SAVED				
								Opps to Advance	Extra Bases	Pct	Kills	Outs Made	Plays Saved	Plays Saved Shallow	Medium	Deep	Bases Saved	R/P	Throws	GFP/ DME	Total	Rank
Year	Team	G	Inn	TC	E	Pct	GFP	DM														
2014	Hou	31	261.1	73	2	.973	5	4	16	7	.438	2	68	+7	+8	+1	-2	+7	5	1	0	6	-

Scout's Defensive Rating: 0 plays saved in 2014

Jake Marisnick's Scouting Report can be found on page 270.

Nick Markakis

		BASIC						THROWING				RANGE AND POSITIONING						RUNS SAVED				
								Opps to Advance	Extra Bases	Pct	Kills	Outs Made	Plays Saved	Plays Saved Shallow	Medium	Deep	Bases Saved	R/P	Throws	GFP/ DME	Total	Rank
Year	Team	G	Inn	TC	E	Pct	GFP	DM														
2006	Bal	126	913.1	248	1	.996	17	16	102	50	.490	5	240	+1	-3	+3	+1	+3	2	0	3	5	8
2007	Bal	161	1399.2	318	2	.994	38	16	157	75	.478	10	303	-6	-3	-3	0	-5	-3	2	5	4	12
2008	Bal	156	1367.0	347	3	.991	41	12	153	67	.438	14	329	+7	+7	+2	-2	+11	6	10	6	22	2
2009	Bal	161	1402.0	317	6	.981	36	25	136	66	.485	10	299	-13	-4	-3	-6	-22	-12	2	2	-8	29
2010	Bal	159	1402.1	342	3	.991	34	22	151	66	.437	5	332	-12	-3	-2	-7	-18	-10	0	1	-9	32
2011	Bal	157	1389.2	325	0	1.000	38	18	137	68	.496	9	312	-6	-2	-2	-2	-10	-5	2	7	4	6
2012	Bal	102	926.0	192	2	.990	9	10	82	38	.463	1	187	-7	-1	-3	-3	-13	-7	0	0	-7	30
2013	Bal	155	1381.0	319	0	1.000	35	12	120	60	.500	4	312	-16	-7	-7	-2	-21	-12	0	5	-7	29
2014	Bal	147	1314.1	306	0	1.000	34	11	132	56	.424	5	295	-7	+2	-3	-6	-11	-6	3	4	1	15
		1324	11495.1	2714	17	.994	282	142	1170	546	.467	63	2609	-59	-14	-15	-30	-86	-47	19	33	5	-

Scout's Defensive Rating: 5 plays saved in 2013, 4 plays saved in 2014

Markakis is slowly but surely declining as a right fielder, and an overrated one at that. He flashed immense promise early on, but quickly lost a step, then another, and now rates as a below average defender. His arm, which threw 94-mph fastballs in the 2004 Olympics, is now below average as well. Still good for a good catch here and there, his routes are getting slower and more and more often he's coming up short of balls in the gaps or over his head. His Gold Gloves were presumably awarded more for his spectacular arm than his poor range.

J.D. Martinez

		BASIC						THROWING				RANGE AND POSITIONING						RUNS SAVED				
								Opps to Advance	Extra Bases	Pct	Kills	Outs Made	Plays Saved	Plays Saved Shallow	Medium	Deep	Bases Saved	R/P	Throws	GFP/ DME	Total	Rank
Year	Team	G	Inn	TC	E	Pct	GFP	DM														
2011	Hou	1	9.0	1	0	1.000	0	0				0	1	0	0	0	0	0	0	0	0	0	-
2013	Hou	25	186.0	35	1	.971	1	5	14	12	.857	0	33	-2	-1	+1	-2	-5	-2	-2	-1	-5	-
2014	Det	34	242.2	49	0	1.000	5	3	23	5	.217	0	49	-1	0	-1	+1	0	0	1	-1	0	-
		60	437.2	85	1	.988	6	8	37	17	.459	0	83	-3	-1	0	-1	-5	-2	-1	-2	-5	-

Scout's Defensive Rating: -2 plays saved in 2013, 2 plays saved in 2014

J.D. Martinez's Scouting Report can be found on page 252.

Brandon Moss

		BASIC						THROWING				RANGE AND POSITIONING						RUNS SAVED				
								Opps to Advance	Extra Bases	Pct	Kills	Outs Made	Plays Saved	Plays Saved Shallow	Medium	Deep	Bases Saved	R/P	Throws	GFP/ DME	Total	Rank
Year	Team	G	Inn	TC	E	Pct	GFP	DM														
2007	Bos	4	12.0	1	0	1.000	0	0	1	1	1.000	0	1	0	0	0	0	0	0	0	0	0	-
2008	2 tms	32	234.0	64	0	1.000	6	6	36	18	.500	4	58	-4	0	-3	-1	-7	-4	2	0	-2	-
2009	Pit	79	665.0	180	1	.994	13	8	72	30	.417	6	171	+6	+5	+2	-1	+3	3	2	2	7	10
2010	Pit	5	27.0	4	0	1.000	0	0				0	4	0	0	0	0	-1	0	0	0	0	-
2011	Phi	1	4.0	2	0	1.000	0	0	1	1	1.000	0	2	+1	+1	+1	0	+2	1	0	0	1	-
2012	Oak	13	98.0	27	1	.963	4	3	10	2	.200	1	25	-1	-1	+1	-1	-3	-1	1	0	0	-
2013	Oak	27	176.2	46	1	.978	3	2	17	7	.412	0	44	-4	-2	0	-2	-4	-3	-1	0	-4	-
2014	Oak	34	245.1	52	0	1.000	6	2	18	6	.333	4	48	-1	-3	+1	+2	+1	0	3	1	4	-
		195	1462.0	376	3	.992	32	21	155	65	.419	15	353	-3	0	+2	-3	-9	-4	7	3	6	-

Scout's Defensive Rating: -1 plays saved in 2013, -1 plays saved in 2014

Drafted as a second baseman but deployed in the outfield for the majority of his pro career, Moss is the rare player who has defied the defensive spectrum by playing better in the outfield corners than at first base. He is not particularly adept at catching off-target throws from infielders, and he allows too many hard grounders to get past him down the first base line. Furthermore, Moss's best defensive tool, his arm, is of little use at first base. The A's began deploying him in the

Right Fielders

outfield more often in 2014, and he rewarded them with six baserunner kills between left field and right field. His range isn't going to impress anyone, but the outfield seems to be the most reasonable place to stash him while his bat does the talking.

David Murphy

Year	Team	BASIC							THROWING				RANGE AND POSITIONING						RUNS SAVED				
		G	Inn	TC	E	Pct	GFP	DM	Opps to Advance	Extra Bases	Pct	Kills	Outs Made	Plays Saved	Plays Saved Shallow	Medium	Deep	Bases Saved	R/P	Throws	GFP/DME	Total	Rank
2006	Bos	2	9.1	2	0	1.000	0	0	0	0	-	0	2	0	0	0	0	0	0	0	0	0	-
2007	2 tms	15	80.0	18	0	1.000	2	0	9	4	.444	2	14	0	-1	0	0	0	0	1	1	2	-
2008	Tex	56	407.1	109	1	.991	6	5	47	20	.426	1	107	+7	+3	+2	+2	+11	6	-2	0	4	-
2009	Tex	10	74.0	23	1	.957	0	2	7	3	.429	2	20	-2	0	0	-2	-3	-2	1	0	-1	-
2010	Tex	51	381.1	83	0	1.000	9	5	33	21	.636	1	80	+1	+2	-2	+1	0	0	-2	1	-1	-
2011	Tex	32	247.1	48	0	1.000	3	3	20	8	.400	1	47	+3	0	0	+3	+5	3	0	0	3	-
2012	Tex	17	110.0	20	0	1.000	1	2	11	7	.636	0	20	-1	0	-1	0	0	0	-1	0	-1	-
2013	Tex	1	8.0	4	0	1.000	0	2	1	1	1.000	0	4	-1	-1	0	0	-1	-1	0	0	-1	-
2014	Cle	120	989.0	213	3	.986	12	17	85	43	.506	3	204	-6	+5	-1	-9	-17	-7	-3	-2	-12	34
		304	2306.1	520	5	.990	33	36	213	107	.502	10	498	+1	+8	-2	-5	-5	-1	-6	0	-7	-

Scout's Defensive Rating: 0 plays saved in 2013, 0 plays saved in 2014

David Murphy is an outfielder who has the skills that play very well in left field, but do not translate to right field, where Cleveland had him playing for a majority of the time in 2014. When he is out in left field, Murphy has shown great range in all directions, especially on balls that are hit deep. Murphy's arm is the weakest part of his defensive game, which can be hidden in left field. When forced into right field duty, Murphy has cost his teams four runs with his arm and 14 runs overall in the past three years. At times he struggles with balls over his head and off the wall, as there have been 15 occasions since 2012 where he has misplayed balls off the wall allowing opponents to take an extra base. A team can be comfortable with Murphy in left field, but his weaknesses are exacerbated in right.

Wil Myers

Year	Team	BASIC							THROWING				RANGE AND POSITIONING						RUNS SAVED				
		G	Inn	TC	E	Pct	GFP	DM	Opps to Advance	Extra Bases	Pct	Kills	Outs Made	Plays Saved	Plays Saved Shallow	Medium	Deep	Bases Saved	R/P	Throws	GFP/DME	Total	Rank
2013	TB	72	604.2	119	0	1.000	9	11	50	22	.440	0	118	-1	0	-1	0	-4	-1	-2	0	-3	20
2014	TB	78	674.1	170	4	.976	10	4	62	28	.452	1	160	-5	-2	+1	-4	-9	-5	-2	-1	-8	29
		150	1279.0	289	4	.986	19	15	112	50	.446	1	278	-6	-2	0	-4	-13	-6	-4	-1	-11	-

Scout's Defensive Rating: -2 plays saved in 2013, 2 plays saved in 2014

Myers began his minor league career as a catcher before switching to the outfield full time in 2011. With a background as an offense-first catcher, Myers displays just average speed and often takes poor routes to the ball. Myers has played center field at the big league level, but doesn't possess the necessary speed desired for a starting center fielder. Myers fits in more comfortably at the corner outfield position where his best attributes, such as his plus arm, can be put to good use. While his defense is a work in progress, Myers projects well in right field and has plenty of room for improvement as he learns to read flyballs and line drives.

Daniel Nava

Year	Team	BASIC							THROWING				RANGE AND POSITIONING						RUNS SAVED				
		G	Inn	TC	E	Pct	GFP	DM	Opps to Advance	Extra Bases	Pct	Kills	Outs Made	Plays Saved	Plays Saved Shallow	Medium	Deep	Bases Saved	R/P	Throws	GFP/DME	Total	Rank
2012	Bos	4	20.1	4	0	1.000	0	0	1	0	.000	0	4	0	0	0	0	+1	0	0	0	0	-
2013	Bos	69	493.2	92	1	.989	9	5	40	21	.525	2	88	-5	-2	-2	-1	-3	-3	0	1	-2	19
2014	Bos	69	501.2	131	2	.985	14	9	59	28	.475	5	122	+9	+1	+4	+4	+17	9	3	1	13	3
		142	1015.2	227	3	.987	23	14	100	49	.490	7	214	+4	-1	+2	+3	+15	6	3	2	11	-

Scout's Defensive Rating: -1 plays saved in 2013, 2 plays saved in 2014

Daniel Nava was one of the most improved defensive players in baseball in 2014. After years of subpar play in the outfield, Nava displayed much greater range in 2014, covering Fenway Park's spacious right field with aplomb. Nava has always had a decent arm, but he showed improved arm strength and accuracy last season, leading to six Kills and five Outfield Arm Runs Saved. Besides his outfield duty, Nava has played 30 games at first base between 2013 and 2014 and has proven to be an adequate fill-in when needed. With the crowded Boston outfield, this might have to become a

Right Fielders

larger part of his repertoire moving forward. Overall Nava had a spectacular defensive season in 2014 and could continue as an average or better corner outfielder if given continued chances.

Chris Parmelee

		BASIC							THROWING				RANGE AND POSITIONING						RUNS SAVED				
Year	Team	G	Inn	TC	E	Pct	GFP	DM	Opps to Advance	Extra Bases	Pct	Kills	Outs Made	Plays Saved	Shallow	Medium	Deep	Bases Saved	R/P	Throws	GFP/ DME	Total	Rank
2012	Min	18	132.0	27	0	1.000	0	0	18	8	.444	0	26	0	0	+1	-1	0	0	-1	0	-1	-
2013	Min	68	525.0	113	2	.982	18	5	61	26	.426	5	105	-3	+2	-4	-1	-4	-2	4	2	4	13
2014	Min	33	249.1	65	1	.985	1	7	23	13	.565	0	63	-2	-1	+1	-2	-4	-2	-2	-1	-5	-
		119	906.1	205	3	.985	19	12	102	47	.461	5	194	-5	+1	-2	-4	-8	-4	1	1	-2	

Scout's Defensive Rating: 3 plays saved in 2013, -2 plays saved in 2014

Gerardo Parra

		BASIC							THROWING				RANGE AND POSITIONING						RUNS SAVED				
Year	Team	G	Inn	TC	E	Pct	GFP	DM	Opps to Advance	Extra Bases	Pct	Kills	Outs Made	Plays Saved	Shallow	Medium	Deep	Bases Saved	R/P	Throws	GFP/ DME	Total	Rank
2009	Ari	9	60.2	12	0	1.000	0	1	8	5	.625	1	12	-2	0	-1	-1	-3	-2	0	0	-2	-
2010	Ari	36	255.0	68	1	.985	11	4	27	6	.222	1	65	+1	+1	+2	-2	-2	0	2	1	3	-
2011	Ari	14	73.0	19	0	1.000	3	1	4	1	.250	0	19	+4	0	+2	+1	+6	3	0	0	3	-
2012	Ari	17	127.1	35	0	1.000	4	3	11	5	.455	2	32	+4	+2	0	+2	+7	4	1	0	5	-
2013	Ari	123	1042.1	274	3	.989	40	24	107	33	.308	14	260	+23	+4	+10	+9	+39	20	10	2	32	1
2014	2 tms	109	921.0	205	4	.980	19	18	94	44	.468	6	193	0	-1	+2	-1	+3	1	2	-1	2	11
		308	2479.1	613	8	.987	77	51	251	94	.375	24	581	+30	+6	+15	+8	+50	26	15	2	43	

Scout's Defensive Rating: 6 plays saved in 2013, 2 plays saved in 2014

In 2014, Parra didn't show the range that he had shown in past seasons when he was a regular as one of the best defensive outfielders in the league. Parra has always had a strong reputation for his arm, but often tried to overcompensate for other mistakes with his throws, resulting in offline throws uncharacteristic for him. Flyballs that were hit in the medium to deep range gave Parra the most trouble; too frequently he was slow reading the trajectory of the ball and missed opportunities for outs. Parra also seemed to have difficulty with understanding where he was on the field and anticipating the wall, odd difficulties for an outfielder of his abilities. Previously an asset in any outfield position, Parra will look to rebound to his 2013 Fielding Bible Award form.

Hunter Pence

		BASIC							THROWING				RANGE AND POSITIONING						RUNS SAVED				
Year	Team	G	Inn	TC	E	Pct	GFP	DM	Opps to Advance	Extra Bases	Pct	Kills	Outs Made	Plays Saved	Shallow	Medium	Deep	Bases Saved	R/P	Throws	GFP/ DME	Total	Rank
2007	Hou	14	115.2	38	2	.947	1	0	11	6	.545	0	36	+1	0	0	0	+1	1	-1	0	0	-
2008	Hou	156	1366.1	357	1	.997	27	27	116	46	.397	11	341	+5	+6	+1	-3	-2	-1	8	2	9	8
2009	Hou	157	1375.2	337	5	.985	29	29	132	53	.402	9	317	+18	+11	+6	0	+17	12	6	1	19	1
2010	Hou	155	1370.1	355	6	.983	22	30	141	64	.454	5	341	+11	+5	+7	-1	+7	6	-1	-1	4	11
2011	2 tms	153	1342.2	301	6	.980	28	33	137	59	.431	7	285	0	+6	-1	-4	-6	-2	5	-1	2	11
2012	2 tms	159	1408.1	289	7	.976	26	31	117	61	.521	8	271	-6	0	+4	-10	-17	-7	3	-2	-6	28
2013	SF	162	1431.1	383	7	.982	26	32	143	69	.483	2	374	+2	0	+5	-3	+1	1	-6	-3	-8	30
2014	SF	161	1425.0	322	5	.984	23	23	108	57	.528	7	308	0	+6	-6	0	-6	-2	0	1	-1	20
		1117	9835.1	2382	39	.984	182	205	905	415	.459	49	2273	+31	+34	+16	-21	-5	8	14	-3	19	

Scout's Defensive Rating: -3 plays saved in 2013, -5 plays saved in 2014

One of the most unorthodox players in Major League Baseball, Hunter Pence is embraced by the city of San Francisco for this exact reason. At 6'4", Pence is adept at using his long legs to chase down balls in the gap. This is especially important for him at home in San Francisco with "Triples Alley" in right-center field. Pence has decent speed, but he has a bit of an awkward approach to a lot of flyballs towards him. Specifically, anything that is hit directly at him on a line or that involve him going back can be a bit of a roller coaster for him. In 2014, he had 11 Defensive Misplays and Errors that involved breaking in the wrong direction, bad routes, failing to anticipate the wall, and failed dives for line drives. These are all DMs related to judgment that Pence had issues gauging the ball on. This definitely contributes to his poor Scout's Defensive Rating, which ranks as the second lowest of all right fielders. Like his swing, his throwing motion is awkward, almost a bit of a push rather than a throw. However, it's been effective for him over the years, usually nabbing 5-10 baserunners per season. Though Pence has proven to be one of the most durable players in baseball, he should not be considered any better than an average right fielder at this point.

Right Fielders

David Peralta

	BASIC							THROWING				RANGE AND POSITIONING						RUNS SAVED				
Year Team	G	Inn	TC	E	Pct	GFP	DM	Opps to Advance	Extra Bases	Pct	Kills	Outs Made	Plays Saved	Plays Saved Shallow	Medium	Deep	Bases Saved	R/P	Throws	GFP/DME	Total	Rank
2014 Ari	40	357.0	81	1	.988	11	6	35	15	.429	5	75	-1	-4	+1	+3	+3	1	4	1	6	-

Scout's Defensive Rating: 1 plays saved in 2014

David Peralta's storybook journey to the major leagues culminated in a fine rookie season with the Diamondbacks in 2014. Having only converted from pitcher to full-time position player in 2011, Peralta showed an impressive natural ability to play the outfield after being called up in June, seeing time at all three outfield positions over 88 games as a rookie. Peralta did well defending deep balls at all three outfield positions. His best tool, as you might expect from a former pitcher, is his arm. Peralta had five baserunner kills and saved four runs right, which is amazing considering he played just 357 innings at the position. Furthermore, Peralta's defense improved as the season went on, an encouraging development for a player who appears to still have plenty of room to grow as a defender.

Gregory Polanco

	BASIC							THROWING				RANGE AND POSITIONING						RUNS SAVED				
Year Team	G	Inn	TC	E	Pct	GFP	DM	Opps to Advance	Extra Bases	Pct	Kills	Outs Made	Plays Saved	Plays Saved Shallow	Medium	Deep	Bases Saved	R/P	Throws	GFP/DME	Total	Rank
2014 Pit	83	619.0	151	2	.987	13	14	55	30	.545	5	144	-6	-3	+1	-3	-11	-6	2	2	-2	22

Scout's Defensive Rating: -4 plays saved in 2014

Gregory Polanco had an up-and-down rookie season patrolling right field at PNC Park. Many fielders have trouble with PNC's odd dimensions in right, and Polanco was no exception, occasionally letting a ball bounce over his head or drop for a hit. Additionally, Polanco lost four balls in the sun/lights in just 619 innings on defense. Moreover, Polanco tied Hunter Pence for fourth among right fielders in dropped balls off his glove, with five, despite playing roughly 800 fewer innings. On the other hand, Polanco excelled with his arm in 2014, recording five kills and only allowing runners to take an extra base just 55 percent of the time. Polanco certainly has the speed and arm to play right field well, but his routes were often unsure. At just 23 years of age, Polanco is still raw, and one should expect his defense to improve in 2015.

Yasiel Puig

	BASIC							THROWING				RANGE AND POSITIONING						RUNS SAVED				
Year Team	G	Inn	TC	E	Pct	GFP	DM	Opps to Advance	Extra Bases	Pct	Kills	Outs Made	Plays Saved	Plays Saved Shallow	Medium	Deep	Bases Saved	R/P	Throws	GFP/DME	Total	Rank
2013 LAD	93	773.1	160	4	.975	27	18	59	27	.458	4	148	+7	0	0	+7	+13	7	1	1	9	8
2014 LAD	91	790.2	158	1	.994	15	25	60	23	.383	6	152	-2	-3	0	0	-3	-2	4	-2	0	19
	184	1564.0	318	5	.984	42	43	119	50	.420	10	300	+5	-3	0	+7	+10	5	5	-1	9	-

Scout's Defensive Rating: 3 plays saved in 2013, 2 plays saved in 2014

One of the most electric and controversial players in recent memory, Puig immediately demanded attention from MLB fans with his defensive wizardry in his first week in the big leagues in 2013. A large chunk of Puig's career on the field to date has been defined by laser throws to the infield, crashing full speed into walls, and full extension dives in order to snag flyballs out of the air, and rightly so. However, another large part is defined by his rawness. While he was rated as having saved nine runs in right field in his rookie season, good for eighth in the league, he fell back to average in 2014 and he wasn't any better in the 442.1 innings he racked up in center field either thanks to an inverted Good Plays/Misplays ratio. Puig seems good for an ugly wasted throw at least once a month and still struggles with reading fly balls consistently. He sometimes will throw inexplicably to the wrong base and dives for balls he had no chance at. But don't let the negatives completely overwhelm the positives. He is still an exceptional athlete who, at just 23 years old, *should* improve on the mental part of his game to complement his natural physical talents.

Right Fielders

Josh Reddick

		BASIC						THROWING				RANGE AND POSITIONING						RUNS SAVED				
								Opps to	Extra			Outs	Plays	Plays Saved			Bases			GFP/		
Year	Team	G	Inn	TC	E	Pct	GFP	DM	Advance	Bases	Pct	Kills	Made	Saved	Shallow	Medium	Deep	Saved	R/P	Throws	DME	Total	Rank
2009	Bos	10	35.0	10	1	.900	1	1	4	2	.500	0	9	-1	-1	0	0	-2	-1	0	0	-1	-
2010	Bos	15	66.2	13	0	1.000	2	3	7	5	.714	1	12	+1	0	+1	0	+2	1	0	0	1	-
2011	Bos	56	432.2	111	4	.964	5	9	35	22	.629	3	103	+8	+1	+2	+5	+15	8	-1	-1	6	3
2012	Oak	136	1179.2	294	5	.983	31	21	102	47	.461	11	275	+9	-2	+3	+8	+22	10	6	2	18	1
2013	Oak	113	966.1	258	5	.981	32	14	88	45	.511	8	244	+10	+3	+5	+2	+12	7	3	3	13	5
2014	Oak	107	873.1	203	5	.975	18	8	67	32	.478	4	194	+7	-2	+2	+8	+19	8	2	0	10	4
		437	3553.2	889	20	.978	89	56	303	153	.505	27	837	+34	-1	+13	+23	+68	33	10	4	47	-

Scout's Defensive Rating: 6 plays saved in 2013, 4 plays saved in 2014

Early in his career Josh Reddick played all three outfield positions, but by 2012 he had found a home in right field, where is has done nothing but excel. Each of the last four years, Josh Reddick had been ranked in the top five in Defensive Runs Saved, including a league-leading total of 18 in 2012. His major strength is his speed and ability to track deeps balls heading toward the wall or gap. He was one of the best right fielders in tracking down deep balls. Another strongpoint of Josh Reddick's abilities is his arm strength. In the three years from 2012 to 2014, he saved 11 runs via his arm. Only the elite arms in the game (Jose Bautista and Gerrado Parra) had more Outfield Arm Runs Saved than Reddick over that period. The only downside to Reddick's game are his struggles on shallow line drives. There are moments when he seems to get a poor jump on the ball coming off the bat and will either come up short or dive and have the ball roll by him. While he could help himself by cheating further in, this might prove detrimental as additional extra-base hits might fall in over his head. Without changing a thing, Reddick is certainly capable continuing as one of the premier defensive right fielders in baseball.

Alex Rios

		BASIC						THROWING				RANGE AND POSITIONING						RUNS SAVED				
								Opps to	Extra			Outs	Plays	Plays Saved			Bases			GFP/		
Year	Team	G	Inn	TC	E	Pct	GFP	DM	Advance	Bases	Pct	Kills	Made	Saved	Shallow	Medium	Deep	Saved	R/P	Throws	DME	Total	Rank
2004	Tor	108	943.2	230	2	.991	15	13	103	41	.398	8	209	+9	+10	+1	-1	+12	7	7	-1	13	4
2005	Tor	138	1056.2	254	2	.992	15	13	113	42	.372	4	246	+1	+1	+2	-1	+1	1	4	2	7	9
2006	Tor	124	953.0	226	1	.996	12	12	92	27	.293	5	218	+11	+7	+2	+3	+16	9	8	1	18	1
2007	Tor	147	1250.0	258	5	.981	16	19	123	48	.390	6	243	+4	-2	+3	+3	+12	7	6	1	14	3
2008	Tor	93	820.0	175	1	.994	11	14	62	22	.355	3	170	+11	+5	+3	+3	+16	9	3	0	12	4
2009	2 tms	110	982.0	235	3	.987	13	20	101	33	.327	1	228	-2	+1	0	-4	-9	-3	4	0	1	19
2012	CWS	156	1369.0	349	7	.980	24	23	147	81	.551	5	333	+6	+8	+3	-4	+7	5	-1	3	7	8
2013	2 tms	155	1365.2	339	3	.991	26	16	115	52	.452	5	327	-10	-6	+2	-6	-15	-8	2	2	-4	25
2014	Tex	114	962.1	262	6	.977	13	15	120	62	.517	3	250	+2	-2	+4	0	+5	2	-4	-2	-4	24
		1145	9702.1	2328	30	.987	145	155	976	408	.418	40	2224	+32	+22	+20	-7	+45	29	29	6	64	-

Scout's Defensive Rating: -6 plays saved in 2013, -5 plays saved in 2014

At one time Alex Rios was one of the best defensive outfielders in baseball, even winning the Fielding Bible Award for right field in 2007. While he certainly isn't at that elite level anymore, he is still capable of covering enough ground to be an everyday outfielder. Rios has a long, athletic build and appears to glide around the outfield. Rios continues to possess above average range moving from side to side, but has some difficulty coming in for shallow balls or heading back for deep shots. One area where Rios has long struggled is in getting good reads off the bat, at times leading him to misjudge flyballs. Rios still displays plus arm strength that has consistently held runners in check over his nine-year career. Although his best days are clearly behind him and he isn't the defensive asset he once was, Rios should be able to play around a league average right field for at least a couple of more seasons.

Stefen Romero

		BASIC						THROWING				RANGE AND POSITIONING						RUNS SAVED				
								Opps to	Extra			Outs	Plays	Plays Saved			Bases			GFP/		
Year	Team	G	Inn	TC	E	Pct	GFP	DM	Advance	Bases	Pct	Kills	Made	Saved	Shallow	Medium	Deep	Saved	R/P	Throws	DME	Total	Rank
2014	Sea	42	294.1	66	1	.985	4	5	22	12	.545	0	64	+1	0	-1	+2	+2	1	-2	-1	-2	-

Scout's Defensive Rating: 0 plays saved in 2014

Right Fielders

Justin Ruggiano

Year	Team	G	Inn	TC	E	Pct	GFP	DM	Opps to Advance	Extra Bases	Pct	Kills	Outs Made	Plays Saved	Plays Saved Shallow	Medium	Deep	Bases Saved	R/P	Throws	GFP/ DME	Total	Rank
2007	TB	1	1.0	1	0	1.000	0	0	0	0	-	0	1	0	0	0	0	0	0	0	0	0	-
2008	TB	15	87.0	22	1	.955	1	1	9	1	.111	0	21	+1	0	+1	0	+3	2	1	0	3	-
2011	TB	6	38.0	9	0	1.000	0	2	1	0	.000	0	9	0	0	0	-1	-1	0	0	0	0	-
2012	Mia	15	99.2	17	0	1.000	0	1	8	4	.500	0	17	-1	0	0	0	-1	-1	0	0	-1	-
2013	Mia	5	38.0	8	0	1.000	0	0	2	1	.500	0	8	0	0	0	0	0	0	0	0	0	-
2014	ChC	34	258.0	52	0	1.000	3	7	21	11	.524	0	52	-5	-1	-3	-1	-9	-4	-1	-1	-6	-
		76	521.2	109	1	.991	4	11	41	17	.415	0	108	-5	-1	-2	-2	-8	-3	0	-1	-4	-

Scout's Defensive Rating: 0 plays saved in 2013, -1 plays saved in 2014

Michael Saunders

Year	Team	G	Inn	TC	E	Pct	GFP	DM	Opps to Advance	Extra Bases	Pct	Kills	Outs Made	Plays Saved	Plays Saved Shallow	Medium	Deep	Bases Saved	R/P	Throws	GFP/ DME	Total	Rank
2012	Sea	5	31.0	6	0	1.000	0	1	3	2	.667	0	6	+1	+1	0	0	+1	1	-1	0	0	-
2013	Sea	34	246.2	61	0	1.000	5	3	21	13	.619	1	60	+3	0	0	+2	+5	2	-1	0	1	-
2014	Sea	68	480.2	105	0	1.000	7	2	42	19	.452	1	104	+6	+2	+3	+2	+9	5	0	2	7	8
		107	758.1	172	0	1.000	12	6	66	34	.515	2	170	+10	+3	+3	+4	+15	8	-2	2	8	-

Scout's Defensive Rating: 1 plays saved in 2013, 0 plays saved in 2014

Michael Saunders has a knack for getting to the baseball, and he was an exceptional defender in the 68 games he played in right field this year. At first glance you might just notice a taller outfielder with long limbs, but Saunders has an effortless glide about his run that has helped him get to balls the average right fielder doesn't reach. Nicknamed "The Condor" because of his size and build, Saunders gets excellent reads on flyballs off the bat. He doesn't look that fast because of his calm strides, but don't be fooled. He compliments his defensive range with a strong arm, though it is pushed to its limit in right field. He didn't have many outfield assists but wasn't tested often by baserunners. He gets to hits quickly in right field, which often allows him to prevent any further runner advancement. After struggling in center in the previous two seasons, Saunders should remain an asset in either outfield corner.

Nate Schierholtz

Year	Team	G	Inn	TC	E	Pct	GFP	DM	Opps to Advance	Extra Bases	Pct	Kills	Outs Made	Plays Saved	Plays Saved Shallow	Medium	Deep	Bases Saved	R/P	Throws	GFP/ DME	Total	Rank
2007	SF	30	229.1	49	1	.980	4	5	20	12	.600	0	48	+4	+1	0	+3	+8	5	-2	-1	2	-
2008	SF	19	161.2	41	0	1.000	7	3	17	12	.706	0	40	+4	+1	+1	+2	+9	5	-2	0	3	-
2009	SF	86	597.2	147	2	.986	17	17	55	26	.473	7	136	+9	+3	+3	+3	+13	7	2	0	9	4
2010	SF	109	542.1	126	1	.992	14	20	46	20	.435	6	118	+3	+1	+1	+1	+2	2	4	0	6	10
2011	SF	96	703.2	152	2	.987	13	13	64	30	.469	4	142	-9	-2	-4	-3	-16	-8	1	0	-7	31
2012	2 tms	80	489.1	101	1	.990	4	7	40	18	.450	0	100	+4	+3	0	+2	+8	4	-1	-1	2	14
2013	ChC	126	1041.0	250	3	.988	19	15	85	47	.553	4	244	+5	+6	-1	0	+3	3	-3	1	1	15
2014	2 tms	87	733.1	167	0	1.000	9	6	56	33	.589	4	159	+9	+4	0	+4	+12	8	1	1	10	4
		633	4498.1	1033	10	.990	87	86	383	198	.517	25	987	+29	+17	0	+12	+39	26	0	0	26	-

Scout's Defensive Rating: 1 plays saved in 2013, 0 plays saved in 2014

Schierholtz has put together a nice career in Major League Baseball. He does not have blazing speed, nor does he have a rocket arm, but Schierholtz plays right field well for the most part. He gets nice jumps on flies and liners in any direction. He doesn't have the range that he had when he broke into the league with San Francisco, but he has made up for it with improved reads and routes. His arm is above average and can hold its own in right field, nabbing a handful of runners per year despite limited time. After making a career as the defensively sound half of a platoon, Schierholtz has shown no signs of slowing down.

Right Fielders

Moises Sierra

		BASIC						THROWING				RANGE AND POSITIONING						RUNS SAVED				
Year	Team	G	Inn	TC	E	Pct	GFP	DM	Opps to Advance	Extra Bases	Pct	Kills	Outs Made	Plays Saved	Plays Saved Shallow	Medium	Deep	Bases Saved	R/P	Throws	GFP/DME	Total	Rank
2012	Tor	39	316.0	70	0	1.000	4	6	42	16	.381	1	67	-7	-3	-3	-1	-13	-7	0	1	-6	-
2013	Tor	29	221.2	53	2	.962	4	4	15	9	.600	0	51	+1	+1	-1	+1	+2	1	-1	-1	-1	-
2014	2 tms	70	372.1	85	3	.965	10	6	42	19	.452	2	79	-1	0	-2	+1	0	0	0	2	2	-
		138	910.0	208	5	.976	18	16	99	44	.444	3	197	-7	-2	-6	+1	-11	-6	-1	2	-5	

Scout's Defensive Rating: 0 plays saved in 2013, 1 plays saved in 2014

Grady Sizemore

		BASIC						THROWING				RANGE AND POSITIONING						RUNS SAVED				
Year	Team	G	Inn	TC	E	Pct	GFP	DM	Opps to Advance	Extra Bases	Pct	Kills	Outs Made	Plays Saved	Plays Saved Shallow	Medium	Deep	Bases Saved	R/P	Throws	GFP/DME	Total	Rank
2014	2 tms	26	219.0	33	1	.970	1	5	18	9	.500	0	32	0	-2	0	+2	+3	1	-1	-1	-1	-

Scout's Defensive Rating: 0 plays saved in 2014

Seth Smith

		BASIC						THROWING				RANGE AND POSITIONING						RUNS SAVED				
Year	Team	G	Inn	TC	E	Pct	GFP	DM	Opps to Advance	Extra Bases	Pct	Kills	Outs Made	Plays Saved	Plays Saved Shallow	Medium	Deep	Bases Saved	R/P	Throws	GFP/DME	Total	Rank
2007	Col	1	2.0	0	0	-	0	0				0	0	0	0	0	0	0	0			0	-
2008	Col	14	86.0	19	0	1.000	3	2	14	8	.571	0	18	-1	-1	0	0	-1	-1	-1	-1	-3	-
2010	Col	33	223.2	50	1	.980	4	6	27	15	.556	0	48	+2	+2	0	-1	+1	1	-2	-2	-3	-
2011	Col	107	867.1	188	5	.973	13	21	80	49	.613	0	182	0	-4	0	+4	+2	1	-5	-2	-6	29
2012	Oak	13	75.2	14	1	.929	0	1	5	4	.800	0	13	+1	0	+1	0	+1	1	-1	0	0	-
2013	Oak	9	65.0	13	0	1.000	1	1	7	5	.714	0	13	0	0	0	0	0	0	-1	0	-1	-
2014	SD	43	294.1	65	0	1.000	4	4	36	19	.528	3	62	0	-2	-1	+3	+5	1	0	1	2	-
		220	1614.0	349	7	.980	25	35	169	100	.592	3	336	+2	-5	0	+6	+8	3	-10	-4	-11	

Scout's Defensive Rating: 0 plays saved in 2013, 1 plays saved in 2014

Seth Smith's Scouting Report can be found on page 254.

Travis Snider

		BASIC						THROWING				RANGE AND POSITIONING						RUNS SAVED				
Year	Team	G	Inn	TC	E	Pct	GFP	DM	Opps to Advance	Extra Bases	Pct	Kills	Outs Made	Plays Saved	Plays Saved Shallow	Medium	Deep	Bases Saved	R/P	Throws	GFP/DME	Total	Rank
2008	Tor	7	60.0	11	0	1.000	2	1	6	2	.333	0	11	+2	0	0	+2	+4	2	0	2	4	-
2009	Tor	21	173.1	39	3	.923	1	4	18	11	.611	0	36	-1	-2	-1	+2	0	0	-2	-1	-3	-
2010	Tor	29	245.0	48	0	1.000	6	9	19	11	.579	1	47	-2	0	+1	-2	-4	-2	-1	-1	-4	-
2011	Tor	3	24.0	3	0	1.000	0	1				0	3	0	0	0	0	0	0	0	0	0	-
2012	Pit	33	233.1	59	0	1.000	5	7	25	12	.480	0	58	+2	-2	+1	+3	+6	3	-1	0	2	-
2013	Pit	79	494.0	118	1	.992	6	9	39	22	.564	4	112	-1	-2	0	+1	0	0	1	0	1	16
2014	Pit	64	386.0	70	1	.986	9	6	39	19	.487	3	64	-7	-1	-1	-5	-11	-6	1	1	-4	-
		236	1615.2	348	5	.986	29	37	146	77	.527	8	331	-7	-7	0	+1	-5	-3	-2	1	-4	

Scout's Defensive Rating: -2 plays saved in 2013, -1 plays saved in 2014

Jorge Soler

		BASIC						THROWING				RANGE AND POSITIONING						RUNS SAVED				
Year	Team	G	Inn	TC	E	Pct	GFP	DM	Opps to Advance	Extra Bases	Pct	Kills	Outs Made	Plays Saved	Plays Saved Shallow	Medium	Deep	Bases Saved	R/P	Throws	GFP/DME	Total	Rank
2014	ChC	24	205.0	48	2	.958	4	1	28	14	.500	2	44	0	0	-1	+1	+2	1	0	0	1	-

Scout's Defensive Rating: 1 plays saved in 2014

George Springer

		BASIC						THROWING				RANGE AND POSITIONING						RUNS SAVED				
Year	Team	G	Inn	TC	E	Pct	GFP	DM	Opps to Advance	Extra Bases	Pct	Kills	Outs Made	Plays Saved	Plays Saved Shallow	Medium	Deep	Bases Saved	R/P	Throws	GFP/DME	Total	Rank
2014	Hou	71	618.0	152	7	.954	20	10	79	39	.494	3	139	+2	0	+1	+1	+4	2	-1	-1	0	17

Scout's Defensive Rating: 2 plays saved in 2014

Right Fielders

Bursting onto the major league scene with gawdy offensive numbers for the Astros, George Springer was equally impressive as a defender in his first year. Coming up through the minor leagues, Springer played mostly center field, but saw most of his major league action in 2014 in right field, where he is likely to end up in the future. At 6'3", he is very fast considering his large, athletic build. While his speed could lend itself to playing center, he doesn't always take the most effective routes to the ball and too often takes risks deep into the gap. His skill set, including an above average arm, profiles very well into a corner outfield spot. The balls that he misplayed can largely be explained as growing pains for a young defender. As he becomes more comfortable in right field, it is not unreasonable to think that he could grow into an above average corner outfielder.

Giancarlo Stanton

	BASIC							THROWING				RANGE AND POSITIONING						RUNS SAVED				
Year Team	G	Inn	TC	E	Pct	GFP	DM	Opps to Advance	Extra Bases	Pct	Kills	Outs Made	Plays Saved	Plays Saved Shallow	Medium	Deep	Bases Saved	R/P	Throws	GFP/DME	Total	Rank
2010 Fla	98	854.2	233	4	.983	25	16	102	48	.471	8	219	+6	-2	+1	+8	+17	7	2	1	10	4
2011 Fla	142	1219.0	296	6	.980	25	43	120	51	.425	5	280	+8	+6	-1	+3	+9	6	2	-5	3	8
2012 Mia	117	1034.1	270	7	.974	24	30	98	44	.449	5	257	+12	+7	0	+5	+19	10	2	-3	9	7
2013 Mia	116	1031.1	248	8	.968	18	31	108	53	.491	5	233	+4	+8	-3	-1	-1	1	-2	-5	-6	26
2014 Mia	143	1262.1	332	6	.982	28	23	132	54	.409	6	320	+8	-1	+2	+7	+13	7	0	-1	6	9
	616	5401.2	1379	31	.978	120	143	560	250	.446	29	1309	+38	+18	-1	+22	+57	31	4	-13	22	-

Scout's Defensive Rating: -4 plays saved in 2013, -1 plays saved in 2014

By and large, Stanton's routes were very efficient and he rarely made a poor read. Stanton has decent range for a massive, bat-first outfielder, allowing him to track down challenging flyballs. He was rewarded with 16 Good Fielding Plays of this subtype, which ranked fifth among regulars in right field. The power of Stanton's throwing arm was also on full display in right field. Cannon, rocket, laser...pick your metaphor. Whatever you call it, it's hanging from his right shoulder and he's using it to torment baserunners. Rarely needing assistance from the ground to get the ball to the infield, Stanton possesses one of the most powerful arms in the majors. In 2014, he tied for the third-most baserunner kills for regulars in right field, throwing out six baserunners without the use of a cutoff man. There is an issue here, however: his overaggressiveness leads to more mistakes than most at the position. Stanton ranked very highly in two different Defensive Misplay and Error subtypes: first in failed dives with five and tied for first in mishandling base hits with seven. It may be hard for Stanton to tame his aggressiveness without sacrificing the abilities that make him an above average outfielder in the first place, but with his bat, I'm sure the Marlins don't need him to change a thing.

Ichiro Suzuki

	BASIC							THROWING				RANGE AND POSITIONING						RUNS SAVED				
Year Team	G	Inn	TC	E	Pct	GFP	DM	Opps to Advance	Extra Bases	Pct	Kills	Outs Made	Plays Saved	Plays Saved Shallow	Medium	Deep	Bases Saved	R/P	Throws	GFP/DME	Total	Rank
2003 Sea	159	1367.0	351	2	.994	-	-	140	53	.379	8	333	+7	+1	+2	+4	+15	9	6	-	15	2
2004 Sea	158	1405.1	387	3	.992	25	15	146	55	.377	7	367	+22	+16	+3	+4	+32	19	6	5	30	1
2005 Sea	158	1388.1	392	2	.995	34	11	168	88	.524	6	383	+7	+4	+5	-1	+10	6	-5	6	7	8
2006 Sea	121	1061.2	260	2	.992	13	9	119	55	.462	4	250	+7	0	+1	+6	+14	8	1	1	10	2
2008 Sea	91	788.1	186	4	.978	24	14	93	39	.419	6	176	+7	+3	+3	+1	+13	8	3	1	12	5
2009 Sea	145	1291.0	326	4	.988	31	14	124	58	.468	2	317	+7	+3	+6	-2	+9	5	-5	3	3	16
2010 Sea	160	1412.0	365	4	.989	28	22	144	74	.514	4	353	+3	0	+6	-3	+3	2	-5	2	-1	20
2011 Sea	151	1333.0	274	4	.985	23	10	127	71	.559	5	263	-3	-2	+4	-5	-3	-2	-3	2	-3	23
2012 2 tms	132	1072.1	244	1	.996	30	6	103	41	.398	2	239	+11	+5	+5	+2	+15	8	0	2	10	5
2013 NYY	128	993.1	225	3	.987	29	7	92	38	.413	2	217	+7	+10	+2	-5	+6	4	1	3	8	10
2014 NYY	119	811.2	178	1	.994	13	8	68	36	.529	1	173	+6	+4	+2	0	+7	4	-2	-1	1	13
	1522	12924.0	3188	30	.991	250	116	1324	608	.459	47	3071	+81	+44	+39	+1	+121	71	-3	24	92	-

Scout's Defensive Rating: 8 plays saved in 2013, 3 plays saved in 2014

A savvy veteran of the outfield, Ichiro Suzuki continues to be a steady defensive option well into his 40s. Ichiro still uses his natural talents of tracking fly balls with relative ease, rarely misreading a ball as it enters the outfield. Where he does tend to get into trouble is when flyballs approach the outfield wall. In his youth, he would climb and crash into the fence with reckless abandon, but now with his advanced age, he seems less certain to make an aggressive play. He will always feel most comfortable in right field, but now has been asked to play left and center as a defensive replacement, and his unfamiliarity shows. Throughout his career, Ichiro has been known for his powerful and accurate arm, and while he still is capable of throwing runners out, his reputation has served as a warning to baserunners who choose to not test the seasoned vet. It is obvious he is past his prime years as an elite level defender, but Ichiro keeps such excellent care of his body he could conceivably keep playing at average or better defense for a few more years.

Right Fielders

Jose Tabata

		BASIC							THROWING				RANGE AND POSITIONING		Plays Saved				RUNS SAVED		GFP/		
Year	Team	G	Inn	TC	E	Pct	GFP	DM	Opps to Advance	Extra Bases	Pct	Kills	Outs Made	Plays Saved	Shallow	Medium	Deep	Bases Saved	R/P	Throws	DME	Total	Rank
2011	Pit	15	106.0	15	0	1.000	0	4	16	8	.500	0	15	-2	0	+1	-3	-5	-2	-1	0	-3	-
2012	Pit	77	496.0	114	3	.974	8	9	42	24	.571	2	107	+1	-4	+3	+2	+5	2	0	0	2	16
2013	Pit	50	340.2	55	0	1.000	8	3	35	12	.343	0	55	-2	+2	+2	-6	-8	-3	0	0	-3	-
2014	Pit	37	211.2	38	0	1.000	4	4	17	6	.353	2	35	-1	0	-1	0	-4	-2	1	0	-1	-
		179	1154.1	222	3	.986	20	20	110	50	.455	4	212	-4	-2	+5	-7	-12	-5	0	0	-5	-

Scout's Defensive Rating: 3 plays saved in 2013, -2 plays saved in 2014

Oscar Taveras

		BASIC							THROWING				RANGE AND POSITIONING		Plays Saved				RUNS SAVED		GFP/		
Year	Team	G	Inn	TC	E	Pct	GFP	DM	Opps to Advance	Extra Bases	Pct	Kills	Outs Made	Plays Saved	Shallow	Medium	Deep	Bases Saved	R/P	Throws	DME	Total	Rank
2014	StL	62	479.0	101	1	.990	3	6	36	19	.528	2	95	-4	-6	+1	+1	-8	-4	0	0	-4	25

Scout's Defensive Rating: 0 plays saved in 2014

Will Venable

		BASIC							THROWING				RANGE AND POSITIONING		Plays Saved				RUNS SAVED		GFP/		
Year	Team	G	Inn	TC	E	Pct	GFP	DM	Opps to Advance	Extra Bases	Pct	Kills	Outs Made	Plays Saved	Shallow	Medium	Deep	Bases Saved	R/P	Throws	DME	Total	Rank
2009	SD	68	493.2	126	1	.992	10	7	56	21	.375	2	123	+6	+2	-1	+5	+13	6	0	-1	5	11
2010	SD	89	600.1	148	3	.980	7	16	54	24	.444	1	144	+9	+2	+8	0	+12	7	0	-1	6	9
2011	SD	91	662.2	151	2	.987	10	9	44	21	.477	2	147	+8	+4	+2	+2	+10	6	0	-1	5	4
2012	SD	114	737.1	178	6	.966	12	16	69	41	.594	1	171	+7	+1	-2	+7	+15	7	-4	-4	-1	21
2013	SD	97	594.0	144	2	.986	13	10	68	37	.544	2	139	0	+6	-1	-5	-4	-1	-3	1	-3	20
2014	SD	75	443.1	105	0	1.000	9	6	36	23	.639	0	104	+10	+2	+5	+4	+17	9	-3	1	7	7
		534	3531.1	852	14	.984	61	64	327	167	.511	8	828	+40	+17	+11	+13	+63	34	-10	-5	19	-

Scout's Defensive Rating: 2 plays saved in 2013, 3 plays saved in 2014

Will Venable's Scouting Report can be found on page 276.

Dayan Viciedo

		BASIC							THROWING				RANGE AND POSITIONING		Plays Saved				RUNS SAVED		GFP/		
Year	Team	G	Inn	TC	E	Pct	GFP	DM	Opps to Advance	Extra Bases	Pct	Kills	Outs Made	Plays Saved	Shallow	Medium	Deep	Bases Saved	R/P	Throws	DME	Total	Rank
2011	CWS	21	163.0	28	0	1.000	2	3	23	6	.261	1	26	-1	+1	-2	0	-1	-1	2	0	1	-
2014	CWS	84	649.1	144	4	.972	8	10	61	30	.492	2	137	-6	-2	-3	-1	-12	-6	-1	-1	-8	31
		105	812.1	172	4	.977	10	13	84	36	.429	3	163	-7	-1	-5	-1	-13	-7	1	-1	-7	-

Scout's Defensive Rating: -7 plays saved in 2014

To put it bluntly, Dayan Viciedo is one of the worst defensive corner outfielders in baseball. Both visual evidence of well below average athleticism and Viciedo's poor defensive numbers indicate that he is unable to cover ground at an acceptable level. His Scout's Defensive Rating ranked dead last in right and fourth-worst in left despite limited time at both. Viciedo possesses a canon for an arm that can even hold its own in right field, but it proved less effective in 2014 than previously. Now 26, Viciedo is running out of time for his offensive upside to materialize before his defensive skills become unemployable.

Shane Victorino

		BASIC							THROWING				RANGE AND POSITIONING		Plays Saved				RUNS SAVED		GFP/		
Year	Team	G	Inn	TC	E	Pct	GFP	DM	Opps to Advance	Extra Bases	Pct	Kills	Outs Made	Plays Saved	Shallow	Medium	Deep	Bases Saved	R/P	Throws	DME	Total	Rank
2003	SD	3	12.1	3	0	1.000	-	-	3	2	.667	0	3	0	+1	0	-1	0	0	0	-	0	-
2005	Phi	3	5.0	0	0	-	0	0	0	0		0							0	0	0	0	-
2006	Phi	21	156.0	41	0	1.000	5	5	11	6	.545	3	38	+1	+2	+1	-2	-1	-1	2	0	1	-
2007	Phi	114	918.2	242	3	.988	20	27	95	31	.326	9	229	+10	+9	+5	-4	+9	5	11	0	16	2
2008	Phi	5	40.0	14	0	1.000	1	0	3	1	.333	0	14	-1	-1	+1	-1	-1	-1	0	0	-1	-
2012	LAD	1	1.0	0	0	-	0	0				0								0	0	0	-
2013	Bos	110	913.1	276	3	.989	28	21	81	33	.407	8	264	+21	+15	0	+7	+33	18	4	1	23	2
2014	Bos	30	263.2	57	0	1.000	2	1	19	10	.526	0	56	+2	+2	0	0	+2	1	-1	1	1	-
		287	2310.0	633	6	.991	56	54	212	83	.392	20	604	+33	+28	+7	-1	+42	22	16	2	40	-

Scout's Defensive Rating: 4 plays saved in 2013, -1 plays saved in 2014

Right Fielders

In his first year in Boston, Shane Victorino proved to be a great fit for the spacious right field of Fenway Park. After years of playing in center field, Victorino was second in the majors in 2013 with 23 Defensive Runs Saved among right fielders. Victorino plays a shallow right field which allows him to take away hits on shallow balls, but he still has the speed and closing ability of a center fielder to get back on deep balls. Victorino possesses an exceptional throwing arm, which, along with his shallow positioning, helps prevent runners from taking extra bases on him. Injuries slowed Victorino down in 2014, but there is nothing that should keep him from bouncing back as a high level defender. The Red Sox have a bit of a log jam in the outfield entering the 2015 season, but Victorino's defensive prowess should help him continue to get his bat in the lineup.

Jayson Werth

		BASIC						THROWING					RANGE AND POSITIONING						RUNS SAVED				
Year	Team	G	Inn	TC	E	Pct	GFP	DM	Opps to Advance	Extra Bases	Pct	Kills	Outs Made	Plays Saved	Plays Saved Shallow	Medium	Deep	Bases Saved	R/P	Throws	GFP/DME	Total	Rank
2003	Tor	19	99.0	22	0	1.000	-	-	14	7	.500	1	16	-1	-1	0	0	-1	-1	1	-	0	-
2004	LA	14	74.0	19	0	1.000	2	1	2	2	1.000	0	19	+1	-1	0	+1	+1	1	-1	0	0	-
2005	LAD	43	291.0	74	0	1.000	3	3	24	11	.458	3	71	+3	+4	0	0	+2	1	2	1	4	-
2007	Phi	58	446.0	118	2	.983	17	8	47	13	.277	3	109	+3	+1	0	+2	+7	4	5	2	11	4
2008	Phi	88	661.1	150	0	1.000	12	10	50	20	.400	6	143	+2	+3	+1	1	0	0	4	2	6	10
2009	Phi	146	1288.2	341	4	.988	16	26	119	49	.412	6	327	+11	+5	+6	0	+17	9	3	-4	8	8
2010	Phi	135	1171.0	261	4	.985	33	24	96	32	.333	5	249	-3	+4	+4	-10	-15	-6	5	2	1	16
2011	Was	134	1172.2	305	8	.974	31	29	141	62	.440	8	288	-7	0	-2	-4	-11	-6	3	-1	-4	26
2012	Was	76	608.2	156	0	1.000	8	15	54	26	.481	3	152	-5	-2	0	-3	-10	-5	-1	0	-6	27
2013	Was	126	1072.0	244	2	.992	16	11	105	46	.438	2	235	0	-3	+1	+1	+4	1	-2	1	0	17
2014	Was	139	1220.2	260	5	.981	18	20	116	50	.431	5	248	-5	0	-5	0	-8	-5	1	0	-4	26
		978	8105.0	1950	25	.987	156	147	768	318	.414	42	1857	-1	+10	+5	-14	-14	-7	20	3	16	-

Scout's Defensive Rating: -3 plays saved in 2013, -5 plays saved in 2014

While his offensive contributions have not disappointed, Werth's defense has failed to live up to the high expectations set for him after signing his nine-figure contract. He will make the easy play consistently but comes up short on most tough plays in right field. Werth's lack of productivity on defense was particularly alarming in 2014, as he failed to make even 50 percent of plays graded as Moderate difficulty by BIS Video Scouts, completing just 44 percent of such plays against the league average of 64 percent. Werth was not signed to be a Fielding Bible Award contender, but entering his age 35 season in 2015 with a history of hamstring problems, Werth will need to find a way to minimize his defensive detriment to a competitive Nationals team.

Pitchers Register and Scouting Reports

Year	Fielding Bible Award Winner	Runner Up	Third Place
2006	Greg Maddux	Kenny Rogers	Mark Buehrle
2007	Johan Santana	Greg Maddux	Chien-Ming Wang
2008	Kenny Rogers	Greg Maddux	Jesse Litsch
2009	Mark Buehrle	Zack Greinke	Johan Santana
2010	Mark Buehrle	Zack Greinke	Trevor Cahill
2011	Mark Buehrle	R.A. Dickey	Jake Westbrook
2012	Mark Buehrle	Jake Westbrook	Zack Greinke
2013	R.A. Dickey	Zack Greinke	Mark Buehrle
2014	Dallas Keuchel	Clayton Kershaw	Henderson Alvarez

Pitchers

Cody Allen

Year	Tm	Inn	TC	E	GFP	DM	Rng	SB	CCS	PCS/PPO	CS%	R/P	SB	Bnt	GFP/DME	Tot	Rnk
			BASIC					HOLDING				RUNS SAVED					
2012	Cle	29	5	0	0	0	-1	2	2	1	.50	-1	1	0	0	0	-
2013	Cle	70	8	3	0	1	-1	6	0	0	.00	0	-1	-1	0	-2	-
2014	Cle	70	4	0	1	1	0	4	1	0	.20	0	0	0	0	0	-
		169	17	3	1	2	-2	12	3	1	.20	-1	0	-1	0	-2	

Henderson Alvarez

Year	Tm	Inn	TC	E	GFP	DM	Rng	SB	CCS	PCS/PPO	CS%	R/P	SB	Bnt	GFP/DME	Tot	Rnk
2011	Tor	64	19	1	2	0	+4	1	2	0	.67	3	1	0	0	4	-
2012	Tor	187	54	4	6	5	+3	2	0	0	.00	3	1	-1	0	3	29
2013	Mia	103	34	1	3	5	+1	2	0	0	.00	1	0	1	0	2	39
2014	Mia	187	56	2	7	3	+8	8	3	1	.33	6	0	0	0	6	3
		540	163	8	18	13	16	13	5	1	.32	13	2	0	0	15	

Chase Anderson

Year	Tm	Inn	TC	E	GFP	DM	Rng	SB	CCS	PCS/PPO	CS%	R/P	SB	Bnt	GFP/DME	Tot	Rnk
2014	Ari	114	26	1	1	0	+1	2	1	1	.50	1	1	0	0	2	46

Chris Archer

Year	Tm	Inn	TC	E	GFP	DM	Rng	SB	CCS	PCS/PPO	CS%	R/P	SB	Bnt	GFP/DME	Tot	Rnk
2012	TB	29	6	1	0	0	0	1	1	1	.67	0	1	-1	0	0	-
2013	TB	129	21	2	2	2	+1	16	2	0	.11	1	-2	0	0	-1	104
2014	TB	195	31	4	4	4	-5	14	4	1	.26	-4	0	0	0	-4	169
		352	58	7	6	6	-4	31	7	2	.23	-3	-1	-1	0	-5	

Jake Arrieta

Year	Tm	Inn	TC	E	GFP	DM	Rng	SB	CCS	PCS/PPO	CS%	R/P	SB	Bnt	GFP/DME	Tot	Rnk
2010	Bal	100	23	2	2	2	+1	11	1	2	.08	1	0	-1	0	0	85
2011	Bal	119	28	3	0	1	+4	11	4	0	.27	3	-1	0	0	2	39
2012	Bal	115	25	3	1	3	-2	9	3	0	.25	-1	0	-1	0	-2	137
2013	2 tms	75	28	1	1	1	+4	7	2	0	.22	3	-1	1	0	3	-
2014	ChC	157	39	2	3	3	0	24	4	1	.17	0	-3	0	0	-3	156
		566	143	11	7	10	7	62	14	3	.19	6	-5	0	0	0	

Bronson Arroyo

Year	Tm	Inn	TC	E	GFP	DM	Rng	SB	CCS	PCS/PPO	CS%	R/P	SB	Bnt	GFP/DME	Tot	Rnk
2003	Bos	17	2	0	-	-	-	0	0	0	-					0	-
2004	Bos	179	42	2	1	0	-3	4	5	0	.56	-2	1	0	0	-1	116
2005	Bos	205	44	2	1	0	-4	4	3	1	.43	-3	1	1	0	-1	134
2006	Cin	241	62	0	4	5	0	5	5	0	.50	0	1	0	0	1	65
2007	Cin	211	39	1	2	4	+1	3	6	2	.67	1	3	-1	0	3	34
2008	Cin	200	50	0	2	2	+2	5	1	2	.29	2	1	2	0	5	9
2009	Cin	220	51	2	3	1	+2	12	5	1	.33	2	0	1	1	4	12
2010	Cin	216	49	0	6	0	+8	6	2	0	.25	6	0	1	1	8	7
2011	Cin	199	56	4	3	3	+3	9	4	0	.31	2	0	2	0	4	18
2012	Cin	202	47	0	2	0	+4	7	4	2	.42	3	1	0	0	4	16
2013	Cin	202	45	1	4	0	0	3	4	1	.57	0	1	1	0	2	46
2014	Ari	86	25	1	0	1	0	5	5	0	.50	0	0	0	0	0	90
		2177	512	13	28	16	13	63	44	9	.43	11	9	7	2	29	

Scott Atchison

Year	Tm	Inn	TC	E	GFP	DM	Rng	SB	CCS	PCS/PPO	CS%	R/P	SB	Bnt	GFP/DME	Tot	Rnk
2004	Sea	31	8	0	0	0	0	3	0	0	.00	0	0	0	0	0	-
2005	Sea	7	1	0	0	0	0	1	1	0	.50			0	0	0	-
2007	SF	31	8	0	3	1	+1	4	0	0	.00	1	-1	0	0	0	-
2010	Bos	60	13	0	1	0	-1	6	2	0	.25	-1	0	1	0	0	-
2011	Bos	30	6	1	0	1	+1	1	3	0	.75	1	1		-1	1	-
2012	Bos	51	18	0	0	1	+3	2	0	0	.00	2	0	0	0	2	-
2013	NYM	45	19	1	2	0	+2	6	0	0	.00	1	-1	0	0	0	-
2014	Cle	72	19	1	1	2	+2	4	2	0	.33	1	0		0	1	-
		327	92	3	7	5	8	27	8	0	.23	5	-1	1	-1	4	

Burke Badenhop

Year	Tm	Inn	TC	E	GFP	DM	Rng	SB	CCS	PCS/PPO	CS%	R/P	SB	Bnt	GFP/DME	Tot	Rnk
2008	Fla	47	12	0	0	0	+3	4	3	0	.43	2	0	0	0	2	-
2009	Fla	72	15	0	1	1	0	4	0	0	.00	0	0	1	0	1	-
2010	Fla	68	23	1	0	2	+1	2	1	2	.67	1	0	-1	0	1	-
2011	Fla	64	13	0	1	0	-2	2	1	1	.33	-1	1	0	0	0	-
2012	TB	62	9	2	0	0	-1	1	0	0	.00	-1	0		0	-1	-
2013	Mil	62	18	2	3	1	+2	3	4	0	.57	2	1	0	0	3	-
2014	Bos	71	21	2	1	1	+1	5	1	0	.17	1	0	0	0	1	-
		446	111	7	6	5	4	20	11	1	.35	4	3	1	-1	7	

Homer Bailey

Year	Tm	Inn	TC	E	GFP	DM	Rng	SB	CCS	PCS/PPO	CS%	R/P	SB	Bnt	GFP/DME	Tot	Rnk
2007	Cin	45	7	1	0	0	-1	9	0	1	.00	-1	-1	0	0	-2	-
2008	Cin	36	6	1	0	1	-1	8	1	0	.11	-1	-1	0	0	-2	-
2009	Cin	113	26	2	1	2	0	10	5	1	.33	0	0	0	1	1	69
2010	Cin	109	22	1	0	2	-2	10	6	1	.38	-2	0	0	0	-2	145
2011	Cin	132	26	1	2	2	-1	9	2	1	.18	-1	0	-1	0	-2	136
2012	Cin	208	43	3	4	1	+5	16	7	0	.30	4	0	0	0	4	14
2013	Cin	209	47	1	9	4	0	14	2	1	.18	0	-1	1	1	1	65
2014	Cin	146	30	0	2	1	+1	4	3	2	.50	1	1	0	0	2	46
		998	207	10	18	13	1	80	26	7	.26	0	-2	0	2	0	

Scott Baker

Year	Tm	Inn	TC	E	GFP	DM	Rng	SB	CCS	PCS/PPO	CS%	R/P	SB	Bnt	GFP/DME	Tot	Rnk
2005	Min	54	11	0	1	0	-1	0	3	1	1.00	-1	1	0	0	0	-
2006	Min	83	11	0	0	0	-1	5	3	0	.38	-1	0	0	0	-1	111
2007	Min	144	21	2	1	3	0	11	4	0	.27	0	-1	2	0	1	73
2008	Min	172	22	1	3	0	-1	8	5	0	.38	-1	0	0	0	-1	118
2009	Min	200	26	0	5	2	+1	10	3	1	.23	1	0	0	1	2	43
2010	Min	170	29	1	0	1	0	3	6	1	.67	0	2	0	0	2	50
2011	Min	135	17	0	1	2	-2	4	5	0	.56	-2	1	-1	0	-2	144
2013	ChC	15	3	0	0	0	-1	0	1	0	1.00	-1	0	0	0	-1	-
2014	Tex	81	7	0	0	0	-1	5	2	0	.29	0	0	0	0	0	90
		1053	147	4	11	8	-5	46	32	3	.41	-5	3	1	1	0	

Grant Balfour

Year	Tm	Inn	TC	E	GFP	DM	Rng	SB	CCS	PCS/PPO	CS%	R/P	SB	Bnt	GFP/DME	Tot	Rnk
2003	Min	26	4	0	-	-	+1	2	1	0	.33	1	0	0	-	1	-
2004	Min	39	7	0	0	0	-1	2	2	0	.50	-1	0	0	0	-1	-
2007	2 tms	25	6	0	0	2	-2	3	0	2	.25	-2	1	-1	0	-2	-
2008	TB	58	5	0	0	1	0	2	1	0	.33	0	0	0	0	0	-
2009	TB	67	4	0	0	1	-1	6	1	0	.14	-1	0	1	0	0	-
2010	TB	55	4	0	1	0	0	2	2	0	.50	0	0	0	0	0	-
2011	Oak	62	6	0	0	0	-1	1	0	0	.00	0	0	0	0	0	-
2012	Oak	75	13	0	0	0	+2	3	3	0	.50	1	0	0	0	1	-
2013	Oak	63	7	1	0	1	+1	1	0	0	1.00	1	0	0	0	1	-
2014	TB	62	6	0	0	0	0	6	2	0	.25	0	0	0	0	0	-
		532	62	1	1	5	-1	26	11	3	.32	-1	1	0	0	0	

Antonio Bastardo

Year	Tm	Inn	TC	E	GFP	DM	Rng	SB	CCS	PCS/PPO	CS%	R/P	SB	Bnt	GFP/DME	Tot	Rnk
2009	Phi	24	2	0	0	0	0	2	0	1	.33	0	0		0	0	-
2010	Phi	19	2	0	1	1	0	0	0	0	-	0	0	0	0	0	-
2011	Phi	58	4	1	0	1	+1	2	0	0	.00	1	0	-1	0	0	-
2012	Phi	52	3	1	0	0	-1	7	1	0	.13	0	-1		0	-1	-
2013	Phi	43	2	0	0	1	0	3	1	0	.40	-1	0	-1	0	-2	-
2014	Phi	64	3	1	0	2	0	3	0	0	.00	0	0	-1	-1	-2	-
		259	16	3	1	5	-1	17	2	2	.19	0	-1	-3	-1	-5	

Trevor Bauer

Year	Tm	Inn	TC	E	GFP	DM	Rng	SB	CCS	PCS/PPO	CS%	R/P	SB	Bnt	GFP/DME	Tot	Rnk
2012	Ari	16	6	2	0	0	+1	4	0	0	.00	0	-1	-1	0	-2	-
2013	Cle	17	4	0	1	0	+1	4	1	0	.20	1	0	0	0	1	-
2014	Cle	153	22	1	1	1	+1	19	6	2	.27	0	-1	0	0	-1	111
		186	32	3	2	1	3	27	7	2	.23	1	-2	-1	0	-2	

Pitchers

Josh Beckett

Year	Tm	BASIC Inn	TC	E	GFP	DM	Rng	HOLDING SB	CCS	PCS/PPO	CS%	RUNS SAVED R/P	SB	Bnt	GFP/DME	Tot	Rnk
2003	Fla	142	25	1	-	-	-2	5	5	0	.50	-2	1	0	0	-1	127
2004	Fla	157	23	2	2	2	+1	5	5	0	.50	1	1	-1	0	1	58
2005	Fla	179	38	1	1	2	-1	6	6	1	.54	-1	1	0	0	0	99
2006	Bos	205	38	0	1	2	-2	15	5	0	.06	-2	-2	0	0	-4	165
2007	Bos	201	32	2	2	4	-3	14	6	1	.30	-2	0	0	-1	-3	153
2008	Bos	174	35	2	3	0	-1	7	4	1	.42	-1	1	0	0	0	97
2009	Bos	212	27	2	1	5	0	15	3	0	.17	0	-1	0	0	-1	115
2010	Bos	128	30	1	0	3	+3	18	1	0	.05	2	-3	-1	0	-2	129
2011	Bos	193	36	3	3	2	-1	31	4	0	.11	-1	-4	0	0	-5	166
2012	2 tms	170	33	1	2	3	-1	19	3	1	.14	-1	-2	-1	0	-4	162
2013	LAD	43	10	1	1	0	0	3	2	0	.40	0	0	0	0	0	-
2014	LAD	116	18	2	0	2	0	12	6	0	.33	0	-1	0	0	-1	111
		1919	345	18	16	25	-7	150	46	4	.24	-7	-9	-3	-1	-20	

Erik Bedard

Year	Tm	BASIC Inn	TC	E	GFP	DM	Rng	HOLDING SB	CCS	PCS/PPO	CS%	RUNS SAVED R/P	SB	Bnt	GFP/DME	Tot	Rnk
2004	Bal	137	19	0	1	1	-3	10	3	0	.23	-2	-1	0	1	-2	131
2005	Bal	142	29	1	2	2	+4	8	2	2	.33	3	0	-2	0	1	57
2006	Bal	196	34	1	2	3	+3	4	2	0	.33	2	0	0	0	2	38
2007	Bal	182	23	0	1	1	+2	5	2	0	.29	2	0	0	0	2	42
2008	Sea	81	10	0	1	0	+2	5	1	0	.17	2	0	0	1	3	27
2009	Sea	83	10	0	1	0	+1	5	2	1	.38	1	0	0	0	1	60
2011	2 tms	129	15	1	0	2	-1	3	2	2	.50	0	2	-1	0	1	74
2012	Pit	126	14	0	2	3	-1	6	0	0	.00	0	0	-1	0	-1	114
2013	Hou	151	15	3	0	2	0	5	1	0	.17	0	0	-2	0	-2	131
2014	TB	76	7	0	0	0	0	1	0	0	.00	0	0	0	0	0	-
		1303	176	6	10	14	7	52	15	5	.27	8	1	-6	2	5	

Ronald Belisario

Year	Tm	BASIC Inn	TC	E	GFP	DM	Rng	HOLDING SB	CCS	PCS/PPO	CS%	RUNS SAVED R/P	SB	Bnt	GFP/DME	Tot	Rnk
2009	LAD	71	12	1	2	3	-2	6	1	0	.14	-2	-1	0	0	-3	-
2010	LAD	55	13	0	1	0	0	2	0	0	.00	0	0	0	0	0	-
2012	LAD	71	19	1	2	2	+2	4	1	0	.20	1	0	0	1	2	-
2013	LAD	68	23	2	4	4	-3	4	2	0	.33	-2	0	0	0	-2	-
2014	CWS	66	11	0	0	1	-1	5	0	0	.00	0	-1	0	0	-1	-
		331	78	4	9	10	-4	21	4	0	.16	-3	-2	0	1	-4	

Matt Belisle

Year	Tm	BASIC Inn	TC	E	GFP	DM	Rng	HOLDING SB	CCS	PCS/PPO	CS%	RUNS SAVED R/P	SB	Bnt	GFP/DME	Tot	Rnk
2003	Cin	9	2	0	-	-	-1	0	0	0	-	-1	0	0		-1	-
2005	Cin	86	18	2	1	1	-1	7	2	0	.22	-1	0	0	0	-1	120
2006	Cin	40	6	0	0	1	0	1	0	0	.00	0	0	-1	0	-1	-
2007	Cin	178	30	0	3	1	-2	11	6	0	.35	-2	0	0	0	-2	138
2008	Cin	30	8	1	0	0	0	3	1	0	.25	0	0	0	0	0	-
2009	Col	31	8	0	1	0	0	4	0	0	.00	0	-1	0	0	-1	-
2010	Col	92	16	2	1	1	0	2	1	0	.33	0	0	0	0	0	107
2011	Col	72	13	0	1	1	0	0	3	1	1.00	0	1	0	0	1	-
2012	Col	80	14	1	2	0	-3	1	0	0	.00	-2	0	-1	0	-3	152
2013	Col	73	21	0	1	2	+2	3	0	0	.00	2	0	0	0	2	-
2014	Col	65	19	1	2	1	0	4	1	0	.20	0	0	1	0	1	-
		754	155	7	12	8	-5	36	14	1	.29	-4	0	-2	0	-6	

Dellin Betances

Year	Tm	BASIC Inn	TC	E	GFP	DM	Rng	HOLDING SB	CCS	PCS/PPO	CS%	RUNS SAVED R/P	SB	Bnt	GFP/DME	Tot	Rnk
2011	NYY	3	0	0	0	0	0	1	0	0	.00	0	0	0		0	-
2013	NYY	5	0	0	0	1	0	0	0	0	-	0	0	0		0	-
2014	NYY	90	14	2	1	0	-1	12	2	1	.20	-1	-1	0		-2	146
		97	14	2	1	1	-1	13	2	1	.19	-1	-1	0		-2	

Brad Boxberger

Year	Tm	BASIC Inn	TC	E	GFP	DM	Rng	HOLDING SB	CCS	PCS/PPO	CS%	RUNS SAVED R/P	SB	Bnt	GFP/DME	Tot	Rnk
2012	SD	28	3	3	0	0	-1	5	0	1	.17	-1	0	0		-1	-
2013	SD	22	6	0	0	0	0	1	2	1	.67	0	1	0	0	1	-
2014	TB	65	6	0	0	2	-1	4	2	1	.33	-1	0	-1	0	-2	-
		114	15	3	0	2	-2	10	4	3	.33	-2	1	-1	0	-2	

Brad Brach

Year	Tm	BASIC Inn	TC	E	GFP	DM	Rng	HOLDING SB	CCS	PCS/PPO	CS%	RUNS SAVED R/P	SB	Bnt	GFP/DME	Tot	Rnk
2011	SD	7	0	0	0	0	0	0	0	0		0	0			0	-
2012	SD	67	10	2	0	0	-2	11	1	1	.15	-1	-1	0	0	-2	-
2013	SD	31	7	0	0	0	+1	1	1	0	.14	1	-1	0		0	-
2014	Bal	62	11	3	0	0	0	5	2	1	.38	0	0	-1	0	-1	-
		167	28	5	0	0	-1	22	4	2	.21	0	-2	-1	0	-3	

Zach Britton

Year	Tm	BASIC Inn	TC	E	GFP	DM	Rng	HOLDING SB	CCS	PCS/PPO	CS%	RUNS SAVED R/P	SB	Bnt	GFP/DME	Tot	Rnk
2011	Bal	154	32	2	1	2	-1	7	3	0	.30	-1	0	-3	0	-4	161
2012	Bal	60	12	1	2	4	-1	1	2	0	.67	0	1	0	-1	0	-
2013	Bal	40	5	0	1	3	-3	2	0	1	.33	-2	0	0	0	-2	-
2014	Bal	76	20	0	1	1	+3	2	0	0	.00	2	0	0	0	2	-
		331	69	3	5	10	-1	12	5	1	.33	-1	1	-3	-1	-4	

David Buchanan

Year	Tm	BASIC Inn	TC	E	GFP	DM	Rng	HOLDING SB	CCS	PCS/PPO	CS%	RUNS SAVED R/P	SB	Bnt	GFP/DME	Tot	Rnk
2014	Phi	118	28	3	0	1	-1	4	1	1	.20	-1	0	0	1	0	100

Clay Buchholz

Year	Tm	BASIC Inn	TC	E	GFP	DM	Rng	HOLDING SB	CCS	PCS/PPO	CS%	RUNS SAVED R/P	SB	Bnt	GFP/DME	Tot	Rnk
2007	Bos	23	5	1	1	2	-1	0	0	1	-	-1	1	-1	-1	-2	-
2008	Bos	76	9	0	0	2	-3	3	2	1	.40	-2	1	0	-1	-2	-
2009	Bos	92	17	1	2	0	-1	6	0	0	.00	-1	-1	0	0	-2	138
2010	Bos	174	47	2	3	4	-1	8	4	3	.43	-1	2	0	-1	0	101
2011	Bos	83	30	1	2	1	+2	6	2	1	.33	2	0	0	0	2	41
2012	Bos	189	46	3	1	4	+1	9	2	1	.18	1	0	0	-1	0	89
2013	Bos	108	32	2	1	2	-2	6	6	0	.50	-1	1	0	0	0	95
2014	Bos	170	37	1	3	0	-3	6	5	0	.45	-2	1	0		-1	134
		915	223	11	13	15	-8	44	21	7	.35	-5	5	-1	-4	-5	

Mark Buehrle

Year	Tm	BASIC Inn	TC	E	GFP	DM	Rng	HOLDING SB	CCS	PCS/PPO	CS%	RUNS SAVED R/P	SB	Bnt	GFP/DME	Tot	Rnk
2003	CWS	230	53	0	-	-	-3	1	2	5	.80	-2	3	1	-	2	55
2004	CWS	245	72	4	9	3	+7	5	2	10	.62	5	4	0	1	10	3
2005	CWS	237	60	2	8	1	+2	8	1	5	.27	2	2	1	0	5	10
2006	CWS	204	45	1	0	2	+5	4	3	10	.64	4	5	-1	0	8	4
2007	CWS	201	48	1	3	2	+2	2	0	5	.80	2	3	1	0	6	4
2008	CWS	219	52	0	2	3	0	5	2	7	.58	0	4	0	1	5	11
2009	CWS	213	55	1	7	2	+9	4	0	8	.50	7	3	0	0	10	1
2010	CWS	210	50	0	5	2	+8	3	3	11	.50	6	5	1	0	12	2
2011	CWS	205	56	1	1	2	+6	3	3	6	.70	4	4	-1	0	7	5
2012	Mia	202	60	0	5	2	+8	5	0	5	.38	6	2	2	2	12	1
2013	Tor	204	49	2	5	5	0	4	1	6	.56	0	3	0	1	4	19
2014	Tor	202	42	1	5	5	0	1	0	4	.75	0	2	1	-1	2	55
		2573	642	13	50	29	44	48	15	82	.56	34	40	5	4	83	

Madison Bumgarner

Year	Tm	BASIC Inn	TC	E	GFP	DM	Rng	HOLDING SB	CCS	PCS/PPO	CS%	RUNS SAVED R/P	SB	Bnt	GFP/DME	Tot	Rnk
2009	SF	10	3	0	1	0	+1	0	0	0	-	1	0	0	0	1	-
2010	SF	111	14	1	2	1	0	8	1	1	.20	0	0	0	0	0	88
2011	SF	205	32	3	1	4	-4	12	8	4	.48	-3	2	0	-1	-2	147
2012	SF	208	45	2	2	0	+2	27	5	5	.27	2	-1	-1	1	1	61
2013	SF	201	43	3	3	1	+6	8	1	6	.47	4	2	-2	1	5	10
2014	SF	217	36	2	3	5	-2	7	1	9	.59	-1	4	-2	0	1	75
		952	173	11	12	11	3	62	16	25	.39	3	7	-5	1	6	

Pitchers

A.J. Burnett

		BASIC					HOLDING				RUNS SAVED					
Year	Tm	Inn	TC	E	GFP	DM	Rng	SB	CCS	PCS/PPO	CS%	R/P	SB	Bnt	GFP/DME	Tot	Rnk
2003	Fla	23	7	0	-	-	0	1	1	0	.50	0	0			0	-
2004	Fla	120	28	0	2	4	+3	14	4	2	.26	2	-1	1	0	2	36
2005	Fla	209	31	2	2	4	-3	24	6	1	.20	-2	-2	0	0	-4	164
2006	Tor	136	23	1	3	3	-2	18	4	1	.18	-2	-2	1	0	-3	160
2007	Tor	166	34	2	2	4	-1	31	0	0	.00	-1	-5	0	0	-6	171
2008	Tor	221	54	7	3	2	-2	22	5	5	.29	-2	0	-1	0	-3	151
2009	NYY	207	28	3	1	3	+1	23	10	4	.34	1	1	0	0	2	43
2010	NYY	187	29	4	5	6	-1	37	3	4	.12	-1	-4	-1	-1	-7	174
2011	NYY	190	38	5	0	2	-6	24	5	5	.23	-4	0	0	1	-3	159
2012	Pit	202	58	1	2	3	+2	38	0	4	.05	1	-4	0	0	-3	148
2013	Pit	191	33	2	3	5	-2	22	2	1	.08	-1	-2	-1	0	-4	164
2014	Phi	214	35	1	1	0	-4	33	8	3	.21	-3	-2	0	0	-5	172
		2065	398	28	24	36	-15	287	48	30	.18	-12	-21	-1	0	-34	

Jared Burton

		BASIC					HOLDING				RUNS SAVED					
Year	Tm	Inn	TC	E	GFP	DM	Rng	SB	CCS	PCS/PPO	CS%	R/P	SB	Bnt	GFP/DME	Tot	Rnk
2007	Cin	43	7	1	1	2	-2	4	1	1	.20	-2	0		0	-2	-
2008	Cin	59	16	1	1	0	+4	4	1	0	.20	3	0		0	3	-
2009	Cin	59	11	2	0	1	-1	4	0	1	.00	-1	0	1	0	0	-
2010	Cin	3	1	0	0	0	0	1	0	0	.00		0		0	0	-
2011	Cin	5	0	0	0	0	0	2	0	0	.00	0	0			0	-
2012	Min	62	14	1	0	1	+3	6	0	0	.00	2	-1	0	0	1	-
2013	Min	66	17	1	0	4	+1	14	3	0	.18	1	-2	0	0	-1	-
2014	Min	64	10	0	0	0	-2	10	0	1	.00	-2	-1	0	0	-3	-
		361	76	6	2	8	3	45	5	3	.10	1	-4	1	0	-2	-

Trevor Cahill

		BASIC					HOLDING				RUNS SAVED					
Year	Tm	Inn	TC	E	GFP	DM	Rng	SB	CCS	PCS/PPO	CS%	R/P	SB	Bnt	GFP/DME	Tot	Rnk
2009	Oak	179	36	1	2	0	+3	17	8	2	.37	2	0	1	1	4	12
2010	Oak	197	61	1	8	0	+12	15	2	5	.25	9	1	0	1	11	3
2011	Oak	208	45	1	3	3	+1	28	7	3	.22	1	-2	-2	0	-3	151
2012	Ari	200	52	5	3	5	+1	12	7	0	.37	1	0	-1	0	0	89
2013	Ari	147	40	0	2	1	+4	16	0	2	.06	3	-1	1	0	3	22
2014	Ari	111	18	1	2	1	-1	17	3	1	.19	0	-2	-1	0	-3	156
		1040	252	9	20	10	20	105	27	13	.25	16	-4	-2	2	12	-

Matt Cain

		BASIC					HOLDING				RUNS SAVED					
Year	Tm	Inn	TC	E	GFP	DM	Rng	SB	CCS	PCS/PPO	CS%	R/P	SB	Bnt	GFP/DME	Tot	Rnk
2005	SF	46	4	1	0	0	0	1	1	0	.50	0	0	0		0	-
2006	SF	191	35	3	1	3	-2	15	3	0	.17	-2	-1	1	0	-2	142
2007	SF	200	31	0	4	4	-2	8	5	0	.38	-2	1	1	0	0	102
2008	SF	218	38	0	1	4	-2	13	10	0	.43	-2	1	1	0	0	103
2009	SF	218	39	0	2	6	0	11	9	0	.45	0	1	0	-1	0	86
2010	SF	223	35	2	2	0	+2	19	7	3	.34	1	0	1	0	2	43
2011	SF	222	40	3	3	3	+2	18	5	0	.22	2	-1	1	-1	1	61
2012	SF	219	36	2	3	3	+1	18	9	0	.33	1	-1	0	1	1	68
2013	SF	184	38	1	4	1	+1	17	3	1	.19	1	-2	1	1	1	54
2014	SF	90	26	2	2	0	0	8	4	1	.38	0	0	0	0	0	90
		1811	322	14	22	24	0	128	56	5	.32	-1	-2	6	0	3	-

Chris Capuano

		BASIC					HOLDING				RUNS SAVED					
Year	Tm	Inn	TC	E	GFP	DM	Rng	SB	CCS	PCS/PPO	CS%	R/P	SB	Bnt	GFP/DME	Tot	Rnk
2003	Ari	33	10	1	-	-	+2	3	0	2	.00	2	0		0	2	-
2004	Mil	88	19	0	1	1	+1	1	0	6	.50	1	3	0	0	4	24
2005	Mil	219	48	4	2	2	-4	2	3	12	.82	-3	6	0	1	4	25
2006	Mil	221	47	2	6	3	+2	1	1	6	.75	2	3	0	1	6	7
2007	Mil	150	38	1	7	2	+2	6	0	2	.00	2	1	2	1	6	4
2010	Mil	66	12	0	0	0	+2	1	0	0	.00	1	0	0	0	1	-
2011	NYM	186	35	0	4	3	0	9	2	3	.36	0	1	0	0	1	74
2012	LAD	198	33	1	8	5	+4	6	1	4	.33	3	2	-1	0	4	16
2013	LAD	106	19	0	1	3	-1	2	1	0	.33	-1	0	0	0	-1	115
2014	2 tms	97	13	1	2	1	+1	1	0	1	.50	1	1	0	0	2	46
		1365	274	10	31	20	9	32	8	36	.42	8	17	1	3	29	-

David Carpenter

		BASIC					HOLDING				RUNS SAVED					
Year	Tm	Inn	TC	E	GFP	DM	Rng	SB	CCS	PCS/PPO	CS%	R/P	SB	Bnt	GFP/DME	Tot	Rnk
2011	Hou	28	8	0	0	0	+1	1	0	0	.00	1	0	1	0	2	-
2012	2 tms	32	4	0	0	0	-1	3	0	0	.00	0	0	0	0	0	-
2013	Atl	66	4	0	0	1	0	5	4	0	.44	0	0		-1	-1	-
2014	Atl	61	11	1	1	1	0	1	1	0	.50	-1	0	0	0	-1	-
		186	27	1	1	2	-1	10	5	0	.33	0	0	1	-1	0	-

Carlos Carrasco

		BASIC					HOLDING				RUNS SAVED					
Year	Tm	Inn	TC	E	GFP	DM	Rng	SB	CCS	PCS/PPO	CS%	R/P	SB	Bnt	GFP/DME	Tot	Rnk
2009	Cle	22	9	1	0	2	+1	3	1	3	.50	1	1		-1	1	-
2010	Cle	45	8	0	1	0	+2	5	6	0	.55	1	0	0	0	1	-
2011	Cle	125	19	0	1	2	+1	6	1	2	.33	1	1	0	0	2	44
2013	Cle	47	12	2	0	1	0	3	0	1	.00	0	0	-1	0	-1	-
2014	Cle	134	26	2	1	1	+2	9	4	1	.31	1	0	0	0	1	65
		372	74	5	3	6	6	26	12	7	.38	4	2	-1	-1	4	-

Scott Carroll

		BASIC					HOLDING				RUNS SAVED					
Year	Tm	Inn	TC	E	GFP	DM	Rng	SB	CCS	PCS/PPO	CS%	R/P	SB	Bnt	GFP/DME	Tot	Rnk
2014	CWS	129	19	0	2	0	-1	7	4	0	.36	-1	0		1	0	100

Andrew Cashner

		BASIC					HOLDING				RUNS SAVED					
Year	Tm	Inn	TC	E	GFP	DM	Rng	SB	CCS	PCS/PPO	CS%	R/P	SB	Bnt	GFP/DME	Tot	Rnk
2010	ChC	54	16	0	1	1	+3	5	2	0	.29	2	0	0	0	2	-
2011	ChC	11	1	0	0	0	0	0	0	0		0	0		0	0	-
2012	SD	46	13	0	0	0	-1	12	2	0	.14	-1	-2	0	0	-3	-
2013	SD	175	48	1	7	1	+7	16	5	1	.24	5	-1	0	1	5	8
2014	SD	123	24	1	0	2	+3	8	3	0	.27	3	0	1	0	4	12
		409	102	2	8	4	12	41	12	1	.23	9	-3	1	1	8	-

Jhoulys Chacin

		BASIC					HOLDING				RUNS SAVED					
Year	Tm	Inn	TC	E	GFP	DM	Rng	SB	CCS	PCS/PPO	CS%	R/P	SB	Bnt	GFP/DME	Tot	Rnk
2009	Col	11	2	0	0	0	0	3	1	0	.25	0	0		0	0	-
2010	Col	137	22	1	1	0	+1	7	3	0	.30	1	0	1	0	2	43
2011	Col	194	69	4	0	2	+9	4	7	1	.64	6	2	-1	0	7	3
2012	Col	69	21	3	2	2	+2	2	1	2	.50	2	1	0	-1	2	-
2013	Col	197	38	1	2	1	+1	6	2	1	.33	0	1	1	0	2	46
2014	Col	63	13	1	1	1	0	2	1	0	.33	0	0	0	1	1	-
		672	165	10	6	7	13	24	15	4	.41	9	4	2	-1	14	-

Joba Chamberlain

		BASIC					HOLDING				RUNS SAVED					
Year	Tm	Inn	TC	E	GFP	DM	Rng	SB	CCS	PCS/PPO	CS%	R/P	SB	Bnt	GFP/DME	Tot	Rnk
2007	NYY	24	1	0	0	0	0	1	0	0	.00	0	0		0	0	-
2008	NYY	100	16	0	3	2	-1	8	3	1	.33	-1	0	1	0	0	97
2009	NYY	157	38	2	1	2	-1	26	7	1	.24	-1	-2	1	0	-2	138
2010	NYY	72	8	0	1	1	0	10	1	0	.09	0	-1		0	0	-
2011	NYY	29	7	0	0	0	0	2	1	0	.33	0	0		0	0	-
2012	NYY	21	2	0	0	0	0	4	0	0	.00	0	-1		0	-1	-
2013	NYY	42	7	0	1	0	+1	9	1	0	.10	1	-1	0	0	0	-
2014	Det	63	11	0	1	0	-1	7	2	0	.22	-1	-1	0	0	-2	-
		507	90	2	7	5	-2	67	15	2	.20	-2	-6	2	0	-6	-

Jesse Chavez

		BASIC					HOLDING				RUNS SAVED					
Year	Tm	Inn	TC	E	GFP	DM	Rng	SB	CCS	PCS/PPO	CS%	R/P	SB	Bnt	GFP/DME	Tot	Rnk
2008	Pit	15	4	0	0	0	0	3	0	0	.00	0	0	0	0	0	-
2009	Pit	67	11	0	2	0	+1	3	0	0	.00	1	0		1	2	-
2010	2 tms	63	9	0	0	0	-1	1	1	0	.50	0	0	0	0	0	-
2011	KC	8	0	0	0	0	0	1	0	0	.00	0	0		0	0	-
2012	2 tms	25	3	1	0	0	0	0	0	0		0	0	-1	0	-1	-
2013	Oak	57	14	0	2	3	-1	1	0	0	.00	-1	0	0	0	-1	-
2014	Oak	146	15	0	1	2	-3	4	2	1	.43	-3	1		0	-2	154
		380	56	1	5	5	-4	13	3	1	.24	-3	1	-1	1	-2	-

Pitchers

Wei-Yin Chen

Year	Tm	Inn	TC	E	GFP	DM	Rng	SB	CCS	PCS/PPO	CS%	R/P	SB	Bnt	GFP/DME	Tot	Rnk
2012	Bal	193	39	1	4	2	+3	11	1	2	.21	2	0	2	-1	3	31
2013	Bal	137	20	0	3	0	+4	4	2	1	.43	3	1	0	0	4	14
2014	Bal	186	31	0	3	3	+4	5	0	1	.17	3	0	-1	0	2	36
		515	90	1	10	5	11	20	3	4	.26	8	1	1	-1	9	

Tony Cingrani

Year	Tm	Inn	TC	E	GFP	DM	Rng	SB	CCS	PCS/PPO	CS%	R/P	SB	Bnt	GFP/DME	Tot	Rnk
2012	Cin	5	2	1	0	0	-1	0	0	0	-	-1	0		0	-1	
2013	Cin	105	22	0	1	1	+1	5	0	6	.55	1	2	0	0	3	27
2014	Cin	63	4	1	0	0	-2	2	0	2	.33	-1	1	0	0	0	
		173	28	2	1	1	-2	7	0	8	.50	-1	3	0	0	2	

Steve Cishek

Year	Tm	Inn	TC	E	GFP	DM	Rng	SB	CCS	PCS/PPO	CS%	R/P	SB	Bnt	GFP/DME	Tot	Rnk
2010	Fla	4	2	0	1	0	0	0	0	0	-	0		0		0	
2011	Fla	55	13	4	0	1	0	5	0	0	.00	0	-1	-2	0	-3	
2012	Mia	64	15	1	0	0	0	3	0	0	.00	0	0	-1	0	-1	
2013	Mia	70	16	1	0	0	-1	1	2	0	.67	0	1		0	1	
2014	Mia	65	9	2	2	0	-3	5	3	1	.44	-2	0	0	0	-2	
		257	55	8	3	1	-4	14	5	1	.30	-2	0	-3	0	-5	

Tyler Clippard

Year	Tm	Inn	TC	E	GFP	DM	Rng	SB	CCS	PCS/PPO	CS%	R/P	SB	Bnt	GFP/DME	Tot	Rnk
2007	NYY	27	4	0	0	0	0	5	0	0	.00	0	-1		0	-1	
2008	Was	10	0	0	0	0	0	0	0	0		0	0			0	
2009	Was	60	9	0	0	0	0	1	1	0	.50	0	0	1	0	0	
2010	Was	91	5	0	0	1	1	5	1	1	.17	-1	0	0	0	-1	116
2011	Was	88	8	0	0	1	0	3	4	1	.63	0	1	0	0	1	74
2012	Was	73	13	2	0	0	+1	8	0	0	.00	1	-1	0	0	0	
2013	Was	71	8	0	1	0	0	2	0	0	.00	0	0		0	0	
2014	Was	70	8	0	0	0	+2	4	2	0	.33	1	0		0	1	
		491	55	2	1	2	2	28	8	2	.24	1	-1	1	0	1	

Alex Cobb

Year	Tm	Inn	TC	E	GFP	DM	Rng	SB	CCS	PCS/PPO	CS%	R/P	SB	Bnt	GFP/DME	Tot	Rnk
2011	TB	53	12	1	0	5	0	11	0	0	.00	0	-2	0	0	-2	
2012	TB	136	46	1	1	9	+9	19	1	1	.10	7	-2	0	0	5	10
2013	TB	143	28	1	1	3	+1	12	2	2	.25	1	0	0	0	1	54
2014	TB	166	33	4	4	1	+1	12	1	0	.14	1	0	0	0	1	65
		498	119	7	6	11	11	54	5	5	.13	9	-4	0	0	5	

Gerrit Cole

Year	Tm	Inn	TC	E	GFP	DM	Rng	SB	CCS	PCS/PPO	CS%	R/P	SB	Bnt	GFP/DME	Tot	Rnk
2013	Pit	117	21	1	0	1	0	9	5	0	.36	0	0	0	0	0	86
2014	Pit	138	33	2	3	1	+2	21	5	1	.19	2	-2	0	0	0	81
		255	54	3	3	2	2	30	10	1	.25	2	-2	0	0	0	

Josh Collmenter

Year	Tm	Inn	TC	E	GFP	DM	Rng	SB	CCS	PCS/PPO	CS%	R/P	SB	Bnt	GFP/DME	Tot	Rnk
2011	Ari	154	24	0	1	1	-1	4	7	0	.64	0	1	0	0	1	74
2012	Ari	90	16	0	1	0	0	3	4	0	.57	0	1	1	0	2	53
2013	Ari	92	15	0	2	0	0	4	3	0	.43	0	0	0	0	0	86
2014	Ari	179	36	0	3	1	0	9	6	0	.40	0	0	1	0	1	71
		516	91	0	6	3	-1	20	20	0	.50	0	2	2	0	4	

Bartolo Colon

Year	Tm	Inn	TC	E	GFP	DM	Rng	SB	CCS	PCS/PPO	CS%	R/P	SB	Bnt	GFP/DME	Tot	Rnk
2003	CWS	242	31	3	-	-	-2	1	6	1	.86	-2	2	0	-	0	106
2004	Ana	208	41	3	6	1	-1	3	6	1	.67	-1	2	1	0	2	56
2005	LAA	223	24	0	1	5	-3	2	4	0	.67	-2	1	0	0	-1	127
2006	LAA	56	12	1	0	1	0	1	3	0	.75	0	1	0	0	1	-
2007	LAA	99	12	1	0	2	-4	2	2	0	.50	-3	1	0	0	-2	147
2008	Bos	39	8	2	1	1	-2	0	0	0	-	-2	0	0	0	-2	
2009	CWS	62	14	1	0	0	0	0	0	1	-	0	1	0	0	1	
2011	NYY	164	29	1	4	0	0	5	3	1	.38	0	1		0	1	74
2012	Oak	152	28	4	0	3	+2	1	0	0	.00	2	1	-3	0	0	88
2013	Oak	190	29	1	1	9	-2	7	1	2	.22	-1	-1	-1	-1	-2	136
2014	NYM	202	43	5	2	4	+1	3	1	1	.40	0	1	0	0	2	55
		1639	271	22	15	26	-11	25	26	7	.53	-9	12	-2	-1	0	

Kevin Correia

Year	Tm	Inn	TC	E	GFP	DM	Rng	SB	CCS	PCS/PPO	CS%	R/P	SB	Bnt	GFP/DME	Tot	Rnk
2003	SF	39	7	0	-	-	0	4	2	0	.33	0	0	0		0	
2004	SF	19	3	0	0	2	-1	3	0	0	.00	-1	0	-1	0	-2	
2005	SF	58	4	0	0	0	-2	4	2	0	.33	-2	0	-1	0	-3	
2006	SF	70	6	2	0	0	-1	3	2	1	.50	-1	1		0	0	
2007	SF	102	17	0	1	1	-2	10	3	0	.23	-2	-1	0	0	-3	153
2008	SF	110	21	1	0	0	-2	4	6	1	.64	-2	2	-1	0	-1	121
2009	SD	198	46	2	3	2	0	7	6	1	.50	0	1	-2	0	-1	115
2010	SD	145	28	2	0	0	+1	11	5	0	.31	0	0	0	0	0	88
2011	Pit	154	33	0	4	2	+2	6	5	1	.50	2	1	-1	0	2	41
2012	Pit	171	47	1	2	0	0	7	3	1	.36	0	1	-1	0	0	93
2013	Min	185	36	2	1	1	-5	6	4	1	.45	-4	1	-1	0	-4	169
2014	2 tms	154	35	4	3	0	-1	7	2	0	.22	-1	0	-1	1	-1	120
		1405	283	12	16	8	-11	72	40	6	.39	-11	6	-9	1	-13	

Jarred Cosart

Year	Tm	Inn	TC	E	GFP	DM	Rng	SB	CCS	PCS/PPO	CS%	R/P	SB	Bnt	GFP/DME	Tot	Rnk
2013	Hou	60	14	0	3	0	+1	5	3	0	.38	1	0			1	2
2014	2 tms	180	49	0	3	4	+1	6	4	0	.40	0	1	0	-1	0	90
		240	63	0	6	4	2	11	7	0	.39	1	1	0		2	

Neal Cotts

Year	Tm	Inn	TC	E	GFP	DM	Rng	SB	CCS	PCS/PPO	CS%	R/P	SB	Bnt	GFP/DME	Tot	Rnk
2003	CWS	13	2	0	-	-	0	0	0	0	-	0	0	0	-	0	
2004	CWS	65	10	1	0	1	+2	5	1	0	.17	2	0	0	0	2	
2005	CWS	60	16	0	1	0	+2	2	0	1	.33	2	0	0	0	2	
2006	CWS	54	13	0	1	2	+1	2	0	0	.00	1	0	1	-1	1	
2007	ChC	17	2	0	0	0	0	1	0	1	.50	0	0	0	0	0	
2008	ChC	36	8	2	0	1	-1	3	0	0	.00	-1	0	0	0	-1	
2009	ChC	11	2	0	0	0	+1	0	0	0	-	0	1	0		1	
2013	Tex	57	10	0	1	1	+1	3	1	0	.25	1	0	-1	0	0	
2014	Tex	67	10	0	0	1	0	3	0	1	.25	0	0	1	0	1	
		380	73	3	3	6	6	20	2	3	.20	6	0	1	-1	6	

Johnny Cueto

Year	Tm	Inn	TC	E	GFP	DM	Rng	SB	CCS	PCS/PPO	CS%	R/P	SB	Bnt	GFP/DME	Tot	Rnk
2008	Cin	174	34	3	1	3	-1	7	6	1	.46	-1	1	0	0	0	97
2009	Cin	171	21	2	2	4	+1	3	3	2	.71	1	2	0	-1	2	49
2010	Cin	186	42	2	2	1	0	3	2	3	.57	0	2	0	0	2	50
2011	Cin	156	46	5	2	1	+1	1	4	2	.80	1	2	0	-1	2	44
2012	Cin	217	68	5	3	2	0	5	5	10	.90	0	6	1	1	8	3
2013	Cin	61	16	1	1	0	+2	2	2	0	.50	2	0	0	0	2	
2014	Cin	244	63	3	2	3	+5	6	4	4	.50	4	2	0	0	6	4
		1208	290	21	13	14	8	22	26	22	.62	7	15	1	-1	22	

Brandon Cumpton

Year	Tm	Inn	TC	E	GFP	DM	Rng	SB	CCS	PCS/PPO	CS%	R/P	SB	Bnt	GFP/DME	Tot	Rnk
2013	Pit	31	3	0	0	0	-2	1	2	0	.67	-1	0	0	0	-1	
2014	Pit	70	12	0	2	0	+2	6	1	1	.25	1	0	0	0	1	
		100	15	0	2	0		7	3	1	.36	0	0	0	0	0	

Pitchers

John Danks

Year	Tm	Inn	TC	E	GFP	DM	Rng	SB	CCS	PCS/PPO	CS%	R/P	SB	Bnt	GFP/DME	Tot	Rnk
2007	CWS	139	23	1	2	0	+2	10	0	2	.09	2	0	0	0	2	42
2008	CWS	195	40	0	2	3	+2	23	2	6	.26	2	0	1	1	4	16
2009	CWS	200	42	2	2	4	+2	18	3	6	.28	2	1	0	-1	2	36
2010	CWS	213	40	0	7	4	+3	6	2	4	.50	2	2	1	-1	4	20
2011	CWS	170	34	0	2	1	-1	15	2	7	.35	-1	2	2	0	3	38
2012	CWS	54	19	3	3	0	+3	1	1	0	.50	2	0	1	0	3	-
2013	CWS	138	21	0	3	1	0	2	3	1	.60	0	1	0	0	1	65
2014	CWS	194	29	1	1	0	+2	12	2	2	.20	1	0	0	0	1	65
		1303	248	7	22	13	13	87	15	28	.30	10	6	5	-1	20	-

Yu Darvish

Year	Tm	Inn	TC	E	GFP	DM	Rng	SB	CCS	PCS/PPO	CS%	R/P	SB	Bnt	GFP/DME	Tot	Rnk
2012	Tex	191	33	0	0	3	+2	23	4	0	.15	1	-2	-1	0	-2	132
2013	Tex	210	23	0	1	4	0	18	7	0	.28	0	-1	1	0	0	86
2014	Tex	144	22	0	1	0	+3	10	0	0	.00	2	-1	0	1	2	38
		545	78	0	2	7	5	51	11	0	.18	3	-4	0	1	0	-

Wade Davis

Year	Tm	Inn	TC	E	GFP	DM	Rng	SB	CCS	PCS/PPO	CS%	R/P	SB	Bnt	GFP/DME	Tot	Rnk
2009	TB	36	5	0	0	0	0	4	1	0	.20	0	0			0	-
2010	TB	168	37	2	1	0	-3	13	4	2	.28	-3	0	1	0	-2	146
2011	TB	184	29	0	2	0	-1	2	3	2	.67	-1	2	1	0	2	57
2012	TB	70	11	1	1	1	+1	4	2	0	.33	1	0	0	0	1	-
2013	KC	135	26	1	1	3	-2	5	3	1	.38	-1	1	0	-1	-1	115
2014	KC	72	8	1	0	1	-1	4	1	0	.20	-1	0			-1	-
		666	116	5	5	5	-6	32	14	5	.33	-5	3	2	-1	-1	-

Jorge de la Rosa

Year	Tm	Inn	TC	E	GFP	DM	Rng	SB	CCS	PCS/PPO	CS%	R/P	SB	Bnt	GFP/DME	Tot	Rnk
2004	Mil	23	5	1	0	0	+1	2	1	0	.33	1	0			1	-
2005	Mil	42	8	1	1	1	-1	4	0	0	.00	-1	0	-1	0	-2	-
2006	2 tms	79	10	1	0	3	0	10	0	1	.09	0	-1	-1	0	-2	-
2007	KC	130	17	1	1	2	-1	6	2	2	.40	-1	1	-1	0	-1	113
2008	Col	130	19	0	0	0	-1	13	2	3	.28	-1	0	1	0	0	97
2009	Col	185	38	5	0	2	+1	16	1	2	.16	1	-1	-1	0	-1	110
2010	Col	122	22	0	2	2	+2	6	2	1	.33	2	0	1	1	4	20
2011	Col	59	12	0	0	0	0	10	2	0	.17	0	-1	0	0	-1	-
2012	Col	11	0	0	0	0	0	1	0	0	.00	0	0			0	-
2013	Col	168	38	1	2	1	+5	13	5	5	.43	4	2	0	-1	5	10
2014	Col	184	31	2	2	5	0	14	1	2	.18	0	-1	0	0	-1	111
		1132	200	12	8	16	6	95	16	16	.25	5	-1	-2	0	2	-

Rubby de la Rosa

Year	Tm	Inn	TC	E	GFP	DM	Rng	SB	CCS	PCS/PPO	CS%	R/P	SB	Bnt	GFP/DME	Tot	Rnk
2011	LAD	61	18	2	1	2	-1	9	4	0	.31	-1	-1	0	-1	-3	-
2012	LAD	1	0	0	0	0	0	1	0	0	.00		0			0	
2013	Bos	11	3	1	0	1	0	2	0	0	.00	0	0	0	0	0	-
2014	Bos	102	24	1	2	0	0	4	3	0	.43	0	0	1	0	1	71
		174	45	4	3	3	-1	16	7	0	.30	-1	-1	1	-1	-2	-

Samuel Deduno

Year	Tm	Inn	TC	E	GFP	DM	Rng	SB	CCS	PCS/PPO	CS%	R/P	SB	Bnt	GFP/DME	Tot	Rnk
2010	Col	3	0	0	0	0	0	0	0	0	-	0	0			0	-
2011	SD	3	2	0	0	0	0	2	0	0	.00	0	0	0	0		-
2012	Min	79	26	2	2	1	0	8	1	2	.11	0	0	-1	0	-1	114
2013	Min	108	35	1	0	4	-1	5	2	0	.29	-1	0	0	-1	-2	136
2014	2 tms	101	30	3	0	0	-3	13	1	0	.07	-2	-2	0	0	-4	163
		293	93	6	2	5	-4	28	4	2	.13	-3	-2	-1	-1	-7	-

Jacob deGrom

Year	Tm	Inn	TC	E	GFP	DM	Rng	SB	CCS	PCS/PPO	CS%	R/P	SB	Bnt	GFP/DME	Tot	Rnk
2014	NYM	140	26	0	2	3	-1	8	4	0	.33	-1	0	1	-1	-1	120

Randall Delgado

Year	Tm	Inn	TC	E	GFP	DM	Rng	SB	CCS	PCS/PPO	CS%	R/P	SB	Bnt	GFP/DME	Tot	Rnk
2011	Atl	35	10	0	1	0	0	2	1	0	.33	0	0	0	0	0	-
2012	Atl	93	22	0	2	0	-1	1	3	1	.80	-1	1	1	0	1	83
2013	Ari	116	17	1	1	3	0	1	1	0	.50	0	0	1	0	1	65
2014	Ari	78	16	1	2	1	-1	5	0	0	.00	-1	-1	0	0	-2	-
		321	65	2	6	4	-2	9	5	1	.40	-2	0	2	0	0	-

Odrisamer Despaigne

Year	Tm	Inn	TC	E	GFP	DM	Rng	SB	CCS	PCS/PPO	CS%	R/P	SB	Bnt	GFP/DME	Tot	Rnk
2014	SD	96	27	3	2	4	0	11	3	1	.27	0	-1	1	0	0	90

Ross Detwiler

Year	Tm	Inn	TC	E	GFP	DM	Rng	SB	CCS	PCS/PPO	CS%	R/P	SB	Bnt	GFP/DME	Tot	Rnk
2007	Was	1	0	0	0	0	0	0	0	0	-					0	-
2009	Was	76	18	0	1	0	+1	6	0	3	.33	1	1	0	0	2	-
2010	Was	30	8	0	2	0	-1	4	1	1	.33	-1	0	0	0	-1	-
2011	Was	66	9	1	0	1	-1	3	2	0	.40	-1	0	-1	0	-2	-
2012	Was	164	31	1	2	1	0	3	2	1	.40	0	1	0		1	75
2013	Was	71	11	0	3	2	-3	2	0	0	.00	-2	0	1	0	-1	-
2014	Was	63	14	0	2	2	-3	3	1	1	.40	-2	0	-1	0	-3	-
		471	91	2	10	6	-7	21	6	6	.34	-5	2	-1	0	-4	-

R.A. Dickey

Year	Tm	Inn	TC	E	GFP	DM	Rng	SB	CCS	PCS/PPO	CS%	R/P	SB	Bnt	GFP/DME	Tot	Rnk
2003	Tex	117	20	0	-	-	+3	7	2	1	.22	2	0	0	0	2	36
2004	Tex	104	31	2	1	1	-1	6	5	4	.45	-1	2	0	0	1	71
2005	Tex	30	10	0	0	0	+3	3	0	0	.00	2	0	0	0	2	-
2006	Tex	3	0	0	0	0	0	0	0	0	-		0			0	-
2008	Sea	112	29	0	1	0	+2	6	3	5	.54	2	2	0	0	4	16
2009	Min	64	15	1	0	2	-1	5	1	1	.17	-1	0	0	0	-1	-
2010	NYM	174	61	0	5	1	+8	9	2	1	.25	6	0	1	1	8	7
2011	NYM	209	67	2	3	1	+8	7	2	5	.30	6	2	1	1	10	1
2012	NYM	234	60	4	2	4	+4	4	2	5	.43	3	3	0	0	6	5
2013	Tor	225	53	2	5	2	+6	8	3	2	.27	5	1	1	0	7	2
2014	Tor	216	42	2	2	2	+5	3	1	2	.40	4	1	0	0	5	5
		1487	388	13	21	11	37	58	21	26	.33	28	11	3	2	44	-

Jake Diekman

Year	Tm	Inn	TC	E	GFP	DM	Rng	SB	CCS	PCS/PPO	CS%	R/P	SB	Bnt	GFP/DME	Tot	Rnk
2012	Phi	27	6	2	0	0	-1	5	0	1	.17	-1	0	0	0	-1	-
2013	Phi	38	7	2	1	2	0	2	0	0	.00	0	0	-1	-1	-2	-
2014	Phi	71	12	0	0	3	-2	5	2	1	.38	-2	0	0	-1	-3	-
		136	25	4	1	5	-3	12	2	2	.25	-3	0	-1	-2	-6	-

Sean Doolittle

Year	Tm	Inn	TC	E	GFP	DM	Rng	SB	CCS	PCS/PPO	CS%	R/P	SB	Bnt	GFP/DME	Tot	Rnk
2012	Oak	47	6	2	0	1	-2	5	0	1	.17	-1	0	0	0	-1	-
2013	Oak	69	7	0	0	1	-2	6	1	2	.33	-1	0	0	0	-1	-
2014	Oak	63	5	0	0	0	0	6	1	0	.14	0	-1	0	0	-1	-
		179	18	2	0	2	-4	17	2	3	.23	-2	-1	0	0	-3	-

Felix Doubront

Year	Tm	Inn	TC	E	GFP	DM	Rng	SB	CCS	PCS/PPO	CS%	R/P	SB	Bnt	GFP/DME	Tot	Rnk
2010	Bos	25	6	3	0	0	0	1	1	0	.50	0	0			0	-
2011	Bos	10	2	0	0	0	0	2	2	0	.60	0	1			1	-
2012	Bos	161	25	1	3	5	-2	19	2	1	.14	-1	-2	0	0	-3	151
2013	Bos	162	24	1	3	2	0	15	1	4	.25	0	0	0	0	0	86
2014	2 tms	80	15	1	1	0	-1	10	1	0	.09	0	-1	0	0	-1	111
		438	72	6	7	7	-3	47	8	5	.22	-1	-2	0	0	-3	-

Pitchers

Danny Duffy

		BASIC						HOLDING				RUNS SAVED					
Year	Tm	Inn	TC	E	GFP	DM	Rng	SB	CCS	PCS/PPO	CS%	R/P	SB	Bnt	GFP/DME	Tot	Rnk
2011	KC	105	17	0	1	1	-2	11	2	7	.45	-1	2	1	0	2	57
2012	KC	28	2	0	0	0	0	2	0	2	.33	0	1		0	1	1
2013	KC	24	3	0	0	0	0	2	1	0	.33	0	0		1	1	1
2014	KC	149	21	5	0	2	-2	5	2	6	.38	-1	3	-3		-1	120
		306	43	5	1	3	-4	20	6	15	.41	-2	6	-2	1	3	

Roenis Elias

		BASIC						HOLDING				RUNS SAVED					
Year	Tm	Inn	TC	E	GFP	DM	Rng	SB	CCS	PCS/PPO	CS%	R/P	SB	Bnt	GFP/DME	Tot	Rnk
2014	Sea	164	24	0	1	0	+1	3	1	1	.40	1	1	0	0	2	46

Nathan Eovaldi

		BASIC						HOLDING				RUNS SAVED					
Year	Tm	Inn	TC	E	GFP	DM	Rng	SB	CCS	PCS/PPO	CS%	R/P	SB	Bnt	GFP/DME	Tot	Rnk
2011	LAD	35	8	0	0	0	+2	2	0	2	.33	2	1		0	3	
2012	2 tms	119	23	0	1	3	0	4	2	1	.33	0	1	0	0	1	75
2013	Mia	106	30	2	2	1	-2	1	0	1	.00	-1	1	0	1	1	79
2014	Mia	200	52	1	1	1	0	1	2	2	.80	0	2	1	1	4	22
		460	113	3	4	5	0	8	4	6	.47	1	5	1	2	9	

Robbie Erlin

		BASIC						HOLDING				RUNS SAVED					
Year	Tm	Inn	TC	E	GFP	DM	Rng	SB	CCS	PCS/PPO	CS%	R/P	SB	Bnt	GFP/DME	Tot	Rnk
2013	SD	55	6	0	0	0	+1	6	1	1	.25	1	0		0	1	
2014	SD	61	8	0	1	0	-1	2	0	0	.00	-1	0		0	-1	
		116	14	0	1	0		8	1	1	.20	0	0		0	0	

Marco Estrada

		BASIC						HOLDING				RUNS SAVED					
Year	Tm	Inn	TC	E	GFP	DM	Rng	SB	CCS	PCS/PPO	CS%	R/P	SB	Bnt	GFP/DME	Tot	Rnk
2008	Was	13	3	0	0	1	0	0	1	0	1.00	0	0			0	
2009	Was	7	0	0	0	0	0	0	0	0	-	0	0			0	
2010	Mil	11	3	0	0	0	0	3	0	0	.00	0	-1			-1	
2011	Mil	93	16	0	0	0	-1	8	2	1	.20	-1	0	0		-1	123
2012	Mil	138	20	0	1	3	-1	15	5	2	.25	-1	0	0		-1	118
2013	Mil	128	15	1	4	0	-3	9	1	0	.10	-2	-1			-3	153
2014	Mil	151	27	0	3	1	+5	15	7	1	.32	3	-1	0	1	3	23
		541	84	1	8	5	0	50	16	4	.24	-1	-3	0	1	-3	

Jeurys Familia

		BASIC						HOLDING				RUNS SAVED					
Year	Tm	Inn	TC	E	GFP	DM	Rng	SB	CCS	PCS/PPO	CS%	R/P	SB	Bnt	GFP/DME	Tot	Rnk
2012	NYM	12	3	0	0	1	0	1	2	0	.67	0	0			0	
2013	NYM	11	1	0	0	0	-1	2	0	0	.00	0	0			0	
2014	NYM	77	18	3	1	5	0	7	0	0	.00	0	-1	-2		-3	
		100	22	3	1	6	-1	10	2	0	.17	0	-1	-2		-3	

Danny Farquhar

		BASIC						HOLDING				RUNS SAVED					
Year	Tm	Inn	TC	E	GFP	DM	Rng	SB	CCS	PCS/PPO	CS%	R/P	SB	Bnt	GFP/DME	Tot	Rnk
2011	Tor	2	0	0	0	0	0	0	0	0	-		0			0	
2013	Sea	56	12	0	3	0	+1	3	1	0	.25	0	0			0	
2014	Sea	71	17	0	2	1	0	1	3	1	.75	0	1	0		1	
		128	29	0	5	1	1	4	4	1	.50	0	1	0		1	

Scott Feldman

		BASIC						HOLDING				RUNS SAVED					
Year	Tm	Inn	TC	E	GFP	DM	Rng	SB	CCS	PCS/PPO	CS%	R/P	SB	Bnt	GFP/DME	Tot	Rnk
2005	Tex	9	2	0	0	0	+1	0	1	0	1.00	1	0		0	1	
2006	Tex	41	15	3	0	0	+1	2	1	0	.33	1	0	-1	0	1	
2007	Tex	39	8	0	1	0	+1	6	2	0	.25	1	0	0	0	1	
2008	Tex	151	36	2	1	2	+3	22	5	0	.19	2	-3	-1	0	-2	134
2009	Tex	190	46	4	3	3	+1	15	7	0	.32	1	-1	0	0	0	79
2010	Tex	141	39	0	2	2	+1	16	7	1	.33	1	0	0	0	1	59
2011	Tex	32	10	0	0	0	+2	3	4	0	.57	2	0		0	0	
2012	Tex	124	20	0	1	2	-3	20	3	0	.13	-2	-2	0	0	-4	164
2013	2 tms	182	43	3	4	1	+3	30	3	0	.09	3	-4	1	-1	-1	103
2014	Hou	180	36	0	4	4	-2	35	7	0	.17	-1	-5	0	-1	-7	174
		1089	255	12	12	14	8	149	40	1	.22	9	-15	-1	-2	-9	

Casey Fien

		BASIC						HOLDING				RUNS SAVED					
Year	Tm	Inn	TC	E	GFP	DM	Rng	SB	CCS	PCS/PPO	CS%	R/P	SB	Bnt	GFP/DME	Tot	Rnk
2009	Det	11	0	0	0	0	0	0	0	0	-		0			0	
2010	Det	3	2	0	0	0	0	0	0	0	-		0	0		0	
2012	Min	35	3	0	0	0	0	3	0	0	.00	0	0	0		0	
2013	Min	62	10	0	1	1	+1	5	1	0	.17	1	0	-1		0	
2014	Min	63	15	0	0	0	0	1	0	0	.00	0	0	0		0	
		174	30	0	1	1	1	9	1	0	.10	1	0	0	-1	0	

Mike Fiers

		BASIC						HOLDING				RUNS SAVED					
Year	Tm	Inn	TC	E	GFP	DM	Rng	SB	CCS	PCS/PPO	CS%	R/P	SB	Bnt	GFP/DME	Tot	Rnk
2011	Mil	2	2	0	0	0	0	1	0	1	.50	0	0			0	
2012	Mil	128	27	5	0	0	+3	10	3	0	.23	3	0	0	0	3	29
2013	Mil	22	7	0	2	0	0	3	0	0	.00	0	0	0	1	1	
2014	Mil	72	15	1	0	0	+2	5	2	1	.29	1	0	0	0	1	
		223	51	6	2	0	5	19	5	2	.24	4	0	0	1	5	

Doug Fister

		BASIC						HOLDING				RUNS SAVED					
Year	Tm	Inn	TC	E	GFP	DM	Rng	SB	CCS	PCS/PPO	CS%	R/P	SB	Bnt	GFP/DME	Tot	Rnk
2009	Sea	61	13	1	2	0	+2	0	1	0	1.00	2	0		1	3	
2010	Sea	171	37	1	1	1	-2	2	2	0	.60	-2	2	1	0	1	83
2011	2 tms	216	58	3	9	6	+5	4	2	0	.33	4	1	-1	0	4	15
2012	Det	162	36	2	0	0	+4	2	2	2	.67	3	2	-3	0	2	41
2013	Det	209	52	0	1	2	0	8	5	1	.38	0	1	0	0	1	65
2014	Was	164	37	1	1	2	+1	0	0	1	1.00	1	1	0	0	2	46
		982	233	8	14	11	10	16	12	6	.50	8	7	-3	1	13	

Yovani Gallardo

		BASIC						HOLDING				RUNS SAVED					
Year	Tm	Inn	TC	E	GFP	DM	Rng	SB	CCS	PCS/PPO	CS%	R/P	SB	Bnt	GFP/DME	Tot	Rnk
2007	Mil	110	26	1	1	0	+2	4	0	2	.20	2	1	0	0	3	27
2008	Mil	24	5	0	0	0	0	1	0	1	1.00	0	0	0	0	0	
2009	Mil	186	27	0	2	0	-1	19	2	0	.10	-1	-2	1	0	-2	138
2010	Mil	185	37	1	1	0	0	11	5	1	.35	0	0	0	0	0	88
2011	Mil	207	44	2	2	0	+3	14	6	1	.33	3	0	0	0	3	25
2012	Mil	204	41	4	3	0		9	3	1	.25	0	1	2	0	3	38
2013	Mil	181	37	1	1	1	0	15	0	1	.00	0	-1	0	0	-1	105
2014	Mil	192	40	0	3	2	-5	9	2	4	.31	-3	1	0	1	-1	137
		1289	257	6	14	6	-1	81	19	10	.23	1	0	3	1	5	

Matt Garza

		BASIC						HOLDING				RUNS SAVED					
Year	Tm	Inn	TC	E	GFP	DM	Rng	SB	CCS	PCS/PPO	CS%	R/P	SB	Bnt	GFP/DME	Tot	Rnk
2006	Min	50	6	0	0	0	-2	2	0	0	.00	-2	0		0	-2	
2007	Min	83	13	2	0	3	-2	1	2	1	.75	-2	1	-2	0	-3	153
2008	TB	185	27	2	0	3	-4	5	1	0	.17	-3	0	-1	0	-4	167
2009	TB	203	22	1	0	4	-2	3	4	0	.57	-2	1	1	0	0	102
2010	TB	205	24	1	2	2	-3	9	3	1	.31	-2	0	0	1	-1	124
2011	ChC	198	32	7	2	3	-3	10	4	1	.33	-2	1	-1	-1	-3	157
2012	ChC	104	19	3	0	2	-2	2	1	2	.60	-2	1	-4	0	-5	167
2013	2 tms	155	26	2	0	1	-4	5	3	0	.38	-4	0	0	0	-4	169
2014	Mil	163	29	3	3	5	-1	6	1	2	.33	0	1	-1	-1	-1	111
		1345	198	21	7	23	-22	43	19	7	.38	-19	5	-8	-1	-23	

Pitchers

Kevin Gausman

Year	Tm	Inn	TC	E	GFP	DM	Rng	SB	CCS	PCS/PPO	CS%	R/P	SB	Bnt	GFP/DME	Tot	Rnk
2013	Bal	48	12	0	1	1	-1	0	0	0	-	0	0	0	0	0	-
2014	Bal	113	16	0	1	1	-1	5	3	1	.38	-1	1	0	0	0	100
		161	28	0	2	2	-2	5	3	1	.38	-1	1	0	0	0	-

Dillon Gee

Year	Tm	Inn	TC	E	GFP	DM	Rng	SB	CCS	PCS/PPO	CS%	R/P	SB	Bnt	GFP/DME	Tot	Rnk
2010	NYM	33	5	0	0	0	+1					1	0	0	0	1	-
2011	NYM	161	30	1	4	3	-2	8	7	0	.47	-1	1	1	0	1	87
2012	NYM	110	27	2	1	1	+1	7	3	0	.30	1	0	0	0	1	68
2013	NYM	199	50	1	6	2	+2	12	4	3	.29	1	1	1	0	3	27
2014	NYM	137	38	0	3	2	+3	7	3	0	.30	2	0	0	0	2	38
		639	150	4	14	8	5	34	17	3	.35	4	2	2	0	8	-

Kyle Gibson

Year	Tm	Inn	TC	E	GFP	DM	Rng	SB	CCS	PCS/PPO	CS%	R/P	SB	Bnt	GFP/DME	Tot	Rnk
2013	Min	51	5	0	0	0	-2	4	2	0	.33	-2	0		0	-2	-
2014	Min	179	57	0	2	2	+2	7	4	2	.36	2	1	0	1	4	17
		230	62	0	2	2	0	11	6	2	.35	0	1	0	1	2	-

Jeanmar Gomez

Year	Tm	Inn	TC	E	GFP	DM	Rng	SB	CCS	PCS/PPO	CS%	R/P	SB	Bnt	GFP/DME	Tot	Rnk
2010	Cle	58	13	0	1	1	-3	7	3	2	.36	-2	0		0	-2	-
2011	Cle	58	17	1	3	1	+3	6	3	1	.40	2	0		0	2	-
2012	Cle	91	18	0	0	3	+3	5	2	1	.29	2	0	-1	0	1	61
2013	Pit	81	20	0	5	1	+2	7	2	0	.22	1	-1	1	0	1	54
2014	Pit	62	14	1	0	0	0	6	4	0	.40	0	0	0	0	0	-
		349	82	2	9	6	5	31	14	4	.34	3	-1	0	0	2	-

Gio Gonzalez

Year	Tm	Inn	TC	E	GFP	DM	Rng	SB	CCS	PCS/PPO	CS%	R/P	SB	Bnt	GFP/DME	Tot	Rnk
2008	Oak	34	6	0	1	0	0	0	0	2	1.00	0	1	1	1	3	-
2009	Oak	99	16	1	3	2	+1	4	0	2	.33	1	1	-1	-1	0	79
2010	Oak	201	41	1	4	2	0	12	5	2	.20	0	0	0	0	1	69
2011	Oak	202	34	1	5	1	-1	19	2	2	.17	-1	-1	0	0	-2	136
2012	Was	199	34	2	3	4	+1	12	1	0	.08	1	-1	-1	0	-1	112
2013	Was	196	23	1	5	3	-4	11	2	3	.31	-3	1	0	0	-2	145
2014	Was	159	26	1	3	3	-1	8	3	3	.43	-1	1	0	-1	-1	120
		1089	180	7	24	15	-4	66	9	14	.26	-3	2	0	-1	-2	-

Miguel Gonzalez

Year	Tm	Inn	TC	E	GFP	DM	Rng	SB	CCS	PCS/PPO	CS%	R/P	SB	Bnt	GFP/DME	Tot	Rnk
2012	Bal	105	10	0	1	0	-2	2	3	0	.60	-1	1	-1	0	-1	118
2013	Bal	171	31	1	3	3	-1	2	3	0	.60	0	1	1	0	2	46
2014	Bal	159	21	1	4	1	-2	12	2	1	.14	-2	-1	0	0	-3	160
		435	62	2	8	4	-5	16	8	1	.33	-3	1	0	0	-2	-

Sonny Gray

Year	Tm	Inn	TC	E	GFP	DM	Rng	SB	CCS	PCS/PPO	CS%	R/P	SB	Bnt	GFP/DME	Tot	Rnk
2013	Oak	64	20	1	2	0	+2	1	1	1	.50	1	1			1	-
2014	Oak	219	62	3	10	0	0	7	3	1	.30	0	1	1	1	3	34
		283	82	4	12	0	2	8	4	2	.33	1	2	1	1	5	-

Shane Greene

Year	Tm	Inn	TC	E	GFP	DM	Rng	SB	CCS	PCS/PPO	CS%	R/P	SB	Bnt	GFP/DME	Tot	Rnk
2014	NYY	79	13	4	1	0	-3	5	3	0	.38	-3	0		0	-3	161

Luke Gregerson

Year	Tm	Inn	TC	E	GFP	DM	Rng	SB	CCS	PCS/PPO	CS%	R/P	SB	Bnt	GFP/DME	Tot	Rnk
2009	SD	75	18	0	3	1	0	1	1	0	.50	0	0	0	0	0	-
2010	SD	78	22	0	1	0	+4	7	0	0	.00	3	-1	0	0	2	-
2011	SD	56	24	2	1	1	+2	5	0	0	.00	2	-1	0	0	1	-
2012	SD	72	24	1	4	2	+2	5	1	0	.17	2	0	-1	0	1	-
2013	SD	66	17	1	2	2	+2	10	0	0	.00	1	-2	1	0	0	-
2014	Oak	72	12	0	1	0	+2	10	0	0	.00	1	-2	0	0	-1	-
		419	117	4	12	6	12	38	2	0	.05	9	-6	0	0	3	-

Zack Greinke

Year	Tm	Inn	TC	E	GFP	DM	Rng	SB	CCS	PCS/PPO	CS%	R/P	SB	Bnt	GFP/DME	Tot	Rnk
2004	KC	145	28	0	1	2	+3	5	3	0	.38	2	0	0	0	2	36
2005	KC	183	44	1	3	2	+2	5	3	1	.38	2	1	1	0	4	22
2006	KC	6	1	0	0	0	0	0	0	0	-	0	0		0	0	-
2007	KC	122	18	0	1	1	0	7	3	1	.30	0	0	1	0	1	73
2008	KC	202	36	1	2	1	+4	2	3	3	.67	3	2	-1	0	4	13
2009	KC	229	47	1	7	1	+2	5	8	2	.64	2	3	2	1	8	2
2010	KC	220	49	1	5	0	+4	12	10	3	.48	3	2	3	1	9	6
2011	Mil	172	35	0	4	2	+2	8	5	1	.43	2	1	1	0	4	18
2012	2 tms	212	53	0	8	2	+4	9	6	5	.44	3	3	0	0	6	5
2013	LAD	178	47	0	5	0	+4	3	4	2	.57	3	2	1	1	7	3
2014	LAD	202	59	1	2	0	+5	6	2	0	.25	4	0	1	0	5	5
		1872	417	5	38	11	30	62	47	18	.46	24	14	9	3	50	-

Justin Grimm

Year	Tm	Inn	TC	E	GFP	DM	Rng	SB	CCS	PCS/PPO	CS%	R/P	SB	Bnt	GFP/DME	Tot	Rnk
2012	Tex	14	5	0	0	0	+1	2	2	0	.50	1	0	-1	0	0	-
2013	2 tms	98	25	2	0	1	0	4	3	2	.50	0	1	-1	0	0	86
2014	ChC	69	10	0	0	0	0	6	0	0	.00	0	-1	0	0	-1	-
		181	40	2	0	1	1	12	5	2	.33	1	0	-2	0	-1	-

Jeremy Guthrie

Year	Tm	Inn	TC	E	GFP	DM	Rng	SB	CCS	PCS/PPO	CS%	R/P	SB	Bnt	GFP/DME	Tot	Rnk
2004	Cle	12	2	0	0	0	0	1	0	0	.00	0	0		0	0	-
2005	Cle	6	3	0	0	1	0	0	0	0	-	0	-1		0	-1	-
2006	Cle	19	5	0	0	0	+2	2	1	0	.33	2	0		0	2	-
2007	Bal	175	38	1	0	3	+1	4	5	1	.56	1	2	0	0	3	34
2008	Bal	191	43	3	2	4	+3	13	4	0	.24	2	-1	-1	-1	1	52
2009	Bal	200	36	1	3	2	+3	9	2	4	.18	2	1	1	0	4	12
2010	Bal	209	48	4	2	2	+2	5	2	0	.29	1	0	0	0	1	59
2011	Bal	208	49	3	5	2	+4	3	5	1	.67	3	2	1	0	6	9
2012	2 tms	182	32	4	1	0	+2	8	4	2	.33	1	1	-1	0	1	68
2013	KC	212	39	0	5	3	-2	9	3	1	.25	-2	0	1	0	-1	126
2014	KC	203	42	6	1	5	-1	10	3	2	.29	-1	1	-1	0	-1	120
		1616	337	22	19	22	14	64	29	11	.33	9	6	1	-1	15	-

Juan Gutierrez

Year	Tm	Inn	TC	E	GFP	DM	Rng	SB	CCS	PCS/PPO	CS%	R/P	SB	Bnt	GFP/DME	Tot	Rnk
2007	Hou	21	2	0	0	1	0	1	1	0	.50	0	0	-1	0	-1	-
2009	Ari	71	7	0	0	0	-2	11	1	1	.08	-2	-1	0	0	-3	-
2010	Ari	57	14	1	0	2	0	8	0	0	.00	0	-1	0	-1	-2	-
2011	Ari	18	3	2	0	0	-2	2	0	0	.00	-2	0		0	-2	-
2013	2 tms	55	8	2	0	1	-7	9	2	0	.18	-6	-1	0	0	-7	-
2014	SF	64	9	0	0	1	-2	7	1	0	.13	-2	-1	0	0	-3	-
		286	43	5	0	5	-13	38	5	1	.12	-12	-4	-1	-1	-18	-

Jesse Hahn

Year	Tm	Inn	TC	E	GFP	DM	Rng	SB	CCS	PCS/PPO	CS%	R/P	SB	Bnt	GFP/DME	Tot	Rnk
2014	SD	73	15	0	0	2	+1	3	1	1	.25	1	0	0	-1	0	-

David Hale

Year	Tm	Inn	TC	E	GFP	DM	Rng	SB	CCS	PCS/PPO	CS%	R/P	SB	Bnt	GFP/DME	Tot	Rnk
2013	Atl	11	2	0	0	0	0	1	0	0	.00	0	0		0	0	-
2014	Atl	87	21	0	0	0	-1	13	3	0	.19	-1	-1	1	0	-1	120
		98	23	0	0	0	-1	14	3	0	.18	-1	-1	1	0	-1	-

Pitchers

Cole Hamels

Year	Tm	Inn	TC	E	GFP	DM	Rng	SB	CCS	PCS/PPO	CS%	R/P	SB	Bnt	GFP/DME	Tot	Rnk
		BASIC						HOLDING				RUNS SAVED					
2006	Phi	132	24	0	2	2	+4	9	2	0	.18	3	-1	1	0	3	22
2007	Phi	183	29	1	5	0	-1	14	0	2	.13	-1	-1	0	1	-1	113
2008	Phi	227	47	3	5	2	+3	15	0	2	.12	2	-1	1	0	2	36
2009	Phi	194	34	0	0	3	-2	18	6	5	.38	-2	1	0	-1	-2	147
2010	Phi	209	37	1	3	0	+3	10	5	1	.38	2	1	0	0	3	26
2011	Phi	216	34	1	4	2	+5	23	5	1	.21	4	-2	-1	0	1	60
2012	Phi	215	39	4	3	2	0	23	6	5	.32	0	0	-2	0	-2	133
2013	Phi	220	39	1	1	4	0	25	5	5	.29	0	-1	0	-1	-2	131
2014	Phi	205	32	0	2	2	+1	19	4	6	.32	0	1	1	0	2	55
		1801	315	11	25	17	13	156	33	27	.27	8	-3	0	-1	4	

Jason Hammel

Year	Tm	Inn	TC	E	GFP	DM	Rng	SB	CCS	PCS/PPO	CS%	R/P	SB	Bnt	GFP/DME	Tot	Rnk
		BASIC						HOLDING				RUNS SAVED					
2006	TB	44	9	0	0	0	0	1	2	1	.67	0	1		0	1	-
2007	TB	85	13	1	1	1	-1	16	3	0	.16	-1	-2		0	-3	149
2008	TB	78	12	0	1	0	0	11	1	0	.08	0	-1	0	0	-1	-
2009	Col	177	31	0	2	1	0	18	2	1	.10	-2	0	0	0	-2	135
2010	Col	178	35	1	3	2	-1	18	4	2	.22	-1	-1	0	0	-2	139
2011	Col	170	39	1	1	1	0	16	5	2	.27	0	0	-1	0	-1	121
2012	Bal	118	28	1	1	2	+4	6	3	1	.40	3	1	0	0	4	16
2013	Bal	139	11	0	0	0	-4	8	3	0	.27	-3	0	0	0	-3	161
2014	2 tms	176	31	2	1	1	0	12	3	2	.20	0	0	-1	0	-1	111
		1165	209	6	10	8	-2	106	26	9	.21	-2	-4	-2	0	-8	

Brad Hand

Year	Tm	Inn	TC	E	GFP	DM	Rng	SB	CCS	PCS/PPO	CS%	R/P	SB	Bnt	GFP/DME	Tot	Rnk
		BASIC						HOLDING				RUNS SAVED					
2011	Fla	60	13	1	0	0	+2	3	1	3	.57	2	1	0	0	3	-
2012	Mia	4	0	0	0	0	-1	2	0	0	.00	-1	0			-1	-
2013	Mia	21	3	0	0	0	0	1	0	0	.00	0	0		0	0	-
2014	Mia	111	32	0	1	2	+3	6	2	0	.25	3	0	1	0	4	12
		195	48	1	1	2	4	12	3	3	.33	4	1	1	0	6	-

J.A. Happ

Year	Tm	Inn	TC	E	GFP	DM	Rng	SB	CCS	PCS/PPO	CS%	R/P	SB	Bnt	GFP/DME	Tot	Rnk
		BASIC						HOLDING				RUNS SAVED					
2007	Phi	4	0	0	0	0	0	0	0	0	-		0			0	-
2008	Phi	32	5	0	0	0	0	1	0	0	.00	0	0	0	0	0	-
2009	Phi	166	26	0	1	2	-1	4	3	1	.50	-1	1	1	0	1	74
2010	2 tms	87	13	0	2	2	0	1	1	2	.75	0	1	0	0	1	69
2011	Hou	156	17	0	1	0	0	11	2	3	.31	0	1	0	0	1	74
2012	2 tms	145	29	0	3	2	-2	10	1	0	.09	-2	0	0	0	-2	141
2013	Tor	93	11	0	1	2	+1	9	0	0	.00	0	-1	0	0	-1	105
2014	Tor	158	20	1	0	1	+6	7	2	1	.30	4	0	0	0	4	11
		840	121	1	8	9	4	43	9	7	.27	1	2	1	0	4	

Aaron Harang

Year	Tm	Inn	TC	E	GFP	DM	Rng	SB	CCS	PCS/PPO	CS%	R/P	SB	Bnt	GFP/DME	Tot	Rnk
		BASIC						HOLDING				RUNS SAVED					
2003	2 tms	76	9	0	-	-	+1	8	2	0	.20	1	-1	0	0	0	-
2004	Cin	161	31	0	2	4	0	7	5	0	.42	0	0	1	0	1	66
2005	Cin	212	30	0	1	5	+1	9	9	0	.50	1	1	-1	-1	0	82
2006	Cin	234	46	2	0	0	-4	16	7	1	.33	-3	0	-1	0	-4	169
2007	Cin	232	31	0	1	4	0	13	8	0	.38	0	0	0	0	0	91
2008	Cin	184	28	1	2	2	-4	17	4	0	.19	-3	-2	0	0	-5	173
2009	Cin	162	20	2	2	2	0	13	3	2	.28	0	0	1	0	1	69
2010	Cin	112	20	1	1	2	-2	3	4	1	.57	-2	1	0	0	-1	124
2011	SD	171	29	4	2	3	+1	24	9	2	.29	1	-1	-2	0	-2	133
2012	LAD	180	43	2	1	2	-1	8	4	0	.33	0	0	0	0	0	93
2013	2 tms	143	25	1	2	1	0	8	1	1	.20	0	-1		0	-1	105
2014	Atl	204	35	0	0	1	-1	19	5	2	.21	-1	0	0	0	-1	120
		2071	347	13	14	26	-9	145	61	9	.31	-6	-3	-2	-1	-12	

Dan Haren

Year	Tm	Inn	TC	E	GFP	DM	Rng	SB	CCS	PCS/PPO	CS%	R/P	SB	Bnt	GFP/DME	Tot	Rnk
		BASIC						HOLDING				RUNS SAVED					
2003	StL	73	8	0	-	-	-1	2	1	0	.33	-1	0	0		-1	
2004	StL	46	10	1	0	0	0	3	0	0	.00	0	0	0	0	0	
2005	Oak	217	42	2	2	5	-2	19	4	1	.21	-2	-2	0	0	-4	164
2006	Oak	223	44	1	1	1	+3	10	4	1	.29	2	0	0	0	2	38
2007	Oak	223	30	1	1	1	-5	20	6	0	.23	-4	-1	1	0	-4	167
2008	Ari	216	29	0	4	1	-2	9	2	0	.18	-2	0	2	0	0	103
2009	Ari	229	43	0	1	3	+4	18	6	0	.25	3	-1	1	0	3	26
2010	2 tms	235	37	1	2	2	-4	19	8	2	.32	-3	0	1	0	-2	146
2011	LAA	238	48	0	2	1	+5	21	2	3	.19	4	-1	0	0	3	24
2012	LAA	177	33	3	0	0	+3	9	2	1	.18	2	0	-1	0	1	61
2013	Was	170	23	0	1	1	-1	11	1	0	.08	-1	-1	0	0	-2	136
2014	LAD	186	38	1	0	1	+2	15	5	0	.25	1	-1	0	0	0	85
		2232	385	10	14	16	2	156	41	8	.23	-1	-7	4	0	-4	

Jeremy Hellickson

Year	Tm	Inn	TC	E	GFP	DM	Rng	SB	CCS	PCS/PPO	CS%	R/P	SB	Bnt	GFP/DME	Tot	Rnk
		BASIC						HOLDING				RUNS SAVED					
2010	TB	36	4	0	0	0	-1	2	0	0	.00	0	0	0	0	0	-
2011	TB	189	31	0	1	2	+1	10	0	3	.09	0	0	0	0	0	99
2012	TB	177	40	2	2	2	0	7	3	1	.30	0	1	1	0	2	53
2013	TB	174	23	0	3	1	-1	6	4	1	.40	-1	0	1	1	1	79
2014	TB	64	11	1	2	2	+1	5	1	0	.17	0	0	-1	0	-1	-
		640	109	3	6	7	0	30	8	5	.23	-1	2	0	1	2	-

Kyle Hendricks

Year	Tm	Inn	TC	E	GFP	DM	Rng	SB	CCS	PCS/PPO	CS%	R/P	SB	Bnt	GFP/DME	Tot	Rnk
		BASIC						HOLDING				RUNS SAVED					
2014	ChC	80	20	0	0	1	+1	4	3	0	.43	1	0	0	0	1	65

Felix Hernandez

Year	Tm	Inn	TC	E	GFP	DM	Rng	SB	CCS	PCS/PPO	CS%	R/P	SB	Bnt	GFP/DME	Tot	Rnk
		BASIC						HOLDING				RUNS SAVED					
2005	Sea	84	27	0	0	0	+2	3	1	2	.40	2	1	0	0	3	27
2006	Sea	191	41	0	0	1	+6	14	4	1	.26	5	0	0	0	5	9
2007	Sea	190	38	1	1	3	-1	10	5	1	.33	-1	1	0	0	0	94
2008	Sea	201	46	1	10	3	+4	19	3	2	.17	3	-1	-1	0	1	51
2009	Sea	239	54	1	4	3	+2	20	7	1	.29	2	-1	0	0	1	57
2010	Sea	250	54	2	2	7	+1	15	5	0	.25	1	0	0	0	1	59
2011	Sea	234	57	2	3	3	-2	31	8	2	.21	-2	-2	-1	0	-5	167
2012	Sea	232	37	2	3	2	-1	17	6	2	.29	0	0	0	0	0	93
2013	Sea	204	24	2	3	4	-3	17	5	0	.23	-2	-1	0	0	-3	153
2014	Sea	236	37	1	2	1	+1	20	4	1	.20	0	-2	0	0	-2	141
		2060	415	12	28	27	9	166	48	12	.25	8	-5	-2	0	-	

Roberto Hernandez

Year	Tm	Inn	TC	E	GFP	DM	Rng	SB	CCS	PCS/PPO	CS%	R/P	SB	Bnt	GFP/DME	Tot	Rnk
		BASIC						HOLDING				RUNS SAVED					
2006	Cle	75	24	0	0	1	+2	10	1	1	.17	2	-1	0	0	1	-
2007	Cle	215	64	2	4	0	0	13	5	2	.28	2	0	1	0	2	57
2008	Cle	121	32	2	2	3	+2	6	1	0	.14	2	0	0	-1	1	52
2009	Cle	125	29	0	3	3	+1	8	4	0	.33	1	0	0	-1	0	79
2010	Cle	210	63	2	3	5	+8	33	6	0	.15	6	-4	0	0	2	35
2011	Cle	189	38	0	1	4	+4	15	6	0	.29	3	-1	0	0	2	39
2012	Cle	14	2	0	0	1	0	1	1	0	.50	0	0	0	0	0	-
2013	TB	151	23	0	0	2	0	18	5	1	.22	0	-1	0	0	-1	105
2014	2 tms	165	34	0	1	2	+1	23	2	0	.15	2	-2	0	0	0	81
		1264	309	6	11	21	18	127	31	6	.21	16	-8	1	-2	7	-

Kelvin Herrera

Year	Tm	Inn	TC	E	GFP	DM	Rng	SB	CCS	PCS/PPO	CS%	R/P	SB	Bnt	GFP/DME	Tot	Rnk
		BASIC						HOLDING				RUNS SAVED					
2011	KC	2	2	0	0	0	0	0	0	0	-	0	0	0	0	0	-
2012	KC	84	17	0	0	2	-1	12	4	0	.25	-1	-1	1	0	-1	118
2013	KC	58	9	1	1	0	0	8	2	0	.20	0	-1		0	-1	-
2014	KC	70	13	0	2	0	0	6	2	0	.25	0	0	0	0	0	-
		214	41	1	3	2	-1	26	8	0	.24	-1	-2	1	0	-2	-

Pitchers

Greg Holland

Year	Tm	Inn	TC	E	GFP	DM	Rng	SB	CCS	PCS/PPO	CS%	R/P	SB	Bnt	GFP/DME	Tot	Rnk
		BASIC						HOLDING				RUNS SAVED					
2010	KC	19	6	0	1	0	0	1	0	0	.00	0	0			0	0
2011	KC	60	4	0	0	0	-1	1	0	0	.00	-1	0	0	0	-1	
2012	KC	67	5	0	1	0	-4	2	2	0	.50	-3	0	1	0	-2	
2013	KC	67	11	0	0	0	0	3	0	0	.00	0	0	0	0	0	
2014	KC	62	9	0	0	0	-3	3	2	0	.40	-2	0	0	1	-1	
		275	35	0	2	0	-8	10	4	0	.29	-6	0	1	1	-4	

J.J. Hoover

Year	Tm	Inn	TC	E	GFP	DM	Rng	SB	CCS	PCS/PPO	CS%	R/P	SB	Bnt	GFP/DME	Tot	Rnk
		BASIC						HOLDING				RUNS SAVED					
2012	Cin	31	1	0	0	0	-1	1	0	0	.00	-1	0		0	-1	
2013	Cin	66	12	1	0	0	-1	1	1	0	.50	-1	0	0	0	-1	
2014	Cin	63	7	0	0	1	-2	0	1	0	1.00	-2	0	0	0	-2	
		159	20	1	0	1	-4	2	2	0	.50	-4	0	0	0	-4	

T.J. House

Year	Tm	Inn	TC	E	GFP	DM	Rng	SB	CCS	PCS/PPO	CS%	R/P	SB	Bnt	GFP/DME	Tot	Rnk
		BASIC						HOLDING				RUNS SAVED					
2014	Cle	102	20	2	1	2	-2	6	0	2	.25	-2	0	0	0	-2	152

Tim Hudson

Year	Tm	Inn	TC	E	GFP	DM	Rng	SB	CCS	PCS/PPO	CS%	R/P	SB	Bnt	GFP/DME	Tot	Rnk
		BASIC						HOLDING				RUNS SAVED					
2003	Oak	240	74	2	-	-	+3	7	6	2	.46	2	2	0		4	15
2004	Oak	189	49	1	3	4	-3	8	4	1	.33	-2	1	-1	0	-2	131
2005	Atl	192	64	1	4	4	+1	10	6	2	.41	1	1	1	0	3	33
2006	Atl	218	47	0	1	4	-1	23	3	2	.15	-1	-2	0	1	-2	136
2007	Atl	224	70	0	3	3	+5	9	4	2	.31	4	1	1	0	6	3
2008	Atl	142	30	1	0	3	+4	6	4	0	.40	3	0	0	0	3	24
2009	Atl	42	7	0	1	1	-1	1	4	0	.80	-1	1		0	0	-
2010	Atl	229	77	3	5	0	+3	11	11	3	.50	2	2	1	1	6	10
2011	Atl	215	46	2	1	2	-1	16	5	0	.24	-1	-1	0	0	-2	136
2012	Atl	179	34	1	0	0	-4	2	5	1	.71	-3	2	0	1	-1	131
2013	Atl	131	22	1	1	1	-3	7	1	0	.13	-2	-1	0	0	-3	153
2014	SF	189	36	2	2	2	-1	15	2	1	.17	-1	-1	0	0	-2	146
		2191	556	14	21	24	2	115	55	14	.34	1	5	2	2	10	

Jared Hughes

Year	Tm	Inn	TC	E	GFP	DM	Rng	SB	CCS	PCS/PPO	CS%	R/P	SB	Bnt	GFP/DME	Tot	Rnk
		BASIC						HOLDING				RUNS SAVED					
2011	Pit	11	4	0	0	0	+1	2	0	0	.00	1	0	0	0	1	-
2012	Pit	76	24	1	0	1	+3	17	0	0	.00	2	-3	0	0	-1	-
2013	Pit	32	10	2	1	0	-1	4	1	1	.33	0	0	0	0	0	-
2014	Pit	64	24	1	1	1	+3	4	4	3	.60	2	2	-1	0	3	-
		183	62	4	2	2	6	27	5	4	.23	5	-1	-1	0	3	

Phil Hughes

Year	Tm	Inn	TC	E	GFP	DM	Rng	SB	CCS	PCS/PPO	CS%	R/P	SB	Bnt	GFP/DME	Tot	Rnk
		BASIC						HOLDING				RUNS SAVED					
2007	NYY	73	14	1	0	0	+1	9	3	0	.25	1	-1	0	0	0	-
2008	NYY	34	5	0	1	0	+1	8	0	0	.00	1	-1	0	1	1	-
2009	NYY	86	9	0	0	0	0	5	2	0	.29	0	0	0	0	0	86
2010	NYY	176	20	0	0	0	-1	10	5	0	.33	-1	0	0	0	-1	116
2011	NYY	75	8	0	0	0	-1	7	0	0	.00	-1	-1	0	0	-1	-
2012	NYY	191	22	1	0	2	-4	4	3	0	.43	-3	1	0	0	-2	145
2013	NYY	146	13	0	0	3	-2	8	3	0	.27	-1	0	0	-1	-2	136
2014	Min	210	19	1	0	3	-8	14	1	0	.07	-6	-1	0	-1	-8	175
		990	110	3	1	8	-14	65	17	0	.21	-10	-3	0	-1	-13	

Tommy Hunter

Year	Tm	Inn	TC	E	GFP	DM	Rng	SB	CCS	PCS/PPO	CS%	R/P	SB	Bnt	GFP/DME	Tot	Rnk
		BASIC						HOLDING				RUNS SAVED					
2008	Tex	11	2	1	0	1	-1	1	0	1	.50	-1	0		0	-1	-
2009	Tex	112	18	1	2	0	-2	9	2	1	.25	-2	0	0	1	-1	129
2010	Tex	128	26	1	3	0	-1	5	1	1	.29	-1	0	0	0	-1	116
2011	2 tms	85	19	1	1	0	+1	6	3	1	.40	0	1	0	0	1	74
2012	Bal	134	37	0	5	0	+2	1	4	0	.80	2	1	0	1	4	22
2013	Bal	86	14	0	2	1	-1	3	4	0	.57	-1	1	0	0	0	95
2014	Bal	61	14	2	1	1	+1	4	1	0	.20	1	0	0	0	0	-
		616	130	7	14	3	-1	29	15	4	.40	-2	3	0	2	2	

Drew Hutchison

Year	Tm	Inn	TC	E	GFP	DM	Rng	SB	CCS	PCS/PPO	CS%	R/P	SB	Bnt	GFP/DME	Tot	Rnk
		BASIC						HOLDING				RUNS SAVED					
2012	Tor	59	9	0	2	0	0	5	1	0	.17	0	0	1	0	1	-
2014	Tor	185	21	1	1	2	-3	22	3	0	.12	-2	-3	1	0	-4	163
		243	30	1	3	2	-3	27	4	0	.13	-2	-3	2	0	-3	

Hisashi Iwakuma

Year	Tm	Inn	TC	E	GFP	DM	Rng	SB	CCS	PCS/PPO	CS%	R/P	SB	Bnt	GFP/DME	Tot	Rnk
		BASIC						HOLDING				RUNS SAVED					
2012	Sea	125	18	1	0	2	0	10	7	0	.41	0	0	0	0	0	93
2013	Sea	220	40	1	3	2	+6	5	2	0	.29	5	0	0	0	5	8
2014	Sea	179	42	1	1	1	0	0	8	0	1.00	0	2	0	0	2	55
		524	100	3	4	5	6	15	17	0	.53	5	2	0	0	7	

Edwin Jackson

Year	Tm	Inn	TC	E	GFP	DM	Rng	SB	CCS	PCS/PPO	CS%	R/P	SB	Bnt	GFP/DME	Tot	Rnk
		BASIC						HOLDING				RUNS SAVED					
2003	LA	22	3	0	-	-	+1	1	0	0	.00	1	0			1	-
2004	LA	25	8	0	0	0	+1	2	1	0	1.00	1	0		0	1	-
2005	LAD	29	7	0	0	0	0	2	1	0	.33	0	0		0	0	-
2006	TB	36	6	0	0	1	0	3	0	0	.00	0	0	0	0	0	-
2007	TB	161	27	2	0	6	-6	17	4	1	.23	-5	-1	0	-1	-7	172
2008	TB	183	31	1	0	1	-2	12	6	1	.33	-2	-1	0	0	-1	121
2009	Det	214	31	4	2	1	-3	23	9	0	.28	-2	-2	0	1	-3	158
2010	2 tms	209	35	5	2	1	-2	19	6	0	.24	-2	-1	-1	0	-4	160
2011	2 tms	200	43	3	1	3	+1	22	1	0	.04	1	-2	-1	0	-2	133
2012	Was	190	40	3	1	2	-1	7	3	2	.42	-1	1	0	0	0	105
2013	ChC	175	44	4	3	3	0	18	2	1	.10	-1	-1	-2	0	-3	147
2014	ChC	141	33	1	0	0	+4	14	5	4	.26	3	1	0	0	4	12
		1584	305	23	9	19	-7	140	37	12	.22	-6	-4	-4	0	-14	

Kenley Jansen

Year	Tm	Inn	TC	E	GFP	DM	Rng	SB	CCS	PCS/PPO	CS%	R/P	SB	Bnt	GFP/DME	Tot	Rnk
		BASIC						HOLDING				RUNS SAVED					
2010	LAD	27	2	0	0	0	-1	5	0	0	.00	0	-1	0	0	-1	-
2011	LAD	54	5	0	0	0	+1	7	0	0	.00	1	-1	1	0	1	-
2012	LAD	65	7	1	0	1	+2	5	0	0	.00	1	-1		0	0	-
2013	LAD	77	4	0	0	0	-2	7	2	0	.22	-1	-1		0	-2	136
2014	LAD	65	9	1	0	1	0	6	2	0	.25	0	0	-1	0	-1	-
		287	27	2	0	2	0	30	4	0	.12	1	-4	0	0	-3	

Kevin Jepsen

Year	Tm	Inn	TC	E	GFP	DM	Rng	SB	CCS	PCS/PPO	CS%	R/P	SB	Bnt	GFP/DME	Tot	Rnk
		BASIC						HOLDING				RUNS SAVED					
2008	LAA	8	4	0	0	0	+1	1	0	0	.00	1	0		0	1	-
2009	LAA	55	11	0	0	1	0	3	0	0	.00	0	0		0	0	-
2010	LAA	59	11	0	0	0	-2	5	2	0	.29	-2	0	1	0	-1	-
2011	LAA	13	3	0	0	0	-1	1	0	0	.00	-1	0		0	-1	-
2012	LAA	45	6	1	0	0	0	4	1	0	.20	0	0	-1	0	-1	-
2013	LAA	36	2	0	0	2	-1	5	0	0	.00	-1	-1		0	-2	-
2014	LAA	65	15	1	0	2	+4	4	1	0	.20	3	0	0	0	3	-
		280	52	2	0	5	1	23	4	0	.15	0	-1	0	0	-1	

Ubaldo Jimenez

Year	Tm	Inn	TC	E	GFP	DM	Rng	SB	CCS	PCS/PPO	CS%	R/P	SB	Bnt	GFP/DME	Tot	Rnk
		BASIC						HOLDING				RUNS SAVED					
2006	Col	8	2	0	0	0	0	2	1	0	.33	0	0		0	0	-
2007	Col	82	25	3	1	0	+1	16	0	0	.00	1	-3	0	0	-2	133
2008	Col	199	52	4	2	0	+1	19	2	3	.14	1	-1	-1	0	-1	110
2009	Col	218	61	2	4	3	+1	15	4	2	.29	1	0	2	0	3	31
2010	Col	222	37	1	1	0	+1	12	13	2	.52	1	2	0	0	3	30
2011	2 tms	188	44	2	0	2	+4	24	6	2	.20	3	-2	-1	0	0	91
2012	Cle	177	29	1	1	0	-1	32	5	0	.14	0	-4	1	0	-3	149
2013	Cle	183	21	2	4	5	-2	16	6	0	.27	-1	-1	-1	-1	-4	164
2014	Bal	125	20	0	1	2	+2	19	6	0	.24	2	-2	-1	1	0	81
		1401	291	15	14	12	7	155	43	9	.23	8	-11	-1		-4	

Tommy Kahnle

Year	Tm	Inn	TC	E	GFP	DM	Rng	SB	CCS	PCS/PPO	CS%	R/P	SB	Bnt	GFP/DME	Tot	Rnk
		BASIC						HOLDING				RUNS SAVED					
2014	Col	69	15	2	0	2	-1	10	1	0	.09	-1	-1	0	0	-2	

Pitchers

Scott Kazmir

		BASIC						HOLDING				RUNS SAVED					
Year	Tm	Inn	TC	E	GFP	DM	Rng	SB	CCS	PCS/PPO	CS%	R/P	SB	Bnt	GFP/DME	Tot	Rnk
2004	TB	33	6	1	0	0	0	5	2	2	.38	0	0			0	-
2005	TB	186	27	3	3	2	-2	7	8	2	.56	-2	2	1	0	1	75
2006	TB	145	17	1	1	4	-2	15	1	5	.17	-2	0	1	0	-1	118
2007	TB	207	28	3	0	4	-6	12	6	3	.40	-5	2	0	0	-3	162
2008	TB	152	16	2	0	2	-2	7	1	4	.30	-2	1	0	0	-1	121
2009	2 tms	147	18	0	1	3	-2	4	1	2	.43	-2	1	0	0	-1	129
2010	LAA	150	33	2	5	2	+1	12	2	4	.29	1	1	1	0	3	30
2011	LAA	2	1	0	0	0	+1	2	0	0	.00	1	0		0	1	-
2013	Cle	158	25	3	2	1	+1	6	2	0	.25	0	0	0	1	1	65
2014	Oak	190	23	3	0	1	+1	18	1	1	.10	1	-2	0	0	-1	109
		1370	194	18	12	19	-10	88	24	23	.30	-10	5	3	1	-1	-

Joe Kelly

		BASIC						HOLDING				RUNS SAVED					
Year	Tm	Inn	TC	E	GFP	DM	Rng	SB	CCS	PCS/PPO	CS%	R/P	SB	Bnt	GFP/DME	Tot	Rnk
2012	StL	107	32	2	1	2	+2	8	5	2	.38	1	1	0	0	2	47
2013	StL	124	32	3	1	3	+1	2	1	0	.33	0	0	-1	0	-1	105
2014	2 tms	96	11	0	0	1	-2	7	1	0	.13	-2	0		0	-2	152
		327	75	5	2	6	1	17	7	2	.29	-1	1	-1	0	-1	-

Kyle Kendrick

		BASIC						HOLDING				RUNS SAVED					
Year	Tm	Inn	TC	E	GFP	DM	Rng	SB	CCS	PCS/PPO	CS%	R/P	SB	Bnt	GFP/DME	Tot	Rnk
2007	Phi	121	27	0	2	2	+1	8	2	0	.20	1	0	0	0	1	64
2008	Phi	156	43	1	5	1	+7	15	4	1	.25	5	-1	-1	1	4	12
2009	Phi	26	5	1	0	0	0	0	0	0	-	0	0		0	0	-
2010	Phi	181	45	3	3	2	+5	4	4	1	.50	4	1	-1	0	4	16
2011	Phi	115	25	1	1	6	0	3	3	0	.50	0	1	-1	0	0	99
2012	Phi	159	34	1	1	2	+2	8	3	0	.27	2	0	0	0	2	42
2013	Phi	182	58	2	11	3	+4	10	2	0	.17	3	-1	2	0	4	14
2014	Phi	199	49	2	3	1	+4	5	6	1	.58	3	2	-1	1	5	8
		1138	286	11	26	17	23	53	24	3	.33	18	2	-2	2	20	-

Ian Kennedy

		BASIC						HOLDING				RUNS SAVED					
Year	Tm	Inn	TC	E	GFP	DM	Rng	SB	CCS	PCS/PPO	CS%	R/P	SB	Bnt	GFP/DME	Tot	Rnk
2007	NYY	19	2	0	1	0	+1	1	1	0	.50	1	0		0	1	-
2008	NYY	40	7	0	1	0	+1	5	2	1	.29	1	0	0	0	1	-
2009	NYY	1	0	0	0	0	0	0	0	0	-	0			0	0	-
2010	Ari	194	38	1	0	0	+2	12	5	1	.33	2	0	1	0	3	26
2011	Ari	222	36	0	1	2	+1	6	0	1	1.00	1	0	1	0	2	44
2012	Ari	208	35	4	2	3	-1	4	3	0	.43	-1	1	0	0	0	105
2013	2 tms	181	27	0	2	3	-3	2	4	0	.67	-2	2	1	-1	0	99
2014	SD	201	30	0	1	2	-1	15	7	2	.35	-1	0	1	0	0	100
		1066	175	5	8	10	0	45	22	5	.35	1	3	4	-1	7	-

Clayton Kershaw

		BASIC						HOLDING				RUNS SAVED					
Year	Tm	Inn	TC	E	GFP	DM	Rng	SB	CCS	PCS/PPO	CS%	R/P	SB	Bnt	GFP/DME	Tot	Rnk
2008	LAD	108	20	1	5	2	0	5	0	2	.29	0	0	1	0	1	69
2009	LAD	171	27	0	2	3	-2	6	3	7	.54	-2	3	0	0	1	77
2010	LAD	204	36	1	0	2	0	8	1	8	.50	0	3	1	-1	3	34
2011	LAD	233	47	0	5	6	+2	14	2	9	.39	1	3	1	0	5	14
2012	LAD	228	51	0	3	2	+2	8	3	11	.60	1	5	0	0	6	9
2013	LAD	236	35	1	4	1	0	5	1	7	.44	0	3	1	0	4	19
2014	LAD	198	41	2	2	1	+8	5	2	4	.44	6	2	-1	0	7	2
		1378	257	5	21	17	10	51	12	48	.47	6	19	3	-1	27	-

Dallas Keuchel

		BASIC						HOLDING				RUNS SAVED					
Year	Tm	Inn	TC	E	GFP	DM	Rng	SB	CCS	PCS/PPO	CS%	R/P	SB	Bnt	GFP/DME	Tot	Rnk
2012	Hou	85	29	2	1	0	+4	9	1	1	.18	3	-1	-2	0	0	87
2013	Hou	154	31	0	3	0	+3	7	4	0	.36	2	0	0	1	3	25
2014	Hou	200	66	1	3	2	+10	1	2	1	.75	7	1	1	1	10	1
		439	126	3	7	2	17	17	7	2	.35	12	0	-1	2	13	-

Craig Kimbrel

		BASIC						HOLDING				RUNS SAVED					
Year	Tm	Inn	TC	E	GFP	DM	Rng	SB	CCS	PCS/PPO	CS%	R/P	SB	Bnt	GFP/DME	Tot	Rnk
2010	Atl	21	1	1	0	1	-1	3	0	0	.00	0	0		0	0	-
2011	Atl	77	11	0	1	0	0	1	2	1	.75	0	1		0	1	74
2012	Atl	63	5	0	1	0	0	8	1	0	.11	0	-1	0	0	-1	-
2013	Atl	67	7	0	0	2	-1	3	2	0	.40	-1	0		0	-1	-
2014	Atl	62	10	0	0	0	0	5	1	0	.17	0	0	0	0	0	-
		289	34	1	2	3	-2	20	6	1	.26	-1	0	0	0	-1	-

Corey Kluber

		BASIC						HOLDING				RUNS SAVED					
Year	Tm	Inn	TC	E	GFP	DM	Rng	SB	CCS	PCS/PPO	CS%	R/P	SB	Bnt	GFP/DME	Tot	Rnk
2011	Cle	4	0	0	0	0	0	0	0	0	-		0			0	-
2012	Cle	63	14	0	0	1	0	15	3	0	.17	0	-2	0	0	-2	-
2013	Cle	147	31	1	0	2	0	6	3	0	.33	0	0	1	0	1	65
2014	Cle	236	31	0	0	1	-2	8	9	0	.53	-2	2	0	0	0	106
		450	76	1	0	4	-2	29	15	0	.34	-2	0	1	0	-1	-

Tom Koehler

		BASIC						HOLDING				RUNS SAVED					
Year	Tm	Inn	TC	E	GFP	DM	Rng	SB	CCS	PCS/PPO	CS%	R/P	SB	Bnt	GFP/DME	Tot	Rnk
2012	Mia	13	1	0	0	0	0	0	0	0	-		0	0		0	-
2013	Mia	143	32	1	2	3	-1	5	5	2	.50	-1	2	-1	-1	-1	115
2014	Mia	191	36	0	0	1	-1	13	6	0	.32	-1	0	0	0	-1	120
		347	69	1	2	4	-2	18	11	2	.38	-2	2	-1	-1	2	

Hiroki Kuroda

		BASIC						HOLDING				RUNS SAVED					
Year	Tm	Inn	TC	E	GFP	DM	Rng	SB	CCS	PCS/PPO	CS%	R/P	SB	Bnt	GFP/DME	Tot	Rnk
2008	LAD	183	58	2	5	6	+4	7	2	2	.22	3	1	-1	1	4	13
2009	LAD	117	21	1	1	3	-2	10	0	1	.00	-2	0	0	1	-3	158
2010	LAD	196	30	3	1	5	-1	14	7	1	.33	-1	0	0	1	2	139
2011	LAD	202	51	0	5	2	+6	9	4	1	.36	5	1	1	0	7	4
2012	NYY	220	42	0	1	1	+2	17	8	1	.32	1	0	0	1	2	47
2013	NYY	201	37	0	6	1	+5	6	6	2	.50	4	2	0	0	6	6
2014	NYY	199	35	1	1	2	-3	4	2	1	.33	-2	1	0	0	-1	134
		1319	280	7	20	20	11	67	29	9	.31	8	4	0	1	13	-

John Lackey

		BASIC						HOLDING				RUNS SAVED					
Year	Tm	Inn	TC	E	GFP	DM	Rng	SB	CCS	PCS/PPO	CS%	R/P	SB	Bnt	GFP/DME	Tot	Rnk
2003	Ana	204	38	3	-	-	0	14	7	1	.36	0	0	-2	-	-2	133
2004	Ana	198	36	1	1	2	-2	15	7	1	.32	-2	0	-1	0	-3	148
2005	LAA	209	33	3	1	1	-3	11	7	2	.42	-2	1	1	0	0	108
2006	LAA	218	35	0	0	3	+5	12	4	0	.25	4	0	1	0	5	10
2007	LAA	224	49	2	0	0	-3	19	5	2	.24	-2	0	0	0	-2	138
2008	LAA	163	24	5	2	2	-4	11	2	1	.21	-3	0	-1	0	-4	167
2009	LAA	176	37	2	5	0	+1	13	3	0	.19	1	-1	0	0	0	79
2010	Bos	215	46	3	0	2	-2	26	8	2	.28	-2	-2	0	0	-4	160
2011	Bos	160	38	2	2	1	-2	33	3	0	.08	-1	-5	0	0	-6	172
2013	Bos	189	49	2	5	0	-1	36	7	0	.16	-1	-5	1	0	-5	171
2014	2 tms	198	30	3	1	2	-3	17	3	0	.15	-2	-2	-1	0	-5	171
		2155	417	26	17	14	-13	207	56	9	.23	-10	-14	-2	0	-26	-

Mat Latos

		BASIC						HOLDING				RUNS SAVED					
Year	Tm	Inn	TC	E	GFP	DM	Rng	SB	CCS	PCS/PPO	CS%	R/P	SB	Bnt	GFP/DME	Tot	Rnk
2009	SD	51	6	0	0	2	0	4	3	0	.43	0	0		-1	-1	-
2010	SD	185	30	1	2	2	-2	7	0	1	1.00	-1	0	1	0	0	101
2011	SD	194	39	1	4	2	+2	25	7	1	.24	1	-2	0	0	-1	118
2012	Cin	209	40	0	1	1	0	17	2	1	.15	0	-1	1	0	0	93
2013	Cin	211	47	1	2	4	+1	14	5	0	.26	1	-1	0	-1	-2	130
2014	Cin	102	22	0	0	1	0	7	2	0	.22	0	0	0	0	0	90
		952	184	3	9	12	1	74	19	3	.22	1	-4	1	-2	-4	

Pitchers

Brandon League

Year	Tm	Inn	TC	E	GFP	DM	Rng	SB	CCS	PCS/PPO	CS%	R/P	SB	Bnt	GFP/DME	Tot	Rnk
2004	Tor	5	0	0	0	0	0	0	0	0	-	0	0			0	-
2005	Tor	36	8	1	0	0	0	0	0	0	-	0	0		0	0	-
2006	Tor	43	18	2	0	2	0	1	1	0	.50	0	0	-1	0	-1	-
2007	Tor	12	5	1	1	1	+1	0	1	0	1.00	1	0		0	1	-
2008	Tor	33	12	0	0	0	-1	0	0	0	-	-1	0		0	-1	-
2009	Tor	75	16	2	0	1	-2	9	1	0	.10	-2	-1	-2	0	-5	-
2010	Sea	79	17	0	1	1	-2	5	5	0	.50	-1	1	1	0	1	79
2011	Sea	61	8	3	0	1	-4	5	1	0	.17	-3	0	-1	0	-4	-
2012	2 tms	72	12	1	0	0	-1	11	3	0	.21	-1	-1	-1	0	-3	-
2013	LAD	54	14	2	1	3	-3	2	2	0	.50	-2	0	0	-1	-3	-
2014	LAD	63	16	3	1	2	-2	4	3	0	.43	-1	0	-2	0	-3	-
		532	126	15	4	11	-14	37	17	0	.31	-10	-1	-6	-1	-18	-

Mike Leake

Year	Tm	Inn	TC	E	GFP	DM	Rng	SB	CCS	PCS/PPO	CS%	R/P	SB	Bnt	GFP/DME	Tot	Rnk
2010	Cin	138	43	3	2	1	0	5	3	1	.38	0	1	0	0	1	69
2011	Cin	168	40	0	3	3	+3	5	2	2	.29	2	1	1	0	4	18
2012	Cin	179	57	2	4	1	+4	8	6	1	.43	3	1	1	1	6	5
2013	Cin	192	55	1	5	1	+8	9	4	0	.31	6	0	0	0	6	4
2014	Cin	214	60	4	2	1	+3	12	4	2	.25	2	1	0	0	3	26
		891	255	10	16	7	18	39	19	6	.33	13	4	2	1	20	-

Cliff Lee

Year	Tm	Inn	TC	E	GFP	DM	Rng	SB	CCS	PCS/PPO	CS%	R/P	SB	Bnt	GFP/DME	Tot	Rnk
2003	Cle	52	7	1	-	-	0	4	2	0	.33	0	0	-1	-	-1	-
2004	Cle	179	12	0	0	2	-2	9	4	1	.36	-2	0	0	0	-2	131
2005	Cle	202	18	3	1	4	-4	7	4	0	.36	-3	0	0	-1	-4	170
2006	Cle	201	23	1	1	0	-2	7	1	2	.30	-2	1	0	0	-1	118
2007	Cle	97	13	1	0	1	-3	4	1	0	.20	-2	0	0	0	-2	138
2008	Cle	223	31	1	4	2	-4	3	0	0	.00	-3	0	0	0	-3	158
2009	2 tms	232	42	2	2	1	-3	7	1	2	.30	-2	1	1	0	0	102
2010	2 tms	212	28	4	2	3	-5	4	3	0	.43	-4	1	0	0	-3	158
2011	Phi	233	34	1	5	2	-1	11	2	2	.27	0	0	0	1	1	74
2012	Phi	211	31	3	2	4	-4	4	1	2	.43	-3	1	1	-1	-2	145
2013	Phi	223	36	1	1	2	+2	3	1	1	.40	1	1	0	0	2	39
2014	Phi	81	12	0	2	1	0	4	1	1	.33	0	0	0	0	0	90
		2146	287	18	20	22	-26	67	21	11	.32	-20	5	1	-1	-15	-

Dominic Leone

Year	Tm	Inn	TC	E	GFP	DM	Rng	SB	CCS	PCS/PPO	CS%	R/P	SB	Bnt	GFP/DME	Tot	Rnk
2014	Sea	66	8	0	0	1	0	6	5	1	.45	0	0	0	0	0	-

Jon Lester

Year	Tm	Inn	TC	E	GFP	DM	Rng	SB	CCS	PCS/PPO	CS%	R/P	SB	Bnt	GFP/DME	Tot	Rnk
2006	Bos	81	11	0	0	0	-1	9	1	6	.40	-1	2	-1	0	0	93
2007	Bos	63	11	1	2	0	-2	4	1	1	.33	-2	0		0	-2	-
2008	Bos	210	42	2	0	2	-2	8	2	3	.38	-2	1	1	0	0	103
2009	Bos	203	33	2	1	3	+3	19	0	6	.24	2	0	-2	0	0	78
2010	Bos	208	43	3	0	3	+4	22	1	6	.24	3	0	-1	0	2	36
2011	Bos	192	29	1	2	2	-2	14	8	4	.46	-1	2	0	0	1	87
2012	Bos	205	37	2	0	3	+2	13	3	0	.19	1	0	-1	0	0	89
2013	Bos	213	32	2	3	3	-3	12	3	1	.25	-2	0	0	-1	-3	153
2014	2 tms	220	26	2	0	4	-1	16	4	1	.24	-1	-1	0	-1	-3	158
		1596	264	15	8	20	-2	117	23	28	.30	-3	4	-4	-2	-5	-

Colby Lewis

Year	Tm	Inn	TC	E	GFP	DM	Rng	SB	CCS	PCS/PPO	CS%	R/P	SB	Bnt	GFP/DME	Tot	Rnk
2003	Tex	127	21	0	-	-	0	5	6	0	.55	0	1	0	-	1	73
2004	Tex	15	3	0	0	0	0	1	0	0	.00	0	0	0	0	0	-
2006	Det	3	0	0	0	0	0	0	0	0	-	0			0	0	-
2007	Oak	38	4	0	0	0	0	1	0	0	.00	0	0	0	0	0	-
2010	Tex	201	25	5	2	1	-5	13	4	0	.24	-4	-1	0	0	-5	169
2011	Tex	200	20	4	1	1	0	10	7	0	.41	0	1	-1	0	0	99
2012	Tex	105	13	2	1	3	-1	8	3	0	.27	-1	0	0	0	-1	118
2014	Tex	170	14	1	1	0	-1	18	8	0	.31	-1	-1	-2	0	-4	162
		859	100	12	5	5	-7	56	28	0	.33	-6	0	-3	0	-9	-

Tim Lincecum

Year	Tm	Inn	TC	E	GFP	DM	Rng	SB	CCS	PCS/PPO	CS%	R/P	SB	Bnt	GFP/DME	Tot	Rnk
2007	SF	146	24	0	0	2	-2	10	2	0	.17	-2	-1	0	0	-3	153
2008	SF	227	26	0	4	3	-3	20	3	0	.13	-2	-2	0	-1	-5	172
2009	SF	225	40	2	2	4	-4	20	5	0	.20	-3	-2	0	0	-5	171
2010	SF	212	27	2	3	3	-4	27	3	0	.10	-3	-3	0	0	-6	171
2011	SF	217	40	1	3	0	-1	23	12	2	.38	-1	0	1	0	0	109
2012	SF	186	37	0	2	1	0	25	2	1	.07	0	-3	1	0	-2	133
2013	SF	198	32	4	0	3	-3	21	2	0	.09	-3	-3	-1	-1	-8	176
2014	SF	156	24	1	0	1	0	22	4	2	.21	0	-2		0	-2	141
		1567	250	10	10	18	-17	168	33	5	.18	-14	-16	1	-2	-31	

Francisco Liriano

Year	Tm	Inn	TC	E	GFP	DM	Rng	SB	CCS	PCS/PPO	CS%	R/P	SB	Bnt	GFP/DME	Tot	Rnk
2005	Min	24	5	0	0	0	0	3	0	1	.25	0	0		0	0	-
2006	Min	121	10	1	0	3	-3	9	0	0	.00	-2	-1	-1	0	-4	165
2008	Min	76	13	0	0	1	-2	6	0	3	.33	-2	1	0	0	-1	-
2009	Min	137	16	0	3	0	-1	15	3	6	.38	-1	1	0	0	0	96
2010	Min	192	29	1	5	4	-3	12	1	2	.20	-2	0	-1	-1	-4	160
2011	Min	134	22	0	1	1	+1	9	2	3	.36	1	1	0	0	2	44
2012	2 tms	157	29	0	3	2	+3	16	0	3	.11	2	0	0	0	2	42
2013	Pit	161	38	1	2	6	+7	7	2	2	.36	5	1	-1	-1	4	13
2014	Pit	162	29	3	1	3	+2	19	4	1	.21	2	-2	1	-1	0	81
		1163	191	6	15	20	4	96	12	21	.25	3	1	-2	-3	-1	-

Jeff Locke

Year	Tm	Inn	TC	E	GFP	DM	Rng	SB	CCS	PCS/PPO	CS%	R/P	SB	Bnt	GFP/DME	Tot	Rnk
2011	Pit	17	5	0	0	0	+1	3	0	1	.25	1	0	0	0	1	-
2012	Pit	34	4	0	0	0	-2	4	1	1	.33	-2	0	-1	0	-3	-
2013	Pit	166	46	1	2	2	0	8	2	6	.47	0	2	0	0	2	46
2014	Pit	131	18	0	0	1	-1	7	1	5	.46	0	2	0	0	2	55
		348	73	1	2	3	-2	22	4	13	.42	-1	4	-1	0	2	-

Kyle Lohse

Year	Tm	Inn	TC	E	GFP	DM	Rng	SB	CCS	PCS/PPO	CS%	R/P	SB	Bnt	GFP/DME	Tot	Rnk
2003	Min	201	38	1	-	-	-3	12	3	1	.20	-2	0	-1	-	-3	155
2004	Min	194	34	0	1	4	-1	16	5	4	.33	-1	1	-1	0	-1	109
2005	Min	179	40	0	3	0	-2	3	3	4	.67	-2	2	0	0	0	108
2006	2 tms	127	36	0	0	0	0	2	2	2	.60	0	1	1	0	2	51
2007	2 tms	193	34	1	3	1	+1	12	8	1	.40	1	1	-1	0	1	64
2008	StL	200	49	0	5	4	-2	9	2	1	.25	-2	0	1	0	-1	121
2009	StL	118	34	1	1	0	+2	4	1	0	.20	2	0	0	0	2	36
2010	StL	92	27	1	0	1	-1	1	2	1	.75	-1	1	1	1	2	55
2011	StL	188	51	0	2	3	0	6	1	0	.67	0	1	0	0	1	74
2012	StL	211	43	0	2	0	0	6	4	1	.40	0	1	0	0	1	75
2013	Mil	199	23	0	1	1	0	8	1	0	.11	0	0	1	0	1	65
2014	Mil	198	35	1	2	4	+3	10	4	1	.33	2	0	1	-1	2	38
		2099	444	5	20	18	-3	84	37	16	.36	-3	8	2	0	7	-

Aaron Loup

Year	Tm	Inn	TC	E	GFP	DM	Rng	SB	CCS	PCS/PPO	CS%	R/P	SB	Bnt	GFP/DME	Tot	Rnk
2012	Tor	31	9	0	0	0	-1	3	0	3	.50	-1	1	0	0	0	-
2013	Tor	69	31	3	2	2	+2	3	2	5	.70	2	2	-1	-1	2	-
2014	Tor	69	21	1	1	1	+5	8	0	1	.11	4	-1	0	-1	2	-
		168	61	4	3	3	6	14	2	9	.44	5	2	-1	-2	4	-

Jordan Lyles

Year	Tm	Inn	TC	E	GFP	DM	Rng	SB	CCS	PCS/PPO	CS%	R/P	SB	Bnt	GFP/DME	Tot	Rnk
2011	Hou	94	24	1	1	2	+1	4	0	1	.00	1	0	0	0	1	64
2012	Hou	141	27	1	1	0	-2	10	4	0	.29	-2	0	0	0	-2	141
2013	Hou	142	31	1	5	2	+3	5	3	0	.38	2	0	0	0	2	34
2014	Col	127	31	1	1	0	+3	6	0	0	.00	2	-1	1	0	2	38
		503	113	4	8	4	5	25	7	1	.22	3	-1	1	0	3	-

Pitchers

Lance Lynn

Year	Tm	Inn	TC	E	GFP	DM	Rng	SB	CCS	PCS/PPO	CS%	R/P	SB	Bnt	GFP/DME	Tot	Rnk
2011	StL	35	4	0	0	1	-2	2	1	0	.33	-2	0	0	1	-2	-
2012	StL	176	22	1	0	2	0	9	8	2	.50	0	2	0	-1	1	75
2013	StL	202	41	1	3	7	-7	7	7	1	.50	-5	2	1	-1	-3	163
2014	StL	204	37	1	0	7	+4	1	3	0	.75	3	1	0	-1	3	23
		616	104	3	3	17	-5	19	19	3	.51	-4	5	1	-3	-1	

Jean Machi

Year	Tm	Inn	TC	E	GFP	DM	Rng	SB	CCS	PCS/PPO	CS%	R/P	SB	Bnt	GFP/DME	Tot	Rnk
2012	SF	7	2	0	0	0	0	0	0	0		0	0	0		0	-
2013	SF	53	15	1	2	1	+2	4	0	1	.00	2	0	0		2	-
2014	SF	66	22	2	3	0	+2	3	2	2	.50	1	1	1		3	-
		126	39	3	5	1	4	7	2	3	.30	3	1	1	0	5	

Paul Maholm

Year	Tm	Inn	TC	E	GFP	DM	Rng	SB	CCS	PCS/PPO	CS%	R/P	SB	Bnt	GFP/DME	Tot	Rnk
2005	Pit	41	7	0	1	1	+2	2	2	0	.50	2	0			2	-
2006	Pit	176	53	2	0	2	+1	13	3	9	.46	1	3	2	-1	5	13
2007	Pit	178	37	1	3	2	0	11	5	1	.35	0	0	-1	0	-1	108
2008	Pit	206	39	2	1	3	+3	5	4	3	.58	2	2	1	0	5	9
2009	Pit	195	50	2	5	2	+3	15	3	4	.29	2	1	0	1	4	12
2010	Pit	185	48	3	2	3	0	8	1	2	.20	1	0	0	0	1	69
2011	Pit	162	38	1	2	3	+3	7	1	3	.30	2	1	0	0	3	26
2012	2 tms	189	33	2	0	4	+1	6	3	4	.50	1	2	-1	-1	1	68
2013	Atl	153	26	1	2	2	+1	10	1	1	.17	0	0	0	0	0	86
2014	LAD	71	18	1	2	1	+1	3	0	1	1.00	1	0	0	1		
		1556	349	15	18	23	15	80	23	28	.36	11	10	1	-1	21	

Seth Maness

Year	Tm	Inn	TC	E	GFP	DM	Rng	SB	CCS	PCS/PPO	CS%	R/P	SB	Bnt	GFP/DME	Tot	Rnk
2013	StL	62	16	0	1	0	-1	2	0	0	.00	-1	0	0		-1	-
2014	StL	80	32	2	4	1	+6	1	3	0	.75	4	1	0	0	5	5
		142	48	2	5	1	5	3	3	0	.50	3	1	0	0	4	

Carlos Martinez

Year	Tm	Inn	TC	E	GFP	DM	Rng	SB	CCS	PCS/PPO	CS%	R/P	SB	Bnt	GFP/DME	Tot	Rnk
2013	StL	28	7	0	1	4	-2	1	1	0	.50	-1	0	0	-1	-2	-
2014	StL	89	35	1	2	0	+3	5	3	0	.38	2	0	1	0	3	26
		117	42	1	3	4	1	6	4	0	.40	1	0	1	-1	1	

Nick Martinez

Year	Tm	Inn	TC	E	GFP	DM	Rng	SB	CCS	PCS/PPO	CS%	R/P	SB	Bnt	GFP/DME	Tot	Rnk
2014	Tex	140	22	0	2	1	-2	4	3	1	.50	-1	1	1	0	1	75

Justin Masterson

Year	Tm	Inn	TC	E	GFP	DM	Rng	SB	CCS	PCS/PPO	CS%	R/P	SB	Bnt	GFP/DME	Tot	Rnk
2008	Bos	88	14	1	1	0	+2	9	1	0	.10	2	-1	0	0	1	52
2009	2 tms	129	28	2	1	3	-3	15	5	1	.29	-3	-1	0	0	-4	168
2010	Cle	180	61	5	4	3	0	13	6	2	.38	0	1	0	1	2	50
2011	Cle	216	49	2	1	4	-3	14	13	2	.50	-2	2	0	0	0	113
2012	Cle	206	59	1	3	4	+5	25	7	0	.22	4	-2	-2	1	1	59
2013	Cle	193	49	1	1	2	+2	9	3	1	.25	1	0	0	0	1	54
2014	2 tms	129	31	1	0	2	+3	5	2	0	.29	2	0	0	0	2	38
		1141	291	13	11	18	6	90	37	6	.31	4	-1	-2	2	3	

Daisuke Matsuzaka

Year	Tm	Inn	TC	E	GFP	DM	Rng	SB	CCS	PCS/PPO	CS%	R/P	SB	Bnt	GFP/DME	Tot	Rnk
2007	Bos	205	34	0	5	3	0	18	7	0	.28	0	-1	0	1	0	91
2008	Bos	168	36	1	2	3	+3	15	5	0	.25	2	-1	-1	-1	-1	109
2009	Bos	59	7	0	1	1	-1	7	0	0	.00	-1	-1	1	0	-1	-
2010	Bos	154	22	2	4	4	+2	25	7	0	.22	1	-3	-1	0	-3	151
2011	Bos	37	2	0	0	0	-1	6	0	0	.00	-1	-1		0	-2	-
2012	Bos	46	8	0	0	0	-1	11	0	1	1.00	-1	-1	0	0	-1	-
2013	NYM	39	5	0	2	1	0	5	1	0	.17	0	-1	0	0	-1	-
2014	NYM	83	11	0	0	1	+1	12	1	2	.14	1	-1	0	0	0	85
		790	125	3	14	13	3	99	21	3	.18	2	-10	-1	0	-9	

Tyler Matzek

Year	Tm	Inn	TC	E	GFP	DM	Rng	SB	CCS	PCS/PPO	CS%	R/P	SB	Bnt	GFP/DME	Tot	Rnk
2014	Col	118	27	2	1	5	-1	5	2	1	.38	-1	0	-1	0	-2	146

Brandon Maurer

Year	Tm	Inn	TC	E	GFP	DM	Rng	SB	CCS	PCS/PPO	CS%	R/P	SB	Bnt	GFP/DME	Tot	Rnk
2013	Sea	90	16	0	3	1	+1	6	5	0	.45	1	0	0	0	1	54
2014	Sea	70	7	0	0	0	-2	3	0	0	.00	-1	0	0	0	-1	-
		159	23	0	3	1	-1	9	5	0	.36	0	0	0	0	0	

Zach McAllister

Year	Tm	Inn	TC	E	GFP	DM	Rng	SB	CCS	PCS/PPO	CS%	R/P	SB	Bnt	GFP/DME	Tot	Rnk
2011	Cle	18	2	1	0	0	-3	1	1	1	.50	-2	1		0	-1	-
2012	Cle	125	10	1	0	1	-4	18	1	0	.05	-3	-2	-1	0	-6	174
2013	Cle	134	16	2	0	1	-2	7	2	0	.22	-2	0	-1	0	-3	153
2014	Cle	86	10	2	1	1	-2	9	3	0	.25	-2	-1	-1	0	-4	163
		363	38	6	1	3	-11	35	7	1	.17	-9	-2	-3	0	-14	

Brandon McCarthy

Year	Tm	Inn	TC	E	GFP	DM	Rng	SB	CCS	PCS/PPO	CS%	R/P	SB	Bnt	GFP/DME	Tot	Rnk
2005	CWS	67	7	0	0	0	0	2	0	0	.00	0	0	0	0	0	-
2006	CWS	85	15	0	1	2	-1	8	3	0	.27	-1	-1	0	0	-2	136
2007	Tex	102	18	2	0	2	-1	17	5	0	.23	-1	-2	0	0	-3	149
2008	Tex	22	1	0	0	0	0	6	1	0	.14	0	-1		0	-1	-
2009	Tex	97	18	1	0	1	0	5	2	0	.29	0	0	0	0	0	86
2011	Oak	171	38	4	0	3	-2	11	3	1	.27	-1	0	-1	0	-2	136
2012	Oak	111	21	0	3	1	-1	13	3	0	.19	-1	-1	0	0	-2	137
2013	Ari	135	24	0	3	0	-2	2	0	0	.00	-2	0	0	0	-2	142
2014	2 tms	200	31	0	0	1	+2	17	4	1	.23	1	-1	0	0	0	85
		989	173	7	7	10	-5	81	21	2	.22	-5	-6	-1	0	-12	

Jake McGee

Year	Tm	Inn	TC	E	GFP	DM	Rng	SB	CCS	PCS/PPO	CS%	R/P	SB	Bnt	GFP/DME	Tot	Rnk
2010	TB	5	1	0	0	0	0	0	0	0	-	0	0	0	0	0	-
2011	TB	28	3	0	0	0	0	4	0	0	.00	0	-1	0	0	-1	-
2012	TB	55	9	0	2	0	+1	0	0	0	-	1	0	0	0	1	-
2013	TB	63	6	0	1	1	-1	3	0	0	.00	0	0	0	0	0	-
2014	TB	71	8	1	0	1	-2	2	0	1	.33	-1	0	1	0	0	-
		222	27	1	2	2	-2	9	0	1	.10	-1	-1	1	0	-1	

Dustin McGowan

Year	Tm	Inn	TC	E	GFP	DM	Rng	SB	CCS	PCS/PPO	CS%	R/P	SB	Bnt	GFP/DME	Tot	Rnk
2005	Tor	45	8	1	1	2	0	7	2	1	.30	0	0	-1	0	-1	-
2006	Tor	27	4	0	0	0	-1	3	1	0	.25	-1	0	0	0	-1	-
2007	Tor	170	50	4	1	3	+5	29	1	0	.03	4	-4	1	0	1	60
2008	Tor	111	25	3	5	1	-1	12	4	0	.25	-1	-1	0	0	-2	139
2011	Tor	21	2	0	0	1	0	4	0	0	.00	0	-1		0	-1	-
2013	Tor	26	10	2	2	3	+1	2	1	0	.33	1	0	0	0	1	-
2014	Tor	82	14	0	2	0	0	6	1	1	.25	0	0	1	0	1	71
		482	113	10	11	10	4	63	10	2	.16	3	-6	1	0	-2	

Collin McHugh

Year	Tm	Inn	TC	E	GFP	DM	Rng	SB	CCS	PCS/PPO	CS%	R/P	SB	Bnt	GFP/DME	Tot	Rnk
									BASIC			HOLDING			RUNS SAVED		
2012	NYM	21	3	0	0	0	+1	2	2		.50	0	0			0	-
2013	2 tms	26	9	0	0	0	-1	6	0	0	.00	0	-1	0	0	-1	-
2014	Hou	155	35	2	3	4	+2	6	5	0	.45	1	1	0	-1	1	65
		202	47	2	3	4	2	14	7	0	.33	1	0	0	-1	0	

Jenrry Mejia

Year	Tm	Inn	TC	E	GFP	DM	Rng	SB	CCS	PCS/PPO	CS%	R/P	SB	Bnt	GFP/DME	Tot	Rnk
2010	NYM	39	12	0	0	0	-1	3	1	0	.25	-1	0		0	-1	-
2012	NYM	16	3	1	0	0	-4	2	0	0	.00	-3	0	-1	0	-4	-
2013	NYM	27	3	0	1	0	-2	1	0	0	.00	-1	0		0	-1	-
2014	NYM	94	13	0	0	1	-5	8	0	0	.00	-3	-1	0	0	-4	167
		176	31	1	1	1	-12	14	1	0	.07	-8	-1	-1	0	-10	

Mark Melancon

Year	Tm	Inn	TC	E	GFP	DM	Rng	SB	CCS	PCS/PPO	CS%	R/P	SB	Bnt	GFP/DME	Tot	Rnk
2009	NYY	16	5	0	1	0	+1	2	0	0	.00	1	0		0	1	-
2010	2 tms	21	6	0	0	0	0	0	0	0	-	0	0		0	0	-
2011	Hou	74	18	1	0	1	0	6	2	0	.25	0	0	0	0	0	-
2012	Bos	45	13	0	2	1	+1	0	1	0	1.00	1	0	0	0	1	-
2013	Pit	71	18	0	0	1	+2	3	0	0	.00	2	0	0	0	2	-
2014	Pit	71	18	1	1	0	+1	1	1	0	.50	1	0	0	0	1	-
		299	78	2	4	3	5	12	4	0	.25	5	0	0	0	5	

Wade Miley

Year	Tm	Inn	TC	E	GFP	DM	Rng	SB	CCS	PCS/PPO	CS%	R/P	SB	Bnt	GFP/DME	Tot	Rnk
2011	Ari	40	6	1	0	1	-1	3	1		.40	-1	0	-1	0	-2	-
2012	Ari	195	31	1	1	0	+2	3	2	4	.67	2	3	0	0	5	12
2013	Ari	203	38	0	2	1	-4	5	2	5	.50	-3	2	0	0	-1	128
2014	Ari	201	37	3	2	2	-1	4	4	5	.60	-1	3	0	0	2	61
		638	112	5	5	4	-4	15	9	15	.56	-3	8	-1	0	4	

Andrew Miller

Year	Tm	Inn	TC	E	GFP	DM	Rng	SB	CCS	PCS/PPO	CS%	R/P	SB	Bnt	GFP/DME	Tot	Rnk
2006	Det	10	1	0	0	0	0	0	0	0	-	0	0		0	0	-
2007	Det	64	12	2	1	2	-2	10	1	0	.09	-2	0	0	0	-3	-
2008	Fla	107	14	1	2	4	-2	13	2	1	.19	-2	-1	0	0	-3	151
2009	Fla	80	15	1	0	0	0	13	3	0	.19	0	-1	1	0	0	86
2010	Fla	33	5	0	1	1	-1	4	0	0	.00	-1	-1	0	0	-2	-
2011	Bos	65	13	2	0	1	-2	8	1	0	.11	-1	-1	-1	0	-3	-
2012	Bos	40	4	1	0	0	-1	0	0	0	-	-1	0		0	-1	-
2013	Bos	31	5	1	1	1	-2	2	1	0	.33	-1	0	-1	0	-2	-
2014	2 tms	62	9	1	1	2	-1	2	1	0	.33	0	0	0	0	0	-
		492	78	9	6	11	-10	52	9	1	.16	-8	-5	-1	0	-14	

Shelby Miller

Year	Tm	Inn	TC	E	GFP	DM	Rng	SB	CCS	PCS/PPO	CS%	R/P	SB	Bnt	GFP/DME	Tot	Rnk
2012	StL	14	1	0	0	0	0	0	0	0	-	0	0		0	0	-
2013	StL	173	24	1	2	0	-2	9	4	0	.31	-2	0	-1	0	-3	153
2014	StL	183	27	1	2	1	-1	14	5	1	.30	-1	0	0	1	0	100
		370	52	2	4	1	-3	23	9	1	.30	-3	0	-1	1	-3	

Tommy Milone

Year	Tm	Inn	TC	E	GFP	DM	Rng	SB	CCS	PCS/PPO	CS%	R/P	SB	Bnt	GFP/DME	Tot	Rnk
2011	Was	26	5	0	0	0	+1	1	0	1	.50	1	0	0	0	1	-
2012	Oak	190	24	1	0	2	+1	8	4	6	.56	1	3	-1	0	3	36
2013	Oak	156	18	1	2	4	0	9	1	2	.25	0	0	-1	0	-1	105
2014	2 tms	118	24	1	3	2	+1	7	0	2	.22	2	0	-1	0	1	64
		490	71	3	5	8	3	25	5	11	.39	4	3	-3	0	4	

Mike Minor

Year	Tm	Inn	TC	E	GFP	DM	Rng	SB	CCS	PCS/PPO	CS%	R/P	SB	Bnt	GFP/DME	Tot	Rnk
2010	Atl	41	4	0	0	0	-1	3	0	2	.40	-1	0	0	0	-1	-
2011	Atl	83	12	0	0	3	-1	2	2	0	.50	-1	1	0	0	0	109
2012	Atl	179	24	0	1	2	0	10	0	2	.17	0	0	0	0	0	93
2013	Atl	205	25	0	3	0	+1	4	7	1	.67	1	2	0	0	3	27
2014	Atl	145	19	0	1	6	-3	9	1	1	.10	-2	0	-1	-1	-4	163
		652	84	0	5	11	-4	28	10	6	.35	-3	3	-1	-1	-2	

Franklin Morales

Year	Tm	Inn	TC	E	GFP	DM	Rng	SB	CCS	PCS/PPO	CS%	R/P	SB	Bnt	GFP/DME	Tot	Rnk
2007	Col	39	11	0	0	0	+1	4	1	1	.20	1	0	0	0	1	-
2008	Col	25	5	0	0	0	+1	5	0	0	.00	1	-1	0	0	1	-
2009	Col	40	6	0	0	1	0	1	1	0	.50	0	1	0	0	1	-
2010	Col	29	1	0	0	0	0	1	0	0	.00	0	0		0	0	-
2011	2 tms	46	9	0	1	0	0	6	0	4	.00	0	1	0	0	1	-
2012	Bos	76	12	1	0	2	0	8	0	0	.20	0	1	0	-1	0	-
2013	Bos	25	5	0	0	0	-1	1	1	3	.50	-1	1		0	0	-
2014	Col	142	31	5	2	1	0	9	1	0	.10	0	-1	0	0	-1	111
		423	80	6	3	4	1	35	4	13	.15	1	2	0	-1	2	

Bryan Morris

Year	Tm	Inn	TC	E	GFP	DM	Rng	SB	CCS	PCS/PPO	CS%	R/P	SB	Bnt	GFP/DME	Tot	Rnk
2012	Pit	5	2	0	0	0	0	2	0	0	.00	0	0		0	0	-
2013	Pit	65	15	0	3	1	+1	1	2	0	.67	0	1		0	1	-
2014	2 tms	64	11	1	1	0	+1	1	0	2	.00	1	1	-1	0	1	-
		134	28	1	4	1	2	4	2	2	.33	1	2	-1	0	2	

Charlie Morton

Year	Tm	Inn	TC	E	GFP	DM	Rng	SB	CCS	PCS/PPO	CS%	R/P	SB	Bnt	GFP/DME	Tot	Rnk
2008	Atl	75	10	0	0	1	0	7	1	1	.22	0	0	0	0	0	-
2009	Pit	97	18	0	1	2	0	9	3	1	.31	0	0	0	0	0	86
2010	Pit	80	21	3	1	1	-2	12	1	2	.14	-1	-1	0	0	-2	139
2011	Pit	172	39	1	1	0	-1	16	5	2	.27	-1	0	1	0	0	109
2012	Pit	50	12	3	0	1	-1	4	0	0	.00	-1	0	0	-1	-2	-
2013	Pit	116	17	0	1	1	-1	11	6	0	.35	-1	0	0	0	-1	115
2014	Pit	157	33	1	0	0	+2	14	3	4	.22	2	1	0	1	4	17
		746	150	8	4	6	-3	73	19	10	.25	-2	0	1	0	-1	

Edward Mujica

Year	Tm	Inn	TC	E	GFP	DM	Rng	SB	CCS	PCS/PPO	CS%	R/P	SB	Bnt	GFP/DME	Tot	Rnk
2006	Cle	18	2	0	0	0	-1	0	0	1	1.00	-1	0		0	-1	-
2007	Cle	13	0	0	0	0	0	1	0	0	.00	0	0		0	0	-
2008	Cle	39	4	0	2	0	+1	0	1	0	1.00	1	0		0	1	-
2009	SD	94	14	0	2	2	+1	3	3	0	.50	1	1	0	0	2	43
2010	SD	70	10	0	0	1	0	2	0	1	.33	0	0	0	0	0	-
2011	Fla	76	22	2	4	0	+1	7	1	2	.13	0	0	1	1	2	52
2012	2 tms	65	19	1	1	0	+2	1	1	0	.50	2	0	0	0	2	-
2013	StL	65	15	0	1	0	+1	2	2	0	.50	0	0	0	1	1	-
2014	Bos	60	10	1	0	1	+1	4	2	0	.33	1	0	-1	0	0	-
		499	96	4	10	4	5	20	10	4	.38	4	1	0	2	7	

Jimmy Nelson

Year	Tm	Inn	TC	E	GFP	DM	Rng	SB	CCS	PCS/PPO	CS%	R/P	SB	Bnt	GFP/DME	Tot	Rnk
2013	Mil	10	1	0	0	1	+1	2	0	0	.00	0	0		0	0	-
2014	Mil	69	9	1	1	0	-3	7	0	0	.00	-2	-1	-1	0	-4	-
		79	10	1	1	1	-2	9	0	0	.00	-2	-1	-1	0	-4	

Pitchers

Pat Neshek

Year	Tm	Inn	TC	E	GFP	DM	Rng	SB	CCS	PCS/PPO	CS%	R/P	SB	Bnt	GFP/DME	Tot	Rnk
2006	Min	37	3	0	0	1	-1	3	2	0	.40	-1	0	0	0	-1	-
2007	Min	70	11	0	1	0	+1	1	2	0	.67	1	1	0	0	2	-
2008	Min	13	3	0	1	0	0	0	0	0	-	0	0	0	0	0	-
2010	Min	9	2	0	0	0	0	1	0	1	.50	0	0		0	0	-
2011	SD	25	2	0	0	0	+1	3	0	0	.00	1	0		0	1	-
2012	Oak	20	1	0	0	0	0	2	0	0	.00	0	0		0	0	-
2013	Oak	40	5	0	1	0	0	2	1	0	.33	0	0	0	0	0	-
2014	StL	67	10	0	0	2	+1	2	1	0	.33	0	0	1	0	1	-
		281	37	0	3	3	2	14	6	1	.33	1	1	1	0	3	

Juan Nicasio

Year	Tm	Inn	TC	E	GFP	DM	Rng	SB	CCS	PCS/PPO	CS%	R/P	SB	Bnt	GFP/DME	Tot	Rnk
2011	Col	72	21	1	1	3	+1	7	0	1	.13	1	-1	0	0	0	-
2012	Col	58	11	0	0	0	-2	3	4	2	.63	-1	2	0	0	1	-
2013	Col	158	24	0	2	1	-1	8	3	0	.27	-1	0	0	0	-1	115
2014	Col	94	18	1	0	0	-1	6	2	0	.25	0	0	-1	0	-1	111
		381	74	2	3	4	-3	24	9	3	.31	-1	1	-1	0	-1	

Jon Niese

Year	Tm	Inn	TC	E	GFP	DM	Rng	SB	CCS	PCS/PPO	CS%	R/P	SB	Bnt	GFP/DME	Tot	Rnk
2008	NYM	14	4	0	1	0	0	0	0	0	-	0	0	0	0	0	-
2009	NYM	26	4	0	1	1	-1	1	1	1	.67	-1	1	0	0	0	-
2010	NYM	174	34	1	0	4	+2	0	3	1	1.00	2	2	-1	-1	2	40
2011	NYM	157	40	0	2	1	+3	7	1	0	.13	2	0	1	0	3	26
2012	NYM	190	33	2	3	2	+3	8	0	2	.20	2	1	0	0	3	31
2013	NYM	143	33	2	2	6	-2	2	0	1	.33	-2	1	1	-1	-1	126
2014	NYM	188	39	4	0	1	+3	9	4	2	.40	2	1	0	0	3	26
		891	187	9	9	15	8	27	9	7	.37	5	6	1	-2	10	

Hector Noesi

Year	Tm	Inn	TC	E	GFP	DM	Rng	SB	CCS	PCS/PPO	CS%	R/P	SB	Bnt	GFP/DME	Tot	Rnk
2011	NYY	56	8	0	0	0	+1	6	3	0	.33	1	0	-1	0	0	-
2012	Sea	107	15	1	2	0	-2	6	4	1	.45	-1	1	0	0	0	105
2013	Sea	27	4	1	2	1	0	1	1	0	.50	0	0	0	0	0	-
2014	3 tms	172	27	1	0	0	+3	7	2	0	.22	2	0	0	0	2	38
		362	54	3	4	1	2	20	10	1	.35	2	1	-1	0	2	

Ricky Nolasco

Year	Tm	Inn	TC	E	GFP	DM	Rng	SB	CCS	PCS/PPO	CS%	R/P	SB	Bnt	GFP/DME	Tot	Rnk
2006	Fla	140	25	4	0	4	-1	6	6	0	.50	-1	1	-1	0	-1	111
2007	Fla	21	2	0	0	0	-2	2	1	0	.33	-2	0	-1	0	-3	-
2008	Fla	212	29	0	1	6	-2	7	5	0	.42	-2	1	1	-1	-1	121
2009	Fla	185	31	0	1	2	-1	13	3	1	.24	-1	-1	0	0	-2	138
2010	Fla	158	30	3	3	2	-1	5	4	2	.55	-1	1	-2	0	-2	139
2011	Fla	206	34	1	0	3	0	12	2	0	.14	0	-1	-2	0	-3	152
2012	Mia	191	44	1	1	0	-4	14	4	0	.22	-3	-1	-1	0	-5	169
2013	2 tms	199	43	2	0	1	0	9	5	2	.40	0	1	-1	0	0	86
2014	Min	159	21	0	0	3	-2	16	3	2	.24	-1	-1	1	-1	-2	146
		1471	259	11	6	21	-13	84	33	7	.32	-11	0	-6	-2	-19	

Bud Norris

Year	Tm	Inn	TC	E	GFP	DM	Rng	SB	CCS	PCS/PPO	CS%	R/P	SB	Bnt	GFP/DME	Tot	Rnk
2009	Hou	56	4	0	0	0	-1	1	0	1	.00	-1	1		0	0	-
2010	Hou	154	36	3	5	1	+2	12	5	1	.29	2	0	1	1	4	20
2011	Hou	186	54	3	4	4	+2	16	6	3	.27	1	0	0	-1	0	92
2012	Hou	168	35	2	3	1	+1	13	9	2	.43	1	1	0	0	2	47
2013	2 tms	177	31	1	7	3	+2	16	5	2	.24	1	0	2	-1	2	39
2014	Bal	165	25	1	5	3	0	15	9	0	.38	0	0	0	-1	-1	111
		905	185	10	24	12	6	73	34	9	.32	4	2	3	-2	7	

Vidal Nuno

Year	Tm	Inn	TC	E	GFP	DM	Rng	SB	CCS	PCS/PPO	CS%	R/P	SB	Bnt	GFP/DME	Tot	Rnk
2013	NYY	20	2	0	0	0	0	0	0	0	-	0	0	0	0	0	-
2014	2 tms	162	23	0	1	2	+2	4	1	2	.43	2	1	0	0	3	26
		181	25	0	1	2	2	4	1	2	.43	2	1	0	0	3	

Brett Oberholtzer

Year	Tm	Inn	TC	E	GFP	DM	Rng	SB	CCS	PCS/PPO	CS%	R/P	SB	Bnt	GFP/DME	Tot	Rnk
2013	Hou	72	10	0	2	0	+1	1	4	0	.80	1	1	0	0	2	-
2014	Hou	144	23	1	2	7	-1	10	2	1	.17	-1	0	-1	0	-2	146
		215	33	1	4	7	0	11	6	1	.35	0	1	-1	0	0	-

Darren O'Day

Year	Tm	Inn	TC	E	GFP	DM	Rng	SB	CCS	PCS/PPO	CS%	R/P	SB	Bnt	GFP/DME	Tot	Rnk
2008	LAA	43	13	1	0	0	-1	2	1	0	.33	-1	0	0	0	-1	-
2009	2 tms	59	7	0	0	2	+1	7	4	0	.36	1	0	0	0	1	-
2010	Tex	62	10	1	1	0	+1	3	1	0	.25	1	0	-1	0	0	-
2011	Tex	17	5	1	1	0	0	4	0	0	.00	0	-1	0	0	-1	-
2012	Bal	67	9	0	2	0	0	4	1	1	.33	0	0	0	0	0	-
2013	Bal	62	8	1	0	0	0	6	4	0	.40	0	0	0	0	0	-
2014	Bal	69	16	1	1	2	0	4	0	1	.20	0	0	0	0	0	-
		378	68	5	5	4	1	30	11	2	.30	1	-1	-1	0	-1	

Jake Odorizzi

Year	Tm	Inn	TC	E	GFP	DM	Rng	SB	CCS	PCS/PPO	CS%	R/P	SB	Bnt	GFP/DME	Tot	Rnk
2012	KC	7	3	0	1	0	0	2	0	0	.00	0	0	0	0	0	-
2013	TB	30	7	0	0	0	+1	0	0	0	-	1	0	0	0	1	-
2014	TB	168	18	0	0	3	-3	4	5	2	.60	-2	2	0	0	0	106
		205	28	0	1	3	-2	6	5	2	.50	-1	2	0	0	1	-

Dan Otero

Year	Tm	Inn	TC	E	GFP	DM	Rng	SB	CCS	PCS/PPO	CS%	R/P	SB	Bnt	GFP/DME	Tot	Rnk
2012	SF	12	3	0	0	0	0	1	1	0	.50	0	0		0	0	-
2013	Oak	39	8	0	1	2	0	1	0	0	.00	0	0	0	-1	-1	-
2014	Oak	07	29	0	1	1	+3	3	2	1	.50	2	1	0	0	3	26
		138	40	0	2	3	3	5	3	1	.44	2	1	0	-1	2	

Adam Ottavino

Year	Tm	Inn	TC	E	GFP	DM	Rng	SB	CCS	PCS/PPO	CS%	R/P	SB	Bnt	GFP/DME	Tot	Rnk
2010	StL	22	4	0	0	0	-1	2	1	0	.33	-1	0	0	0	-1	-
2012	Col	79	15	0	1	2	0	16	1	0	.06	0	-2	0	-1	-3	149
2013	Col	78	17	1	0	1	-3	11	2	0	.15	-3	-1	1	0	-3	161
2014	Col	65	8	0	0	1	0	3	1	0	.25	0	0	0	0	0	-
		244	44	1	1	4	-4	32	5	0	.14	-4	-3	1	-1	-7	

Jonathan Papelbon

Year	Tm	Inn	TC	E	GFP	DM	Rng	SB	CCS	PCS/PPO	CS%	R/P	SB	Bnt	GFP/DME	Tot	Rnk
2005	Bos	34	5	0	0	0	0	1	4	0	.80	0	1		0	1	-
2006	Bos	68	8	1	0	0	-1	4	1	0	.20	-1	0		0	-1	-
2007	Bos	58	4	0	0	0	-1	4	0	0	.00	-1	0		0	-1	-
2008	Bos	69	13	3	0	2	-5	2	0	1	.00	-4	0	0	0	-4	-
2009	Bos	68	6	1	0	0	0	10	1	0	.09	0	-1		0	-1	-
2010	Bos	67	10	1	1	0	-2	11	0	0	.00	-1	-2	0	0	-3	-
2011	Bos	64	6	1	0	0	-1	6	0	0	.00	-1	-1	0	0	-2	-
2012	Phi	70	10	0	0	2	-1	8	2	1	.27	-1	0	1	-1	-1	-
2013	Phi	62	7	0	0	0	-2	6	0	1	.14	0	0	0	0	0	-
2014	Phi	66	6	0	0	0	-2	4	2	0	.33	-2	0	0	0	-2	-
		627	75	7	2	6	-14	56	10	3	.18	-11	-3	1	-1	-14	

James Paxton

Year	Tm	Inn	TC	E	GFP	DM	Rng	SB	CCS	PCS/PPO	CS%	R/P	SB	Bnt	GFP/DME	Tot	Rnk
2013	Sea	24	5	0	0	1	+1	0	0	0	-	0	0	0	0	0	-
2014	Sea	74	11	3	0	1	-2	7	2	0	.22	-2	-1	-1	-1	-5	-
		98	14	3	0	2	-1	7	2	0	.22	-2	-1	-1	-1	-5	

Pitchers

Brad Peacock

Year	Tm	Inn	TC	E	GFP	DM	Rng	SB	CCS	PCS/PPO	CS%	R/P	SB	Bnt	GFP/DME	Tot	Rnk
2011	Was	12	1	0	0	0	-1	0	0	0	-	0	0	0		0	-
2013	Hou	83	15	1	2	0	+1	12	1	0	.08	0	-2	0	0	-2	131
2014	Hou	132	16	2	3	2	-1	10	1	0	.09	-1	-1	0	0	-2	146
		227	32	3	5	2	-1	22	2	0	.08	-1	-3	0	0	-4	

Jake Peavy

Year	Tm	Inn	TC	E	GFP	DM	Rng	SB	CCS	PCS/PPO	CS%	R/P	SB	Bnt	GFP/DME	Tot	Rnk
2003	SD	195	40	3	-	-	-1	7	1	0	.13	-1	-1		-	-1	120
2004	SD	166	35	1	6	3	+1	16	1	0	.06	1	-2	1	1	1	58
2005	SD	203	35	1	1	1	+2	19	5	1	.21	2	-2	0	0	0	77
2006	SD	202	44	2	2	3	+1	25	6	0	.19	1	-3	0	1	0	104
2007	SD	223	48	0	3	5	+5	21	2	1	.09	4	-2	0	0	2	41
2008	SD	174	40	2	6	0	0	18	8	1	.33	0	-1	1	1	1	69
2009	2 tms	102	19	1	4	1	+1	9	2	0	.18	1	-1	0	1	0	60
2010	CWS	107	24	0	2	2	0	12	1	3	.20	0	0	0	0	0	88
2011	CWS	112	16	1	2	1	-4	10	5	0	.33	-3	0	1	0	-2	147
2012	CWS	219	37	1	4	2	+3	9	8	1	.47	2	2	0	0	4	22
2013	2 tms	145	20	0	2	2	+1	9	6	1	.40	0	0	0	-1	-1	105
2014	2 tms	203	50	2	2	4	+2	8	6	1	.43	2	1	0	-1	2	38
		2050	408	14	34	24	11	163	51	9	.25	9	-9	4	2	6	

Joel Peralta

Year	Tm	Inn	TC	E	GFP	DM	Rng	SB	CCS	PCS/PPO	CS%	R/P	SB	Bnt	GFP/DME	Tot	Rnk
2005	LAA	35	7	0	0	0	0	1	1	2	.67	0	1	0	0	1	-
2006	KC	74	10	0	0	2	-3	4	1	0	.20	-2	0	0	0	-2	-
2007	KC	88	11	0	0	0	-1	8	0	1	1.00	-1	-1		0	-2	136
2008	KC	53	5	0	0	2	-2	3	1	0	.25	-2	0	0	0	-2	-
2009	Col	25	6	1	1	0	0	2	0	1	1.00	0	0	1	0	1	-
2010	Was	49	5	0	1	0	-1	3	0	1	1.00	0	0	0	0	0	-
2011	TB	68	9	0	0	0	0	5	2	1	.29	0	0	0	0	0	-
2012	TB	67	8	0	0	0	-1	3	1	0	.25	0	0	0	0	0	-
2013	TB	71	7	0	1	0	0	2	1	0	.33	0	0	0	0	0	-
2014	TB	63	7	0	0	1	+1	5	0	0	.00	1	0	0	0	0	-
		591	75	1	3	5	-7	36	7	6	.18	-4	-1	1	0	-4	

Wily Peralta

Year	Tm	Inn	TC	E	GFP	DM	Rng	SB	CCS	PCS/PPO	CS%	R/P	SB	Bnt	GFP/DME	Tot	Rnk
2012	Mil	29	9	1	1	0	0	1	3	0	.75	0	1	0	0	1	-
2013	Mil	183	30	1	4	5	-6	8	5	1	.38	-4	1	1	1	-1	129
2014	Mil	199	43	0	2	1	-2	19	5	1	.21	-1	-1	1	0	-1	120
		411	82	2	7	6	-8	28	13	2	.32	-5	1	2	1	-1	

Glen Perkins

Year	Tm	Inn	TC	E	GFP	DM	Rng	SB	CCS	PCS/PPO	CS%	R/P	SB	Bnt	GFP/DME	Tot	Rnk
2006	Min	6	1	0	0	0	0	0	0	0	-	0	0	0		0	-
2007	Min	29	3	0	0	1	0	1	1	0	.50	0	0	0		0	-
2008	Min	151	28	1	3	2	+3	3	1	3	.57	2	2	0	0	4	16
2009	Min	96	12	1	1	2	-3	7	0	0	.00	-2	-1	0	0	-3	158
2010	Min	22	10	0	1	0	+1	2	0	1	.33	1	0	0	0	1	-
2011	Min	62	11	1	2	1	-1	3	1	1	.40	-1	0	1	0	0	-
2012	Min	70	16	1	1	1	+1	2	1	2	.60	0	1	0	-1	0	-
2013	Min	63	7	0	0	0	0	0	0	0	-	0	0	0	0	0	-
2014	Min	62	10	0	2	0	+2	2	1	1	.50	2	1	0	0	3	-
		559	98	4	10	7	3	20	5	8	.39	2	3	1	-1	5	

Yusmeiro Petit

Year	Tm	Inn	TC	E	GFP	DM	Rng	SB	CCS	PCS/PPO	CS%	R/P	SB	Bnt	GFP/DME	Tot	Rnk
2006	Fla	26	2	0	0	0	0	0	2	0	1.00	0	1	0		1	-
2007	Ari	57	5	0	0	0	-1	4	0	0	.00	-1	0	0	0	-1	-
2008	Ari	56	7	0	0	0	-1	2	1	0	.33	-1	0	0	0	-1	-
2009	Ari	90	14	1	1	1	0	9	1	0	.10	0	-1	0	0	-1	115
2012	SF	5	2	0	0	0	+1	1	2	1	.67	1	1	0		2	-
2013	SF	48	6	0	1	0	+1	2	1	0	.33	0	0	0	0	0	-
2014	SF	117	14	2	0	0	-4	15	4	0	.21	-3	-2		0	-5	172
		399	50	3	2	1	-4	33	11	1	.25	-4	-1	0	0	-5	

Jake Petricka

Year	Tm	Inn	TC	E	GFP	DM	Rng	SB	CCS	PCS/PPO	CS%	R/P	SB	Bnt	GFP/DME	Tot	Rnk
2013	CWS	19	4	0	1	1	+1	1	1	0	.50	1	0	0		1	
2014	CWS	73	13	0	1	0	-2	2	3	1	.67	-1	1	1	0	1	-
		92	17	0	2	1	-1	3	4	1	.63	0	1	1	0	2	

David Phelps

Year	Tm	Inn	TC	E	GFP	DM	Rng	SB	CCS	PCS/PPO	CS%	R/P	SB	Bnt	GFP/DME	Tot	Rnk
2012	NYY	100	17	3	1	0	-2	3	1	3	.25	-2	2	0	0	0	108
2013	NYY	87	23	1	0	1	-1	3	3	3	.50	0	2	0	0	2	46
2014	NYY	113	28	0	2	1	+1	7	4	3	.46	1	1	1	0	3	32
		299	68	4	3	2	-2	13	8	9	.43	-1	5	1	0	5	

Michael Pineda

Year	Tm	Inn	TC	E	GFP	DM	Rng	SB	CCS	PCS/PPO	CS%	R/P	SB	Bnt	GFP/DME	Tot	Rnk
2011	Sea	171	26	1	1	3	-3	10	10	0	.50	-2	1	0	0	-1	128
2014	NYY	76	12	1	0	1	0	5	3	1	.44	0	0	0	-1	-1	-
		247	38	2	1	4	-3	15	13	1	.48	-2	1	0	-1	-2	

Yohan Pino

Year	Tm	Inn	TC	E	GFP	DM	Rng	SB	CCS	PCS/PPO	CS%	R/P	SB	Bnt	GFP/DME	Tot	Rnk
2014	Min	60	12	0	0	2	0	3	1	1	.25	0	0	0	-1	-1	-

Drew Pomeranz

Year	Tm	Inn	TC	E	GFP	DM	Rng	SB	CCS	PCS/PPO	CS%	R/P	SB	Bnt	GFP/DME	Tot	Rnk
2011	Col	18	1	0	0	0	0	1	1	0	.50	0	0	0		0	-
2012	Col	97	21	1	0	1	-2	10	1	1	.17	-2	-1	0	0	-3	152
2013	Col	22	2	0	0	0	+1	3	0	0	.00	1	0	0		1	-
2014	Oak	69	9	0	1	0	+1	6	0	0	.00	1	-1	0	0	0	-
		205	33	1	1	1	0	20	2	1	.13	0	-2	0	0	-2	

Rick Porcello

Year	Tm	Inn	TC	E	GFP	DM	Rng	SB	CCS	PCS/PPO	CS%	R/P	SB	Bnt	GFP/DME	Tot	Rnk
2009	Det	171	38	2	1	7	-2	8	2	1	.20	-2	0	0	-1	-3	158
2010	Det	163	25	1	3	2	-5	10	5	0	.33	-4	0	0	0	-4	166
2011	Det	182	38	2	2	2	-1	16	4	0	.20	-1	-1	1	0	-1	123
2012	Det	176	47	5	1	5	+1	18	5	1	.22	1	-1	0	0	0	89
2013	Det	177	37	1	2	2	-4	12	4	2	.29	-3	0	0	-1	-4	168
2014	Det	205	39	4	2	1	-1	7	7	0	.50	-1	1	0	0	0	100
		1073	224	15	11	19	-12	71	27	4	.28	-10	-1	1	-2	-12	

David Price

Year	Tm	Inn	TC	E	GFP	DM	Rng	SB	CCS	PCS/PPO	CS%	R/P	SB	Bnt	GFP/DME	Tot	Rnk
2008	TB	14	1	0	0	0	0	0	0	0	-	0	0	0		0	-
2009	TB	128	23	1	2	3	0	8	3	3	.43	0	1	0	0	1	69
2010	TB	209	30	0	2	0	-1	13	4	3	.35	-1	1	1	1	2	55
2011	TB	224	40	4	5	2	-1	20	4	1	.20	-1	-1	1	0	-1	123
2012	TB	211	37	3	4	2	+5	11	10	1	.48	3	2	-1	1	5	11
2013	TB	187	32	0	4	0	+1	11	6	5	.48	1	2	0	1	4	18
2014	2 tms	248	23	1	2	2	-2	12	3	2	.25	-1	1	-1	0	-1	120
		1221	186	9	19	9	2	75	30	15	.36	1	6	2	1	10	-

Jose Quintana

Year	Tm	Inn	TC	E	GFP	DM	Rng	SB	CCS	PCS/PPO	CS%	R/P	SB	Bnt	GFP/DME	Tot	Rnk
2012	CWS	136	29	1	1	4	+1	7	2	2	.36	0	1	0	-1	0	93
2013	CWS	200	29	2	3	4	+1	7	0	5	.42	1	2	0	0	3	27
2014	CWS	200	29	0	4	1	+3	9	3	2	.36	2	1	0	1	4	17
		536	87	3	8	9	5	23	5	9	.38	3	4	0	0	7	-

Pitchers

Erasmo Ramirez

Year	Tm	Inn	TC	E	GFP	DM	Rng	SB	CCS	PCS/PPO	CS%	R/P	SB	Bnt	GFP/DME	Tot	Rnk
2012	Sea	59	12	0	3	0	+1	4	0	0	.00	0	0	0	1	1	
2013	Sea	72	9	0	1	1	+1	3	0	0	.00	1	0	0	0	1	
2014	Sea	75	10	0	1	0	-1	6	1	1	.25	-1	0	0	0	-1	
		206	31	0	5	1	1	13	1	1	.13	0	0	0	1	1	

A.J. Ramos

Year	Tm	Inn	TC	E	GFP	DM	Rng	SB	CCS	PCS/PPO	CS%	R/P	SB	Bnt	GFP/DME	Tot	Rnk
2012	Mia	9	1	0	0	0	0	0	1	0	1.00	0	0		0	0	-
2013	Mia	80	16	2	1	2	0	7	1	1	.30	-1	0	0	-1	-2	136
2014	Mia	64	8	0	1	0	-2	7	3	0	.30	-2	0	0	0	-2	
		153	25	2	2	2	-3	14	6	1	.33	-3	0	0	-1	-4	

Cesar Ramos

Year	Tm	Inn	TC	E	GFP	DM	Rng	SB	CCS	PCS/PPO	CS%	R/P	SB	Bnt	GFP/DME	Tot	Rnk
2009	SD	15	4	0	0	0	0	3	0	1	.25	0	0	-1	0	-1	-
2010	SD	8	1	0	1	0	0	1	0	0	.00	0	0		0	0	-
2011	TB	44	12	0	0	0	+2	4	0	0	.00	1	0		0	1	-
2012	TB	30	9	0	0	0	0	3	0	0	.00	0	0		0	0	-
2013	TB	67	15	0	0	0	0	6	0	0	.00	0	-1		1	0	-
2014	TB	83	14	2	1	1	-1	3	0	0	.00	-1	0	0	0	-1	120
		246	55	2	2	1	1	20	0	1	.05	0	-1	-1	1	-1	

Todd Redmond

Year	Tm	Inn	TC	E	GFP	DM	Rng	SB	CCS	PCS/PPO	CS%	R/P	SB	Bnt	GFP/DME	Tot	Rnk
2012	Cin	3	2	1	0	1	-1	2	0	0	.00	0	0		0	0	-
2013	Tor	77	10	1	0	3	0	8	0	0	.00	0	-1		0	-1	105
2014	Tor	75	6	2	0	0	-3	7	6	0	.46	-2	0		0	-2	-
		155	18	4	0	4	-4	17	6	0	.26	-2	-1		0	-3	

Garrett Richards

Year	Tm	Inn	TC	E	GFP	DM	Rng	SB	CCS	PCS/PPO	CS%	R/P	SB	Bnt	GFP/DME	Tot	Rnk
2011	LAA	14	5	0	0	0	0	1	1	1	.50	0	1		0	1	-
2012	LAA	71	7	1	0	1	-2	8	2	0	.20	-1	-1	0	0	-2	-
2013	LAA	145	39	2	6	4	-1	10	5	0	.33	-1	0	0	0	-1	115
2014	LAA	169	26	3	2	2	-1	10	3	0	.23	-1	0	0	0	-1	120
		398	77	6	8	7	-4	29	11	1	.28	-3	0	0	0	-3	

Andre Rienzo

Year	Tm	Inn	TC	E	GFP	DM	Rng	SB	CCS	PCS/PPO	CS%	R/P	SB	Bnt	GFP/DME	Tot	Rnk
2013	CWS	56	19	1	1	2	+2	1	0	1	1.00	1	0		-1	0	-
2014	CWS	65	17	3	0	0	0	3	0	0	.00	0	0	-2	0	-2	-
		120	36	4	1	2	2	4	0	1	.00	1	0	-2	-1	-2	

Tanner Roark

Year	Tm	Inn	TC	E	GFP	DM	Rng	SB	CCS	PCS/PPO	CS%	R/P	SB	Bnt	GFP/DME	Tot	Rnk
2013	Was	54	14	1	2	0	-1	1	0	0	.00	-1	0	0	0	-1	-
2014	Was	199	36	2	2	1	+1	8	5	1	.38	1	1	2	0	4	21
		252	50	3	4	1	0	9	5	1	.36	0	1	2	0	3	

David Robertson

Year	Tm	Inn	TC	E	GFP	DM	Rng	SB	CCS	PCS/PPO	CS%	R/P	SB	Bnt	GFP/DME	Tot	Rnk
2008	NYY	30	4	0	0	0	-2	4	3	0	.43	-2	0		0	-2	-
2009	NYY	44	3	0	0	0	-3	2	1	1	.50	-2	0		0	-2	-
2010	NYY	61	5	0	0	2	-1	6	1	0	.14	-1	0		0	-1	-
2011	NYY	67	7	1	0	1	-1	16	2	0	.11	-1	-2	0	0	-3	-
2012	NYY	61	5	0	1	0	-1	8	1	0	.11	-1	-1		0	-2	-
2013	NYY	66	8	0	0	0	-1	7	1	0	.13	0	-1	0	0	-1	-
2014	NYY	64	9	0	0	0	0	8	1	0	.11	0	-1		0	-1	-
		393	41	1	1	3	-8	51	10	1	.18	-7	-5	0	0	-12	

Fernando Rodney

Year	Tm	Inn	TC	E	GFP	DM	Rng	SB	CCS	PCS/PPO	CS%	R/P	SB	Bnt	GFP/DME	Tot	Rnk
2003	Det	30	3	0	-	-	-1	10	1	0	.09	-1	-2	0		-3	
2005	Det	44	7	1	0	0	+1	4	1	0	.33	1	0		0	1	
2006	Det	72	15	1	0	0	0	5	3	1	.44	0	1	0	0	1	
2007	Det	51	15	1	1	2	0	6	2	0	.25	0	0	-1	0	-1	
2008	Det	40	6	0	0	1	0	4	0	0	.00	0	0	0	0	0	
2009	Det	76	16	0	0	0	-3	2	0	0	.00	-2	0	0	0	-2	
2010	LAA	68	17	0	0	1	-1	13	0	1	.07	-1	-2	0	0	-3	
2011	LAA	32	6	1	0	3	-2	5	0	0	.00	-2	-1		-1	-4	
2012	TB	75	26	0	4	1	-1	2	1	0	.33	-1	0	1	1	1	
2013	TB	67	13	2	1	3	0	9	2	0	.18	0	-1		0	-1	
2014	Sea	66	10	1	1	1	-1	6	0	1	.14	-1	0	0	-1	-1	
		619	134	7	7	12	-8	64	10	3	.17	-7	-5	0	-1	-13	

Francisco Rodriguez

Year	Tm	Inn	TC	E	GFP	DM	Rng	SB	CCS	PCS/PPO	CS%	R/P	SB	Bnt	GFP/DME	Tot	Rnk
2003	Ana	86	15	0	-	-	0	6	3	1	.40	0	0	0		0	86
2004	Ana	84	14	0	2	1	0	4	2	0	.33	0	0	1	0	1	66
2005	LAA	67	12	1	0	0	-1	2	0	0	.00	-1	0	0	0	-1	
2006	LAA	73	10	0	0	1	+1	2	1	1	.33	1	1	0	0	2	
2007	LAA	67	6	0	0	0	-1	12	1	0	.08	-1	-2	0		-3	
2008	LAA	68	12	2	1	1	0	8	0	0	.00	0	-1	-1	0	-2	
2009	NYM	68	8	0	0	0	-1	7	2	0	.22	-1	-1	0	0	-2	
2010	NYM	57	9	0	0	0	-2	4	1	1	.20	-2	0	0	0	-2	
2011	2 tms	72	12	0	0	0	-3	11	1	0	.08	-2	-1	0	0	-3	
2012	Mil	72	5	0	0	2	-3	12	0	1	.00	-2	-1	0	0	-3	
2013	2 tms	47	6	0	0	0	-1	3	1	1	.25	1	1	0	0	-2	
2014	Mil	68	9	0	1	1	+1	7	1	0	.13	1	-1	1	0	-1	
		829	118	3	5	7	-10	78	13	5	.15	-8	-5	1	0	-12	

Hector Rondon

Year	Tm	Inn	TC	E	GFP	DM	Rng	SB	CCS	PCS/PPO	CS%	R/P	SB	Bnt	GFP/DME	Tot	Rnk
2013	ChC	55	17	0	2	0	+1	4	1	0	.20	1	0	0	0	1	-
2014	ChC	63	19	0	2	0	+3	6	1	0	.14	2	-1		0	1	-
		118	36	0	4	0	4	10	2	0	.17	3	-1	0	0	2	

Trevor Rosenthal

Year	Tm	Inn	TC	E	GFP	DM	Rng	SB	CCS	PCS/PPO	CS%	R/P	SB	Bnt	GFP/DME	Tot	Rnk
2012	StL	23	2	0	0	0	0	1	1	0	.50	0	0		0	0	-
2013	StL	75	10	1	0	1	-3	2	0	1	1.00	-2	1	-1	0	-2	-
2014	StL	70	12	1	1	2	-1	2	0	0	.00	-1	0		0	-1	-
		168	24	2	1	3	-4	3	3	1	.50	-3	1	-1	0	-3	

Robbie Ross

Year	Tm	Inn	TC	E	GFP	DM	Rng	SB	CCS	PCS/PPO	CS%	R/P	SB	Bnt	GFP/DME	Tot	Rnk
2012	Tex	65	16	0	2	2	0	1	1	0	.50	0	0	0	0	0	-
2013	Tex	62	15	0	2	0	+4	1	0	0	.00	3	0	0	0	3	-
2014	Tex	78	12	2	1	0	0	2	2	0	.50	0	1	0	0	1	-
		205	43	2	5	2	4	4	3	0	.43	3	1	0	0	4	

Tyson Ross

Year	Tm	Inn	TC	E	GFP	DM	Rng	SB	CCS	PCS/PPO	CS%	R/P	SB	Bnt	GFP/DME	Tot	Rnk
2010	Oak	39	10	0	0	0	+1	2	0	0	.00	1	0	0	0	1	-
2011	Oak	36	7	1	2	0	0	1	0	0	.00	0	0	0	1	1	-
2012	Oak	73	24	0	1	1	0	10	2	1	.23	0	-1	1	0	0	-
2013	SD	125	31	2	1	0	0	11	6	1	.29	0	0	1	0	1	65
2014	SD	196	56	3	2	6	+3	31	9	2	.24	2	-2	-1	-1	-2	140
		469	128	6	6	8	4	55	17	4	.27	3	-3	1	0	1	

Hyun-Jin Ryu

Year	Tm	Inn	TC	E	GFP	DM	Rng	SB	CCS	PCS/PPO	CS%	R/P	SB	Bnt	GFP/DME	Tot	Rnk
2013	LAD	192	37	0	1	2	+1	1	1	1	.67	1	1	0	0	2	39
2014	LAD	152	33	1	1	1	+4	2	1	0	.33	3	0	0	0	3	23
		344	70	1	2	3	5	3	2	1	.50	4	1	0	0	5	

Pitchers

Danny Salazar

Year	Tm	Inn	TC	E	GFP	DM	Rng	SB	CCS	PCS/PPO	CS%	R/P	SB	Bnt	GFP/DME	Tot	Rnk
2013	Cle	52	5	0	0	1	-1	3	0	0	.00	-1	0	0	0	-1	-
2014	Cle	110	9	0	0	2	-2	3	2	1	.40	-1	1	1	0	1	75
		162	14	0	0	3	-3	6	2	1	.25	-2	1	1	0	0	-

Chris Sale

Year	Tm	Inn	TC	E	GFP	DM	Rng	SB	CCS	PCS/PPO	CS%	R/P	SB	Bnt	GFP/DME	Tot	Rnk
2010	CWS	23	1	0	0	0	-1	0	0	0	-	-1	0	0	0	-1	-
2011	CWS	71	20	0	0	3	0	3	1	3	.57	0	1	1	0	2	-
2012	CWS	192	34	1	2	4	-3	14	4	6	.42	-2	2	0	-1	-1	128
2013	CWS	214	25	1	1	2	-2	19	2	1	.10	-1	-2	0	0	-3	149
2014	CWS	174	17	0	1	2	+1	4	3	1	.50	0	1	0	0	1	71
		674	97	2	4	11	-5	40	10	11	.33	-4	2	1	-1	-2	-

Jeff Samardzija

Year	Tm	Inn	TC	E	GFP	DM	Rng	SB	CCS	PCS/PPO	CS%	R/P	SB	Bnt	GFP/DME	Tot	Rnk
2008	ChC	28	7	0	1	1	0	5	0	1	.17	0	0	0	0	0	-
2009	ChC	35	9	1	0	0	0	3	1	0	.25	0	0	-1	0	-1	-
2010	ChC	19	3	0	0	0	0	4	1	0	.20	0	0	0	0	0	-
2011	ChC	88	15	1	1	1	-1	16	2	0	.11	-1	-2	0	0	-3	155
2012	ChC	175	40	2	3	4	+4	15	5	0	.25	3	-1	0	-1	1	60
2013	ChC	214	42	3	4	4	-7	15	7	0	.32	-5	0	-1	0	-6	174
2014	2 tms	220	43	3	4	2	-1	19	7	2	.30	-1	0	0	0	-1	120
		777	159	10	13	12	-5	77	23	3	.25	-4	-3	-2	-1	-10	-

Anibal Sanchez

Year	Tm	Inn	TC	E	GFP	DM	Rng	SB	CCS	PCS/PPO	CS%	R/P	SB	Bnt	GFP/DME	Tot	Rnk
2006	Fla	114	29	1	0	5	+2	6	1	0	.14	2	0	0	-1	1	58
2007	Fla	30	12	2	0	1	0	1	0	0	.00	0	0	0	0	0	-
2008	Fla	52	11	4	1	0	-1	7	0	1	.00	-1	-1	-1	0	-3	-
2009	Fla	86	18	2	0	1	+1	11	1	0	.08	1	-1	0	0	-1	110
2010	Fla	195	44	5	1	2	-6	11	3	0	.21	-4	0	2	0	-2	150
2011	Fla	196	45	1	4	1	+1	15	2	2	.12	1	0	1	0	2	44
2012	2 tms	196	44	2	6	3	+1	23	4	1	.15	1	-2	2	0	1	68
2013	Det	182	37	1	5	2	-4	25	1	2	.04	-3	-3	0	0	-6	173
2014	Det	126	29	0	1	4	+1	13	3	1	.19	1	-1	0	-1	-1	109
		1177	269	18	18	19	-5	112	15	7	.12	-2	-8	3	-2	-9	-

Ervin Santana

Year	Tm	Inn	TC	E	GFP	DM	Rng	SB	CCS	PCS/PPO	CS%	R/P	SB	Bnt	GFP/DME	Tot	Rnk
2005	LAA	134	20	0	0	0	0	8	4	1	.38	0	0	0	0	0	88
2006	LAA	204	27	2	0	2	-2	5	8	1	.64	-2	2	0	0	0	99
2007	LAA	150	19	0	0	0	-1	11	3	0	.21	-1	0	0	0	-1	113
2008	LAA	219	32	0	2	3	-5	16	4	0	.20	-4	-1	1	0	-4	170
2009	LAA	140	16	1	1	3	-2	15	5	0	.25	-2	-1	0	0	-3	158
2010	LAA	223	32	0	3	2	-5	36	8	1	.18	-3	-4	1	0	-6	171
2011	LAA	229	36	5	3	0	-2	28	5	0	.15	-2	-3	-2	1	-6	174
2012	LAA	178	34	1	0	6	0	16	2	1	.11	0	-1	0	-1	-2	133
2013	KC	211	42	1	2	3	+2	13	8	0	.38	1	0	-1	0	0	83
2014	Atl	196	38	1	2	2	+2	7	6	1	.46	1	1	0	0	2	46
		1882	296	11	13	21	-13	155	53	5	.26	-12	-7	-1	0	-20	-

Hector Santiago

Year	Tm	Inn	TC	E	GFP	DM	Rng	SB	CCS	PCS/PPO	CS%	R/P	SB	Bnt	GFP/DME	Tot	Rnk
2011	CWS	5	1	0	0	0	0	0	0	0	-	0	0		0	0	-
2012	CWS	70	12	0	0	0	+1	10	1	0	.09	1	-1		0	0	-
2013	CWS	149	26	1	7	2	+7	9	5	1	.40	5	1	-1	1	6	5
2014	LAA	127	22	2	1	0	+1	10	1	6	.41	1	2	0	0	3	32
		352	61	3	8	2	9	29	7	7	.33	7	2	-1	1	9	-

Max Scherzer

Year	Tm	Inn	TC	E	GFP	DM	Rng	SB	CCS	PCS/PPO	CS%	R/P	SB	Bnt	GFP/DME	Tot	Rnk
2008	Ari	56	10	1	2	0	0	0	1	0	1.00	0	0	0	0	0	-
2009	Ari	170	35	2	2	2	-2	10	5	1	.38	-2	1	-1	0	-2	147
2010	Det	196	30	2	2	3	-2	17	12	1	.43	-1	0	0	-1	-2	139
2011	Det	195	23	0	2	1	-6	12	6	3	.43	-5	2	1	0	-2	150
2012	Det	188	22	1	2	1	-7	15	8	3	.38	-5	1	1	0	-3	160
2013	Det	214	41	3	2	2	0	14	6	3	.36	0	1	-1	1	1	65
2014	Det	220	27	0	1	0	-5	13	10	0	.43	-4	1	-1	0	-4	169
		1239	188	10	13	9	-22	81	48	11	.41	-17	6	-1	0	-12	-

Bryan Shaw

Year	Tm	Inn	TC	E	GFP	DM	Rng	SB	CCS	PCS/PPO	CS%	R/P	SB	Bnt	GFP/DME	Tot	Rnk
2011	Ari	28	13	1	0	1	0	1	1	1	.67	0	1	0	0	1	-
2012	Ari	59	12	1	0	1	+1	3	3	1	.50	1	-1	0	0	1	-
2013	Cle	75	11	2	2	2	-1	4	2	0	.33	-1	0	-1	0	-2	-
2014	Cle	76	11	0	2	2	-1	11	2	0	.15	-1	-1	0	0	-1	-
		239	47	4	4	6	-1	19	8	2	.32	-1	1	-1	0	-1	-

James Shields

Year	Tm	Inn	TC	E	GFP	DM	Rng	SB	CCS	PCS/PPO	CS%	R/P	SB	Bnt	GFP/DME	Tot	Rnk
2006	TB	125	29	0	0	0	0	7	2	4	.36	0	1	1	0	2	51
2007	TB	215	55	1	4	2	+2	9	6	0	.40	2	1	0	0	3	27
2008	TB	215	39	1	2	0	-1	7	1	6	.46	-1	1	1	0	1	77
2009	TB	220	43	2	4	4	-1	5	2	1	.29	-1	1	0	0	0	96
2010	TB	203	39	4	2	4	-5	10	3	2	.23	-4	1	-1	0	-4	166
2011	TB	249	54	3	2	4	+1	6	4	13	.45	0	6	1	0	7	7
2012	TB	228	42	5	4	6	-2	14	2	3	.13	-2	0	0	-1	-3	152
2013	KC	229	35	3	1	3	-3	5	5	3	.50	-2	2	1	0	1	99
2014	KC	227	52	4	3	3	-3	6	5	4	.45	-2	3	0	0	1	80
		1910	388	23	22	26	-12	69	35	31	.36	-10	16	3	-2	7	-

Matt Shoemaker

Year	Tm	Inn	TC	E	GFP	DM	Rng	SB	CCS	PCS/PPO	CS%	R/P	SB	Bnt	GFP/DME	Tot	Rnk
2013	LAA	5	1	0	0	0	+1	1	0	0	.00	1	0		0	1	-
2014	LAA	136	22	3	1	2	+2	7	3	2	.30	1	1	0	0	2	46
		141	23	3	1	2	3	8	3	2	.27	2	1	0	0	3	-

Alfredo Simon

Year	Tm	Inn	TC	E	GFP	DM	Rng	SB	CCS	PCS/PPO	CS%	R/P	SB	Bnt	GFP/DME	Tot	Rnk
2008	Bal	13	7	0	0	0	-1	1	0	0	.00	-1	0		0	-1	-
2009	Bal	6	2	0	1	0	+1	1	1	0	.50	1	0		0	1	-
2010	Bal	49	9	0	0	0	-2	5	2	0	.29	-2	0		0	-2	-
2011	Bal	116	24	1	3	0	+1	10	8	0	.44	1	0	0	0	1	64
2012	Cin	61	13	1	1	1	0	6	3	0	.33	0	0	0	0	0	-
2013	Cin	88	18	0	1	0	+1	3	4	1	.57	1	1	0	0	2	39
2014	Cin	196	43	2	2	2	+5	15	8	1	.35	3	0	1	0	4	12
		529	116	4	8	3	5	41	26	2	.39	3	1	1	0	5	-

Tyler Skaggs

Year	Tm	Inn	TC	E	GFP	DM	Rng	SB	CCS	PCS/PPO	CS%	R/P	SB	Bnt	GFP/DME	Tot	Rnk
2012	Ari	29	8	0	1	2	+1	0	0	1	1.00	1	1	0	0	2	-
2013	Ari	39	6	0	0	1	0	2	1	0	.33	0	0	0	0	0	-
2014	LAA	113	20	1	0	4	-1	9	3	4	.44	-1	1	-2	-1	-3	158
		181	34	1	1	7	0	11	4	5	.45	0	2	-2	-1	-1	-

Joe Smith

Year	Tm	Inn	TC	E	GFP	DM	Rng	SB	CCS	PCS/PPO	CS%	R/P	SB	Bnt	GFP/DME	Tot	Rnk
2007	NYM	44	11	0	1	2	0	5	1	0	.17	0	0		0	0	-
2008	NYM	63	21	0	3	0	+4	6	2	0	.25	3	0	1	0	4	-
2009	Cle	34	12	0	2	0	+3	1	0	0	.00	2	0		0	2	-
2010	Cle	40	9	0	2	1	+2	6	0	1	.14	1	0		0	1	-
2011	Cle	67	26	1	2	0	+7	4	2	3	.43	5	1	0	0	6	-
2012	Cle	67	17	1	1	2	+1	2	1	1	.50	0	1	0	0	2	-
2013	Cle	63	11	1	0	1	+1	1	1	2	.67	1	1	-1	-1	0	-
2014	LAA	75	15	0	2	1	+1	3	0	0	.00	1	0	0	0	1	-
		453	128	3	14	6	18	28	7	7	.28	13	3	1	-1	16	-

Pitchers

Will Smith

Year	Tm	Inn	TC	E	GFP	DM	Rng	SB	CCS	PCS/PPO	CS%	R/P	SB	Bnt	GFP/DME	Tot	Rnk
2012	KC	90	10	0	1	1	-4	8	2	1	.27	-3	0	0	0	-3	156
2013	KC	33	7	1	0	0	0	1	0	1	.50	0	0	-1	0	-1	-
2014	Mil	66	8	1	0	1	-2	2	1	1	.50	-1	1	0	0	0	-
		188	25	2	1	2	-6	11	3	3	.35	-4	1	-1	0	-4	

Drew Smyly

Year	Tm	Inn	TC	E	GFP	DM	Rng	SB	CCS	PCS/PPO	CS%	R/P	SB	Bnt	GFP/DME	Tot	Rnk
2012	Det	99	18	3	0	3	+2	8	4	2	.43	2	1	-1	0	2	42
2013	Det	76	12	0	0	1	0	8	1	1	.20	0	-1	0	0	-1	-
2014	2 tms	153	26	1	2	4	0	15	2	7	.38	0	1	-1	0	0	90
		328	56	4	2	8	2	31	7	10	.35	2	1	-2	0	1	

Rafael Soriano

Year	Tm	Inn	TC	E	GFP	DM	Rng	SB	CCS	PCS/PPO	CS%	R/P	SB	Bnt	GFP/DME	Tot	Rnk
2003	Sea	53	6	0	-	-	0	4	1	0	.20	0	0	-	-	0	
2004	Sea	3	1	1	0	0	0	0	0	0	-	0	0	0	0	0	
2005	Sea	7	0	0	0	0	-1	0	0	0	-	-1	0			-1	
2006	Sea	60	5	0	0	2	0	7	2	0	.22	0	-1	0	0	-1	
2007	Atl	72	5	1	0	0	0	7	2	0	.22	0	-1	-1	0	-2	
2008	Atl	14	2	0	0	0	0	1	1	0	.50	0	0		0	0	
2009	Atl	76	11	0	0	0	+1	3	0	0	.00	1	0	1	0	2	
2010	TB	62	4	1	0	0	-1	3	0	0	.00	-1	0		0	-1	
2011	NYY	39	3	0	0	1	-2	6	2	0	.25	-2	0	0	0	-2	
2012	NYY	68	6	1	1	1	-1	3	1	0	.25	-1	0	-1	0	-2	
2013	Was	67	9	0	0	0	0	3	0	0	.00	0	0	0	0	0	
2014	Was	62	6	0	1	0	0	3	2	0	.40	0	0	0	0	0	
		583	58	4	2	5	-4	40	11	0	.22	-4	-2	-1	0	-7	

Craig Stammen

Year	Tm	Inn	TC	E	GFP	DM	Rng	SB	CCS	PCS/PPO	CS%	R/P	SB	Bnt	GFP/DME	Tot	Rnk
2009	Was	106	18	0	1	1	+1	17	2	0	.11	1	-2	0	0	-1	110
2010	Was	128	32	4	2	2	-1	4	1	0	.20	0	0	0	0	0	88
2011	Was	10	3	0	0	0	+1	1	0	0	.00	1	0		0	1	
2012	Was	88	14	1	0	0	+1	12	1	0	.08	1	-2		0	-1	112
2013	Was	82	8	0	0	2	-2	9	3	0	.25	-2	-1	0	-1	-4	166
2014	Was	73	10	1	0	0	0	5	1	0	.17	0	0	-1	0	0	
		486	85	6	3	5	0	48	8	0	.14	1	-5	-1	-1	-6	

Tim Stauffer

Year	Tm	Inn	TC	E	GFP	DM	Rng	SB	CCS	PCS/PPO	CS%	R/P	SB	Bnt	GFP/DME	Tot	Rnk
2005	SD	81	16	0	1	0	0	1	2	0	.67	0	0		0	0	88
2006	SD	6	0	0	0	0	0	0	1	0	1.00	0	0			0	
2007	SD	8	0	0	0	0	0	0	0	0	-	0	0			0	
2009	SD	73	13	0	1	0	0	1	2	0	.67	0	1	1	0	2	
2010	SD	83	12	0	1	1	+1	1	2	0	.67	1	1	0	0	2	43
2011	SD	186	65	1	4	0	+4	5	7	1	.62	3	2	1	0	6	9
2012	SD	5	1	0	0	1	0	1	1	0	.50	0	0		0	0	
2013	SD	70	16	0	2	3	0	0	3	0	1.00	0	1	0	-1	0	
2014	SD	64	12	0	1	1	-2	1	2	0	.67	-2	1	0	0	-1	
		575	135	1	10	6	3	10	20	1	.68	2	6	2	-1	9	

Stephen Strasburg

Year	Tm	Inn	TC	E	GFP	DM	Rng	SB	CCS	PCS/PPO	CS%	R/P	SB	Bnt	GFP/DME	Tot	Rnk
2010	Was	68	8	1	0	0	-3	2	1	0	.33	-2	0		0	-2	
2011	Was	24	3	0	0	0	0	1	0	0	.00	0	0		0	0	
2012	Was	159	28	0	0	2	-1	14	1	1	.13	-1	-1	0	0	-2	137
2013	Was	183	28	0	0	3	-3	13	5	0	.28	-2	-1	0	0	-3	153
2014	Was	215	42	4	0	1	+2	13	6	0	.32	2	0	1	0	3	26
		649	109	5	0	6	-5	43	13	1	.25	-3	-2	1	0	-4	

Marcus Stroman

Year	Tm	Inn	TC	E	GFP	DM	Rng	SB	CCS	PCS/PPO	CS%	R/P	SB	Bnt	GFP/DME	Tot	Rnk
2014	Tor	131	26	0	3	1	+1	4	1	1	.20	1	0		0	1	65

Pedro Strop

Year	Tm	Inn	TC	E	GFP	DM	Rng	SB	CCS	PCS/PPO	CS%	R/P	SB	Bnt	GFP/DME	Tot	Rnk
2009	Tex	7	1	0	0	0	0	0	0	0	-	0	0		0	0	
2010	Tex	11	1	0	0	0	0	1	0	0	.00	0	0	0	0	0	
2011	2 tms	22	3	0	0	0	0	3	0	0	.00	0	0	-1	0	-1	
2012	Bal	66	18	0	0	2	0	1	1	0	.50	0	0	0	0	0	
2013	2 tms	57	7	0	1	4	0	1	0	0	.00	0	0	-2	0	-2	
2014	ChC	61	6	0	1	2	0	1	1	0	.50	0	0	-1	0	-1	
		224	36	0	2	8	0	7	2	0	.22	0	0	-4	0	-4	

Eric Stults

Year	Tm	Inn	TC	E	GFP	DM	Rng	SB	CCS	PCS/PPO	CS%	R/P	SB	Bnt	GFP/DME	Tot	Rnk
2006	LAD	18	4	1	0	0	0	0	0	0	-	0	0	-1	0	-1	
2007	LAD	39	7	0	2	0	+1	3	0	0	.00	1	0	0	0	1	
2008	LAD	39	7	1	0	0	0	2	1	0	.33	0	0	0	0	0	
2009	LAD	50	12	0	1	1	0	3	2	1	.50	0	1	0	0	1	
2011	Col	12	1	0	0	0	0	0	0	0	-	0	0		0	0	
2012	2 tms	99	19	0	1	1	+2	8	2	1	.27	2	0	0	0	2	42
2013	SD	204	39	2	3	3	+6	6	2	0	.25	4	0	-1	0	3	21
2014	SD	176	40	2	4	3	+3	15	3	1	.17	2	-1	0	1	2	38
		635	129	6	11	8	12	37	9	3	.24	9	0	-2	1	8	

Anthony Swarzak

Year	Tm	Inn	TC	E	GFP	DM	Rng	SB	CCS	PCS/PPO	CS%	R/P	SB	Bnt	GFP/DME	Tot	Rnk
2009	Min	59	7	0	1	0	0	1	2	0	.67	0	1		0	1	-
2011	Min	102	10	0	0	2	0	3	3	0	.50	0	1	0	0	1	74
2012	Min	97	15	0	1	1	-2	1	1	0	.50	-1	0	1	1	1	83
2013	Min	96	16	1	0	0	-1	3	3	1	.57	0	1	0	0	1	65
2014	Min	86	15	0	1	1	0	2	0	0	.00	0	0	0	0	0	90
		439	63	1	2	4	-3	10	9	1	.50	-1	4	0	1	4	-

Masahiro Tanaka

Year	Tm	Inn	TC	E	GFP	DM	Rng	SB	CCS	PCS/PPO	CS%	R/P	SB	Bnt	GFP/DME	Tot	Rnk
2014	NYY	136	26	0	4	1	+2	6	0	1	.14	2	0	0	2	4	17

Junichi Tazawa

Year	Tm	Inn	TC	E	GFP	DM	Rng	SB	CCS	PCS/PPO	CS%	R/P	SB	Bnt	GFP/DME	Tot	Rnk
2009	Bos	25	1	0	0	0	0	1	0	0	.00	0	0		0	0	-
2011	Bos	3	0	0	0	0	0	0	0	0	-	0	0			0	-
2012	Bos	44	6	0	0	0	+1	4	1	0	.20	1	0		0	1	-
2013	Bos	68	8	0	0	0	0	3	2	0	.40	0	0	0	0	0	-
2014	Bos	63	10	3	0	1	+1	0	0	1	-	1	1	0	0	2	-
		203	25	3	0	1	2	8	3	1	.27	2	1	0	0	3	-

Julio Teheran

Year	Tm	Inn	TC	E	GFP	DM	Rng	SB	CCS	PCS/PPO	CS%	R/P	SB	Bnt	GFP/DME	Tot	Rnk
2011	Atl	20	6	0	0	0	0	3	0	0	.00	0	0		0	0	-
2012	Atl	6	2	0	0	0	0	0	0	1	-	0	0		0	0	-
2013	Atl	186	37	0	3	2	+3	7	1	8	.13	2	3	0	1	6	7
2014	Atl	221	48	0	1	3	+1	14	4	6	.26	1	2	2	0	5	10
		432	93	0	4	5	4	24	5	15	.20	3	5	2	1	11	-

Nick Tepesch

Year	Tm	Inn	TC	E	GFP	DM	Rng	SB	CCS	PCS/PPO	CS%	R/P	SB	Bnt	GFP/DME	Tot	Rnk
2013	Tex	93	16	0	0	1	-1	5	0	1	.00	-1	0	0	0	-1	115
2014	Tex	126	24	0	2	1	-4	4	3	4	.60	-3	2	0	0	-1	137
		219	40	0	2	2	-5	9	3	5	.40	-4	2	0	0	-2	-

Pitchers

Dale Thayer

Year	Tm	Inn	TC	E	GFP	DM	Rng	SB	CCS	PCS/PPO	CS%	R/P	SB	Bnt	GFP/DME	Tot	Rnk
2009	TB	14	1	0	0	0	-1	1	0	0	.00	-1	0		0	-1	-
2010	TB	2	0	0	0	0	0	0	0	0	-	0				0	-
2011	NYM	10	4	0	0	0	0	1	0	0	.00	0			0	0	-
2012	SD	58	4	0	0	0	-2	12	1	0	.08	-2	-2	0	0	-4	-
2013	SD	65	9	1	1	0	0	7	0	1	.13	0	-1	-1	0	-2	-
2014	SD	65	8	0	3	1	-2	9	2	0	.18	-2	-1	0	0	-3	-
		214	26	1	4	1	-5	30	3	1	.12	-5	-4	-1	0	-10	-

Chris Tillman

Year	Tm	Inn	TC	E	GFP	DM	Rng	SB	CCS	PCS/PPO	CS%	R/P	SB	Bnt	GFP/DME	Tot	Rnk
2009	Bal	65	6	0	2	0	0	1	5	0	.83	0	1		0	1	-
2010	Bal	54	14	1	0	0	0	3	1	0	.25	0	0		0	0	-
2011	Bal	62	8	0	1	2	-4	5	3	0	.38	-3	0	0	0	-3	-
2012	Bal	86	10	1	0	0	-1	4	2	0	.33	-1	0	0	0	-1	118
2013	Bal	206	26	0	1	0	-3	1	7	1	.89	-2	3	1	0	2	52
2014	Bal	207	31	2	2	1	0	3	3	1	.75	0	2	-1	1	2	55
		680	95	4	6	3	-8	15	21	2	.59	-6	6	0	1	1	-

Shawn Tolleson

Year	Tm	Inn	TC	E	GFP	DM	Rng	SB	CCS	PCS/PPO	CS%	R/P	SB	Bnt	GFP/DME	Tot	Rnk
2012	LAD	38	4	0	0	0	0	1	0	1	.00	0	0	0	0	0	-
2013	LAD	0	0	0	0	0	0	0	0	0	-					0	-
2014	Tex	72	11	0	1	2	-1	4	2	0	.33	-1	0	0	-1	-2	-
		109	15	0	1	2	-1	5	2	1	.29	-1	0	0	-1	-2	-

Josh Tomlin

Year	Tm	Inn	TC	E	GFP	DM	Rng	SB	CCS	PCS/PPO	CS%	R/P	SB	Bnt	GFP/DME	Tot	Rnk
2010	Cle	73	13	0	1	1	+2	2	3	0	.60	1	1	0	0	2	-
2011	Cle	165	43	2	1	1	+1	0	0	1	-	1	1	-1	0	1	64
2012	Cle	103	22	0	0	0	+1	3	2	0	.40	0	1	0	0	1	75
2013	Cle	2	0	0	0	0	0	0	0	0	-	0	0			0	-
2014	Cle	104	22	2	1	0	-1	1	2	0	.67	-1	1	1	0	1	75
		447	100	4	3	2	3	6	7	1	.54	1	4	0	0	5	-

Carlos Torres

Year	Tm	Inn	TC	E	GFP	DM	Rng	SB	CCS	PCS/PPO	CS%	R/P	SB	Bnt	GFP/DME	Tot	Rnk
2009	CWS	28	5	0	0	0	0	4	1	0	.20	0	0	1	0	1	-
2010	CWS	14	3	1	0	0	0	0	0	1	1.00	0	0	1	0	1	-
2012	Col	53	11	1	0	1	-2	5	1	1	.17	-1	0	0	0	-1	-
2013	NYM	86	14	0	1	2	0	4	1	0	.20	0	0	1	0	1	65
2014	NYM	97	13	1	3	0	-5	5	0	0	.00	-4	0	1	1	-2	155
		278	46	3	4	3	-7	18	3	2	.18	-5	1	3	1	0	-

Jacob Turner

Year	Tm	Inn	TC	E	GFP	DM	Rng	SB	CCS	PCS/PPO	CS%	R/P	SB	Bnt	GFP/DME	Tot	Rnk
2011	Det	13	1	0	0	2	0	7	0	0	.00	0	-1		0	-1	-
2012	2 tms	55	11	0	0	0	+1	2	2	0	.50	2	0	0	0	2	-
2013	Mia	118	40	5	3	3	-1	18	3	4	.22	-1	0	-2	0	-3	149
2014	2 tms	113	28	0	2	1	-5	17	2	2	.15	-3	-1	0	0	-4	167
		298	80	5	5	6	-5	44	7	6	.19	-2	-2	-2	0	-6	-

Koji Uehara

Year	Tm	Inn	TC	E	GFP	DM	Rng	SB	CCS	PCS/PPO	CS%	R/P	SB	Bnt	GFP/DME	Tot	Rnk
2009	Bal	67	5	0	2	0	0	4	0	1	.00	0	0	0	0	0	-
2010	Bal	44	5	0	0	1	0	1	0	0	.00	0	0	1	0	1	-
2011	2 tms	65	6	0	0	0	0	0	0	1	-	0	0		0	0	-
2012	Tex	36	6	1	1	0	0	1	0	0	.00	0	0		0	0	-
2013	Bos	74	9	0	0	0	0	1	1	0	.50	0	0	0	0	0	-
2014	Bos	64	10	0	1	2	-1	1	1	1	.50	0	1	0	-1	0	-
		350	41	1	4	3	-1	8	2	3	.20	0	1	1	-1	1	-

Jason Vargas

Year	Tm	Inn	TC	E	GFP	DM	Rng	SB	CCS	PCS/PPO	CS%	R/P	SB	Bnt	GFP/DME	Tot	Rnk
2005	Fla	74	15	0	0	0	+2	11	0	1	.00	2	-1	0	0	1	-
2006	Fla	43	8	0	1	2	+2	6	0	0	.00	2	-1	0	-1	0	-
2007	NYM	10	0	0	0	1	-1	2	0	0	.00	-1	0		0	-1	-
2009	Sea	92	16	0	2	1	+2	2	5	2	.75	2	2	0	0	4	12
2010	Sea	193	26	0	7	3	+1	9	1	1	.10	1	0	0	0	1	59
2011	Sea	201	29	1	1	3	+2	18	3	2	.22	1	-1	0	0	0	92
2012	Sea	217	37	2	1	2	+4	10	6	0	.38	3	1	1	-1	4	16
2013	LAA	150	27	1	0	0	-5	12	1	4	.25	-4	1	0	1	-2	146
2014	KC	187	31	2	2	4	+6	14	3	0	.18	5	-1	-2	0	2	35
		1166	189	6	14	16	13	84	19	10	.23	11	0	-1	-1	9	-

Yordano Ventura

Year	Tm	Inn	TC	E	GFP	DM	Rng	SB	CCS	PCS/PPO	CS%	R/P	SB	Bnt	GFP/DME	Tot	Rnk
2013	KC	15	4	1	0	0	+1	0	0	0	-	1	0		0	1	-
2014	KC	183	48	2	3	2	+1	1	1	0	.50	1	1	0	0	2	46
		198	52	3	3	2	2	1	1	0	.50	2	1	0	0	3	-

Justin Verlander

Year	Tm	Inn	TC	E	GFP	DM	Rng	SB	CCS	PCS/PPO	CS%	R/P	SB	Bnt	GFP/DME	Tot	Rnk
2005	Det	11	5	1	0	0	0	1	0	0	.00	0	0		0	0	-
2006	Det	186	38	3	1	2	+1	4	4	8	.83	1	5	0	0	6	8
2007	Det	202	24	0	1	2	-2	4	1	2	.20	-2	1	0	0	-1	124
2008	Det	201	33	2	2	1	+4	8	8	2	.53	3	2	0	0	5	7
2009	Det	240	36	2	2	1	-3	9	15	3	.64	-2	4	1	0	3	35
2010	Det	224	51	2	5	1	+4	24	7	3	.23	3	-1	0	0	2	36
2011	Det	251	50	5	2	0	+5	10	4	2	.33	4	1	-1	1	5	11
2012	Det	238	53	4	1	0	+3	16	4	1	.20	2	0	2	1	5	12
2013	Det	218	38	0	3	0	0	21	4	3	.16	0	-1	0	0	-1	105
2014	Det	206	39	6	1	0	+1	13	4	0	.24	1	0	-1	0	0	85
		1978	367	27	15	10	13	107	51	24	.34	10	11	1	2	24	-

Carlos Villanueva

Year	Tm	Inn	TC	E	GFP	DM	Rng	SB	CCS	PCS/PPO	CS%	R/P	SB	Bnt	GFP/DME	Tot	Rnk
2006	Mil	54	11	0	0	0	+3	2	0	0	.00	2	0		0	2	-
2007	Mil	114	11	0	0	1	-2	6	2	1	.33	-2	0	1	0	-1	124
2008	Mil	108	22	1	0	2	+1	5	2	0	.29	1	0	0	0	1	60
2009	Mil	96	20	0	1	2	+1	5	1	0	.17	1	0	1	0	2	43
2010	Mil	53	6	0	0	0	0	8	1	0	.11	0	-1	0	0	-1	-
2011	Tor	107	17	1	0	1	+3	13	1	0	.07	2	-2	-2	0	-2	132
2012	Tor	125	18	0	2	1	-3	6	5	0	.45	-2	1	1	0	0	108
2013	ChC	129	18	0	3	0	+1	10	5	1	.38	1	0	1	0	0	83
2014	ChC	78	15	0	1	2	+2	12	1	0	.08	1	-2	-1	-1	-3	-
		863	138	2	7	9	6	67	18	2	.23	4	-4	-1	-1	-2	-

Ryan Vogelsong

Year	Tm	Inn	TC	E	GFP	DM	Rng	SB	CCS	PCS/PPO	CS%	R/P	SB	Bnt	GFP/DME	Tot	Rnk
2003	Pit	22	7	1	-	-	-1	1	0	0	.00	-1	0		-	-1	-
2004	Pit	133	22	0	0	1	-2	5	1	0	.17	-2	0	0	0	-2	131
2005	Pit	81	13	0	0	0	-1	3	1	0	.25	-1	0	0	0	-1	120
2006	Pit	38	14	0	0	0	+3	6	1	0	.14	2	-1	1	0	2	-
2011	SF	180	32	0	0	2	+1	12	3	1	.20	0	0	0	0	0	99
2012	SF	190	26	0	1	4	+1	10	8	1	.47	1	1	1	-1	2	47
2013	SF	104	17	0	1	0	-1	5	4	0	.44	-1	0	0	0	-1	115
2014	SF	185	32	2	0	3	+4	12	6	1	.33	3	0	-1	0	2	36
		932	163	3	2	10	4	54	24	3	.32	1	0	1	-1	1	-

Edinson Volquez

Year	Tm	Inn	TC	E	GFP	DM	Rng	SB	CCS	PCS/PPO	CS%	R/P	SB	Bnt	GFP/DME	Tot	Rnk
2005	Tex	13	1	0	0	0	-1	1	0	0	.00	-1	0		0	-1	-
2006	Tex	33	6	0	0	0	0	4	1	0	.20	0	0		0	0	-
2007	Tex	34	2	0	0	0	-2	2	0	0	.00	-2	0		0	-2	-
2008	Cin	196	35	1	1	3	+1	21	12	0	.36	1	-1	0	-1	-1	110
2009	Cin	50	13	2	0	0	+2	2	0	-1	.00	2	0	-1	0	1	-
2010	Cin	63	12	0	1	1	+1	4	1	0	.20	1	0	1	0	2	-
2011	Cin	109	16	2	0	1	-2	16	4	0	.20	-2	-2	-1	0	-5	167
2012	SD	183	27	0	2	2	-6	22	9	1	.31	-4	-1	0	0	-5	171
2013	2 tms	170	32	0	3	4	-3	24	2	0	.08	-2	-3	-2	0	-7	175
2014	Pit	193	38	3	2	1	-1	9	6	1	.44	-1	0	0	0	-1	75
		1042	182	8	9	13	-11	105	35	2	.26	-8	-6	-2	-1	-17	-

Pitchers

Michael Wacha

Year	Tm	Inn	TC	E	GFP	DM	Rng	SB	CCS	PCS/PPO	CS%	R/P	SB	Bnt	GFP/DME	Tot	Rnk
2013	StL	65	10	1	0	0	-1	1	0	0	.00	0	0	0	0	0	-
2014	StL	107	25	0	4	0	-2	0	1	1	1.00	-1	1	1	1	2	61
		171	35	1	4	0	-3	1	1	1	.67	-1	1	1	1	2	

Tsuyoshi Wada

Year	Tm	Inn	TC	E	GFP	DM	Rng	SB	CCS	PCS/PPO	CS%	R/P	SB	Bnt	GFP/DME	Tot	Rnk
2014	ChC	69	12	0	2	0	+1	0	0	1	1.00	1	1		1	3	-

Adam Wainwright

Year	Tm	Inn	TC	E	GFP	DM	Rng	SB	CCS	PCS/PPO	CS%	R/P	SB	Bnt	GFP/DME	Tot	Rnk
2005	StL	2	0	0	0	0	0	2	0	0	.00	0				0	-
2006	StL	75	11	1	0	1	0	3	0	0	.00	0	0	1	0	1	-
2007	StL	202	43	2	1	3	-1	6	7	1	.57	-1	2	0	1	2	59
2008	StL	132	28	1	0	1	+2	2	2	2	.67	2	1	0	0	3	27
2009	StL	233	56	0	3	7	-1	12	4	1	.29	-1	0	1	1	1	74
2010	StL	230	58	1	3	2	+3	8	5	1	.38	2	1	0	0	4	20
2012	StL	199	35	1	2	1	-2	2	3	0	.60	-1	1	-1	0	-1	118
2013	StL	242	61	0	6	4	+3	3	3	0	.50	2	1	1	0	4	17
2014	StL	227	51	1	1	1	+4	6	2	0	.25	3	1	0	1	5	8
		1541	343	7	16	20	8	44	26	5	.41	6	6	4	3	19	

Adam Warren

Year	Tm	Inn	TC	E	GFP	DM	Rng	SB	CCS	PCS/PPO	CS%	R/P	SB	Bnt	GFP/DME	Tot	Rnk
2012	NYY	2	0	0	0	0	-1	1	0	0	.00	-1	0			-1	-
2013	NYY	77	16	0	1	1	+1	2	0	1	.00	1	0	0	0	1	54
2014	NYY	79	10	2	0	0	0	1	2	0	.67	0	1	-1	0	0	90
		158	26	2	1	1	0	4	2	1	.33	0	1	-1	0	0	

Tony Watson

Year	Tm	Inn	TC	E	GFP	DM	Rng	SB	CCS	PCS/PPO	CS%	R/P	SB	Bnt	GFP/DME	Tot	Rnk
2011	Pit	41	11	0	0	1	+1	8	0	1	.11	1	-1	1	0	1	-
2012	Pit	53	11	2	1	0	+1	9	0	1	.10	1	-1	1	0	1	-
2013	Pit	72	14	0	1	1	+2	3	0	1	.25	1	0	0	0	1	-
2014	Pit	77	19	1	1	0	0	4	2	0	.33	0	0	0	0	0	-
		243	55	3	2	3	4	24	2	3	.17	3	-2	2	0	3	

Jered Weaver

Year	Tm	Inn	TC	E	GFP	DM	Rng	SB	CCS	PCS/PPO	CS%	R/P	SB	Bnt	GFP/DME	Tot	Rnk
2006	LAA	123	17	2	0	2	0	11	3	0	.21	0	-1	0	0	-1	107
2007	LAA	161	29	2	4	1	-3	19	2	1	.10	-2	-2	0	0	-4	164
2008	LAA	177	23	2	2	3	-2	20	5	2	.20	-2	-1	0	0	-3	151
2009	LAA	211	30	1	3	1	+1	19	5	3	.24	1	0	0	0	1	60
2010	LAA	224	28	0	2	0	0	27	3	3	.13	0	-2	0	0	-2	133
2011	LAA	236	34	2	0	2	-1	10	6	6	.41	-1	3	0	0	2	57
2012	LAA	189	26	0	1	2	-1	9	7	2	.47	0	2	1	-1	2	53
2013	LAA	154	12	1	3	2	-2	13	1	0	.07	-1	-2	0	0	-3	149
2014	LAA	213	39	2	1	1	+2	25	5	3	.17	-1	-1	-1	1	0	85
		1688	238	12	16	14	-6	153	37	20	.21	-4	-4	0	0	-8	

Daniel Webb

Year	Tm	Inn	TC	E	GFP	DM	Rng	SB	CCS	PCS/PPO	CS%	R/P	SB	Bnt	GFP/DME	Tot	Rnk
2013	CWS	11	0	0	0	0	0	0	0	0	-	0	0			0	-
2014	CWS	68	13	3	1	1	-2	7	1	0	.13	-1	-1		0	-2	-
		79	13	3	1	1	-2	7	1	0	.13	-1	-1		0	-2	

Zack Wheeler

Year	Tm	Inn	TC	E	GFP	DM	Rng	SB	CCS	PCS/PPO	CS%	R/P	SB	Bnt	GFP/DME	Tot	Rnk
2013	NYM	100	6	0	0	2	-2	10	2	0	.17	-2	-1	0	-1	-4	166
2014	NYM	185	34	2	1	2	-3	7	3	1	.30	-3	1	1	0	-1	137
		285	40	2	1	4	-5	17	5	1	.23	-5	0	1	-1	-5	

Chase Whitley

Year	Tm	Inn	TC	E	GFP	DM	Rng	SB	CCS	PCS/PPO	CS%	R/P	SB	Bnt	GFP/DME	Tot	Rnk
2014	NYY	76	13	0	0	0	-2	5	6	0	.55	-1	1			0	-

Tom Wilhelmsen

Year	Tm	Inn	TC	E	GFP	DM	Rng	SB	CCS	PCS/PPO	CS%	R/P	SB	Bnt	GFP/DME	Tot	Rnk
2011	Sea	33	8	1	0	0	+1	3	0	1	.25	1	0	0	0	1	-
2012	Sea	79	14	2	0	2	-3	12	1	0	.08	-2	-2	0	0	-4	164
2013	Sea	59	10	1	0	1	-1	5	0	0	.00	-1	-1	0	0	-2	141
2014	Sea	79	17	1	1	1	0	14	0	0	.00	-2	-2	0	0	-2	141
		250	49	5	1	4	-3	34	1	1	.06	-2	-5	0	0	-7	

Jerome Williams

Year	Tm	Inn	TC	E	GFP	DM	Rng	SB	CCS	PCS/PPO	CS%	R/P	SB	Bnt	GFP/DME	Tot	Rnk
2003	SF	132	29	3	-	-	-1	9	3	1	.31	-1	0	-1		-2	137
2004	SF	129	32	2	2	3	+1	8	1	2	.20	1	0	-1	-1	-1	104
2005	2 tms	123	34	1	1	2	0	7	1	4	.22	0	1	1	0	2	51
2006	ChC	12	5	1	0	0	-1	1	1	0	.50	-1	0			0	-
2007	Was	30	5	1	0	0	-2	2	0	0	.00	-2	0			-2	-
2011	LAA	44	8	2	0	1	-3	3	1	1	.40	-2	0			-2	-
2012	LAA	138	29	0	2	0	+1	14	3	2	.18	1	0		0	1	68
2013	LAA	169	32	1	3	1	+1	9	7	1	.44	1	1	-1	0	1	54
2014	3 tms	115	19	0	0	4	-2	5	2	1	.29	-1	0	0	0	-1	120
		892	190	11	8	11	-6	58	19	12	.28	-4	2	-2	-1	-5	

C.J. Wilson

Year	Tm	Inn	TC	E	GFP	DM	Rng	SB	CCS	PCS/PPO	CS%	R/P	SB	Bnt	GFP/DME	Tot	Rnk
2005	Tex	48	12	0	0	0	0	1	0	0	.00	0	0	0	0	0	-
2006	Tex	44	7	0	1	1	0	5	2	1	.38	0	0	0	0	0	-
2007	Tex	68	17	1	0	1	-1	8	0	0	.00	-1	0	0	0	-1	-
2008	Tex	46	13	1	2	2	+1	1	1	0	.50	1	0	0	0	1	-
2009	Tex	74	18	2	3	2	+1	4	2	0	.33	1	0	-1	0	0	-
2010	Tex	204	35	2	3	3	0	21	7	1	.28	0	-1	-1	0	-2	133
2011	Tex	223	30	1	1	3	0	24	7	0	.23	0	-2	0	-1	-3	152
2012	LAA	202	42	2	2	2	+3	22	7	5	.35	2	1	0	0	3	31
2013	LAA	212	34	1	5	5	+1	15	1	1	.12	1	-1	0	0	0	83
2014	LAA	176	34	3	5	5	+5	13	7	1	.35	3	0	-1	-1	1	63
		1298	242	13	22	21	10	108	34	9	.28	7	-3	-3	-2	-1	

Justin Wilson

Year	Tm	Inn	TC	E	GFP	DM	Rng	SB	CCS	PCS/PPO	CS%	R/P	SB	Bnt	GFP/DME	Tot	Rnk
2012	Pit	5	1	0	0	0	0	2	0	0	.00	0	0	0	0	0	-
2013	Pit	74	15	0	0	0	-1	7	2	1	.30	-1	0	0	1	0	-
2014	Pit	60	5	1	0	0	-3	7	0	1	.13	-2	-1	0	0	-3	-
		138	21	1	0	0	-4	16	2	2	.20	-3	-1	0	1	-3	

Alex Wood

Year	Tm	Inn	TC	E	GFP	DM	Rng	SB	CCS	PCS/PPO	CS%	R/P	SB	Bnt	GFP/DME	Tot	Rnk
2013	Atl	78	13	0	1	0	+1	3	2	3	.50	1	2	0	0	3	27
2014	Atl	172	30	2	1	1	-3	7	3	5	.36	-2	2	0	0	0	106
		249	43	2	2	1	-2	10	5	8	.41	-1	4	0	0	3	

Travis Wood

Year	Tm	Inn	TC	E	GFP	DM	Rng	SB	CCS	PCS/PPO	CS%	R/P	SB	Bnt	GFP/DME	Tot	Rnk
2010	Cin	103	13	3	2	0	+2	0	0	0	-	1	0	0	0	1	59
2011	Cin	106	19	0	1	0	+1	5	2	3	.50	1	1	1	0	3	33
2012	ChC	156	34	2	4	0	+1	6	1	0	.14	1	0	1	0	2	47
2013	ChC	200	35	1	5	1	0	4	2	1	.43	0	1	0	0	1	65
2014	ChC	174	24	0	5	3	+4	10	3	0	.23	3	0	1	0	4	12
		738	125	6	17	4	8	25	8	4	.32	6	2	3	0	11	

Pitchers

Brandon Workman

		BASIC						HOLDING				RUNS SAVED					
Year	Tm	Inn	TC	E	GFP	DM	Rng	SB	CCS	PCS/PPO	CS%	R/P	SB	Bnt	GFP/DME	Tot	Rnk
2013	Bos	42	1	0	0	0	-1	10	2	1	.17	-1	-1		0	-2	-
2014	Bos	87	14	1	1	0	0	13	7	0	.35	0	-1	-1	0	-2	141
		128	15	1	1	0	-1	23	9	1	.28	-1	-2	-1	0	-4	

Vance Worley

		BASIC						HOLDING				RUNS SAVED					
Year	Tm	Inn	TC	E	GFP	DM	Rng	SB	CCS	PCS/PPO	CS%	R/P	SB	Bnt	GFP/DME	Tot	Rnk
2010	Phi	13	4	0	0	0	+1	0	1	0	1.00	1	0	0	0	1	-
2011	Phi	132	24	0	3	1	+2	2	0	0	.00	1	0	0	0	1	64
2012	Phi	133	27	1	0	1	-2	5	6	0	.55	-2	1	0	0	-1	128
2013	Min	49	14	1	1	3	+1	1	2	0	.67	0	1	0	0	1	-
2014	Pit	111	17	1	1	1	-2	0	3	0	1.00	-2	1	0	0	-1	134
		437	86	3	5	6	0	8	12	0	.60	-2	3	0	0	1	-

Jamey Wright

		BASIC						HOLDING				RUNS SAVED					
Year	Tm	Inn	TC	E	GFP	DM	Rng	SB	CCS	PCS/PPO	CS%	R/P	SB	Bnt	GFP/DME	Tot	Rnk
2003	KC	25	4	0	-	-	0	5	0	1	.00	0	0	0	-	0	-
2004	Col	79	25	0	0	1	+2	13	2	4	.13	2	0	1	0	3	-
2005	Col	171	37	2	1	3	-2	25	7	6	.22	-2	0	-2	0	-4	164
2006	SF	156	40	2	0	3	-7	13	3	7	.38	-5	2	0	0	-3	164
2007	Tex	77	20	1	3	0	+1	4	4	1	.50	1	1	0	0	2	-
2008	Tex	84	35	2	5	2	+1	9	1	2	.10	1	0	-1	0	0	88
2009	KC	79	19	2	0	0	+1	7	3	2	.30	1	1	0	0	2	43
2010	2 tms	58	21	0	0	1	+3	13	0	1	.00	3	-2	-1	0	0	-
2011	Sea	68	18	1	0	0	-2	8	2	2	.27	-2	0	0	0	-2	-
2012	LAD	68	24	5	2	0	-2	10	0	2	.09	-2	-1	-2	1	-4	-
2013	TB	70	21	0	1	0	-1	16	2	3	.16	0	-1	0	0	-1	-
2014	LAD	70	17	0	1	1	-1	4	0	0	.00	-1	0	0	0	-1	-
		1006	281	15	13	11	-7	127	24	31	.20	-4	0	-5	1	-8	-

Chris Young

		BASIC						HOLDING				RUNS SAVED					
Year	Tm	Inn	TC	E	GFP	DM	Rng	SB	CCS	PCS/PPO	CS%	R/P	SB	Bnt	GFP/DME	Tot	Rnk
2004	Tex	36	6	1	0	0	0	4	0	1	.20	0	0	0	0	0	-
2005	Tex	165	20	0	1	5	+2	13	6	0	.32	2	-1	0	0	1	59
2006	SD	179	20	0	2	4	-2	41	4	1	.09	-2	-6	1	0	-7	175
2007	SD	173	21	1	0	5	-1	44	0	2	.00	-1	-7	0	0	-8	173
2008	SD	102	16	1	1	0	0	15	2	1	.12	0	-2	0	0	-2	135
2009	SD	76	18	0	0	1	+1	20	0	1	.00	0	-3	1	0	-1	-
2010	SD	20	3	0	1	0	0	2	0	0	.00	0	0		0	0	-
2011	NYM	24	2	0	0	0	-1	4	0	1	.20	0	0	0	0	0	-
2012	NYM	115	15	1	1	4	-4	19	3	1	.14	-3	-2	0	0	-5	169
2014	Sea	165	18	1	0	3	0	13	4	0	.24	0	-1	-1	0	-2	141
		1055	139	5	6	22	-5	175	19	8	.11	-3	-22	1	0	-24	-

Brad Ziegler

		BASIC						HOLDING				RUNS SAVED					
Year	Tm	Inn	TC	E	GFP	DM	Rng	SB	CCS	PCS/PPO	CS%	R/P	SB	Bnt	GFP/DME	Tot	Rnk
2008	Oak	60	14	0	1	2	+2	1	0	2	.00	2	1	1	0	4	-
2009	Oak	73	23	0	0	5	-1	3	1	1	.25	-1	0	1	-1	-1	-
2010	Oak	61	16	1	0	2	+5	2	1	0	.33	3	0	1	0	4	-
2011	2 tms	58	23	3	1	1	0	6	3	0	.33	0	0	-1	0	-1	-
2012	Ari	69	25	1	4	0	+6	1	0	0	.00	4	0	0	0	4	-
2013	Ari	73	26	2	2	1	+4	2	0	1	.33	3	0	1	-1	3	-
2014	Ari	67	24	2	1	0	+1	1	0	0	.00	1	0	0	1	2	-
		460	151	9	9	11	17	16	5	4	.27	12	1	3	-1	15	-

Jordan Zimmermann

		BASIC						HOLDING				RUNS SAVED					
Year	Tm	Inn	TC	E	GFP	DM	Rng	SB	CCS	PCS/PPO	CS%	R/P	SB	Bnt	GFP/DME	Tot	Rnk
2009	Was	91	24	1	3	1	+3	8	4	2	.38	2	1	0	0	3	28
2010	Was	31	5	2	0	0	+1	3	1	0	.25	1	0		0	1	-
2011	Was	161	36	0	1	4	-1	3	6	3	.67	0	3	0	-1	2	52
2012	Was	196	42	2	7	1	+3	10	2	0	.17	2	0	1	0	3	31
2013	Was	213	42	2	5	2	+1	14	3	2	.26	1	0	1	1	3	27
2014	Was	200	33	1	2	0	+1	3	4	0	.57	1	1	0	0	2	46
		892	182	8	18	8	8	41	20	7	.36	7	5	2	0	14	-

METHODOLOGIES

Baseball Info Solutions' Data Collection

Bill James and John Dewan have been collecting baseball data together for many years. At STATS, Inc., they sent scorers to each major league stadium to sit in the press box and record information about each play. Scorers recorded trajectory information for each ball in play as well as the "zone" to which the ball was hit.

When forming Baseball Info Solutions (BIS) in 2002, they decided to start recording a litany of information from video. In addition to pitch type, velocity and location data, they began recording each batted ball location as a pixel on a computer screen, rather than as a zone. Using recorded video gave their video scouts the ability to rewind as many times as necessary to record accurate information.

In the BIS database, we record the pixel coordinate of each recorded batted ball location. We also translate these (x,y) coordinates into a "Vector" and "Distance," which are more intuitive for certain types of analysis. The Vector and Distance coordinates reflect a polar coordinate system. Vector refers to the degree-wide angle of the recorded location, with 135 representing the first base line, 180 as straight-away center field, and 225 as the third base line. Distance refers to the distance from home plate, rounded to the nearest foot.

In the early years of BIS, each batted ball was classified by velocity (soft, medium, hard) and type (groundball, line drive, flyball or bunt). Combining this information with hit locations, John Dewan and cohorts developed the original Range and Positioning System for evaluating defenders.

In 2006, the company added a more detailed description of the trajectory of each batted ball for clients. We added a new trajectory, "fliner", to describe the balls higher than a typical line drive but lower than an average flyball. BIS decided to split line drives and flyballs into four distinct categories: line drives, fliner-liners, fliner-flies and flyballs. In the Range and Positioning system, the two categories of fliners were grouped together.

Around that time, Bill James developed a new system for tracking previously-unrecorded details about defensive play. We now know this information as Good Fielding Plays and Defensive Misplays. BIS has been able to record this information back to 2004, marking every ball scooped out of the dirt and every missed cutoff man, among other things.

The following year, Baseball Info Solutions began tracking balls hit off outfield walls. No longer would left fielders be penalized for flyballs that hit 20 feet up the Green Monster.

In 2010, BIS began tracking the location of the catcher's target before every pitch.

After completing *The Fielding Bible—Volume II*, BIS decided to record even more information about every ball in play. Now, BIS video scouts put a stop watch to every batted ball, giving us a more objective description of the ball's speed and trajectory. Groundballs are timed from contact with the bat until they are touched by a fielder or cross into the outfield grass, whichever comes first. Flyballs and line drives are timed until they are caught or land untouched.

While expanding the variety of data collected in an effort to satisfy the desire for more data, the company has also increased its expectations of data quality. In addition to automated quality control checks and auditing reports, BIS video scouts now complete a minimum of three passes through each major league game.

For the 2014 season, BIS introduced the frame-by-frame timing process, which is a more accurate way of timing particular events from a game. The events timed frame-by-frame include runner advancements from first to third, first to home, and second to home; long throws from an outfielder; pitcher delivery times; catcher pop times; stolen base times; pickoff attempts to first base; and max effort home-to-first times such as bunt-for-hit attempts and ground-into-double-play opportunities. The frame-by-frame timing capabilities help BIS collect more consistent and precise data, as well as eliminate any instances where a timed event may be inaccurate due to camerawork.

As technology and video feeds have improved, so has our data quality. By no means do we believe that our most-recent data is perfect. It's possible, even likely, that there are other forms of bias or error that we haven't even considered yet. Fortunately, we've also begun to collect more objective data, such as the batted ball timer, to reduce the room for error. Stronger data collection will ultimately produce better analysis and improve our understanding and appreciation for Major League Baseball.

Methodology:
The Run Matrix

Through four volumes of *The Fielding Bible*, we've developed metrics which significantly improve our understanding of defense in baseball. In order to make these metrics more meaningful, we have converted our nine separate evaluation systems into a common currency: runs.

Baseball is all about runs. Runs determine the score and consequently the winner of each game. Runs are all over the statistics. How many runs did he drive in? What's his earned run average? Now, we can add, "How many runs did he save (or cost) his team defensively?" In order to convert each rating system into runs, we made use of a tool developed in the 1970's called the 24 States Run Matrix.

24 States Analysis (or The Run Matrix)

Take your pick. What do you want to call it? Sometimes it's called "24 States Analysis." I'm a big fan of *The Matrix* movie series so I'll go with "The Run Matrix." It sounds like a complicated concept, but in reality it's not that difficult. The basic premise is simple: at any point in an inning (defined by the current baserunners and number of outs), how many runs can we expect the offense to score, on average, before the third out is made?

Well, we can figure that out, can't we? There are eight combinations of men on base: none on, man on first, man on second, man on third, men on first and second, men on first and third, men on second and third, and bases loaded. There can be either zero, one, or two

outs at any point in the inning, so three options there. Eight base-situations times three out-situations gives you 24 states. For each of these situations, we can count how many runs scored through the end of that half inning. The end result is a chart that tells you, at any point in time, how many runs we can expect the offense to score by the end of the inning. Here's the Run Matrix for 2011:

The Run Matrix (2011)

Runners	0 Outs	1 Out	2 Outs
None	0.477	0.258	0.099
First only	0.839	0.500	0.220
Second only	1.061	0.647	0.317
Third only	1.453	0.944	0.312
First & Second	1.402	0.867	0.421
First & Third	1.750	1.146	0.476
Second & Third	1.932	1.334	0.543
Bases Loaded	2.142	1.475	0.763

The number in the chart corresponding to nobody on and no outs is 0.477. That simply means that anytime this situation occurred in an inning during 2011, an average of 0.477 runs were scored from that point until the end of the inning. Sometimes the offense scored one run, sometimes two, sometimes ten, and often zero. But on average, 0.477.

Or, take the bases loaded with one out, when the run expectancy is 1.475. Considering every one of these situations in 2011, we find that 1.475 runs scored on average after a team had the bases loaded and one out.

The key way that we use this chart is to look at it before and after a play. Let's say there's a man on first with one out. The expected runs at that point are 0.500.

The next play is a groundball to the shortstop. He boots it for an error and we now have men on first and second with one out. The expected runs went from 0.500 to 0.867. That's an increase of 0.367 runs; thus, the error cost the defensive team an expected 0.367 runs. We don't have to follow it through and count the rest of the inning. We know what the value of the ending state is and can use it.

Let's go back to that first situation: a runner on first base with one out. What if, rather than making an error, the shortstop got the forceout at second base? The starting run expectancy is still 0.500, but with two outs and a runner on first (the batter, after reaching on the fielder's choice) the run expectancy drops to 0.220, a difference of -0.280 runs. According to Newton's Third Law, for every force there is an equal and opposite reaction. Similarly, that fielder's choice groundball affected the offense -0.280 expected runs while helping the defense +0.280 runs.

What if the defense turned a double play? This result (three outs) ends the half inning and the offense's chance to score. While the offense was expected to score an average of 0.500 runs before the end of the inning, they scored none. The run value of the play, the change in run expectancy, is -0.500. The difference between turning a double play (+0.500 from the defense's perspective) and booting the ball (-0.367) is huge: 0.867, almost a full run! If a particular shortstop turns 20 errors or base hits into outs over the course of the season, you can see how the runs will start to add up.

It's important to note that every error isn't going to be worth exactly +0.367 runs, and every double play isn't worth -0.500 runs. With the bases loaded and nobody out, an error will be more costly (and a double play will be more valuable) than with the bases empty. If we wanted to find the run value of the average error made, we could compare the run expectancy states from before and after every error made last season. The average change in run expectancy is the approximate run value of an error.

We can apply similar logic to estimate the run impact of any baseball event, including doubles, double plays, fly outs, sacrifice bunts, baserunner kills, and stolen bases. We use these average run values in our various Defensive Runs Saved components to determine the appropriate run effect on each aspect of defensive play.

Methodology:
Range and Positioning

The Range and Positioning System is the primary component of Defensive Runs Saved, responsible for rating each fielder's success at turning batted balls into outs. The basic premise of the system is to approximate the proportion of the league's fielders who would have successfully made any given play, then to appropriately reward or penalize each fielder for his efforts.

The system indirectly measures several skills which are crucial to a fielder's ability to record outs. Each outfielder's positioning, reactions, reads, routes, range/speed and hands, are important elements to catching flyballs. Infielders need those same skills plus a quick and smooth glove-to-hand transfer as well as a strong and accurate throw to successfully turn groundballs into groundouts. The combination of these individual skills determines whether a particular fielder can make the plays to help his team.

A play is considered "made" by the fielder if he gets a putout or assist on the batted ball. This includes catching the ball on the fly, throwing out the batter at first or retiring a runner via force out (among other things). A play is considered "not made" when the fielder doesn't get a putout or assist on the play AND no other fielder had the first putout, assist or error. For example, if the third baseman fields a groundball towards the third base/shortstop hole, we don't count this play for or against the shortstop. We assume that he didn't have an opportunity to make the play and award no credit or penalty.

Let's say we're watching a Yankees game, and Jacoby Ellsbury is patrolling center field. We might estimate that a particular play is made by the league's center fielders 42 percent of the time (we'll come back to

the details of that calculation later). If Ellsbury makes this play, it's a nice play. A sizable 58 percent of center fielders did NOT make the play. We reward him for this; specifically, we reward him 0.58 Range and Positioning points, or Plays Saved. If Ellsbury does not make the play, we penalize him according to the proportion of fielders who did make the play, 0.42. In this case, Ellsbury would get -0.42 Plays Saved on the play.

Because giving up doubles and triples is obviously more costly than allowing singles, we also calculate Bases Saved to estimate how many bases a fielder saved or cost his team on these plays. When this particular play was not made, the batter got an average of 1.50 bases on the play. Since the center fielders who made this play were rewarded with 0.58 Plays Saved, and each play saved 1.50 bases, we can say that a center fielder saved $0.58 * 1.50 = 0.87$ bases by making the catch.

If center fielder Ellsbury did not make the play, he is penalized by 0.42 plays times the number of bases he allowed the batter to reach. If he doesn't make the catch but plays it well and holds the batter to a single, he's penalized $-0.42 * 1 = -0.42$ bases. If he lollygags and allows the batter a double, he is penalized $-0.42 * 2 = -0.84$ bases. If he completely overruns the ball and turns it into a triple, he'll be docked 1.26 bases.

Lastly, we estimate how many runs a player saved or cost his team. The way that we do this varies based on the position that a player plays. We calculate, for each infield position, the average number of runs that each Bases Saved point is worth, then multiply the Bases Saved credit or penalty on a play by the runs factor for the position. For infielders, the overwhelming majority of groundball and infield line drive hits are simply singles, so each play corresponds to about one base, and each base corresponds to about 0.75 runs. See the table below for the run factors associated with each infield position.

Range and Positioning Runs Saved Factors

Position	Factor
Pitcher	0.75
First Base	0.73
Second Base	0.76
Third Base	0.76
Shortstop	0.76

Note that the Runs Saved Factors reflect the run value per Based Saved, not the per Play Saved.

For outfielders, we convert Plays Saved to Runs Saved based on each batted ball. (We recently changed some details of this calculation, with a full explanation covered in the chapter called Range and Positioning Accounting Change: Shallow vs. Deep on page 113.) Using the 24 Run Expectancy states (see Run Matrix Methodology on page 322), we grouped balls hit to the outfield according to their depth, direction, and outcome (single, double, triple, inside-the-park home run, or flyout) and calculated the average number of runs that each is worth. If the outfielder successfully makes an out, we take the run value of a flyout for that depth/direction grouping and subtract the average run expectation for hits in that grouping, and we multiply the resulting number by the Plays Saved credit for that play. If the outfielder does not make the play, then we take the run value of the resulting hit type, subtract the run value of a flyout, and multiply that number by the Plays Saved penalty for not making that play. We call the final result Range and Positioning Runs Saved.

For example, on a deep flyball to center field, an out would be worth -0.22 runs on average, while a single would be worth 0.48 runs, a double 0.76 runs, and a triple 1.03 runs. If Jacoby Ellsbury lets the ball drop for a double, we penalize him the value of the double (0.76) minus the value of the out (-0.22), multiplying the difference by the Plays Saved penalty (-0.42 from our earlier example), or (0.76-[-0.22])*-0.42 = 0.98*(-0.42) = -0.41 Range and Positioning Runs Saved. If he does make the play, we calculate the average run value of hits in that particular bucket (50/50 singles and doubles, so 0.48*0.50+0.76*0.50 = 0.62 runs per hit), subtract the

value of an out (-0.22) and multiply the difference (0.84) by the Plays Saved credit (0.58), resulting in 0.49 Range and Positioning Runs Saved.

We then add up the credits and penalties from every play over the course of the entire season to arrive at a rating for any particular fielder. We use different units to cite a fielder's Range and Positioning rating, including plays, bases and runs. The average fielder will have a rating of 0 plays, 0 bases and 0 runs.

We might quote a player's Plays Saved as +20, meaning the fielder made about 20 more plays than we'd expect from the average fielder at his position. Another fielder might cost his team 24 bases, translating to a -24 Bases Saved score. Depending on the plays and the position, the first fielder might finish the season with 15 Range and Positioning Runs Saved, meaning we estimate that his team allowed 15 fewer runs than they would have with a league-average fielder at the position thanks to this fielder's range and ability to convert batted balls into outs. On the other hand, -15 Range and Positioning Runs Saved means the fielder cost the team 15 runs due to his inability to record outs.

Approximating the difficulty of an individual play is part science and part art. To do so, we take into account a number of factors, including the location, trajectory and velocity of the given batted ball. We also account for a few specific factors that affect each position differently.

Infield Groundball Range and Positioning

We rate pitchers, first basemen, second basemen, third basemen, and shortstops on their ability to field groundballs.

The original Range and Positioning System, introduced in *The Fielding Bible* (2006), used two primary components, "vector" and "velocity," to approximate the difficulty of each play. "Vector" is the term for a one degree-wide angle at which the groundball was hit. "Velocity" refers to the recorded speed of the groundball, either soft, medium, or hard. (For more information on vector, velocity, and BIS data collection, see page 320.)

In 2011, there were 408 medium groundballs marked at Vector 206, 19 degrees off of the third base line (roughly 45 feet) and towards the shortstop side of the hole. We'll say that these 408 groundballs comprise one "bucket" of very similar grounders which we'll consider together. Out of those 408 plays, the shortstop made 192 of them, roughly 47 percent. We'd expect to see good shortstops make this play more often than not, but a poor shortstop will rarely convert the out.

First basemen have a unique challenge in that they typically stand right next to first base when holding a runner close. This greatly restricts their range on groundballs, through little fault of their own. Therefore, when there is a runner on first base with second base open, we make the assumption that the first baseman was likely holding the runner at the base. Accordingly, for first basemen, we consider these plays separately from all other groundballs by grouping them in separate buckets.

As one of baseball's oldest strategies, hit-and-run plays usually affect middle infielders. We consider any play where the runner on first is breaking towards second a hit-and-run play. It may have been intended as a straight steal, but if the batter hits the ball, it becomes a hit-and-run in practice, at least from the standpoint of the defense. The Range and Positioning System also considers these plays separately from other groundballs.

Lastly, while corner infielders can make plays down the lines to save potential doubles and triples, pitchers and middle infielders are going for balls that almost always turn into simple singles. For shortstops, second basemen and pitchers, we assume that every groundball saved or cost the team one base. Therefore, we don't calculate a separate Bases Saved score for them.

For infielders, the Range and Positioning System remained unchanged through *The Fielding Bible—Volume II*. However, for *Volume III*, we reevaluated the system and implemented a few changes and enhancements to the system, reflected in the 2010-present numbers.

When Baseball Info Solutions began collecting batted ball timer data for groundballs, we wanted to incorporate this more objective information to get a more accurate measure of how hard each batted ball was hit. BIS Video Scouts record the time from when the ball makes contact with the bat until either the point a fielder first touches the ball or when it passes by the infield/outfield dirt/grass cutoff (whichever comes first). The Range and Positioning System then divides the distance the ball traveled to that point (in feet) by the time (in seconds) and converts to miles per hour (mph).

It's certainly true that groundballs lose some of their speed while bouncing through the infield, and their average speed will decline as they progress. However, the difference in the average speed of a single groundball when fielded at different distances is relatively small when compared to the overall variance among groundball speeds.

We take each groundball's average speed and group it into one of six timer groups (see chart).

Timer Groups for Groundballs

Timer Group	Min (mph)	Max (mph)
1	0	25
2	25	45
3	45	55
4	55	65
5	65	75
6	75	-

As you might expect, the slowest and fastest groundballs give fielders the most trouble. Infielders have the easiest time with groundballs which travel between 25 and 45 miles per hour. Infielders can range far to both sides, and they usually have enough time left that a good throw will retire the batter or runner. The harder a ball is hit, however, the more a fielder's range is limited. Unless it's hit right at him, he won't have the time to get to the ball before it passes through the infield.

With the batted ball timer data, we moved to a rolling two-year base to increase the sample size of plays considered in each bucket. Increasing the size of the buckets is a tradeoff between accuracy and precision; we want to increase the sample size to decrease the random noise within each bucket, but at the same time we want to keep the buckets small so that the included plays are as similar as possible, and we're getting precise estimates of a play's difficulty. We feel more confident with the accuracy and precision of the new base.

As a result of the multi-year base, the average fielder isn't guaranteed to sit exactly at zero when initially calculated; therefore, we re-center the league so that a rating of zero represents the average fielder at the position for each season.

We also compared out rates on groundballs from right-handed batters to those from left-handed batters. We found that the out rates shifted over a few vectors for opposite-handed hitters, due to fielders' leaning and/or positioning themselves differently. As a result of that analysis, we elected to treat groundballs from right-handed and left-handed hitters separately by forming distinct buckets.

Lastly, in reviewing the hit-and-run groundballs, we decided to group each set of three vectors together to increase the sample size when evaluating the difficulty of these plays, giving us more accurate assessments of each play.

Infield Flyball Range and Positioning

We also rate first basemen, second basemen, third basemen and shortstops on their ability to field flyballs and line drives.

As of *The Fielding Bible—Volume II*, the Range and Positioning System considered infield flyballs based on type (liner, fliner, fly), velocity (soft, medium, hard), and location (grouped into roughly 3 feet by 3 feet zones).

For 2010-present Range and Positioning numbers, we made two changes. First, we replaced the recorded type and velocity information with hang-time data, and divided the plays into six hang-time groups. We also reviewed the system and found that zones of roughly 8 feet by 8 feet gives us more plays in each bucket and therefore a better approximation of the difficulty of each play.

Outfield Range and Positioning

We measure each outfielder's success at catching flyballs and line drives. The system introduced in The Fielding Bible utilized three pieces of information to assess each play's difficulty: type (flyball or line drive), velocity (soft, medium, hard) and location.

In 2006, Baseball Info Solutions began tracking a category of plays between line drives and flyballs, termed "fliners," to further separate the easy outs (high flyballs) from sure hits (hard liners).

In 2007, BIS began tracking balls hit unreachably high off outfield walls, and the Range and Positioning System correspondingly added the "Manny Adjustment." Outfielders have no chance on balls high off the Green Monster, for example, where no fielder could reach without a cape and the ability to leap tall buildings in a single bound. Our system appropriately removes these plays from consideration.

In 2009 we incorporated the new hang-time data for outfield flyballs, replacing type and velocity information. Each flyball or line drive is split into one of six Timer Groups based on its hang-time. Obviously, the longer a ball hangs in the air, the more likely it will be caught for an out

Timer Groups for Flyballs (Center Fielders)

Timer Group	Min (sec)	Max (sec)
1	0.0	2.7
2	2.7	3.0
3	3.0	3.5
4	3.5	4.2
5	4.2	5.0
6	5.0	-

While we formerly considered each flyball within a region of about 5 feet by 5 feet (5 feet deep by one vector wide), for 2010-present we switched to roughly 10 by 10 regions (10 feet by two vectors). We also moved to a rolling two-year base. As mentioned previously, we believe this increases the accuracy of our estimates without compromising the precision of smaller buckets.

As a result of the unadjusted multi-year base, the average fielder isn't guaranteed to sit exactly at zero when initially calculated; therefore, we re-center the league so that a rating of zero represents the average fielder at the position for each season.

Methodology:
Outfield Arm Runs Saved

Under the old system of evaluating outfield throwing arms, we examined three types of plays: first to third on a single, second to home on a single, and first to home on a double. We counted the results of these plays. We break these results into three categories:

1) Moved: Anytime a runner takes an extra base on a hit (i.e. two bases on a single, three bases on a double), we say that the runner has "Moved."

2) Did Not Move: If the runner goes station-to-station on the hit, we call that "Did Not Move."

3) Thrown Out: If the runner gets thrown out trying to take the extra base, that's "Thrown Out."

We look at the frequencies of these events, and then we add a fourth category, Miscellaneous Kills. A Miscellaneous Kill is anytime a runner is thrown out on the basepaths by an outfielder (without a relay) that doesn't involve a base hit. For example, a runner who is thrown out trying to score on a flyout would be a Miscellaneous Kill. The four categories put together comprise an player's Outfield Arm Runs Saved.

Now, we dig a little deeper. While we still examine the same three key types of plays: first to third on a single, second to home on a single, or first to home on a double, we felt that, for example, all first to third advancements are not created equal. Let's look at two plays to understand why all first to third plays are not the same. The first play is a bloop single to shallow right field near the foul line with two outs and a runner on first. The old system treats this the same as our second play, a medium-distance line drive single toward the right-center

field gap with no one out and a runner on first.

2011 First to Third Plays

Play	Moved	Did Not Move	Thrown Out
Bloop Single	90%	10%	0%
Line Drive	38%	62%	0%

Our old system grouped these two plays together for our evaluations. The information in the chart above shows that these two plays are very different. On the bloop single, the runner advances 90 percent of the time. This makes sense because there were two outs, so the runner should be more aggressive, and the ball landed in a spot a bit far from the right fielder. There's little the right fielder can do to prevent the advancement. The line drive was hit to medium right-center, much closer to the right fielder, and there were no outs, so it made sense for the runner to be more cautious. In this situation, runners only advanced 38 percent of the time.

These two plays highlight our additional classifications for each ball in play. First, we separate flyballs from grounders and use a slightly different technique for each. If the ball in play was a flyball, we then determine if there are two outs. With two outs, we would expect a runner to be more aggressive, and he is.

2011 First to Third Plays:
Line Drive to Medium Right-Center

Play	Moved	Did Not Move	Thrown Out
Two Outs	62%	38%	0%
Less Than Two Outs	38%	62%	0%

Using our medium-distance line drive to right-center, we find that the Moved percentage and the Did Not Move percentage flip. That's the reason we isolate two-out plays.

Next, we establish the location of the ball in play. On flyballs, each outfield position is split into nine zones that resemble a tic-tac-toe board. Three are shallow, three are medium, and three are deep.

If we group all flyballs based on outs and location, we have 18 categorizations, or buckets, for flyballs for each situation (first to third, second to home, first to home) and each outfield position. We use a rolling one year of data to get our league average Moved percentage, Did Not Move percentage and Thrown Out percentage for each bucket in each situation for each position. When tabulating Thrown Out numbers, we only give the outfielder half credit for relay outs, i.e. runners that were Thrown Out with the help of a relay man.

The next step is calculating a player's opportunities. To get his opportunities, we add the number of times baserunners Moved against him to the number of times they Did Not Move to the number of times a runner was Thrown Out. Relay outs are counted as half an opportunity. His opportunities are multiplied by the league average percentages in each bucket to get his expected Moved, Did Not Move and Thrown Out numbers. The difference between the expected numbers and the player's actual numbers are multiplied by the run value of each play. Add that up and we have his Throwing Arm Runs Saved for flyballs, but that's only half the equation.

The other half of the equation is groundballs, where we get to showcase our batted ball timer data. We don't separate two-out balls in play from non-two-out balls in play for groundballs, nor do we use distance for ground balls. Rather than use distance, which the fielder has some control over, we split the field into slices of pie that start from home plate. Each position gets six slices of pie (mmm...yummy!) for first to third and second to home situations. Let's compare two grounders of the same velocity hit to right field, one toward the middle of right field and the other down the line, to show why location is still important for grounders.

2011 Grounders to Right Field 55 to 65 MPH

Play	Moved	Did Not Move	Thrown Out
Mid-Right	62%	38%	0%
Down the Line	100%	0%	0%

Just as we saw with flyballs, the location matters. Everyone advanced from first to third on grounders hit down the line, while not as many advanced on balls hit to the middle of right field.

In first to third and second to home situations, we also group the balls in play by velocity. There are four velocity groups: 0 to 45 MPH, 45 to 55 MPH, 55 to 65 MPH and 65+ MPH. Let's look at that same grounder to mid-right but with two different MPH groupings.

2011 Grounders to Mid-Right Field

Play	Moved	Did Not Move	Thrown Out
45 to 55 MPH	71%	25%	4%
65+ MPH	55%	44%	1%

This makes sense. A hard-hit ball is likely to get picked up quicker by a fielder than a soft-hit ball. That reduces the chances of a baserunner advancing from first to third on a single. Using both velocity and vector creates 24 buckets for each outfield position on both first to third and second to home situations, respectively.

First to home situations on grounders are the odd-ball, the cousin Oliver from the Brady Bunch. They just don't belong. We classified only four grounders as first to home plays for center fielders for 2011. We obviously can't split those four balls into 24 buckets. The dearth of grounders that produce first to home situations led us to significantly alter the methodology for these situations. First, the velocity doesn't matter here, so we threw it out. Then we had to address the location buckets. For center field, we merged all 24 buckets to create one super bucket. We don't care about the location because there are so few plays. For corner outfielders, instead of six buckets, we have three asymmetrical buckets. Think about it for a second. Where would a groundball need to be hit in order for the runner to try to take two extra bases? The answer is down the line. Anything could happen on a grounder down the line. A fielder would have to run a significant distance to get to the ball and/or it could rattle around in the corner to give the runner extra time to advance. For each corner outfield position, we put a bucket on each side of the foul line and a catch-all bucket for everything else toward the middle of the field.

To get the groundball share of an outfielder's Throwing Arm Runs Saved, we perform a calculation similar to that for flyballs. First, we use balls from a rolling one year of data to get our league average Moved percentage, Did Not Move percentage and Thrown Out percentage for each bucket in each situation for each position. The league numbers are then multiplied by a player's opportunities (Moved + Did Not Move + Thrown Out) in each bucket to get his expected Moved,

Did Not Move and Thrown Out. We still only give outfielders half credit for relay outs, and we only count those plays as half of an opportunity. The difference between the expected and the individual player's actual numbers are multiplied by the run value of each play. Add that up to get the grounders portion of his throwing Runs Saved.

So that's both halves of our Throwing Arm Runs Saved, but there's actually a third half. Yes, a third half. We have to reward outfielders for the runners they throw out, unassisted, that is not a first to third, second to home, or first to home situation. These plays we group into a category called Miscellaneous kills. Under our original Throwing Arm Runs Saved methodology, we rewarded an outfielder with 0.75 Runs Saved for each Miscellaneous Kill. We're still going to do that this time, but we're going to compare a player's Miscellaneous Kills to his expected number. We first calculate the league average Miscellaneous Kills per touch which is the sum of Miscellaneous Kills over the total number of touches. We take the league number and multiply that by a player's touches. That gives us an expected number for the fielder. The difference between the player's actual total and the expected total is multiplied by our run value (0.75) to get a player's Miscellaneous Kills Runs Saved.

A player's total Outfield Arm Runs Saved is then the sum of our three halves: flyballs Runs Saved + groundballs Runs Saved + Miscellaneous Kills Runs Saved.

Methodology:
Double Play Runs Saved

Our original GDP system measured double play conversion rates, compared each player to the average, and converted to Runs Saved. This system worked well considering its simplicity, highlighting double play savants like Mark Grudzielanek and pointing out the weak links like Jeff Kent. But we wanted to do better.

Utilizing our batted ball timer data, we developed a new system for evaluating double play groundballs. We implemented this new double plays system for seasons in which BIS batted ball timer data is available (2009 to the present); for previous seasons, we continue to use the original GDP Runs Saved system introduced in *The Fielding Bible—Volume II.*

Original System (used for 2008 and prior)

Using the definitions from the original Fielding Bible:

GDPs: How many times the player was involved in a groundball double play, either starting the double play or as the "pivot" man.

GDP Opps: How many times the player was involved in a fielding play on a groundball in a double play situation (man on first with less than two outs). This includes DPs, force outs, errors, etc.

Pivots: How many times the player made the double play pivot (for second basemen: 6-4-3, 5-4-3, 1-4-3, etc.).

Pivot Opps: How many times the player accepted a force out at second in a situation that could have been a double play (for second basemen: 6-4, 5-4, 1-4, etc.).

Pivots and Pivot Opps are included in GDPs and GDP Opps, but are also listed separately because of the different set of skills required. We include a pivot rating for shortstops as well as second basemen (yeah, I know, a shortstop doesn't usually pivot physically like a second basemen does, but you get the idea).

Now we need to determine the run value of the successful and unsuccessful double play. It turns out the changes in base-out run expectancies are very close for both positions:

**Average Run Expectancy Change
on Double Play Attempts**

	Shortstop	Second Baseman
DP	0.80	0.81
Missed DP	0.23	0.23
DP %	59%	51%

By Run Expectancy Change (RE), we mean, for example, that on a completed double play involving the shortstop, the number of expected runs that the offense will score in the inning has dropped by 0.80 runs. If the fielder doesn't get the double play and only gets a force out, the run expectancy only drops by 0.23 runs. (For more details on run expectancy and the 24 States Run Matrix, see page 322.)

Note that shortstops converted a higher percentage of DP Opps into double plays. The offense's run expectancy based on all GDP Opps (whether completed or not) drops by an average of 0.80 * 0.59 + 0.23 * (1 - 0.59) = 0.57 runs on a GDP Opp fielded by an average shortstop, but only 0.51 runs when fielded by an average second baseman. Since we are putting Runs Saved on an above-average scale, the run value awarded to each play will subtract out the average run expectancy change on GDP Opps. For shortstops, a completed DP is worth 0.80 - 0.57 = 0.23 runs, and a Missed DP is 0.23 - 0.57 = -0.34 runs.

However, we're not quite through. A typical double play involves more than one fielder to complete. A 6-4-3 double play requires both the shortstop and the second baseman. In fact, by awarding the full run value we are double-counting all such double plays. How much credit should we give to each? Let's split it 50/50 and call it even:

Run Values Applied on Double Play Attempts

	Shortstop	Second Baseman
DP	0.12	0.15
Missed DP	-0.17	-0.15

These are the values we apply to each player's DPs and Missed DPs to find out how many runs each middle infielder helped or hurt his team on double play opportunities.

New Timer System (used from 2009 to the present)

We recently redesigned our system to measure the approximate difficulty level of each double play opportunity. First, we redefined double play opportunities slightly so we can better measure a fielder's performance on traditional chances. Then we consider both the angle (Batted Ball Vector) and speed (the time it took to reach the original fielder) to form the basis of the

play's difficulty. Each set of six degrees (vectors) and three-tenths of a second are grouped together to form buckets of similar plays.

The accounting works very similar to the Range and Positioning System. For example, 87 percent of the double play opportunities that reached the shortstop at vector 192 in 1.8 seconds (right at the normal shortstop in double play depth) were converted successfully. On these double plays, we award 1 - 0.87 = 0.13 points, split between the original fielder and the pivot man. If only the force out was recorded, we debit the fielders -0.87 points, again split between the two.

By comparison, a 2.1-second groundball about 20 feet further to the shortstop's right (vector 204) is converted for a double play just 17 percent of the time. The double play and pivot man split 1 - 0.17 = 0.83 points for a successful double play. If only the force out was recorded, we dock the fielders -0.17 points, or -0.085 each.

From there, we multiply by the average run value difference between failed and successful double plays. Across all positions, we found that the average difference between successful and failed double plays was 0.58 runs.

In the new system, we also measure the run impact of corner infielders' double play opportunities. While corner infielders rarely function as the middle man on a double play, they still have an opportunity to get the ball to second base quickly and cleanly and should be rewarded or penalized appropriately. As you might expect, the range between the best and worst corner infielders on double play attempts is small.

Lastly, we apply a minor adjustment to ensure that the average player at each position centers at exactly zero Double Plays Runs Saved. This new Timer Double Plays system is in place from 2009 to the present.

Methodology:
Bunts Runs Saved

In the Bunt Runs Saved system, each bunt event is first classified as a sacrifice bunt attempt or a non-sacrifice bunt attempt based on the game situation. We consider a bunt a sacrifice attempt if there is at least one runner on base with less than two outs. It is obviously possible for a player to decide on his own to try to bunt for a hit in what would otherwise be considered a sacrifice situation, but without the ability to know exactly what the batter intended, these classifications provide a pretty sturdy basis from which to work.

Each bunt is then further classified according to three other parameters:

- the direction the ball is hit
- the defensive position of the player who fields the ball
- whether the batter was a pitcher or not

The direction of the bunt is measured as a vector coming off of home plate, with the vectors grouped into six equally sized zones that span between the first base line and the third base line. This basically creates six equally sized pie slices of the infield between the first base line and the third base line, where the center of the pie is at home plate.

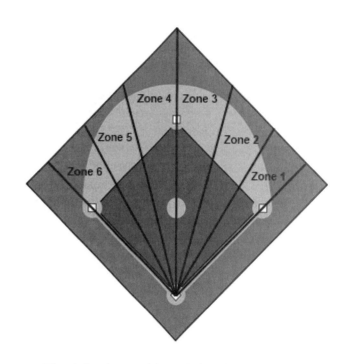

The defensive position of the player who fields the ball is self-explanatory. Third base, first base, catcher, or pitcher.

We found that when pitchers bunt for a sacrifice, the defense had a much easier time converting the out than on non-pitcher bunts. Presumably, pitchers are easier to retire because they jog to first to conserve their stamina for the mound, or they simply don't bunt as well as position players. For this reason, we evaluate pitcher bunts separately.

We group bunts into different sets, or "buckets,"

based on these distinct qualities: sacrifice/non-sacrifice, direction, fielder position, and pitcher/non-pitcher batting. Within each bucket, the bunt attempts are then categorized as one of the following bunt outcomes.

Sacrifice Bunt Attempts:

- *Sac Out* - The player that fields the ball is credited with a putout or an assist, no baserunners are out on the play, and at least one baserunner advances. Using the 24 States Run Matrix (see page 322), these plays are worth -0.18 runs on average.

- *Out No Advance* - The player that fields the ball is credited with a putout or an assist, no baserunners are out on the play, and no baserunners advance. This includes situations where the fielder catches the bunt in the air or otherwise retires the batter without allowing baserunner advancement. These plays are worth -0.43 runs on average.

- *Fielder's Choice* - The player that fields the ball is credited with a putout or an assist, the batter safely reaches base, and a baserunner is out on the play. On average, these plays were worth -0.45 runs.

- *Bunt DP* - A bunt play on which the batter is out and at least one baserunner is out OR the batter reaches safely and two baserunners are out. These plays cost the offense an average of -0.85 runs.

- *All Safe* - The player that fields the ball does not record a putout or an assist. This includes base hits (batter beats out the throw), fielder's choices where all the runners are safe, plays on which the fielder makes a fielding error, and plays on which the fielder makes a throwing error. These plays help the offense increase their run expectation an average of 0.63 runs.

Non-Sacrifice Bunt Attempts:

- *Pure Out* - The player that fields the ball is credited with a putout or an assist in a non-sacrifice situation. The offense's run expectancy decreases an average of -0.21 runs on these plays.

- *All Safe* - The player that fields the ball does not record a putout or an assist. This includes bunt hits, fielder's choices with two outs where all the runners are safe, plays on which the fielder makes a fielding error, and plays on which the fielder makes a throwing error. These plays are worth an average of 0.32 runs.

Note: if the fielder makes a play but no out is recorded due to another fielder's error, we give the original fielder credit for making the play successfully.

Using our play-by-play data going back to 2003, we determined the likelihood of each bunt outcome occurring within each bucket.

For example, for the bucket represented by:
- A sacrifice bunt attempt
- Hit to Zone 1 (near the first base line)
- Fielded by the first baseman
- With a non-pitcher batting

The results look like this:
- 74 percent of the time the fielder records a Sac Out
- 12 percent of the time everyone is safe (All Safe)
- 7 percent of the time the fielder records an Out No Advance
- 6 percent of the time the fielder records a Fielder's Choice
- 1 percent of the time the fielder records a Double Play

Within each bucket, a player is debited or credited based on the actual plays he makes compared to what was expected based on the percentages. The aggregate of those debits and credits are then converted to runs based on the run values (as determined by changes in run expectancy) associated with each bunt event type.

If we multiply each bunt outcome's frequency by the corresponding run value, we find the average run value for this particular bunt (-0.12). Let's say our first baseman completed the sacrifice out on this play. Because a sacrifice out is worth -0.18 runs for the offense, we can attribute the small decrease in run expectancy [-0.18 - (-0.12) = -0.06 runs for the offense, or +0.06 runs for the defense] to the first baseman for getting the out.

Instead of recording the sacrifice out, what if the first baseman had gotten the lead runner for a fielder's choice? We can subtract the run expectation for the play (-0.12) from the run value of a fielder's choice (-0.45) to find that the play cost the offense -0.45 - (-0.12) = -0.33 runs. In other words, the first baseman saved a third of a run by nabbing the lead runner.

The same is done for each play that a fielder faces over the course of the season. Each bunt classification bucket has its own set of percentages and expected run value; the difference between the bunt outcomes and expectations yields a fielder's total Bunt Runs Saved.

Throwing errors, while captured in the two All Safe categories and the Out No Advance category, require a secondary run value adjustment due to additional baserunner advancement. This adjustment is handled similarly to the other bunt type events. For each bucket, there is an associated likelihood of a throwing error occurring. A fielder's actual number of throwing errors is compared to his expected number of throwing errors, for which he receives a debit or a credit, and that difference is then converted to runs based on the run value of the throwing error. The run value of the throwing error has been calculated with the run value of the All Safe or Out No Advance removed so that there is no double counting.

So let's go back to the example that we were using earlier—a sacrifice bunt attempt, bunted by a non-pitcher, bunted to zone 1, and fielded by the first baseman. Let's say that this time the first baseman tries to throw out the lead runner going to second base, but throws the ball away. This would be categorized as an All Safe because all baserunners will have advanced safely. We subtract the expected run value from the play (-0.12)

from the run value of an All Safe outcome (0.63) to find that the play helped the offense an expected 0.75 runs, so we penalize the first baseman three-quarters of a run.

Now, if this had been a case where the runner simply beat the throw to the bag, we would be done. However, the first baseman also made a throwing error, which likely means that runners were able to advance further. In this situation there is a 1 percent likelihood of a throwing error occurring. Therefore, the first baseman has made 1 − 0.01 = 0.99 more throwing errors than expected. The ADDITIONAL change in run expectancy of making the throwing error (on top of the run value of the All Safe) is 0.35 runs for the offense. This means that the first baseman has cost his team an additional 0.99 x 0.35 = 0.3465 runs. So with the All Safe plus the throwing error, the first baseman cost his team a total of 0.75 + 0.35 = 1.10 runs on this play.

Because we are using a multi-year base for evaluating bunts, there is no guarantee that any individual season will center with the average fielder at each position at zero Runs Saved when initially calculated. Therefore, we make an additional adjustment to force the league average to zero for each season.

Methodology:
Good Play/Misplay Runs Saved

The release of *The Fielding Bible—Volume II* featured Defensive Runs Saved (DRS), the "next generation" of defensive evaluations. DRS took the Range and Positioning System, which must seem like an antique by now, and other elements of fielding—an outfielder's throwing arm, a pitcher's ability to control the running game, etc.— and translated these metrics into runs. Another cornerstone of that book was the introduction of Bill James' Defensive Misplays and Good Fielding Plays system. Good Fielding Plays (GFP) and Defensive Misplays (DM) were defined by James as "a very specific observation of a very narrowly defined event, created in such a way as to keep the scorer's use of judgment to an absolute minimum." Examples of these specific observations would be a catcher blocking the ball in the dirt, an outfielder robbing a home run, or a player losing the ball in the lights and allowing a catchable ball to drop in for a hit. We treat errors the same as we treat Misplays. Rather than classify an error vaguely as an error, we get a little more specific. An error could be a "groundball through infielder" or "bad throw," among other types.

We dipped our toe in the water of converting Good Fielding Plays and Defensive Misplays and Errors to Runs Saved with home run robberies back in *Volume II*, but since the publication of *Volume II*, we have converted our other GFP and DM data to the familiar Runs Saved scale, adding another layer to our defensive evaluations. Let's take a look behind the curtain and see how it's done.

We have over 80 total GFP/DM types. Some of these types are not converted to Runs Saved. This was done purposefully because including them would result in a play getting unreasonably double-counted. For instance, we have a Misplay type "Groundball Through Infielder." Let's say a batter hits a ball down the first base line. Let's call the first baseman Bill Buckner. If the ball, which should be fielded easily, gets through Buckner (which, let's face it, isn't likely), he gets penalized via the Range and Positioning System for not cleanly fielding the ball and recording the out. We felt that penalizing Buckner a second time for his Misplay would be egregious. He simply did not field the ball. There was no boneheaded play (like kicking the ball) that resulted in Buckner not fielding the ball or no unusual event that prevented him from making the play.

The flip side of the Buckner play is the Good Fielding Play "robs home run." Robbing a home run requires an extraordinary effort that goes above and beyond what is necessary to record a standard flyball out. In the 2002 All-Star Game, Torii Hunter leaped and caught a sure home run off the bat of Barry Bonds. Hunter's elbow was at the top of the Milwaukee center field wall, so his glove was more than a foot above that. That was no ordinary out. Had Hunter's catch been made in the regular season, he would have been rewarded for making the play in the Range and Positioning System, but it would look like an ordinary fly out. He gets additional credit for robbing a home run through Good Play/Misplay Runs Saved.

"Robs home run" was its own Runs Saved category in *Volume II*, and we rewarded each robbery with 1.6 Runs Saved. In *Volume III*, we rolled home run robberies back into Good Play/Misplay Runs Saved where they belong and updated the methodology a bit to center the data. Many of the Good Play/Misplay types we converted to DRS use a similar methodology.

Each GFP/DM type that we convert to Runs Saved is centered at zero, meaning if you add up the home run robbery Runs Saved over every player at a particular position for a particular season, you get zero. Good Plays and Misplays center on opportunities, usually a player's fielding touches or innings, depending on the specific type of Good Play or Misplay. We compare a player's actual number of GFPs and DMs to an expected number based on his touches or innings. The difference, multiplied by the run value of the play, is his Runs Saved for that category.

If we are trying to calculate the home run robbery portion of Torii Hunter's Good Play/Misplay Runs Saved for 2011, we take the following steps:

- Find the league average home run robbery per opportunity for right fielders in 2011. All we do here is add up the number of home run robberies across the league for right fielders in 2011 and divide by the total number of touches by those same players. This is our league average home run robbery rate.

- We multiply the league average home run robbery rate by Hunter's touches to get his expected number of home run robberies for 2011. Because of the infrequency of home run robberies, this number is 0.14.

- Then, we use the expected number of home run robberies and compare that to Hunter's actual home run robberies. Hunter, in his old age, didn't rob any home runs this year.

- We find that his actual robberies minus expected robberies is -0.14.

- Multiply -0.14 by the run value of robbing a home run (still 1.6 runs) and we get -0.22, which is Hunter's home run robbery Runs Saved.

We repeat this process for the other Good Play, Misplay and error types, except the three involved in first basemen scoops and the three involved with catchers preventing wild pitches and passed balls, which are handled a bit differently. Let's go over our methodology to estimate Runs Saved for making difficult catches on throws. Most of these kind of catches are scoops on throws in the dirt made by first basemen, so we often refer to this in shorthand as Scoops.

A scoop is really two different plays—a bad throw and a nice play that saves a throwing error. We developed our methodology for the scoops portion of Good Play/Misplay Runs Saved with this in mind.

The first half of a scoop play is the throw. In the Range and Positioning System, an infielder gets rewarded for plays that he makes—even if that made play was a result of his own bad throw that was scooped by a first baseman. If a first baseman is saving his team runs picking throws out of the dirt, the corresponding fielder that was making poor throws deserves to be penalized. Since the thrower gets credit for making the play in the Range and Positioning System, we dock a portion of his Plays Saved credit, relative to the scoop percentage on the play, as part of his Good Play/Misplay Runs Saved. Since we penalize bad throws, we also need to credit the thrower on failed scoops. We do this in the same way, based on the Plays Saved on the play, relative to the league average scoop percentage.

The second half of the play is the scoop itself. If a first baseman (or usually the first baseman, any fielder can have to manage a bad throw) picks a low throw out of the dirt or lunges to save a wild throw from giving runners a shot at extra bases, we give him credit with a Good Fielding Play for handling a difficult throw or catching a wild throw. However, if the ball is within the fielder's reach and he doesn't come up with it, he receives a Defensive Misplay for failing to catch the throw. To measure the receiving fielder's credit, we calculate the percentage of each of these three plays where he handled a difficult throw, caught a wild throw, or failed to catch the throw. Our denominator would be the sum of all three of these type of plays. We compare a player to the league average to get his scoop Runs Saved.

Once we have a player's Runs Saved number for each Good Play/Misplay type, we add that all up to get his GFP/DME Runs Saved.

Methodology:
Catcher Stolen Base Runs Saved

In the discussion of a pitcher's control over the running game on page 340, we illustrate how pitchers vary wildly in their ability to prevent stolen bases. Consequently, when evaluating a catcher's effect on baserunners we need to adjust for the pitcher's impact on each potential stolen base.

To do so, we revisit the pitcher's entire history of allowing stolen bases. We credit the catcher for every stolen base better (or worse) than the pitcher's career rate.

We'll walk through the example of 2011 Fielding Bible Award winner Matt Wieters. The young Oriole caught 1,150 innings behind the plate, nabbing 32 of 90 potential basestealers. (We ignore "Pitcher Caught Stealing," when the runner is thrown out without a pitch to the plate, since the catcher had no part in the play.) The league threw out 23 percent of basestealers in 2011, so Wieters' 36 percent certainly stands out. Further, when you compare each pitcher's career caught-stealing rate with their rate when Wieters caught them in 2011, you see that Wieters threw out a higher percentage more often than not.

	With Wieters, 2011			With All Catchers, Career
Player	SB	CCS	CS Pct	CS Pct
Alfredo Simon	8	5	38%	39%
Jake Arrieta	7	4	36%	19%
Zach Britton	6	3	33%	30%
Kevin Gtregg	6	2	25%	19%
Jeremy Guthrie	2	5	71%	34%
Tommy Hunter	3	3	50%	22%
Chris Tillman	3	3	50%	50%
Jim Johnson	3	2	40%	33%
Jeremy Accardo	5	0	0%	16%
Mike Gonzalez	4	0	0%	8%
Brad Bergesen	2	1	33%	43%
Chris Jakubauskas	1	2	67%	43%
Brian Matusz	2	1	33%	11%
Willie Eyre	1	1	50%	56%
Pedro Strop	2	0	0%	0%
Jason Berken	1	0	0%	0%
Jo-Jo Reyes	1	0	0%	13%
Mark Worrell	1	0	0%	0%

Let's walk through the Wieters-Guthrie case. Over his career, Guthrie has allowed 37 stolen bases in 56 attempts, a 66 percent stolen base success rate. With Wieters in 2011, however, Guthrie allowed just 2 steals in 7 attempts. Based on his career rate, we would have expected $7 * 0.66 = 4.6$ successful steals; instead, Wieters allowed just 2. The difference, 2.6, is the number of stolen bases Wieters saved with Guthrie on the mound.

Repeating this calculation for every pitcher Wieters

caught in 2011, we find that Wieters saved about 6.8 stolen bases for Orioles pitchers.

Utilizing the 24 States Run Matrix (see page 322), we found the run value of a stolen base to be about 0.22 runs and catcher caught stealing plays (excluding pitcher caught stealing) to be worth about -0.48 runs. Because each stolen base saved is the difference between a successful stolen base and a catcher caught stealing, we attribute the 0.70 run difference to the catcher. In Wieters' case, we multiply the 6.8 stolen bases saved by 0.70 to get approximately 5 runs saved on stolen base attempts.

Additionally, many catchers fire directly to a base after a pitch in an effort to catch runners napping. Each pickoff is worth approximately 0.46 runs. While Wieters did not pick off any runners in 2011, Dioner Navarro led the league with five catcher pickoffs.

Methodology:
Pitcher Stolen Base Runs Saved

The toughest pitcher to run against since 2002 was Kenny Rogers. Though he retired after 2008, opposing baserunners only attempted 10 stolen bases with Rogers on the mound over 2006-08 and were successful only twice, for a 80 percent caught stealing rate. On the other hand, there is Chris Young, who was not able to stop the run. Over six years he has allowed 126 stolen bases in 133 attempts, a 5 percent caught stealing rate. Rogers' rate is an incredible 75 percentage points higher than Young's, while the gap between the best and worst catchers (Yadier Molina and Josh Bard, at 37 percent and 13 percent, respectively) is just 24 percentage points.

The mission is to convert pitcher stolen base data into runs saved. To do this, we need to break it into two components, caught stealing rate and stolen base frequency.

The first component of Pitcher Stolen Base Runs Saved is calculated based on how often runners were caught by way of a catcher caught stealing, pitcher caught stealing, or pitcher pickoff. The second component is based on how often runners attempt to steal on the pitcher.

Using the 24 States Run Matrix (see page 322), we found the average run value of a stolen base was 0.19 runs (obviously a positive event for the offense), while the average run value of a pickoff or caught stealing was -0.43 runs.

Based on the relative variance in their caught stealing rates, we then assigned 65 percent of the responsibility for stolen bases and catcher caught stealing to the pitcher and 35 percent to the catcher. Pitcher caught stealing and pickoff plays were credited entirely to the pitcher. Stolen bases are counted as $-0.19 * 0.65 = -0.1235$ runs per occurrence (restated as a negative because we're evaluating Runs Saved from the perspective of the pitcher). Catcher caught stealing are $0.43 * 0.65 = 0.2795$ runs per occurrence. Pitcher caught stealing and pickoffs are 0.43 runs per occurrence.

For example, Mark Buehrle allowed three steals in six attempts as well as four pitcher caught stealings and two pickoffs. This amounts to $(3 * -0.19 * 0.65) + (3 * 0.43 * 0.65) + (4 * 0.43) + (2 * 0.43) = 3.05$ runs saved on these twelve plays.

On the other hand, Tommy Hanson allowed 30 steals in 32 attempts, with one pitcher caught stealing. He receives $(30 * -0.19 * 0.65) + (2 * 0.43 * 0.65) + (1 * 0.43) + (0 * 0.43) = -2.72$ runs saved on these 33 plays.

Additionally, we examine how often opposing baserunners attempted stolen bases in the first place. For example, Kenny Rogers limited opposing baserunners to a 20 percent success rate, but only 10 runners were foolish enough to even try to run against him in three seasons. What about those other would-be basestealers who were afraid to try in the first place? Rogers and similar pitchers should be credited for that, too.

We counted the number of stolen base opportunities (defined as any situation with a runner on first and second base open) against each pitcher. We then compared the number of stolen base attempts to the average number of stolen base attempts in the same number of opportunities. For every stolen base attempt allowed less than average, we credit him with the average run value of a stolen base attempt (as calculated from the 24 States Run Matrix).

For example, runners had 222 opportunities to steal bases against Mark Buehrle in 2011. An average pitcher in Buehrle's shoes would have allowed 21.6 stolen base attempts, but the lefty allowed just 6. He allowed 21.6 - 6 = 15.6 attempts fewer than expected, the most in Major League Baseball. Including both successful steals and failed attempts, the average stolen base was worth about 0.047 runs last year. We award Buehrle 15.6 * 0.047 = 0.73 additional runs of credit, bringing his total to 3.78 Runs Saved.

If a pitcher allowed more stolen base attempts than league average, they lose the other 35 percent of the runs we were attributing to the catcher for attempts above league average. For example, Tommy Hanson allowed 32 stolen base attempts in 111 stolen base opportunities last year. Given that many opportunities, we would have expected 10.8 attempts, 21.2 fewer than he actually allowed (the biggest difference in baseball last year). We've already penalized Hanson for 65 percent of all 32 stolen base attempts; we additionally penalize him $21.2 / 32 * (30 * -0.19 * 0.35) = -1.32$ for the additional stolen bases and $21.2 / 32 * (2 * 0.43 * 0.35) * -1 = -0.20$ to remove credit for the additional caught stealing. This additional -1.52 penalty, on top of the -2.72 runs saved from the first part, means that Hanson cost himself about 4.2 runs on stolen base attempts in 2011.

Lastly, we apply a small adjustment so the league average pitcher centers at exactly zero Stolen Base Runs Saved.

Methodology:
Adjusted Earned Runs Saved

The evaluation of catcher defense, specifically the handling of the pitching staff, has been the subject of much debate over the years. Craig Wright introduced Catcher ERA in his book *Diamond Appraised*, comparing catchers on the same team to gauge pitchers' effectiveness when throwing to different pitch callers. Many analysts, including Keith Woolner formerly of Baseball Prospectus and now with the Cleveland Indians, have questioned the validity of Catcher ERA and similar statistics.

In *The Fielding Bible—Volume II*, we introduced a method called Adjusted Earned Runs Saved. Our goal is to assess each catcher's ability to handle the pitching staff, saving runs with intelligent pitch calling and anything else he can do to help each pitcher be more effective. The idea is similar to Catcher ERA, with some very important adjustments.

First, we park-adjust each pitcher's seasonal ERA. For example, let's take a look at Tim Hudson from 2011. The former Auburn Tiger allowed 77 earned runs and a 3.22 ERA; however, Hudson pitched primarily in pitcher-friendly Turner Field that year. We park adjust his total by dividing his earned runs allowed in each ballpark by its park factor, then adding them up to get 82.4 adjusted earned runs and a 3.45 Adjusted ERA.

We then look specifically at each pitcher's performance with each catcher. We perform the same park adjustment calculation to find how many adjusted earned runs the pitcher allowed with each catcher. Brian McCann caught Hudson for 118 innings that year and allowed 49 earned runs. Those 49 earned runs turn into 53.3 adjusted earned runs after applying the park factors.

Next, we take the pitcher's full season Adjusted Earned Run Average, multiply by the number of innings thrown to that particular catcher, and divide by nine to get the expected number of (adjusted) earned runs allowed by that pitcher/catcher duo. We then subtract the actual number of adjusted earned runs for that tandem to find the number of adjusted earned runs saved for that catcher. Back to our Hudson/McCann example, Hudson's full season Adjusted ERA was 3.45, multiply by 118 and divide by nine to get...45.2. They actually allowed 53.3 adjusted earned runs, a difference of -8.1 adjusted earned runs.

We do the same calculation for every pitcher-catcher combination in baseball, then add up the adjusted earned runs saved for each catcher. For Brian McCann, this amounts to -6.5 adjusted earned runs saved.

There's one final adjustment. The scale of adjusted earned runs can vary quite a bit, especially in smaller sample sizes. There is a lot of random noise in a single season of pitcher ERA, let alone the variation between catchers. If a pitcher has a bad day and gives up six runs in six innings for one particular backup catcher, that might be three runs more than expected. However, those extra three runs could be attributed to any number of things that have nothing to do with the catcher. The wind might be blowing out that day, the pitcher could be going through a dead-arm period and not have his best stuff, or he might have forgotten to eat his Wheaties for breakfast. Because of all the variables outside of the catcher's control, we apply a credibility factor. We take the catcher's adjusted earned runs saved, multiply by the number of innings he caught that year, then divide by three times the number of innings caught in a full season behind the plate. For 2011, this number was 1,451. For McCann, we multiply -6.5 * 1,083 / (1,451 * 3) = -1.6, which rounds to -2 Adjusted Earned Runs Saved.

Methodology:
Strike Zone Runs Saved

The following pages provide an in-depth explanation of our research and methodology for Strike Zone Plus/Minus. There is evidence to suggest that some players may have more of a knack than others for getting these borderline pitches called strikes. In order to better quantify how much value a player is able to provide to his team, we developed a system for measuring the contribution each player is able to make in getting more or fewer strikes called than average.

For the sake of clarity, throughout this section the word "players" will be used to refer to all four of the pitcher, the catcher, the batter, and the umpire. Obviously the umpire is an officiant, not a player of the game. But we are treating all four as active participants in this context, and it will be less confusing if we simply use a single word that applies to all of them.

Determining Significant Variables

There are many factors that contribute to a pitch being called a ball or a strike. In addition to the identities of the pitcher, the catcher, the batter, and the umpire, there are many variables related to the context that the pitch was thrown in. In order to determine the individual contributions of each of the active participants on a given pitch, first we have to start by isolating their contribution as a group from the context of the pitch. There are seven contextual variables that we thought would most affect the outcome of a pitch, so we investigated each of the seven to determine their significance. Those seven variables, listed in no particular order, are:

- Pitch Location
- Batter Handedness
- Pitcher Handedness
- Ball/Strike Count
- Command: how close the pitcher was to hitting the catcher's target
- Pitch Type
- Home/Road: whether the pitcher/catcher play for the home team or road team

While other methodologies have attempted to account for some of these variables to varying degrees, our approach is unique in that we can incorporate our command data into the methodology. In addition to the pitch charting operation that we have had in place since the company's inception, in 2010 we began charting the location of where the catcher sets his target before each pitch. This allows us to measure how close the pitcher came to hitting his target and to determine how much that might affect the umpire's call.

In calculating Strike Zone Plus/Minus for a given pitch, the first thing we need to know is the expected strike percentage for that pitch. How we determine that expected strike percentage depends on which of the above variables we choose to consider. Ideally, we would account for them all. However, the more factors that we include in defining the expected strike percentage, the more we increase the likelihood of running into sample size issues - i.e., the more discretely defined our buckets for classifying each pitch become, the fewer pitches we will have in each bucket.

For this study, we used all pitch data going back to 2010. Of these variables, we wanted to determine which are the most important. To do this, we went through the following process.

Since it is the underlying basis for whether a pitch is called a ball or a strike in the first place, we began by bucketing pitches just by their Pitch Location according to a grid that is approximately one inch by one inch. Then we went through the other variables one by one to see how much variation in Plus/Minus there was for each.

The two variables that showed the most significant variation were Count and Command. For example, pitches were 5.6 percent more likely than average to be called strikes in a 3-0 count, while pitches were 3.2 percent less likely to be called strikes in 0-1 counts.

Count (Balls-Strikes)	Plus/Minus Strike Pct
3-0	5.6%
2-0	4.2%
1-0	2.5%
3-1	1.6%
0-0	1.3%
2-1	0.1%
1-1	-1.5%
3-2	-1.8%
2-2	-2.1%
1-2	-2.7%
0-2	-2.9%
0-1	-3.2%

Because of these significant differences between counts, we decided to include Count as a major variable and to separate each count before calculating the expected strike percentage for every pitch.

For Command, we found that the difference in horizontal distance between where the catcher set up and where the pitch location ended up mattered more than the vertical difference in terms of the expected strike percentage. Therefore, we grouped pitches by their horizontal distance from the catcher's target. Pitches closest to the glove were called strikes 2.8 percent more often than average, while pitches farthest from the glove were called strikes 8.6 percent less often than average.

Command (Horiz Dist from Target)	Plus/Minus Strike Pct
Group 1 (closest to the glove)	2.8%
Group 2	-0.3%
Group 3	-2.9%
Group 4 (farthest from the glove)	-8.6%

Given these significant differences based on command after accounting for pitch location, we added Command as a second significant variable.

The other variables - Batter Handedness, Pitcher Handedness, Pitch Type, and Home/Road - did not show as much variation.

Bat Side	Plus/Minus Strike Pct
LHB	0.1%
RHB	-0.1%

Pitch Side	Plus/Minus Strike Pct
RHP	0.2%
LHP	-0.4%

Pitch Type	Plus/Minus Strike Pct
Fastball	0.3%
Offspeed	-0.4%
Breaking Ball	-0.5%

Home/Road	Plus/Minus Strike Pct
Home	0.2%
Road	-0.2%

Given these results, we knew that we wanted to bucket pitches by Count and Command. However, despite the fact that Batter Handedness and Pitcher Handedness did not show a large variation, we suspected that they might show a larger effect if we focus on specific pitch locations. In other words, if we look at the plate from the pitcher's perspective, we thought that pitches on the left half of the plate might show a large variation in their Plus/Minus depending on the batter's handedness, with a similar but opposite skew on the right half of the plate. Both might show a large variation individually, but taken together they might cancel each other out, thereby masking the significance of Batter Handedness as a variable. And there could be a similar effect for Pitcher Handedness.

To test this, we calculated the Plus/Minus for pitches on each side of the plate separately. In each case, there was a more significant variation for Batter Handedness and for Pitcher Handedness than those variables showed with all pitches taken together. The results are shown in the tables below.

Plate Side (Pitcher's POV)	Bat Side	Plus/Minus Strike Pct
Left Half	LHB	1.7%
	RHB	-4.0%
Right Half	LHB	2.0%
	RHB	-2.8%

Plate Side (Pitcher's POV)	Pitch Side	Plus/Minus Strike Pct
Left Half	LHP	1.1%
	RHP	-0.4%
Right Half	LHP	0.7%
	RHP	-1.7%

While the effect was strong for Batter Handedness, the effect was less so for Pitcher Handedness. Therefore, we knew that the next significant variable that we would add to the bucketing criteria would be Batter Handedness.

After bucketing for Pitch Location, Count, Command, and Batter Handedness, we reached the point where the size of our buckets is about as small as we want them to get given our set of four years worth of pitch data. The remaining variables—Pitcher Handedness, Pitch Type, and Home/Road—still suggest that they might have some effect, but the effect of each has either been reduced or remained small after the addition of these initial variables. See the tables below.

Plate Side (Pitcher's POV)	Pitch Side	Plus/Minus Strike Pct
Left Half	LHP	0.9%
	RHP	-0.3%
Right Half	LHP	0.4%
	RHP	-1.0%

Pitch Type	Plus/Minus Strike Pct
Breaking Ball	0.2%
Offspeed	0.0%
Fastball	-0.1%

Home/Road	Plus/Minus Strike Pct
Home	0.2%
Road	-0.2%

Therefore, we are confident that we are adjusting for all of the most significant variables.

The Basis for Determining the Strike Zone Plus/Minus of Each Pitch

After we categorize each pitch by its location, the count the pitch was thrown in, the proximity of the pitch to the catcher's target, and the batter's handedness, we can determine the percent likelihood that each pitch is to be called a strike. The full array of these strike percentages represents our Strike Zone Plus/Minus Basis, i.e., the basis by which we assign credit if the pitch is called a strike or debit if the pitch is called a ball.

Because the baseball environment is constantly in flux, we want to be sure that our basis remains current. As we pointed out in the previous section, we used four years of data to determine how to bucket our pitches, adding levels of complexity to the bucketing up to the point that we were still comfortable that the number of pitches that fit into each bucket was meaningful. In order to balance the need for both recency and for legitimate sample sizes, we will be using a rolling four-year basis moving forward. That means that the strike percentages used to determine Strike Zone Plus/Minus will always be reflective of pitch results going back exactly four years from the current date.

Calculating Strike Zone Plus/Minus

The basic idea behind calculating Strike Zone Plus/Minus is pretty straight forward. If a pitch is called a strike, there is positive credit to be awarded (plus) to the players involved. If a pitch is called a ball, there is negative credit to be assigned (minus). The amount of positive or negative credit given depends on how likely that pitch was to be called a strike in the first place, which we know from the Basis that we previously calculated.

For example, if a pitch is thrown that is one inch off the outside edge of the plate and 10 inches off the ground, to a left handed batter, in a 2-1 count, and misses the catcher's target by 6 inches, we estimate there to be a 43 percent chance that the pitch will be called a strike. Therefore, if the umpire calls the pitch a strike, then there are plus-0.57 Strike Zone Plus/Minus points (or "extra strikes") to be allotted to the participants on the pitch. However, if the umpire is not so moved and he calls the pitch a ball, then there are minus-0.43 points to be divvied up among the four parties.

The notion of determining a Plus/Minus for a pitch is fairly common throughout the majority of methodologies that strive to assign credit for getting more or fewer strikes called than average. However, most of these methodologies are constrained by the idea of measuring "catcher framing". They operate under the preconceived assumption that getting extra strikes called is primarily the responsibility of the catcher. The entire Plus/Minus credit for a pitch is assigned to the catcher, and then the the pitcher, the umpire, and the batter get treated as context that needs to be adjusted for. In the batter's case, most don't even give him a thought. And for methodologies that attempt to quantify the pitcher's ability to get extra strikes called, they have to run a separate model where the entire Plus/Minus credit for a pitch is assigned to the pitcher, with adjustments then made for the catcher and others.

With our methodology, we treat all four of the pitcher, the catcher, the batter, and the umpire as active participants on each pitch. We have divided the Plus/ Minus credit for each pitch among all four according to their individual abilities, and we run a single model to be able to evaluate all of the participants individually.

The approach that we take is an iterative one. Iterative techniques are widely used throughout sports, from football to baseball, from the highest professional level down through college and even high school sports. Some of the more notable ratings systems based on iterative approaches include the BCS college football computer ratings as well as Jeff Sagarin's ratings for various sports published by USA Today.

In the case of Strike Zone Plus/Minus, in order to determine every player's value for a given season, each iteration of the process consists of going through every taken pitch of that season and calculating how much credit to assign each player on each pitch (using the four-year rolling Basis as our frame of reference for the strike percentages). We begin by making certain assumptions for the first iteration, followed by an evaluation of every pitch. The results that we get from the first iteration are used to inform the second iteration, and then we go through the whole season's worth of pitches again. Using the results from the second iteration, we run a third iteration on every pitch. We keep doing this until the changes in the results from one iteration to the next become very small.

To begin, without any initial knowledge about the abilities of any individual to get extra strikes called, we simply start by going through each pitch and dividing the Plus/Minus credit evenly between all four players. So let's go back to the example pitch that we mentioned earlier, and let's say the pitch was called a strike. Therefore, the overall Plus/Minus for that pitch is plus-0.57. And let's say that James Shields was pitching to Salvador Perez with Oswaldo Arcia batting and Dana DeMuth behind the plate calling balls and strikes. All four would be given plus-0.1425 credit for the pitch.

Once we have done this for every pitch, we add up all the credits and debits that a player has received to get an initial indication of his Strike Zone Plus/Minus. If a player's initial Plus/Minus is positive, it suggests that he has the ability to get more strikes called than average. If his Plus/Minus is negative, it suggests that he gets fewer strikes (more balls) called than average. However, we do not really know either of these things for sure at this point. We know better than to think that each player is equally responsible for the outcome of a given pitch. We also know that each player interacts within a unique combination of environments over the course of the season. Salvador Perez catches James Shields often, but Perez will also catch a number of other pitchers on the Royals' staff, each with a different style. And both Shields and Perez will be paired with an uneven distribution of hitters and umpires over time as well.

What if, on a particular pitch, there is a pitcher, a catcher, and a batter all prone to getting extra strikes called, but an umpire who is working against them? We don't want that umpire getting the same credit as the other three. So we begin to make iterative adjustments.

For our second iteration, we want to separate the individual tendencies of the players on each pitch from the portion of the Plus/Minus that is attributable to a neutral environment. We start by dividing each player's total initial Strike Zone Plus/Minus from the first iteration by the number of pitches that they were involved in to get their Plus/Minus Per Pitch. This number represents the contribution that each player brings to an individual pitch.

Returning to our example, let's say that after the first iteration Shields had achieved plus-0.018 Plus/Minus Per Pitch, meaning that there were 1.8 percent more strikes than average called while he was pitching. And let's say Perez was worth plus-0.002 (0.2 percent more strikes than average), Arcia was worth plus-0.015 (1.5 percent more strikes than average), and DeMuth was worth minus-0.005 (0.5 percent fewer strikes than average) - these numbers being entirely hypothetical. Combined, they get an additional 0.030 more strikes than expected per pitch. When we subtract this from the plus-0.57 Plus/Minus of the pitch, we are left with plus-0.54.

This plus-0.54 represents the portion of the Plus/Minus of the pitch attributable to a neutral environment. All four players can lay equal claim to it. Therefore, we can distribute this evenly among the four players, which means assigning plus-0.135 to each.

We then add each player's share of the neutral portion (the plus-0.135) to his individual contribution (his Plus/Minus Per Pitch). Therefore, instead of the plus-0.1425 that each received after the first iteration, now Shields gets 0.135 + 0.018 = 0.153 credit for this pitch. Likewise, Perez gets 0.137, Arcia gets 0.150, and DeMuth gets 0.130. By doing the same thing for every other pitch and adding up the results, we now have a new Strike Zone Plus/Minus total for each player.

Having done this second iteration, we are closer to having an accurate reflection of each player's ability to get extra strikes called, but we are still not that far removed from having given everyone equal credit to begin with. There is actually a pretty large change in Strike Zone Plus/Minus for most players from the first iteration to the second. Therefore, to continue refining how accurately our numbers reflect each player's skill, we repeat the process that we did for the second iteration again and again. With each iteration, the change in Strike Zone Plus/Minus for each player gets smaller. We stop iterating once the change has become so small that we know we have converged on a true reflection of each player's abilities. Normally, this takes about 10 iterations.

The final step we take is to include an adjustment to help smooth out the small pitch samples of some players. We do this by regressing each player's Strike Zone Plus/Minus by a certain number of league average pitches. Based on our research, adding 250 league average pitches to each player's actual total of pitches is the optimal number.

Run Value

In order to state each player's impact in terms of the runs that he saves or costs his team (or, in the umpire's case, the runs he saves or costs all teams), we need to know what the run value of converting a ball into a strike is. Therefore, we took our pitch results from the same 2010-13 time period, calculated the run expectancy associated with each ball/strike count, and then found the difference in the change in run expectancy between the next pitch being called a ball and the next pitch being called a strike. Because we did not find any evidence that any given player is putting more or less effort into getting an extra strike called depending on the count, we felt comfortable averaging all the changes in run expectancy into a single run value. The average difference in run expectancy between a ball and a strike amounts to .1189 runs, which we will apply as the final step.

Independence Test

One of the main concerns of trying to assign credit for getting extra strikes called is that the players involved do not all interact with each other with the same frequency. In particular, pitchers and catchers are likely to have significant overlap in their pitch samples. So if a pitcher has a positive Strike Zone Plus/Minus, is that because he himself is good at getting extra strikes, or is it because he throws the majority of his pitches to a good catcher?

In order to determine whether our system is adequately accounting for these interaction effects, we performed a couple of variations on a "with or without you" correlation test. To do this, we looked at each pitcher with a specific catcher and with all other catchers. If our system is measuring the performance of each player independently, then the correlation of the pitcher's performance with a specific catcher to the pitcher's performance with all other catchers should be high (i.e., the pitcher's performance is consistent no matter who the catcher is). Conversely, the correlation of the performance of that catcher to the performance of all other catchers with that same pitcher should be low (i.e., each catcher is unique).

For each pitcher, we calculated his Plus/Minus Per

Pitch on the pitches he threw to a specific catcher, and then separately calculated his Plus/Minus Per Pitch on the pitches he threw to all other catchers. For example, within the last four years, Eric Stults has thrown 1205 pitches to Nick Hundley that have either been a called ball or a called strike, and he has thrown 1411 such pitches to all other catchers. When paired with Hundley, he has managed 0.020 extra strikes per pitch. With all other catchers, he has managed 0.019 extra strikes per pitch. We did this for every pitcher/catcher pair, and then calculated the correlation between the two sets of numbers—the values with the specific catcher and the values with all other catchers.

If we limit our sample to pitcher/catcher pairs where the pitcher had thrown at least 100 pitches to both the catcher in question and to all other catchers so as to eliminate small sample effects, the correlation comes out to 0.80. That's pretty strong. That suggests that our system is measuring very consistent performance for pitchers no matter who the catcher is. If we increase the threshold to 500 pitches thrown with and without the catcher, the correlation comes out to 0.91. That's even stronger. And as we continue to increase the threshold, the relationship continues to strengthen. Therefore, the first part of our test has us confident that our system is truly measuring the performance of each player independently.

For the second part of our test, we looked at the same pitcher/catcher pairings, but instead calculated the Plus/Minus Per Pitch that the catcher in question achieved with that pitcher, as well as the Plus/Minus Per Pitch that all those other catchers accumulated with that pitcher. Turning back to our Stults/Hundley example, Hundley had a minus-0.007 Plus/Minus Per Pitch when he caught Stults, whereas all the other catchers that caught Stults had a plus-0.016 Plus/Minus Per Pitch when they were paired with him. As before, we did this for all pitcher/catcher pairs, and we calculated the correlation between the two sets of numbers. This time, when the threshold was set to 100 pitches and 500 pitches with and without the catcher, the correlation came out to minus-0.04 and minus-0.03 respectively. This suggests no evidence of a relationship between the performances of the various catchers that caught the same pitcher as measured by our system. This adds to our confidence that our system is truly measuring the performances of each player independently.

Just to drive the point home, we did the same exercise, but instead of using our iteratively calculated

Strike Zone Plus/Minus numbers, we used the numbers that one would get if the Plus/Minus credit for each pitch were simply divided evenly between each player. With the threshold set to 100 pitches, both the correlation of the pitchers' numbers and the correlation of the catchers' numbers came out to 0.19. As we expected, the pitchers' correlation is much stronger than this after our iterative adjustments, and the catchers' correlation is much weaker. Therefore, we know that we have significantly improved the accuracy of our measurement by using our iterative approach.

Even/Odd Year Correlation Test

In order to test that our new Strike Zone Plus/Minus metric is measuring something meaningful, we performed an even/odd year correlation. If we are measuring a meaningful ability for a player to get extra strikes called, then we would expect his numbers to be consistently high or low from year to year. To do this, we added the Strike Zone Plus/Minus Runs Saved from 2010 and 2012 together and compared them to the subtotal of 2011 and 2013 taken together for all players that were involved in at least 500 called pitches in both sets of years. The table below shows the correlation for each of four player types.

Player Type	Even/Odd Year Correlation
Pitchers	0.46
Catchers	0.86
Batters	0.50
Umpires	0.77

The even/odd year correlation for Catchers is extremely high. In fact, it is stronger than for any of our other defensive metrics regardless of position. The correlation for Umpires is quite high as well. It is not very surprising that Catchers and Umpires would have the highest correlations between even and odd years considering that they are generally involved in many more pitches than Pitchers and Batters over the course of a season. However, despite showing less consistency between even and odd years, the correlations for Pitchers and Batters are still strong enough to inspire confidence. Overall, these results demonstrate that Strike Zone Plus/Minus is doing an excellent job of measuring a meaningful skill.

Methodology:
Shift Runs Saved

In 2012, Baseball Info Solutions conducted an investigation into the effect of the Ted Williams shift on the Range and Positioning component of Defensive Runs Saved numbers. We found that the tremendous increase in shifting, and in the variety of shift defenses used, had skewed individual player totals, most notably Brett Lawrie's. The Blue Jays employed the second-most defensive shifts in baseball in 2012, and the way they positioned Lawrie was something special.

The Lawrie Defense is like a normal Ted Williams Shift against a lefty swinger, but the unique aspect is that the third baseman moves all the way over to short right field where the second baseman would normally play in the shift. This alignment was rare in years prior, but, with shift usage nearly doubling that year, positioning a third baseman or shortstop in short right field became much more common.

Our Range and Positioning System was making Lawrie look incredibly good due to the fact that he was making plays in short right field that other third basemen weren't making. However, it wasn't as if he had other-worldly range or that he was smarter about how he positioned himself than other third basemen. It was his team telling him to go stand in short right field. To address this, the Range and Positioning System now removes all shift plays from the calculation for individual players. The result is that a player like Lawrie will not receive credit for making a play well beyond his normal range while in a full-scale defensive shift. At the same time, other third basemen will not be penalized for failing to make a play which Lawrie or another fielder made due to the shift.

However, we still wanted a way to estimate a team's Runs Saved on shift plays. It is the team's decision whether to use a shift or not and where to position each fielder, and we needed a way to measure how effectively each team was utilizing its shifts. So we created Shift Runs Saved. It works similarly to the Range and Positioning System (for details, see page 324), but instead of looking at each fielder individually, the new system treats the entire infield as one collective unit. It considers how hard the ball was hit and what direction the ball was hit, and then it compares how often a team was able to make an out on that type of ball in play while using a defensive shift to how often the league as a whole was able to make an out on that type of ball in play, shift or no shift. Positive credit is assigned for successful plays made and negative credit is given for plays not made, which we then convert to Runs Saved.

For example, let's say the Blue Jays are playing the Lawrie Defense against David Ortiz. Big Papi hits a hard groundball that averages 70 miles an hour through the infield at an angle 17 degrees off the first base line. This play might only be made 25 percent of the time across all of baseball; however, the Blue Jays have Brett Lawrie standing right there, and he makes the play easily. In our new system, the Blue Jays' infield will get a collective credit for making the play, and that credit is then converted into a run value.

We have implemented this change for historical data going back to 2010.

Acknowledgments

First of all, we need to recognize the BIS Research & Development team of Scott Spratt and Joe Rosales. These two have worked extremely hard on this book and everything leading up to it and should be considered co-authors. Though this is their first *Fielding Bible* book as full-time staff members (Joe worked with us on *Volume III* as an R&D Intern), they have jointly driven the proprietary research that we shared with team clients over the past three years and we now publish in this book. Their hard work over the past three years is irreplaceable.

Thanks to our R&D Interns over the past three years, including Glenn DuPaul, Dan Lependorf, Doug Wachter, and Dan Foehrenbach. They each contributed to the analytical and editorial content of this book through their contributions to the R&D department. We are thrilled to report they are all doing well in the world, with Dan L. and Doug moving on to opportunities with MLB teams, Dan F. joining the BIS full-time staff, and Glenn now serving as the Director of Analytics for the Brooklyn Nets.

Next, we want to thank the rest of the BIS staff, old and new. The expanded Operations department, which leads our data collection efforts, includes Dan Casey, Tim Kwilos, Kevin Morrissey, Mike Piekarski, Todd Radcliffe, Jim Swavely, Jon Vrecsics, and the new additions James Mehall and Dan Foehrenbach. The IT department, led by newcomer Rob Dougherty, was eager to help out in any way possible. Thanks to Rob, Patrick Coyle, Greg Thomas, and Ben Stanczak. Thanks also to Carol Olsen, who keeps things running smoothly at the BIS office. Special thanks to Andy Johnson, Eric Nehs, and Jeff Spoljaric, who moved on from BIS in the past year.

A number of other video scouts contributed scouting reports to the book: Joe Brehm, Dan Edwards, Dan Foehrenbach, Josh Hofer, Andy Houk, Ryan Klimek, Keanan Lamb, Spencer Moody, Chris Mosch, Jon Presser, Tucker Stobbe, Josh Tuchman, Zeke Turrentine, and Ezra Wise. Full-timers Andy Johnson and Kevin Morrissey contributed excellent scouting reports of their own, and Kevin was especially helpful by writing several additional reports when we came to him at the last minute.

When we came to Bill James a month before this book's deadline and asked him if he could contribute, he came back two weeks later with a 57-page article that we were forced to trim down to fit into this book. Bill's work always inspires and challenges us to be better analysts and writers. Please check out his writing about baseball and many other topics at BillJamesOnline.com. We eagerly await the next installment of "The Man on the Train".

Jim Capuano is our Director of Business Development, helping to bring the results of our research to a larger audience. Thanks to our partners at ESPN, FanGraphs, and Baseball-Reference for helping to create that larger audience.

Thanks to our friends at ACTA Sports (ACTASports.com), including Greg Pierce, Mary Doyle, Emily Heath, Mary Eggert, Isz, Patricia Lynch, Abby Pierce, Hugh Spector, and Tom Wright.

Finally, thank you to all of our friends and families who've had to put up with our baseball obsessions year-round, but especially during the weeks leading up to this book's deadline. Amy Jedlovec has been through five Handbooks and two *Fielding Bibles* now, and Juliet has now been through one of each. Sue Dewan has been with John through enough books to fill a library, helping with a number of them herself. We don't know how to thank you enough for your patience with us every time we are approaching a deadline.

Baseball Info Solutions

Baseball Info Solutions (BIS) opened its doors back in 2002 and has been on the leading edge of the advanced analytical study of baseball ever since. The company's mission is to provide the most accurate, in-depth, timely professional baseball data, including cutting-edge research and analysis, striving to educate major league teams and the public about baseball analytics.

BIS employs a staff of expert baseball analysts and an army of highly trained video scouts who conduct several passes of each game, recording everything from basic box score data to times and locations of balls in play, pitch types and locations, defensive shifts, and much more.

The company's analysts and programmers dissect the data, producing a variety of predictive studies and analytics, including, for example, Defensive Runs Saved. Defensive Runs Saved estimates the number of runs a defender saves or costs his teams because of his ability to convert balls in play into outs, defend bunts, turn double plays, prevent baserunner advancements, and several other factors. A couple of the more recent advancements are Strike Zone Plus/Minus—which measures the number of extra strikes drawn from umpires due to the specific skills and characteristics of catchers, pitchers, batters, and the umpires themselves—and Stolen Base Red Light/Green Light—which predicts baserunner success rates on stolen bases against various pitcher-catcher combinations, even if they have never faced each other.

Baseball Info Solutions was co-founded by John Dewan, who has been a leader in baseball analytics for more than 25 years. From his first partnership with Bill James as the Executive Director of Project Scoresheet to co-founding STATS, Inc. and his 15-year tenure there as CEO, John has continually broken new ground in sports data and analytics. Through products and publications such as *The Bill James Handbook* and *The Fielding Bible*, John, Bill, and BIS have continued that tradition to this day.

For data inquiries, potential job openings, or additional information, please contact BIS at:

Baseball Info Solutions
41 S. 2nd Street
Coplay, PA 18037
610-261-2370
info@baseballinfosolutions.com
www.baseballinfosolutions.com